GEORGE STUBBS

1724–1806

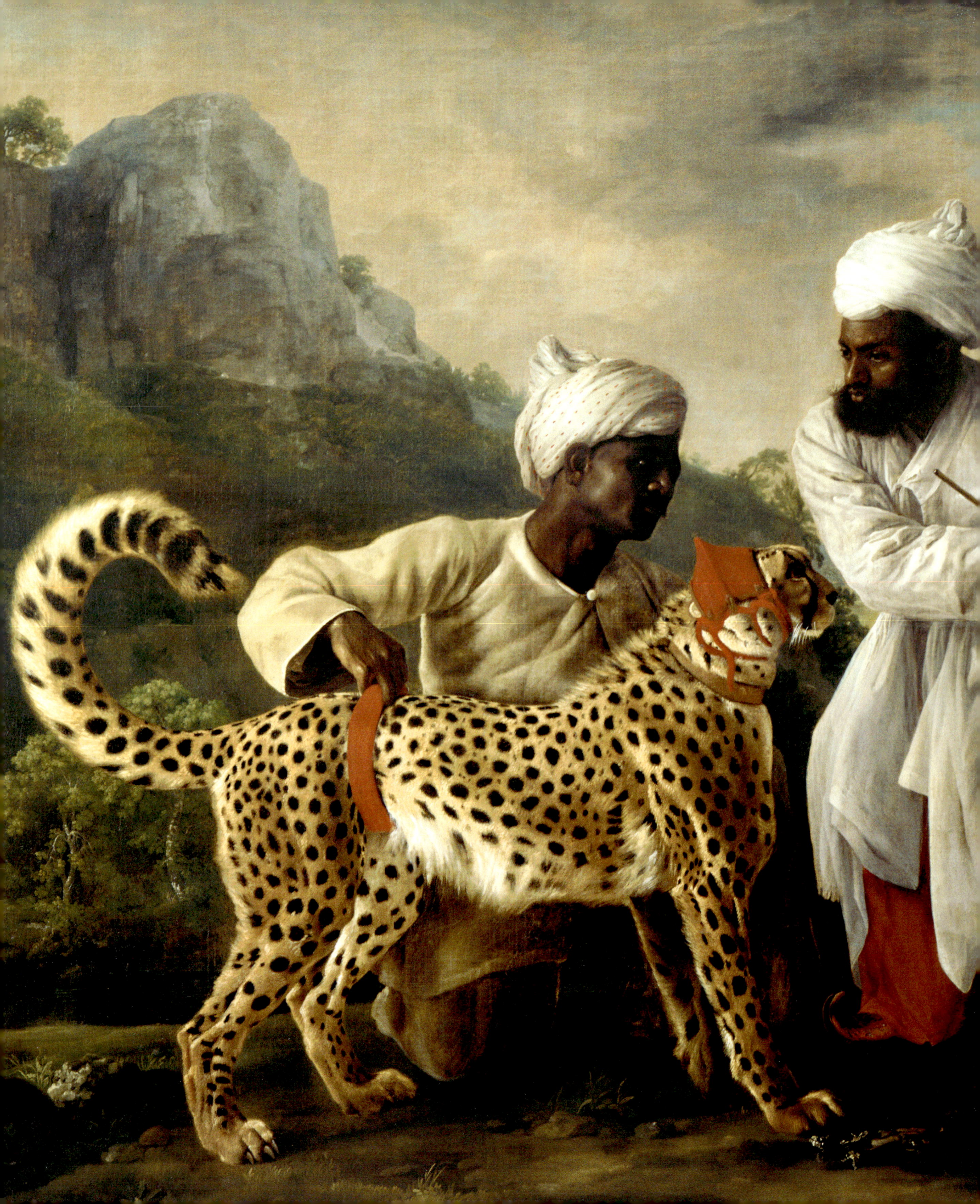

GEORGE STUBBS

1724–1806 SCIENCE INTO ART

Edited by Herbert W. Rott

With contributions by Brian Allen, Werner Busch,
Tim Clayton, Sophie Goldhagen, Oliver Kase, Martin Myrone,
Herbert W. Rott and Francis Russell

PRESTEL
MUNICH · LONDON · NEW YORK

BAYERISCHE STAATSGEMÄLDESAMMLUNGEN
MUNICH · NEUE PINAKOTHEK

FOREWORD

ESSAYS

8	Martin Myrone	*George Stubbs—Between Market, Nature and Art*
22	Werner Busch	*Stubbs's Aesthetics*
42	Oliver Kase	*"Make the Knife go with the Pencil"—Science and Art in George Stubbs's "Anatomy of the Horse"*
60	Tim Clayton	*Stubbs and the Print*
78	Francis Russell	*Stubbs and his Patrons*
88	Brian Allen	*George Stubbs—A Critical Afterlife 1806–2012*
94	Herbert W. Rott	*Some Early German Collectors of British Art*

CATALOGUE

104 THE ANATOMY OF THE HORSE

120 PAINTINGS

194 PRINTS

210 PRINTS AFTER STUBBS

APPENDIX

234 George Stubbs—Biographical Notes

237 Bibliography

239 Lenders to the Exhibition

Klaus Schrenk

FOREWORD

Exhibiting the works of a painter like George Stubbs in Germany may perhaps seem like an extravagant indulgence. His name is hardly one of those which draw huge crowds or inspire high levels of public interest in this country. Lovers of art and animals know him as the creator of extraordinary equine portraits, yet that this man numbered among one of the most exceptional artists of his age has still to be discovered in Germany. This exhibition with its accompanying catalogue gives a German audience the opportunity to do just this.

The Neue Pinakothek is home to one of the most important collections of eighteenth- and nineteenth-century British paintings in continental Europe. The collection was initiated around 1800 when the first paintings arrived in Munich from the British Isles. One of these was George Stubbs's *Spanish Pointer,* perhaps the first painting by this artist ever to leave the island's shores. To this day this portrait of a dog remains one of very few works by him on the continent and the only one in a German museum. It was only in around 1900 and then in the 1970s and 1980s that the inventory of British painting in Munich was considerably expanded. Today the key artists of the epoch—from Hogarth to Reynolds, from Gainsborough to Lawrence, and from Constable to Turner—are represented in the form of major pieces. Created over a period of some 200 years, this historic collection provides a foil against which the works by the outsider Stubbs can be unfolded.

Pictures by George Stubbs are testimony to a specifically British way of life. Horses and hounds—the subjects of the so-called *sporting art*—mirror the interests and ethos of the eighteenth-century British nobility. This group cultivated and honed the idea of living in harmony with nature on their country seats as an alternative to urban civilization. Animals played an important role in this, not least horses, the breeding and keeping of which was at the same time a passion, a science and a pastime. The English Thoroughbred, as captured by Stubbs in masterly portraits of its most important specimens, stands for both the new commercial world of sport and pleasure and the evolutionary advancement of nature according to the Enlightenment belief in progress. These paintings, however, also demonstrate the new ideals of speed and elegance, not to mention confidence and modernity as the outward expression of British society's success and the high self-esteem in which it held itself during the period in which England, with its new ideal of art true to nature, was soon to set the tone across Europe.

Equally exceptional is the foundation of Stubbs's art in empiricism, which was more pronounced in England than in any other European country at this time. Pictures were created that were rooted in the observation of nature; the process of cognition was guided by vision. In order to gain experience in these areas Stubbs went further than almost any other artist before or after him. *The Anatomy of the Horse* is based on drawings and studies which Stubbs produced through close contact with its animal subjects. The idea that he himself dispatched with, dissected and drew animals at a farmstead somewhere out in the far-flung provinces perhaps seems quite nightmarish to today's beholder. His way of going about things, however, reveals the categorical desire to get to the truth and to subject everything to the piercing gaze that is characteristic of his artistic approach. Whether the etchings illustrating his treatise or his portraits of horses and other animals, his artistic qualifications are clear in his rendering of this knowledge in carefully composed, highly aesthetic images. Empiricism and aesthetics are rarely found to be as closely united in the history of European art as they are in the work of George Stubbs.

The articles in this catalogue highlight these interrelationships from different perspectives. Martin Myrone sums up the unusual career of this largely successful, but later forgotten artist, positioning him against the background of the English art market which was especially vital from around 1750 onwards. Werner Busch outlines the two poles—truth to nature and claims to art—between which Stubbs sought to pitch his oeuvre. Oliver Kase vividly describes the special position occupied by his treatise on equine anatomy—a work aesthetically rooted in the most merciless empiricism—among early modern publications of this kind. Tim Clayton turns his attention to prints, an important facet of Stubbs's work, and discusses both reproductive prints after his paintings and the etchings from his own hand which belong to the most beautiful works produced in this field in eighteenth-century England. Francis Russell illuminates the tight network of contacts and personal relationships woven by the patrons of this artist. Brian Allen reports on the vicissitudes of Stubbs's reputation, which was subject to greater oscillations than that of any other British artist of his calibre. And finally Herbert Rott looks at the links between Germany and England in the late eighteenth century, when the first collections of British art were formed. All authors are thanked for their contributions which introduce this artist to a German audience for the first time.

This publication was inspired by the exhibition of George Stubbs's drawings, prints and paintings in the Neue Pinakothek. We are grateful to the lenders for their willingness to relinquish these precious works to us temporarily. The great museums and collections in Britain—the Royal Collection, the National Gallery, the British Museum, the Tate in London and the National Gallery of Scotland—were open-minded and co-operative from the moment they heard of our intentions. In lending their wonderful *Cheetah and Stag,* the Manchester Art Gallery is also sharing one of the institution's most important works with Munich. Furthermore, we are indebted to the helpfulness of the Royal Academy in London which, in lending us a selection of the anatomical drawings by Stubbs in their possession, allows us to illustrate the empirical basis and scientific components of the artist's work. We are also beholden to the important collections of natural history in Glasgow and London founded by the brothers William and John Hunter, for whom Stubbs painted exotic animals. Borrowed from collections in Aschaffenburg, Coburg and Nuremberg, reproductive prints made after Stubbs's paintings document the contemporary collecting of English prints in Germany.

Many of Stubbs's most beautiful, not to mention most important, paintings can still be found in private hands, owned by the descendants of those collectors and patrons who bought the paintings from Stubbs himself more than two centuries ago. It was crucial to the success of this venture that pictures like those painted for Lord Rockingham and the Duke of Rutland could be borrowed. Our particular thanks go to Lady Juliet Tadgell for her helpful support and also to the owners of the immensely valuable and rarely—or indeed never—exhibited paintings which have made the journey from Belvoir Castle in Leicestershire, Grimsthorpe Castle in Lincolnshire, Mount Stuart in Scotland, Bodrhyddan Hall in North Wales and Squerryes Court in Kent. Finally, the fact that we are able to show major works from the collection of the man whose name is so closely connected with the re-discovery and re-evaluation of George Stubbs in the twentieth century, Paul Mellon, is a particular pleasure. His works come to us from their home at the Yale Center for British Art in New Haven, Connecticut.

Mere good will and resolve here in Munich would never have been enough to bring this exhibition into being. The backing of our British colleagues, who were always forthcoming with both words and deeds, was essential. Judy Egerton, the authority on Stubbs's work and author of a truly laudable catalogue raisonné, lent her enthusiastic and affectionate support from the start. Though she and we both would have wished it otherwise, her health sadly prevented her from being able to contribute to the catalogue and exhibition. In not only giving her encouragement but also volunteering her advice she has nevertheless been of tremendous assistance. Equally important was Francis Russell, who contacted lenders, opened doors and was always a ready advisor and respondent. Nicholas Penny offered his indispensable help; and David Moore-Gwyn and Emmeline Hallmark likewise assisted in the mediation of the loans. We thank each and every one of these colleagues wholeheartedly. Special thanks, however, must go to Sir Ronald Grierson for his support in preparing the exhibition.

As the initiator and curator responsible for this exhibition Herbert Rott used his considerable powers of persuasion and pressed ahead with this project, becoming the first to draw George Stubbs's works together and present them in a German museum. Only very few major examples of eighteenth- and nineteenth-century British art can be found in museums and galleries in Germany and with this exhibition of the work of George Stubbs we would like to focus on one of the most important English artists of the 1700s. Thanks to the generous support of the lenders Herbert Rott was able to transform an excellent concept into an exceptional exhibition. My great thanks are due to him and he has my heartfelt appreciation for his intensive work in the months leading up to this and his unfailing commitment to making this ambition a reality. He was supported by one young colleague in particular, Sophie Goldhagen, who contributed inestimably to the preparations for both the exhibition and catalogue.

This catalogue became the beautiful object it is thanks to Prestel, in particular the inexhaustible and precise Anja Besserer. It was the idea of the publishing house, an idea for which we are very grateful, that an English catalogue should be produced parallel to the German publication. Here Rachel King is to be thanked for her valuable input in respect of the English translations. We would like to note our gratitude to the Paul Mellon Centre for Studies in British Art for having made a grant to help with the cost of the images.

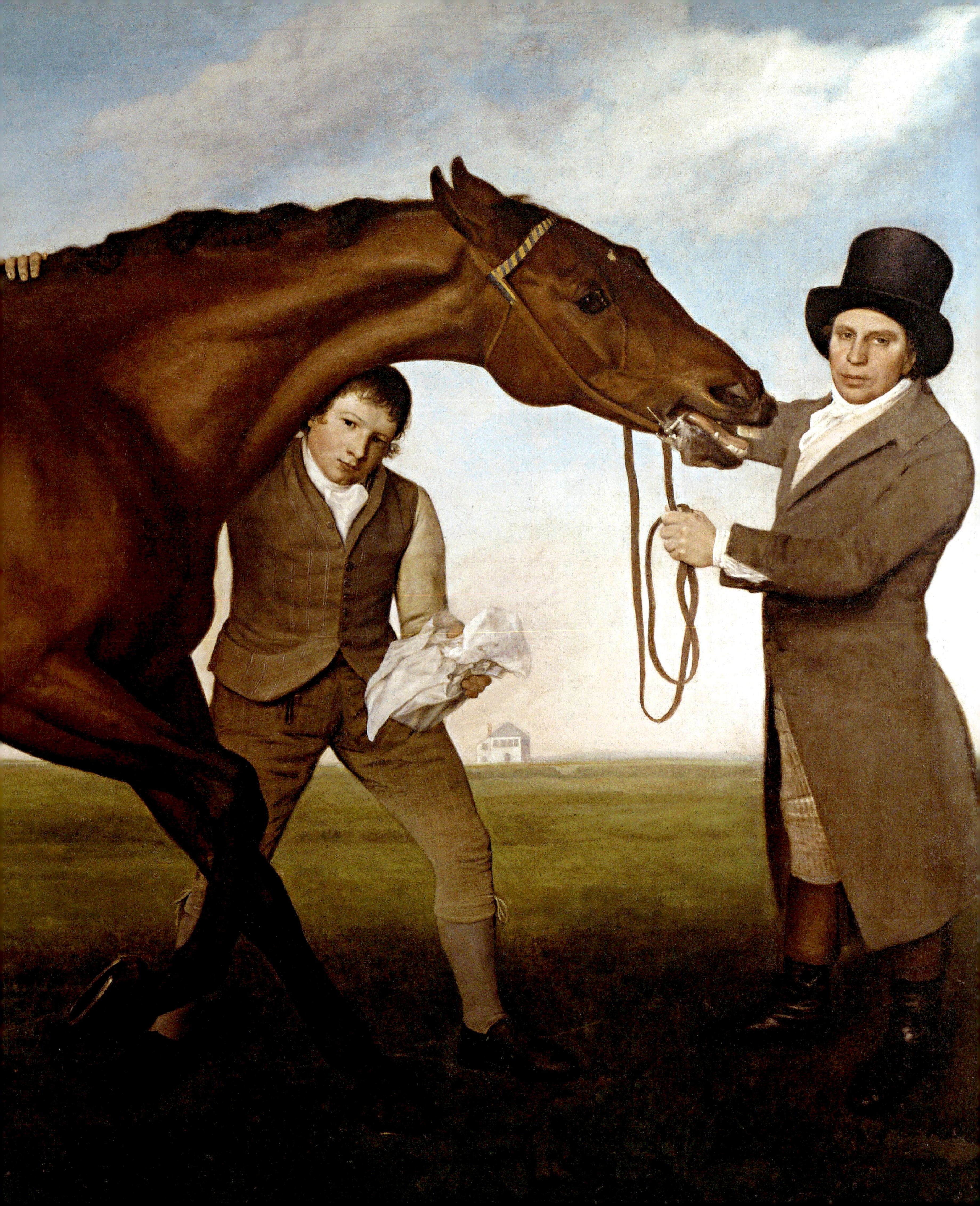

Martin Myrone

GEORGE STUBBS—BETWEEN MARKET, NATURE AND ART

Stubbs is one of a small handful of eighteenth-century British artists whose name may be readily recognized beyond the English-speaking world. Along with the works of William Hogarth (1697–1764), Joshua Reynolds (1723–1792) and Thomas Gainsborough (1727–1788), and perhaps George Romney (1734–1802) and Joseph Wright of Derby (1734–1797), the most famous of Stubbs's paintings have attained the status of being "iconic". The sale in July 2011 of one of his most elaborate and accomplished exercises in horse painting, *Gimcrack on Newmarket Heath*, for a record price of over £20 million, has confirmed his stature at least among wealthy collectors. Such pictures have been reproduced and discussed not only as representative of the output and outlook of this individual artist, but as potent visualizations of the values of the era which produced them. Whereas Hogarth's robust portrait images of his contemporaries and his subject pictures seem to reveal vividly the social life of early-eighteenth century London, the glamorous portraits of Reynolds, Gainsborough and Romney are taken to embody high society's flattering image of itself. On the other hand, Gainsborough's pictures of peasants in a luminous English countryside offer an alternative view of Britain, as a place of rural abundance and overwhelming natural beauty. Stubbs's images have traditionally been cast similarly, as offering an insight into the more exclusive world of horse-racing. His pristine vision of racing horses, their handlers and jockeys, and other fine beasts including cattle and exotics, are often considered as exemplary of the main passions of the British social élite: dogs, horses and rural sports.

As with any artist who has entered the canon of "great masters", George Stubbs has attracted sustained scholarly scrutiny and critical attention from a number of perspectives. The conclusions which have been drawn about his work have been various and sometimes contradictory. Stubbs has, certainly, long been held in esteem as the finest sporting artist of the eighteenth century, and indeed of all time. But that reputation for supremacy in a distinct genre of art has also been married to an appreciation of the painter in somewhat different terms: as a clear-sighted documenter of the natural world. As Werner Busch discusses in his essay in this catalogue, the very baldness and clarity of Stubbs's treatment of natural forms may seem to lead to an approach towards art which eschews aesthetic concerns. Together with Joseph Wright of Derby, Stubbs has been positioned as a leading proponent in the visual arts of the great project of Enlightenment—eighteenth-century Europe's drive towards secular reason, empiricism and political freedom. Wright's most famous images of industry and science seem to point towards a fresh and novel apprehension of the reality of the modern age, and suggest an excitement about the future. Stubbs's great anatomical projects and paintings like *Whistlejacket* seem similarly to engage with a new way of looking at the world and offer a vision of nature both precise and monumental.

Both versions of Stubbs's art—the one emphasizing his ability to convey an enticing vision of British nature and the sporting scene which flattered his patrons, the other proposing that his was an heroically single-minded intellect unencumbered by tradition—have much to recommend them. But both can also be tested out somewhat. The idea of Enlightenment has been made more complicated through recent scholarship: what was a monolithic movement towards modern rationalism has now been accounted for as a complex and multi-faceted phenomenon, taking in many local variations around Europe. There are Scottish and English enlightenments as well as French enlightenments, each of which has a quite distinct character; there is no single model. Also, historians query how far any kind of Enlightenment was about rationalism in a simply positive sense; was there a dark underbelly of this progress towards science and reason? And as for Stubbs as representative of a mythically cohesive British identity, those very motifs which perhaps once seemed to represent a lost golden age of peace and calm and simple pleasures have become controversial to a degree previously unknown. Blood sports and property rights in the countryside are hot political topics.

Faced with these contradictory features within Stubbs's art, there has been a tendency to emphasize the artist's singularity, and to refer to his personality as the guiding factor in his art. Judy Egerton, the leading authority on Stubbs's art, the author of the masterful *catalogue raisonné*, and a scholar whose name is, quite naturally, evoked repeatedly in this present publication, has concluded that the painter's greatest quality lay in "having followed his own bent, unswayed by the prevailing grand manner or by sensationalism, remaining faithful to his preferred subject-matter despite awareness that it was deemed to occupy only a lowly place in the academic hierarchy; and, in pursuing his own projects, unconcerned with making money."[1] This insight helps us appreciate something of the specificity of Stubbs's career, in strictly biographical terms. However, as the essays gathered here testify, Stubbs's art cannot be detached from the political culture and artistic and intellectual preoccupations of his age.

HUMBLE BEGINNINGS

The artist's father, John Stubbs, was a Liverpool leatherworker. Apart from a short time, perhaps only weeks, when he worked with the provincial artist Hamlet Winstanley copying pictures at Knowsley Hall near Liverpool in 1741, Stubbs was self-trained. This brief period with Winstanley exposed him to a rather undistinguished quarter of the art market: Winstanley was a provincial portrait painter who also acted as an artistic odd-job man for the 10th Earl of Derby at Knowsley House. Although biographical accounts abound with stories of his early heroic interest in art, Stubbs's early years would suggest that he was destined to join Winstanley among the ranks of now-forgotten provincial artists. We know that, having split perhaps acrimoniously from Winstanley, he spent a few years at home, drawing and studying anatomy. His intention, according to Humphry's *Memoir*, was "to qualify himself for painting Rural, Pastoral & familiar subjects in History as well as Portraiture."[2] It was, though, the art of portraiture that was to occupy him. He spent periods in Wigan and Leeds and then went to York, where he stayed for a number of years. There he studied anatomy at the hospital, and with a swiftness that we today might find alarming, became an anatomy teacher. He was still only in his early twenties by this point. However, he was commissioned to design the illustrations for a new book by the man-midwife Dr John Burton, who had worked at York Hospital. The illustrations for Burton's *An Essay Towards a Complete New System of Midwifery, Theoretical and Practical* published in 1751 are technically crude (see p. 56, fig. 16). Stubbs had not been trained in printmaking; having picked up the basics of etching from a house painter at Leeds, he nonetheless lacked the proper tools for the task. Instead of a professional etching tool, he reputedly used a domestic sewing needle stuck into the handle of a skewer. With this makeshift tool he scratched away at wax-coated metal plates, so that when they were plunged into acid the lines he had drawn would be etched into their surface. To strengthen the design, he engraved directly into the plate, now using sharp tools borrowed from a local clockmaker.

These are the earliest dated works by Stubbs; the point to highlight here is that while they show an artist engaging very directly in contemporary scientific enquiry, they remind us also of the dark, even gruesome, side of eighteenth-century science; and also the controversial and commercial aspects of scientific publication. The growth of male midwives has been seen as an attempt to assert a professional, paid, male presence in the field of human reproduction, previously an exclusively female arena. If they were not now associated with the name of Stubbs, the small and technically awkward plates for Burton's *Essay* would certainly be more readily and accurately dismissed as hasty products of the highly commercialized (and potentially exploitative) world of eighteenth-century medicine, rather than as the penetrating insights into natural form which they are now occasionally described as being.

In 1751 or 1752, Stubbs moved again, this time to Hull, "always practising Portrait Painting and dissection."[3] Then, in 1754, Stubbs went briefly to Italy. A period in Italy was emerging as crucial for the more ambitious kinds of artists, both for the art training which could be acquired there and perhaps still more importantly for the chance to network among the aristocratic Grand Tourists who frequented Italy, and particularly Rome. There were, at this time, examples of the transformative effect an Italian trip had had on an artist's career, most spectacularly with the case of Reynolds. The latter left England in 1749 as a promising young portrait painter with mainly provincial connections, but returned from Italy in 1752 with an influential network of artists and patrons, and his mind full of new ideas which helped set the tone for British art for the next thirty years. Stubbs was part of a generation of British artists which included, besides Reynolds, the sculptor Joseph Wilton, the architect William Chambers and the landscape painter Richard Wilson, who all went to Italy around this time and who went on to play leading roles in the rapidly developing British art world. But whereas these other men focused their ambitions on the new Royal Academy of Arts, eventually founded in London in 1768, Stubbs long kept his distance from that élitist institution, associating himself instead with the more democratic Society of Artists until as late as 1780.

The Royal Academy and the artists associated with it promoted an idealistic version of art, one rooted in antique values and the visual and theoretical traditions of seventeenth-century French and Italian art. The experience of travelling to Italy and copying the exemplars of art was meant to be the foundation for the high-minded elevation of the aspiring artist. But Stubbs's first biographer makes a point of stating that "whilst he resided in Rome he [n]ever Copied one picture or even design'd one subject for an Historical Composition; nor did he make one drawing or model from the antique".[4] Successive commentators have concluded that this simply could not have been the case, and that he must have studied classical sculpture with some attention. The treatment of the "Horse and Lion" theme, which Stubbs addressed from 1762 through a series of paintings, prints and in Wedgwood pottery, undoubtedly refers in some fashion to the near life-size antique group of the *Lion and Horse* which was on view at the Palazzo dei Conservatori when he was in Rome, although this group was also popular as a reproduction among Grand Tourists and Stubbs could easily have come across a version of it back in England. But if that is a matter of rather technical art-historical dispute, it is more certain that Stubbs's travels did not transform his fortunes. As Francis Russell points out, he did not appear to make contact with his future patrons Lord Bolingbroke and the 3rd Duke of Grafton at that time, although they were on their Grand Tours. Their patronage only occurred a few years later. Instead, Stubbs spent the period after his time in Italy (1754–56) back in Liverpool, without making any significant advances in his career.

In 1756, however, when his prospects were really looking no better than they had been a decade before, he began the project that was to transform his reputation. Accompanied by Mary Spencer, his life-long companion, partner in art, and mother of his children, Stubbs retired to a barn in Lincolnshire. There, over a period of eighteen months, he dissected a succession of horses, working on each animal corpse for weeks, making detailed drawings and notes that would form the basis for a publication on the anatomy of the horse. He devised an elaborate system for preserving and suspending each body, which he described in some detail to Humphry:

> The first subject that he procured, was a horse that was bled to death by the jugular vein; after which the arteries & veins were injected. —A Bar of Iron was then suspended from the ceiling of the room by a Teagle to which Iron Hooks of various sizes & lengths were fixed. —Under this bar a plank was swung about 18 inches wide for the horses feet to rest upon and the animal was suspended to the Iron Bar by the above mentioned Hooks which were fastened into the opposite off side of the horse to that which was intended to be designed; by passing the Hooks thro' the Ribs & fastening them under the Back bone and by these means the Horse was fixed in the altitude to which these points represent & continued hanging in the posture six or seven lengths or as long as they were fit for use.[5]

With the horse suspended in position, Stubbs would proceed by "stripping off the skin & cleaning & preparing as much of the subject as he concluded would employ a whole day to prepare, design, & describe". Working through layers of muscles and discarding internal organs until he came to the bone, he would move around the body section by section until the whole animal was reduced to a skeleton. He would then proceed onto a new subject. Over the eighteen months Stubbs must have produced numerous drawings, perhaps hundreds: forty-two survive (cat. nos. 1–15).

This was a truly original project, as Werner Busch and Oliver Kase discuss in more detail in this catalogue. The only real equivalent was Carlo Ruini's horse anatomy of 1598 which was illustrated with relatively schematic woodcut prints. This had been frequently plagiarized and hardly rivalled by the numerous veterinarian tracts of a more modest nature produced in the eighteenth century. With his *Anatomy of the Horse* Stubbs introduced into animal anatomy an intensive technical care found only in human anatomy. As well as original, this was, in truth, a rather bizarre and certainly a rather dangerous undertaking. In an era before effective disinfectants, anatomists often fell prey to diseases which could prove fatal. But he hoped that this would make his reputation; he brought the drawings to London in 1758 or 1759, and when professional engravers refused to undertake such a complex project, engraved the drawings himself, finally publishing the *Anatomy of the Horse* to great acclaim in 1766.

"MR STUBBS, THE HORSE PAINTER"

Stubbs must have calculated that the time was right for this move into the specialized field of depicting horses. The market for horse painting was ready to be exploited. The genre appeared to be at a low point, with the Swiss artist André Rouquet in 1755 lamenting the poor standards in the art: "As soon as a race horse has acquired some fame, they have him immediately drawn to the life: this for the most part is a dry profile, but in other respects bearing a good resemblance; they generally clap the figure of some jockey or other

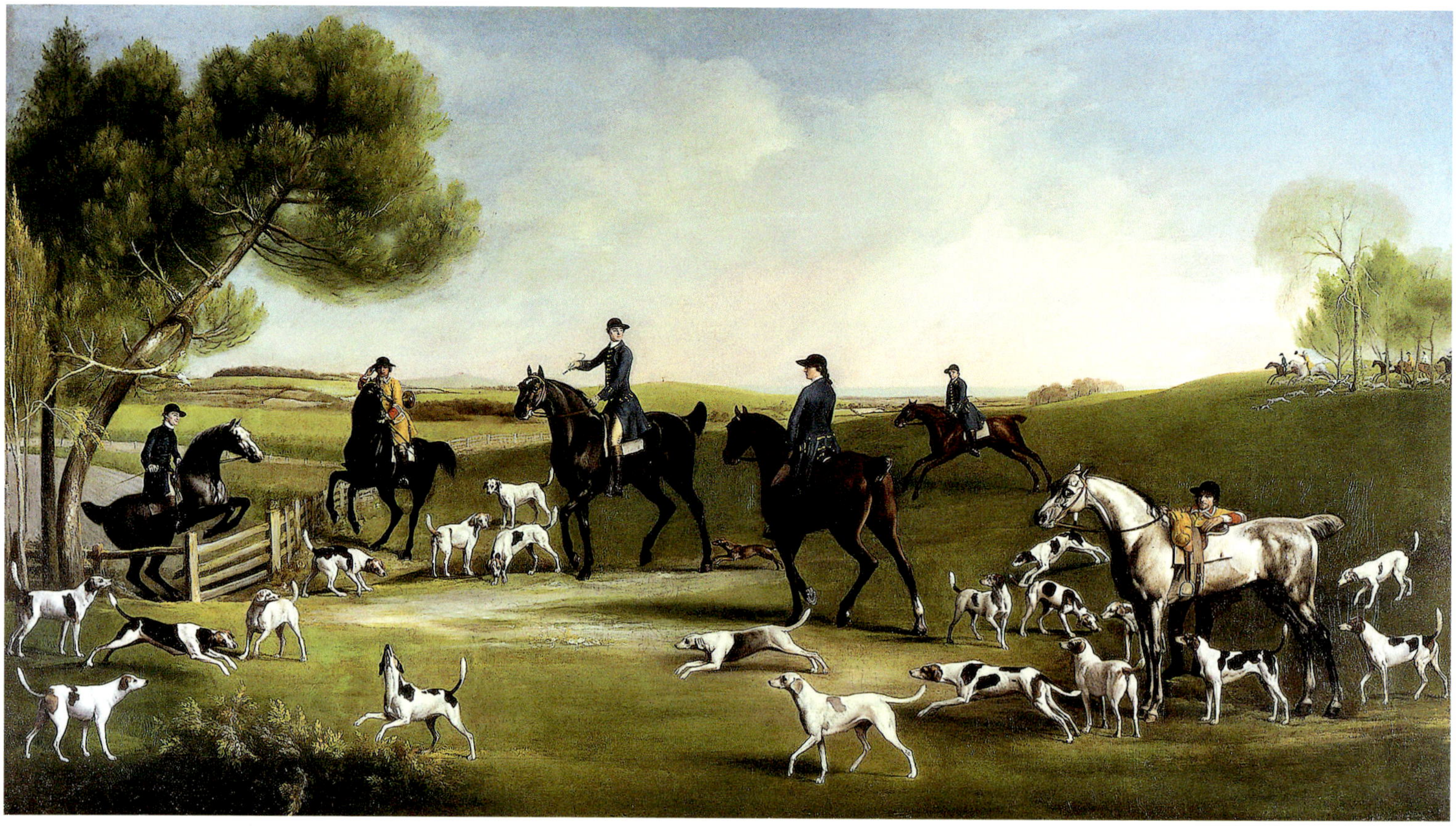

1 George Stubbs, *The 3rd Duke of Richmond with the Charlton Hunt*, c. 1759, oil on canvas, 139.5 x 247.5 cm
Trustees of the Goodwood Collection, Goodwood House, West Sussex

upon his back, which is but poorly done."[6] Among the leading practitioners of sporting art, John Wootton (?1682–1764) had given up sporting art to focus on landscape painting, and James Seymour (?1702–1752) had died a few years previously. The field was relatively clear and with his long and unusual experience of anatomical studies Stubbs was able to bring new and distinctive skills to the art of painting sporting pictures.

With his technical precision and intellectual ambition amply demonstrated by the drawn studies of the *Anatomy*, Stubbs was able swiftly to acquire well-born patrons who were, arguably, looking for something new in the painting of sporting life. In 1759 he was commissioned to produce three large canvases of sporting scenes for Charles Lennox, 3rd Duke of Richmond (figs. 1–2). Still only in his twenties, the Duke had studied at the progressive university at Leyden, been on his Grand Tour (in 1755), was a member of the scientific Royal Society, and had opened his gallery of casts after classical sculpture in London to art students. He was part of a more youthful generation of art patrons who were turning away from the collecting of standard Old Masters towards the promotion of the nascent "British School" of art. Further significant patrons appeared in the persons of the 3rd Duke of Grafton, Lord Spencer, Lord Bolingbroke and Lord Rockingham, among others. As Francis Russell discusses in this catalogue, these men enjoyed close (sometimes intimate) personal, family and political links, being all landowners and members of the Whig political opposition; they were also patrons of Joshua Reynolds, who may well have played a pivotal role in establishing Stubbs's reputation. As a wider context for their patronage of an emerging British artist we could also consider Britain's involvement

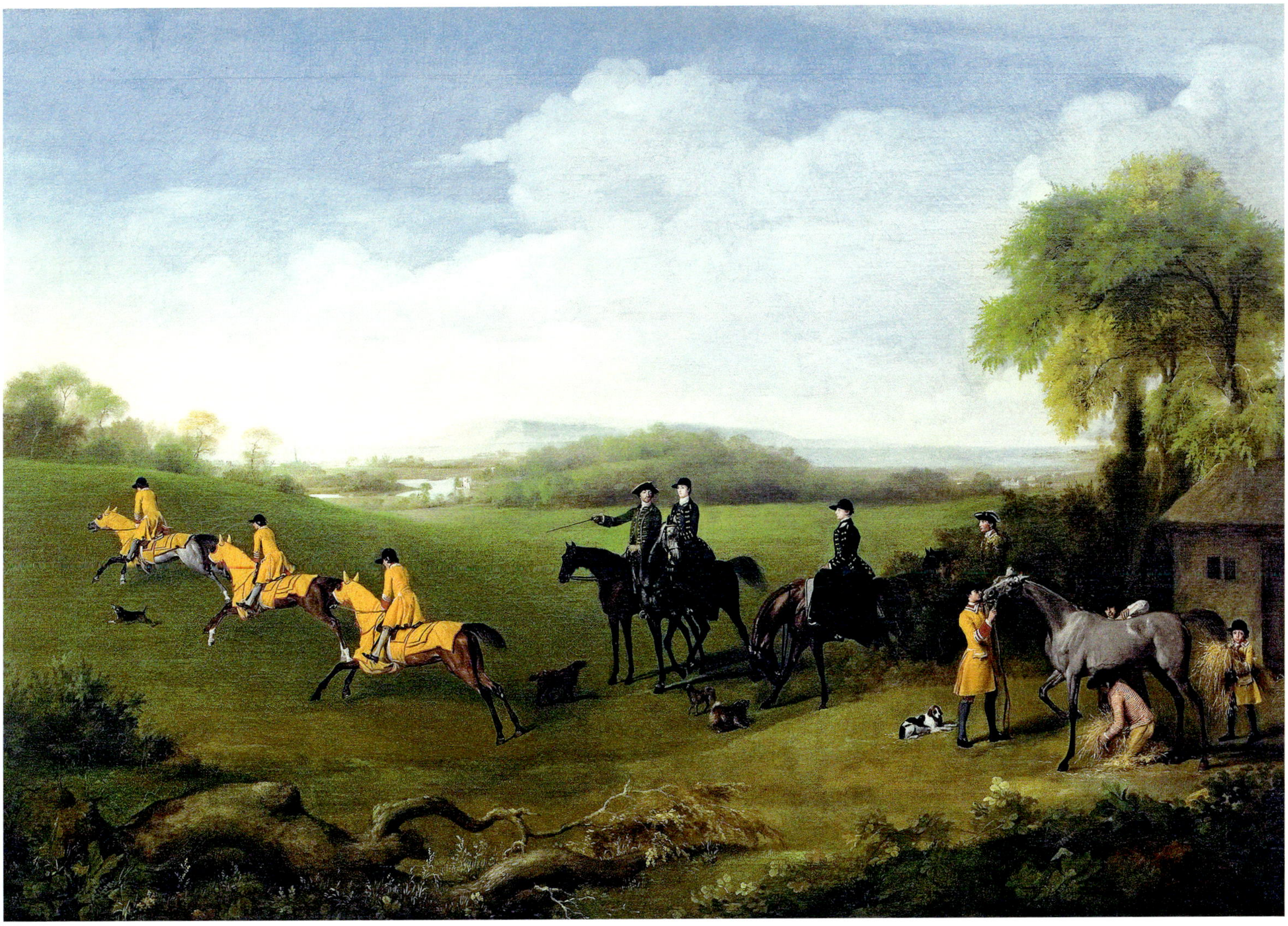

2 George Stubbs, *The Duchess of Richmond and Lady Louisa Lennox Watching Racehorses in Training at Goodwood*, c. 1760, oil on canvas, 139.5 x 204.5 cm
Trustees of the Goodwood Collection, Goodwood House, West Sussex

in the Seven Years' War (1756–63) and the upsurge of national pride and expectation over the course of the conflict.

Through the 1760s Stubbs became preoccupied with sporting pictures. He worked mainly for this tightly-knit sporting fraternity made up of aristocratic landowners, but encompassing also some of the self-made men of the racecourse such as William Wildman, a Smithfield meat trader who had risen to fame and fortune through his investments in racing. Wildman was the initial owner of Gimcrack, selling the horse to Viscount Bolingbroke before its victory at Newmarket. When Gimcrack won a further victory at Newmarket in July 1765, Stubbs was again asked to produce a painting to commemorate the event, this time for Viscount Bolingbroke, who either shared ownership with Wildman or had taken it over. This time, Stubbs created a more elaborate image, with Gimcrack being rubbed down while the race he has just won is played out, simultaneously, on the right hand side of the canvas (fig. 3). This is the painting that sold for a record-breaking price in 2011. When Gimcrack changed hands again, and was sold to Lord Grosvenor, the image was reproduced as an exact replica for this patron (now in the Jockey Club).

This is a very literal instance of Stubbs repeating himself by creating a replica of his own picture. There are further instances of Stubbs producing multiple versions of the same image, sometimes

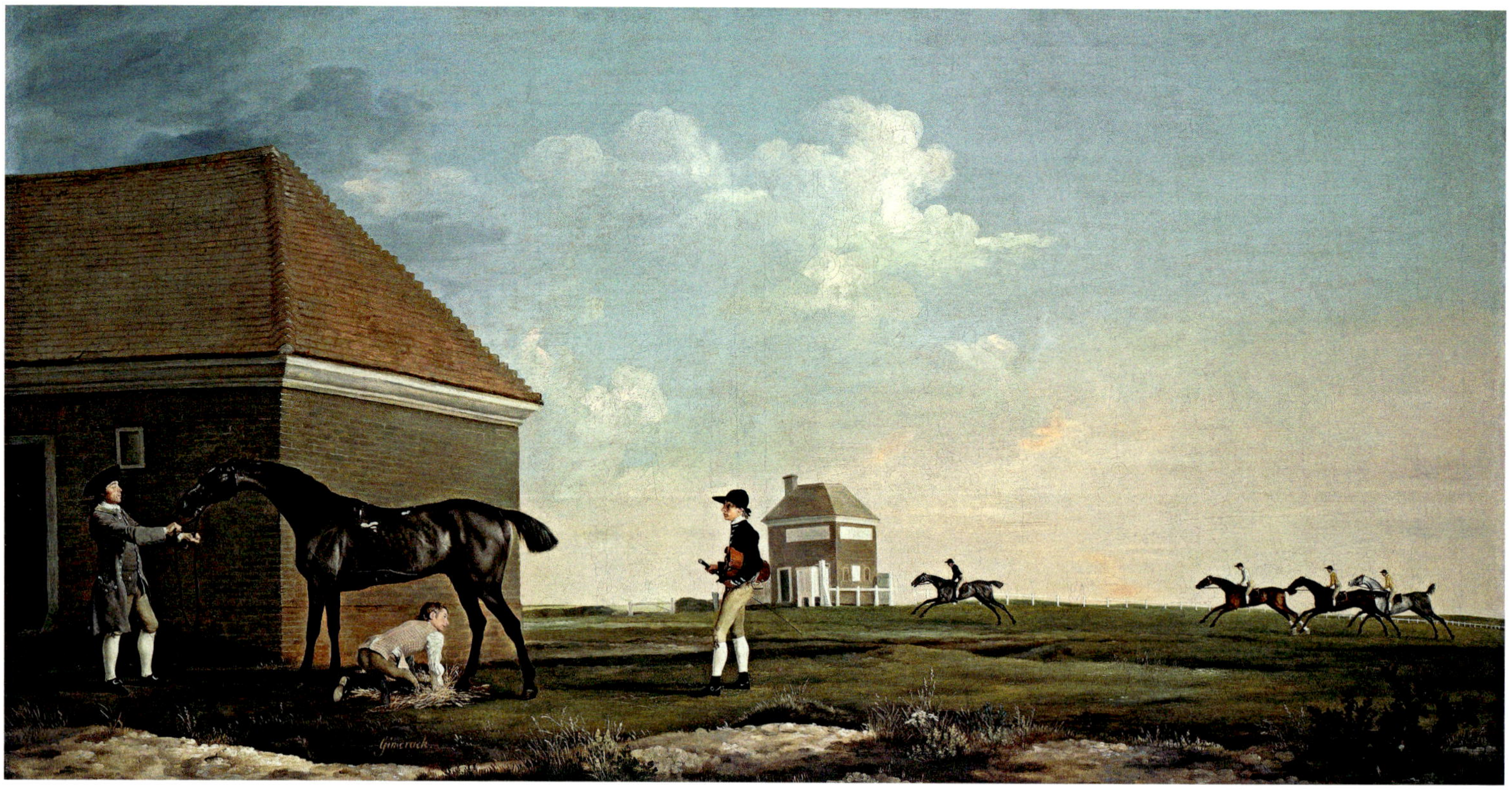

3 George Stubbs, *Gimcrack on Newmarket Heath*, c. 1765, oil on canvas, 101.6 x 193.2 cm
Private collection

for reasons which remain unclear. But it is true, also, that the artist worked with a relatively limited number of pictorial formulae, which he applied time and time again, albeit with subtly important adjustments. The recurrence of the Rubbing-down House at Newmarket in numerous sporting pictures, including three in this exhibition, is one visible sign of the painter repeating himself, in compositions which were designed to serve a very similar purpose for very similar patrons. What Stubbs produced, whether it was for an entrepreneur like Wildman or the horse owners of inherited fortunes like Bolingbroke, was an image of the racecourse as a place of almost chilling calm. We know from written accounts of horse races of the time, and other sporting pictures, that this is far removed from the realities of the racecourse. These were crowded, dirty, noisy places, where people from across the social classes mixed and gambled and played (fig. 4). Much of the appeal of horse-racing seems to have been the social liberties it provided: gentlemen could parade their mistresses openly, fritter their money away, and watch and bet on boxing matches and cock-fights. The normal rules that divided adult from childish behaviour, the wealthy from the worker were, if only temporarily and partly, dissolved in a maelstrom of rough activity. Pierre-Jean Grosley, who was in England for a few weeks in 1765 but still managed to publish a three-volume account of the country, reported that: "Many gentlemen of fortune ruin themselves by these pleasures … I saw, with the utmost astonishment, how greatly the spectators of all ranks seem to interest themselves in Cock-fights, which, after all, are no more than children's play … There are neither lists nor barriers at these races: the horses run in the midst of the crowd, who leave only a space sufficient for them to pass through; at the same time, encouraging them by gestures and loud shouts. The victor, when he has arrived at the goal, finds it a difficult matter to disengage himself from the crowd, who congratulate, caress, and embrace him, with an effusion of heart, which it is not easy to form an idea of, without having seen it."[7] Earlier in the century, Daniel Defoe had noted the "great concourse of nobility and gentry" that gathered at Newmarket for the races, but also reported that "they were all so intent, so eager, so busy upon the sharping part of the sport, their wagers and bets, that to me they seemed just as so many horse-coursers in Smithfield, descending (the greatest of them) from their high dignity and quality, to picking one another's pockets."[8] So the racecourse was something of a topsy-turvy world, where the rich acted like wide-boys or played like children, and the poor had an uncommonly good time. The eighteenth-century racecourse was a site of what the influential cultural theorist Mikhail Bakhtin termed "the carnivalesque", where social norms were suspended and the world, at least briefly, turned upside down.[9]

The defining quality of Stubbs's racing pictures could be said to be the complete absence of any hint of this "carnivalesque" disorder (see cat. nos. 23, 25, 26). The crowds are simply absent from the picture frame. His is an abstracted image of the racecourse, abstracted from the realities of the race as a social event, but abstracted also in its management of a limited repertoire of elements which are rearranged repeatedly into a series of 'new' compositions which all resemble one another. What we can trace across these canvases is not really the documentation or commemoration of individual races, or even particular horses, but a celebration of the power of art to project an image of order which seems to exist above and beyond specific circumstances. It was an image that his patrons, as a class, and encompassing (a few) of the self-made men of the racecourse as well as those with inherited wealth, could subscribe to.

In that sense, Stubbs's images participate in the ordering and regulation of racing itself that emerged in this period. By the middle of the eighteenth century there was increasing concern about the unruliness and social disruption of races. Laws were passed regulating gambling more closely, and around 1750 the aristocratic Jockey Club was established, as a self-elected regulatory body. They introduced a system of jockey's colours and authorized publications documenting race meetings and the genealogies of horses. The racecourse was being rationalized, at once providing increasing amounts of accurate information for the public at large, and re-affirming the authority of the aristocratic class. The race meeting might still be a rough and ready place on the day, but the principles for keeping the race itself in order were in place. With his paintings, Stubbs (many of whose patrons were members of the Jockey Club) was similarly putting his house in order. In his art, as in the printed records and rules of the races, horses were being ennobled and classified according to a highly formalized system.

Stubbs's images of the sporting world tread an uncertain line between rarefied aesthetic precision and descriptive bluntness. Depending on one's point of view, they are either exquisite renderings of natural beauty far elevated above the banal circumstances of their production, or merciless dissections of optical reality. It is quite possible, of course, to try to combine, or to waver between, these positions, and Stubbs's troubled position in art history, discussed more fully by Brian Allen in his essay in this catalogue, must suggest that this has been the case.

Quite aside from the art-historical questions that would be raised about Stubbs's art and the nature of his achievement long after his death, the artist faced more immediate challenges. This was a period of much greater formality in the art world. Stubbs's generation could only get art training by joining an artist's studio (at home or abroad); there was a drawing school in London but this was very informally run until the 1760s, when an effort, led by artists including Reynolds, sought royal patronage and stricter organization, the end result being the foundation of the Royal Academy in 1768. This was an institution which Stubbs (like Wright of Derby and Gainsborough) had a rather "semi-detached" relationship with, being made an Associate in 1780 and a full Royal Academician in 1782, but never submitting a painting to the Academy as the representative Diploma Work which would have formalized his membership. Stubbs's support of the rival Society of Artists up to that date has been read as the demonstration of a degree of antagonism towards the more élitist and rarefied aesthetic values promoted by the Academy.

4 John Nixon, *Brighton Races*, 1805, watercolour, 51.4 x 67.9 cm
New Haven, Yale Center for British Art, Paul Mellon Collection

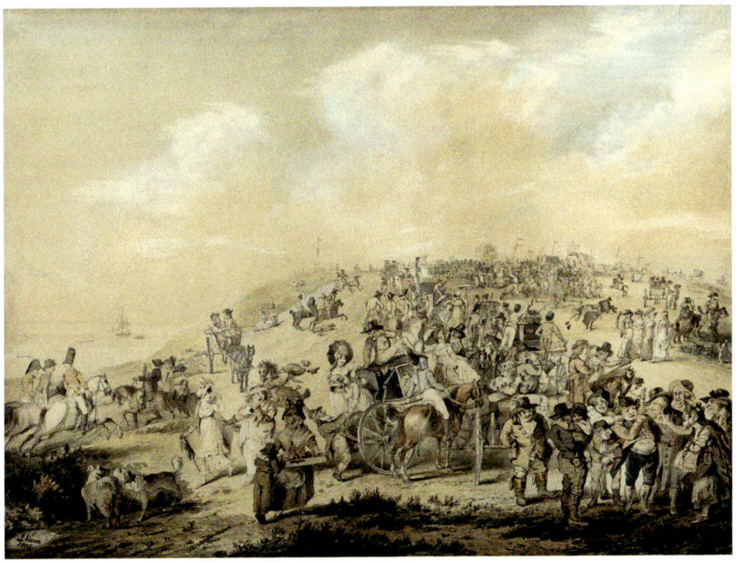

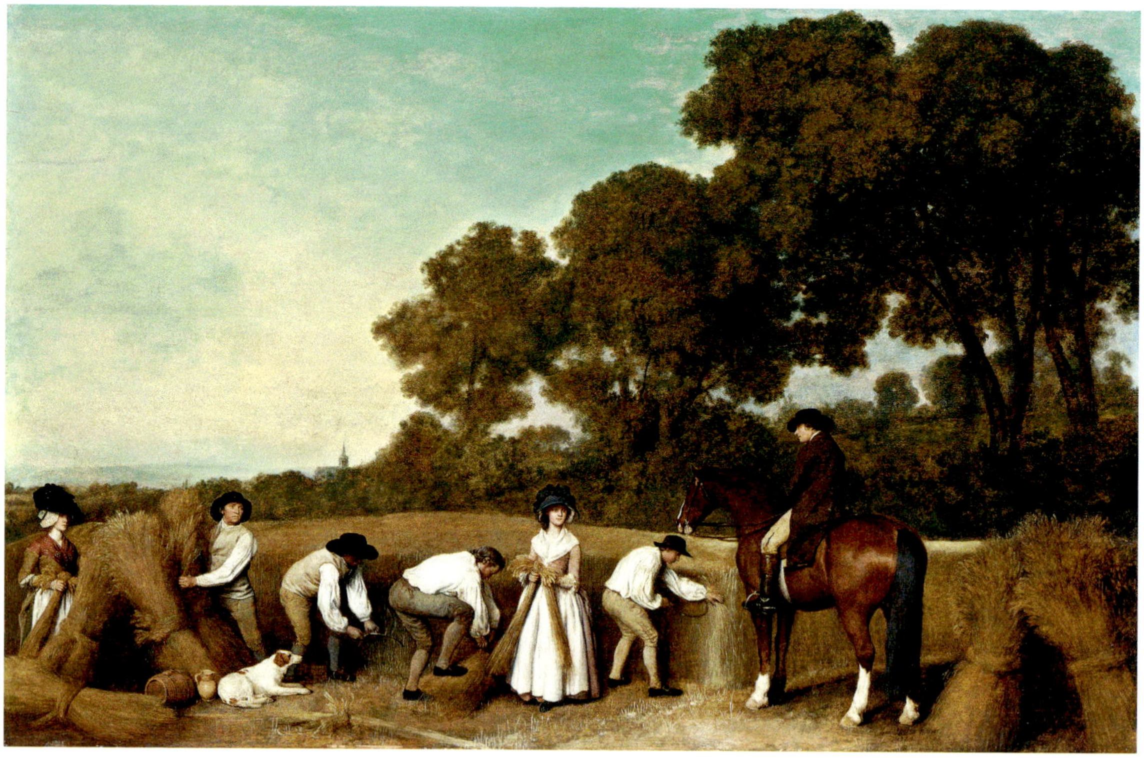

5 George Stubbs, *Haymakers*, 1785, oil on panel, 89.5 x 135.3 cm London, Tate

Nonetheless, we find Stubbs making some efforts to fit in with contemporary aesthetic demands, particularly as the patronage of the horse-owning Whigs began to decline through the 1760s. This was most apparent in the series of images of a horse being attacked and devoured by a lion. Starting with a huge canvas created for the Marquess of Rockingham in 1762, Stubbs created a series of paintings and prints depicting a violent encounter between a horse and a lion that stretched right through to the 1790s (cat. nos. 40–42). It was a series intended to appeal far beyond the little network of his sporting patrons, to an audience generated after 1760 by the new art exhibitions and the print market. With versions of the subject exhibited by Stubbs with the Society of Artists in 1763, 1764, 1768 and 1770, the publication of prints after his paintings, his design of a version of the theme for ceramic plaques created by Wedgwood and the subsequent incorporation of the motifs into decorative wares by manufacturers, the 'Lion and Horse' was the most enduringly popular of Stubbs's creations.

Such works also testify to Stubbs's awareness that horse painting, with its lowly history and supposed lack of intellectual content, was generally looked down upon. Within academic art theory, so resolutely revived by the creation of the Royal Academy in 1768, the painting of animals was the lowest rank of the arts. Accordingly, Stubbs tried repeatedly to become something other than a sporting artist, even painting a number of subjects from classical mythology. From among these, only versions of *Phaeton attempting to drive the Horses of the Sun* survive, in oil and in Wedgwood, but we know that he also painted and exhibited large oils of *Hercules and Achelous* (1770) and *Hercules Saving Dejanira from the Centaur Nessus* (1772), and a *Judgement of Hercules* which appeared in his studio sale. If these paintings had survived, we might be required to adjust our usual assumption that Stubbs absolutely eschewed the idealizing grand manner which was so strongly associated with the Royal Academy. The documentary evidence pointing towards the existence of such pictures must indicate that Stubbs was prepared to tackle the grand manner on occasion: meanwhile, the fact that so few pictures of this kind are recorded, must suggest that he considered these efforts unsuccessful in one way or another.

EXPANDING TECHNIQUE AND SUBJECT MATTER

Stubbs extended his repertoire in more obviously successful ways by establishing a reputation as the prime painter of exotic animal specimens. The arrival of new animals in the country was the occasion for tremendous public interest in the late eighteenth century. The first zebra arrived in England in 1762 and was put on show at

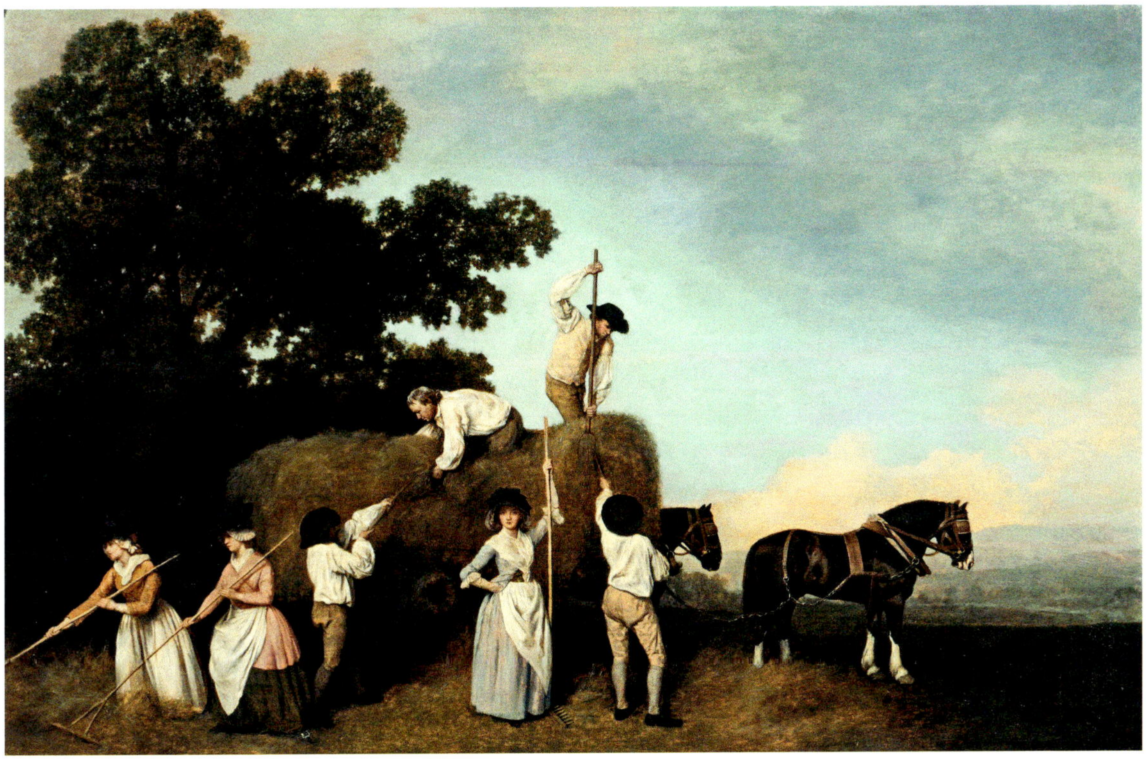

6 George Stubbs, *Reapers*, 1785, oil on panel, 89.9 x 136.8 cm London, Tate

Buckingham House before touring the country; Stubbs painted its picture and exhibited it at the Society of Artists (cat. no. 45). When the first moose arrived from Canada in 1770, the anatomist and physician William Hunter commissioned Stubbs to paint that as well to demonstrate the distinctness of this species from the extinct Irish elk (the antlers of which are introduced at the left of the canvas to make the point) (cat. no. 46). The thrill of the exotic stretched across and brought together the worlds of popular street shows, serious science, and the more trite kind of sportsman's entertainment parading as an experiment in natural history. Stubbs's art could operate equally in each context; removed from the context of their creation, each of these images can be admired in the same way, for their remarkable attention to the specificities of colour and texture and physical structure, their ability to monumentalize these creatures, and to create an evocative natural context for them. In each case Stubbs's ability to create an image of factuality, which disqualified him from consideration as a serious artist, is brought into service in the transformation of nature into a visual spectacle. The culture of Enlightenment, with its desire to identify, classify and reveal, was also a culture of commodification.

Stubbs also branched out into human portraiture, albeit with limited success, at least as far as one of his most important patrons in this regard, Josiah Wedgwood, was concerned. The association with Wedgwood arose through Stubbs's experiments in painting with enamel on Wedgwood-manufactured plaques. The artist repeated efforts to work with a more permanent medium than oil paint on a more secure surface than canvas, starting with enamel on copper (cat. no. 41) and expanding to experiments with painting on ceramic plaques (cat. no. 39). Although the individual paintings which resulted can be counted among the most brilliant and best-preserved by the artist, the process was hugely risky and never entirely satisfactory. Stubbs's forays into printmaking, and his use of print as a creative and original medium, are, as Timothy Clayton details in this catalogue, a further aspect of the artist's experimental outlook.

The most sustained effort to widen his skills came with the *Haymaker* and *Reaper* images. The pictures were his sole exhibits at the Royal Academy in 1786, the first of the artist's works to be shown with the institution since 1782 (figs. 5–6). He exhibited them again, at the exhibition held in Liverpool by the Society for Promoting Painting and Design in 1787, and in 1788 the artist announced that the subjects would be among a group of new prints he was planning to publish. These prints were eventually issued in 1791 (see cat. nos. 62–63), and in 1794–95 he repeated the subjects in three oval enamel paintings (*Haymakers* and *Haycarting* in the Lady Lever Art Gallery, Liverpool, and *Reapers* in the Yale Center for British Art, New Haven). With the *Haymakers* and *Reapers* Stubbs was hoping to address the wider audience for art that was developing in these years. Prints of rural scenes, very often using the soft tonalities available with stipple engraving (the technique used for Stubbs's 1791 reproductions of these pictures) always sold well. What is important to note is that these exhibitions and prints were primarily aimed at an urban audience. These rural images offered them a mythical, idealized vision of the countryside as the location of sure and timeless values and an assurance of the heartiness of country living.

But where mainstream images of rural labour tended to stress something of the raggedness of the workers, offering their ragged clothes as both a confirmation of the "naturalness" of the scene, and for their "picturesque" interest, Stubbs's labourers are strikingly clean and tidy. The men wear buckled shoes and breeches that would have proved uncomfortable to bend down in, and the women are fashionably dressed. We know from contemporary accounts that farm labourers might be better dressed than we would anticipate, and that women who worked seasonally might come on to the land in the costumes they would normally wear for their other work, for instance in service, which would have required a degree of smartness. But even so, Stubbs's workers have a cleanliness that is improbable given the work they are undertaking, and which certainly does not provide for the sentimental response from city-dwellers that such imagery was meant to elicit.

They are, instead, organized into almost mechanical rhythms. In the *Haymakers* the workers are organized into a tidy pyramid, each figure taking up a role in a neat sequence of events; in the *Reapers*, they are choreographed into a gently undulating wave of activity, with the church spire, and the mounted farm overseer, and the row of towering, ancient-looking oaks, combining to establish the presence of the economic, religious and temporal authorities that ruled over their lives. Both pictures contrive an image of strict order, perhaps too strict and unreal for contemporary tastes. Stubbs may have calculated that in a time of rising rural problems, his urban audience would have wanted to know that agricultural labourers were sternly disciplined. If so, he miscalculated.

The original exhibition of the *Haymakers* and *Reapers* in 1786 drew a great deal of criticism. The critic of *The Morning Post* (6 May 1786) had the quite opposite opinion: "In horses this artist stands unrivalled; as to his reapers, no injury would have been done to his fame, had they been entirely omitted. How difficult to persuade a man to pursue his forte". While the critic of *The Daily Universal Register* (17 May 1786) praised the artist for "returning to his associated brethren, and conquering his resentments" by choosing to exhibit at the Academy after several years, he also noted that "Animals are the forte of this master; undoubtedly the figures want taste in their disposition, and the arrangement has too Gothic an appearance". "Gothic" here means an antiquated formality, associated with what we would characterize as pre-Renaissance and Early Renaissance art, but is also employed more generally to conjure associations with a dry precision that resulted in a formal awkwardness which fell outside academic aesthetic regulations whose proclaimed aim was a more poetic breadth reflecting the intellect of the painter. The 'Gothic' artifice of these scenes meant that if these subjects were an attempt to address a market, they failed.

The criticisms of the *Haymakers* and *Reapers* in Stubbs's own day show that the public and art patrons were simply unwilling to consider Stubbs as anything other than as a painter of sporting life. As Brian Allen discusses in the catalogue, Stubbs's identity as 'only' a painter of horses has dogged his art-historical reputation even in later centuries. But the other criticism contained here, that Stubbs's paintings appeared unnatural, may be harder to understand. However, such accusations towards the artist did appear during that period. For instance, a newspaper reviewer responding to a Stubbs painting of cattle exhibited in 1768 similarly complained that he thought the picture showed "unnatural, cold and clayey scenes".[10] It is tempting to overlook such comments or to dismiss them as simply prejudiced or ignorant. But what we are reminded of here, is that there is no universal standard of "naturalism" in art, either now or, certainly, in the eighteenth century. For critics and commentators who adhered to a more academic definition of painterly realism, one which required natural forms to be refined and idealized to fit timeless ideals of perfection, Stubbs's attention to surface details, to texture and the effects of light, would make his paintings seem "unnatural", even ugly and distracting.

DECLINE

So although Stubbs received patronage from the élite, and critical acclaim in many quarters, there were doubts about the nature of his art and the limitations of the genre he was most strongly identified with—sporting painting. The critics and the public repeatedly showed themselves to be unwilling to consider Stubbs as anything other than "only" a painter of horses and dogs.

Given the tendency to see Stubbs as an heroic proponent of Enlightenment naturalism, defying convention and the need to make money, it is a little surprising to find him deeply involved in a commercial art project later in his life. This was the 'Turf Gallery', initiated in 1790. The research of David Oldrey, communicated by Judy Egerton, has identified the prime movers behind the project as the principal heirs of Colonel Denis O'Kelly (the owner of the famous horse Eclipse).[11] The intention was that the gallery would display paintings by Stubbs of famous horses, attracting subscrip-

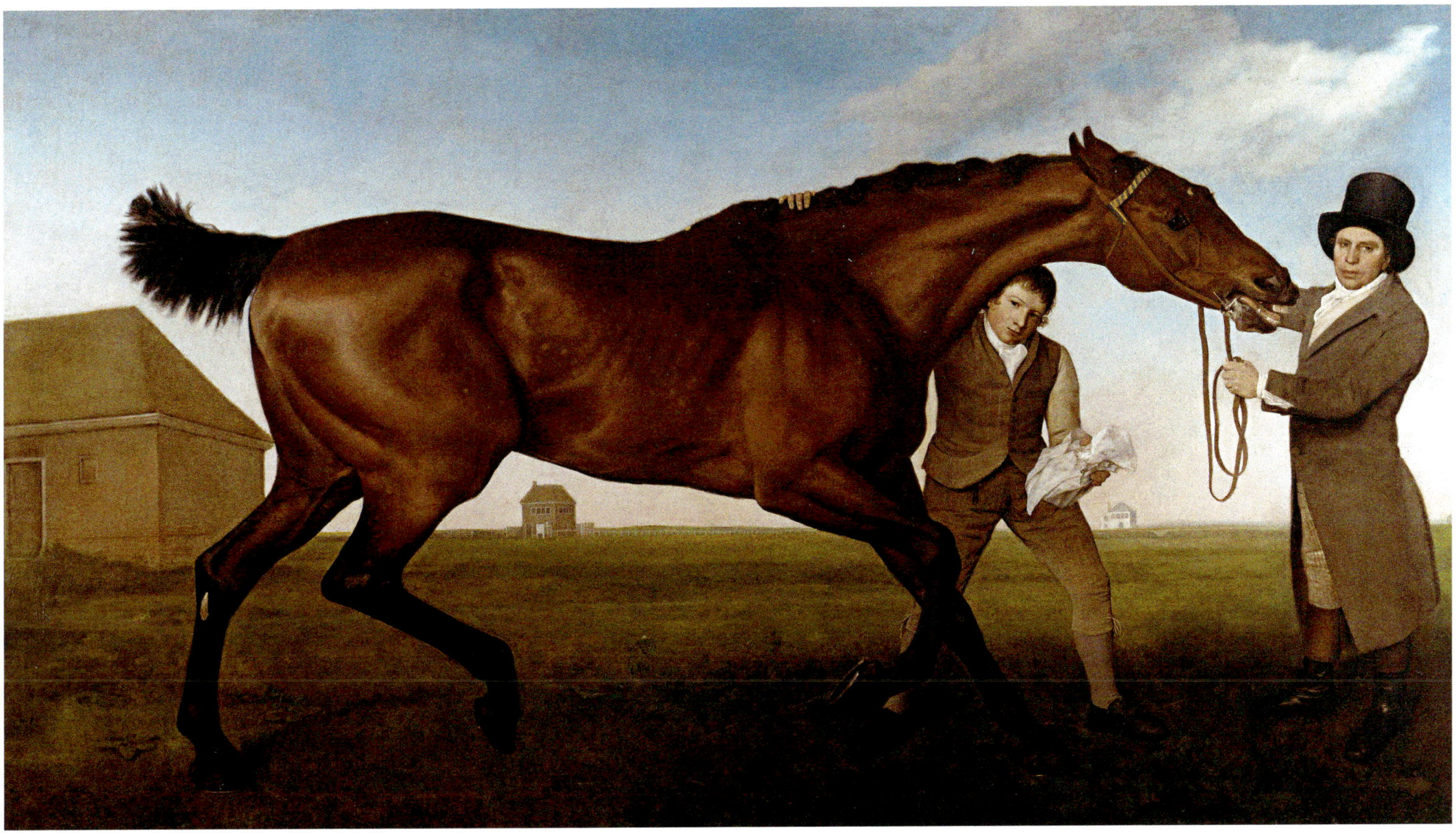

7 George Stubbs, *Hambletonian, Rubbing Down*, 1800, oil on canvas, 209 x 367 cm
Mount Stewart House and Garden, County Down, Northern Ireland (The National Trust)

tions for a series of prints of those paintings by Stubbs's son, George Townley Stubbs: the original aim was that the series would stretch to 145 separate images, accompanied by a text describing the history of horse-racing. The project was a preoccupation for Stubbs during the early 1790s. He failed to exhibit at the Royal Academy from 1791 through to 1799, so when the Turf Gallery finally opened in Conduit Street in 1794 the *Sporting Magazine* welcomed the exhibition as an opportunity finally to see his works again. There had been a number of comparable projects over recent years. Most significant were the various galleries of paintings on patriotic literary and historical themes set up at the end of the 1780s by the publishers John Boydell, Robert Bowyer and Thomas Macklin, which were similarly meant to create interest for the sale of prints reproducing pictures on show there. Although the gallery was warmly welcomed and extensively covered by the *Sporting Magazine*, it does not seem to have gathered much wider interest. It closed in 1798, with only a handful of the proposed prints published. The explanation offered by Humphry's *Memoir* was that the current war with France had made the export of prints impossible and the scheme unworkable. But there may be an indication here, too, of the commercial limitations of sporting art. While enthusiasts for the racecourse may have taken an interest in these images, it is not clear that there was a larger market of people with more general tastes to support such an ambitious project.

In the first modern biographical account of Stubbs, by Joseph Mayer (1876), it was remarked that it was solely by the presence of his name on prints found in "old country inns of Yorkshire" that he was remembered, if at all. Art critics, according to Mayer, knew of his reputation only as "a man who painted racehorses".[12] Stubbs was, arguably, never able to escape the sporting world. In 1799 the young and rakish Sir Henry Vane-Tempest commissioned Stubbs to paint his horse, which had won a race for him at Newmarket

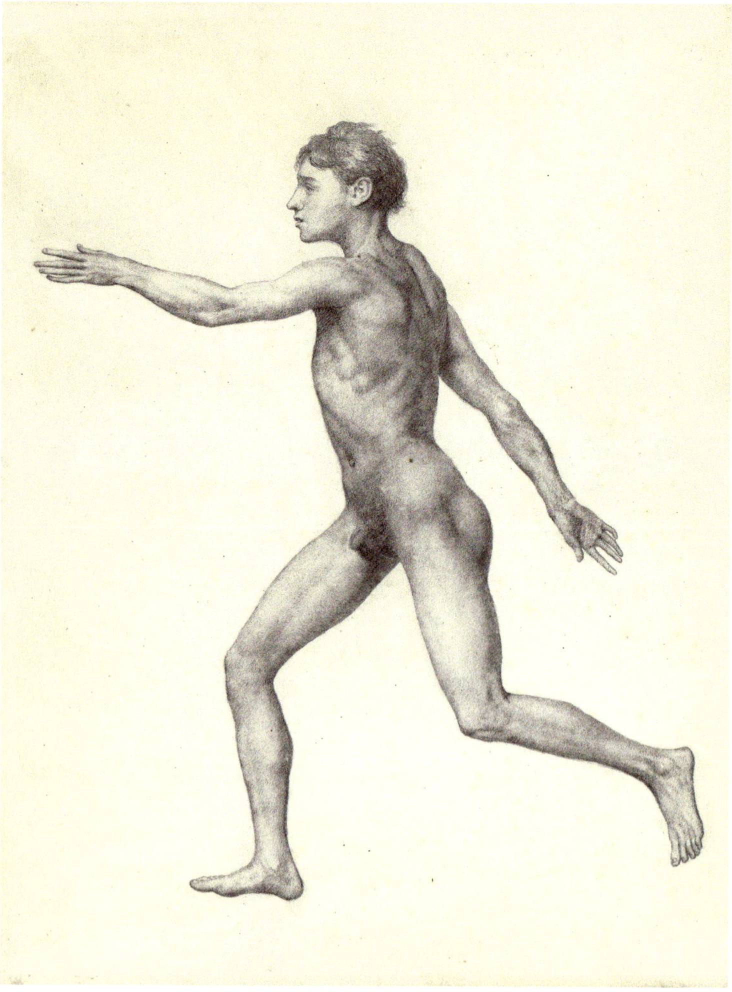

8 George Stubbs, *A Comparative Anatomical Exposition of the Human Body with that of a Tiger and a Common Fowl,* 1795–1806, Human Figure, lateral view, graphite, 54.6 x 40.6 cm
New Haven, Yale Center for British Art, Paul Mellon Collection

9 George Stubbs, *A Comparative Anatomical Exposition of the Human Body with that of a Tiger and a Common Fowl,* 1795–1806, Human Skeleton in Crawling Posture, Finished Study, 44.8 x 27.9 cm
New Haven, Yale Center for British Art, Paul Mellon Collection

10 George Stubbs, *A Comparative Anatomical Exposition of the Human Body with that of a Tiger and a Common Fowl,* 1795–1806, Tiger Skeleton, Finished Study, 28.3 x 41.6 cm
New Haven, Yale Center for British Art, Paul Mellon Collection

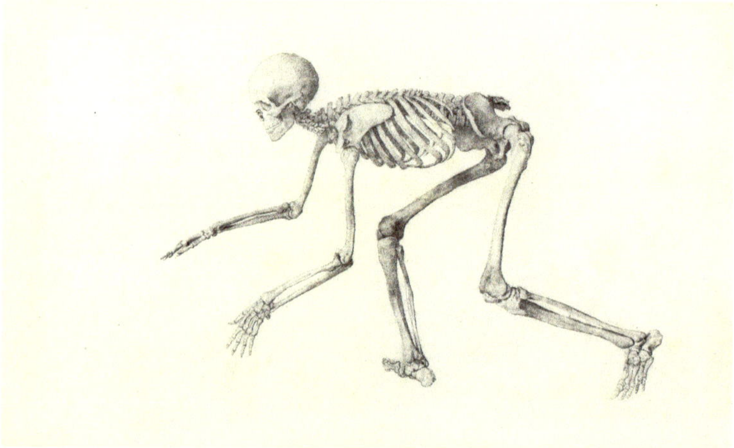

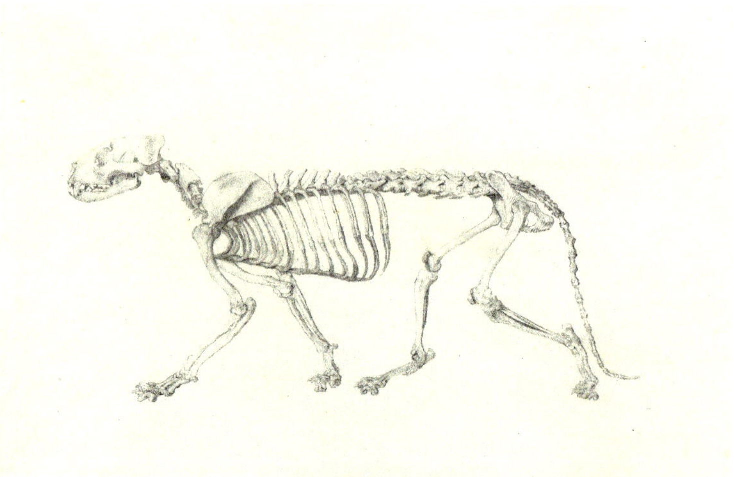

in March against Joseph Cookson's Diamond for a huge wager. According to contemporary reports, the race was vicious, with both horses being whipped and goaded until they bled. Hambletonian won by just half a neck. The resulting, vast painting was exhibited at the Royal Academy, but was not well received (fig. 7). Certainly, the work drew little comment in the press, the *Morning Herald* noting, unusually for this artist, that the human figures were better conceived than the horse which is "calculated to give but a very slender idea of the superior swiftness of his speed". For reasons still unknown, Vane-Tempest refused to pay the price demanded by Stubbs. The case went to court, with George Garrard, Ozias Humphry and the portrait painter Thomas Lawrence presenting evidence on Stubbs's side while John Opie and John Hoppner were "very violent against the claim."[13] While Stubbs won his case, the affair may have damaged his professional reputation, Farington noting shortly afterwards that when he was asked by a potential patron who might be suitable to paint his horse "I recommended Garrard, as I concluded Stubbs wd. be too expensive."[14]

Stubbs's last great project was the series of drawings of dissected tigers, chickens and humans that would provide the basis of the engravings illustrating a huge work of comparative anatomy, "shewing the analogy between the Human frame, the Quadruped and the fowl, giving also an accurate description of the bones, cartilages, muscles, fascias, ligaments &c &c (which he intended to have carried on to the vegetable world)."[15] Over 120 drawings and four volumes of text (two in French) survive, revealing the gigantic scale of the publication he had in mind. The human, the tiger and the chicken are shown in closely comparable positions, from the front, from the side and from behind, with their skin, stripped of their skin and reduced to a skeleton. Quite how the project would have been extended to "the vegetable world" remains unclear.

Stubbs died in July 1806 without seeing the *Comparative Anatomy* published in full. His last words, according to Humphry, were "I fear not death, I have no particular wish to live. I had indeed hoped to have finished my Comparative Anatomy eer I went, but for other things I have no anxiety."[16] A professional artist for some sixty years, he still appears to have been substantially in debt at his death, in particular to Lady Isabella Saltonstall. The monies raised by the sale of his works had to go to her, and the diarist Joseph Farington noted that "It is understood that after Her debt is paid there will be little left."[17] This may be taken as evidence of personal disinterest, of how Stubbs dedicated himself to his art regardless of the question of making money. But it is more likely an indication of how the painter struggled to match his skills and interests to a complex and changing marketplace. In the sale of Stubbs's studio contents the enamels and pictures of exotics sold well, but the more mainstream Turf Gallery portraits of horses sold badly, and the prints, which should have served the artist commercially, attracted little interest.

The *Comparative Anatomy* should have been Stubbs's great, final artistic monument. But the publication of the prints went largely unnoticed. The idea of examining comparatively the anatomies of men and animals was very current, but he was by this date an isolated figure and the images remain, today, strange and disconcerting. Like Stubbs's art as a whole, they can certainly be explained as expressions of a singular artistic vision. His illustrations propose a complete fusion of the aesthetic and the scientific. Each figure in the *Comparative Anatomy* is animated, as if alive, lit and posed not just as an object of study, but as an object of beauty (figs. 8–10). Viewed in historical perspective, this may be a final monument to the Enlightenment belief in the power of visual experience to persuade us of truth. The limits of Stubbs's commercial success, and the questions raised about his reputation as an artist in his lifetime and since, may, however, indicate something more complex: a mismatch between his personal artistic ideals, artistic realities, and the intellectual and aesthetic requirements of, variously, his patrons, the ordinary consumers of culture, and competing professional groups. Given the pristine character of Stubbs's paintings, it may seem simply wilful or perverse to point to the "failure" of his art. But it is the "failure" of his art, its strangeness and, from some perspectives, incoherence, which has ensured that it has endured and continues to fascinate.

1 Egerton, *George Stubbs*, 2007, pp. 97 f.
2 For the history of Ozias Humphry's *Memoir* of George Stubbs, which was based on conversations with the artist in the latter part of his life, see Egerton, *George Stubbs* 2007, p. 10. The text used here is the edited version, published in Exhib. Cat. *Fearful Symmetry*, 2000, pp. 195–212 (p. 201 quoted).
3 Ibid., p. 202.
4 Ibid., p. 202.
5 Ibid., p. 211.
6 André Rouquet, *The Present State of the Arts in England*, London 1755, p. 58.
7 Pierre-Jean Grosley, *A Tour to London*, trans. Thomas Nugent, 2 vols., London 1772, vols. 2, pp. 156-8.
8 Daniel Defoe, *A Tour Through the Whole Island of Great Britain*, Harmondsworth 1971, p. 98.
9 For the application of Bakhtin's notion of "carnival" to eighteenth-century Britain, see Peter Stallybrass and Allon White, *The Politics and Poetics of Transgression*, London 1986.
10 Quoted in Egerton, *George Stubbs*, 2007, no. 107.
11 Ibid., p. 547.
12 Joseph Mayer, *Early Exhibitions of Art in Liverpool with Some Notes for a Memoir of George Stubbs*, Liverpool 1876, p. 93.
13 Kenneth Garlick et al. (eds.), *The Diary of Joseph Farington*, 17 vols., New Haven and London 1978–98, vol. 4, p. 1536.
14 Ibid., vol. 4, p. 1574.
15 Quote in Exhib. Cat. *Fearful Symmetry*, 2000, p. 207.
16 Ibid., p. 208.
17 *The Diary of Joseph Farington* (see note 13), vol. 8, p. 3056.

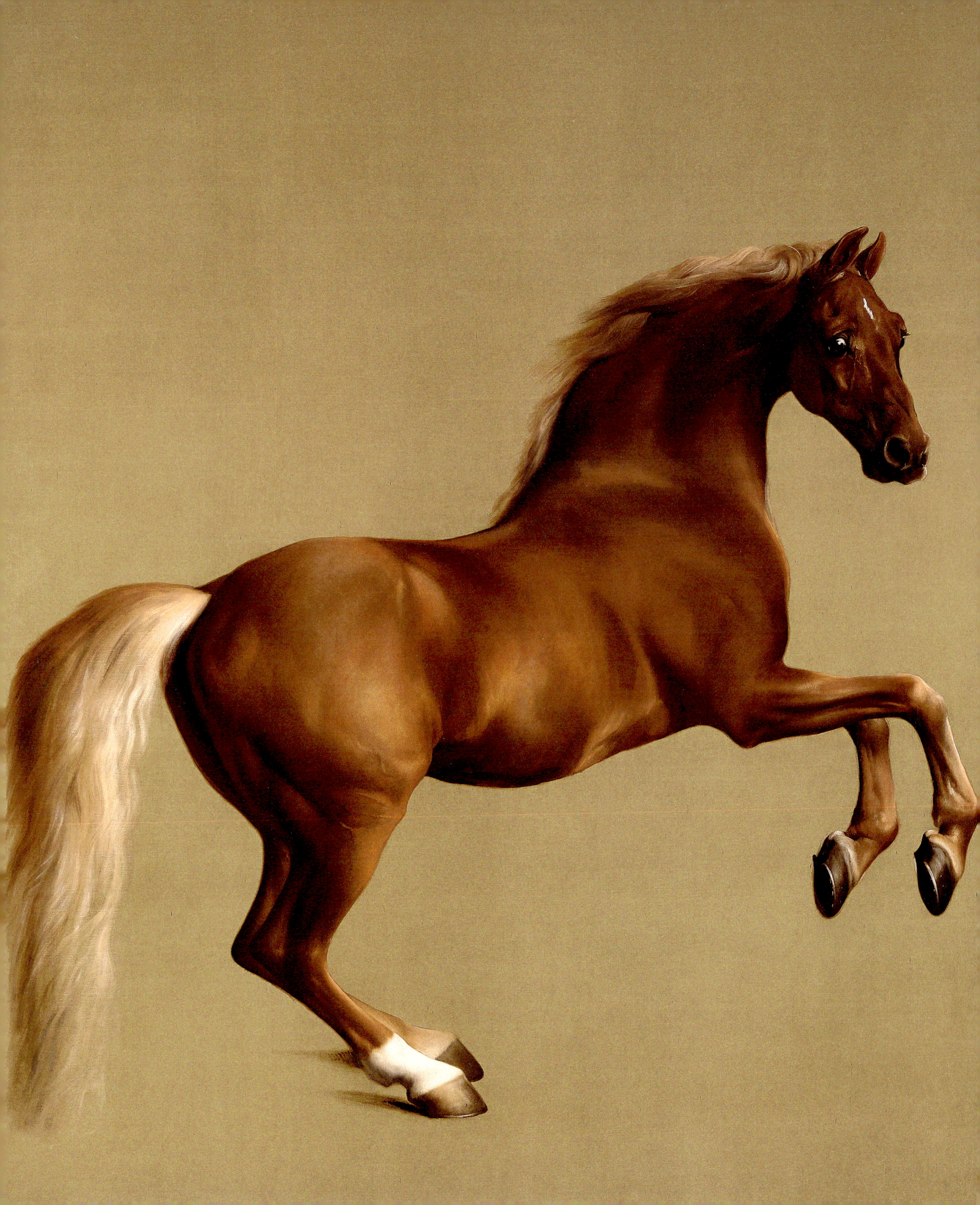

Werner Busch

STUBBS'S AESTHETICS

Aesthetics? Can it ever be meaningful to talk about aesthetics when speaking about an artist who is held to be little more than a painter of horses; a painter who reproduced things exactly as they appeared, guaranteeing their scientific value in doing so? When confronted with his paintings is not our impression rather that they are just an agglomeration of precise observations; that they are a mere catalogue of juxtapositions? Why ask about aesthetics anyway? Can that which has simply been documented have an aesthetic at all?

Regardless of what one's own opinion might be, today's concept of aesthetics is not only classical but also idealized. It says that pictures should be compositionally balanced, but not stiff and lacking in movement. It wants them to tell a story: to have a beginning, to develop, to reach a climax and to come to an end. They should have a centre—both in the intellectual as well as in the physical sense. This spiritual and actual focal point should not, however, be aligned with the vertical central axis, for placing the said centre in the middle of the picture effectively impedes any movement. Instead, and in accordance with the conventions of reading now established in Europe, it should be located slightly off to the right. Everything else in the picture should relate to it and, in turn, take its meaning from it. Thus a picture should be composed of both a super- and subordination, and the depicted should harmonize with this order as much as is possible. The concept also says that pleasing pictures develop spatially, are suffused with ambience, and seamlessly integrate everything within them.

Admittedly modern art often contradicts these rules. When it comes to the art of the past, however, we expect the elements which go to make up a picture to be animated. What is more, the way in which these components relate to one another not only determines how we conceive of a painting but also of art. Stubbs's contemporaries thought that his works only fulfilled these requirements in part. They had a simple reason at the ready to dismiss his work and one justified entirely by classical theories of art: Mr. Stubbs was no more than a parrot of nature, and he and his art were to be looked down upon. This argument was underpinned by the notion that real art does not just replicate nature as it actually is, but rather shows it as it should be in an idealized form. This idealized form depends on a certain understanding of beauty. The artist can take either Aristotle or Plato as his mentor and either distil an idealized version of beauty from the wide range available in reality, or be divinely inspired and spiritually sensitive to the essence of beauty and apply this in his work. The first type develops 'a posteriori' and is the result of experience and study. The second comes to the inspired artist 'a priori' and is expressed in a creative flush.

The artist who simply copies, on the other hand, proceeds in a mechanical, uninspired, unintellectual, and purely manual manner. Faced with an object, he renders it accurately—like-for-like, no more, no less—which is to say accurately according to the classical concept. Perhaps more importantly still, classical theory also promoted a hierarchy of objects and accordingly genres of painting. Closely bound up with the above notion of beauty, this system of ranking was not set in stone until surprisingly late, although it had essentially been applied since the sixteenth century at the latest. The preface to André Félibien's *Seven Conferences* of 1668 documents debates concerning certain outstanding paintings that took place at the French Royal Academy of Arts and were led by its president Charles Le Brun. Félibien progresses from subjects considered low to those seen as higher, he moves from the inanimate to the animate, and he grades them in their importance. Still life is ranked most lowly; indeed the French term 'nature morte' refers expressly to the genre's lack of life. Landscape painting, itself also fundamentally static, follows. Next are depictions of animals, which do little to awaken the interest of the viewer despite dealing with living things. Only the human being can do this and the reproduction of a person in a portrait is confirmation enough that the painter is on the path to higher things. Yet even where the portrait shows a tendency to improve upon nature, it is still first and foremost imitation of it, for a portrait is ultimately a question of resemblance. Accordingly Félibien argues that only the artist who can undertake the transition from the single figure to the group of figures holds the key to the door of perfection. This can be

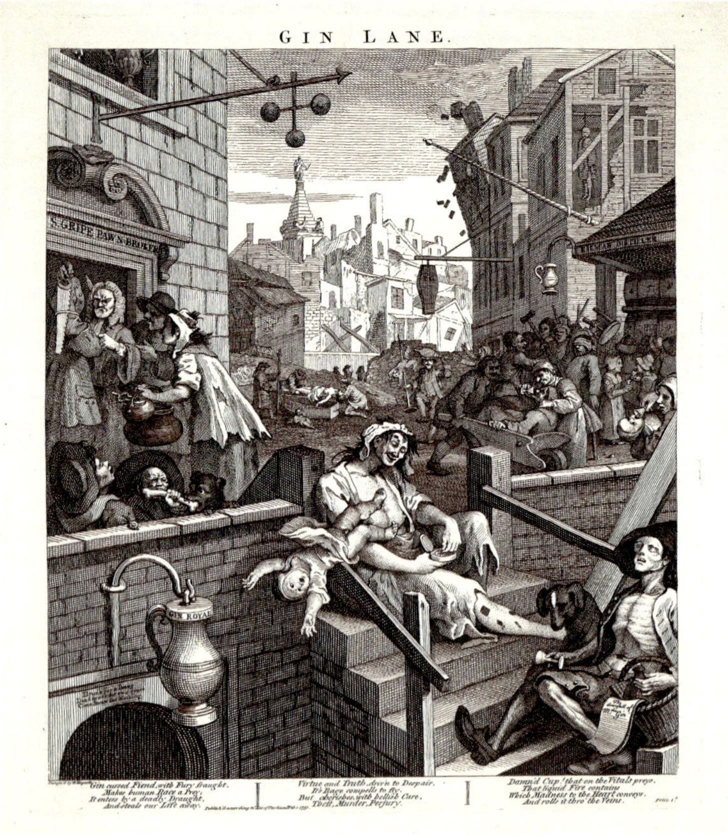

1 William Hogarth, *Gin Lane*, 1751, engraving with etching, 38.5 x 32.0 cm London, The British Museum

achieved by embedding the figures in scenery or recounting a story of exemplary character—a story which is historically important or poetically pleasing. Félibien, however, also goes beyond the classical hierarchy of genres in which history, myth and poetry are given the highest status, for Félibien still subordinates exemplary histories to fables which have been allegorically rendered and to tales from mythology which invoke and exult the ruler and his virtues by casting him in a symbolic light. Portrayed as the new Apollo or Alexander, Louis XIV inherited their qualities and honours. And so it is that the typified ruler can rise above the earthly realm and be released from any claims that he be judged according to the criteria of men and society. He is represented thus in the image of God. The summit of the hierarchical pyramid is made manifest in the figure of the absolutist ruler and in the world of art as much as in terms of the state.[1]

England in the eighteenth century posed a challenge to the validity of this politically-dressed hierarchy of the genres. In 1690 John Locke had argued for the separation of powers. In the early 1700s the monarchy, which had already suffered an early and radical blow from Oliver Cromwell, became a constitutional monarchy with political parties. These parties could debate issues for and against, and took turns in taking on the responsibilities of government. We can add to this that George I and George II not only hailed from Hanover but also spoke hardly a word of English. The realm was in a fragile state and its purely representative function became apparent. In the newly-formed Great Britain, art ceased to play the legitimizing role for which it had long been employed. Two cultures took root: the culture of the nobility and that of the middle classes. The first imported so-called High Art from Italy and disdained national artistic activities. In fact, the art of the court had long been a European import and the successors of Anthony van Dyck were continuing to come from abroad to be painters to the king. There was virtually no native tradition of the arts and certainly no tradition whatsoever of English art theory; nor was there an institution dedicated to these matters. The culture of the middle classes grew up around 1700. Land reforms bolstered the power of larger landowners and concentrated land ownership in the hands of a few. The development of the canal and banking systems accelerated the opening up of the countryside and centuries-old structures were dismantled. Outside the towns the population suffered and an unstoppable exodus to the metropolis of London began. Those fleeing the country faced considerable problems in the city, not the least of which was finding and knowing their place in the capital. London was not a place of production, but of service; hordes of apprentices, clerks and domestic servants sought a foothold there. Disaster al-

2 William Hogarth, *Captain Thomas Coram*, 1740,
oil on canvas, 94 x 58 cm
London, Foundling Museum, Thomas Coram Foundation

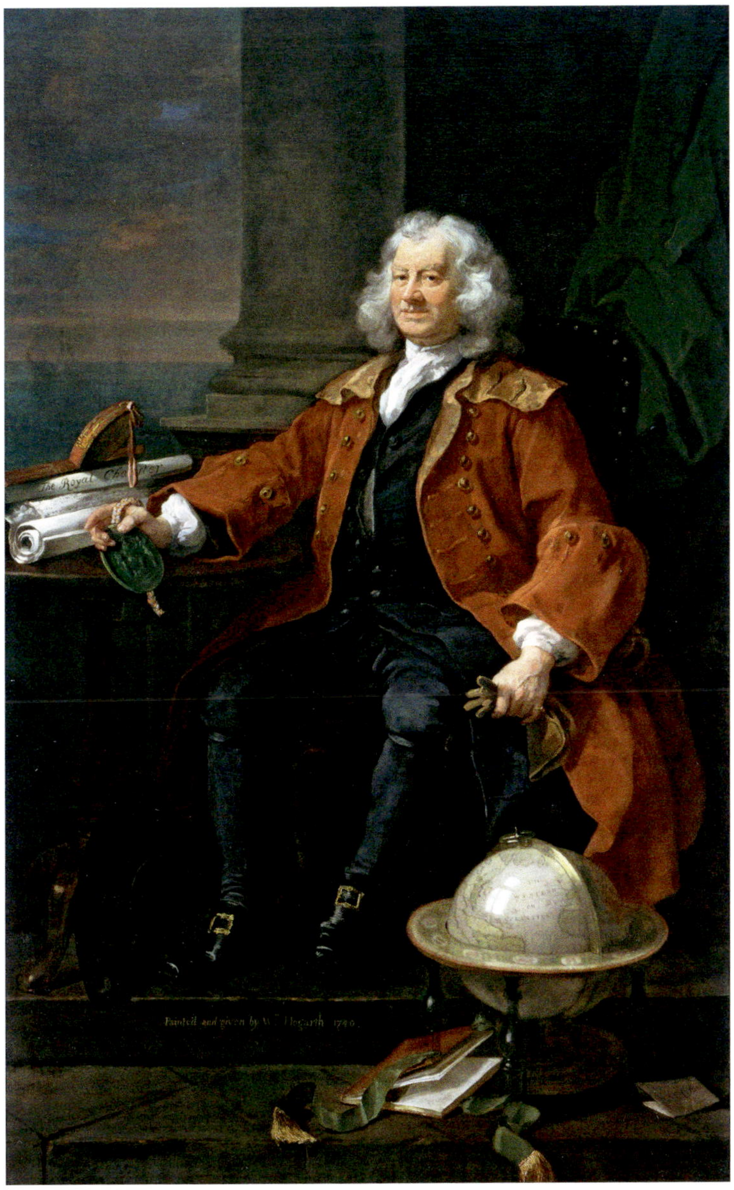

ways loomed around the next corner and the problem of alcohol abuse was immense, fuelled by unlicensed gin stills that happily bought up the poorest quality grain from the landed gentry. For a time one house in five in London was a gin-shop. William Hogarth and Henry Fielding's ultimately successful anti-gin campaign of 1750/51 sprang from innumerable futile attempts to regulate the abuse of gin by legal means (fig. 1).[2]

The church, especially the so-called Latitudinarians who belonged to the Low Church, introduced social reforms and the initiatives of private citizens, themselves rooted in a widely preached middle-class morality, also initiated change. These initiatives found their expression early on in moralizing weekly magazines like the *The Spectator*, *Tatler* or *The Guardian* but also to a lesser extent in breviaries aimed at apprentices. The results of statistical surveys successfully allowed pressure to be applied to the government to take up against those who drew their power from owning land. Private individuals denounced the intolerable conditions in hospitals, foundling homes and orphanages as well as prisons and asylums and founded new institutions. A new kind of 'middle-class' art allied itself to this area of culture. William Hogarth took up the possibilities for creativity it offered with vigour. As governor of St Bartholomew's Hospital he painted murals in the stairwell leading to the Great Hall for no fee in the 1730s. Not long afterwards he would go on to support the Foundling Hospital, to welcome abandoned children into his own home and to encourage fellow artists to donate suitable history paintings creating the first public exhibition of art in England there. Hogarth also immortalized its founder, Captain Coram, in a life-size portrait, adapting the trappings of a court portrait for middle-class sitters and viewers in doing so (fig. 2).[3]

The nobility were able to accept art taking on the role of a social reformer as long as its activities remained restricted to the didactic medium of prints. When it came to paintings, however, they saw an attack on their own codes of High Art and sought to neutralize any claims of this type. The artists for their part banded together in private academies. These were not much more than study groups of equals in fact, such as Hogarth's St Martin's Lane Academy. They also created their own exhibiting institutions like the Society of Artists which was organized along non-hierarchical lines and would play an important role in Stubbs's life. These private academies took on commissions for the decoration of interior spaces. For example, the insides of the small dining pavilions in Vauxhall Gardens—the so-called supper boxes—were fitted out by the St Martin's Lane Academy. At the centre of London's largest pleasure gardens there also stood a similarly furnished music pavilion intended for concerts. This pavilion provided the backdrop for a monument to George Frideric Handel erected in 1738 by Hogarth's friend and member of his Academy, the sculptor Louis-François Roubiliac (fig. 3). The statue was the first monument ever to be dedicated to a living artist or philosopher. It took more than thirty years for a second—addressed to Voltaire—to be produced. Roubiliac's *Handel* stands out because it consciously places the composer in a context in which he himself would have felt completely alien. He is represented without

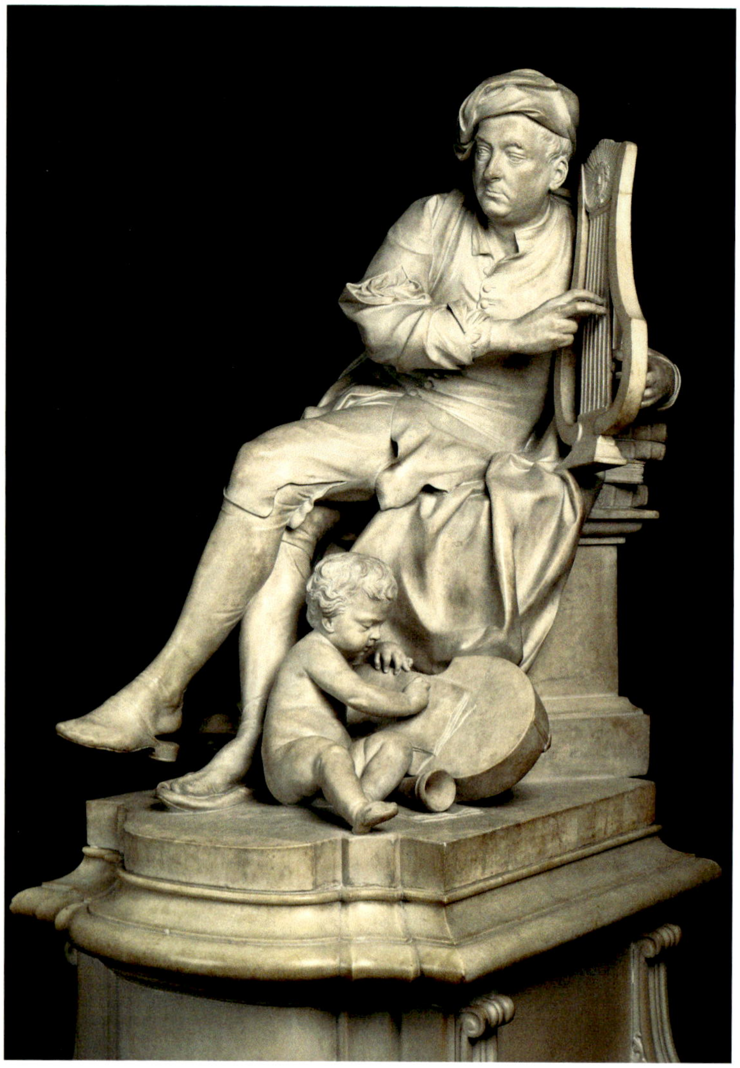

3 Louis-François Roubiliac, *George Frideric Handel*, 1738, marble, h. 135.3 cm
London, Victoria and Albert Museum

the full-bottomed wig he always wore in public and wears an indoor cap instead. His knee-breeches are not correctly tied and he is wearing slippers, one of which he has even taken off and is using as a comfortable foot-rest. This was completely unheard of for a public monument. Yet Handel is also playing a lyre and is attended by a *putto* who is capturing the tune as a musical score; Handel is thus portrayed as an Apollo or Orpheus. The high and the low come together in a curious mixture, making the elevated master of Italian opera accessible to the wider, entertainment-seeking public. Much as this must have irritated Handel, he was quick to learn from it, turning his attention to a new market beyond aristocratic opera. Like Hogarth he became a governor of the Foundling Hospital, donating an organ, simply in order to be able to give recitals there.[4]

This coexistence of two parallel, only occasionally converging cultures continued relatively untroubled until 1768. This was the year of the founding of the Royal Academy of Arts with the soon-to-be ennobled Joshua Reynolds as president. The event split the artistic community. The Academy sought to ally itself with the norms of European High Art, and Reynolds was to provide the theoretical armature with his *Discourses*. This was a contradictory and essentially belated undertaking since European aesthetics had been pursuing other directions for some time. The French Salon, founded in 1737, had even permitted non-Academicians to exhibit. Disagreements between the Rubenists and the Poussinists as to the sovereignty of line or colour, part of the so-called 'querelle des anciens et des modernes,' ended in favour of colour. This was an attack on the classical concept of art in the academy insofar as colour had traditionally been considered a painterly quirk when compared to the act of drawing through which the subject was conclusively captured. At the same time, the elevation of colour signalled the strengthening of painting's appeal to the senses and provoked the investigation of the ways in which art can take effect. However, this focus on effect also reduced art's intellectual claims. With the sensory in the foreground, the complexity of theme faded into the background and a wider audience gained access to works. In the French Salon a plethora of paintings competed with one another for the attention of the viewer on the crowded exhibition walls. The institution was thus responsible for compelling the painter to seek ways to strengthen the appeal of a picture if he wanted it to be able to hold its own among the masses. Making a powerful impact through the heightening of emotions, for example, made it easier to address the viewer. Art criticism emerged in parallel, offering assistance to the public in dealing with paintings and affording the visitor the possibility of debating the paintings he saw. Paintings began to be created for a wider market and the importance of the state and church as patrons declined.[5]

While the French state of affairs is only partly applicable to England, it certainly becomes clear against this backdrop that the English were trying to turn back the clock with the founding of the Royal Academy. It propagated a type of art that put history painting on a pedestal and that was to be achieved by establishing a national school of history painting with not only Homer as a source of inspiration but also Shakespeare and Milton. This attempt to place England within the tradition of European High Art was not very fruitful, not least because when it came to national art, cultured patrons (basically the nobility) continued to demand the portrait. Reynolds attempted to glorify this genre by portraying his sitters in classical roles and applying formulae from the tradition of High Art to their characterization (not without justification the French call this 'portrait historié'). It was hoped that by doing so the portrait would share in the status of history painting and take on the high ranking of Italian classical history paintings collected by the nobility on their Grand Tours.[6]

ART BETWEEN EMPIRICAL KNOWLEDGE AND ACADEMIC IDEALISM

Where, then, does George Stubbs fit into this context and how can we explain his distinctive approach to reality in art-theoretical terms? Or to put it more simply: can his works claim to be art at all? Stubbs notably achieved his critical artistic breakthrough in the 1760s and chalked up his greatest successes just before the foundation of the Royal Academy, at a time characterized by pronounced debates on the progress of English art. His fellow artists were mostly members of the Society of Artists. This institution had no single focus and allowed both the graphic and applied arts to be exhibited. There was still no dominant, idealizing standard, but there certainly were factions. Nationally-oriented artists squared up to those with an international bent, who, like Reynolds, had travelled to Italy early on and were trying to import Italian norms and standards to England. There was also the issue of the provinces versus the city, and it is in considering this rivalry that we come closer to understanding Stubbs's own situation.

Stubbs came from Liverpool. His colleague Joseph Wright of Derby, who was ten years younger but in many ways very similar, hailed, as his name suggests, from Derby. Both were thus from England's truly industrial region where industrial development and advancements in scientific knowledge were inextricably entwined. Research into the natural sciences may well have had its traditional centre at the Royal Society in London, but in the nation's capital it largely lacked the basis in reality which was part and parcel of practice in the industrialized provinces. Thus private provincial scientific societies were formed in Bristol, Bath, Peterborough, Spalding, Manchester, Birmingham, Derby and Newcastle for example. The most important of these was the Lunar Society in Birmingham. A precondition for their rise was the establishment of provincial educational establishments. Primarily founded by dissenters hailing from strictly organized communities these so-called 'dissenting academies' did not teach the antiquated, classical canon of Oxbridge, but rather tangible, useful subjects—modern languages,

4 John Burton, *An Essay Towards a Complete New System of Midwifery*, London 1751, pl. 18, etching by George Stubbs, 18.4 x 10.2 cm
New Haven, Yale Centre for British Art, Paul Mellon Collection

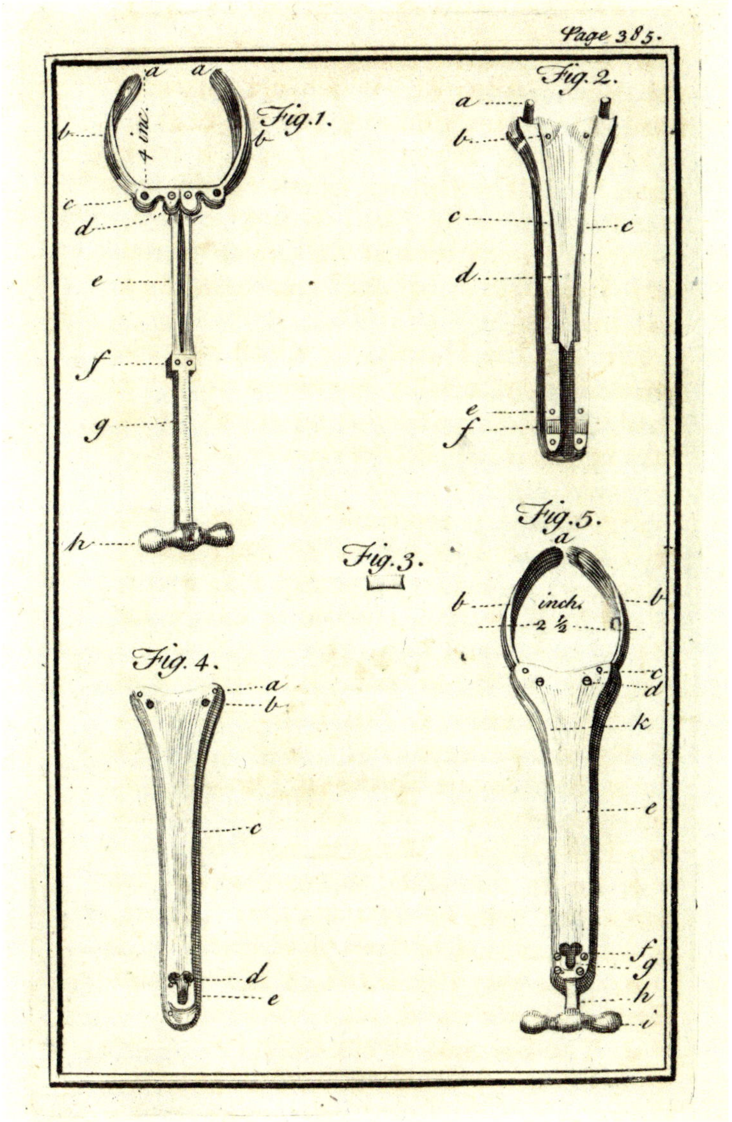

mathematics and the experimental natural sciences—and above all they promoted knowing by doing. The provinces organized themselves independently, rapidly and on a massive scale.

Though comparatively small, the Lunar Society in Birmingham, then the most important private scientific society, was highly active and achieved remarkable revolutionary results.[7] Both Stubbs and Wright of Derby had fairly close contact with a number of its members. They were very well acquainted with the porcelain manufacturer Josiah Wedgwood, who, together with his Society colleagues, experimented with new materials, firing processes and products. The doctor Erasmus Darwin, grandfather of the evolutionary scientist Charles Darwin, was also a member and was already deliberating evolutionary models. His *Botanic Garden* is the most comprehensive (and incidentally rhyming) summation of the eighteenth-century knowledge in the natural sciences, complimented by endless references which furnish proof of Darwin's own mastery of the sources.[8] The great chemist Joseph Priestley was also associated with the Society and so too were Matthew Boulton and James Watt, famous for inventing the steam engine, and at some remove even Benjamin Franklin, father of the lightning rod among other things. Most importantly there was also an unrelenting pan-European exchange of ideas with other societies and individual researchers. The avowed aim of the Society was to make the results of research immediately useful to industry and to aid its development thereby. To this end members also included makers of scientific instruments, such as John Whitehurst from Derby, who simultaneously pursued geological research and clock-making and was a close friend of Wright of Derby. Instrument-makers also had a further function. The most famous of them, Benjamin Martin and James Ferguson for example, travelled the country with huge batteries of instruments, going particularly to the industrial regions and giving lectures—sometimes even courses lasting several days—which were advertised to subscribers in the regional press. In one twelve-part lecture series they taught "the properties of matter, motion, machines (Lever, Pulley etc.), hydrostatics, hydraulics, pneumatics, winds and sounds, light and colours, vision and optical instruments, the solar system and the use of globes." To be able to reach a public that was not at all or only basically educated in mathematics required the use of clear, purposeful language and, above all, extreme clarity when conducting experiments. The travelling scholars did not shy away from sideshow effects in order to make an impressive impact. These ambulant experimenters also published their lectures in the form of treatises which were written in just as understandable a style so that their results could be referred to by others. The importance of these lecturers for the education and development of provincial England can hardly be overestimated and all the more so because regional scientific organizations were enthusiastically engaging with Martin and Ferguson in a vigorous exchange of ideas.[9]

It is only against this background that we can comprehend what Stubbs, coming from a modest social situation, was undertaking to do. After an unsatisfactory and short initial apprenticeship as a painter, Stubbs taught himself until, at the age of twenty, he went to York. Though he painted portraits there, he primarily studied anatomy under Charles Atkinson at the town's County Hospital. This was such a success that he soon began to teach anatomy to the medical students and did so until he was invited by the doctor John Burton to produce eighteen illustrations based in part on post mortems of the female body for the latter's treatise *An Essay Towards a Complete New System of Midwifery*. Burton insisted not only that Stubbs should draw for him but also that he learn how to engrave, and the treatise appeared in 1751. Burton was particularly proud of the new birthing forceps which he had personally developed and which Stubbs illustrated in his last plate (fig. 4). In his *Tristram Shandy*, Laurence Sterne created a malicious parody of Dr Burton in the figure of Dr Slop, whose new forceps left Tristram Shandy disfigured for life by crushing his poor nose during the birth. Though perhaps not particularly professional and confident in their execution, Stubbs's etchings are nonetheless extremely vivid representations.[10]

It must have been while still at York that the idea to follow up the obstetrical illustrations with a separate treatise on the anatomy of the horse was mooted. Before beginning this, however, Stubbs obviously thought it necessary at least to have seen Italy and its art, and thus he set off on a short Italian trip in 1754. Today opinions in the literature on Stubbs continue to diverge here: was Stubbs influenced by what he saw in Italy, or did he really fully reject his experience there on account of his decidedly non-classical conception of art? In the following we will try to provide an answer to this question. First, however, the scientific standard of Stubbs's horse anatomy requires attention. After having stayed in Italy for only a few months, Stubbs settled in Liverpool, painting portraits and, it is said, various animals. It is likely that he also began dissecting here.

Then, in 1756, he was offered the chance to dissect horses in a barn made available to him in Horkstow, Lincolnshire, apparently encouraged by Lady Nelthorpe, whose own portrait and that of her family he had previously painted. Stubbs undertook these dissec-

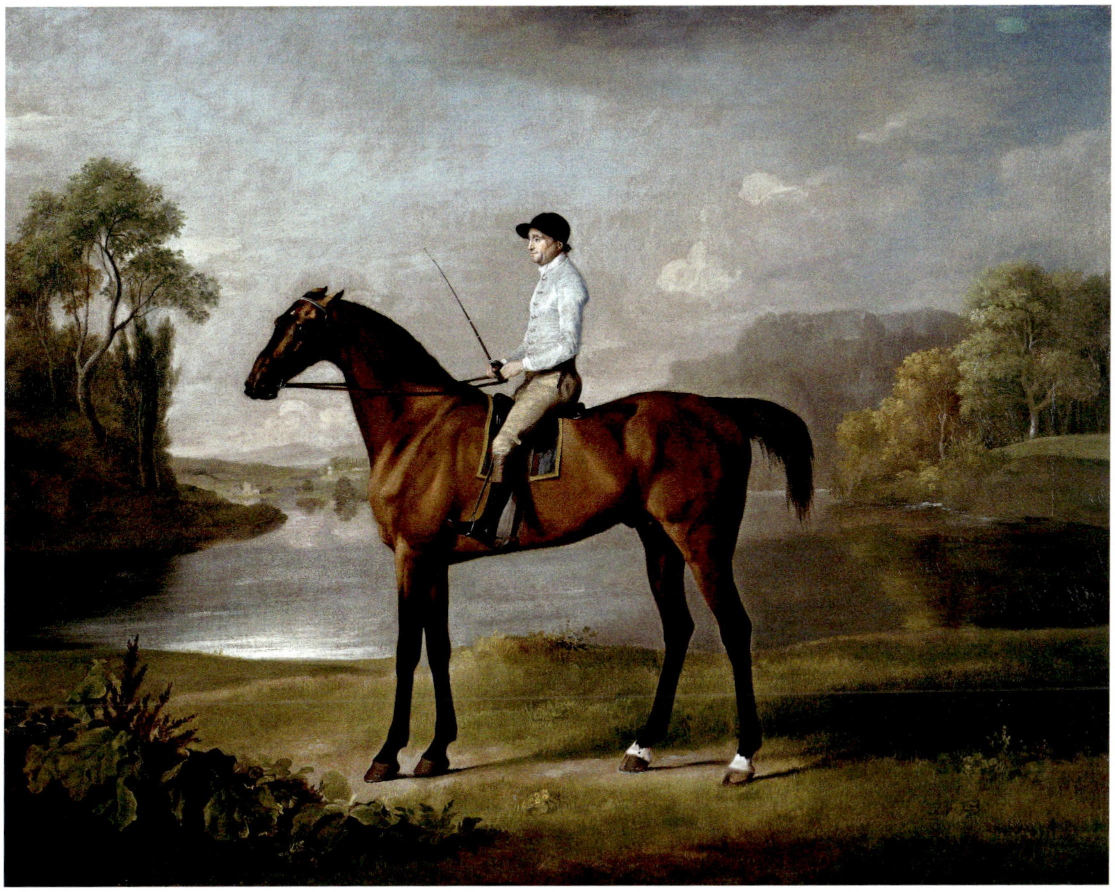

5 George Stubbs, *Scrub, with John Singleton up*, 1762, oil on canvas, 100.4 x 125.7 cm
The Trustees of the Rt. Hon. Olive, Countess Fitzwilliam's Chattels Settlement, by permission of Lady Juliet Tadgell

tions alone but for his common-law wife, Mary Spencer, with whom he stayed until his death. For between sixteen and eighteen months he cut apart and drew horse after horse. The process apparently took up to seven weeks each time—which must have meant that an unbearable smell developed. But when he was young Stubbs had assisted his father in his work with fresh leather still reeking of tannic acid, and had thus been 'toughened up' from childhood onwards. It was all unbelievably laborious since—so says the title page of the final published treatise—all bones, cartilages, muscles, fascias, ligaments, nerves, arteries, veins and glands were to be recorded in exacting detail.[11]

Stubbs followed the *Tabulae Sceleti et Musculorum Corporis Humani* published by Bernhard Siegfried Albinus and illustrated by Jan Wandelaar in his work. This famous treatise had first been published at Leiden in 1747 and then in London two years later, when the English translation had been accompanied by new engravings by Charles Grignion and others. Albinus's human anatomy looked back over a long tradition of progressively more scientific investigations. In the case of equine anatomy, however, there was only one precedent: Carlo Ruini's 1598 *Dell'anatomia et dell'infirmità del cavallo,* the woodcuts of which seem rough and highly simplified when compared to Stubbs's *Anatomy*. Stubbs adopted from Ruini the idea of depicting the horse right down to its skeleton and in movement. Albinus proceeded in a similar way in his human anatomy. Representing the dead as if they were alive is certainly disturbing, yet it makes sense nonetheless since it allows both the organisation of and different functions played by the parts of the body—muscles, veins etc.—to be shown. It has rightly been said that since Leonardo's work on horse anatomy no one has ever been able to rival Stubbs in the accuracy of representing the body of the horse, and that Stubbs, as far as his systematic approach is concerned, eclipses all previous artists (see the article by Oliver Kase in the present catalogue). After almost two years of uninterrupted activity in Horkstow, Stubbs took his drawings to London in 1758. He hoped to find an engraver capable of transferring the works to engraving plates in the capital. Charles Grignion, engraver of the English edition of Albinus's human anatomy, seems to have been the first to whom he spoke. Grignion, however, appears to have declined the offer. Equally the other engravers approached by Stubbs—Arthur Pond's name is mentioned for example—considered themselves unable to take the project on. Apparently they felt that they were no match for the extraordinary complexity and detail of Stubbs's drawings.

In the first instance, what is known about Stubbs's life and work goes back to Stubbs's friend and colleague Ozias Humphry who, following exhaustive conversations with the elderly Stubbs, recorded the artist's reminiscences in his *Memoir*. Later we will return to ask whether these can be taken at face value or whether they are connected to the idea of the 'artist' arising from the literary tradition of artists' lives and, moreover, a certain art-historical standpoint.[12] Whichever is the case, for the moment Stubbs's efforts resulted in him taking it upon himself to produce the engravings of the drawings. Many years would pass as he only worked on the plates early in the morning and late at night. The result is a reproduction of remarkable precision and astonishing contrast, even in its graphic tonality. This is not a case of schematic depiction according to which the represented is nominally identifiable, it (and this cannot be stressed strongly enough) is a case of the reproduction of the appearance of the lit body at each stage of dissection. The bodies are illuminated and shaded with no loss of detail. They are not only astonishingly lively but the viewer can also experience them spatially, indeed almost haptically.

Stubbs's *Anatomy of the Horse* first appeared in 1766, published by J. Purser in London. A great success, it was reprinted many times and Stubbs apparently sold individual sheets from it until his death. Letters, such as those from the famous Dutch anatomist Petrus Camper in 1771, express a wholehearted enthusiasm for the work,[13] demonstrating just how well known Stubbs's publication was among other natural scientists. Camper hoped that Stubbs might now turn his attention to the internal organs of the horse in order to serve veterinary surgeons even better. Stubbs rejected this, saying that he had fulfilled his task: the *Anatomy* had been produced for artists first and foremost and only for horse owners and breeders in the second instance.

6 William Hogarth, *Heads of Six of Hogarth's Servants*, c. 1750–55, oil on canvas, 63.0 x 75.5 cm
London, Tate

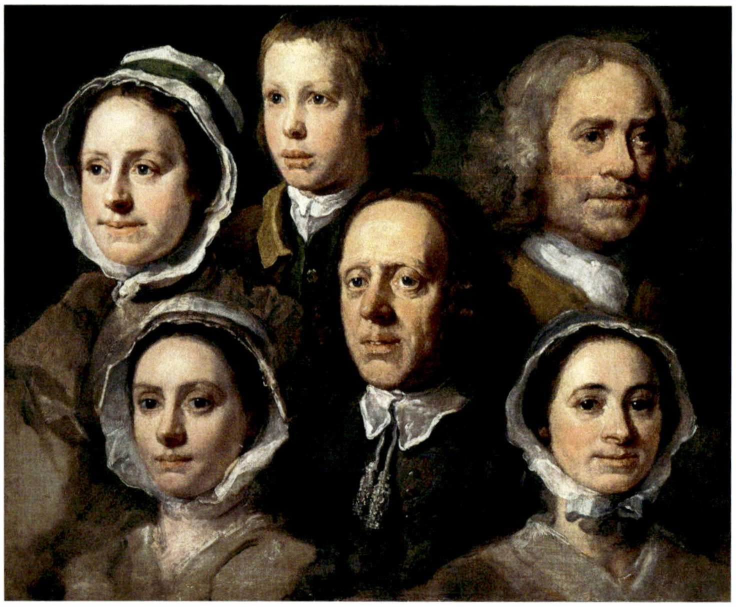

STUBBS'S SPORTING ART AS A MIRROR OF SOCIAL RELATIONSHIPS

In horse-owning and horse-breeding circles especially, Stubbs's success was certainly phenomenal. He must have shown the drawings to some English noblemen after coming to London in 1758, triggering a wave of commissions for painted horse portraits. This admittedly had the result that the 1760s saw Stubbs experience an early peak in his career. This wealth of commissions also explains why it took so long to complete the eighteen horse anatomy plates. The astonishing precision of his drawings of the equine anatomy aside, why did these meet with such immediate success among an entire group of the nobility? Joshua Reynolds was apparently responsible, or at least partially responsible for providing the contacts. It is a notable fact that each of the noblemen and women employing Stubbs at the beginning of the 1760s was also being immortalized by Reynolds—who having returned from Italy had become the most important English portrait painter.

The group of clients to whom Stubbs appealed had three things in common: they were young, extremely rich and held similar political convictions. They were Whigs, who, finding themselves in opposition, pined for political influence. Known as the 'Whigs in waiting', they were holding out for their political break and had returned to their country seats where certain pastimes had become popular. They renovated, or rather reconstructed their stately piles according to the latest fashions. Having been on their Grand Tour to Italy, they bought art to furnish their town and country houses. They went hunting. They transformed their gardens on a grand scale, abandoning the formal, strict French style of garden in favour of the more relaxed English style. The more serious among the Whigs took an interest in agricultural reforms. Above all, however, they devoted themselves to breeding racehorses and this they did with untamed gusto. They erected immense stables, preferred and bought Arabian horses, entered their best horses in races and wa-

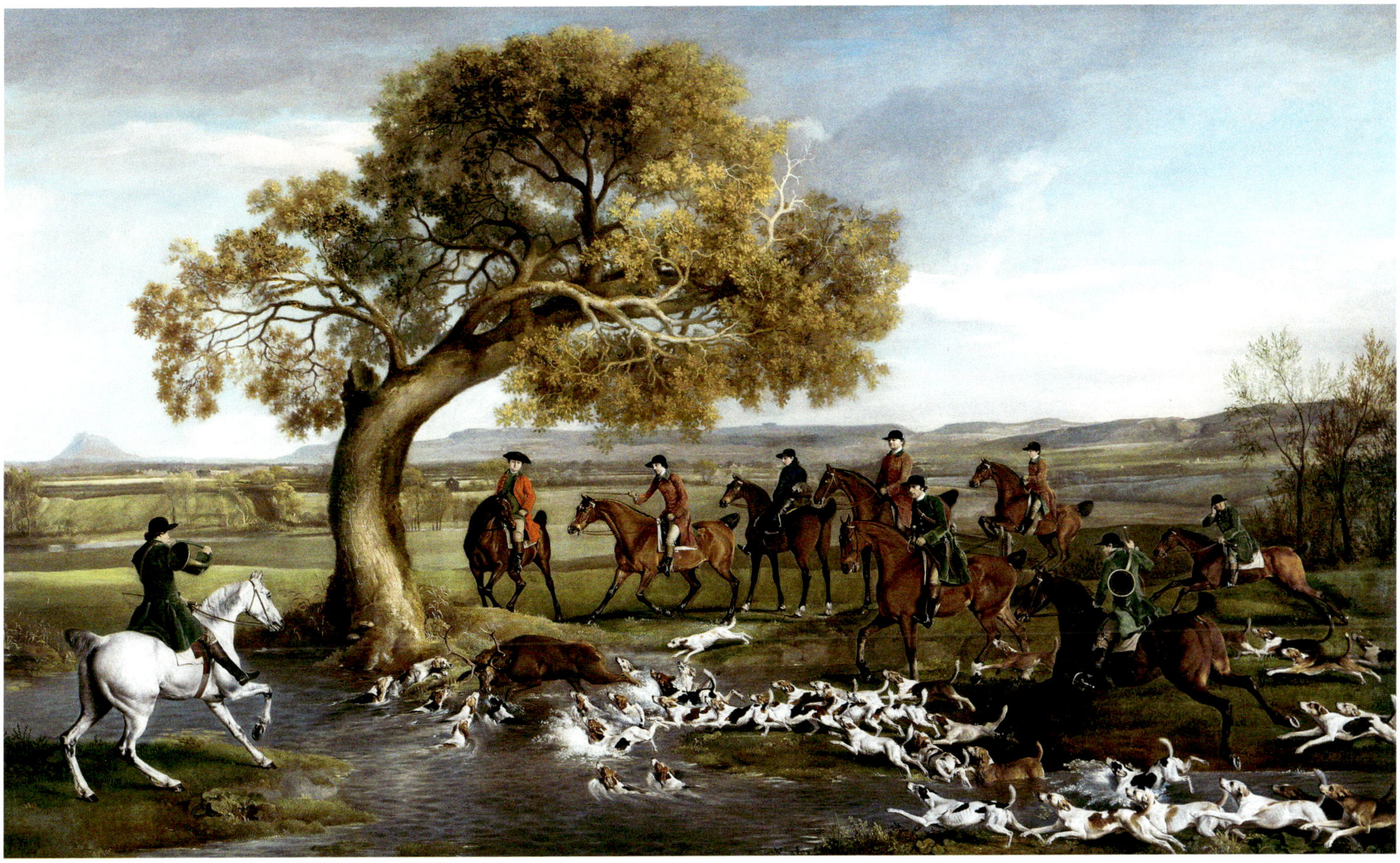

7 George Stubbs, *The Grosvenor Hunt*, 1762, oil on canvas, 149 x 241 cm
Private collection

gered huge amounts on them, leading to the ruin of one or two of the owners.

Stubbs's (and Reynolds's) patrons were the 1st Baron, later 1st Earl Richard Grosvenor; the Viscounts Torrington and Bolingbroke; the Dukes of Richmond, Portland and Grafton; John Spencer of Althorp, soon-to-be Earl Spencer; and above all the Marquess of Rockingham. The latter was also considered to be the ringleader of this group which was known as 'the Rockingham Whigs.' He was briefly prime minister twice—including for a short period in 1765, despite a dislike of the royal court and sympathy for America. Rather unusually for a nobleman, the 3rd Duke of Richmond had received a university education in the natural sciences and had studied in Leiden. Richmond founded the Ordnance Survey which mapped the country in full, an exercise without which there would have been no Industrial Revolution. When the other Young Whigs took an interest in the sciences, it was in zoology and anatomy, for they not only bred dogs and horses on their estates but they also assembled entire menageries as proof of their exclusivity. Priority went, however, to horse-breeding and horse-racing and the group founded the Jockey Club–which still exists–in the 1750s. An exact record was kept of each mating and these pedigree lists are still maintained today. The larger stables were given their own colours, allowing the jockeys to be instantly recognized during the running, thereby adding to the prestige of the horse owners. The Jockey Club drew up mandatory racing regulations and established an equally binding calendar of meets. In short, the sport of horse-racing was transformed into a semi-professional system dominated by these noblemen and a few others.[14]

Yet it was not the owners who were immortalized in paintings, but primarily the great race winners. Such winners dominated the

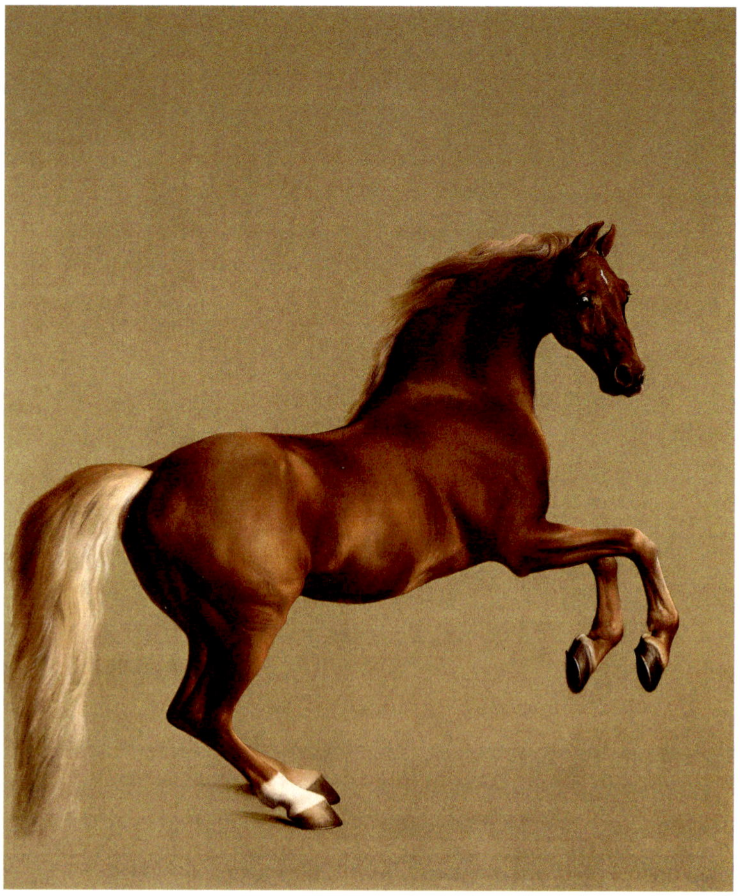

8 George Stubbs, *Whistlejacket*, c. 1762, oil on canvas, 292 x 246 cm
London, The National Gallery

turf for a while before their talents determined that they would be put out to stud to pass on their qualities to the next generations. All the same, the individual horse was irreplaceable and was to be admired as such. There was no one better suited to capture this than Stubbs, whose extraordinary anatomical studies were clearly a match for all scientific standards in the subject. So it was that Stubbs painted Romulus for Lord Spencer, Hollyhock and Lustre for Lord Bolingbroke, Baudy for Lord Grosvenor, and Scrub for the Marquess of Rockingham. The latter was portrayed with the jockey mounted in the saddle, as the charming expression has it "John Singleton up" (fig. 5).

It was not only jockeys who were painted alongside the horse, but also frequently the groom or the trainer–the people who looked after the animal and who, together with it, formed a virtually symbiotic unit. Depicting these people alongside the horse as a team was, for the owner, proof of the care he took in horse-breeding. The grooms, who were often experienced breeders and who are better thought of as stud masters, are–like the jockeys–often named. They belonged to the household and were painted by Stubbs with the same care and accuracy as the horses with which they were entrusted. This has the interesting consequence that just as he unmistakably captured the individuality of the horse, so too their carers appear as individuals in Stubbs's pictures. Grooms, trainers and jockeys can be seen to have been valuable subjects in Stubbs's eyes and he afforded them something akin to social justice by depicting them. His precursor in this was William Hogarth, who had famously portrayed his six servants as studies of heads with obvious sympathy (fig. 6). But as with works by Stubbs, the role that Hogarth's picture was destined to play meant that the emancipation of his employees was little more than a side effect. Rendered in a relaxed painterly style, it hung in Hogarth's studio where it was intended to demonstrate his artistic and representational capabilities to potential clients.[15] Incidentally, it is not particularly surprising that an eighteenth-century artist who primarily earned his living by making prints should have been able to afford six servants. The flight from the countryside had created a surplus of cheap labour in London–people who were happy to be taken on and looked after in a household in return for a modest income.

The aforementioned horse portraits–and there would be many more–were all created between 1761 and 1763. In this short period Stubbs also developed three more painting types: the dog portrait, showing the same preoccupation with the individuality of the animal subjects; the hunt painting, famous examples of which are the *Charlton Hunt* for the 3rd Duke of Richmond and the

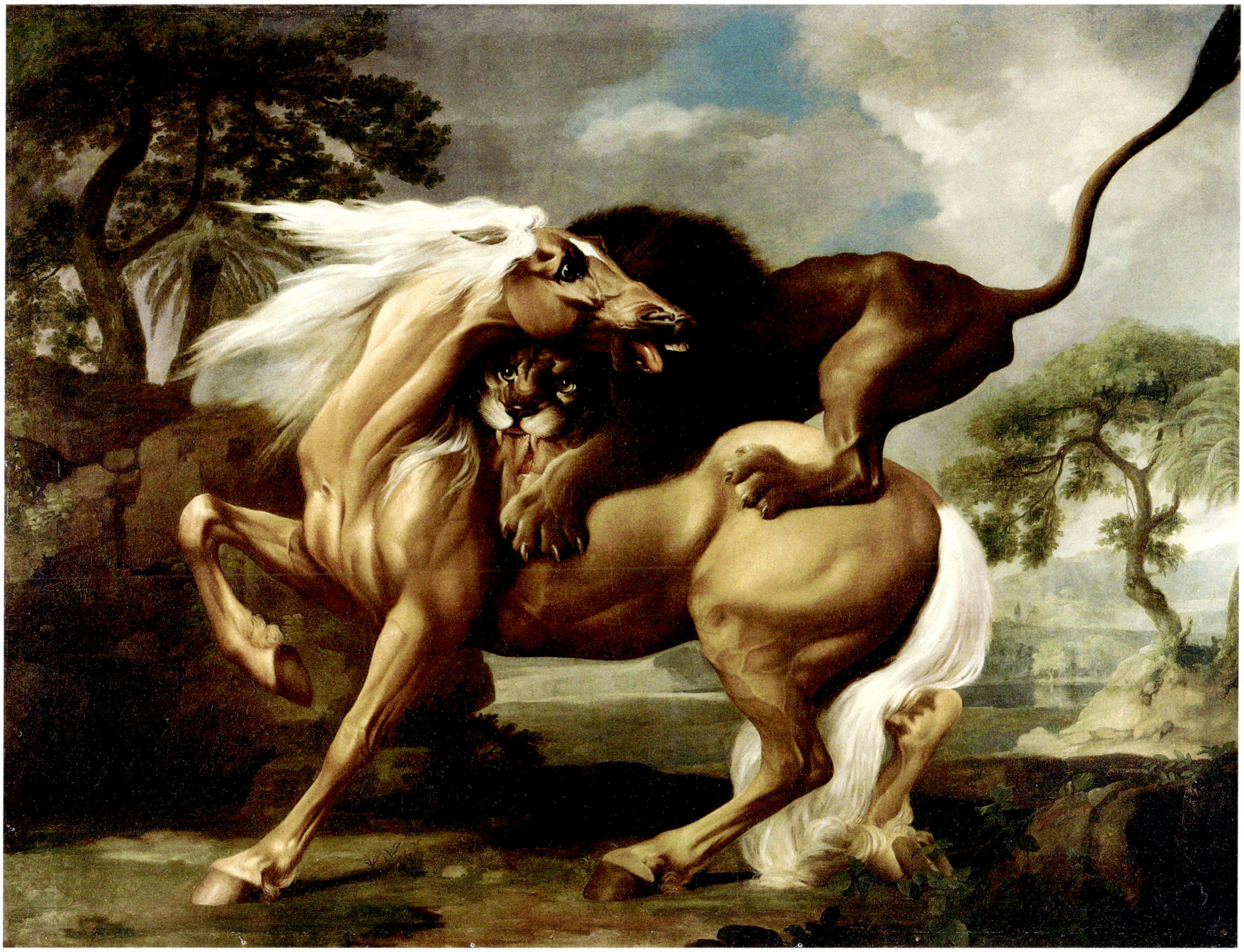

9 George Stubbs, *Lion Attacking a Horse*, 1762,
oil on canvas, 244 x 333 cm
New Haven, Yale Center for British Art, Paul Mellon Collection

Grosvenor Hunt (fig. 7);[16] and the so-called "mares-and-foals" type in which, lined up as if in a frieze, brood mares and their foals are presented.

A painting belonging to this last type made for the 2nd Viscount Bolingbroke is certainly among the leaders of the field. But the highlight without doubt is the group painted for the 2nd Marquess of Rockingham in 1762, for here the group of horses is not embedded in a surrounding landscape but appears before a neutral, ochre-brown coloured background (cat. no. 20).[17] Small shadows are cast by the horses's hooves, giving the animals the appearance of being grounded. Nevertheless, only the horses's bodies themselves create a sense of space. This happens indirectly thanks to the uniform rendering of light and shade. Rockingham seems to have been particularly taken with this form, which allows for the complete concentration on the horses represented, for a further painting showing the three stallions Whistlejacket, Godolphin Hunter and Godolphin Colt from the Rockingham stud on a neutral background was produced in the same year. Whistlejacket, the most fa-

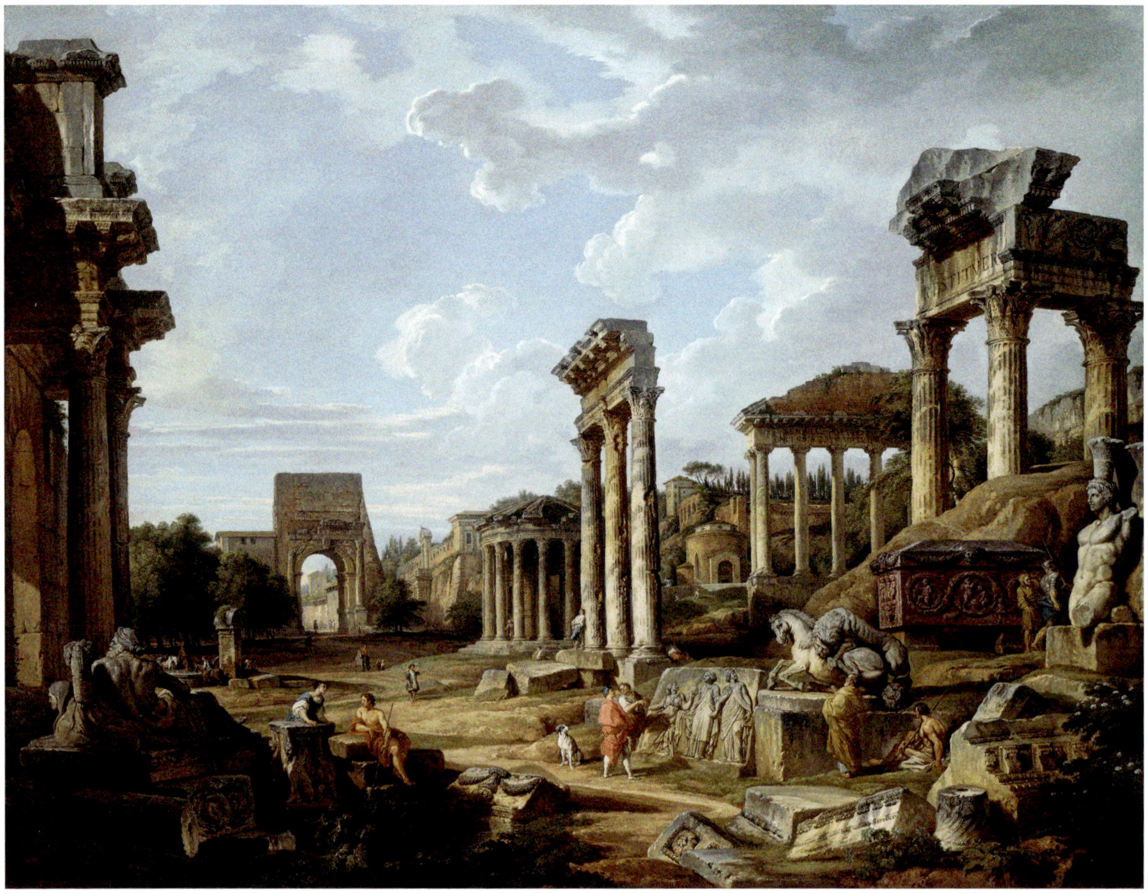

10 Giovanni Paolo Pannini, *A Capriccio of the Roman Forum* with the 'horse-and-lion' group, 1741, oil on canvas, 170.8 x 217.8 cm
Yale University Art Gallery, Stephen Carlton Clark, B.A., 1903, Fund

mous of the three, is being held by Rockingham's head groom, Mr Cobb (cat. no. 19)[18] who–since the horse is unsaddled–stands pressed up close against him. The groom wears Rockingham's livery. Placed against the same neutral background but also represented with a recognizable kindness while looking at the viewer, this juxtaposition generates a paradoxical tension between abstract space and tangible figure, increasing the attentiveness of the viewer.

Whistlejacket, the famous Arabian stallion, was also immortalized by the artist in an enormous individual portrait, measuring almost three by two-and-a-half metres (fig. 8). He owes his fame not so much to his successes as a racehorse or breeding stallion, but primarily to George Stubbs. This is unquestionably one of the most important British paintings of the eighteenth century and is certainly the most important image of a horse ever to be created.[19] It made its triumphant entry into the National Gallery only a few years ago (1997) and today it catches the visitor's eye, hanging at the end of an enfilade. In its quivering vibrancy, its monumentality is quite stunning. Whistlejacket turns his body to the right. His head, with its large shining eyes, is turned slightly towards the viewer, and he rears up in a *levade*. Precisely this latter detail has led to extensive discussions, for the *levade* pose appertains to the mounted ruler or army commander and is a sign of his triumphant superiority–the expression of majestic dignity. One only needs to think of the paintings of Velázquez and Rubens, the equestrian portraits of Philip IV, his court favourites the Count Duke of Olivares or the Cardinal-Infante Ferdinand, Philip's representative and governor of the Spanish Netherlands, or George Villiers, Duke of Buckingham. It has been supposed that Rockingham had originally commissioned Stubbs to leave the horse's back empty for King George III, who had ascended the throne in 1760. A second artist was to have painted the king, and a third the landscape background. Whether this story, which Stubbs provided for Humphry's *Memoir*, really relates to *Whistlejacket* remains unclear.[20] Rockingham is said to have finally broken with the king for political reasons in December 1762, leaving the horse bare backed. In all his beauty Whistlejacket was now given a neutral background. Writing of *Whistlejacket* in 1772, Horace Walpole perpetuated the myth: "It was to have had a figure of George 3d until Lord Rockingham went into opposition."[21] We might ask whether Rockingham was really still thinking of honouring the king when he commissioned this painting. Immediately after ascending the throne in 1760 George III had entrusted his faithful mentor, Lord Bute, with absolute power and the latter remained a convinced Tory and prime minister until 1763. Even if it was only first in December 1762 that Rockingham officially broke with the king, the circumstances had surely already fundamentally changed before this.

THE IMITATION OF NATURE AND THE IDEAL OF ANTIQUITY

Because even more legends have sprung up around the powerful image of Whistlejacket, now is the appropriate moment to comment in more detail on Humphry's account of George Stubbs's life, his *Memoir*. Humphry noted that Whistlejacket was originally supposed to bear George III and that the painting was to have been the product of three genre specialists. Probably in order to justify why the picture remained in its 'unfinished' state and to explain why this state itself accounts for the painting's particular artistic quality, Humphry recited the following story: when Stubbs had almost finished the painting, for which the horse, accompanied by a groom familiar to it (the only groom able to keep the extremely nervous horse in check), was posing as a model, Stubbs moved the canvas from where he was working and placed it against the wall to consider its impact. In doing this he turned his back on Whistlejacket. Suddenly, the groom, who was holding the horse, cried out. Highly agitated, Whistlejacket was staring wildly at his portrait and seemed to want to attack it. The groom held him back with force, but was hurled into the air. Stubbs eventually managed to frighten it off with his maulstick and palette and Whistlejacket was led back to its stable with effort, after having glanced confusedly once again at the painting. The Marquess of Rockingham appeared shortly afterwards and when he heard of the events he was so convinced of the impact of the painting that he ordered that it should remain in this state with the horse alone against a neutral background.[22] One recent author still considered this story to be credible despite being aware of Walpole's differing explanation for this decision.[23] It seems that the nature of this story as a topos escaped him. Regardless of whether they are formulated by the artist himself or by some associated person after his death, written accounts of artists' lives in the eighteenth and nineteenth centuries not only form a specific literary genre with their own rules, they are also totally clad in rhetoric.[24] They aim to eloquently express the artist's particular, ultimately art-theoretical position and they lend this position more power by using figures of speech. It is perhaps telling that many accounts of English lives bear the title *Anecdotes*. The word anecdote means nothing other than a rhetorical figure and its use lends this figure a putative authority on the basis of being told from life. Humphrey has a single aim when recalling anecdotes–there is a whole series of them, almost indistinguishably mixed up with historical facts–and this is to justify Stubbs's particular approach to reality by repeatedly recalling it, as well as to stress an original, special artistic quality in Stubbs's work that is on a par with a classical, idealized concept of art. This has a long tradition and in this way a Titian or a Rembrandt were raised to the rank of a Raphael or Rubens.[25]

This model of justification had a noble provenance and had its roots in classical antiquity. If classical, idealized art theory draws upon Aristotelian or Platonic philosophy, then the second tradition, whose proponents painted so realistically that their images seem to come to life, to breathe and to move, has its *locus classicus* in Pliny's *Natural History*, the 35th book of which is dedicated to famous painters of antiquity such as Apelles, Zeuxis and Protogenes, Parrhasius and Nicias. Because their works no longer survive, they live on in Pliny's anecdotes and these revolve almost exclusively around the deceptive imitation of nature as a particular quality. The best artist is he who most convincingly succeeds in making things appear living. If the artist is understood as someone who brings things to life, he can be assigned almost divine powers of creation; he is the creator of a second nature. This concept is also found in the Christian tradition: as God had created man from clay, a dead material, then breathed *pneuma*–the breath of life–into him, so the artist proceeds correspondingly. Although completely paradoxical to us today, classical art theory also recourses to these anecdotes and in doing so becomes entangled in two fundamentally contradictory art forms: the realistic imitation of nature and the imitation of nature which idealizes reality. Here too the rhetorical topos formulated in Humphry's argument is evident. The sole purpose is the ennobling of the artist in question, who can then be located within the genealogy of the great artistic heroes of antiquity.[26]

In the case of Stubbs, the origin of the anecdote can be identified precisely. We might think firstly and generally of the famous anecdotes in Pliny, for example the one in which the sparrows try to peck at Zeuxis's painted grapes, or the one in which (much closer to our example) a stallion tries to mount a painted mare, or even the one where quails try to fly towards a quail painted just on the edge of a work by Protogenes–the model is always the same.[27] Yet Humphry's version takes us back more specifically to Vasari and his *Lives of the Artists* of 1550 and 1568. In England these were also the most widely-known accounts of artists' lives. One story tells of a horse that was painted by Bramantino in such a lifelike manner that it was attacked by another horse.[28] Humphry, for his part, clearly elaborated upon and embellished this.

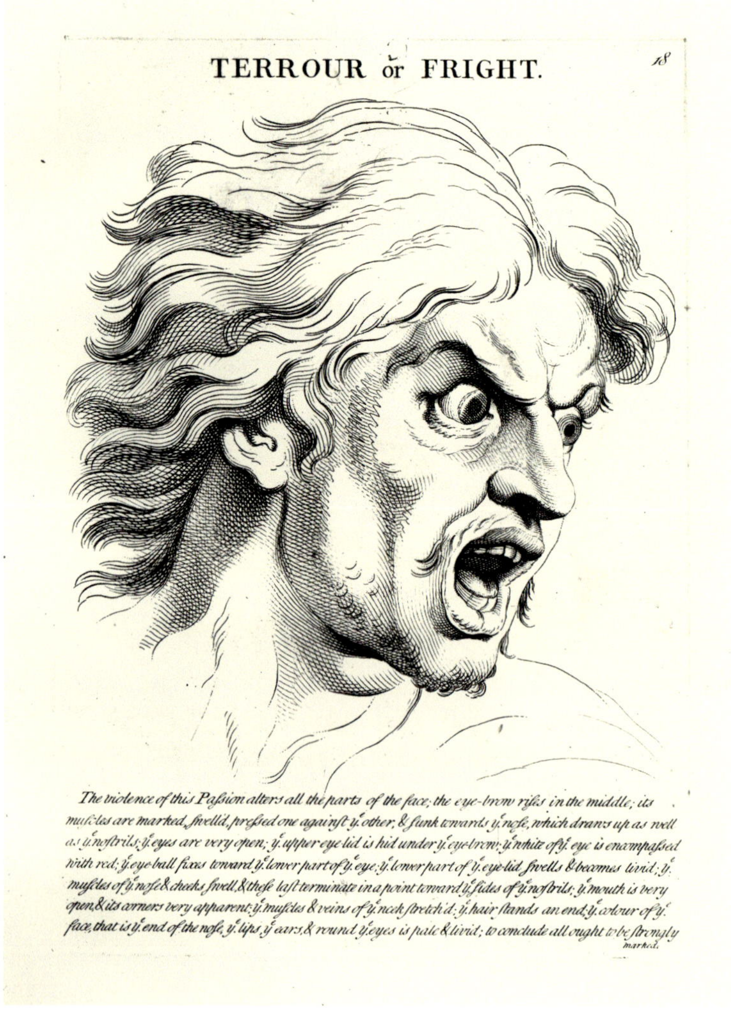

11 Charles Le Brun, *Terror or Fright*,
from *Heads Representing the Various Passions of the Soul*, 1765,
engraving, 28.6 x 18.4 cm
London, The British Museum

All other stories produced by Humphry belong to the same category: like the statement that Stubbs was determined that nature only could serve as a model and should thus be reproduced as faithfully as possible. Writing on Stubbs has taken all of this literally, as if it were a case of objective facts. This not only obscures scholarship's view of the art-historical dimension behind that which is quoted, it also prevents the recognition of that which truly motivated Stubbs, since his thoughts were in no way completely taken up with trying to represent nature exactly. Like many artists before him, he made use of a topos which he saw as the only available alternative to the classical, idealistic scheme and which could artistically hold its own in the face of this tradition. Stubbs completed his short Italian trip in 1754 and Humphry is intent—current research once again agrees with him on this issue—on giving the impression that art in Rome had not the slightest influence on him. According to Humphry, in discussions with fellow artists in Rome, Stubbs was alone in being of a completely different opinion, which can only mean that he argued against the entire classical, idealizing philosophy and with it questioned what the art of Rome stood for.[29] The anti-classical position is also a topos, which—whether represented by Hogarth, Thomas Gainsborough or John Constable—is commonly characterized by its proponent's complete rejection of the idea and practice of travelling to Italy.[30] Stubbs did, however, go to Italy and thus the point is to minimize the impact of this country entirely, although we know that Stubbs owned works by Italian artists. According to his theoretically consistent idea of a topos Humphry must reject the Italian influence on all levels, even in the practice of art itself. At the very beginning of his *Memoir* he writes that Stubbs would "for the future look into nature for himself and consult & study her only; and to this determination he steadily adhered during the course of his long life, for he never copied one picture whatever for his improvement either in Italy or elsewhere."[31] In the context of the trip to Rome Humphry summarizes that Stubbs "was to convince himself that nature was & is always superior to art whether Greek or Roman;–and having renew'd this conviction he immediately resolved upon returning home."[32] Accordingly, if Stubbs learnt one thing from his Italian journey it was that if nature is to be one's only teacher there is no need for the model of classical art and antiquity.

THE 'HORSE-AND-LION' PAINTINGS AND THEIR CLAIM TO HIGH ART

Although the scientific basis of Stubbs's studies of the natural world should not be doubted, the question certainly arises as to whether or not this idea of a topos really holds true for the artist. Here, an anecdote which emerged later than Humphry's text and which can possibly be traced back to Stubbs's common-law wife Mary Spencer is revealing. Appearing in the *Sporting Magazine* of May 1808, just two years after Stubbs's death, it is also an anecdote which has largely misled scholars, despite the quite absurd touches it displays. Stubbs made a whole series of horse-and-lion paintings in which either a horse, catching sight of a lion, rears up in fright, or in which the lion has already pounced onto the horse's back to tear it to pieces. In the latter case, the horse is sometimes still standing or has already collapsed. The pictures were clearly a success as Stubbs had to repeat them many times. Stubbs's contemporaries, in particular those noblemen familiar with Italy, must have immediately recognized that the paintings showing a horse and lion in combat (cat. no. 42) were a blatant paraphrase of an important sculpture from antiquity exhibited in the Palazzo dei Conservatori (fig. 10). Especially admired by Michelangelo, this had been copied since the sixteenth century and many variations had been made, such as the small bronze from the circle of Giambologna and the life-size copy made in 1743 for the garden at Rousham by Peter Scheemakers, one of the most important sculptors in England. A smaller marble version was also in the collection of Henry Blundell, who owned a version of Stubbs's horse-and-lion group. Lord Rockingham too was in possession of one of the many bronzes and, in 1762, he gave Stubbs the commission for the largest-ever version of the horse-and-lion group, which measured the not inconsiderable 2.44 x 3.33 metres (fig. 9). There is therefore no doubt that the model for these works was not only immediately recognizable, but indeed that it was intended to be recognized.[33]

Yet the anecdote, in the sense of the topos applied to Stubbs with its art-theoretical ulterior motive, attempts to divert attention from this sculpture as a model at all costs. The story goes that in the Mediterranean on his return from the Eternal City to England, Stubbs met an educated African man who had also spent time in Rome on board of his ship. The latter invited Stubbs to his house in Morocco with the aim of showing him a lion in the wild. They landed in Ceuta. One evening from the city walls, the painter saw with delight how a lion actually attacked a white 'Barbary horse', that is an Arabian stallion, not 200 yards away. A lion crept up and suddenly pounced on the creature which flinched in terror, but, rigid with fear, could not escape. The lion leapt on the horse's back, brought it down and ripped out its entrails.[34] Even recent research on Stubbs accepts this story, posing the rhetorical question: if the story were not true, why would it have been invented?[35] Others express mild scepticism because the story was not recounted by Humphry, but find it nonetheless plausible.[36] This too is an amazing argument which, given the nature of Humphry's text, is unintentionally droll. Let us look a little closer, then, not least because Humphry again unproblematically subsumes the horse-and-lion images into Stubbs's distinctive understanding of nature. He also informs us that Stubbs had studied lions in Lord Shelbourne's menagerie on a number of occasions, where he had also been able to observe lions pouncing on their prey.[37] Stubbs apparently captured these impressions with quick outline sketches in black and white chalks. And so it is that the stories compete with one another whilst also being bound to one and the same art-theoretical goal.

An appraisal of the circumstances surrounding the commission of the large horse-and-lion picture for Lord Rockingham should allow us to get close to what was really motivating Stubbs. Two huge pictures were commissioned in parallel: *Whistlejacket* and the horse-and-lion picture. But the pictures, as research has revealed with a certain amount of regret, were never displayed together. Therefore this is not a case of pendant pictures.[38] Indeed they are not pendants, but rather antithetical pictures. From the very beginning the horse-and-lion picture hung in Rockingham's town house, while *Whistlejacket* hung in his country residence. Stubbs was clearly able to distinguish what should belong where. The city was the place for a picture with pretensions to history, one that demonstrated a clear reference to antiquity and which, by nature, needed to be more than the mere reproduction of reality. How, then, does this work go beyond being indebted to the real world? It does this in two ways: in the anthropomorphization of the horse—the exaggeration of its natural appearance—which deviates from the model of nature and in a *concetto* that has been subtly worked into the image. The latter turns the work into the art of ideas and thus satisfies its pretensions to history painting. Stubbs studied the classical concept of the passions. He owned nineteen engravings of Le Brun's expressions of the emotions, a further series of twenty-three "coloured Prints of the Passions", and he had made four of his own sketches showing the expression of the emotions: laughter, crying, sadness and terror or fright (engraved in 1800 by his son). The sketches were published in the *écorché*, that is without the skin, making it possible to understand each movement of the muscles in the face.[39] They clearly show that his approach was predicated on science. Here, we might suppose that Stubbs is indebted, as was William Hogarth before him, to the tradition of James Parsons's 1747 lecture to the Royal Society entitled *Human Physiognomy Explain'd* and Benjamin Ralph's 1759 *The School of Raphael or, the*

Student's Guide to Expression in Historical Painting.[40] Both take a more medical approach, as they refer to the movements of the muscles in order to be able to explain differences in expression.

In his 1988 book on *Sporting Art* Stephen Deuchar correctly observed that Stubbs used Le Brun's expression of the emotion 'terreur' (fig. 11) for the facial expression of his horse attacked by a lion and even adopts those details where Le Brun departs from nature in order to intensify the persuasive power of this expression. Stubbs may have taken it from the 1701 English edition of Le Brun's treatise.[41] The images correspond with one another in their wide-open mouths, one might speak of jaws, exposing the upper and lower teeth and tongue; in their eyes widened in horror; in the powerful, bulging brows; and finally in the hair which is being whisked around as if by furies in a storm. The metaphor of hair standing on end comes to mind. Similarly, running path-like down the body of the animal, the neck muscle—made prominent by exertion—is also clearly exaggerated by Stubbs. This has little to do with the representation of nature; this is expressional code. For each of versions of his horse-and-lion group still known to us today, Stubbs selected his own mode of representation indebted to the aesthetics of the sublime.

A poem by Horace Walpole, which he composed after being inspired by a variation on the horse being terrified by the lion exhibited at the Society of Artists in 1763, confirms that this constitutes a recognizable approach. Published in the *Public Advertiser* on 4 November 1763, its existence is somewhat surprising as Walpole had previously paid no attention to Stubbs's horse portraits. He clearly saw immediately that the approach taken by this work was more than to merely copy and that it sought to do justice to the classical conception of art. Alone the title of the poem identifies this: *On Seeing the Celebrated Startled Horse, Painted by the Inimitable Mr. Stubbs.* Walpole pursues the horse's range of expression, invokes the extreme effect of its emotions on the viewer, sees the absorption of all of its feelings in the horse's flared nostrils, terror and fear pulsing through every vein, invokes the sublime, feels his own blood surging, and advises the great actor Garrick to study this representation of expression, ending with the couplet: "Thy pencil Stubbs no rival need to fear / not mimic art but life itself is here."[42] Though Walpole may still invoke the Plinian topos of bringing to life, the artist significantly did not achieve this through imitation alone. If it is possible to invest a horse with a soul—which Walpole quite clearly intends to do by merging the horse's physiognomy with Le Brun's expressions of passion—then it is by this means that Stubbs makes humans able to sympathize with the horse.

STUBBS'S NEO-CLASSICISM

Stubbs took a step further down the path towards classical art by depicting a few mythological themes, albeit themes which remain connected to the subject of the horse. Representations of Phaeton who borrowed Apollo's quadriga of the sun and rushed headlong to disaster having lost control of the horses (cat. no. 69) can be found in a number of different media. It is not the usual plummet situation known to pictorial tradition that Stubbs presents, but the moment just before when the wildly galloping horses go off course. They too appear seized by madness, their expressions and movements exaggerated beyond the bounds of nature.[43]

Stubbs, it seems, wanted to demonstrate his command over both the classical and the non-classical. Even Humphry cannot avoid quoting the enthusiastic comment of the Swedish sculptor Tobias Sergel when the latter set eyes on one version of Phaeton. After a long stay in Rome, Sergel had stopped off in England on his way back home. He declared "that the focus and expressions, as well as the fiercy [sic] & animated motion of the animals placed them upon a footing with the finest sculptures of the ancients."[44] Did Sergel intend to admire the sculpture's nearness to life or Stubbs's ability to adapt the style of classical antiquity? Sergel had spent the years 1767 to 1778 in Rome in close contact with the group surrounding Henry Fuseli, who was founding an anti-Winckelmannian form of classicism at exactly this time. Fuseli grafted the heightened expression of the passions onto the stylized forms of classicism. This was not only completely alien to Winckelmann's dictum of "noble simplicity" and "quiet grandeur" but also especially unusual for sculpture.[45] Sergel must have recognized a kindred spirit in Stubbs as far as his classical style was concerned. In this respect it seems correct to attribute a neo-classical outlook to Stubbs's art and certainly the same is probably also true of the way in which he represented reality. Thus, we might finally have arrived at Stubbs's own aesthetic as expressed in a distinct system of images. And thus at the *concetto* character of Stubbs's horse-and-lion pictures.

Two minor observations are useful here. First, unlike the ancient sculptural group—which was incidentally radically restored in 1694, the whole head being reconstructed and turned to face forwards in a rather staid way[46]—and also unlike the small bronzes from the workshop of Giambologna, which show the head turned expressively backwards and which are thus Stubbs's primary model.[47] Stubbs always showed his attacked horses unshod. In the groups from antiquity, including in particular the small bronzes, which show the horse broken, the individual nails in the horseshoe can clearly be seen. Stubbs does not omit to trace the horseshoes in his horse portraits and therefore we might assume that this omission is deliberate.[48] Second, Stubbs's horses in the horse-and-lion groups have pronounced tufts of hair on the back of the hock which have been clearly trimmed on the horses in the horse portraits. We are obviously meant to see the horses in the horse-and-lion groups as primeval creatures from an era before civilization. Accordingly, the Arab in a racehorse's blood should be seen as pre-historical and prototypical, in opposition to the Greco-Roman. England, or rather London, was understood to be a new Rome, a stronghold of civilization. And a particular expression of that civilization was horse-breeding, especially that based on sophisticated methods pursued by the nobility.

A further detail underscores the fact that this interpretation is moving in the right direction. In the 1760s Stubbs got to know the unspoiled region of Creswell Crags, not far from Welbeck Abbey on the Nottinghamshire–Derbyshire border, near to the River Wellow. It is a region distinguished by dramatic chalk cliffs, but most notably by prehistoric caves in which the bones of primeval animals had been found. Stubbs's horse-and-lion groups play out against this backdrop above all.[49] In the second half of the century a form of tourism focusing on geology grew up. Previously unheeded because of their ruggedness, rocky areas like the Lake District and, further south, Matlock Dale as well as Dovedale in Derbyshire were opened up, immortalized in the painting of Wright of Derby. At the heart of this development was firstly the prospecting for new minerals which individuals such as Wedgwood would be able to use in their manufactories and secondly—perhaps more importantly—the issue of the age of the Earth and ancient rocks.[50] In this regard it is clear that for Stubbs, justified by the aesthetic theory of the sublime, it was all about illustrating the primitive state of things. And in this state the passions too found their unfettered expression. In order to make this internally coherent *concetto* perceptible to the viewer, Stubbs both alienated the appearance of things and attempted to adhere to a classical concept at the same time.

In the face of the jarring faithfulness to reality shown by Stubbs's horse portraits, it is easy to overlook the fact that a pronounced stylization underlies these images too, albeit a stylization that is merely formal in nature and thus in conscious tension with the claims to reality made by the subject. This formal stylization, which is a feature of the large majority of Stubbs's paintings whether portraits or history paintings, is best demonstrated by his most beautiful mares-and-foals portrait: that with the neutral background painted in 1762 for the 2nd Marquess of Rockingham (cat. no. 20). Arranged in a row as if in a frieze, the horses are painted with crystalline clarity and the background has a cool yellow-green ochre tone. The light falls into the picture from the left and illuminates the horses' bodies, creating logical shadows which are heightened by the light shadows cast by the hooves on the neutral ground. This, in concert with the arrangement in a row, unites the horses, each of which has been carefully allotted its own space. The horses' bodies spatially unfold, even if only along a narrow, stage-like strip, with just as much logic. Yet more important still for the overall impression is the abstract ordering of surfaces. This makes an impact on the viewer by getting under his skin and has thus an aesthetic inescapability. The withers of all five mares, that is the raised parts of their backs, trace the horizontal central axis of the picture. At the same time, the pricked-up ears of the attentive second mare from the left, which fix the highest point of the horses, lie exactly on the upper line of the horizontal golden mean. The lower horizontal runs through the middle of the horses' bodies. It is as if they are strung together on a thread. The two vertical lines of the golden mean, in contrast, mark precisely the highest point of the withers of the second and third mares from the left. The golden mean, also known as the divine proportion since the sixteenth century, is an indiscernible effective organizational schema which appeals to the human eye. It has been found in Greek temples but also in nature, in the nautilus shell for example.[51] Such an imperceptibly-perceptible, abstract aesthetic order can be felt when contemplating all of Stubbs's pictures. This order is intensified by the distinctive stylization in the relationship between form and object. It is also a stylistic marker of neo-classicism, which distinguishes itself from the classical order (this locates objects in an atmospherically developing space) by making objects seem free-standing, finding their place less in the space of illusion than tangibly on the surface of the image like an abstract pattern. We trace their form and perceive them as surface phenomena.

At first sight, the extremely spirited subject can seem frozen or fixed, as each object is seen for itself and the context is only established in an abstract way. But if we get closer to a Stubbs painting, for example the conversation piece showing the Milbanke and Melbourne families (cat. no. 35) created at the end of the 1760s, we suddenly realize that the figures are far from clearly delineated. In fact, they exhibit an infinitely subtle outline of light, which gives the impression of a slight vibration, a sense of bodies breathing. Then we also recognize that this extraordinarily fine veil of light has been drawn over all of the subjects, filling the fields of colour with a delicate sense of life. Objects are presented as appearances. This phenomenon is more than can be illustrated by Leonardo's *sfumato* technique or a sketched rendering. It is an optical mastery of phenomena which seems to presuppose knowledge of Newtonian laws. Furthermore, it is only possible to paint such a visual phenomenon when it has actually already been observed. The place of its perception and the place where it was seen in an intensified way in the eighteenth century was the milky glass plate of the *camera obscura*, which both focused the light and allowed it to be perceived as a surface phenomenon at the same time.[52] Stubbs must have used one.

---

1 On these themes see Werner Busch, *Das sentimentalische Bild. Die Krise der Kunst im 18. Jahrhundert und die Geburt der Moderne*, Munich 1993, pp. 19–24. On individual genres see Stefan Germer, *Kunst – Macht – Diskurs. Die intellektuelle Karriere des André Félibien im Frankreich von Louis XIV.*, Munich 1997, esp. pp. 356–79; Thomas Kirchner, *Der epische Held. Historienmalerei und Kunstpolitik im Frankreich des 17. Jahrhunderts*, Munich 2001, esp. pp. 103–17, 179–317.

2 On the gin campaign see Berthold Hinz, *William Hogarth. Beer Street und Gin Lane. Lehrtafeln zur britischen Volkswohlfahrt*, Frankfurt am Main 1984; Busch 1993 (see note 1), pp. 264–94.

3 Ronald Paulson, *Hogarth*, vol. 2, *High Art and Low, 1732–1750*, New Brunswick, N.J. 1992, St. Bartholomew's Hospital: pp. 77–103; Foundling Hospital: pp. 323–41.

4 Werner Busch, "Händel und der Wandel der Konversation," in: ibid., *Englishness. Beiträge zur englischen Kunst des 18. Jahrhunderts von Hogarth bis Romney*, Berlin and Munich 2010, pp. 9–31.

5 On the "querelle" see Hans Robert Jauß, "Ästhetische Normen und geschichtliche Reflexion in der 'Querelle des Anciens et des Modernes,'" in: *Charles Perrault, Parallèle des anciens et des modernes en ce qui regarde les arts et les sciences*, Munich 1964, pp. 8–64; on the drawing versus colour dispute see Thomas Puttfarken, *Roger de Piles' Theory of Art*, New Haven and London 1985; Max Imdahl, *Farbe. Kunsttheoretische Reflexionen in Frankreich*, Munich 1987.

6 Robert Rosenblum, "Reynolds in an International Milieu," in: Nicholas Penny (ed.), *Reynolds*, Exhib. Cat. Royal Academy of Arts, London 1986; Busch 1993 (see note 1), pp. 394–411.

7 Robert E. Schofield, *The Lunar Society of Birmingham. A Social History of Provincial Science and Industry in Eighteenth-Century England*, Oxford 1963; Jenny Uglow, *The Lunar Men. The Friends who Made the Future*, London 2002.

8 Erasmus Darwin, *The Botanic Garden. A Poem in two Parts*, London 1789 and 1791.

9 For an extensive discussion of individual instrument makers see Werner Busch, "Materie und Geist. Die Rolle der Kunst bei der Popularisierung des Newtonschen Weltbildes," in: *Mehr Licht. Europa um 1770. Die bildende Kunst der Aufklärung*, Exhib. Cat. Städelsches Kunstinstitut und Städtische Galerie, Frankfurt am Main 2000, pp. 401–18 with further literature.

10 John Burton, *An Essay Towards a Complete New System of Midwifery Theoretical and Practical*, London 1751; Venetia Morrison, *The Art of George Stubbs*, London 1989, pp. 12–19 (with six illustrations from the treatise); Exhib. Cat. *Fearful Symmetry*, 2000, p. 154, no. 35 and pl. 35; Egerton, *George Stubbs*, 2007, pp. 17–19 (with eight illustrations from the treatise).

11 Exhib. Cat. *George Stubbs*, 1984/85, nos. 6–25; Exhib. Cat. *Stubbs and the Horse*, 2004/05, pp. 18–41; reduced-size reprint of the late edition of George Stubbs, *The Anatomy of the Horse*, London 1853 (first edn. 1766) with complete text and original plates, London 2005; for the drawings see Egerton, *George Stubbs*, 2007, pp. 112–29, no. 7.

12 Ozias Humphry's *Memoir* in the copy by William Upcott with reminiscences by Mary Spencer transcribed in: Exhib. Cat. *Fearful Symmetry*, 2000, pp. 200–09.

13 Camper's letter of 1771 and an extract from a letter of 1772, ibid., p. 210.

14 For more detail see Egerton, *George Stubbs*, 2007, pp. 36–44.

15 Busch 1993 (see note 1), pp. 425–29; Giles Waterfield, Anne French and Matthew Craske (eds.), *Below Stairs. 400 Years of Servant's Portraits*, Exhib. Cat. National Portrait Gallery, London 2003, on Hogarth's domestic staff see pp. 108–10.

16 Egerton, *George Stubbs*, 2007, nos. 11 and 29.

17 Ibid., nos. 17 (Bolingbroke), 30 (Rockingham); on Rockingham's painting see also Exhib. Cat. *Stubbs and the Horse*, 2004/05, no. 37.

18 Egerton, *George Stubbs*, 2007, no. 31; Exhib. Cat. *Stubbs and the Horse*, 2004/05, no. 38.

19 Egerton, *George Stubbs*, 2007, no. 34; Exhib. Cat. *Stubbs and the Horse*, 2004/05, no. 39.

20 Exhib. Cat. *Fearful Symmetry*, 2000, p. 205.

21 Horace Walpole, "Journals of visits to country seats, & c.," edited by Paget Toynbee, in: *Walpole Society* 16, 1927–28, p. 71.

22 Exhib. Cat. *Fearful Symmetry*, 2000, p. 205.

23 Exhib. Cat. *Stubbs and the Horse*, 2004/05, p. 178.

24 Ernst Kris and Otto Kurz, *Die Legende vom Künstler. Ein geschichtlicher Versuch*, Frankfurt am Main 1980 (first edn., Vienna 1934); Ernst Kris, *Psychoanalytic Explorations in Art*, New York 1964 (first edn. 1952), chapter 2, pp. 64–84.

25 On this tradition see Werner Busch, *Das unklassische Bild. Von Tizian bis Constable und Turner*, Munich 2009.

26 Pliny the Elder, *Natural History*, vol. IX: books 33–35, trans. H. Rackham, Loeb Classical Library, Cambridge, MA 1952.

27 On the grapes: Pliny, Book 35, 65; on the stallion painted by Apelles: Book 35, 95; on the quail painted by Protogenes: Book 35, 121; see Kris and Kurz 1980 (see note 24), p. 90.

28 Giorgio Vasari, *Vite de più eccellenti pittori, scultori, ed architetti*, 9 vols., edited by Gaetano Milanesi, Florence 1878–85, vol. 2, p. 493, also quoted in Kris and Kurz 1980 (see note 24), p. 90, note 2.

29 Exhib. Cat. *Fearful Symmetry*, 2000, p. 201.

30 Werner Busch, "Zur Topik der Italienverweigerung," in: Hildegard Wiegel (ed.), *Italiensehnsucht. Kunsthistorische Aspekte eines Topos*, Munich and Berlin 2004, p. 203–10.

31 Exhib. Cat. *Fearful Symmetry*, 2000, p. 201.

32 Ibid., p. 202.

33 The tradition is pursued most extensively in ibid., nos. 6–17, 19 and text pp. 13–15, 19–21, 24 and Egerton, *George Stubbs*, 2007, pp. 26–30, 294 and nos. 36–39, 112–14, 120, 121.

34 *Sporting Magazine*, vol. 32, May 1808, p. 55, quoted in full in Morrison 1989 (see note 10), pp. 15, 19 and in Exhib. Cat. *Stubbs and the Horse*, 2004/05, pp. 108 f.

35 Morrison 1989 (see note 10), p. 19; there is also total conviction in Exhib. Cat. *Stubbs and the Horse*, 2004/05, pp. 109, 179.

36 Basil Taylor, "George Stubbs. 'The Lion and Horse' Theme," in: *The Burlington Magazine* 107, 1965, pp. 81–86; Exhib. Cat. *Stubbs and the Horse*, 2004/05, p. 121, note 21. Discussed *passim* in Barnaby Rogerson, "Did Stubbs go to Morocco," in: *Country Life* 194, 2 March 2000, pp. 60 f.

37 Exhib. Cat. *Fearful Symmetry*, 2000, p. 206.

38 Egerton, *George Stubbs*, 2007, pp. 170, 175; Exhib. Cat. *Stubbs and the Horse*, 2004/05, p. 109.

39 Exhib. Cat. *Stubbs and the Horse*, 2004/05, p. 108; p. 197, no. 62.

40 Werner Busch, *Nachahmung als bürgerliches Kunstprinzip. Ikonographische Zitate bei Hogarth und in seiner Nachfolge* (*Studien zur Kunstgeschichte*, vol. 7), Hildesheim and New York 1977, pp. 161 f.

41 Morrison 1989 (see note 10), p. 112; Stephen Deuchar, *Sporting Art in Eighteenth Century England. A Social and Political History*, New Haven and London 1988, pp. 107 ff.; Exhib. Cat. *Fearful Symmetry*, 2000, p. 24; Exhib. Cat. *Stubbs and the Horse*, 2004/05, pp. 108, 121, note 17. The human typology of the passions as transferred to horses in the English context are quoted here. Thomas Kirchner has kindly alerted me to the fact that in France, soon after Stubbs's use of the typologies, corresponding comparisons were made in French treatises: see Antoine-François Vincent, *Essai sur l'expression des diverses passions du cheval, considerées dans les trois principaux instans de leur progrès*, Paris 1787, and Thomas Kirchner, *L'expression des passions. Ausdruck als Darstellungsproblem in der französischen Kunst und Kunsttheorie des 17. und 18. Jahrhunderts* (*Berliner Schriften zur Kunst*, vol. 1), Mainz 1991, pp. 323–25, for two expressions of passions in the context of horses' heads, *L'amour* and *La colère*, see pp. 326 and 327 (figs. 83 and 84).

42 Walpole's poem is reprinted in Egerton, *George Stubbs*, 2007, p. 50 and Exhib. Cat. *Stubbs and the Horse*, 2004/05, pp. 106 f., for the quoted lines see p. 107; previously it read (p. 106): "How apprehension, horror, hatred, fear, / In one expression, are concenter'd there!" This evokes Le Brun's typology of mixed passions.

43 For the most extensive discussion of this see Exhib. Cat. *Fearful Symmetry*, 2000, pp. 120–35, nos. 25–29.

44 Ibid., p. 209: Humphry in a memorandum of 31 August 1803; Egerton, *George Stubbs*, 2007, p. 404, no. 200; Exhib. Cat. *Stubbs and the Horse*, 2004/05, p. 69 (quotation not quite correct) and p. 199, no. 64.

45 Werner Busch, “Gegen Winckelmann. Die Neukonzeption des Klassizismus im römischen Künstlerkreis um Johann Heinrich Füßli,” in: *Idea. Jahrbuch der Hamburger Kunstsammlungen 2005–2007* (published 2009), pp. 40–60.

46 Francis Haskell and Nicholas Penny, *Taste and the Antique. The Lure of Classical Sculpture 1500–1900*, New Haven and London, 2nd edn. 1982, pp. 250 f., no. 54.

47 Egerton, *George Stubbs*, 2007, p. 27, fig. 4; Exhib. Cat. *Fearful Symmetry*, 2000, pp. 82–85, no. 11.

48 This was first noted, but no conclusions were drawn, in Morrison 1989 (see note 10), p. 110.

49 Exhib. Cat. *Stubbs and the Horse*, 2004/05, pp. 110 f.; Judy Egerton, “George Stubbs and the Landscape of Creswell Crags,” in: *The Burlington Magazine* 126, 1984, pp. 738–43; Egerton, *George Stubbs*, 2007, p. 177 and nos. 38, 39, 48, 49, 50, 50A, 82, 89, 90, 95.

50 Uglow 2002 (see note 7), chapter 13, Derbyshire Explorata, pp. 138–54.

51 Albrecht Beutelspacher and Bernhard Petri, *Der Goldene Schnitt*, 2nd edn., Heidelberg et al. 1996. A whole series of Stubbs's paintings uses this ideal relationship in their proportions. See Busch 1993 (see note 1), pp. 426–29 on Stubbs's *Hambletonian* (Egerton no. 336). Stubbs uses other extremely stylized geometric structures in *Haymakers*, *Reapers* (Egerton nos. 248–251) and in the very late paintings for the Prince of Wales (Egerton nos. 306–307).

52 Translations of the optical experience of the *camera obscura* in terms of concentration and blurring could first be seen in England in the works of Canaletto, who spent time in England during the Seven Years' War (1756–63), since the Grand Tourists, his clients, did not travel to Italy. On Canaletto and the *camera obscura* see Werner Busch, “Die Wahrheit des Capriccio – die Lüge der Vedute,” in: Ekkehard Mai (ed.), *Das Capriccio als Kunstprinzip*, Exhib. Cat. Wallraf-Richartz-Museum, Cologne; Kunsthaus, Zurich; Kunsthistorisches Museum in the Palais Harrach, Vienna, Milan 1996, pp. 95–101; John H. Hammond, *The Camera Obscura. A Chronicle*, Bristol 1981.

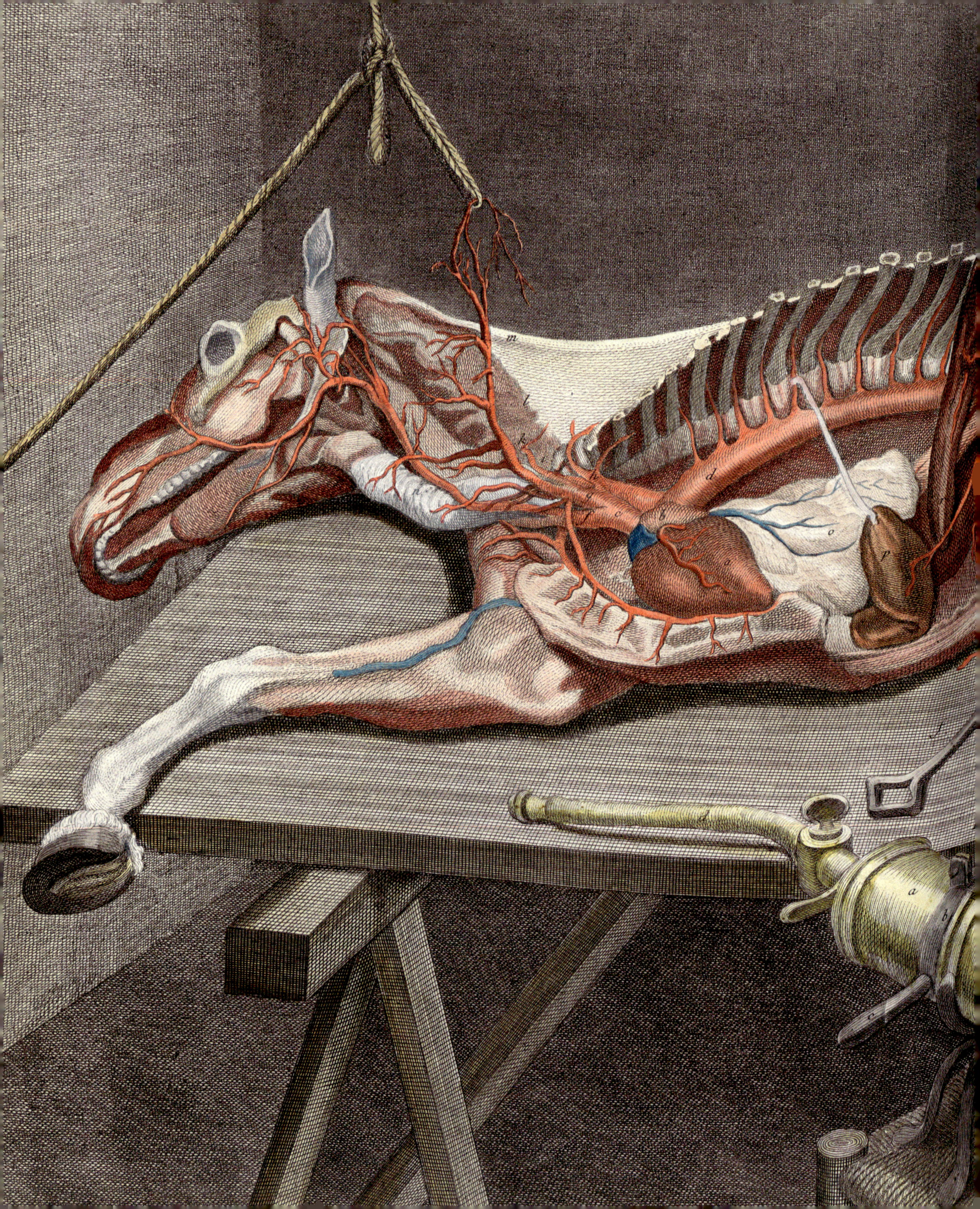

Oliver Kase

"MAKE THE KNIFE GO WITH THE PENCIL"[1]— SCIENCE AND ART IN GEORGE STUBBS'S "ANATOMY OF THE HORSE"

Children in the eighteenth century played with wooden dolls or hobbyhorses; George Stubbs played with bones. Ozias Humphry recalled in his *Memoir* that Stubbs, as a child in Liverpool of barely eight years old, was given bones and preserved specimens by a neighbouring doctor so that he could undertake his own small-scale anatomical research. On his deathbed, Stubbs, by then eighty-one, regretted not being able to complete his work the *Comparative Anatomical Exposition of the Human Body with that of a Tiger and a Common Fowl.*[2] As a theme, the study of anatomy repeated itself with such consistency and frequency in Stubbs's artistic life that we might still ask today "whether most to admire the artist as a *dissector*, or as a *painter* of animals" as the *Gentleman's Magazine* in 1806 did.[3] The quandary is no different when we are faced with his most famous anatomical project: the *Anatomy of the Horse*. The idea of publishing an atlas of equine anatomy probably took seed in the circle of Stubbs's surgical colleagues at the York County Hospital, where he was performing anatomical dissections and giving lectures by the time he was twenty.[4] It was not, however, until 1756 that Stubbs took up the project in earnest, having returned from a short sojourn in Italy. Humphry relates that Stubbs, largely alone but also with the occasional assistance of his common-law wife Mary Spencer, spent eighteen months dissecting, drawing and describing horses in a farmhouse or barn in Horkstow in Lincolnshire.[5] The eighteen highly polished drawings made by him there on the basis of twenty-four (still surviving) working sketches after dissecting approximately a dozen horses are timeless masterpieces of animal anatomy. They show the horse as a skeleton first, in lateral, anterior, and posterior views (cat. nos. 7–9) and, then, the horse's musculature from the same three perspectives. Stubbs lays the horse bare in no less than five steps. Beginning with the subcutaneous tissue, Stubbs drills down into the deepest muscle layers, illustrating the position and paths of the ligaments on the skeleton as well as the deep blood vessels and nerves (cat. nos. 10–15). These drawings still impress today in terms of their artistic just as much as their scientific achievement. Their exceptional elegance, clarity, and graphic precision contrast hugely with the reality of the bloody, dirty and physically draining work that Stubbs must have carried out amid the stink of rotting cadavers and in constant fear of infection.

In his search for qualified engravers who would be able to transpose the project into print, Stubbs brought the drawings to London in 1758, where they quickly became known on account of their outstanding quality.[6] The story goes that even the most established engravers and printers, for example Arthur Pond and Charles Grignion, turned down the task of rendering the accomplished drawings for the press.[7] Stubbs subsequently spent six years etching the printing plates himself, working in the early mornings and at night, until they finally appeared in 1766 as an anatomical atlas—supplemented by comprehensive descriptive texts from his own hand. So accomplished were the etchings that we can speak of his ingenious translation of the drawings into prints. The anatomist Peter Camper recognized the achievement in a letter to Stubbs in 1772 thus: "I'm amazed to meet in the same person so great an Anatomist, so accurate a Painter & so excellent an Engraver."[8]

The path taken by Stubbs's career is unusual in that before making the drawings for his *Anatomy of the Horse* he was neither an established nor experienced painter of horses but rather had been trying his hand as a portrait painter.[9] His earliest known sketches for paintings of horses date to about 1759. Stubbs's anatomical studies

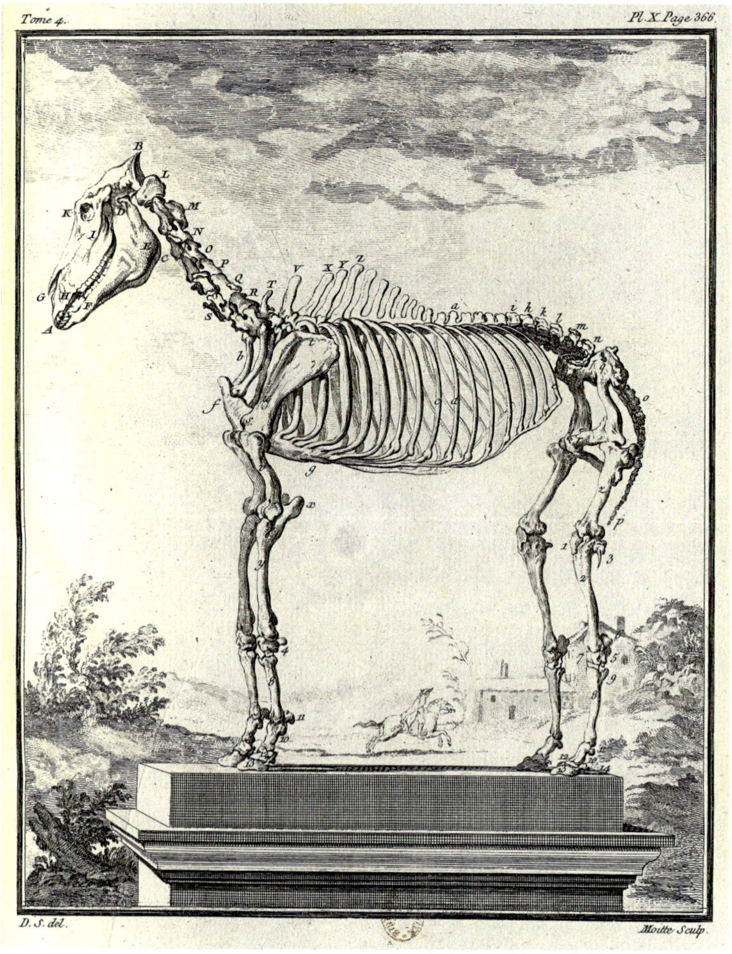

1 Georges-Louis Leclerc de Buffon, *Histoire naturelle générale et particulière*, vol. 4, Paris 1753, pl. x, Skeleton of a Horse, engraving
Paris, Bibliothèque nationale de France

thus not only enriched and improved his work as a painter and portrayer of horses, but actually gave it its impulse. The fact that Stubbs received a whole series of commissions for prestigious equine portraits and hunting scenes from 1760/61 onwards and was rapidly elevated to the leading painter of horses to the English nobility can only be explained by the early success of his anatomical drawings. Two aspects are worthy of note here: in terms of his artistic practice Stubbs's approach testifies to an uncompromising 'critical' (in the Enlightenment sense of the term) approach, in which painting is conceived of as a science and its subjects are examined through their reduction to their fundamental principles. Yet the reasons for which Stubbs's studies were successful still require explanation, for it was thanks to these studies that Stubbs was able to establish himself primarily as a horse painter, rather than as an anatomical draughtsman. The question of how anatomical knowledge was translated into painting, a process which in itself is hardly self-evident, apparently did not pose itself for his patrons. To his contemporaries, Stubbs's aesthetic anatomical drawings must have appeared as the promising beginnings of a new scientifically-founded horse painting. At the same time, the situation was favourable for Stubbs: the leading painters of the older generation in this field, such as James Seymour (1702–1752), were already dead, or, like John Wootton (c. 1682–1764), well advanced in years. Stubbs's drawings, moreover, were well-matched with an interest recently pursued by his potential clients: their systematic attempts in the area of horse-breeding chimed perfectly with Stubbs's analytical investigation of the body of the horse.

ANATOMY AND ITS MEANING IN NATURAL HISTORY AND VETERINARY MEDICINE

Stubbs's lifelong enthusiasm for anatomy was more than just an individual interest; it was also the expression of the popularization of anatomy as a discipline in the eighteenth century. The prime goal of the Enlightenment era, the striving to survey and systematize human knowledge in its entirety, meant that public attention was focused above all on natural history. As an overarching discipline, natural history comprised zoology, biology and geology in equal measure. Anatomical description and illustration attained central importance, not least in the recording of the myriad new species of animals then being discovered on Enlightenment research voyages, because anatomical description and illustration authoritatively advocated an understanding of the ways in which animals moved as well as their physique.[10] As a consequence, standardized lateral views of animal skeletons (fig. 1), anatomical plates and meticulous anatomical descriptions also became a constituent part of one of the most successful and comprehensive publishing projects of the eighteenth century: Georges-Louis Leclerc de Buffon's *Histoire naturelle générale et particulière*, which appeared in forty-four volumes between 1749 and 1804. Buffon, the powerful director of the Jardin du Roi in Paris, gave the horse dignity by according it particular attention, putting it before all other animals, and describing its noblesse, temperament and obedient nature. The anthropocentric criteria backed by the author in his way of looking at Nature saw in the horse the animal most akin to man, the most useful and, above all, the most beautiful of all creatures.[11]

It was not only in natural historical publications that the horse enjoyed admiration and attention. Of outstanding economic importance as a working animal in agriculture, and as means of transport and conveyance in both civil and military life, the horse and its care, sustenance and breeding were of great strategic relevance. With the aim of applying the newest scientific standards to these tasks, the first veterinary schools in the world were founded in France in the 1760s. Scholarship to date has overlooked that Stubbs expressly mentioned the French institutes in the foreword to his *Anatomy of the Horse* and showed himself to be well informed about the recent developments in continental Europe.[12] Only five years before the publication of the *Anatomy*, the first state school for veterinary medicine had been founded in Lyon in 1761 by Claude Bourgelat (1712–1779).[13] Also under his aegis the *École royale vétérinaire d'Alfort* commenced operating in 1766 not far from Paris. Bourgelat's students subsequently founded numerous similar establishments across Europe. In England, which lagged far behind France in veterinary medicine, such a school first came about through the endeavours of the exiled Frenchman Charles Vial de Saint-Bel, founder of the Royal Veterinary College in London in 1791.

Both the establishment of veterinary schools and Stubbs's *Anatomy of the Horse* aspired to a science of animal anatomy. In the seventeenth and eighteenth centuries, medical expertise in terms of horses took the form of knowledge gained on the job by farriers, equerries, and horse doctors, knowledge which had been handed down by word of mouth or written down in compendiums of earlier publications. Bourgelat sought to replace these traditions by critically overhauling texts and examining animals empirically, whilst being guided by unshakeable principles and exacting methods.[14] For Bourgelat, anatomy was the most important element in the refounding animal medicine,[15] an element which he had to promote energetically nonetheless. Complexity and disgust were the two fundamental problems of anatomy that Bourgelat faced. Difficulties experienced by beginners in clearly differentiating between and recognising the individual anatomical parts were compounded by the fact that dissection was a dissuasively dirty business.[16]

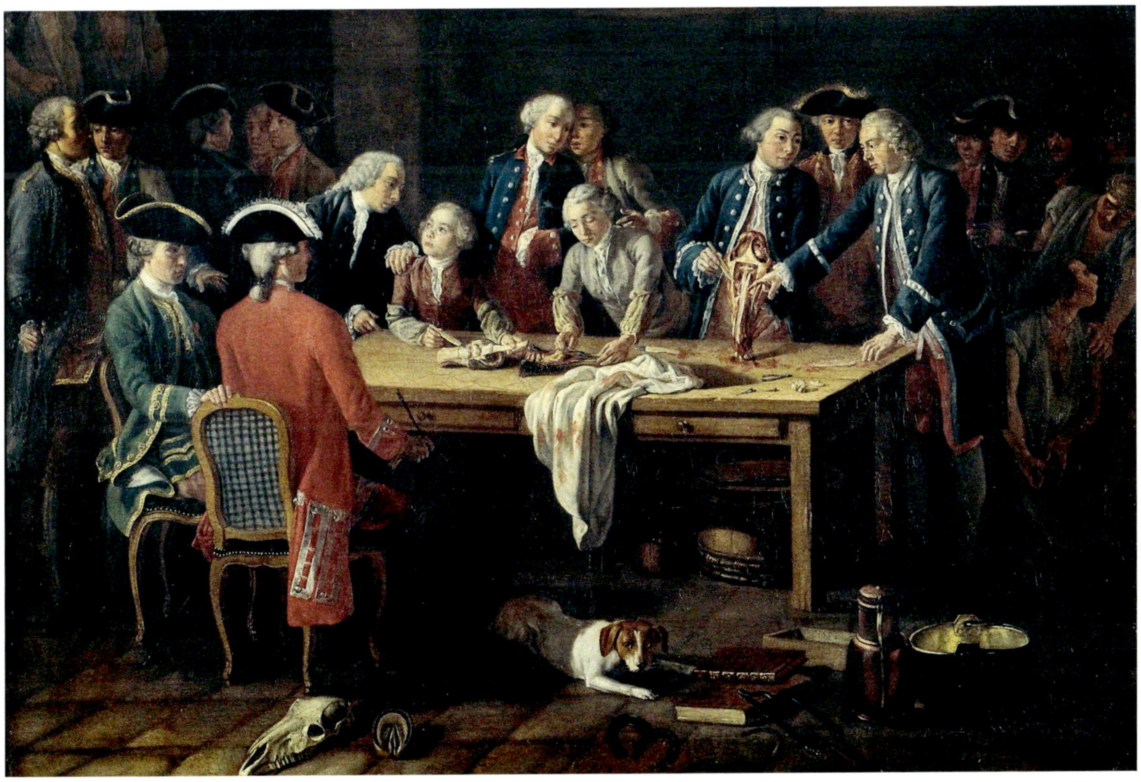

2 Claude-Florentin Sollier, *Anatomy Lecture by Lafosse*, c. 1772, oil on canvas, 88 x 128 cm Maisons-Alfort, École vétérinaire

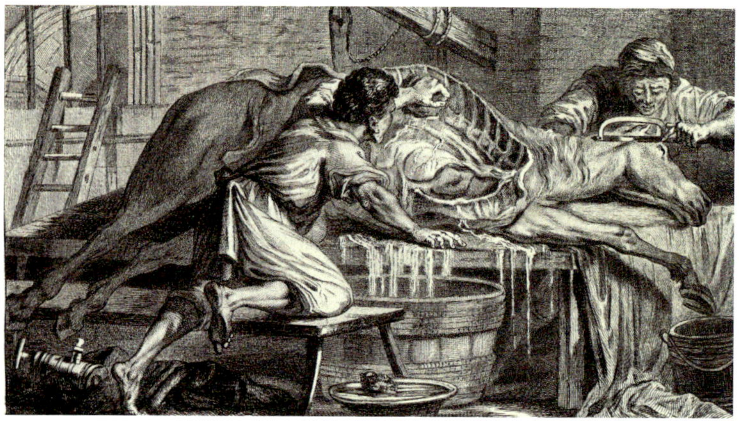

3 Philippe-Etienne Lafosse, *Cours d'hippiatrique*, Paris 1772, pl. XXXVI, Splanchnology (Study of Viscera), engraving
Munich, Bayerische Staatsbibliothek

"THE ANATOMY OF THE HORSE" IN THE CONTEXT OF 'POLITE SCIENCE' AND THE FUNCTIONS OF ANATOMICAL ILLUSTRATION

In the age of Enlightenment, in which the sciences were under increasing pressure to legitimize themselves publically and to address interested laymen, disgust in the face of dead and flayed animals was a challenge which is not to be underestimated. In its complexity and uncensored physicality, anatomy was only partially compatible with the criteria of so-called 'polite science', which was defined by intelligibility, usefulness, sociability, conversation and elegance of verbal presentation.[17] Anatomical demonstrations were certainly now and then part of public scientific practice, but they could not shake off the essential features of being 'impolite', such as the soiling of hands and clothes with blood and secretions, unpleasant smells, decomposition and the violent act of dissecting bodies.[18]

In the case of animals as big as horses, public dissections must have taken on the appearance of a ceremonial slaughter. The frontispiece with which the French horse doctor Philippe-Etienne Lafosse illustrated his *Cours d'hippiatrique* (1772) is a rare depiction of a lecture in veterinary anatomy. The painting produced after the engraved original (fig. 2) similarly shows that the high-ranking participants were spared the sight of an entire horse carcass. They are presented instead with the parts of a hoof and a skull usually hidden beneath the skin, which are being explained by an anatomist standing to the right. This relatively blood-less demonstration contrasts massively with the actual practice of dissection hinted at elsewhere by Lafosse in a vignette illustrating the chapter on splanchnology, in other words the study of the viscera (fig. 3).[19]

Humphry's account of Stubbs's horse dissections in the Horkstow barn, too, is the exact opposite of the public performance of so-called polite science. The anatomy of the horse did not become socially acceptable until the appearance of the atlas and its large-format illustrations. The drawings provided horse-lovers with usually difficult-to-obtain anatomical insights without provoking disgust or horror. Anatomical insights and aesthetic claims contributed to the 'usefulness' of the *Anatomy of the Horse*: the term 'usefulness' was a much repeated central criterion of the enlightened natural sciences, which were preoccupied with being judged on how much they had contributed to social welfare.[20] Thus in his foreword Stubbs also highlighted that his treatise was intended to serve many purposes: it should benefit artists primarily but also horse lovers, horse owners and horse breeders, as well as smiths and horse doctors.[21]

The genesis of the *Anatomy* and the production of the plates document a hermeneutic turning point in which the arts and sciences had equal parts to play around the middle of the eighteenth century. A paradigm shift away from the reading of older texts and towards independent observation, or away from traditional towards rationally verified knowledge, was already evident around 1750 in Bourgelat's *Élémens d'hippiatrique*. Johann Joachim Winckelmann similarly claimed this for both his studies of antiquity and as rationale behind scientific archaeology around 1750. A cult of precise observation and visual immersion grew up which not only transcended the disciplines but also applied to artists and viewers of art as much as it did to natural historians.[22] Because telescopes and microscopes had led to the realization that Nature could not communicate its smallest and most distant elements without mediation, attentive observation was elevated to a much admired exceptional virtue in all of the empirical sciences, to the 'Art of Observation'.[23] The figure of the anatomist, whose gaze bored down into the unknown depths of the body, acquired an especial importance. Louis Jean-Marie Daubenton, who dissected almost two-hundred animals for Buffon's *Histoire naturelle* and composed anatomical descrip-

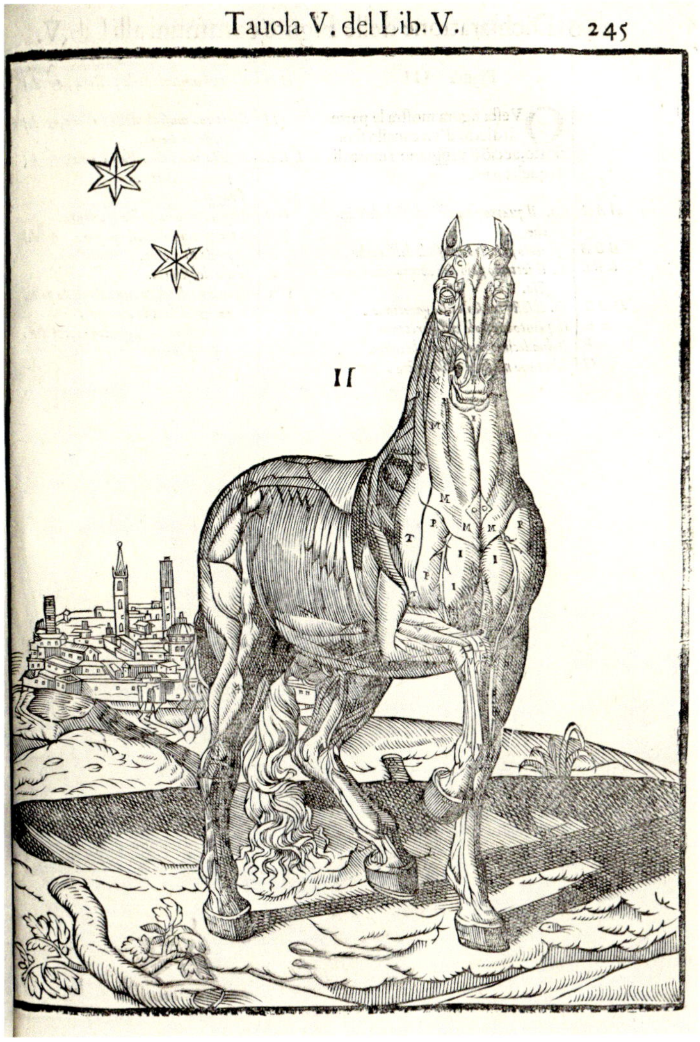

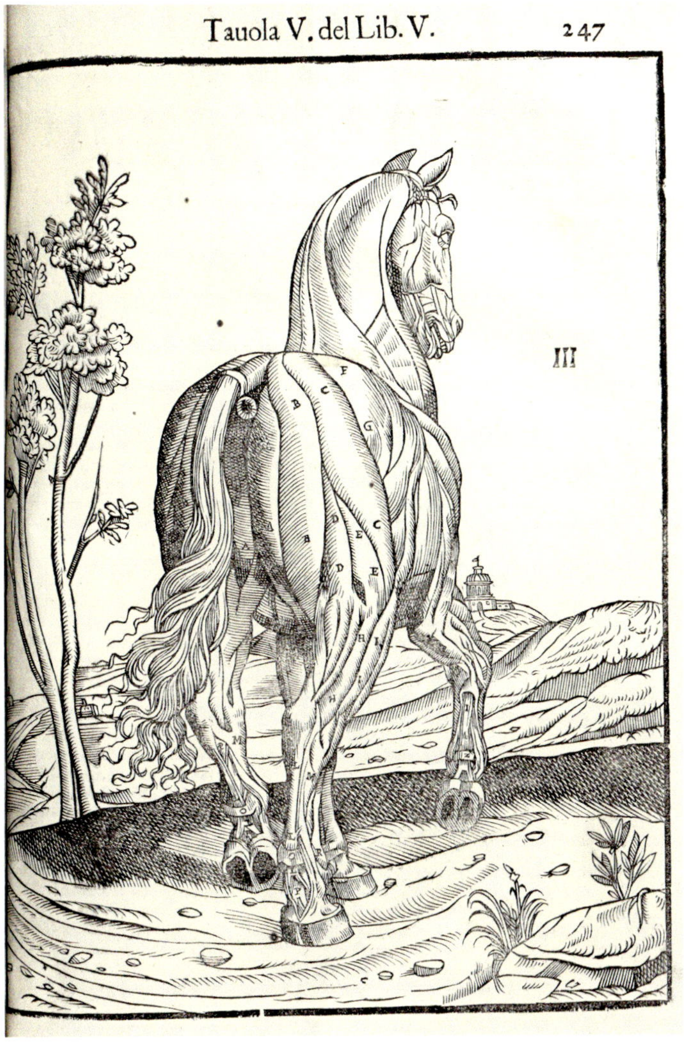

4 Carlo Ruini, *Anatomia del cavallo, infermità, et suoi rimedii*, Venice 1618, vol. v, pl. v/ii, woodcut

5 Carlo Ruini, *Anatomia del cavallo, infermità, et suoi rimedii*, Venice 1618, vol. v, pl. v/iii, woodcut

tions, compared the practice of anatomy to an expedition to the uncharted regions of the world. He followed the anatomist's voyages of discovery with admiration but also not without admonition. In his enthusiasm for detail, wrote Daubenton, the expert could lose sight of the coherency of the body, and, in the unbounded description of minutiae, also his audience, which could no longer keep up with his remarks and or indeed no longer wished to follow them.[24] Stubbs avoided the problem of long-winded or incomprehensible anatomical descriptions by putting large-format drawings at the heart of his project. The sensorial conviction that anatomical knowledge required the guidance of the eye manifests itself herein. Around 1750, the notion that scientific illustration facilitated understanding and should be produced with commensurate care was the basis for Diderot and d'Alembert's *Encyclopédie* and Buffon's *Histoire naturelle*;[25] it was also accepted by the surgeons and anatomists Stubbs knew in York.[26]

There were only a small number of examples in the history of veterinary anatomy on which Stubbs could orient himself for the representation of equine anatomy. Bourgelat's *Élémens d'hippiatrique*

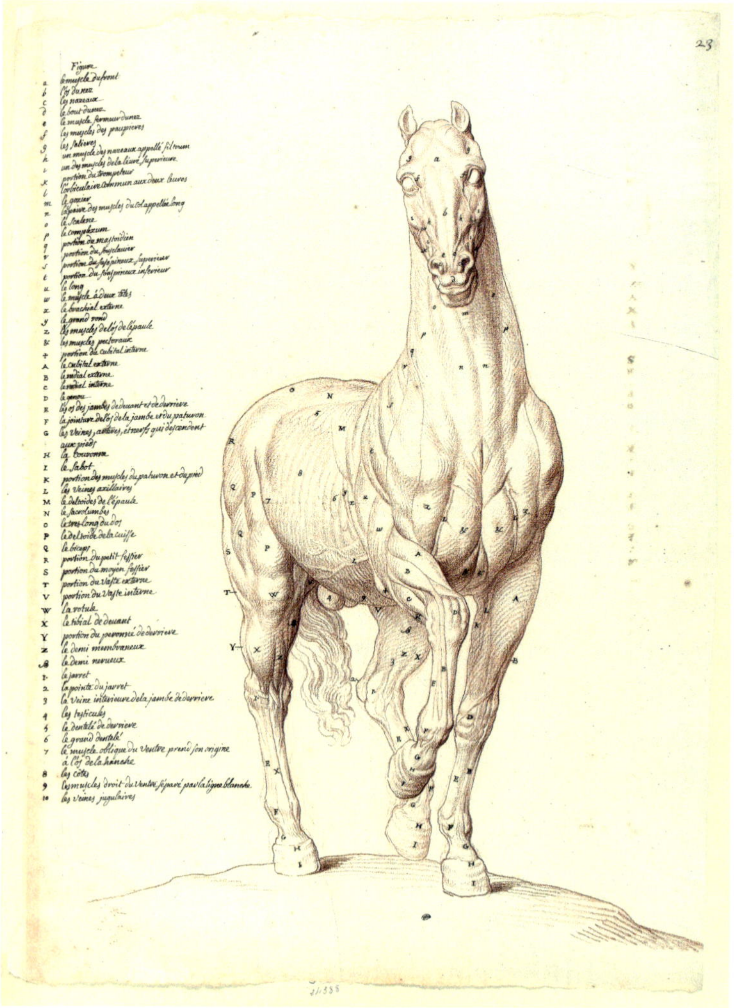

6 Edmé Bouchardon, 'Écorché'-horse, c. 1743/44, brown ink and red chalk, 60 x 44 cm
Paris, Musée du Louvre, Département des arts graphiques

had not been illustrated.[27] The first and last substantial depictions of horse anatomy had been made in the sixteenth century. Carlo Ruini's *Dell'anatomia et dell'infermità del cavallo*, published in 1598, was the first autonomous seminal publication on horse anatomy and medicine. His woodcuts were repeatedly copied in innumerable publications and were still being reproduced in the eighteenth century.[28] Ruini's work was surely among the anatomical treatises which Stubbs consulted for his *Anatomy*, but which he did not name specifically. Stubbs adopted the basic model for the anatomical depiction of horses established by Ruini: the presentation of the beast in its entirety and as if truly alive. Depicted in a gentle trot, the horse is shown in profile, from the front and from behind (figs. 4 and 5). It is also reproduced as a skeleton and the musculature beneath the surface of the skin is shown (as *écorché* or flayed). Just how important these depictions still were in the eighteenth century can be seen in the anatomical sketches of the French sculptor Edmé Bouchardon (fig. 6). Numbering sixty sheets, these might be compared to Stubbs's drawings, if indeed they had also been produced on the basis of Bouchardon's own anatomical research.[29]

Bouchardon's drawings in red chalk, which are to be dated to about 1743/44, were to have been the fundament of a never-published treatise on equine anatomy. His drawings are, however, partly copies of the illustrations of the skeleton and muscles from Ruini's publication.[30] An even greater number of his drawings were produced after a ninety-centimetre-high bronze of the *Flayed Horse* from the Villa Mattei in Rome, which itself was modelled on and cast after Ruini's woodcuts and which was widely found across the European art academies in the form of copies.

The artistic seal of quality 'from Nature', which should be treated with caution given Bouchardon's drawings, was also applied by Stubbs. His Foreword to the *Anatomy* stresses that "all the figures in it are drawn from nature." A brief glance at his drawings and etchings reveals, however, that in contrast to his forerunners, Stubbs was in fact an exacting and autonomous observer of animal anatomy. Bourgelat had already expressed doubts about the anatomical quality of Ruini's woodcuts and descriptions in 1750, but he did not better them with improved illustrations.[31] This is not the case with Stubbs. Stubbs in fact only adopted the position of the horse's body from Ruini's plates. The Italian's rendering of the musculature appears wooden and schematic in comparison with Stubbs's layer-by-layer presentation of the horse.[32] The success of the *Anatomy of the Horse* is surely also evident in the fact that the subtlety and sequence of the drawings and etchings are proof themselves of the success with which Stubbs's anatomical gaze was able to penetrate from skin to the skeleton. The 'Art of Observation' practised by Stubbs not only recognized and differentiated the very smallest of the anatomical elements but also reproduced them in a graphically convincing manner. This 'image-creating' process should therefore be seen as a scientific achievement in itself.[33]

7 Philippe-Etienne Lafosse, *Cours d'hippiatrique,* Paris 1772, pl. xxv, Angiology, Sections of the Aorta, engraving
Munich, Bayerische Staatsbibliothek

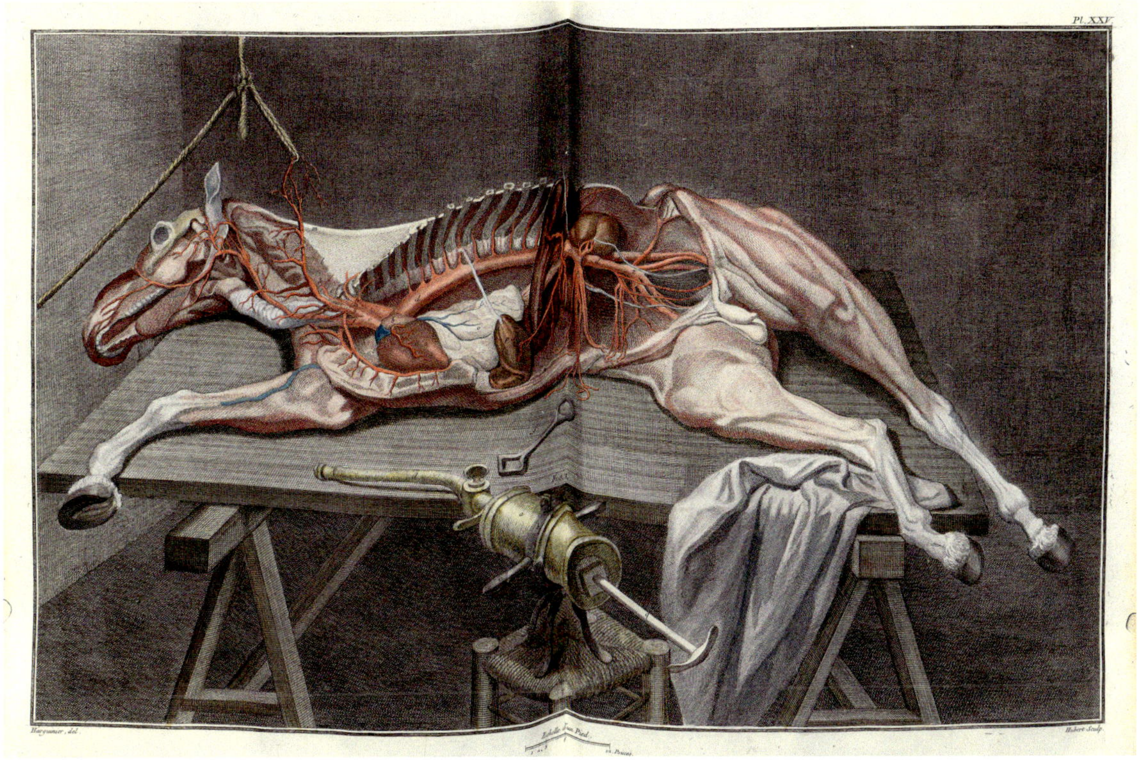

8 Philippe-Etienne Lafosse, *Cours d'hippiatrique*, Paris 1772, pl. xvi, Myology, engraving
Munich, Bayerische Staatsbibliothek

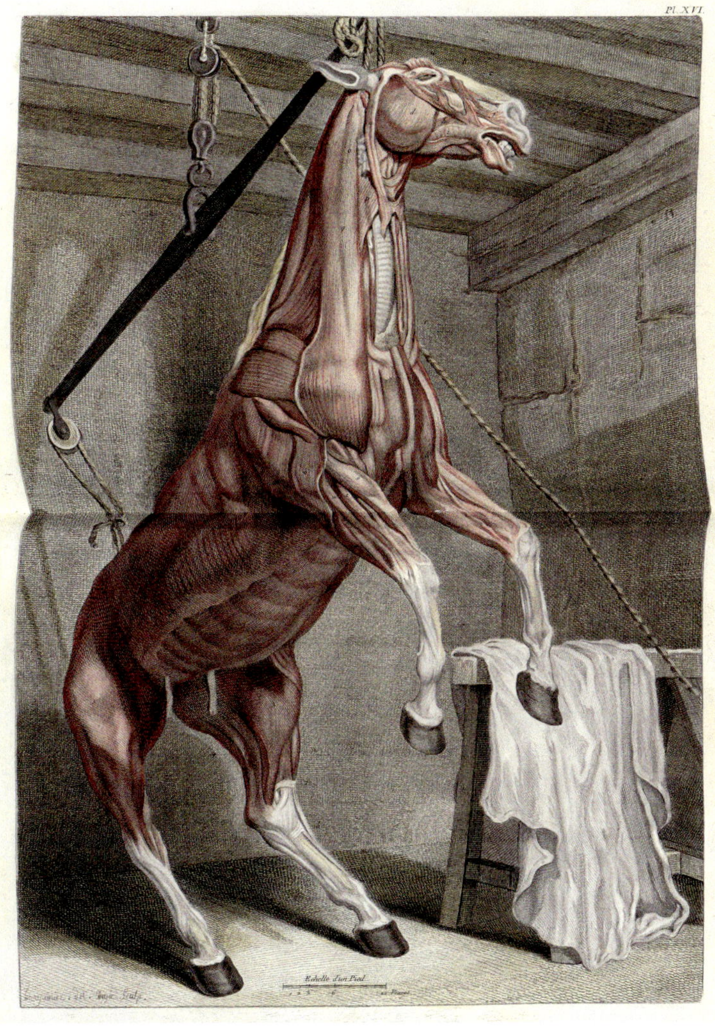

AGAINST AN ICONOGRAPHY OF VIOLENCE—STUBBS'S AESTHETIC PRINCIPLES AND THE 'NATURALISTIC' TRADITION OF REPRESENTATION IN ATLASES OF ANATOMY

The aesthetic merit and originality of Stubbs's *Anatomy of the Horse* is most clearly seen when compared with the most ambitious and extravagant French treatment of horse anatomy to appear in the eighteenth century. The *Cours d'hippiatrique ou traité complet de la médicine des chevaux* by Philippe-Etienne Lafosse (1738–1820), published in folio format in 1772, was a rival to the veterinary medical schools and publications of Claude Bourgelat. Lafosse had begun making anatomical studies of horses at the age of eighteen, roughly about the same time as Stubbs, and between 1767 and 1770 he had taught in an anatomical theatre of his own construction in Paris. With its classification according to the organ systems of the animal, his *Cours*, which he compiled between 1770 and 1772, marked the birth of scientific animal anatomy.[34] Despite his many years of

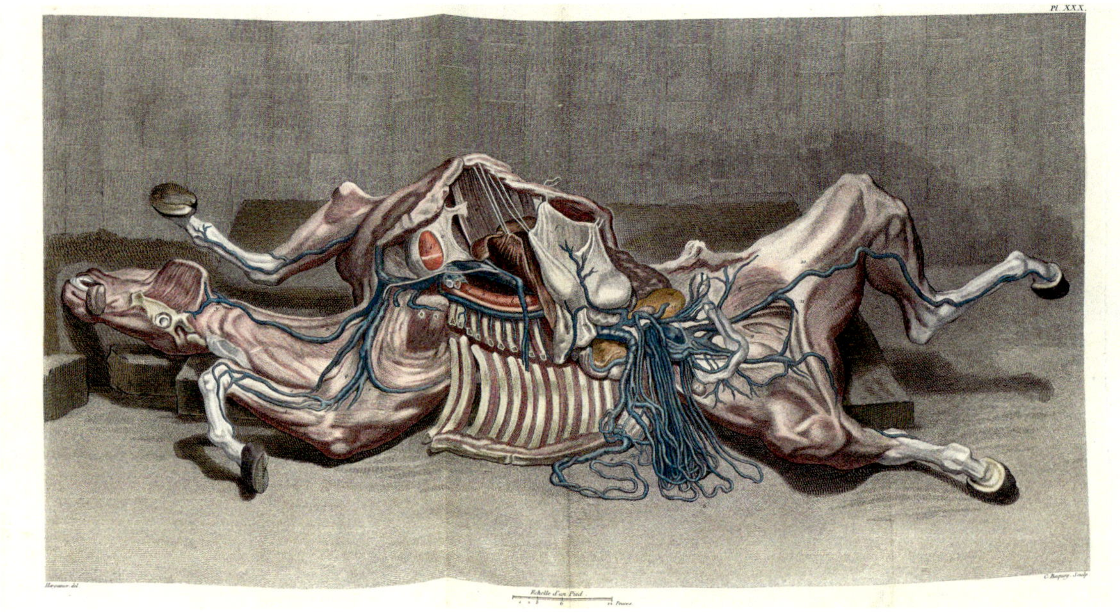

9 Philippe-Etienne Lafosse, *Cours d'hippiatrique*, Paris 1772, pl. xxx, Angiology, Principal Veins, engraving Munich, Bayerische Staatsbibliothek

experience in dissection and comprehensive descriptions, the author was convinced that horse anatomy could only be made intelligible by supplementing the work with illustrations.[35]

With the mutual support of discourse and image in mind, Lafosse commissioned the production of sixty-five engravings, which he also had hand coloured. These have yet to be discussed by scholars of Stubbs, but are highly revealing when set beside the English artist's anatomical plates. Drawn first by Harguinier, Saullier and even Lafosse himself, and then engraved by an array of artists, these plates, which were produced with the investment of both great sums of money and time, show a variety of views of the skeleton and muscles in which Lafosse—like Stubbs—gradually penetrates from the dermis and its musculature down into the depths of the body. Quite differently from the way in which Stubbs represents anatomy, Lafosse depicts places, contraptions, and the real results of the dissections. In the first vascular plate, for example, we see the enormous syringe with which the arteries of the aorta were pumped with a liquid containing wax or tallow in order to make their path more visible (fig. 7). To demonstrate the throat, shoulder and foreleg muscles a horse has been frozen in the rearing 'courbette' pose using a metal bar, hooks, pivots and pulleys (fig. 8).[36] Any suggestion of life preserved in this baroque staging of the horse is lost in the next illustration. In it the left foreleg has already been detached and the head is shown in a sagittal section (sliced from front to back) in order to allow the innermost muscles of the throat and the back muscles which lie further back to be seen. Lafosse had no interest at all in presenting the complete and apparently intact body of a horse. Quite the opposite, for him the presentation of the medical anatomical knowledge was accompanied by the visible and gradual carving up of the body. As is usual in modern anatomy atlases, individual body parts or joints were detached and presented in isolation for the purpose of large-format illustrations. The angiological, neurological and splanchnological plates in which the horse has positively been wrenched open as if the creature had been quartered and the uppermost layers folded back in order to lay the paths of the most important arteries, veins and nerves, as well as blood vessels bare can scarcely be exceeded in their gross clarity and immediacy (fig. 9). This unnatural presentation of multiple perspectives can be explained as an attempt to make the different and hidden aspects of the body visible simultaneously. Nonetheless, such distortions are always a result of the cadaver's traumatic desecration: the horses bodies, which—some with lolling tongue—appear to be laid out as if on the slab, documenting a vexing aesthetic in which violence is depicted anthropomorphically and with relish.

The tradition of 'naturalistic' anatomical illustrations which shock on account of their clinical detachment and refusal to sympathize is comparatively young.[37] It was initiated by Goverd Bidloo in 1685 with his *Anatomia humani corporis*, for which the Netherlandish artist Gérard de Lairesse produced the drawings around 1680. These reproduce preserved specimens prepared by Bidloo in such a way as to make the viewer an eyewitness of the results of the dissections. The bodies are presented as dead, mutilated and spliced open; selected organs and members have been isolated and are shown close up. The layers of skin and muscle are always flung back ostenta-

11 George Stubbs, *The Anatomy of the Horse,* London 1766, The Fifteenth Anatomical Table of the Muscles ... of the Horse, detail
London, The British Museum

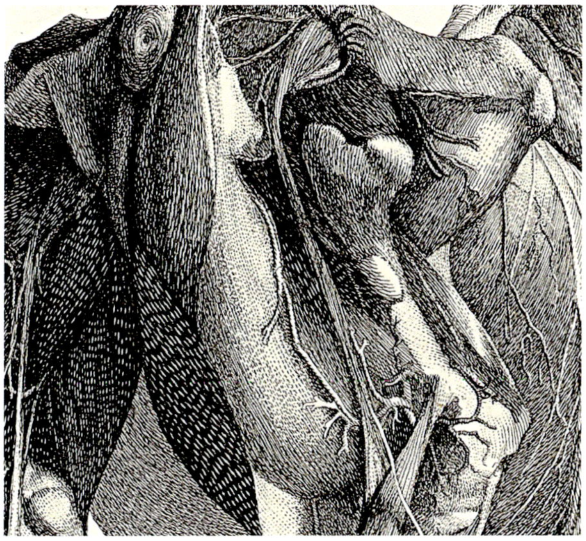

10 Goverd Bidloo, *Anatomia humani corporis,* Amsterdam 1685, pl. 56, engraving
Munich, Bayerische Staatsbibliothek

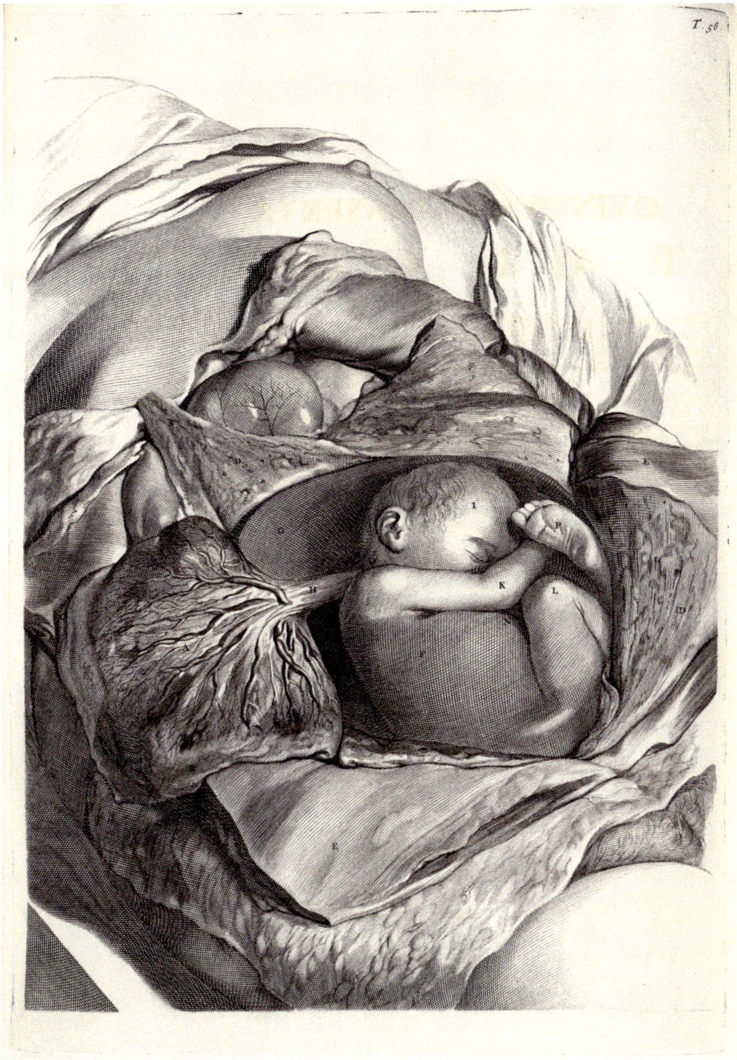

tiously and mechanically secured in place, triumphantly opening the way for the gaze into the inner life of the body (fig. 10). Anatomical tools like rope, nails or stakes as well as tables are an integral part of the pictures. Lafosse may not have named Bidloo as having provided the model for the anatomical plates in his *Cours*, but they are nonetheless clearly to be interpreted as a transferral of the Bidloo'ian style of representation of human anatomy onto the veterinary. Stubbs's highly-sensory and aesthetic approach stands out when confronted with these drastic illustrations. In contrast to any actual anatomical practice, Stubbs's horses are disrobed layer by layer. The physical trauma which manifests itself in slashes, cavities and detached members is suppressed, and the body is never presented in an 'unnatural' or distorted position, raising doubts that the animal was ever once alive. By maintaining the whole and presenting the horse in a slight trot, Stubbs seems to orient himself on Ruini, albeit not without undertaking minor corrections of perspective. In particular, the rear views of Stubbs's horses (cat. nos. 9, 14, 15) demonstrate that they were viewed from a lower viewpoint than they can be seen in Ruini's models (fig. 5). The fact that the viewer looks up at the animal from the height of its hooves ennobles and monumentalizes it.

When his work is compared with Lafosse's plates, Stubbs's devotion to keeping the outer contour of the horse's body intact shows itself to be fundamental. In Lafosse, entrails and vessels frequently dangle out of the body like strings or worms (fig. 9) and abandoned to the gravity of the limp body. This produces a sharp-angled web, diametrically opposed to any neo-classical aesthetic of

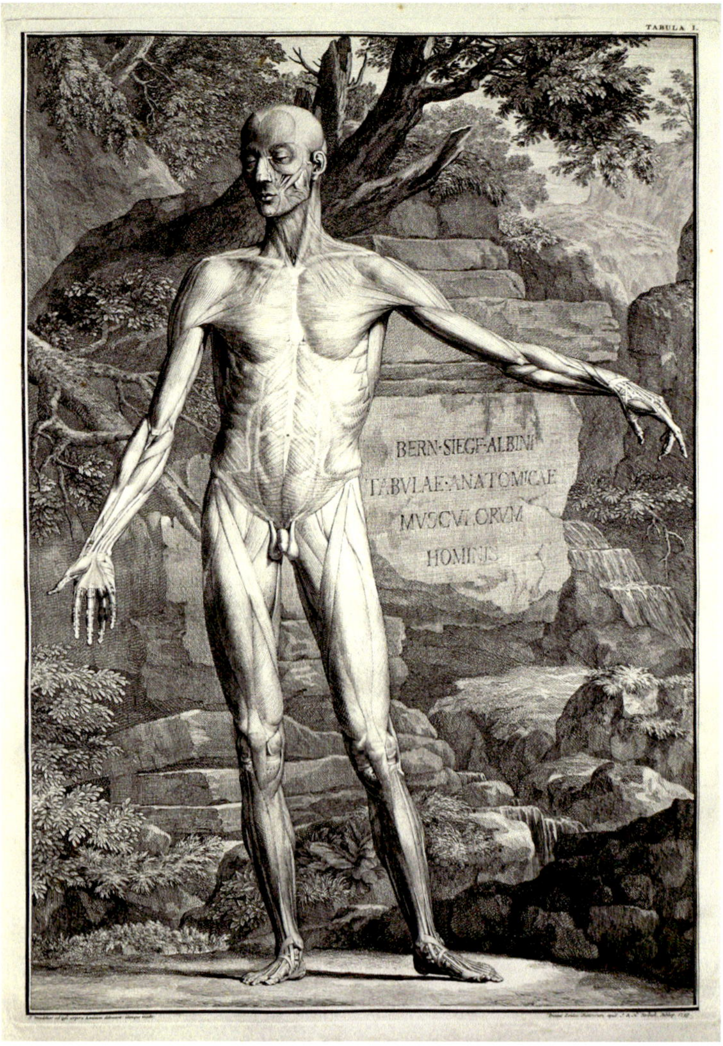

12 Bernhard Siegfried Albinus, *Tabulae sceleti et musculorum corporis humani*, Leiden 1747, pl. I of the Muscles, engraving Humboldt-Universität zu Berlin, Universitätsbibliothek

13 Bernhard Siegfried Albinus, *Tabulae sceleti et musculorum corporis humani*, Leiden 1747, pl. III of the Muscles, engraving Humboldt-Universität zu Berlin, Universitätsbibliothek

14 Bernhard Siegfried Albinus, *Tabulae sceleti et musculorum corporis humani*, Leiden 1747, pl. IV of the Muscles, diagram Humboldt-Universität zu Berlin, Universitätsbibliothek

the curving line. In contrast, Stubbs shows the blood vessels and veins of the horse's body in their functional context as organs. In the lateral view, Stubbs's contour of the horse alludes to Hogarth's "line of grace" and develops in a gentle sweep, which continues over the neck and withers down into the musculature of the tail (cat. nos. 7, 10, 11).[38] Stubbs also expresses the horse's bodily unity by exposing it to a consistent source of light which falls into the frame from the front or from above and by attuning the brightness of each individual bodily element to it. The relief-like modelling and the ever-present suggestion of space are not only aesthetically astounding but also essential for anatomical coherence. Stubbs had to make the ways in which bodily elements spatially overlapped and entwined palpable in two dimensions. We see this process most clearly if we juxtapose Stubbs's plates with those by Lafosse, who applied supplementary colouring to areas of muscles and blood vessels, as well as the paths of the nerves, in order to distinguish certain anatomical parts. Stubbs had complete faith in his ability to differentiate them graphically. In contrast to Lafosse, he renders the overlapping of the muscles, blood vessels and sinews etc. clearly in each of the identical plates, instead of differentiating the illustrations according to the muscular, vascular and nervous systems. This complex approach was made possible by Stubbs's highly variable drawing and engraving technique. He differentiates the various elements by dotting, stippling and using parallel and cross hatching, as well as slender or clearly defined contours (fig. 11). The strong correlation of graphic technique and anatomical element still had to be additionally attuned to the shading of the whole. Issues which are connected with major graphic difficulties in the lateral view of the body are exacerbated in the posterior and anterior views of the horse, where the artist also had to overcome the problem of the foreshortening of the horse's body (cat. nos. 13–15).

IDEALIZED ANATOMICAL ILLUSTRATIONS AND THE ROLE OF THE ARTIST: BERNHARD SIEGFRIED ALBINUS'S "TABULAE" (1747) AS A MODEL FOR STUBBS'S "ANATOMY"

Peter Camper, a contemporary of Stubbs and himself a draughtsman who was acquainted with the problems of representing anatomy, commented enthusiastically about Stubbs's graphic ability, asking "How is it possible that a single man can execute such a plan with so much accuracy and industry? You have certainly had before you the scheme of the great Albinus but even his plates have not that delicacy and fullness, nor the expression of yours."[39]

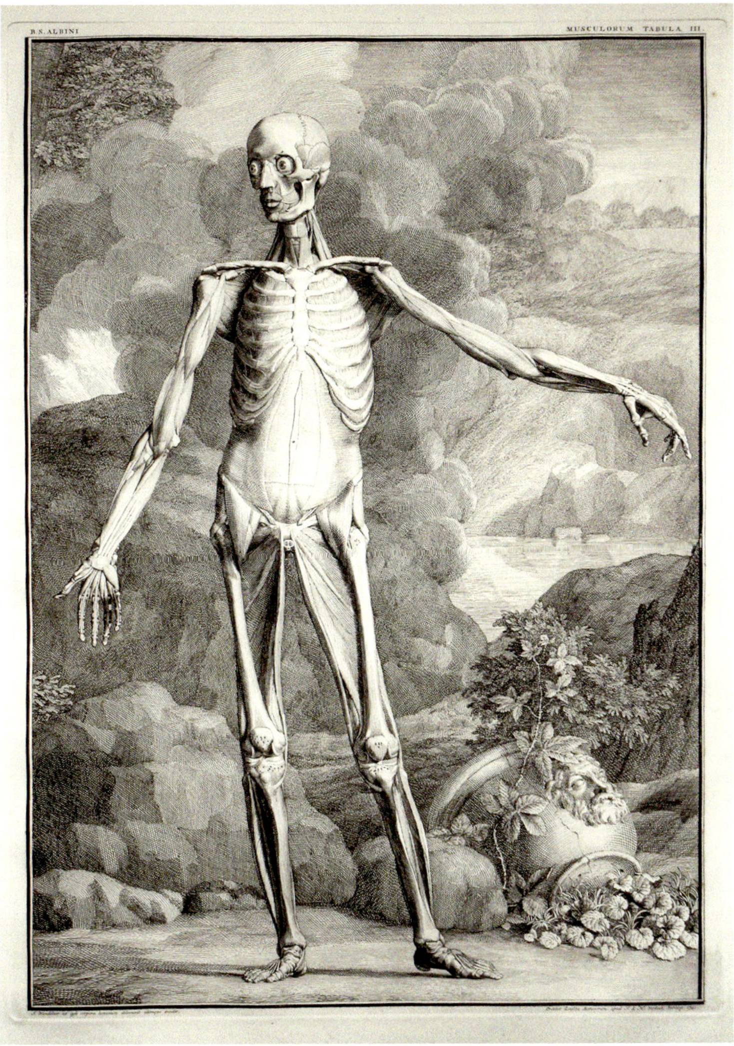

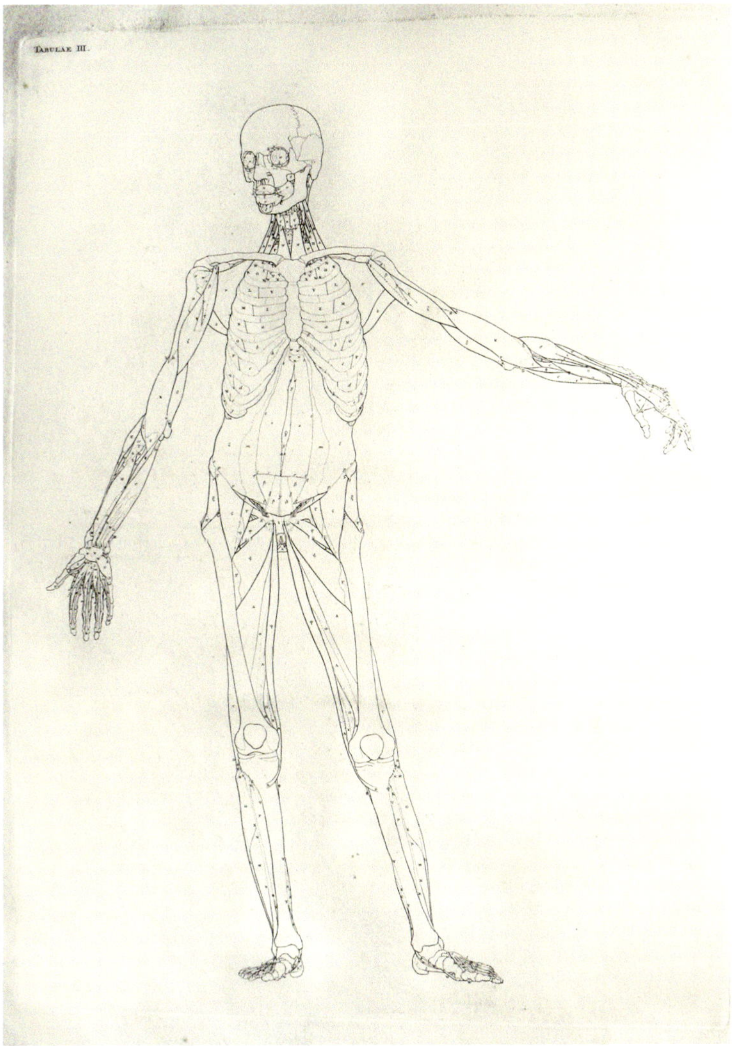

Camper was alluding to the fact that Bernhard Siegfried Albinus's *Tabulae sceleti et musculorum corporis humani*, published in 1747, had served as a reference for Stubbs's *Anatomy*.[40] Albinus had consistently pursued the aestheticization and idealization of human anatomy and had published, with the support of the artist Jan Wandelaar, large-format drawings in his atlas, which had set a new anatomical standard in their clarity, exactitude and beauty.

Albinus served as an example for Stubbs in a number of systematic and technical aspects.[41] He pursued a 'structuralist' model of anatomy in that he saw the skeleton as the architectonic basis for the human physique and dedicated considerable attention to arranging it mechanically in lifelike poses and graphically recording it as correctly as possible.[42] The atlas plates show the body from three viewpoints and undertake the anatomical autopsy, like the *Anatomy of the Horse*, from the outside inwards (figs. 12 and 13). Albinus considered the skeleton to be so important because he wanted to illustrate the connections between the bodily parts and their proportions, and also aimed to show the complete apparatus of movement, how it functioned and was organized.[43] For this reason Albinus attached particular importance to the accuracy of the position and proportions of the muscles and bones, developing a grid system as an aid to graphic transferral which could be positioned at two different distances and which avoided the perspectival distortions and truncations of earlier anatomical atlases.

It was, however, the normative character of Albinus's plates which made them of decisive and fundamental importance for the *Anatomy of the Horse*. Albinus's aim was not to reproduce an individual skeleton with the greatest possible accuracy but rather to recreate the anatomy of, in his opinion, an ideal man—a "homo perfectus". The standard male skeletal frame was unable to fulfil Albinus's ideal

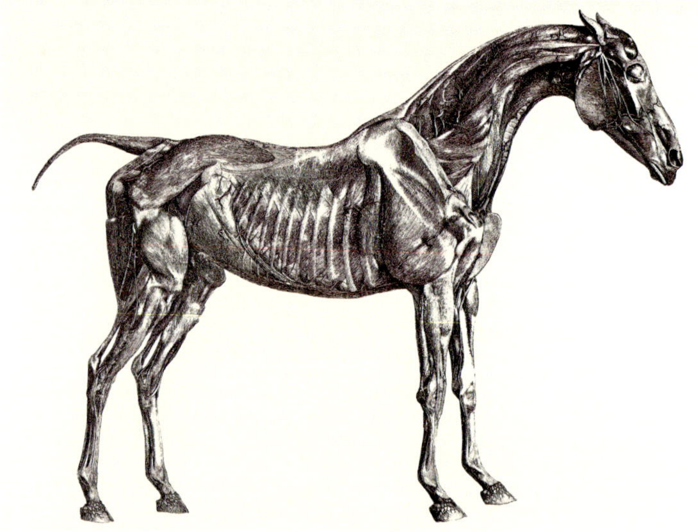

15 George Stubbs, *The Anatomy of the Horse*, London 1766,
The Third Anatomical Table of the Muscles ...
of the Horse, etching

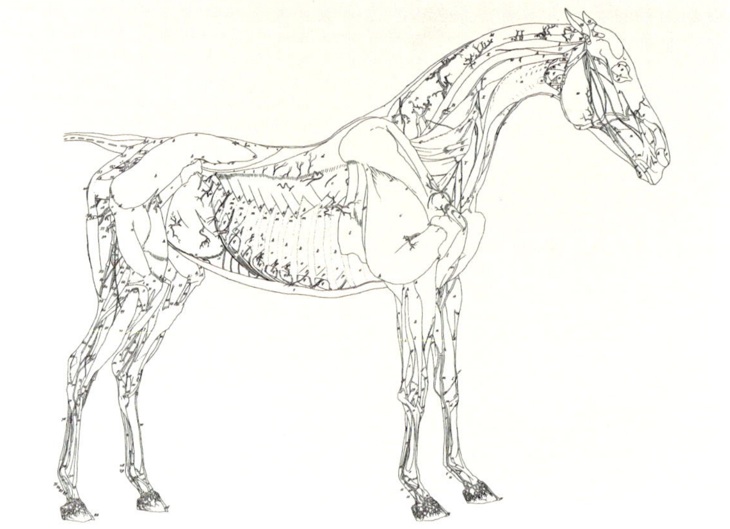

16 George Stubbs, *The Anatomy of the Horse*, London 1766,
The Third Anatomical Table of the Muscles ...
of the Horse, diagram

notions in entirety. Inspired by the paragon of ideal beauty, the Helen created by the ancient Greek painter Zeuxis on the basis of the combined body parts of various women, Albinus attempted to achieve perfect proportions and the complete symmetry of all elements.[44] Here, the artistic conversion of Albinus's imagined ideal was decisive and he conferred the task on Jan Wandelaar. Not only was Wandelaar to attend to the accuracy of the muscles but also to communicate the firmness, elegance, power, grace and harmony of the body.[45] Alongside the stage-like ennobling of the skeleton, landscape backgrounds or drapery were charged with stressing the body's spatial modelling. Albinus did not want to see the serious aestheticization of the anatomical illustration disrupted by the obligatory enumeration of body parts in reference to the anatomical key. He introduced the graphic rendering of the illustrations in the form of diagrams. Explanatory numbers and letters were inserted into the charts which grew from these (fig. 14). Rarely discussed to date, but nonetheless an extremely noteworthy innovation in anatomical illustration, these imply the emancipation of artistic function from that which was scientifically worthy of illustration. The illustration loses its illustrative character and aesthetic pleasure is no longer hampered by a numerical key. Moreover, the increasing importance given to the shading and tonality of the illustration obscures the actual boundaries and relationships between the bones and muscles. The contours of the diagram serve to make these points clear. The tasks are divided: the diagram is conceptually clear and informative, whereas the anatomical illustration is beautiful.[46]

Stubbs transferred Albinus's way of aestheticizing the anatomical illustration to the representation of the horse. At almost the same time as Lafosse was adapting Bidloo's naturalistic process of illustration for his equine anatomy, Stubbs was borrowing Albinus's idealistic schema for his *Anatomy of the Horse*. Stubbs's starting point was similarly a standard skeleton which conceived of an ideal equine anatomy, far removed from individual models. To prevent the disruption of the aesthetic quality of his illustrations, he also employed diagrams of his illustrations after Albinus's model (fig. 16). Like the body in Albinus's work, the horses combine the impression of anatomical correctness with the impression of vitality, elegance and grace. This idealization is not surprising given the audience to which Stubbs mainly hoped to appeal. Horse lovers and breeders were just as keen as painters to find an eminently model example of the species. Albinus's concept also played an inalienable role in the aestheticization of anatomical drawing insofar as he did not—as did Bidloo or Lafosse—show the destruction or dissection of the body, but rather, in the construction of an ideal body on the basis of a standard skeleton and by foregoing the analysis of its components, a process of creation. Artistic categories like imagination and creativity were an essential part of thinking about anatomy when it came to the archetype of a visualized perfect body. With his knowledge about drawing, the fall of light, perspective and composition, it was necessary for the artist to be able to suggest spiritedness and ideal beauty.[47]

With the growing contribution of the aesthetic to the practice of illustrating scientific knowledge, the job of the artist gained in importance in anatomical discourse. The unity of word and image ideally led to recognition for both anatomist and artist.[48] It also resulted, however, in the suppression of the artist by the anatomist. Albinus asserted that his draughtsman Jan Wandelaar was but the 'tool' which he had mastered and manipulated. Albinus had supervised him, corrected him and instructed him throughout.[49] These words confirm a fundamental conflict of authority. As anatomical illustration became idealized the anatomist himself had to put his faith increasingly in the artist's capacity to represent. The aesthetic rules inherent in producing an image simultaneously endangered the anatomical correctness of an illustration. In his *Engravings of the Bones, Muscles and Joints* of 1794 the anatomist John Bell clearly formulated this basic conflict in addition to developing an unusual solution.[50] He simply sketched and engraved his plates himself and, in doing so, proceeded like Stubbs. By eliminating thus the last possible cause of change or incertitude in anatomical illustration—the transferral of sketch to engraving—it was thought that scientific accuracy could be realized seamlessly from specimen to sketch to printed page. Working with the scalpel, the pen and the burin, the most comprehensive anatomical knowledge and artistic powers of expression went thus hand in hand.

WILLIAM HUNTER AND THE QUESTION OF OBJECTIVITY AND REALISM IN ANATOMICAL ILLUSTRATION

In the wake of the publication of Albinus's *Tabulae* a debate grew up around the middle of the eighteenth century as to which sort of illustration should be given precedence in anatomical science. Should one orient oneself—like Albinus—on a synthetically ideal type, or—like Bidloo—prefer a type of illustration that was truer to nature? This issue is not without relevance for Stubbs's anatomical investigations because the debate was sparked by obstetrical treatises for which Stubbs had undertaken his first experiments in drawing and printing when he illustrated Burton's 1751 *Essay Towards a Complete New System of Midwifery*.[51] Furthermore, the Scottish doctor and anatomist William Hunter, who became an important patron of Stubbs from about 1770 onwards, occupied an important corner in the debate. As early as 1751, Hunter had employed highly-finished detailed drawings as a visual aid in his lectures on midwifery.[52] Made by the Dutch artist Jan van Rymsdyk, these drawings only appeared in the form of engravings more than twenty years later, in 1774, in the valuable large-format anatomy atlas *Anatomia uteri humani gravidi tabulis illustrata*. In his foreword, Hunter, who does not mention the artist by name at all in his book, consciously differentiated between two traditions of anatomical illustration. He rejected the idealizing tendency which takes its subjects from the imagination for his purposes because its synthetic character meant that it had no scientific illustrative value.[53] Only the "simple portrait", he wrote, could bear the "mark of truth".

Hunter's trust in the objectivity of graphic reproduction was limitless.[54] For him it was a universal language which he saw as being able to illustrate anatomical specimens with exactitude and accuracy.[55] When compared with Lairesse's drawings, Hunter's attained the utmost importance on account of their still more intensified realism to shocking effect. The mutilated lower torso of a pregnant woman is given the same attention as the foetus itself (fig. 17). The artist dedicates himself to reproducing the layers of skin and tissue of the uterus as well as the foetus with the same meticulousness as he does the stumps of the amputated legs. In Bidloo's plates, the latter were covered with cloths or had not been severed (fig. 10). Skin, tissue, foetus and legs are probably especially intended to emphatically authenticate the objectivity of that which is represented. Why was Hunter so optimistic that his anatomy atlas was able to perfectly reproduce real specimens? The anatomist had demanded that his artist provide the smallest details with the greatest possible graphic finish. In his Foreword he defined this combination as being totally essential for scientific illustration.[56] Rymsdyk knew how to meet Hunter's standards with his captivating graphic representation of texture and structure which, when transformed into prints, developed a hyper real and almost photographic brilliance.

Stubbs doubtless discussed the possibilities of representing the foetus in the womb with Burton in 1751, and probably later with William Hunter too. In comparison to Hunter's *Anatomia uteri*, which is one of the most important anatomical artistic achievements of the eighteenth century, Stubbs's modest illustrations demonstrate a striking degree of abstraction which can be explained by more than just their commitment to tradition.[57] The uterus appears as an abstract circular form in which the foetus lies. Hunter's excessively described layers of flesh and muscle and the texture of the tissue had no role to play at all for Stubbs. Even the position of the womb in the body seems to have been irrelevant. It is only when looking at the image again that one sees that Stubbs illustrated the actual process of childbirth: a barely visible hand pulls the child from the

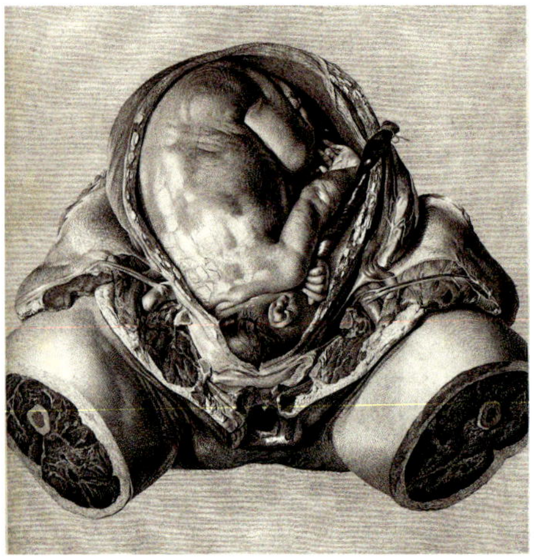

17 William Hunter, *Anatomia uteri humani gravidi tabulis illustrata / The anatomy of the human gravid uterus exhibited in figures*, Birmingham 1774, pl. VI, engraving

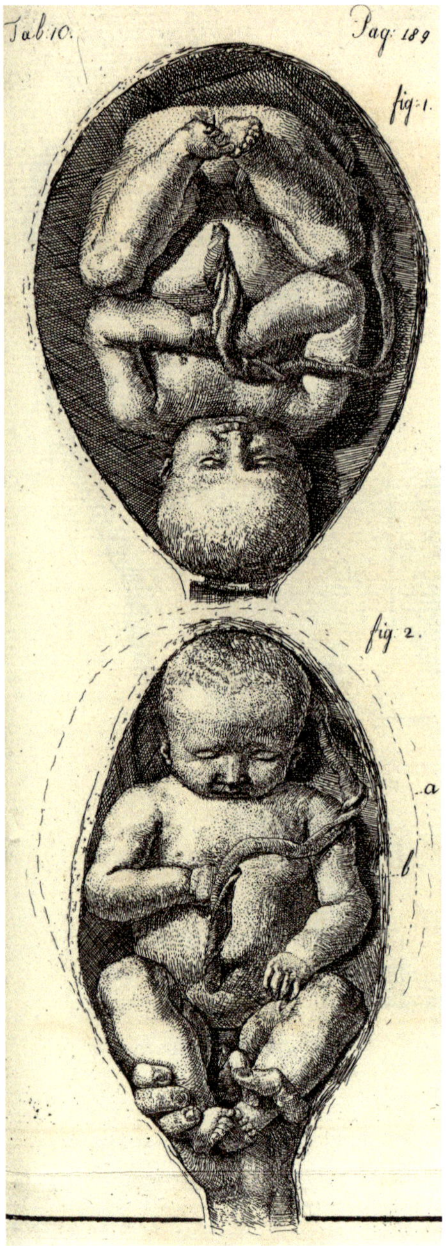

18 John Burton, *An Essay Towards a Complete New System of Midwifery*, London 1751, pl. 10, etching by George Stubbs New Haven, Yale Center for British Art, Paul Mellon Collection

body by its feet (fig. 18). Stubbs's foregoing of the visual depiction of trauma and the abstractional accomplishment of the image should be seen as more than simply inexperience, for these elements are already an early reference to Stubbs's *Anatomy of the Horse.* So too, his fixation with detail never leads to verism à la Bidloo or Hunter. Stubbs's equine anatomies do not display the need to introduce graphic differentiation for the mimetic description of the surfaces. The artist does not use his drawing technique to suggest fleshiness, smoothness, or roughness etc., but only for the clarification of the structural interrelationships between muscles, blood vessels, tendons etc., through which he makes the organisation of the body visible. When set beside Hunters atlas it becomes impressively clear how differing objectives in anatomical science and other objective criteria entail completely different forms of graphic representation.

THE HUMAN ANATOMY AS THE MODEL FOR STUBBS'S "ANATOMY OF THE HORSE"

"The myology—neurology and angiology of men, have not been carried out to such perfection in two ages, as these horses by you."[58] Peter Camper's expert assessment of Stubbs's *Anatomy* deserves attention in closing. On the one hand, his statement names human anatomy as both the reference point and standard used by Stubbs in his equine anatomy. On the other, it stresses that more than just the study of muscles, the achievement of the *Anatomy of the Horse* was the representation of nerves and blood vessels. While it was always taken as a given that the artist would study the structures of the muscles and bones when learning anatomy, the same was not the case for the paths taken by the nerves and the vessels because these barely or never left their mark on the surface of the skin.[59] I mention this specifically here because scholars have long sought to substantiate Stubbs's artistically limited interest in anatomy with the statement that Stubbs, unlike Camper, refused to depict the internal organs on the basis that these were not relevant for him as an artist.[60] Equally, in the meticulousness with which Stubbs illustrated the networks and branches of the nervous and circulatory systems in his anatomical plates, he aimed for much more than artistic usefulness in this appeal to horse owners.[61]

In his first anatomical plates of the subcutaneous layers, Stubbs already shows a white luminescent network of nerve tracts and blood vessels which spread out over the head, neck, rump and flank of the horse like the branches of a river on a map. The deeper levels of dissection, which demonstrate the circulation of blood from the veins down in the hooves up into the head, also aim to represent a highly-developed and complex organism, giving the animal an astonishing dignity, comparable to that of human anatomy. It was precisely the nervous system that contributed decisively to the humanization of the horse in that it furnished evidence for the sensitivity and excitability of the animal by mutually connecting body and spirit.[62] The importance Stubbs gave to the illustration of the hidden connections inside of the animal seems to be a conscious taking up of position against the brutal and reckless treatment of animals which dominated their keeping until well into the eighteenth century. Man and beast became closer in the age of sensibility and anatomical research; comparative anatomy discovered similar structures within both creatures (p. 20, figs. 8–10). In his 1776 treatise *On Duty of Mercy and Sin of Cruelty to Brute Animals* Humphrey Primatt stressed that animals were just as sensitive to pain as human beings due to their sensory organs and nerve system.[63] Stubbs's intention was probably similar when he wrote that his treatise was "a useful Book as a Guide in Comparative Anatomy" in his note to subscribers.

The visual anatomical argument pursued by Stubbs in order to prove the horse's almost human constitution manifests itself in the outward appearance of the book. Large-format anatomical atlases with artfully printed and laboriously produced plates had previously only been used for human anatomy. Just as midwifery had gained in scientific status thanks to anatomical publications in the eighteenth century, so the same happened for veterinary medicine and the artistic representation of the horse, the appeal of which grew concomitantly. For an artist to dedicate the same anatomical attention to the horse as would be given to a human was a striking shift in the norm. Previously, anatomical knowledge had been primarily relevant for history painting, in which the shape and movement of the human body had to be correctly represented. To this end William Hunter also held anatomical lectures freed from medical details for artists which were adopted by the Royal Academy's teaching program in 1768. Hunter emphasized that the position and overall appearance of the body depended on having intimate knowledge of bone and muscle structure. He said that anatomical knowledge would not only produce the impression of accuracy but also of vitality.[64] Thus the analytical dismantling of the body into its individual component parts ultimately only serves composition and its consistency in the treatment of weight, movement and expression.[65]

Stubbs's achievement is to have transferred the contemporary approach of scientifically-rooted painting to the depiction of horses. His *Anatomy of the Horse* was perhaps so successful because it was already triumphantly demonstrating these capacities. In it the art of precisely and anatomically analysing individual elements comes together in an aesthetically convincing composition in which graphic variety, virtuoso perspectival representation and illumination are unified. Thus Stubbs maintains the ambivalence of anatomical illustration in an impressive tension between violent dissection and creative animation, which presents the horse as both anatomical specimen and living creature. Peter Camper demanded that the requisite connection between the exhausting and gross business of animal anatomy with the noblest of all arts, painting, be recognized.[66] Still today, Stubbs's scientific anatomical paintings of horses can be seen as a rare and successful combination of both disciplines.

---

1 Edmund Burke gave the painter James Barry this advice in a letter of 1765: "You ought to make the knife go with the pencil, and study anatomy in real, and, if you can, in frequent dissections." *The Works of the Right Hon. Edmund Burke*, vol. 1, London 1834, p. XI.

2 Humphry's text is reprinted in full in: Exhib. Cat. *Fearful Symmetry*, 2000, pp. 200–12, esp. pp. 211, 208.

3 "Obituary newscutting of George Stubbs," *Gentleman's Magazine* 1806, reprinted in: Exhib. Cat. *Fearful Symmetry*, 2000, p. 198.

4 Egerton, *George Stubbs*, 2007, p. 22.

5 Exhib. Cat. *Fearful Symmetry*, 2000, pp. 202, 211.

6 Exhib. Cat. *George Stubbs*, 1976, pp. 29 f.; see also Werner Busch's essay in the present catalogue.

7 Exhib. Cat. *Fearful Symmetry*, 2000, p. 202; see also Tim Clayton's essay in the present catalogue.

8 On 28 July 1771 to George Stubbs, Exhib. Cat. *Fearful Symmetry*, 2000, p. 210.

9 Egerton, *George Stubbs*, 2007, nos. 1–6.

10 Louis Jean-Marie Daubenton, an anatomist and colleague of Buffon, wrote in his *Histoire naturelle* of 1753: "L'Histoire naturelle n'est pas bornée aux connaissances de l'extérieur, elle s'étend bien plus loin; son objet principal est de développer l'intérieur, et de reconnaître, par l'inspection du dedans, le mécanisme des mouvements qui paraissent au-dehors." Denis Reynaud (ed.), *Buffon, "Discours sur la nature des animaux", suivi de "De la description des animaux" par Daubenton*, Paris 2003, p. 26.

11 "La plus noble conquête que l'homme ait jamais faite est celle de ce fier et fougueux animal ... Le cheval est de tous les animaux celui qui ... a le plus de proportion et d'élégance dans les parties de son corps." See Georges-Louis Leclerc de Buffon, *Histoire naturelle générale et particulière ...*, 44 vols., Paris 1749–88, vol. 4, 1753, pp. 174–76 for the most important passages on the description of the horse. On Buffon's success and other natural-historical publications in the eighteenth century, see Oliver Kase, "'Faire revivre Buffon'. Picassos Tierillustrationen zu Buffons 'Histoire naturelle,' in: Nina Schleif (ed.), Exhib. Cat. *Picasso Künstlerbücher*, Bayerische Staatsgemäldesammlungen, Museum Brandhorst, Munich; Staatliche Kunstsammlungen Dresden, Kupferstichkabinett, Munich 2010, pp. 178–87; Louise E. Robbins, *Elephant Slaves and Pampered Parrots. Exotic Animals in Eighteenth-Century Paris*, Baltimore and London 2002, pp. 169–77. In England too, the horse was celebrated by Pennant as being the most beautiful and useful of all animals: Thomas Pennant, *British Zoology*, 4 vols., London 1768–70, vol. 1, p. 7.

12 "As for Farriers and Horse-Doctors, the Veterinarian School lately established in France shews of what importance their profession is held in this country." George Stubbs, *The Anatomy of the Horse*. Original Text and Modern Paraphrase by J. C. McCunn and C. W. Ottaway. With a New Introduction by Eleanor M. Garvey (Dover Edition), New York 1976, p. 35. The *Gentleman's Magazine* in 1806 acknowledged Stubbs's *Anatomy of the Horse* to be the achievement of an individual in contrast with French state initiatives: Exhib. Cat. *Fearful Symmetry*, 2000, p. 198.

13 Cf. Christophe Degueurce, *Honoré Fragonard et ses écorchés. Un anatomiste au siècle des lumières, avec une contribution de Laure Cadot*, Paris 2010, pp. 21–26; Christophe Degueurce, "La création de l'enseignement et du métier vétérinaires," in: Béatrix Saule and Catherine Arminjon (eds.), Exhib. Cat. *Sciences & Curiosités à la Cour de Versailles*, Château de Versailles, Paris 2010, pp. 131–34; Andrew Cunningham, *The Anatomist Anatomis'd. An Experimental Discipline in Enlightenment Europe*, Farnham, Burlington 2010, p. 341.

14 Claude Bourgelat, *Élémens d'hippiatrique, ou nouveau principes sur la connoissance et sur la médicine des chevaux*, 3 vols., Lyon 1750–53, vol. I, pp. III, IX, XVI, vol. II/1, pp. XV–XXXII.

15 Ibid., vol. II/1, p. 1: "L'anatomie … doit être considérée comme la base & le fondement de l'Hippyatrique." Ibid., p. XLIII: "À mesure que d'une main j'ai découvert avec le scalpel ce que je cherchois, j'ai tracé de l'autre sur le papier ce que j'ai trouvé & ce que j'ai apperçu."

16 Ibid., vol.II/1, pp. XXXIV f.: "L'Anatomie est une science épineuse, rebutante et d'un difficile accès." Ibid., on p. XXXVII the author speaks of the "repugnance qu'il inspire la vue des objets les plus dégoûtans."

17 Oliver Hochadel, *Öffentliche Wissenschaft. Elektrizität in der Aufklärung*, dissertation, Fribourg 2001, Göttingen 2003, pp. 14–28.

18 In 1753 Daubenton wrote (*De la description des animaux*): "La plupart des hommes ont, pour les dissections des cadavres, et pour les descriptions des parties intérieures des animaux, une répugnance naturelle." Reynaud 2003 (see note 10), p. 145; cf. also Martial Guédron, "L'enseignement de l'anatomie artistique en France et la question de la dissection (XVIIIe–XIXe siècles)," in: *Les Cahiers d'histoire de l'art* 2, 2004, pp. 32–40, esp. p. 34.

19 For an extensive discussion of the picture, see Exhib. Cat. Versailles 2010 (see note 13), p. 132.

20 Hochadel 2003 (see note 17), pp. 17–21.

21 Stubbs, *The Anatomy of the Horse*, 1976 (see note 12), p. 35: "If what I have done may in any sort facilitate or promote so necessary a study amongst them [farriers and horse doctors], I shall think my labour well bestowed."

22 Cf. Oliver Kase, *Mit Worten sehen lernen. Bildbeschreibung im 18. Jahrhundert*, dissertation, Heidelberg 2007, Petersberg 2010, pp. 294–97; Wolf Lepenies, "Johann Joachim Winkelmann. Kunst- und Naturgeschichte im 18. Jahrhundert," in: Thomas W. Gaehtgens (ed.), *Johann Joachim Winckelmann 1717–1768*, Hamburg 1986, pp. 221–37, esp. pp. 221–24.

23 This was the title of the book by the Genevan natural scientist Jean Sénébier. The book was his response to a competition announced in 1769, in which the Academy of Sciences in Haarlem sought to investigate the preconditions and aims of the "Art d'Observer": Jean Sénébier, *L'Art d'observer*, 2 vols., Geneva 1775, esp. vol. 1, pp. 147 f., vol. 2, p. 287: "Il semble que la Nature se dévoile au grand Artiste; un Observateur ordinaire n'aura pas une idée juste de la perfection d'un Cheval, que Mr. Falconnet." Cf. also Bourgelat 1750–53 (see note 14), vol. II/1, p. 1.

24 "En ouvrant un animal … on découvre, … un pays nouveau, et on a, pour le reconnaître, tout l'empressement que pourrait avoir un voyageur pour voir une ville qu'il serait allé chercher au bout de monde." Reynaud 2003 (see note 10), p. 145. The anatomist should create a reflection of the animal world which was so exact "qu'il ... croit développer un monde entier. ... il y applique tout son art, … l'anatomiste particularise son sujet dans tous ses points, et descend jusqu'aux plus grandes profondeurs de l'analyse pour le considérer dans ses premiers éléments." Reynaud 2003 (see note 10), pp. 135 f. Cf. also Claude-Henri Watelet and Pierre-Charles Lévesque, *Dictionnaire des arts de peinture, sculpture et gravure*, 5 vols., Paris 1792, vol. 1, lemma 'Anatomie', see p. 73: "L'anatomie est une science profonde. Elle demande, lorsqu'on veut s'en instruire, qu'on étudie, qu'on observe, qu'on médite dans les plus grands détails tout ce qui compose l'organisation des êtres vivans."

25 Sam Smiles, *Eye Witness. Artists and visual documentation in Britain, 1770–1830*, Aldershot 2000, pp. 14–44.

26 John Burton, for whose *Essay Towards a Complete New System of Midwifery* Stubbs contributed drawings and etchings in 1751, emphasized that "Judicious persons must be sensible, that in describing Objects not seen by the Reader will have a better idea of them from a true representation upon a plate, than only from a bare description." Burton 1751, p. XVII.

27 Bourgelat 1750–53 (see note 14), vol. II/1, p. LIV cites the huge costs and the hitherto frequently inadequate representations of horse anatomy as the reason for dispensing with illustrations.

28 Bent Sørensen, "The Enduring Vitality of a Flayed Horse. Carlo Ruini, Bouchardon and others", in: *Apollo* 155, 2002, 481, pp. 30–39, esp. pp. 31 f.

29 Blake, *George Stubbs and the Wide Creation*, 2005, pp. 110 f.; Malcolm Warner, "Stubbs's Classicism", in: Exhib. Cat. *Stubbs and the Horse*, 2004/05, p. 73. The story that these were his own studies from nature goes back to the *Vie d'Edmé Bouchardon* (1762), see Comte de Caylus: Comte de Caylus, *Vies d'Artistes du XVIIIe siècle. Discours sur la peinture et la sculpture. Salons de 1751 et de 1753. Lettre à Lagrenée*, edited by André Fontaine, Paris 1910, pp. 97 f.: A horse belonging to the Baron de Thiers was made available to Bouchardon for his studies. According to Caylus Bouchardon, who was used to pursuing nature down into the smallest details, even lay down beneath the animal to make his drawings.

30 Sørensen 2002 (see note 28) analyses the drawings and names the model (see ibid. p. 35), noting that the caption is taken from Jean Jourdain's *La Vraye cognoissance du cheval* (Paris 1647).

31 Bourgelat 1750–53 (see note 14), vol. I, p. VI f., ibid. vol. II/1, p. XXXV.

32 Peter Camper confirmed the correctness of Stubbs's representations of the skeleton in the eighteenth century, as different to the illustrations of Carlo Ruini, Georges-Louis Leclerc de Buffon, François Robichon de la Guérinière and even when compared with Claude Bourgelat's models of skeletons: "That of Stubbs is masterly and accurate, all the parts are properly placed, are in just positions, and well delineated. In his finished pieces, the muscles are represented with an accuracy that cannot be exceeded. In a word, his skeleton of the horse, and his arrangement of the muscles, exhibit such a master-piece, that the author deserves the highest honours that were ever bestowed upon an artist." Petrus Camper, *The works of the late Professor Camper on the connexion between the science of anatomy and the arts of drawing, painting, statuary, &c.* …, translated from the Dutch by T. Cogan, London 1794, pp. 155 f.

33 Alex Potts, "Natural Order and the Call of the Wild. The Politics of Animal Picturing," in: *Oxford Art Journal* 13, 1990, pp. 12–33, p. 24.

34 Cf. Lafosse: Degueurce 2010 a (see note 13), p. 66 and ibid. 2010 b (see note 13), pp. 131 f.; Louise Lippincott and Andreas Blühm (eds.), Exhib. Cat. *Fierce Friends. Artists and Animals, 1750–1900*, Van Gogh Museum Amsterdam and Carnegie Museum of Art, Pittsburgh, London 2005, pp. 66 f.

35 "Convaincu que les discours & les figures se prêtent un secours mutuel, j'ai osé former l'entreprise d'exposer aux yeux de mes lecteurs des morceaux anatomiques d'un détail immense." Philippe-Étienne Lafosse, *Cours d'hippiatrique ou traité complet de la médecine des chevaux*, Paris 1772, p. X.

36 Astonishingly, this procedure is similar to that related by Humphry in his description of Stubbs's own dissections: Exhib. Cat. *Fearful Symmetry*, 2000, p. 211.

37 An overview of the illustrations in anatomical atlases can be found in Claus Zittel, "Demonstrationes ad oculos. Typologisierungsvorschläge für Abbildungsfunktionen in wissenschaftlichen Werken der frühen Neuzeit," in: Albert Schirrmeister and Mathias Pozsgai (eds.), *Zergliederungen. Anatomie und Wahrnehmung in der Frühen Neuzeit*, Frankfurt am Main 2005 (*Zeitsprünge* 9, 2005, 1/2), pp. 97–135; Mimi Cazort, Monique Kornell and K. B. Roberts, Exhib. Cat. *The Ingenious Machine of Nature. Four Centuries of Art and Anatomy*, National Gallery of Canada, Ottawa and elsewhere, Ottawa 1997; Michael Kemp, "'The Mark of Truth.' Looking and Learning in Some Anatomical Illustrations from the Renaissance and Eighteenth Century," in: William F. Bynum and Roy Porter (eds.), *Medicine and the Five Senses*, Cambridge 1993, pp. 85–121; K. B. Roberts and J. D. W. Tomlinson, *The Fabric of the Body: European Traditions of Anatomical Illustration*, Oxford 1992; Marielene Putscher, *Geschichte der medizinischen Abbildung. Von 1600 bis zur Gegenwart*, Munich 1972; Ludwig Choulant, *Geschichte und Bibliographie der anatomischen Abbildung nach ihrer Beziehung auf anatomische Wissenschaft und bildende Kunst* …, exact reprint of the 1852 Leipzig edition with the addition of the editor's own results initially published in 1858, Wiesbaden 1971; cf. also note 52 below.

38 William Hogarth, *The Analysis of Beauty, written with a view of fixing the fluctuating ideas of taste*, London 1753, p. 140: "Whoever has seen a fine arabian war-horse, unback'd and at liberty, and in a wanton trot, cannot but remember what a large waving line his rising, and at the same time pressing forward, cuts through the air; the equal continuation of which, is varied by his curveting from side to side; whilst his long mane and tail play about in serpentine mouvements."

39 Exhib. Cat. *Fearful Symmetry,* 2000, p. 210.

40 That Albinus served as a model for Stubbs has been stressed on a number of occasions, most recently in Cunningham 2010 (see note 13), pp. 347 f.

41 The Swiss anatomist and natural scientist Albrecht von Haller saw the beginning of the age of "anatomical perfection" in Albinus's activities; cf. Reinhard Hildebrand, "Attic perfection in anatomy: Bernhard Siegfried Albinus (1697–1770) and Samuel Thomas Soemmerring (1755–1830)," in: *Annals of Anatomy* 187, 2005, pp. 555–73, esp. p. 255. On Albinus, see also: Cunningham 2010 (see note 13), pp. 253–62; Reinhard Hildebrand, "Der menschliche Körper als stilisiertes Objekt. Anatomische Präparate, Modelle und Abbildungen im 18. Jahrhundert," in: Rüdiger Schultka and Josef N. Neumann (eds.) in collaboration with Susanne Weidemann, *Anatomie und anatomische Sammlungen im 18. Jahrhundert. Anlässlich der 250. Wiederkehr des Geburtstages von Philipp Friedrich Theodor Meckel (1755–1803)*, Berlin 2007, pp. 197–222, esp. pp. 203–07; Hubert Steinke, "Hallers Anatomie. Spezial-Studien für ein neues Gebäude der Anatomie," in: Schultka / Neumann 2007 (see above), pp. 111–29; Lorraine Daston and Peter Galison, "The Image of Objectivity," in: *Representations* 40, 1992, pp. 81–128, esp. pp. 89–91; Hendrik Punt, "Bernard Siegfried Albinus (1697–1770) und die anatomische Perfektion," in: *Medizinhistorisches Journal* 12, 1977, pp. 325–45.

42 The Foreword to the English edition, *Table of the Skeleton and Muscles of the Human Body* (1749) is reprinted in full in: Terence Doherty, *The Anatomical Works of George Stubbs*, London 1974, Appendix 1.4, pp. 313–18, esp. p. 313.

43 Ibid., p. 313; Hildebrand 2005 (see note 41), p. 557.

44 Doherty 1974 (see note 42), p. 316. Watelet / Lévesque 1792 (see note 24), vol. 5, p. 435 claimed that the selection of ideal individual limbs followed this concept for Antoine Coysevox's (now destroyed) equestrian portrait of Louis XIV. Apparently seventeen of the King's finest horses were employed.

45 Doherty 1974 (see note 42), p. 317.

46 Ibid., p. 318: "In order therefore that the beauty of the figures might not be hurt, it was proper not to add any marks to them … For besides that they would have bespotted the figures, so to speak, they would have obscured several things, … in the outline figures the bound and terminations of the different parts are very readily distinguished."

47 Doherty 1974 (see note 42), p. 317: "The whole figure, though composed of several parts joined together, might nowhere be interrupted, further than nature has observed in those parts, in the symmetry, a certain harmony and equality."

48 Watelet / Lévesque 1792 (see note 24), vol. 1, p. 74 emphasized that the artist was enlightened by the anatomist's knowledge and that, in return, his discoveries could be depicted for the senses: "C'est ainsi que les Sciences & les Arts, … doivent, pour leur mutuel intérêt, s'approcher, se secourir."

49 Doherty 1974 (see note 42), p. 317: Wandelaar was "entirely ruled [by Albinus], as if he was a tool in [his] hands."

50 John Bell, *Engravings explaining the anatomy of the bones, muscles and joints,* London 1794, 1810 (3rd edition), p. III: "Even in the first invention of our best anatomical figures, we see a continual struggle between the anatomist and the painter; one striving for elegance of form, the other insisting upon accuracy of representation."

51 Exhib. Cat. *Fearful Symmetry,* 2000, p. 201. Obstetrics was the subject of heated discussion around 1750. Previously the work of the midwife had been seen as a domestic, female activity, now 'men-midwifes' such as William Smellie and William Hunter tried to establish it as a serious medical subject through their anatomical investigations. Cf. Cunningham 2010 (see note 13), pp. 165–85; Lyle Massey, "Pregnancy and Pathology: Picturing Childbirth in Eighteenth-Century Obstetric Atlases", in: *The Art Bulletin* 87, 2005, pp. 73–91; L. J. Jordanova, "Gender, Generation and Science: William Hunter's Obstetrical Atlas," in: Bynum / Porter 1985, pp. 385–412; Putscher 1972 (see note 37), pp. 110 f.

52 Roberts / Tomlinson 1992 (see note 37), pp. 463 f. Cf. on naturalistic anatomical representations in Bidloo, Hunter and Bell: Cunningham 2010 (see note 13), pp. 270 f.; Hildebrand 2007 (see note 41), pp. 206–208; ibid. 2005 (see note 41), pp. 564–67; Zittel 2005 (see note 37), p. 131; Smiles 2000 (see note 25), pp. 35–41; Kemp 1993 (see note 37), pp. 113–121; Roberts / Tomlinson 1992 (see note 37), pp. 447–66; Daston / Galison 1992 (see note 41), pp. 91–93.

53 William Hunter, *Anatomia uteri humani gravidi tabulis illustrata … The anatomy of the human gravid uterus exhibited in figures,* Birmingham 1774, Preface, n. p.: "Anatomical figures are made in two different ways; one is the simple portrait, in which the object is represented exactly as it was seen, the other is a representation of the object under such circumstances as were not actually seen, but conceived in the imagination. … the one shews the object, or gives perception, the other only describes, or gives an idea of it. A very essential advantage of the first is, that as it represents what was actually seen, it carries the mark of truth, and becomes almost as infallible as the object itself."

54 Ibid., Preface, n. p.: "The art of engraving supplies us … with … an universal language." In his lectures, Hunter also placed great value on graphic clarity: "If a teacher would be of real service, he must take care, not barely to describe but to shew or demonstrate every part." William Hunter, *Two introductory letters to his last course of anatomical lectures at his theatre in Windmill-street …*, London 1784, pp. 87 f.

55 Hunter 1774 (see note 53), Note to Plate VI: "Every part is represented just as it was found; not so much as one joint of a finger having been moved to shew any part more distinctly, or to give a more picturesque effect."

56 Ibid., Preface, n. p.: "Anatomical figures ought to be … well finished. … in anatomy, as in natural history, the subject is supposed to be new, or only imperfectly known, and the smaller parts are to be studied with care, as well as the larger masses. … the greater Part is tolerably well finished, some very highly and delicately." Cf. on Jan van Rymsdyk and the conflict between anatomy's interest in detail and the idealistic art theory of Joshua Reynolds and the Royal Academy: Harry Mount, "Van Rymsdyk and the Nature-Menders. An Early Victim of the Two Cultures Divide," in: *British Journal for Eighteenth-Century Studies* 29, 2006, pp. 79–96.

57 Cunningham 2010 (see note 13), p. 173; R. B. Fountain, "George Stubbs (1724–1806) as an Anatomist," in: *Proceedings of the Royal Society of Medicine* 61, 1968, Nr. 7, pp. 639–46, esp. p. 641 on the thesis that he had created the illustrations on the basis of Albinus's *Seven tables of the uterus of a pregnant woman* of 1748; Doherty 1974 (see note 42), pp. 3 f. also cites John Astruc's *Treatise on all the Diseases of Women* (1743) as another source.

58 Exhib. Cat. *Fearful Symmetry,* 2000, p. 210.

59 Cf. William Hunter in his anatomy lectures for the artists of the Royal Academy: "A painter has not much business with the Vascular System of the human body." In: Peter Black (ed.), Exhib. Cat. *"My Highest Pleasures." William Hunter's Art Collection*, Hunterian Art Gallery, University of Glasgow, London 2007, pp. 168–75, esp. p. 169.

60 Peter Camper to Stubbs on 27 July 1772: "It is a pity you do not like to pursue the viscera of this useful animal." Exhib. Cat. *Fearful Symmetry,* 2000, p. 210.

61 Horse owners should be in a position "to judge of the Structure of the Horse more scientifically, but also to point out the Seat of Diseases, or Blemishes, in that Noble Animal." Stubbs, *The Anatomy of the Horse,* 1976 (see note 12), n. p. ("Proposals for Publishing by Subscription").

62 Hunter on the human nervous system: "The Nerves … convey the influence which the Mind has on the body … Secondly they convey all the influence which the body has on the mind. … The Nervous System, as important as it is in the animal body is not visible in the living bodies," in: Exhib. Cat. Glasgow 2007 (see note 59), p. 169. In his Foreword to Camper's work in 1794 (see note 32), Thomas Cogan stressed (p. VII) the new importance of neurology for the art of anatomy: "Neurology also, which has not been considered as having the most distant relation to the subject, is proved to be of high utility in the representation of the emotions of the mind."

63 "A Brute is an animal no less sensible of pain than a Man. He has similar nerves and organs of sensation, and his cries and groans … are … strong indications to us of his sensibility of pain." Quoted by Malcolm Warner in "Ecce Equus. Stubbs and the Horse of Feeling," in: Exhib. Cat. *Stubbs and the Horse,* 2004/05, p. 5. This is the first clear expression of the humanization and sensitization of the horse in the eighteenth century. For Buffon the sense organs and nervous system were also the basis of the close relationship between humans and mammals: cf. Diana Donald, *Picturing Animals in Britain 1750–1850*, New Haven and London 2007, p. 73. See Cunningham 2010 (see note 13), pp. 295–359 and Donald 2007, pp. 73–76 on comparative anatomy in the eighteenth century.

64 "If there is not a great deal of nature, of Life, of Soul, of Animation in it, the sense will not be properly impressed." In: Exhib. Cat. Glasgow 2007 (see note 59), pp. 171 f.

65 Watelet / Lévesque 1792 (see note 24), vol. 1, p. 75 named these three aspects the three most important results of anatomical knowledge and the "bases positives" of painting. Watelet called for the transference of anatomical knowledge to animal painting in general (p. 73) and to horse painting in particular (p. 610).

66 Camper 1794 (see note 32), pp. 141 f.: "The close connexion there is between the tedious and indelicate employment of dissecting animals, and the most elegant of the arts."

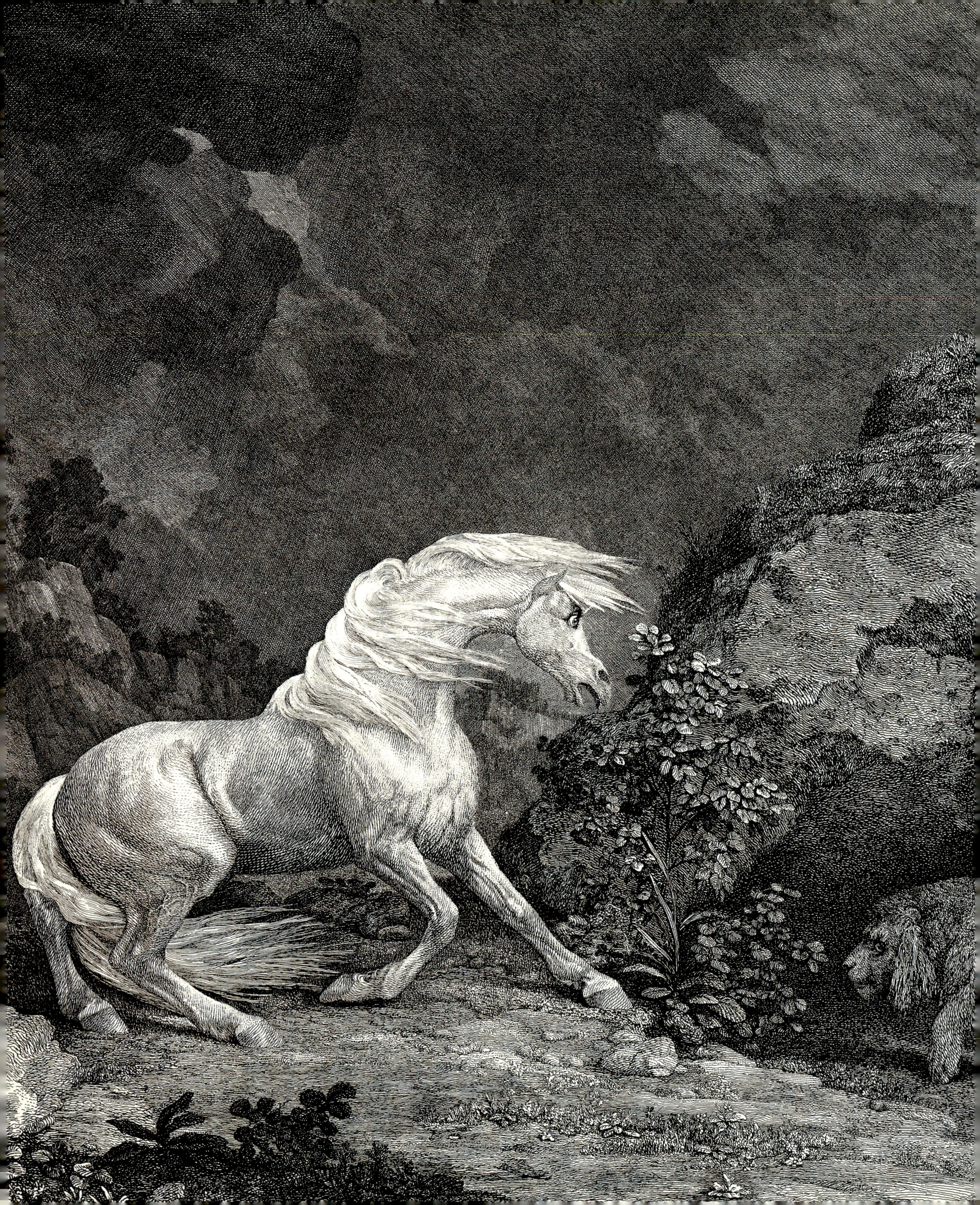

Tim Clayton

STUBBS AND THE PRINT

Before the invention of photography all visual information requiring wide distribution was presented through prints. Prints were made for many purposes—games, fans, visiting cards, maps, plans of battles, images to illustrate and to instruct. They were also made in several grades of quality at a range of prices that reflected this.

The hundreds of prints that reproduced designs by George Stubbs covered several of the principal areas of production. The prints presented in this exhibition were reproductive prints of the highest quality that were intended to record the appearance of paintings. These prints were regarded as works of art in their own right and might be displayed on the wall or might be collected, usually pasted into albums and studied in fine libraries. Stubbs also made prints as anatomical illustrations where clear communication of accurate information was the principal criterion. Several of Stubbs's designs of animals were reproduced for publication as exact records in zoological books or scientific journals. These and other designs were later repeated many times in books of animals for children and similar publications. His horses, dogs and wild animals were included in drawing books that helped teach people to draw. Many other portraits of horses were reproduced relatively cheaply for decoration to be framed or pasted on the walls of homes or inns. Grander prints were made for the *Review of the Turf*, a projected luxury history of British horse breeding and racing. Such 'fine' prints were also frequently used as furniture for the wall—usually pasted on canvas, framed and glazed and sometimes coloured or printed in colours.[1]

EARLY ANATOMICAL PRINTS

Long before anybody engraved a painting by George Stubbs, however, Stubbs made his own first attempts at printmaking. While he was studying and teaching anatomy at York in 1747 or shortly afterwards, Dr John Burton asked Stubbs, twenty-three at that time, to make drawings from dissections to illustrate Burton's *Essay Towards a Complete New System of Midwifery*. His pupils stole the body of a woman who had died in childbirth and Stubbs dissected her corpse in order to make the drawings from nature. He was happy enough to undertake anatomical drawings but he told Burton that he was not competent to engrave them, having no experience whatsoever, and recommended hiring a professional. Burton insisted that Stubbs should do the job.

According to Stubbs, an artist from Leeds who had etched a bit showed him how to do it by covering a halfpenny with etching varnish, smoking it and drawing the design with a sewing needle stuck in a cork. At first attempt Stubbs "found the varnish so hard that when he had the lines to cross, the wax flew off."[2] By trial and error Stubbs learned how to warm a copper plate so that it took an even layer of varnish of the right consistency and how to wash it with acid so that it bit where the needle had exposed the copper. He tried to finish his etchings with fine engraved lines, using burins—the line-engraver's tool—borrowed from a clockmaker. Stubbs was unhappy with the resulting images and refused to put his name to them. They look amateurish and lack the clarity and precision that a fine professional engraver should have provided, but Burton might have been right that Stubbs's understanding of the subject and the quality of his draughtsmanship guaranteed a better result than he might have got from a local engraver.

Stubbs's next published venture in printmaking was to make the plates for his own book, *The Anatomy of the Horse*. Again, he attempted to avoid engraving his drawings himself. Before autumn 1758 he went to London in search not only of an engraver but also of a publisher. He mentions that he approached Arthur Pond, Charles Grignion and others but that "his designs rather excited ridicule than applause."[3] Pond was closely associated with John and Paul Knapton, the publishers of an English edition of Bernhard Siegfried Albinus's *Tabulae sceleti et musculorum corporis humani*, the book that Stubbs had used as a model for the structure of his own. Grignion had led their engraving team, but for this English edition Grignion and his colleagues had merely copied Dutch prints. They had not been required to interpret anatomical drawings. According to Stubbs's own account Grignion and other engravers explained that they "had been unaccustomed to such studies, and, not understanding them, were fearful of being bewildered, and therefore wished to decline undertaking the commission." This was understandable since the job was very complicated and accuracy was vital. Albinus's engraver, Jan Wandelaar, had worked from the dissections under Albinus's personal supervision. It is likely that both Grignion and Pond also pointed out to Stubbs how expensive such a series of such large and detailed engravings would be. Consequently Stubbs decided to make the plates himself in order to ensure that the job was done well while minimizing his financial liability.

It took Stubbs six years to complete the plates, working in the morning and evening around more pressing business. His etching technique had improved out of all recognition by the time that he completed the work and it seems certain that he was given some instruction by a professional.[4] He developed a highly sophisticated vocabulary of etched strokes and dots with which to express the different textures of muscle and bone. He was imitating the visual language of the line engraver but employing it with resounding success in what was more or less pure etching. *The Anatomy of the Horse* was very favourably received by the *Monthly Review* and Stubbs must have been even more delighted to receive a most enthusiastic and effusive letter from Holland: "The myology, neurology, and angiology of men have not been carried to such perfection in two ages, as these horses by you. How is it possible a single man can execute such a plan with so much accuracy and industry? You have certainly had before you the scheme of the great Albinus; but even his plates have not that delicacy and fullness, nor the expression of yours. Give me leave to ask you, was you the engraver?"[5] The highly respected anatomist and natural historian Pieter Camper continued, "You will be curious to be acquainted with a Dutchman who admires with so much ecstasy your Tables. I am public Professor of Medicine, Anatomy and Surgery at Groningen."

Stubbs advertised *The Anatomy of the Horse* "to be published by subscription which indeed he considered was one of the best methods of making himself known."[6] As a method of selling prints, subscription had been introduced at the beginning of the eighteenth century. It was particularly helpful to artists who wished to announce themselves to the public at large and make contact with their admirers while remaining independent of the printsellers who would give them little for their work, make little effort to sell it, and guard the identity of the buyers. Artists were enabled to publish on their own account thanks to the existence of newspaper advertising. They placed advertisements in one or more newspapers announcing the publication of printed proposals for a print and inviting potential subscribers to submit their names and addresses to the artist or his agents. The agents were usually print or booksellers, taking a discount for the impressions they sold on behalf of the artist. Stubbs's distributors included the Liverpool-born bookseller John Almon, a major opposition figure and supporter of John Wilkes, as well as Francis Newbury, James Dodsley, William Owen and John Nourse and the printsellers Ryland & Bryer. A letterpress sheet describing the print and the terms of publication was distributed amongst the print shops and given to subscribers. Publishers often asked for an advance payment to defray the cost of publication and sometimes offered the product more cheaply to subscribers; Stubbs also followed this practice. Subscribers paid two guineas on subscription and a further two on delivery, saving a guinea against the five guineas charged to non-subscribers. Collecting the names of subscribers enabled an artist to identify those willing to buy his product and to contact them directly in future. It was this method of publication that William Hogarth had used to spectacular effect in the *Harlot's Progress* (1732) and later prints, and he was imitated by many other artists.

THE LONDON PRINT MARKET AND THE FIRST PRINTS AFTER STUBBS'S PAINTINGS

In the decades either side of 1750, numerous commentators noted a dramatic increase in the quantity and quality of English prints—a "rapid progress" that could also be traced in painting, sculpture, building, gardening, music and other arts. It was attributed to the immense wealth coming into the country through the success of its manufactures, trade and commerce. Britain's global domination of maritime trade was cemented by the startling victories of the Seven Years War that ended in 1763.

A number of institutional innovations encouraged this advance. The Society for the Encouragement of Arts, Manufactures and Commerce introduced competitions with cash prizes for both young and mature artists, attracting attention to the prizewinning pictures and prints. All the paintings that won the most important prizes were published. In 1760 the Society hosted the first exhibition of contemporary art. The following year there were two exhibitions. The Society of Artists of Great Britain broke away to charge admission to their own exhibition at an auction room in Spring Gardens while the "Free Society" continued to show their work *gratis* through the Society of Arts.[7] As far as the print trade went, a second copyright act encouraged entrepreneurs to publish prints. The first act, secured by William Hogarth in 1735 had granted protection for fourteen years to prints that were published by their designer. The second Copyright Act of 1767 was much more important and far more stimulating to business in that it extended copyright protection to all original publications, so that anybody who arranged to have a copperplate engraved and published could claim copyright, and doubled the period of protection to twenty-eight years.

Through the exhibitions of the 1760s and early 1770s Joshua Reynolds established himself as premier portrait painter in the land, but with numerous rivals including Allan Ramsay, Thomas Gainsborough and George Romney. Johann Zoffany specialised in theatrical portraits. Benjamin West and Angelica Kauffmann established their fame as history painters. Richard Wilson and George Smith were the leaders of a throng of landscape painters. Joseph Wright of Derby made new subject matter out of science and industry and Stubbs became famous as a wonderful new animal painter. Engravers could exhibit and twenty-four became Fellows of the Society on an equal footing with more numerous painters. A number of young engravers emerged as major artists, most notably William Woollett, Robert Strange and William Wynne Ryland as line engravers and Valentine Green, John Dixon, Edward Fisher, William Pether and James Watson as mezzotinters.

Stubbs first showed a painting in 1761 with the Society of Artists. The exhibitions attracted between eleven and twenty-three thousand visitors each year.[8] They soon became part of the print publishing process. Subscriptions for prints were launched during the period of the exhibitions while London was crowded with art lovers. Engravers often exhibited prints that were about to be published. Printsellers chose their projects from among the paintings on exhibition. Painters exhibited pictures that were to be published or that they hoped to sell to a publisher. Thomas Bradford (fl. 1763–1774) became the first Englishman to buy and then publish contemporary paintings, a practice that was common enough in France but new to England.[9] Described in 1763 as a "collector of, and Dealer in Capital Pictures, of which he has a curious collection", Bradford's trade card establishes that he also dealt in prints and drawings and by 1763 he was certainly publishing prints.[10] A number of printsellers and picture dealers followed Bradford's example, among them Ryland & Bryer, John Wesson, Henry Parker and Robert Sayer, in commissioning or buying paintings for publication. John Boydell of Shakespeare Gallery fame later presented himself as the commercial Maecenas behind the British school, but in these early stages other entrepreneurs were much more enterprising than he was. All of the painters listed above had prominent exhibited paintings engraved and published and several print publishers took an interest in Stubbs.

Phaëthon (Lennox-Boyd no. 3) may have been the first of George Stubbs's paintings to be published. It was published by Ryland & Bryer without a date and can thus be placed between their establishment as art dealers and printsellers in 1765 and 1 January 1767, when the new copyright act came into force. The original act had required the date of publication and the name of the publisher to be engraved on the print in order for the owner of the plate to establish copyright. This continued to be a requirement, so from 1 January 1767 prints were invariably dated if copyright was to be claimed. One can only speculate about who took the initiative in publishing *Phaëthon*. It is likely that William Wynne Ryland, engraver to the King, asked Stubbs's permission to publish the print after it was exhibited, but it is also possible that he and Henry Bryer merely acted as distributors, while Stubbs or the engraver Benjamin Green (1739–1798) or both of them together paid for the print.

Gimcrack (Lennox-Boyd no. 2), published in 1766, can be explained with more certainty. Both the painting and the horse it depicted were owned by William Wildman (1718–1784), a very wealthy wholesale meat salesman who eventually compiled the largest single collection of paintings by Stubbs. The print was published by the picture dealer Thomas Bradford. In the writing engraved beneath the picture, Bradford noted wryly that Wildman had offered to sell the horse to him as a hack for 15 guineas just before the salesman discovered his potential as a race horse. Wildman sold Gimcrack for 800 guineas after he had won a number of races.

A third picture dealer who took an interest in Stubbs was John Wesson. His main publications will be described later, but one very rare print of an Arabian horse (Lennox-Boyd no. 18) that possibly belonged originally to a set may date to the mid-1760s.[11]

These isolated publications were followed by a regular series. In May 1767 Benjamin Green exhibited a "Mezzotinto, from Mr Stubbs" with the Society of Artists, of which he was one of the twenty-four engraver Fellows. This was almost certainly *The Horse and Lion* (cat. no. 65), for which proposals were published in the newspapers in late July. By that stage the copper plate was most probably already with the printer for the advertisements promised that impressions would be ready for subscribers in late August. Those who wished to order an impression needed only to send their names either to Benjamin Green at his house, the Golden Head in Little Britain, or to Ryland & Bryer's shop in Cornhill, both in the City of London. For Westminster residents names were taken by Richard Dalton, the King's librarian with a print shop in Pall Mall and by William Austin, engraver, drawing master and printseller in Bond Street.

If Stubbs had a role in promoting himself through publication, it was carefully concealed. It may have been considered somewhat distasteful at this date for artists to promote themselves in this way, although Hogarth had set a conspicuous opposite example and it later became common for painters to involve themselves in the financial gamble of publication. However, it was obviously Stubbs's name that was selling the print. Whereas Green justified his participation with "Fellow of the Society of Artists of Great Britain and Drawing Master of Christ's Hospital", everybody knew who "Mr. Stubbs" was. Green was not particularly well known and this was his first and only venture into showy exhibition mezzotints. He was a sufficiently eccentric choice as the engraver to suggest that the project might have been his initiative. The first clear indication that Stubbs was in some way involved in the enterprise is the footnote that "If encouragement is given, it will be carried on to a Set of six or eight Prints."[12] This could not have been done without some provisional understanding with the painter.

There was perhaps no surer test of public approval or disdain than ordeal by subscription. If the public liked the print, subscribers would flock in. If they did not, the project might be abandoned prior to publication for want of subscribers. The risk of conspicuous rejection was another reason why painters might conceal their association with a publication scheme. However, Stubbs had already sold his *Anatomy of the Horse* by subscription under his own name and he would later do the same with his own prints, so the obvious conclusion is that this was essentially Green's project. Nevertheless, it was normal for a painter and engraver together to supervise the progress of the plate. Progress proofs would be pulled at various stages and it was conventional for the painter to be invited to correct proofs. To some extent, therefore, any authorized engraving of a contemporary painting was a collaborative effort.

THE VALUE OF PUBLICATION TO PAINTERS

Publication brought a painter's work to the public in a far more substantial and permanent way than an exhibition could. "The public always stand much indebted to *Scrapers* and *Engravers*," wrote a journalist in 1772, "as 'tis through the channel of this art that the works of the greatest painters are diffused over the world, and people of moderate fortunes enabled to become possessed of all the spirit of those works, otherwise allotted for the cabinets of the curious."[13] Whereas paintings were seen only occasionally at exhibitions or on visits to the houses of their wealthy owners, prints were widely accessible, the vehicle through which "everyone can enjoy what, without engraving, would be the sole property of one man alone."[14] To make a print of a painting was to publish it in the same way that a good story was published as a book: "Engraving is to fine art what printing is to science and literature."[15] Engraving could give a painter's "masterpieces the same immortality that the art of printing gives to Tasso's *Jerusalem Delivered* and the tragedies of Corneille", wrote a French critic in 1729, introducing a series of prints of the best paintings in France. "The art of engraving … can distribute to all the countries on earth, and transmit to the centuries to come, whatever is most precious and most inspired in the work of outstanding painters. It can give them pupils in places where none of their paintings exists, and could enable the most remote posterity to do justice to their merit and continue to study their work, even if every one of their pictures were to have been destroyed. The number of prints that are taken from a single plate, and the manner in which they are preserved, will ensure that they outlive the majority of the paintings that they reproduce."[16]

The public and painters in particular had three good reasons, therefore, to appreciate skilled engravers. These were that prints enabled people of modest means to possess the designs of artists whose paintings could belong only to the rich; that it was through prints that people in foreign countries got to know about the work of British painters; and that prints preserved the work of artists for posterity: where paintings might accidentally be destroyed, prints usually survived.

The more expensive fine prints were displayed on the walls of the houses of affluent or 'middling' families. Wealthier ladies and gentlemen might also form substantial collections of engravings for perusal in their libraries. It was possible to compile a large collection of fine prints for the price of a single painting. Such collections were used to document the history of art by grouping together the works of great painters or great engravers. By 1700, dictionaries of artists had begun to appear in which the engravings of a painter's work were listed, so that their *oeuvre* was represented by their published output.[17] Thus in the eyes of foreigners and posterity the quality of a painter's work was liable to be judged by the engravings of his paintings. If a painter wanted a widespread or lasting reputation, therefore, it was very much in his interest to have good prints made of his work.

The process, in the simplest terms, involved copying a design by cutting lines into a copper plate, inking the plate so that the ink filled the engraved lines, placing a sheet of paper on top and running paper and plate through a rolling press under pressure so that the ink was transferred from the plate to the paper. This could be done hundreds or thousands of times to produce so many more or less identical images. The procedure was discovered in the fifteenth century and artists quickly appreciated its potential for duplicating and thus promulgating their designs, as a French art historian observed: "Skilful painters who worked for glory, took the opportunity to make use of it to let the world know of their works. Raphael among others employed the burin of the famous Marcantonio to engrave several of his pictures and designs: and these admirable prints worked like so many figures of fame with his trumpet, which carried the name of Raphael to the whole world."[18]

By the eighteenth century engravers had developed highly sophisticated methods for imitating different textures, and many had become highly skilled in translating the particular style of individual painters into their own medium. Up to 1700, Britain had lagged behind France, Italy and Holland with relatively few engravers working in London, fewer still of them Englishmen. The growing wealth of the country in the eighteenth century changed this. The first effect was an influx of foreign prints, chiefly from France and Italy. A number of French engravers were invited to London and they began to teach English pupils. By the time that George Stubbs began to study art, William Hogarth had established himself as a champion of a distinctive modern, English style and his prints had attracted the attention of foreigners to contemporary British design.

By the 1760s there were two preferred methods for reproducing paintings as prints. Mezzotint was chosen for small or unpredictable print runs. Invented as a method for imitating the effects of oil painting, especially in portraits, this tonal process was relatively easy to master and relatively quick to accomplish. The hard work was all in the preparation. To get to the starting point you had to make the surface of a copper plate extremely rough by scratching it all over with a spiked tool called a rocker, dragged first in one direction then another. If the plate were to be inked when completely rocked it would print pure black. Having smoked the surface of the plate, the artist used a scraper to smooth out white highlights (for this reason mezzotinters were known as "scrapers"). Perfectly smooth surfaces held no ink and printed white. Achieving these gradations was easier than it sounds and a number of painters learned how to mezzotint. Mezzotinting was far quicker to accomplish than line engraving or even etching a large plate, and as an early authority noted "its Expeditiousness brings in more money."[19] Its disadvantage was that the burr thrown up by the rocking was delicate and quickly wore away. It took a skilled copperplate printer to get the maximum yield of impressions from a mezzotint. The engraver might well be required to refresh the plate every fifty impressions, since worn impressions lost contrast and became increasingly dull and grey. Even then, the maximum yield might be only 500 impressions or so. At some point the repeatedly reworked copper became too thin and the only way to print more impressions was to scrape a second, duplicate plate. It was not unusual to do this if a plate proved exceptionally popular, as Stubbs's *Horse and Lion* turned out to be. But mezzotint anticipated a relatively small demand, responding quickly and cheaply to a topical subject.

The economics of the publication of a mezzotint were straightforward enough. An edition of 400 copies at 7s 6d would produce £150. Against this the costs were advertising (£1 at most), the copper plate (about £1), the paper (£6 for 480 sheets of dovecote watermarked 'colombier'), the engraver (maybe less than £30 at this date) and letter engraver's fees (about £1) and the printer's fee (about £5), leaving room for more than £100 profit if all were sold. If a mezzotinter published his own plate, his costs were minimal and he risked little more than his own time.

The alternative to mezzotint was line-engraving. In the eighteenth century this always meant a combination of etching with engraving. The design was drawn with an etching needle and bitten into the plate, and then the etching ground was cleaned away and gravers were employed to add depth, neatness and subtlety. With the graver the depth of line could be infinitely varied. Far more delicate effects could be achieved in skies and patterns of engraved lines could be employed to imitate different textures. To engrave a copper plate the surface was once again smoked so that the lines the artist cut appeared orange against black. The engraver rested the plate on a bag of sand and pushed a burin or graver with one hand whilst holding and turning the plate with the other. It took years of practice to master the many skills involved in engraving, and an engraver was at his most productive with a studio of assistants to undertake the less demanding tasks. Fig. 1 shows a fanciful interior of an engraver's studio with the master at work on one plate with his burins beneath a diffusing screen and youthful assistants smoking and biting others. Engraving plates was time-consuming and to make a living an engraver needed to have several in progress simultaneously. The reward was that whereas a mezzotint plate yielded hundreds of impressions an engraved plate yielded thousands.

The economics of a line-engraving were that an edition of say 1,600 copies at 7s 6d would produce £600. Advertising, copper and writing-engraving cost the same as for a mezzotint. Paper might cost £24 and the printer would charge more—perhaps £10 or £15. The engraver might cost considerably more—in 1761, John Boydell paid Woollett £150 to engrave *Niobe*, but a plate with less work might well have cost £100. This might yield a very handsome potential £460 profit—but only if you could sell 1,600 impressions. Moreover, an artist working alone might take a year or more to finish a plate. In the following decades the fees charged by engravers and the price charged for each impression escalated very sharply. Boydell paid James Heath 2 000 guineas to engrave *The Death of Major Pierson* and charged 4 guineas for each impression.[20]

It is hardly surprising that Benjamin Green, though trained as a line engraver, preferred mezzotint for his Stubbs plates. At that time, when prints of contemporary art with unusual subjects were still a novelty, it was far from certain that he would find 500 buyers. Evidently, however, Green felt that he had received sufficient encouragement from subscribers to the *Horse and Lion* to justify a series. In May 1768, during the exhibition, he published *Brood Mares* (cat. no. 67). His mezzotint was on display among the prints in the Society of Artists' rooms and the painting (Egerton no. 89) was probably the 'Brood Mares and Foals' that Stubbs showed in the same exhibition. Green advertised a subscription in early April and publication in mid-May. Displayed at his new house in Christ's Hospital was the painting chosen to be the third in the series, an equestrian portrait of Lord Pigot riding a charger (Egerton no. 78). The publication line lists three major city print-shops as stockists. The advertisements add more and state that the print could be bought at most print shops in town.

For the third print (cat. no. 68), Green employed the same strategy. He exhibited his print with the Society of Artists and published it while it was on public display in May 1769. At his studio subscribers and purchasers could see the painting he was to engrave for the fourth print in the series, "the Lion devouring the Horse, the Property of Luke Scrafton, Esq." (cat. no. 66). In both the last two cases Stubbs had already sold the painting which was borrowed back from the owner in order to be engraved. The last two plates, *Phaeton* (cat. no. 69) and the *Lion and Stag* (cat. no. 70), were neither exhibited nor advertised, presumably because publicity was now superfluous since Green knew who his admirers were.

Green continued to work with Stubbs until 1774, producing a mezzotint of a pointer named *Phyllis* (Lennox-Boyd no. 37) in 1772 and another of *The Horse and Lioness* (cat. no. 71), which he published in 1774 "to complete the Set of Six Prints (the former Plate of the Subject being entirely worn out)."[21] There is no evidence of an earlier *Horse and Lioness*, so by "the former print" Green presumably meant the *Horse and Lion*. The *Horse and Lioness* was another painting belonging to William Wildman to whom Green dedicated the print.

In the early 1770s Green was experimenting with the new process of soft-ground etching, which he was the first to employ in England. It was a process with great appeal to a skilled draftsman. The artist drew on a piece of paper placed on a soft etching ground. When the paper was pulled away the copper was exposed in proportion to the pressure exerted by the pencil, so that when bitten a perfect facsimile of the drawing might be printed. Green used the process to produce *A Drawing Book in Imitation of Chalk* as well as a few larger plates sold singly. One of these reproduced William Wildman's painting of his horse Eclipse (Egerton no. 75; Lennox-Boyd no. 31). Green reduced the design, excluding Wildman and one of his two sons. The chalk drawings are very attractive and include a number of lovely little details from Stubbs, who shared Green's interest in this process, which Green probably taught him, and who later employed it in his own prints.

Green continued his career as a drawing master until his death in 1798, but at some point in 1776 he sold his mezzotint plates and with them the copyright to the printseller Robert Sayer, who was then buying and publishing modern plates greedily. The *Horse and Lion* was indeed so worn that Sayer had it re-engraved from scratch. The image as published by Sayer appears to have been printed from the same plate and continued to carry Green's name, although it was no longer his work. Sayer had the other plates re-engraved and reissued them, evidently reckoning there were still more sales to be had through his much wider-reaching distribution network. It seems that the *Horse and Lion* was always the most popular subject, for a decade later it wore out again. In 1788 Sayer's assistant Robert Laurie engraved a new plate of the image which replaced Green's in the company's catalogues.

STUBBS AND WOOLLETT

Returning to the 1760s, a second series of prints was progressing at the same time as Green's. *The Spanish Pointer* (cat. no. 72) and a set of four prints of *Shooting* (cat. nos. 73–76) were engraved by the young and newly-famous landscape engraver William Woollett (1735–1785; fig. 2) and published between 1768 and 1771 by Thomas Bradford. The dog was the first to appear, published in January 1768 and presented by Bradford as "a Landscape, with a Pointer standing at Game." Woollett, then aged thirty-two, was already famous for his *Niobe* after Richard Wilson (fig. 3) and was well on the way to being widely acknowledged as the best engraver in Europe, a status he had definitely acquired before he died in 1785. When, about this time, Woollett promised to engrave a painting by Thomas Jones, that painter "began to flatter myself with hopes that my reputation would be established and spread abroad through the medium of that celebrated Engraver, as my Master, had in some degree, even his fame extended by the admirable Prints of this Artist after his Pictures."[22] Faced with competition for landscape commissions from George Lambert, Richard Wilson, Francesco Zuccarelli,

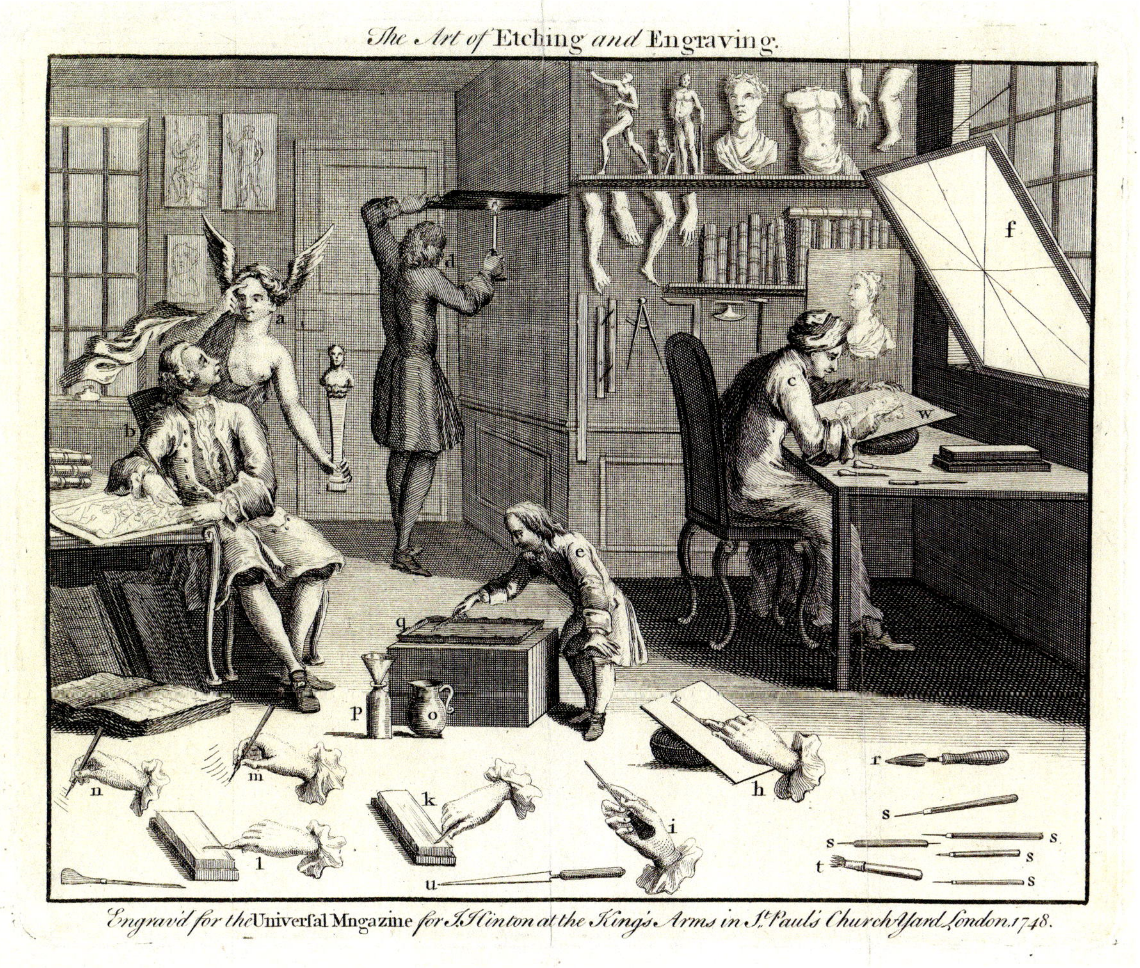

1 *The Art of Engraving and Etching*, etching, 19.6 x 23.4 cm, from John Hinton, ed., *The Universal Magazine*, 1748 London, The British Museum

Thomas Gainsborough, George Barret, John Inigo Richards, William Marlow and Nicholas Thomas Dahl, Jones reckoned it was essential to be "known" and that "nobody was better enabled to make a young Landscape painter known than Woollett." By the time that Stubbs worked with Woollett, Stubbs was already established as a horse painter but wanted to be known as more than just a specialist in horses. Woollett was a fellow Director with Stubbs of the Society of Artists and the two seem to have become personal friends. Stubbs also painted Woollett's own dog and a portrait of the engraver which he kept in his studio.[23]

Stubbs exhibited the first painting in 1767, and Bradford launched a subscription for the set in May 1768, during the exhibition and at much the same time that Green was launching *Brood Mares*. Bradford stated in his subscription proposals and in the writing on the prints that the original pictures were in his possession. A set of paintings was eventually acquired by William Wildman. The story of these paintings is intriguing and has been given a further twist by the discovery of William Wildman's bank account. Between 1764 and 1766 Wildman paid Bradford a total of £1534 13s, presumably for paintings and prints.[24] The last recorded payments by Wildman to Bradford were made in 1766, so that if he bought these paintings from Bradford through his bank account he had bought them by then. If there was only ever one set of paintings (Egerton nos. 82–85), this lends weight to the speculation that one of the sportsmen was Wildman and the other might have been Bradford; that the two of them proposed the series to Stubbs in or before 1766; and that the paintings moved from Bradford's shop to Wildman's house after the completion of the engraving project.[25] One impression of the *Spanish Pointer* has been seen inscribed "Mr Bradford's Dog" and, since he kept the painting until it passed to Robert Sayer at his 1774 sale, it may be that the pointer was Bradford's gundog.[26]

Landscapes were usually engraved in line rather than in mezzotint. Line allowed for far more detail and for delicate effects of light and shade that were beyond the reach of mezzotint. Employing Woollett to engrave five plates was an expensive business, however, and involved considerable risk for Bradford if, as appears on the surface, he paid for both the paintings and the engraving. He claimed that "As the Proprietor will be at a very large Expence in purchasing the Pictures of so great a Master, and employing one of the first Artists in this or, or perhaps any other Country, to engrave the Plates; he flatters himself with Hopes of obtaining the Patronage of the indulgent Public, who of late have so encouraged conspicuous Merit."[27] To offset his capital outlay he treated the set as a whole, costing 1 1/2 guineas, and invited subscribers to pay half when the first plate was delivered and the remainder when the third plate was delivered. When he advertised in May 1768 he expected the first plate to be ready at the end of September. In the event it was published eleven months late in August 1769–not the only occasion on which the good-natured Woollett promised more than he could achieve. When Bradford's plates were sold in 1774 equal shares in the *Shooting* plates were acquired by John Boydell and Robert Sayer. The impressions acquired at some point after 1794 for the collections at Stuttgart and the Veste Coburg were printed from very worn plates, but the set continued to be listed in printsellers' catalogues until 1829 at least. They inspired copies in Britain and abroad and transfer-printed versions of the designs were applied to a range of pottery.

2 William Woollett, *Self-Portrait*, c. 1760, red chalk on paper, 37.7 x 31.7 cm
London, The British Museum

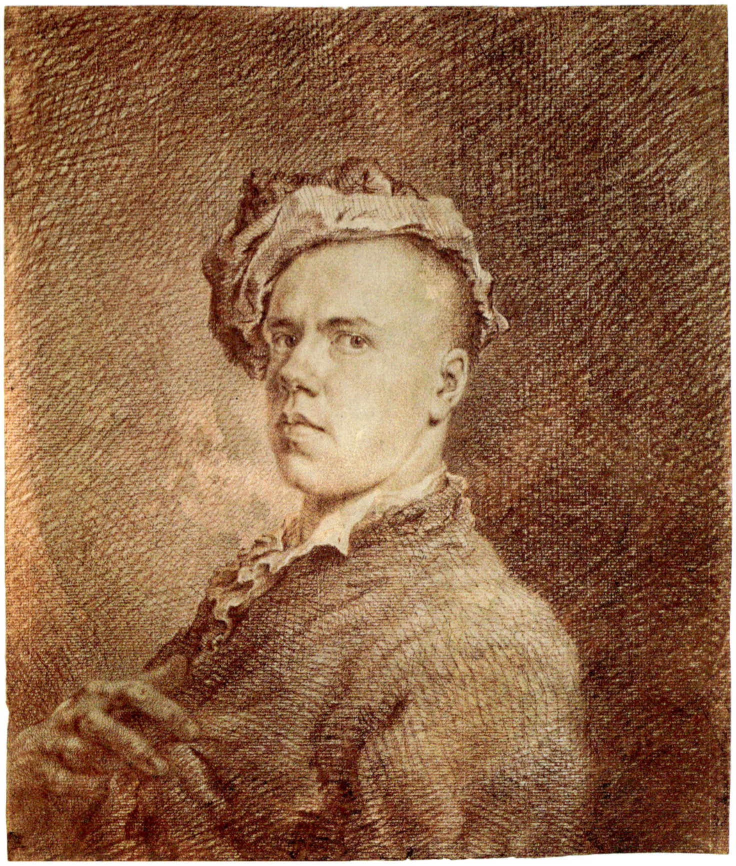

GEORGE TOWNLEY STUBBS AND THE GROWING MARKET

In 1770 Stubbs's twenty-two-year-old son George Townley (1748–before 1816) began to engrave his work. *The Lion and Stag* (Lennox-Boyd no. 15) and *The Horse and Lion* (Lennox-Boyd no. 16) were published by the picture dealer and printseller John Wesson and drew attention to Stubbs's use of a new medium–painting in enamel colours on copper. *Brown Horse Mask* (cat. no. 81), also published by Wesson, served to publicise the stallion that had fathered Eclipse, the racehorse that had just begun to establish a dominance of horse racing that left him as the most famous racehorse ever. Both horses belonged to Stubbs's patron William Wildman and between the two of them Marske and Eclipse made Wildman a second fortune. Wildman bought Eclipse for 75 guineas and sold him in 1770 to the Irish gambler Denis O'Kelly for 1,760 guineas. The famous Eclipse was engraved by Thomas Burke (1749–1815) for Robert Sayer (cat. no. 77).

Up to 1770 Stubbs seems to have attempted to use prints to publicise his grander aspirations–if an animal painter then a painter of the sublime through animals. With his son in the business they, or George Townley, embraced the more commercial world of horse breeding and racing that had provided George with lucrative commissions for paintings, despite his wish to be known for something more glorious. During the 1770s George Townley Stubbs engraved

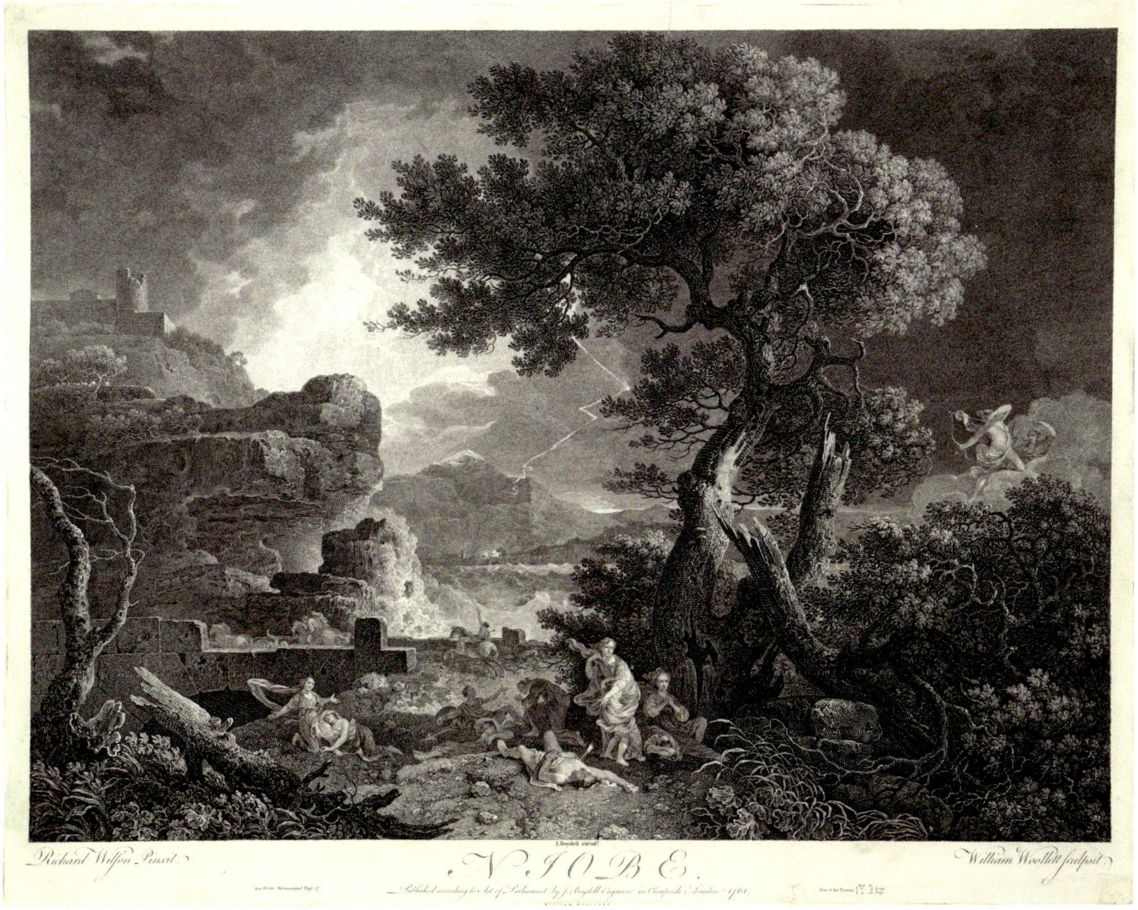

3 William Woollett after Richard Wilson, *Niobe*, 1761, etching, 40.8 x 60.5 cm London, The British Museum

and published a number of small prints of horses and lions. The most ambitious of them was the large mezzotint of a *Stallion and Mare* (cat. no. 82) published in December 1776.

The early 1770s were good years. Stubbs senior and junior sought to build their own business, but the commercial printsellers were very keen to gain rights to Stubbs's images. John Boydell eventually became famous as a commercial patron of contemporary art but around 1770 he had several powerful rivals in the burgeoning market for contemporary art. After Bradford's disappearance it was Robert Sayer who made Stubbs his own, buying the whole or part copyright of Green's plates, Woollett's plates, a set of stallions originally published by Ryland & Bryer, *Brown Horse Mask* and a couple of images that he appears to have originated himself, *The Terrible Horse Trentham* (Lennox-Boyd no. 29) and *Eclipse* (Lennox-Boyd no. 32), both published in 1772. His commercial rivals the Bowles family also published images by Stubbs with the *Sebra* (Lennox-Boyd no. 26) and the *Lion and Lioness* (Lennox-Boyd no. 36). The latter, originally a large and prestigious plate from a painting owned by Sir John Nelthorpe, was cut down when worn to make a pair with the *Sebra*.[28]

The interest of the big merchant printsellers in these plates reflected a growing export trade in prints, chiefly in fine prints to Europe. The boom in British art and print production coincided with and fuelled a period of remarkable enthusiasm for English culture on continental Europe. Printsellers found that there was a very large demand in Europe for contemporary prints to the extent that in 1787 the newspaper *The World* reported that "the calculation in all undertakings is on the foreign sale, being thrice above our own." With English prints reaching Europe in large numbers it was even more pressing that a painter should pay attention to the published record of his work if he was to be seen by foreign connoisseurs and remembered as he would wish.

1772 saw the publication of what became the most admired mezzotint of a Stubbs painting, *A Tigress* by John Dixon (c. 1740–1811; cat. no. 78), taken from a life-size painting of a well-fed female Indian tiger belonging to the Duke of Marlborough. Once again, the publication line is ambiguous as to the identity of the publisher—almost certainly Dixon but conceivably Stubbs. It was issued as a proof in November 1772, although fully lettered impressions are dated 1 February 1773. Dixon exhibited his engraving with the Society of Artists (of which Stubbs was then President and Dixon a director) in April 1773. In 1786 John Chelsum chose it to exemplify how modern mezzotinters had extended their range from portraiture to all kinds of subjects. By 1791 it was hanging with the

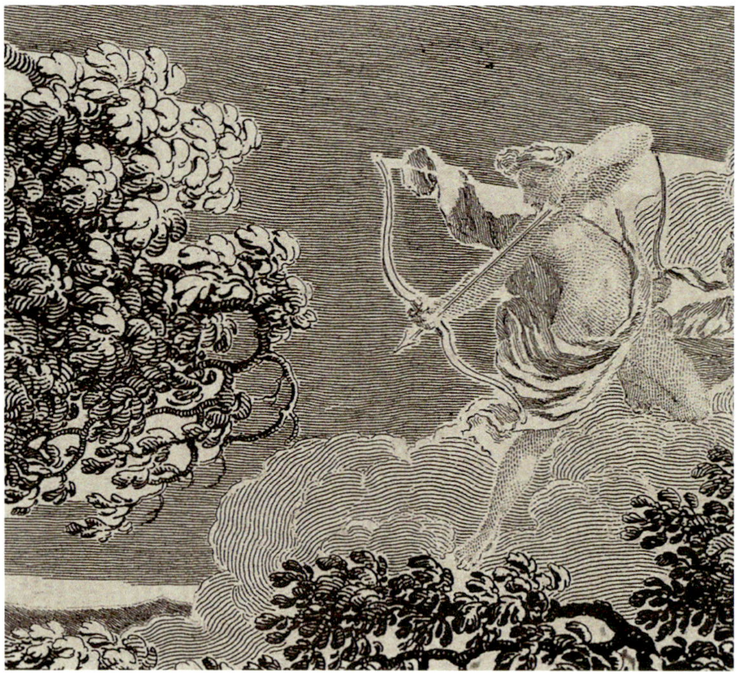

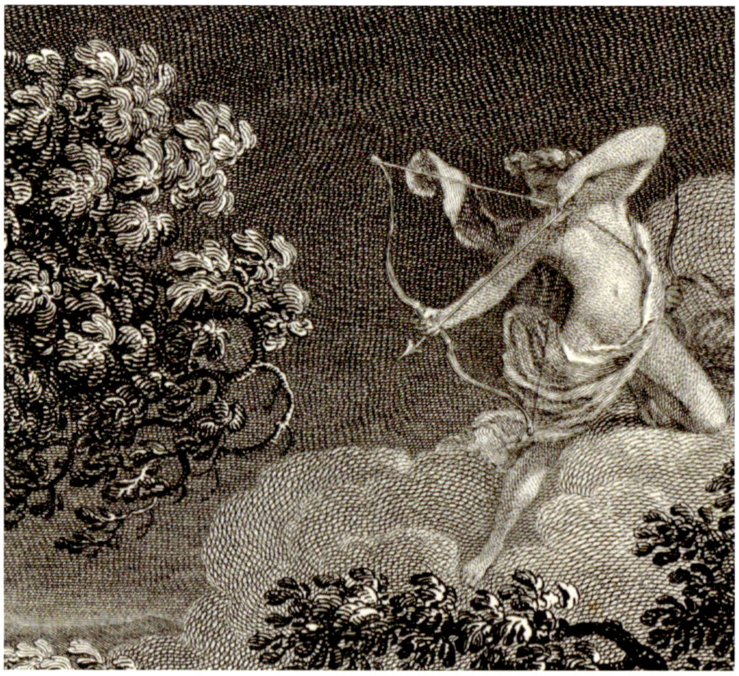

4 William Woollett after Richard Wilson, *Niobe*, 1761, etching, unfinished detail
London, The British Museum

5 William Woollett after Richard Wilson, *Niobe*, 1761, etching, finished detail
London, The British Museum

famous *Death of Wolfe* by Woollett after Benjamin West in the Karlsruhe drawing school to exemplify the achievement of modern English engravers.[29] In 1802 a reviewer in the *Monthly Magazine* gave his opinion that this was "the finest mezzotinto that ever was engraved."[30] By then the print had been out of print for many years, because the plate had been melted in a fire at the printer's premises. As soon as the publisher's 28-year copyright expired in November 1798, Robert Laurie produced an exact copy of "Mr. Dixon's Celebrated Print". A little before that, in July, John Murphy had scraped an authorised version from a painting in Stubbs's possession.

GEORGE STUBBS AS ENGRAVER AND PUBLISHER

In 1777 Stubbs for the first time engraved and published one of his own paintings. It was his signature image, *A Horse Affrighted by a Lion* (cat. no. 52). The large plate is an etching of extraordinary bravado. It is extremely densely worked and must have taken a great many mornings and evenings, assuming Stubbs continued his old practice. If Stubbs had once had problems with the ground coming away from the plate when he attempted cross-hatching he had certainly overcome them by 1777. In this plate he brings to etching the linear language associated with engraving. The strength of the line is matched to the density of object being described and different textures are conveyed with different linear patterns. Thus, the rock is composed of deeply etched worm lines, the sky is a mass of extraordinarily dense and delicate hatching, the grass is wavy lines. Where stormy light falls on the horse Stubbs allows the white of the French 'grand aigle' paper to shine through, fixing the viewer's eye on the white object in the darkness. A comparison of details reveals the difference between conventional engraving and Stubbs's etching technique. Fig. 4 and 5 are details of impressions of Woollett's famous plate *Niobe* in two different states, with different linear patterns expressing different textures and determining the distribution of light. Woollett also uses the white of the paper for bright flashes of stormy light on leaves and the arrowhead. The formality of the linear patterns is relatively restful on the eye. In fig. 6 Stubbs's lines are more densely packed, more agitated and more expressive than Woollett's and the effect of the accumulation of restive detail is to create a disturbed intensity which reflects the emotional charge of the scene.

Three years later Stubbs published a second densely-worked etching, *Tygers at Play* (cat. no. 53), probably after the painting he exhibited with the Royal Academy in 1776. Once again Stubbs showed fascination with the effect of light falling on the playful leopards (at this date all big cats except lions were called tigers) and on the water, contrasted with the gloomy cavern beyond.

The simultaneous publication of twelve prints on 1 May 1788 followed a period between 1782 and 1786 in which Stubbs had declined to exhibit, having fallen out with the Royal Academy. This group of publications signalled a relaunch of his public profile. A pair of big mezzotints by George Townley Stubbs, *Horses Fighting and Bulls Fighting* (Lennox-Boyd nos. 81–82), appeared on the same day. In April Stubbs announced a subscription for the largest of the plates, *The Farmer's Wife and the Raven* (Lennox-Boyd no. 69; fig. 7). It was indeed large—28 by 21 inches (520 x 696 mm)—and it revealed a completely new technique. There was etching in the plate, evident in the trees, but most of it was executed with a variety of roulette wheels and spiked punches and probably mezzotint rockers to create tonal effects of the greatest range and complexity. The tools were those used for prints made in the fashionable "dotted manner" as pioneered by William Wynne Ryland and Francesco Bartolozzi for the neo-classical designs of Angelica Kauffmann and Gianbattista Cipriani, but employed to create quite different and novel effects. Stubbs was not the only engraver to experiment in this way. Apart from his son, who soon showed that he could work in a very similar manner, several leading professional engravers employed similar techniques, notably John Keyse Sherwin (*The Happy Village*, *The Deserted Village*, 1787) and Francis Haward (*Mrs Siddons as the Tragic Muse*, 1787). A detail from *The Happy Village* (figs. 8–9) shows how Sherwin used machine tools in a manner not entirely dissimilar from George Townley Stubbs in his portrait of William Evelyn (figs. 10–11) and George Stubbs in *Labourers* (fig. 12).

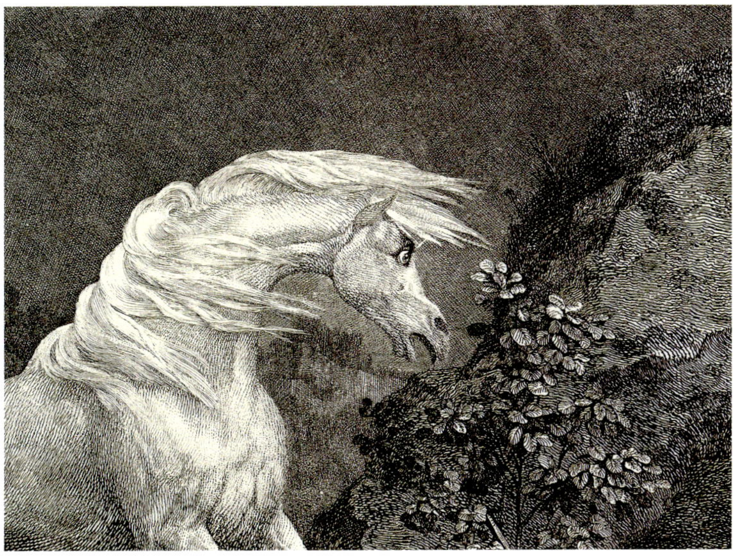

6 George Stubbs, *A Horse Affrighted by a Lion*, 1777, etching, detail
London, The British Museum

Stubbs sold *The Farmer's Wife* by subscription, charging subscribers a guinea, and raising the price to non-subscribers first to £1 6s and later to £1 11s 6d. This sounds expensive compared to the modest 7s 6d charged for Stubbs's earlier etchings (370 x 480 mm) but compares very favourably with the three guineas that John Singleton Copley had charged subscribers to the *Death of Chatham* in 1781 or the four guineas that he charged for the *Siege and Relief of Gibraltar* in 1791. Stubbs evidently saw his prints as collector's items and was well aware that the quality of the impression deteriorated as the plate wore smoother with repeated printing. Thus he promised that "as the prints will be delivered in the order of the names on the list, the earliest subscribers will of course receive the first impressions."[31] For the connoisseur, to whom the promise was addressed, this provided clear and fair incentive to subscribe quickly. Potential subscribers were invited to leave their names at Stubbs's house where they could see the painting and study proofs of the present state of the plate.

The advertisement ended with a note to the effect that "several smaller prints of animals will be finished about the same time", a modest enough introduction to a group of prints currently regarded as some of the best ever produced in Britain. These smaller prints included another version of *A Horse Affrighted at a Lion* (Lennox-Boyd no. 70), this being essentially similar to the composition scraped by his son in mezzotint with the white horse in close-up and the lion emerging from a cavern. A surviving etched proof

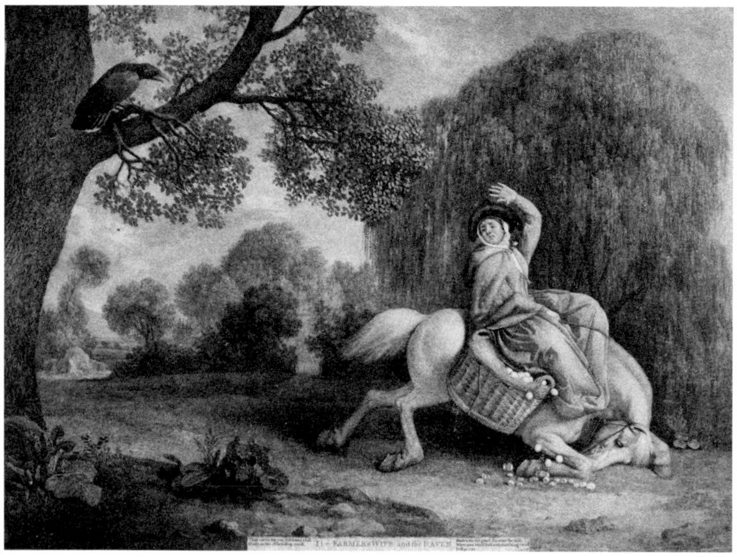

7 George Stubbs, *The Farmer's Wife and the Raven*, 1788, etching with roulette and rocker work, 52.5 x 70 cm
Aschaffenburg Collection,
Staatliche Graphische Sammlung München

of this print provides fascinating insight into the structure of the image. Etched lines radiate from a point behind the lion so that the lion seems to explode from the cave while the horse is sucked into its depths. The companion piece, *A Lion Devouring a Horse* (Lennox-Boyd no. 71), seems to have been made quite differently with much less straight etching, soft-ground etching in the background and much use of roulettes, punches and rockers. *Two Tygers* (cat. no. 60), as an unfinished proof in the Rijksmuseum demonstrates, was heavily dependent on soft-ground etching. The print features Stubbs's own interpretation of the celebrated Blenheim *Tigress*.

The pair of seascapes, *A Lyon* and *A Tyger* (cat. nos. 54–55), were once again mainly etched and in them Stubbs was principally interested in light effects, using machine tools to achieve subtle changes in tone. *Two Dogs* (cat. no. 57) is chiefly soft-ground etching, as is *A Lion* (cat. no. 58). A marvellous proof of this demonstrates that on occasion Stubbs experimented with colour printing, though with a very subtle range of tones. There is no evidence that Stubbs himself owned a copper plate printing press. The sales held after his death mention several engraving tables and tools but no rolling press. Nevertheless, while the evidence points to conventional print runs printed by a professional, it is possible that at least George Townley owned a proofing press.[32] *A Tyger* (cat. no. 59), depicting a sleeping cheetah, was apparently Stubbs's first attempt at pure mezzotint. The three single dogs were all based on soft-ground etching and it is possible that the pencil drawing in Paul Mellon's collection was actually used to make the soft-ground etching.[33] Coloured impressions and impressions coloured with oils exist.

He soon added three more large plates. When he issued subscription proposals for *Hay-Makers* and *Reapers* in September 1788, *Labourers* (Lennox-Boyd no. 86) was already available as a companion piece to the *Farmer's Wife and the Raven*. It is Stubbs's definitive printed version of the design exhibited at the Royal Academy in 1779 and then repeated in enamel for Josiah Wedgwood.

Haymakers and *Reapers* (cat. nos. 62–63) were exhibited at the Royal Academy in 1786 and then at the Society for Promoting Painting and Design at Liverpool in 1787. Stubbs advertised subscription proposals in both London and Liverpool. The prints, priced at £2 10s to subscribers were probably delivered during 1790. Their official publication date was 1 January 1791, after which their price rose to three guineas. The delicate, silvery effects that Stubbs achieves in these plates are quite beautiful, with clever combinations of etching and machine-work to create dappled light on leaves and hazy light in the distance. With these two large plates Stubbs also issued another small one of a sleeping leopard (cat. no. 61).

George Townley Stubbs's *Horses Fighting* and *Bulls Fighting* were published by Benjamin Beale Evans, a publisher who had recently set up on his own account after an apprenticeship to John Boydell. He published a second pair of prints in 1790; these, however, were not engraved by George Townley but instead bear the signature "Henry Birche". Evans published Stubbs's *Labourers* and *Gamekeepers* with the original landscapes on the Torrington estate replaced by fanciful backgrounds painted by Amos Green (Benjamin's cousin). It is unlikely that Stubbs approved of this change and Evans presumably got access to the paintings from their owner Andrew Harrison. Henry Birche has been thought to be a pseudonym for John Boydell's principal engraver, Richard Earlom (1743–1822). It appears, however, in this case at least, to have been a pseudonym for Robert Sayer's principal assistant and engraver, Robert Laurie (c. 1755–1836), or a name used for collaborations between Robert Laurie and Richard Earlom.[34] The name only appears on prints published by Evans and was never used after the death of Robert Sayer in 1793.

George Townley Stubbs now published his own plates. These included an equestrian portrait of William Evelyn and *Two Hacks* and its companion *Two Hunters* (cat. nos. 83–84), from paintings belonging to Henry Utrick Reay of County Durham. These were advertised in the *Newcastle Chronicle*, further illustrating the growing importance of provincial markets. It was common now to offer impressions printed in colours, which meant dabbing on coloured inks in the right places each time the plate went through the press. Coloured impressions were normally twice as expensive as monochrome prints.

The Stubbses launched two ambitious projects during the decade. The *Review of the Turf* was to have been a luxury illustrated history of horse breeding and racing in Britain with biographical entries on a large number of horses arranged alphabetically and fine stipple engravings of a select few in large and small versions for framing and binding. The Stubbses rented the Turf Gallery on Conduit Street as a showroom where the paintings were displayed, and George Townley was installed as manager. The project was backed by an anonymous patron, "Mr Turf", and it collapsed when this patron withdrew. David Oldrey has argued plausibly that "Mr Turf" was Andrew O'Kelly, nephew and co-heir of the wealthy Irish gambler Denis O'Kelly, whose long relationship with the luxury brothel-keeper Charlotte Hayes had not produced children.[35] Andrew, one of the Prince of Wales's fast set, was running a huge stud farm and had an interest in promoting his stallions. The Prince of Wales himself was certainly involved to some degree since the *Review* was dedicated to him and George Townley held an appoint-

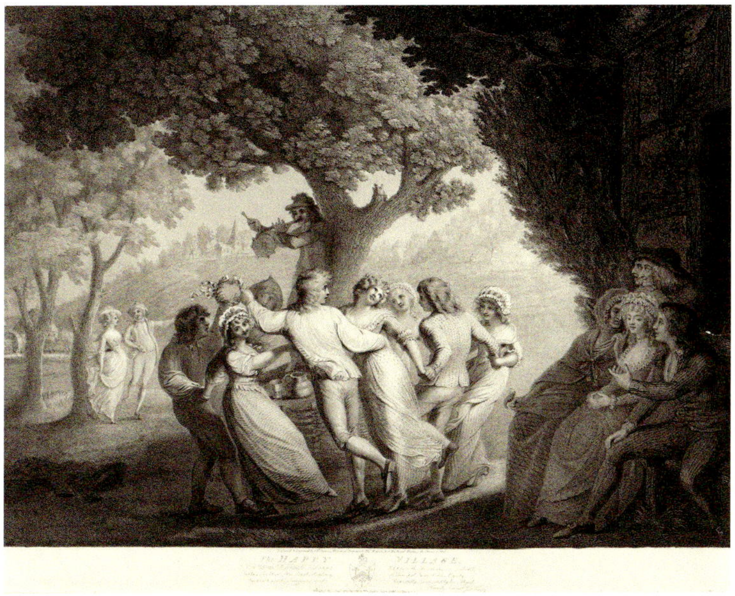

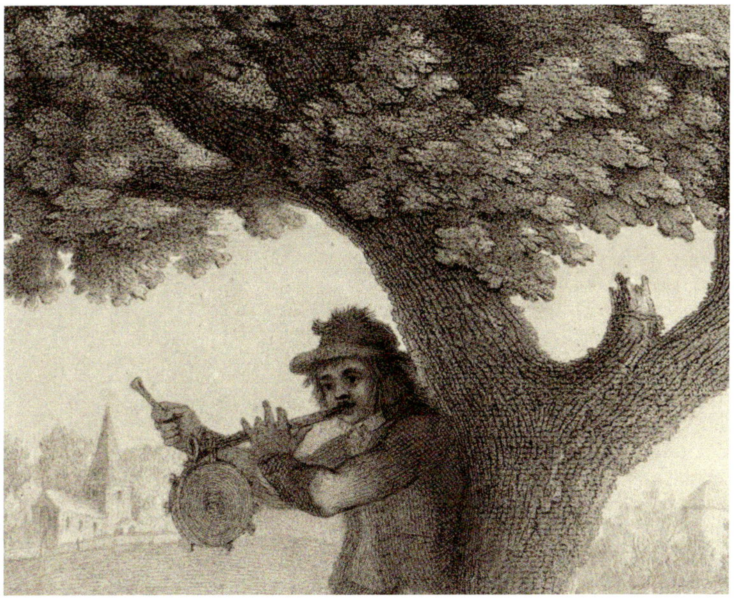

8 John Keyse Sherwin, *The Happy Village*, 1787, etching with stipple, 47.8 x 59.3 cm
London, The British Museum

9 John Keyse Sherwin, *The Happy Village*, 1787, etching with stipple, detail
London, The British Museum

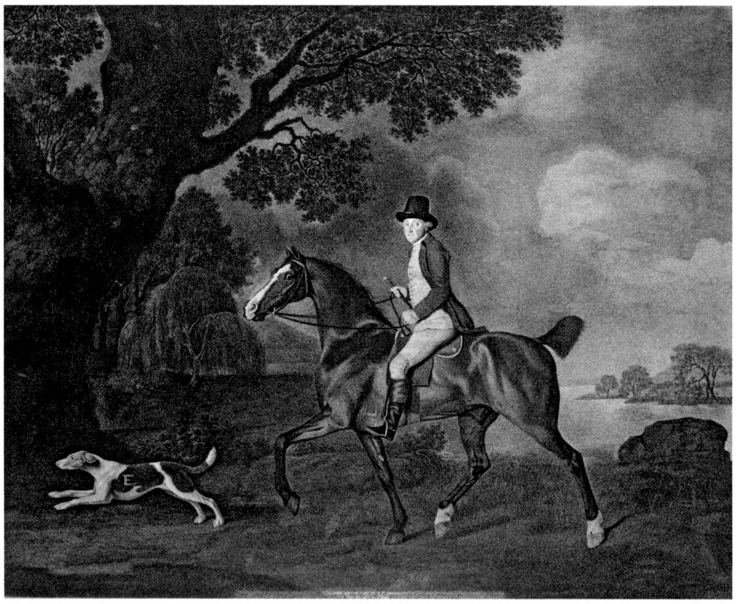

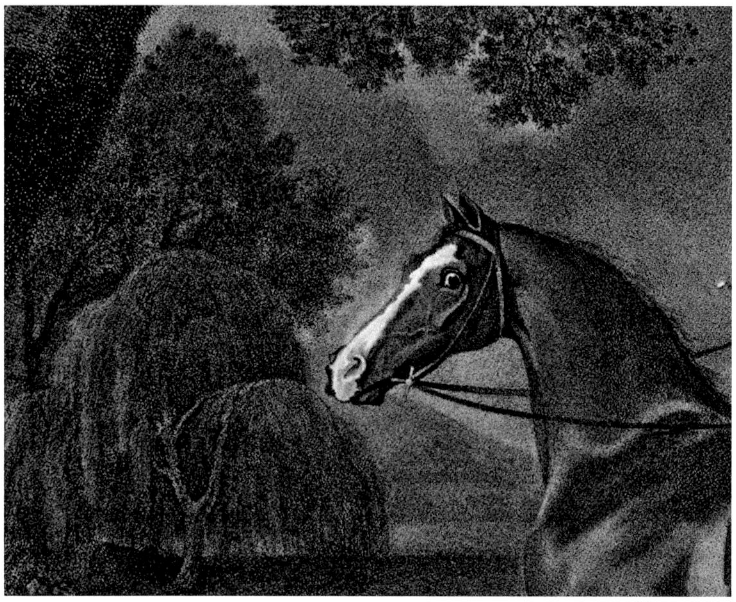

10 George Townley Stubbs, *William Evelyn Esquire*, 1793, roulette work with stipple, 44.9 x 55.3 cm
London, The British Museum

11 George Townley Stubbs, *William Evelyn Esquire*, 1793, roulette work with stipple, detail
London, The British Museum

ment as "Principal Engraver to His Royal Highness the Prince of Wales" on the strength of it. When Mr Turf pulled out, Stubbs, who was also owed over £1000 by the Prince of Wales, found himself in financial trouble and seems to have borrowed £1,900 from Isabella Saltonstall in 1793.[36]

Undaunted, the old man turned back to anatomy, making fifteen engravings for *A Comparative Anatomical Exposition of the Structure of the Human Body, with that of a Tiger and Common Fowl.* He appears to have worked on this up to the time of his death in 1806 and the plates show no decline in quality. A final print, later entitled *Death of the Doe* (cat. no. 64), reproduced a painting exhibited at the Royal Academy in 1801. Its publication line states that it was issued by "G. Stubbs" from Stubbs's house at 24 Somerset Street in 1804. Its authorship is disputed and it is of curiously mixed quality: the animals are better than the human figure and the background. Stubbs was eighty in 1804, but had apparently recently engraved anatomical plates. It is possible that his powers were in sharp decline, but the lack of signature and style of presentation is also most uncharacteristic. I wonder whether the plate might have been incomplete at the time of Stubbs's death, but attribution must remain conjectural until firm evidence emerges.[37]

From the beginning Stubbs took a strong interest in the presentation of his work in print. While there is little evidence to prove the extent of his collaboration with William Woollett and Benjamin Green, it is evident that gradually Stubbs took personal control of his published image until nearly all prints engraved from his paintings were engraved by himself or by his son. All of Stubbs's own prints ostensibly reproduced paintings, so that in one sense they fall naturally into the class of 'reproductive engravings' rather than 'painter's etchings'. Many of them address scenes that Stubbs had treated repeatedly in different media. As Richard Godfrey observed, "In some cases he used the copper to redefine an image on which he had been playing variations for more than 20 years. His prints thus grew out of the tradition of reproductive engraving, but transcended it by virtue of his concentration in reinterpreting his own compositions and the ingenuity with which he deployed conventional engraving tools in unorthodox combinations."[38]

It is reasonable to trace a common motive in Stubbs's search for the permanence and survival of enamel colours and his interest in printmaking.[39] In both cases, according to theory, it was considered probable that the artist's original conception was more likely to survive the rigorous test of time. Experience had already proved that fired enamel colours were more likely to survive in their original form for posterity then oil colours on canvas or some other

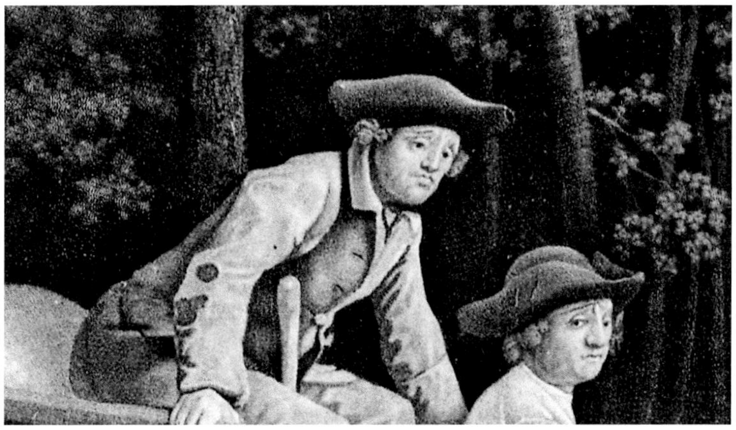

12 George Stubbs, *Labourers*, 1790, stipple with etching, detail
London, The British Museum

perishable support; similarly, prints were supposed to be more likely to preserve a design in pure form than paintings. As Stubbs's contemporary Joseph Strutt argued:

> Wherever a painter has himself handled the graver, his prints are most generally impressed with the same character as his paintings; and are therefore likely to give us a very accurate idea of his style. The prints of Albert Durer, Rembrandt and Salvator Rosa, are all such exact counterparts, that at this time, when the colouring of their pictures is often so far changed, as to answer little further purpose than that of light and shadow, they become in a manner their rivals; and, in the general acceptance of the world, the prints of some of these artists have been as highly valued as their paintings.[40]

It seems likely that the permanence of engravings attracted Stubbs—"the durability of the printed impressions by comparison with the relative frailty of oil painting".[41] He was motivated by the idea that he could pass his own definitive interpretation of his favourite subjects on to posterity, along with the reminder to posterity that he could handle every medium open to an artist. There is no evidence to support the assertions of Basil Taylor and Richard Godfrey that the public was indifferent to Stubbs's prints.[42] On the contrary, the handful of sets in Stubbs's studio sale was presented as one of its highlights. Many impressions have emerged since Taylor wrote and the prints became valuable. However, Stubbs did not use engraving techniques suited to the production of a huge number of impressions, which suggests that commercial considerations were not his highest priority. John Singleton Copley commissioned Francesco Bartolozzi to engrave his painting of the *Death of Chatham* in line and was bitterly disappointed when the plate yielded only 2500 impressions. After 1780 Stubbs made plates that did not lend themselves to retouching and could provide far fewer prints than this. If Stubbs had wanted to make large profits from engraving his work, he would have gone about it differently. What must have mattered was that the prints represented the images that were important to him in the way that he wanted them represented.

I have argued that the painter expected to be known by the published record. For this reason Joshua Reynolds wanted as many of his pictures as possible engraved well and published. There were more prints after Reynolds than any other British artist of the period, but there were not many other painters more fully represented than Stubbs. 146 separate plates appeared in his lifetime (not counting small copies and duplicates and more than seventy anatomical plates). Stubbs shared Reynolds's preoccupation with his published oeuvre, working first with selected artists, then with his son and finally defining a body of work by which to be remembered through his own engravings.

1 For a full account of prints after Stubbs see Lennox-Boyd et al., *George Stubbs*, 1989.
2 Humphry mss, Liverpool Public Library. This was Ozias Humphry's record of what Stubbs had told him of the story of his life.
3 Ibid. The visit took place before Pond's sudden death in September 1758. Grignion's engraving of Nathan Drake's view of York, published in 1756, might have been a connection.
4 Although Basil Taylor (*The Prints of George Stubbs*, 1969, p. 7) was correct to say that after the Leeds etcher there is no evidence that Stubbs's training in engraving methods was anything but a self-education, it seems to me unlikely that he did not compare notes with his friends amongst the professional engravers. Stubbs could have taken lessons from Matthew Darly or William Austin who both taught etching, but it is more likely that he received informal tuition in refined etching techniques from a friend such as William Woollett or the drawing master and engraver Benjamin Green. Richard Godfrey, "George Stubbs as a Printmaker," in: *The Print Collector's Newsletter*, 1982, p. 115 considered it "a fair supposition that it was [Benjamin Green] who instructed Stubbs" in soft-ground etching. He never learned all the arts of the line-engraver, but he did use burins for the finest finishing touches after his plates had been bitten and the varnish removed.
5 Sir Walter Gilbey, *Life of George Stubbs, R. A.*, London 1898, p. 20.
6 Humphry mss.
7 For a fuller account see Timothy Clayton, *The English Print, 1688–1802*, New Haven and London 1997, especially pp. 181–206 and John Brewer, *The Pleasures of the Imagination*, London 1997, especially pp. 201–51.
8 13,000 catalogues were sold for the 1761 exhibition; surviving figures for visitors to the exhibitions of the society of Artists vary between a low of 11,200 in 1763 and a high of 22,906 in 1767. The highest number of visitors to a Royal Academy exhibition was 61,381 for the opening of Somerset House; cf. Brewer 1997 (see note 7), p. 237.

9 See Clayton 1997 (see note 7), pp. 194 f. and note 53.

10 Thomas Mortimer, *The Universal Director*, London 1763; Bradford's trade card illustrated by Lennox-Boyd et al., *George Stubbs*, 1989, p. 5. The earliest publications by Bradford in the British Museum are dated 1 July 1763.

11 Lord Grosvenor's *Arabian* (Lennox-Boyd no. 18). We dated it c. 1770 in that *catalogue raisonné*. I am now inclined to speculate that all undated prints published by Wesson may belong to the years immediately before the 1767 copyright act.

12 *Public Advertiser*, Saturday, 8 August 1767, p. 4 and 11 August, p. 3. The print was also advertised in the *St James's Chronicle*, 25–28 July 1767, p. 3, where Green announced that 'Proposals may be had for publishing five or seven more Prints of Horses, to make a Set'.

13 *Morning Chronicle*, 26 May 1772.

14 Louis Gougenot, *Lettre sur la peinture, la sculpture, et l'architecture*, 2nd edn, Amsterdam 1749, p. 137.

15 Ibid., p. 137.

16 Pierre Crozat, *Recueuil d'estampes d'après les plus beaux tableaux et d'après les plus beaux desseins qui sont en France*, Paris 1729, p. 1; Crozat's book was republished by Pierre-François Basan in 1763.

17 Florent le Comte, *Cabinet de Singularitez*, Brussels 1702; Robert Hecquet, *Catalogue des estampes gravées d'après Rubens; auquel on a joint l'oeuvre de Jordaens, et celle de Visscher*, Paris 1751; Pierre-François Basan, *Dictionnaire des graveurs*, Paris 1767; Carl Heinrich von Heinecken, *Idée générale d'une collection complette d'estampes* and *Dictionnaire des artistes dont nous avons des estampes*, Leipzig 1778; Michael Huber, *Notices générales des graveurs divisés par nations et des peintres rangés par écoles*, Dresden and Leipzig 1787.

18 Roger de Piles, *Abregé de la vie des peintres*, Paris 1699, p. 77.

19 Gerard de Lairesse, *The Art of Painting in all its Branches*, transl. John Frederick Fritsch, London 1738, p. 652.

20 There were twelve pence to a shilling and twenty shillings to a pound. A guinea was one pound and one shilling.

21 *The Daily Advertiser*, Monday, 11 July 1774, p. 1 and following days, quoted Lennox-Boyd et al., *George Stubbs*, 1989, p. 143.

22 "Memoirs of Thomas Jones," A. P. Oppé (ed.), *Walpole Society* 32, 1946–48, p. 19.

23 Lennox-Boyd no. 359, Egerton no. 172; studio sale, second day, lot 48, untraced by Egerton.

24 Robert Fountain, *William Wildman and George Stubbs*, The British Sporting Art Trust Essay no. 44, Autumn 2004, p. 12.

25 The observation that Stubbs's figures were usually portraits justified originally Judy Egerton's speculation (in: Exhib. Cat. *George Stubbs*, 1984/85, p. 111) that the fuller-faced figure might be Wildman, an identification that looks ever more plausible. The suggestion (Lennox-Boyd et al., *George Stubbs*, 1989, p. 93) that the other figure might be Bradford remains more tentative although Wildman and Bradford were evidently doing considerable business with each other at this time.

26 Of the two authentic paintings it seems to me likely that Bradford's was Egerton no. 88 since details of this painting more closely resemble the print and Bradford's painting appears still to have been in England in May 1802 when the dying James Sayer put it (or possibly an engraving of it?) up for sale at Richmond Hill (Burton Frederickson, ed., *The Index of Paintings Sold in the British Isles during the Nineteenth Century*, vol. 1, 1988, p. 714). Egerton takes the opposite view.

27 *The Public Advertiser*, 31 March 1768, p. 4, reprinted Lennox-Boyd et al., *George Stubbs*, 1989, p. 91.

28 Assuming that the *Sebra* was not originally bigger—a possibility since the landscape is more extensive in the original painting. Many of these plates are so rare that it is rash to be too positive.

29 Johann Georg Meusel, *Museum für Künstler und für Kunstliebhaber* 13, 1791, p. 74.

30 *The Monthly Magazine*, February 1802, p. 65.

31 *The Morning Chronicle*, 3 April 1788, reprinted Lennox-Boyd et al., *George Stubbs*, 1989, pp. 184 f.

32 Inking and printing copperplates was a skilled job normally undertaken by specialist copperplate printers. It is most unlikely (*pace* Taylor, *The Prints of George Stubbs*, 1969, p. 12) that Stubbs printed his own plates, though it was common enough for artists to own presses to take proofs. It is, of course, perfectly possible that Mary Spencer retained Stubbs's press along with the plates that she kept until 1817.

33 As Richard Godfrey first speculated, Godfrey 1982 (see note 4) p. 114 and note 6 (Exhib. Cat. *George Stubbs*, 1984/85, no. 170).

34 See Lennox-Boyd et al., *George Stubbs*, 1989, p. 213. The evidence rests solely on a proof print in Liverpool Public Library in which "Engraved by Henry Birche" is followed by a pencil signature "alias R Laurie" with a note in ink in the margin "Finish'd by R Earlom". Whether Birche was Laurie or Earlom or both it represents work done for Evans by engravers who shouldn't have been working for him, probably because they were contracted to work exclusively for others.

35 Egerton, *George Stubbs*, 2007, pp. 246 f.

36 Ibid., p. 547.

37 Taylor, *The Prints of George Stubbs*, 1969, gave the print to Stubbs; Godfrey 1982 (see note 4) p. 116 was uncertain; Lennox-Boyd et al. gave it to George Stubbs with reservations, chiefly surrounding the discovery of a record of a letter (pp. 289 f.) that showed the print was planned in 1801 and that George Townley Stubbs was involved in the process; Egerton attributes it to George Townley, but it would not have been George Stubbs's only poor piece of work.

38 Godfrey 1982 (see note 4), p. 114.

39 Taylor 1984 (see note 4), p. 14.

40 Joseph Strutt, *A Biographical Dictionary; Containing an Historical Account of all the Engravers from the Earliest Period of the Art of Engraving to the Present Time*, 2 vols., London 1785, pp. 2 f.

41 Taylor 1984 (see note 4), p. 14.

42 Ibid., pp. 14 f.; Godfrey 1982 (see note 4), p. 114.

p. 77: Detail from cat. no. 78

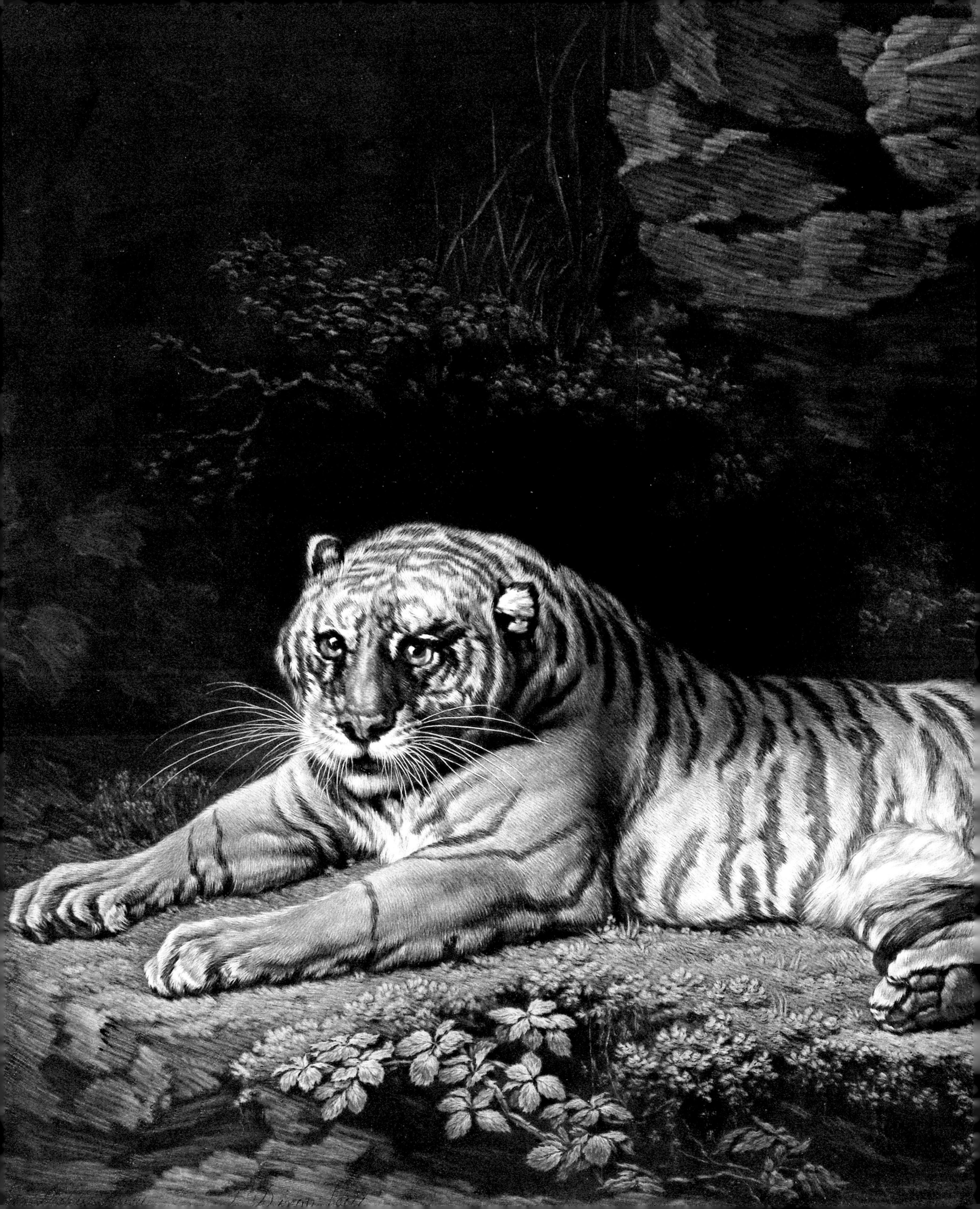

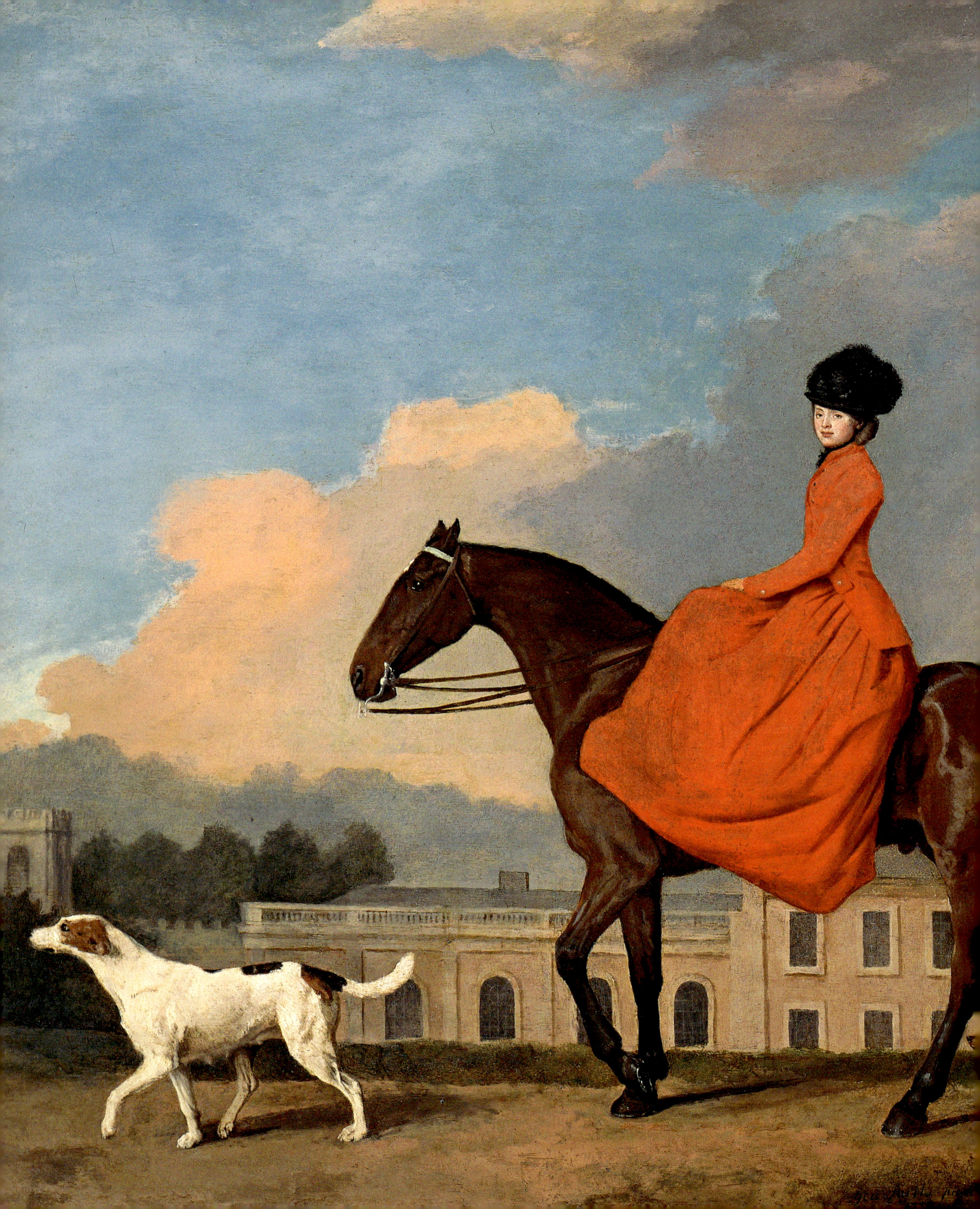

Francis Russell

STUBBS AND HIS PATRONS

This carefully chosen exhibition represents the full range of Stubbs's achievement, and demonstrates why we now recognize that he was not only one of the great artists of his age, but also arguably the most remarkable sporting master in the whole history of European art.[1] The visitor sees how the painter developed, in a sequence of masterpieces commissioned by successive patrons. But we can be confident that these men—and they were almost exclusively men—would be astonished to see the canvasses and panels they ordered in the context of a monographic exhibition. In the exhibitions to which Stubbs himself contributed, at the Society of Arts or, after its foundation in 1768, the Royal Academy, works were arranged in orchestrated picture hangs; and in the houses, whether in the country or in London, for which his pictures were intended, these took their places with other pictures and furnishings in rooms that were often carefully planned.

Stubbs was fortunate. His remarkable abilities fitted him uniquely to work for a number of patrons, many of the most significant of whom belonged to the close-knit world of the Whig plutocracy, the nexus of interrelated families that had supported the so-called Glorious Revolution of 1688 and secured the accession of the House of Hanover on the death of Queen Anne in 1714. Deriving their wealth from territorial estates and their power from control of numerous parliamentary seats and influence over local appointments, the representatives of such families could afford to build or rebuild their houses on a lavish scale. Most were well educated and had gone on from their schools, of which the most fashionable then were Westminster and Eton, to the universities of Oxford or Cambridge, before completing what had been essentially a classical education by making the Grand Tour to Italy. Their architectural tastes were strictly classical, owing much to the influence a generation earlier of Lord Burlington, and sternly rejecting the dramatic extravagances of Sir John Vanbrugh, the chosen domestic architect of some of the more discriminating patrons of the early years of the century. By contrast, their patronage of painters was more conservative. Portraiture predominated. Many of the key families had built up portrait collections over the preceding two centuries, and naturally sought to maintain these, with the result that portraiture was by far the most lucrative activity for any British painter of the time. Portraiture could be paralleled by views of a patron's houses or estates, or by pictures of the animals, most obviously dogs and horses, that had always played an important role in the life of the English landowner. The place of an animal painter may have been a relatively low one in the continental academies of the period; however, we know that Stubbs's major patrons called him in precisely because he was the outstanding animal painter of the day.

To us, Stubbs's work is of an altogether higher order than anything of the kind that had gone before. But just as Reynolds and Gainsborough, and indeed Batoni when he was working for British patrons, knew that they worked in the shadow of Van Dyck and sought at times to allude to this, so Stubbs must have been aware that many of his patrons inherited pictures of horses that had been cherished by their ancestors. Although there are some previous examples, for example the "fair picture of a horse", the life-size grey still at Hatfield, which was recorded there in 1629, the earliest major series of such pictures are the mid-seventeenth-century canvasses of the Duke of Newcastle's manèged horses, which in 1747 were in the Great Hall at Welbeck, and must thus have been familiar to Stubbs's patron, William Cavendish Bentinck, 3rd Duke of Portland from his infancy. Francis Barlow (1626–1704) enjoyed a degree of success as an animal painter after the Restoration of 1660, and in the early decades of the eighteenth century both Peter Tillemans (1684–1734) and James Seymour (1702–1752) specialized in sporting pictures.

Altogether more significant for Stubbs's patrons was the career of John Wootton (1682–1764). Three of the latter's numerous pictures painted for the Duke of Portland's grandparents, the 2nd Earl of Oxford and his wife, Margaret, heiress of the Newcastle estates, were also in the Great Hall at Welbeck by 1747, while others were in the Vestibule. Wootton supplied major series of canvasses for the halls at Badminton, Longleat and Althorp. The son of his patron at Longleat, the 2nd Viscount Weymouth, would marry the sister of

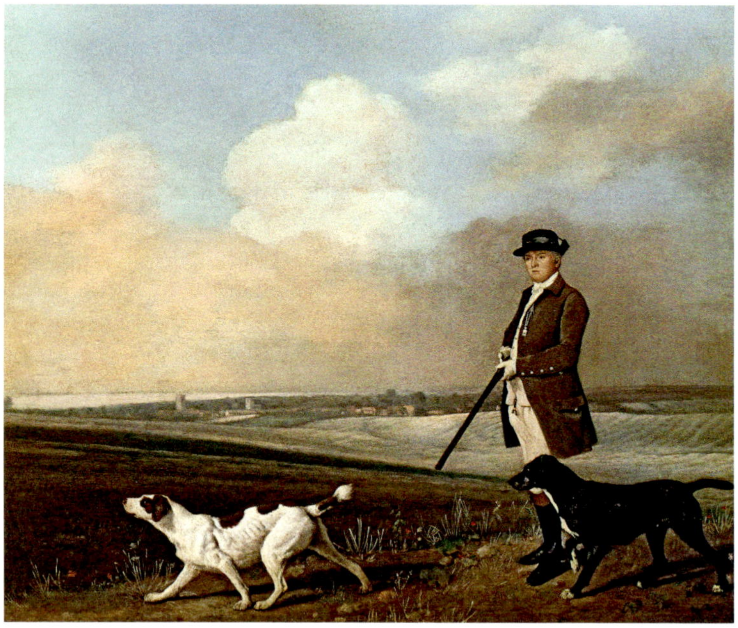

1 George Stubbs, *Sir John Nelthorpe Shooting*, 1776, oil on panel, 61 x 71 cm
Private collection

the 3rd Duke of Portland; while Charles Spencer, 3rd Duke of Marlborough—who commissioned both the pictures in the Hall at Althorp and a sequence of portraits of individual racehorses which were kept at Langley Park in Buckinghamshire—was the father of one patron of Stubbs, George, 4th Duke of Marlborough; the father-in-law of another, Frederick St. John, 2nd Viscount Bolingbroke; and the uncle of a third, John, 1st Earl Spencer. Wootton also worked for Robert Bertie, 1st Duke of Ancaster, grandfather of a client of the artist, and from 1754 for Charles Wentworth Watson, 2nd Marquess of Rockingham, who in the ensuing decade became perhaps the most discriminating of all Stubbs's patrons. Stubbs himself was evidently asked by Rockingham to revise the likeness of the jockey John Singleton in Wootton's canvas of a chestnut, dated 1758, which was formerly at Wentworth Woodhouse.

Patronage by the great Whig families was not obvious in the artist's sights at the outset of his career. He was brought up in Liverpool, and at the age of sixteen (that is in 1740/41) was asked by the doyen of local painters, Hamlet Winstanley, to copy pictures in the collection of the 11th Earl of Derby at Knowsley. The project was abortive, but Stubbs must have had the opportunity of seeing the major group of sporting pictures painted by Tillemans for the 10th Earl of Derby. Surprisingly little is known about Stubbs's early activity as a portraitist. Humphry states that he worked for a Mr. Wilson at Leeds, but the only certain extant pictures of the 1740s are the double portrait of a Lincolnshire landowner, Sir Henry Nelthorpe and his wife of c. 1746 (Egerton no. 2) and the *George Fothergill* (Hull; Egerton no. 3). The latter was painted in York, to which Stubbs had moved in 1744. The Nelthorpes lived at Baysgarth, near Barton-upon-Humber, and his connection with the family was to be of enduring importance to the artist. Further commissions followed, and in 1756–58 Stubbs settled at Horkstow near Barton, where he did the groundwork for the great project that would be published as *The Anatomy of the Horse*. Valentine Knightley of Fawsley in Northamptonshire chose in 1776 to be painted against the view of Barton and the Humber estuary (Egerton no. 182) used for Stubbs's contemporary portrait of his great friend, Sir John Nelthorpe, 6th Baronet (Egerton no. 181; fig. 1), who had succeeded his father in 1746. Sir John's sister, Charlotte, was married to the Rev. Robert Carter Thelwell, who ordered a family group while his neighbour, Charles Anderson Pelham, created Lord Yarborough in 1794, was one of the most loyal patrons of the artist's later years. Thus an association with north Lincolnshire that began in the mid-1740s was maintained until 1804, when Stubbs painted his masterly *Water Spaniel* for Lord Yarborough (Egerton no. 343).

Stubbs's visit to Rome was of considerable importance for his artistic development, but also expanded his acquaintance network. Humphry records that the painter met the architects William Chambers (1723–1796) and Matthew Brettingham the Younger (1725–1803), the agent Thomas Jenkins, the sculptor Simon Vierpyl (*c.* 1725–1810) and the painter Richard Wilson (1713–1782). There is no evidence that he met two future patrons then on the Grand Tour, Lord Bolingbroke or Augustus Fitzroy, 3rd Duke of Grafton, although it is worth noting that the former patronised both Vierpyl and Wilson when in Rome. It may not be a coincidence that Stubbs was to work for a number of Chambers's patrons: the dukes of Richmond, Marlborough and Buccleuch,[2] John Fitzpatrick, 2nd Earl of Upper Ossory, George Brodick, 4th Viscount Midleton, and, rather later, Peniston Lamb, 1st Viscount Melbourne.

When Stubbs returned it was to his native Liverpool, where in 1755 he painted a kinsman of Lord Derby, James Stanley, and, in all probability, William Smythe, who married a member of another Catholic family, Mary Ann Erington, near Liverpool in that year. Their daughter, also called Mary Ann, married Thomas Fitzherbert of Swynnerton as her second husband in 1778. Two years later Stubbs portrayed the two at breakfast, a picture that has sadly not survived. Fitzherbert died in 1781 and in 1785 his widow went through a form of marriage with George, Prince of Wales. The Prince had already commissioned two equestrian portraits of people who worked for him from Stubbs, but only became a major patron of the artist when he and Mrs Fitzherbert were living as man and wife (cat. nos. 50–51).

STUBBS AND THE ROCKINGHAM WHIGS

Stubbs moved to London in 1758 or the following year. He quickly came to the attention of Joshua Reynolds; the latter or Chambers, who had begun to work at Goodwood in 1757, may have recommended him to Charles Lennox, 3rd Duke of Richmond, for whom he painted three major pictures that celebrated the young duke's sporting interests, hunting, shooting and racing in 1759/60. The duke's father was the single most influential patron of Canaletto after his arrival in London in 1746, and the duke himself can be seen to have had a central role in furthering Stubbs's career. His Charlton Hunt drew many friends to Goodwood, including the Countess of Coningsby, whom Stubbs painted in the hunt's livery, and, as Judy Egerton suggests, his first cousin once removed, Augustus Henry (the name by which he was known) Fitzroy, 3rd Duke of Grafton. The latter's horse Patch may have been portrayed at Goodwood. Stubbs was very quickly taken up by other associates of the two dukes: Lord Bolingbroke; Lord Spencer; Peregrine Bertie, 3rd Duke of Ancaster; Richard, 1st Earl Grosvenor; Lord Rockingham; Lord Midleton; and George Byng, 4th Viscount Torrington.

All these men moved in the same circles, belonging to the Jockey Club and to that command post of the Whig interest in London, Brooks's, to which–as Judy Egerton established–no fewer than seventeen of Stubbs's recorded patrons belonged. All, with the exception of Torrington, were patrons of Reynolds, but in the cases of Rockingham, Spencer and Bolingbroke only after they had employed Stubbs. All were extravagant. Bolingbroke owned at least ten pictures by the artist and Torrington owned five, with a sixth to which Stubbs had contributed figures (see below). Both lived far beyond their means, with the ironic result that we only know the scale of the latter's patronage of Stubbs from the catalogue of the auction held after the sale of his Bedfordshire mansion, Southill, in 1778.[3]

Obtaining a divorce necessitated a special act of parliament, and so it is remarkable that three of Stubbs's key patrons secured these–most unusually, because of their own conduct, on terms that permitted their wives to remarry. Bolingbroke was unfaithful to his wife, but their divorce in 1768 gave rise to less public comment than that of the Duke of Grafton in the same year; the latter was Prime Minister at the time. This released Grafton's wife to marry John Fitzpatrick, 2nd Earl of Upper Ossory, another patron of Stubbs. When he found a suitable replacement, the duke in turn released his mistress who subsequently lived in the same capacity with John Frederick, 3rd Duke of Dorset. An unnamed donor gave the latter a picture of one of his own hunters and a groom (Egerton no. 94), painted perhaps not coincidentally in 1768. Two years later Lord and Lady Grosvenor were also divorced. But fractured lives were no bar to influence or public life. However reluctant to take the office, Grafton was as well fitted to serve as Prime Minister as his predecessor Rockingham, although rather less conscientious than another discriminating patron of Stubbs, the Duke of Portland, who held that position in the Whig interest on two occasions.

Stubbs's patrons had differing needs. The Duke of Richmond inherited a distinguished sequence of family portraits, as well as ten of the twenty-four *Monuments to the Remembrance of a Set of British Worthies* commissioned from North Italian artists by Owen MacSwinny which the latter had sold to the 2nd Duke, and views by both Joli and Canaletto. The Duke of Grafton had also inherited fine portraits, and a few outstanding old masters from the collection of his maternal grandfather, Lord Arlington. Lord Spencer had the great collections formed by the earls of Sunderland and by his father's maternal grandmother, Sarah, Duchess of Marlborough. Lord Torrington also inherited a varied collection. By contrast, Lord Grosvenor must have been conscious that his means were not matched by his collection. He had endeavoured to rectify this by retaining Richard Dalton, who was in Italy in 1758/59 searching for

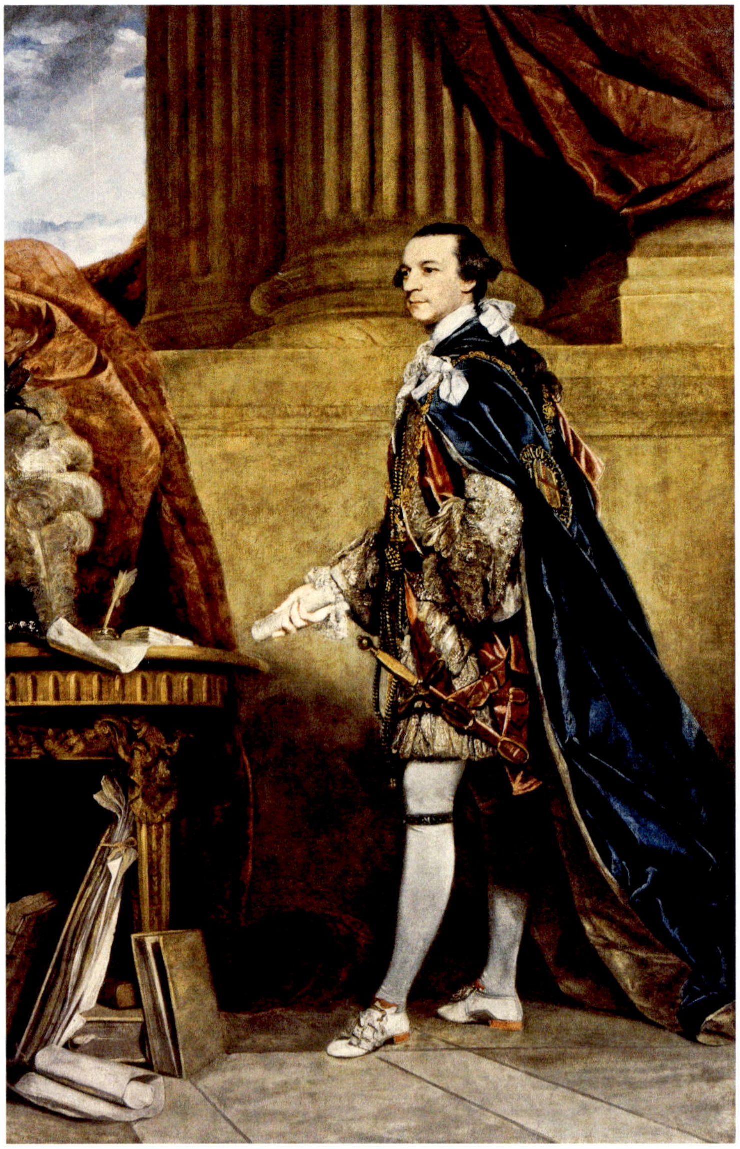

2 Sir Joshua Reynolds, *Charles Watson-Wentworth, 2nd Marquess of Rockingham*, 1766–68, oil on canvas, 239 x 148 cm
The Trustees of the Rt. Hon. Olive, Countess Fitzwilliam's Chattels Settlement, by permission of Lady Juliet Tadgell

medals, drawings and prints on behalf of the Prince of Wales, to purchase pictures there on his behalf. While Stubbs's patrons were deeply interested in the horses and other animals he depicted, the demands placed upon him inevitably reflected the scale of their collections and the demands of the rooms they arranged or rearranged.

STUBBS IN WENTWORTH WOODHOUSE

Often the information at our disposal is tantalizingly incomplete, and we have, alas, no direct evidence as to Stubbs's interaction with his aristocratic patrons. For this reason it is instructive to examine the references to pictures by him in the inventory of the contents of Wentworth Woodhouse prepared after Lord Rockingham's death in 1782 (figs. 2–3).[4] This begins with "Lord Rockingham's Staircase" and continues with his very fully furnished Dressing Room. Four pictures are stated to be by Stubbs (these are here identified with asterisks); his authorship of five others is not noted. Another four horse portraits—a pair of the "Bloud Shouldered Arabian" and the "Hampton Court Arabian", paid for in 1754, and a smaller pair, measuring 40 by 50 inches, including that of the chestnut held by John Singleton—can be identified as by Wootton. A picture of three brood mares and a foal is attributed to the local painter Benjamin Killingbeck. There is no indication as to the authorship of three small horse portraits, or of a picture of "Lap Dogs". In total, there were nine pictures by Stubbs in Lord Rockingham's collection: "A landscape of a Colliery" (Egerton no. 65); "5 Brood Mares and 2 foals" (cat. no. 20); its pendant "Mr. Cobb and 3 horses" (cat. no. 19); "Stag Hounds 5 in number" (cat. no. 28); "Bay Malton at speed rode by Singleton" (Egerton no. 55); "Old Sampson in three Attitudes" (Egerton no. 54); "Thomas Walhead holding a Bay Arabian Horse" and its pendant "Matthew Harrison holding the Horse Solon" (both untraced*); and "A Bay Horse (Scrubb) standing mounted by Jon Singleton" (Egerton no. 32). With its "Library Table" or desk, its maps and instruments to which Rockingham must have referred, the room was clearly much more than the term "Dressing Room" might imply. Off it was Rockingham's "Gun Closet", with two more horse portraits (in one of which Joshua Cobb reappeared) and a large collection of guns.

The circuit continued with "Lord Rockingham's Antichamber", in which there were a picture of "a Buffalo Cow and a Herdsman" and twelve portraits, all of members of Rockingham's family or personal friends, with the exception of Stubbs's *Old Thomas Smith the Banksman* (Egerton no. 67; fig. 4). That this uniquely sensitive

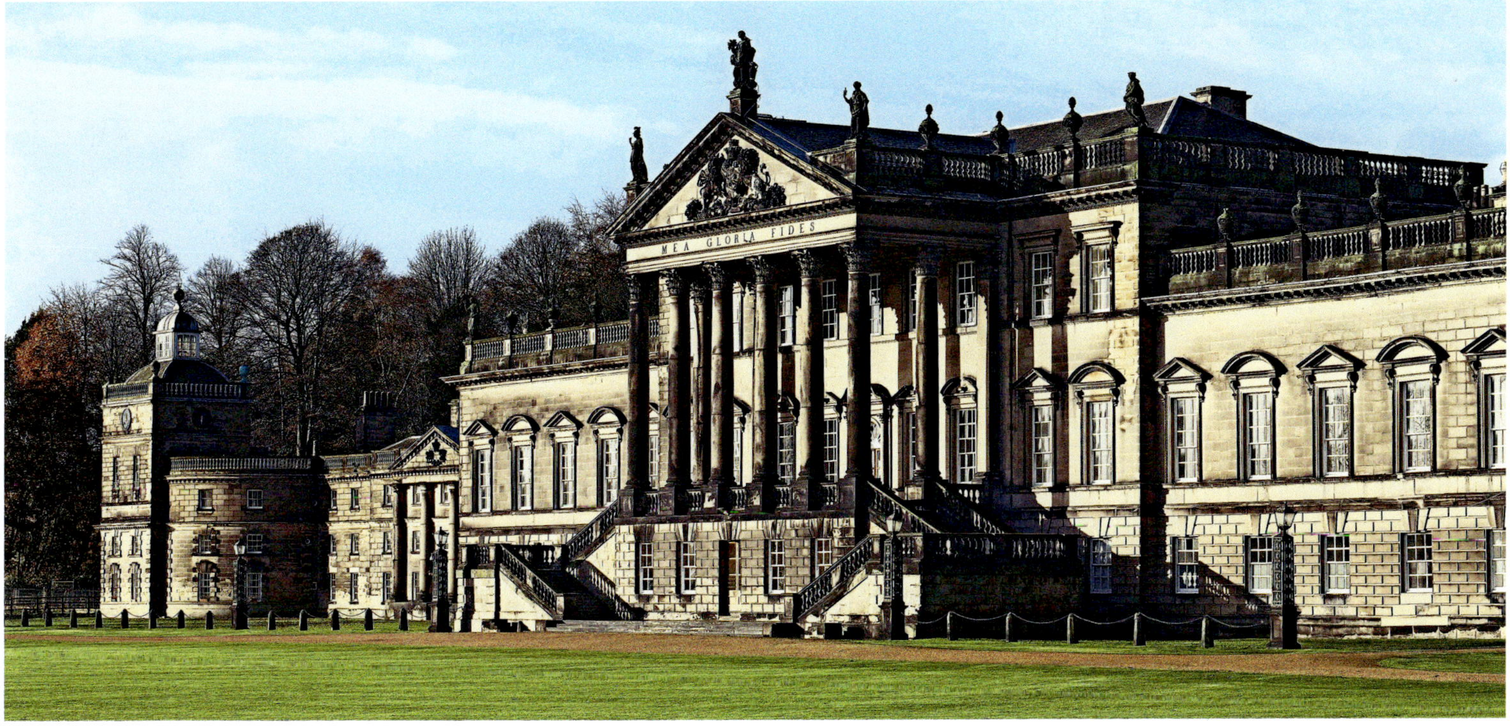

3 View of Wentworth Woodhouse, Yorkshire

servant's portrait was placed in this context casts a telling light on the range of the Marquess's human sympathies. Portraits were mixed with other pictures, including two by West, in the Red Dressing Room, and there were four family portraits and two landscapes in the Red Bed Chamber. Overmantel portraits by Mercier in one of the Waiting Rooms, the Drawing Room and the Supping Room were no doubt installed by the 1st Marquess. There follows the "Pillar'd Hall", with Foggini's *Samson* of 1749, now in the Victoria and Albert Museum. The staircase off this led to the "Dining Room above Stairs", with two large pictures inset in the walls in carved oak frames, an equestrian portrait of King George II and *Whistlejacket* (Egerton no. 34; see p. 32, fig. 8). This pairing must in some way explain the notion that the latter was intended for an equestrian portrait of King George III, which seems improbable for various reasons, most obviously the King's uneasy relationship with Rockingham and his political associates. Nineteen framed pictures and thirty unframed ones, as well as four glazed copies of originals at Rome, were also recorded in the room. Many were portraits, including two major van Dycks of Lord Strafford with his Secretary, and of the three children of the former. But there was also a scattering of old masters and a portrait of the Godolphin Arabian, which is listed as by Stubbs. The Drawing Room, sparsely furnished, contained twenty-one pictures. Here too portraits predominated, with van Dyck's celebrated whole length of Strafford, and Mytens's *Lord Baltimore*. Elsewhere there were other scattered pictures, including a set of nine views of Wentworth Woodhouse by John (?) Ross in the Steward's Room.

Any visitor to Wentworth would have seen how prominently placed *Whistlejacket* was in one of the major rooms of what was the largest of all English Palladian houses. The agriculturalist Arthur Young was shown Rockingham's Antichamber, and noticed the Stubbs portrait there. But the other major pictures Stubbs painted for the Marquess were all placed in the latter's Dressing Room, to which few visitors can have penetrated. Those who did, however, might have wondered why their host went to that plodding local painter, Benjamin Killingbeck for the picture of mares and a foal that also hung in the room. Perhaps there had been some disagreement after the Marquess's rejection of the large portrait of *Scrub* (Halifax Collection; Egerton no. 35); the width of the latter suggests that this may well have been conceived as a pendant to *Whistlejacket* and thus originally intended to replace the equestrian portrait of King George II., as the 1760s progressed, would have seemed increasingly important as a sign of Rockingham's Whig credentials.

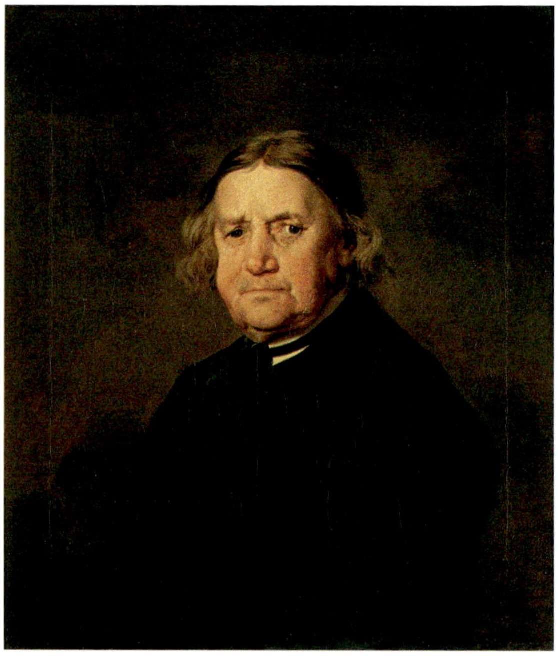

4 George Stubbs, *Thomas Smith*, c. 1765/66, oil on canvas, 71.1 x 62.5 cm
Private collection

CHANGING RELATIONSHIPS

We rightly think of Stubbs as a supreme landscapist. The Duke of Richmond and Lord Grosvenor secured hunting scenes that were also in effect estate portraits of unprecedented distinction. The trio of canvasses that records aspects of the life of Torrington's estate at Southill (Egerton nos. 99–101; cat. nos. 31–32), like the portrait of *The Duke of Portland before the Riding School at Welbeck* (Egerton no. 80) and that of *Lord Bolingbroke's Bay Mare with Lydiard Tregoze in the Background* (Egerton no. 19), must have impressed their owners precisely because of their fidelity and acuity of observation. With other commissions topographical accuracy was clearly irrelevant: Lord Midleton was the only patron who ordered a group of mares and foals that were not specifically owned by him (if we exclude a variant of the Parker composition that may have been painted for either the Duke of Grafton or John Smyth, of Heath Hall, Yorkshire, whom the duke and his former wife considered so unsuitable a son-in-law, Egerton no. 90). Furthermore, col. George Lane Parker was evidently content that his horses should be placed against a cliff reminiscent of Cresswell Crags on the Welbeck estate (Egerton no. 89).

What is remarkable is that a number of the artist's patrons chose on occasion to dispense with Stubbs's services as a landscapist. Lord Rockingham is the most celebrated of these. In the case of *Whistlejacket* the decision was presumably aesthetic, and it is surely significant that two of the largest pictures in his Dressing Room (cat. nos. 19–20) were also on plain buff backgrounds, as was a third (*Old Sampson*; Egerton no. 54), if indeed the landscape was not supplied until after the marquess's death. At least four patrons chose to go to the Irish-born George Barret (1728–1784). He supplied the landscape in both the portrait of the Duke of Grafton's *Antinoüs* and a large, now lost portrait of a dog owned by Portland's brother, Lord Edward Bentinck. As Barret painted a major series of views of the Welbeck estate for the duke in 1765–67, this is hardly surprising. It was no doubt while he was at Welbeck that Barret went to Roche Abbey, some ten miles to the northwest; he painted a number of views, one of which was indeed at Welbeck. This explains the collaboration between the artist and Stubbs recorded in the Torrington sale catalogue of 1778: "A view of Roach Abbey in its present state, in which is introduced the portrait of lady T[orrington]" listed as by "Messrs. Barret and Stubbs". Their names are understandably reversed for two earlier lots: "Portraits of two horses and a poney, belonging to Lord Torrington, remarkably fine", and "Ditto its companion".[5] Unfortunately all three pictures are lost, but the view of Roche, at least, is likely to have been contemporary with Barret's Welbeck views, and thus of c. 1765–67. In 1769–71 Barret exhibited views of the park at Dalkeith, which had been commissioned by Henry Scott, 3rd Duke of Buccleuch and 5th of Queensberry. The unpublished portrait of a horse at Bowhill, for which he supplied the landscape, is presumably also of this period. With the exception of the Duke of Grafton there were thus obvious reasons for Barret's association with these commissions.

There may be a different explanation for the fact that the background of the small portrait of *Hollyhock* painted for Lord Bolingbroke (Egerton no. 20) was left unfinished. Bolingbroke gave the picture to Jean-Louis Monnet in 1766. Presumably he hoped to find a French buyer for the horse itself, and was aware that such a purchaser might not want an English view. In the event the background was painted by Boucher and Vernet. It was perhaps not a coincidence that a pair of pictures by the latter was owned by Bolingbroke. *Hollyhock* subsequently returned to England, to be bought by the Prince Regent in 1810, six years after the death of Stubbs, whom he had come to patronise assiduously. One of Stubbs's earlier patrons, William Wildman, who owned seventeen pictures by him, also bought works on the market: he secured the three Southill pictures at the Torrington sale, and arranged for the background of one to be altered (Egerton no. 100).

If *Hollyhock* was painted as part of what we would now term a marketing campaign, this may have also been the case with other portraits of racehorses, rather in the way that prints by Bartolozzi and other reproductive engravers were used to further the sale of pictures and drawings. Horses were indeed sold with remarkable rapidity. An extreme case is Gimcrack. The animal was acquired by the trainer William Wildman in 1764 and sold in 1765 to Lord Bolingbroke, who commissioned the celebrated picture of him on Newmarket Heath (Egerton no. 70) before selling him on to the comte de Lauraguais (whose interest in horses was equalled by his taste for pictures, but apparently not for those of Stubbs). Sir Charles Bunbury, 6th Baronet, who had married the Duke of Richmond's sister, Lady Sarah Lennox in 1762 and was to be divorced in 1776, bought the horse two years later, selling him to Lord Grosvenor in 1769.[6] Stubbs was the beneficiary; he painted Gimcrack for Wildman (Egerton no. 71), and more than coincidentally used the same composition for a portrait of *Turf* (cat. no. 25) for Bolingbroke, who had purchased that horse in 1764. Some years later, presumably in or after 1769, he was asked to supply the rather automatic replica of the Bolingbroke picture now owned by the Jockey Club for Lord Grosvenor.[7] In the case of Gimcrack the pictures were clearly, as it were, celebratory, but given the turnover in racehorses at the time, we cannot exclude that there was an element of the promotional in some other commissions for portraits of racehorses.

Stubbs's career in the 1760s was dominated by the demands of his great Whig patrons. But he worked for other men as well. The relatively modest portrait of John Warde with his horse is a case in point (cat. no. 37). Warde's eponymous father, who spent a portion of his city fortune on the purchase of Squerryes in Kent, had the sense to retain the existing late-seventeenth-century brick house. For this his son built up a collection of ninety-three works between 1747 and 1774, including the major Frans Hals family portrait now in the Thyssen Collection, for a total of £691 and 8 shillings. As a commission, the Stubbs is not mentioned in Warde's "Catalogue of Pictures of my own Collecting".[8] This, however, records the purchase, in 1758, of "a Bronze of a Lion Seising an Horse", evidently based on the antique prototype that was a source of inspiration to Stubbs. Apart from their interest in the theme, Warde had little in common with the purchaser of the interpretation of this subject shown here (Egerton no. 112; cat. no. 41). Sir Peniston Lamb, 2nd Baronet, of Brocket in Hertfordshire, who in 1770 was created Lord Melbourne in the Irish peerage, was also of a relatively new family. But his marriage in 1769 to Elizabeth, daughter of Sir Ralph Milbanke, 5th Baronet, was to impel him into a very different social sphere. In his group portrait of Lady Melbourne with her father, her brother and her husband (cat. no. 35), Stubbs seems already to have sensed her determination, and no doubt recognized her antennae for the fashionable. The architect James Paine had begun to rebuild Brocket for her father-in-law, and, from 1771, Chambers worked on Melbourne House, Piccadilly, now the Albany. Reynolds painted two portraits of Lady Melbourne in 1770/71, and another of her children, while for furniture Thomas Chippendale was called in.

It was the Melbournes' fate that their elder son, Peniston, would fall in love with an older woman who was already married. Her husband, John Musters, of Colwick Hall, near Nottingham, inherited a substantial estate. But, as with the Melbournes, marriage in 1776 to Sophia Heywood propelled him into a more dynamic social orbit. Colwick was remodelled by John Carr, furniture was bought from Ince and Mayhew and portraits were commissioned from both Reynolds and the equally fashionable George Romney. In 1777/78 Stubbs painted no fewer than seven pictures for Musters: the famous equestrian groups showing the new house and the stables (Egerton nos. 187–88; figs. 5–6); an unpublished equestrian portrait of Musters on his favourite hunter, Pilgrim, with the River Trent behind; the group of Musters's mares with Colwick in the distance, two portraits of Mrs Musters's dogs and another of one of her husband's hunters (Egerton nos. 189–92). These worked on varying levels: as portraits, as records of favourite horses and dogs, and as estate views celebrating the new house with its park. One can understand why the artist was called in to substitute the local vicar for Mrs Musters after she left her husband; her likeness must have been as disturbing to Musters as that of the favourite house terrier in the companion picture (in which the errant wife was merely painted out) was to its less privileged brother—whenever the huntsman brought the dog into the Parlour at Colwick, it "looked up at the picture setting up his bristles, growling, and giving it every challenge in his power", as Humphry relates.[9]

A grander new patron during these same years was Charles Manners, Marquess of Granby and, from 1779, 4th Duke of Rutland, for whom a canvas of two dogs, *Crab and Turk*, was supplied in 1777 (Egerton no. 195), and a more monumental portrait of the latter a year later (cat. no. 48). This is one of the most spirited of Stubbs's dog portraits, and the artist cannot have been ignorant of Granby's serious interest in pictures, an interest which was evidently shared by his wife, who unlike him had been to Italy. Beginning with the purchase of an outstanding Valentin (Toledo Museum of Art), then attributed to Caravaggio, Granby built spectacularly on

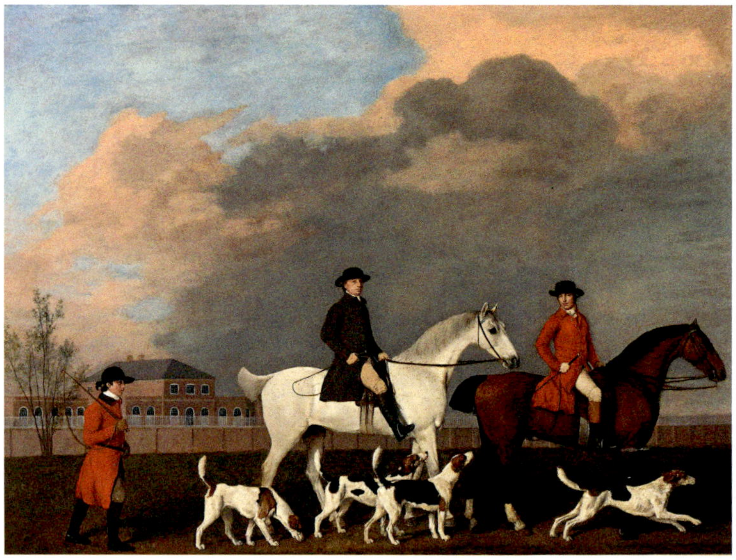

5 George Stubbs, *John Musters and the Rev. Philip Story Riding Out from the Stable Block at Colwick Hall*, 1777, oil on panel, 100.4 x 124.4 cm
Private collection

of Rockingham's pictures by the artist were concentrated in his Dressing Room. The most ambitious of those painted for Musters was in the Parlour rather than the Drawing Room at Colwick.

The Duke of Richmond's three great pictures were, by 1819, in the Billiards Room at Goodwood. George Forbes, 5th Earl of Granard's "picture of 2 favourite horses by Stubs [sic]" was the one painting in his bedroom in his villa at Langley in Buckinghamshire in 1772.[10] Lord Rockingham, who evidently slept in one of the "2 Bedsteds (Mahogany Posts)" in the Summer Bed Chamber at Wentworth, was not alone in keeping pictures by Stubbs in his Dressing Room. When the Duke of Dorset died in 1799, the Stubbs painting of his horse and groom was the only picture in his Dressing Room, which was next to his "Bedchamber" at Knole.[11]

the collection formed by his grandfather, encouraged by various friends and advisors, including Reynolds. The Boccapaduli *Sacraments* of Poussin were his most celebrated acquisitions. Like Wildman, Granby attended the Torrington sale in 1778, buying a major portrait of King Henry VIII, to whom his family owed its earldom. He was already an assiduous patron of British artists, including Mortimer, Marlow, Kaufmann and West. He bought three fine landscapes from Gainsborough and was an outstanding patron of Reynolds. As, ignoring repetitions, the latter painted him twice, his wife on three occasions, and two groups of his children, we should perhaps not be surprised that he wished to have two portraits of what was presumably a cherished dog. The duke's death at the age of 33 in 1787 cut short what had already proved a remarkable collecting career.

Masterpieces as Stubbs's pictures are to us, we must remember that they were painted to record his patrons, their families, their dependants—the servants whom Stubbs observed so sympathetically, and whose special relationships with those who wished to have them portrayed he understood so well—and of course their animals. With notable exceptions such as *Whistlejacket*, these were intended for personal consumption and not for great public rooms. Most

6 George Stubbs, *John and Sophia Musters Riding at Colwick Hall*, 1777, oil on panel, 100.4 x 124.4 cm
Private collection

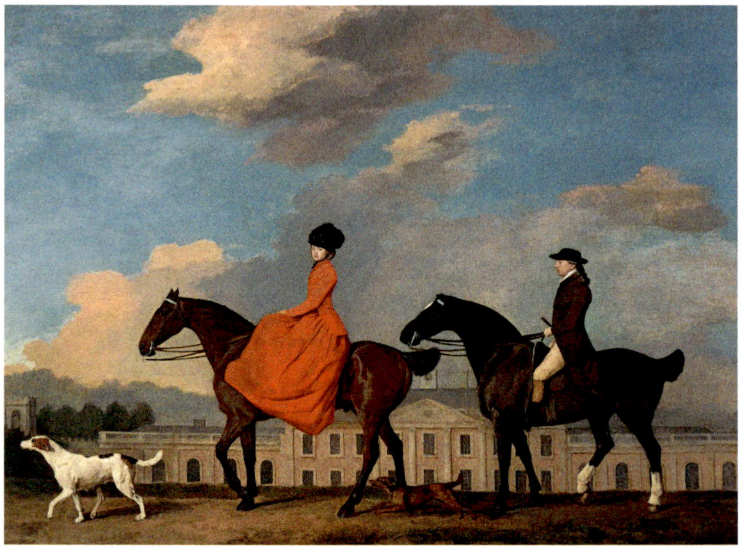

1 As will be obvious to anyone who reads this essay, it draws very extensively on the work of Judy Egerton, to whom it is, most gratefully, dedicated.

2 An overlooked portrait of a horse, with a landscape by Barret, who worked for Henry, 3rd Duke of Buccleuch and 5th of Queensberry is at Bowhill.

3 In addition to the pictures previously associated with Bolingbroke (Egerton nos. 17, 19, 20, 23, 26, and 72), we should add *Molly Long-Legs* (a horse that the viscount bought in 1761; Egerton no. 25), which makes an admirable pair to *Lustre* (Egerton no. 26); the two were presumably the "Portraits of a horse and groom in a landscape" and "Ditto the companion" sold by Bolingbroke at Christie's, 19 March 1779, lots 89 and 90 (which was bought by Sir James Peachey, 4th Baronet and thus presumably went to West Dean). This would mean that *Tristram Shandy* (Egerton no. 23) was the picture sold for Bolingbroke, 10 March 1780, lot 50. The *Mares and Foals* from Lydiard (Egerton no. 17) is evidently the picture bought for twenty-seven guineas by Bolingbroke's son when this was sold on his by then mad father's behalf, Christie's, 11 March 1780. On 20 March 1779 "A landscape with a group of brood mares & horses" and "A ditto the companion" were sold for Bolingbroke as lots 96 and 97 for thirty-six and thirty-five guineas respectively. Does this mean that Bolingbroke bought the *Five Mares at the Duke of Cumberland's stud farm* (Egerton no. 64), which like the Grosvenor *Mares and Foals* is of the same size as the picture formerly at Lydiard (39 by 74 inches /99 x 187 cm; Egerton no. 17), after the duke's death in 1765? Lord Grosvenor himself took an interest in the sale, as Dr John Hunter, also of course a patron of Stubbs, bought another of Bolingbroke's pictures, a landscape by Patel, on his behalf. The 20 March 1779 sale included another Bolingbroke Stubbs that can no longer be identified as lot 69: "A tiger", for which Colonel Pennington paid eight and a half guineas. In addition to these pictures Bolingbroke may have owned a dog portrait first recorded in the possession of a Miss St. John in 1885 (Egerton no. 168).

4 "An inventory of All the Household Goods, Plate, Pictures, Statues and Furniture which were in the late Charles Marquis of Rockingham's Capital Messuage or Mansion called Wentworth … and which are deemed Heir=Looms to be enjoyed according to the direction of his Will", dated "Wentworth 16.th Sept.r 1782" (Sheffield Archives).

5 Torrington sale, Christie's, 25 January 1778, lots 63, 60 and 61 respectively.

6 Lady Sarah's comment on the horse, as "the sweetest little horse there ever was; he is delightful" casts a rather touching light on attitudes of the time, cf. Sheridan Dufferin, *British Sporting Painting 1650–1850*, Exhib. Cat. The Arts Council, London 1974, under no. 43.

7 Inadvertently omitted by Egerton, the picture was sold by the 2nd Earl Grosvenor, Christie's, 2 July 1812, lot 39; the sale also included four portraits of racehorses by Stubbs.

8 Warde Mss., Squerryes Court.

9 As transcribed in Exhib. Cat. *Fearful Symmetry*, 2000, p. 209.

10 As stated in the catalogue of his sale, Christie's, 21 May 1772, lot 21.

11 Posthumous inventory of the 3rd Duke (Knole Ms, f. 12).

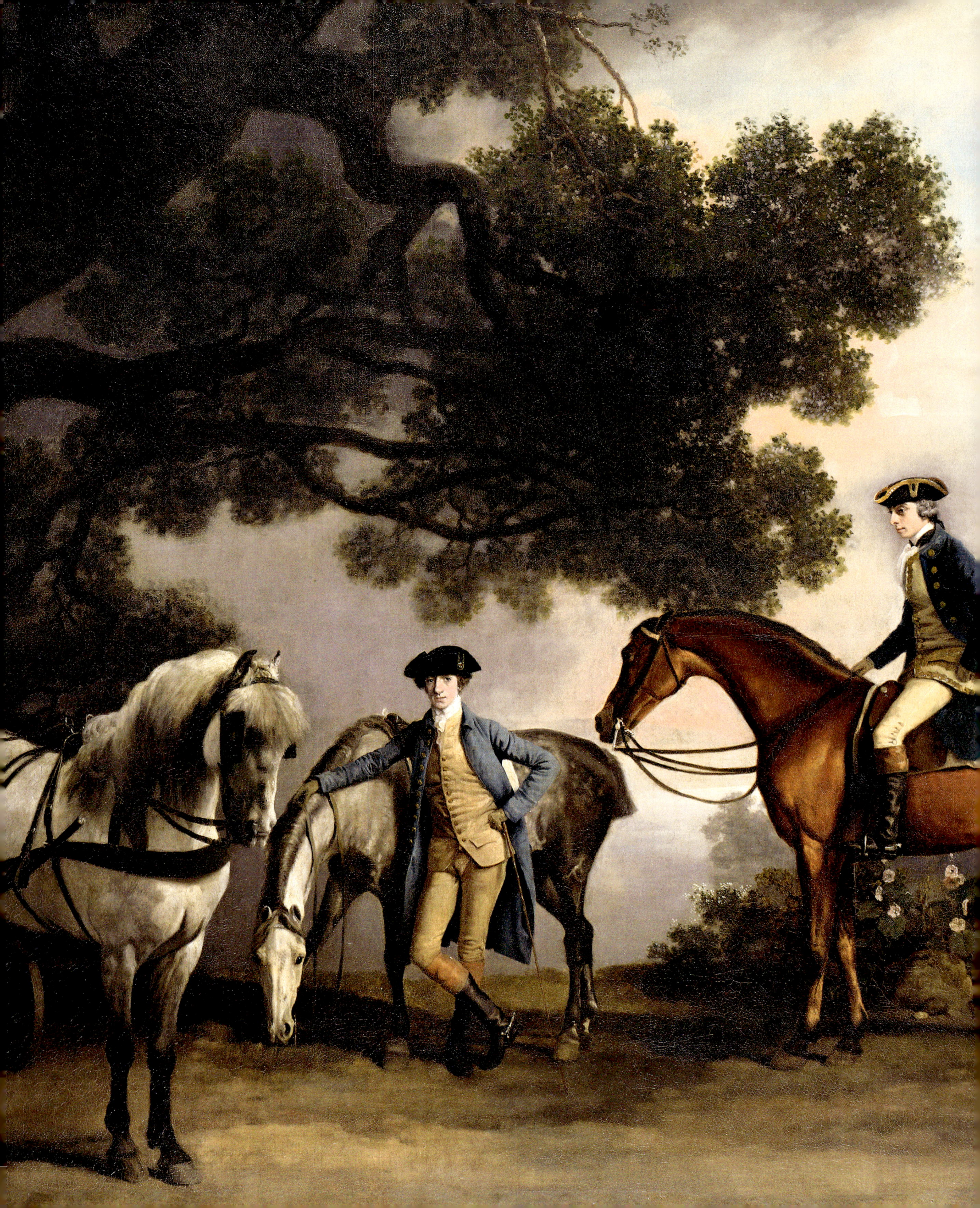

Brian Allen

GEORGE STUBBS
A CRITICAL AFTERLIFE 1806–2012

Writing at the time of the much-acclaimed Stubbs exhibition at the Tate Gallery in London in 1984, the diarist and architectural historian James Lees-Milne (1908–1997) described the artist's work as "England on canvas", yet Stubbs's art has not always been considered quite so synonymous with the country of his birth.[1] It is certainly reasonable to observe, as one eminent French visitor to England did exactly two centuries before Lees-Milne's remark, that the English "have an extraordinary affection for the horse—a passion which is common to the whole country."[2] Even before Stubbs began to paint, the British obsession with horse flesh seems to have mystified foreign observers: "As soon as a race horse has acquired some fame, they have him immediately drawn to the life" observed the Swiss miniaturist André Rouquet (1701–1758), who was resident in London from 1722 to 1752.[3]

It now seems extraordinary that Stubbs lapsed into obscurity so quickly after his death in 1806, not least because he currently holds the record for the most expensive British 'Old Master' painting ever sold at auction and his works are now eagerly sought by the world's great museums and private collectors.[4] Yet, surprisingly, we know less about Stubbs than almost any other eighteenth-century painter of equivalent stature.

Part of the problem with assessing Stubbs's 'afterlife' is the uneasy status of sporting art within the wider canon of British painting. Stephen Deuchar has examined in detail the often hostile responses to this kind of art in eighteenth-century Britain.[5] In essence, as Anna Tietze has pointed out, the Whigs saw sporting art as "symbolic of Toryism, where the urban middle classes criticized it for its celebration of ignorant ruralism, and where artists despised both its technical incompetence and its 'low' subject matter."[6] With the exception of a few gentlemen amateurs, such as Walter Gilbey and Walter Shaw Sparrow, whose contribution is discussed below, very few professional art historians have chosen to work in this field in the twentieth century. Indeed, as recently as the 1950s, the leading historian of British art, Ellis Waterhouse could blithely state that "the general run of sporting painting, although of absorbing interest to the social historian and to the student of the turf is … no business of the historian of art."[7] In more recent times, the political controversy over bloodsports, and fox hunting in particular, has continued to result in the marginalization of sporting art in most major galleries: to the dismay of the British Sporting Art Trust, for instance, through whom they were given, very few of the thirty sporting pictures presented to the Tate Gallery by Paul Mellon in 1979 are ever put on display.

NEGLECT AND REDISCOVERY

It is perhaps less surprising to discover that Stubbs, like a number of his artist contemporaries, died in modest circumstances and that, as the artist and diarist Joseph Farington noted a few weeks after his death, it was thought that he "was but in indifferent circumstances … [but] … had also two or three Houses in Liverpool."[8] Some months later, the art dealer William Seguier (1771–1843) told Farington that "a lady had advanced to Stubbs a considerable Sum of money & Had a bond of Security which gave Her a claim to His pictures &c. These were sold the last week & prices were kept up by Her agents & many articles were bought in. It is understood that after Her debt is paid there will be little left."[9]

Mary Spencer, Stubbs's common-law wife, testified before a magistrate that Stubbs's total assets at his death amounted to under £800. Within a year of his demise his London property (24 Somerset Street, Portman Square), where he had lived since the early 1760s, was auctioned in three sales by Peter Coxe along with its contents and realized £3,484. 5s.[10] It is not known how much was generated by the sale of the artist's library in November 1807 by the bookseller William Stewart.[11]

Stubbs was also unfortunate that he chose in his friend the painter Ozias Humphry (1742–1810) such an errant would-be biographer. Around 1794, when Stubbs was about seventy, he seems to have had one or more conversations with Humphry about his life and career.[12] The notes taken by Humphry, however, were never properly written up and were probably never intended for publication, not least because the blindness that steadily overtook him from 1797 prevented it. At some point after Stubbs's death, the notes were edited and twice transcribed and augmented by Humphry's illegitimate son, the antiquary, book and autograph collector William Upcott (1779–1845), who appears to have been in touch with Stubbs's family. A later biographer of Stubbs, Basil Taylor, believed Upcott was probably the author of the brief obituary that appeared in the *Gentleman's Magazine* in 1806.[13] At some point before her death in 1817, Mary Spencer must have been shown the manuscript by Upcott, since she added a few anecdotes.[14]

The Humphry manuscript remained unpublished; such was Stubbs's comparative anonymity that, less than twenty years after his death, he was not even mentioned in Allan Cunningham's *Lives of the Most Eminent British Painters* (1823). Furthermore, the great Victorian critic and writer John Ruskin (1819–1900) never mentioned him in all his voluminous writings on art.

The revival of Stubbs's reputation did not really begin until the Liverpool silversmith and antiquarian Joseph Mayer (1803–1886) circulated an essay on Stubbs based on Humphry and Upcott's scrappy memoir. It first appeared in a volume privately published in 1876 entitled *Early Exhibitions of Art in Liverpool with some Notes for a Memoir of George Stubbs RA* [sic] and was re-issued three years later as *Memoirs of Thomas Dodd, William Upcott and George Stubbs RA* [sic] (Liverpool, 1879).[15] Coincidentally, this was at about the same time that the French critic Théophile Thoré-Bürger rediscovered that other great 'quiet' master, Jan Vermeer.[16]

As Mayer noted in his opening paragraph, "The name of this eminent artist [Stubbs] is familiar to few people at the present day. In some great mansions the housekeeper will pronounce it, and a visitor who catches that unknown monosyllable in the midst of her drawling roll, may glance with admiration at the big picture overhead, but will probably again forget."[17] Mayer's essay was at least the beginning of a rather slow revival of interest in Stubbs; another two decades were to pass before the appearance of the next work of substance. It was written by the wine merchant, philanthropist and sportsman Sir Walter Gilbey (1831–1914), whose *Life of George Stubbs RA* [sic] was privately printed in a limited edition in 1898. Gilbey did much to improve the breed of English shire horses and wrote extensively on the subject. This doubtless explains, at least in part, his attraction to the work of Stubbs. Gilbey was also an avid collector of paintings by Stubbs and indeed owned more works than any single collector before Paul Mellon. His book included the first attempt at a catalogue of Stubbs's then known works, listing 113 paintings, of which 34 were in his own collection. Like Mayer before him, Gilbey based his text largely on Humphry's manuscript memoir. Although it has long been superseded by more scholarly works, it remains useful since its appendices included acceptably accurate transcriptions of Stubbs's will, the catalogue of his posthumous sale and the prospectus of the *Turf Review* series. Unfortunately, Gilbey rarely gave the sources of his information, with the result that, for instance, the quite detailed account of Stubbs's house in Somerset Street is unusable. In the art-historical writing of the first decades of the twentieth century, Stubbs remained largely ignored except by writers devoted to sporting pursuits such as Walter Shaw Sparrow (1862–1940), whose *British Sporting Artists from Barlow to Herring* (1922), *George Stubbs and Ben Marshall* (1929) and *A Book of Sporting Painters* (1931) added nothing of substance to our knowledge of Stubbs. Although a varied group of works by Stubbs was included in the Royal Academy's enormous exhibition of British Art in 1934, the memorable series of lectures delivered by the celebrated critic and painter Roger Fry (1866–1934) that accompanied the exhibition failed to mention Stubbs, a fact that the art historian Ralph Edwards (1894–1977), writing years later in *Apollo*, considered "an inexplicable lapse." Fry, as Edwards noted, "while persistently proclaiming the vital, indispensable importance of formal values ignored as of no account an artist who clearly by instinct apprehended those values."[18]

It was not until the poet and critic Geoffrey Grigson (1905–1985) published an acutely perceptive and sensitive essay on Stubbs that first appeared in the magazine *Signature* in 1938 that the tide began to turn.[19] "I do not think it is realized how much Stubbs achieved," wrote Grigson. "He could fix cool sensuality and knowledge in exquisite, emotive patches of design. He could express, under control, a peculiarity of his nature in some of the stranger and more disturbing plates in his two *Anatomies*, and … his rhythmical drawing is related to a mind wider, keener, higher, and more inquisitive than the mind of most artists during his time. His work was thorough, and his vision moves us now because it was, at least, uncontaminated, clear, and ordered."[20]

Although scathing about sporting art in general, Grigson's exact contemporary Sir Ellis Waterhouse (1905–1985), the doyen of historians of British art, did at least acknowledge Stubbs as "one of our great masters", going on to state that to classify Stubbs "as a 'sporting painter', as was done in his own lifetime, has been habitual since, and is repeated for convenience in this book is assuredly wrong. He has no links with the sporting painters of the generation of Wootton ... and horse pictures form only part of his work which embraces, in its affectionate study, man, the whole animal kingdom, and nature."[21]

A more sympathetic view of animal painting in general and Stubbs in particular was offered by the highly-rated art historian Basil Taylor (1922–1975), who began to develop an interest in Stubbs as a young man in 1945. In 1955 he published his *Animal Painting in Britain from Barlow to Landseer,* in which he noted "The historian of art whose interests and training have been controlled by a study of continental traditions and the sequence of continental styles ... may well find uninteresting, even unimportant what is, in fact, most characteristic of English art. Stubbs or Marshall have hardly any connexions with Italian, French, or Flemish painting, but they are most typical and important representatives of their own school. A proper history of English animal painting has yet to be written and would require the most laborious and often aesthetically unrewarding research, for, like the explorer among our seventeenth-century portraits, the student would need to have an easy tolerance of inferior pictures. (It is apparently more rewarding to deal with bad human than with bad animal portraits.)"[22] Over the following twenty years until his untimely death in 1975, Basil Taylor made an enormous contribution to the study of Stubbs but never managed to write the major study he apparently planned. In the 'Foreword' to his 1971 monograph on Stubbs Taylor stated "the present essay is not a substitute for the larger study of Stubbs which has occupied me during many years and which may ultimately be published."[23]

The Stubbs exhibition he curated at the Whitechapel Art Gallery in London in 1957 was, however, the first major exhibition of the artist's work in the capital since the loan exhibition at the J & W Vokins Gallery in London in 1885. It certainly demonstrated the full range of the artist's work.[24] This was followed in 1958 by the Arts Council exhibition *George Stubbs: Rediscovered Anatomical Drawings from the Free Public Library, Worcester, Massachusetts.*[25] Over the following years Taylor published important articles on Stubbs in learned journals, but it was his first meeting with Paul Mellon in June 1959 and the establishment of the Paul Mellon Foundation for British Art which followed in 1963 that provided him, as its first Director, with further scholarly opportunities. These included the exhibition in 1969 of *The Prints of George Stubbs* supported by the Paul Mellon Foundation for British Art and *Stubbs in the 1760s,* held at the London dealers Thomas Agnew & Son Ltd in 1970.[26] Taylor's final contribution was the introduction to the 1974 Tate Gallery exhibition *Stubbs and Wedgwood—Unique Alliance between Artist and Potter.*

By this date Judy Egerton, then a Tate curator, had also developed a special interest in Stubbs, largely as a result of her work cataloguing Paul Mellon's collection of sporting paintings.[27] Egerton's first Stubbs exhibition at the Tate was devoted to the anatomical drawings (*George Stubbs—Anatomist and Animal Painter*, 1976), but it was the prelude to the most comprehensive exhibition of the artist's work ever mounted—*George Stubbs 1724–1806*—also held at the Tate Gallery and the Yale Center for British Art in 1984/85. After her retirement from the Tate and following a decade at the National Gallery, where she catalogued the British paintings, Judy Egerton began work on the catalogue raisonné of Stubbs's work as Senior Research Fellow at the Paul Mellon Centre for Studies in British Art; this *opus magnum* was finally published in 2007. As Alex Kidson has put it, this book "changes the landscape of Stubbs scholarship for ever ... [and] completely supercedes earlier literature as the essential starting point for anyone coming to the artist for the first time."[28]

LATE ARRIVAL: STUBBS IN PUBLIC COLLECTIONS

With a few notable exceptions, museum curators and collectors were similarly slow to recognize the merits of Stubbs, perhaps because of lack of familiarity since so many of his best works remained in the private collections for which they had been painted. Interestingly, the first Stubbs to enter a non-British collection appears to be the picture that was the germ of the present exhibition—*The Spanish Pointer* (cat. no. 29)—which was already in Munich by 1810, probably bought by Maximilian Joseph, who became Elector of Bavaria in 1799 and King of Bavaria in 1806. It later entered the Bavarian State Collections and became part of the holdings of the Neue Pinakothek. Indeed, with the notable exception of the Walker Art Gallery in Stubbs's native city Liverpool, museums outside the British Isles seem to have been quicker to appreciate the artist's significance than those in the United Kingdom. As early as 1915 Lord Curzon, the former Viceroy of India, presented the Wedgwood enamel of *Warren Hastings* to the Victoria Memorial Hall in Calcutta (Egerton no. 281). The Philadelphia Museum of Art was bequeathed *Lord Torrington's Brickmakers (Labourers)* by John H. McFadden as early as 1928 (Egerton no. 100). Three paintings by Stubbs were bequeathed to the South African National Gallery by the financier and owner/breeder of racehorses, Sir Abe Bailey (1864–1940) in the 1940s (Egerton nos. 152, 262 and 264); the Felton Bequest at the National Gallery of Victoria in Melbourne purchased *Lion attacking a Horse* in 1949 (Egerton no. 37), and in the same year the Museum of Fine Arts, Boston acquired *Lion and Lioness Resting at the Mouth of a Dark Cave* (Egerton no. 118). Also in 1949, the National Gallery in Washington, D.C. was given *Captain Samuel Sharpe Pocklington with his sister Pleasance and (?) his sister Frances* (Egerton no. 98) whilst *Eclipse with William Wildman and his sons John and James* was bequeathed in 1956 to the Baltimore Museum of Art by William Woodward, Chairman of the American Jockey Club (Egerton no. 75). In 1958, just before the emergence of Paul Mellon as the greatest collector of Stubbs, the Huntington Library and Art Collections was given *Two Saddled Horses, One Ridden by a Groom* (Egerton no. 275). Although Tate Britain now houses fifteen paintings by Stubbs, the first of these to enter the collection, *A Grey Mare Seen Against a Dark Wood* (Egerton no. 228) was not acquired until 1940 and the majority of these works have been given or purchased since the 1970s. The National Gallery's famous *Whistlejacket* (Egerton no. 34) was acquired from the descendants of the Marquess of Rockingham in lieu of death duties as recently as 1997; it was only the third work by Stubbs to enter the Gallery. The other two works are *A Gentleman Driving a Lady in a Phaeton* (Egerton no. 273), bequeathed to the Gallery in 1920 and *The Milbanke and Melbourne Families*, purchased in 1975 (cat. no. 35).

Before the 1940s relatively few great works by Stubbs had been sold out of the collections of his early patrons, and many of Stubbs' greatest works still remain in private hands. One collection worth mentioning is that formed in the first decades of the twentieth century by the whisky magnate and racehorse owner James Buchanan, later the 1st Lord Woolavington and subsequently augmented by his descendants.[29] It was Lord Woolavington's daughter and her husband, Sir Reginald Macdonald-Buchanan, who purchased *Gimcrack on Newmarket Heath* (Egerton no. 70), one of four important paintings commissioned by the 2nd Viscount Bolingbroke in the 1760s which were first sold by Christie's in December 1943.[30] *Gimcrack* was purchased soon after that sale by Walter Hutchinson (1887–1950), the publisher and sportsman who at one time owned eleven works by or attributed to Stubbs. Hutchinson was the founder of the short-lived National Gallery of British Sports and Pastimes, but he did not own *Gimcrack* for long since it was offered for sale again by Christie's in 1951.[31]

In the years that followed a steady trickle of high quality works have come to market, many of them purchased by the American collector and philanthropist Paul Mellon (1907–1999). In 1963 Mellon remarked publicly that "British sporting art has always, blindly and mistakenly, been grossly underrated."[32] He was involved in organizing the exhibition *Sport and the Horse* (Virginia Museum of Fine Arts, 1960) that introduced equestrian art as a new subject to American audiences. Once he began collecting in earnest in 1959, Mellon's collection grew at a staggering pace to become the most comprehensive outside the United Kingdom.[33]

What triggered this compulsion to collect British art, especially sporting paintings? Mellon had spent his early childhood summers in England (his mother was English), and he remarked in his autobiographical memoir that "a great deal of my feeling for the country and horses comes from Mother … and I am therefore partly instinctively English in my love of country. I have lived in England and tasted English life pretty thoroughly, and it came to me naturally and strongly. It is really in my blood … It explains my addiction to English literature, to the English poets, to descriptions of English life, especially sporting and country life, and to the social and emotional aspects of English history … Hunting is another example of the reaction which has set up inside me against business, the city, modern industrial drabness, the suppression of the natural emotions and feelings … It involves the use of the horse, that instinctive animal, and man's mastery of the horse."[34]

After graduating from Yale University in 1929, Mellon moved to England in 1931 to take another undergraduate degree at Cambridge, where he began to collect English sporting and colour plate books. Although his father gave him two of his best paintings by Ben Marshall and two by Sartorius as a wedding present in 1935 he did not acquire his first Stubbs, *Pumpkin with a Stable Lad,* until 1936 (Egerton no. 159). A significant reason for eventually choosing to collect Stubbs and sporting art in general was doubtless to avoid competition with his father, the great financier and collector Andrew W. Mellon (1855–1937), whose remarkable collection of European Old Master paintings was to become the nucleus of the National Gallery of Art in Washington D.C.

After acquiring *Pumpkin*, more than two decades passed before Paul Mellon bought another Stubbs. Nonetheless his introduction to Basil Taylor, the leading Stubbs expert, in June 1959 led to a most productive meeting of minds and, for the next decade, Taylor became Mellon's adviser in forming his collection of British art.[35] Throughout the 1960s and 1970s, when there was still a plentiful supply of excellent pictures coming on to the market, Paul Mellon was able to acquire a vast number of British paintings, including over forty works by Stubbs that were either given in his lifetime or bequeathed to those museums with which he was closely associated. As a result of this greater exposure, it can now perhaps be claimed that Stubbs is no longer seen as an insularly British artist whose appeal lies only in the English-speaking world.[36]

1 James Lees-Milne, *Holy Dread: Diaries 1982–1984*, Michael Bloch (ed.), London 2001, p. 207.
2 François de la Rochefoucauld, *A Frenchman in England*, Jean Marchand (ed.), translated by S. C. Roberts, Cambridge 1933, p. 74. His visit took place in 1784.
3 [André] Rouquet, *The Present State of the Arts in England* (London 1755), facsimile reprint by Cornmarket Press, London 1970, p. 58.
4 *Gimcrack on Newmarket Heath, with a trainer, a jockey and a stable lad* sold for £22,441,250 at Christie's, 5 July 2011 (lot 12).
5 Stephen Deuchar, *Sporting Art in Eighteenth-Century England,* New Haven and London 1988.
6 Anna Tietze, "Artistically or historically important? The reception of the Abe Bailey sporting art collection in South Africa," in: *Journal of the History of Collections* 23, 2011, p. 166.
7 Ellis Waterhouse, *Painting in Britain 1530 to 1790*, Harmondsworth 1953, 3rd edition, 1969, p. 205.
8 Kenneth Garlick et al. (eds.), *The Diary of Joseph Farington,* 17 vols., New Haven and London 1978–98, vol. 8 (July 1806 – December 1807), p. 2854, 19 September 1806.
9 Ibid., p. 3056, 3 June 1807. The lady mentioned was almost certainly Stubbs's benefactor and executor, the unmarried heiress Isabella Saltonstall, whom Stubbs had painted as a child (Egerton, *George Stubbs*, 2007, no. 128).
10 The first sale (26–27 May 1807) took place on the premises; the second sale on 11 June 1807 (no catalogue known); the third sale (house and contents) was held on 12 June 1807; see Egerton, *George Stubbs,* 2007, pp. 94 f.
11 See Blake, *George Stubbs and the Wide Creation,* 2005, p. 293.
12 For Humphry see George C. Williamson, *Life and Works of Ozias Humphry, R.A.*, London 1918.
13 *Gentleman's Magazine* 76, October 1806, pp. 978 f. Basil Taylor first made this suggestion in *Stubbs,* London 1971, p. 8. The obituary is reprinted in Exhib. Cat. *Fearful Symmetry,* 2000, pp. 198 f.
14 Humphry's memoir of Stubbs forms part of the Joseph Mayer papers now in the Record Office and Local History Department of Liverpool City Libraries. The first full transcription of the manuscript by Helen Macintyre was published in Exhib. Cat. *Fearful Symmetry*, 2000, pp. 196–210.
15 Joseph Mayer's essay has been re-published as *A Memoir of George Stubbs by Ozias Humphry and Joseph Mayer*, with an introduction by Anthony Mould, London 2005.
16 See Frances Suzman Jowell, "Vermeer and Thoré-Bürger: Recoveries of Reputation," in: Ivan Gaskell and Michiel Jonker (eds.), *Vermeer Studies*, New Haven and London 1998, pp. 35–57.
17 *A Memoir of George Stubbs by Ozias Humphry and Joseph Mayer* (see note 15), p. 25.
18 Ralph Edwards, "George Stubbs and Contemporary Artists," in: *Apollo* 94, 1971 pp. 519–22.
19 *Signature* 13, 1938, pp. 16–31, republished in: ibid., *The Harp of Aeolus and other Essays on Art Literature and Nature*, London 1947, pp. 13–23.
20 Geoffrey Grigson, "George Stubbs," in: *The Harp of Aeolus*, op. cit., pp. 15, 23.
21 Waterhouse 1969 (see note 7), p. 207. Waterhouse's only other writing on Stubbs was the article "Lord Fitzwilliam's Sporting Pictures by Stubbs," in: *The Burlington Magazine* 83, 1946, p. 199.
22 Basil Taylor, *Animal Painting in England from Barlow to Landseer,* Harmondsworth 1955, p. 13.
23 Basil Taylor, *Stubbs*, London 1971, p. 5.
24 An exhibition of Stubbs works was held at the Walker Art Gallery, Liverpool in 1951. The catalogue of the Vokins exhibition was reprinted in Gilbey's *Life of George Stubbs.*
25 These drawings were purchased by Paul Mellon in 1980 and were presented to the Yale Center for British Art. See Egerton, *George Stubbs,* 2007, no. 327, pp. 566–609.
26 The prints exhibition was held at the Festival Gallery, Aldeburgh, Suffolk and at the Victoria & Albert Museum, London. For an account of the Paul Mellon Foundation see [Brian Allen], *The Paul Mellon Centre for Studies in British Art– A History 1970–2010*, privately printed for the Paul Mellon Centre for Studies in British Art, London 2010, pp. 7–11.
27 Judy Egerton and Dudley Snelgrove, *British Sporting and Animal Paintings 1500–1850 (The Paul Mellon Collection)*, London 1978.
28 Alex Kidson's book review in *The Burlington Magazine* 150, 2008, pp. 835 f.
29 For the Woolavington collection see James Stourton and Emmeline Hallmark, "Art imitating life," in: *Country Life*, 4 June 2008, pp. 150–53.
30 See note 4 above and also "Lord Bolingbroke's Patronage of Stubbs," in: Christie's, *Old Master and British Paintings,* sale catalogue, 5 July 2011.
31 The Gallery of British Sports was housed at Hutchinson House (formerly Derby House) in Stratford Place, off Oxford Street in London. See *The First 600 Selected Pictures–National Gallery of British Sports and Pastimes Founded by Walter Hutchinson, Esquire,* n.d. (1948?), no. 133.
32 Taken from a speech by Paul Mellon delivered on 20 April 1963 at the opening of the exhibition *Painting in England 1700–1850* at the Virginia Museum of Fine Arts. The full text of the speech is published in *Selected Paintings, Drawings, and Books*, New Haven, Yale Center for British Art, 1977, p. XII.
33 Most of Paul Mellon's collection of British art is now housed in the purpose-built Yale Center for British Art in New Haven, Connecticut but other important works by Stubbs were given by him to the two other museums with which he was closely involved: the National Gallery in Washington, D.C. and the Virginia Museum of Fine Arts.
34 Paul Mellon with John Baskett, *Reflections in a Silver Spoon: A Memoir,* London 1992, pp. 151 f.
35 The best account of these events is John Baskett, "Paul Mellon: A Remembrance," in: *Paul Mellon's Legacy – A Passion for British Art. Masterpieces from the Yale Center for British Art,* Exhib. Cat. Yale Center for British Art, New Haven, and Royal Academy of Arts, London 2007, pp. 1–11.
36 Malcolm Cormack, "Paul Mellon and George Stubbs," in: Exhib. Cat. *George Stubbs in the Collection of Paul Mellon,* 1999/2000, pp. 9–13.

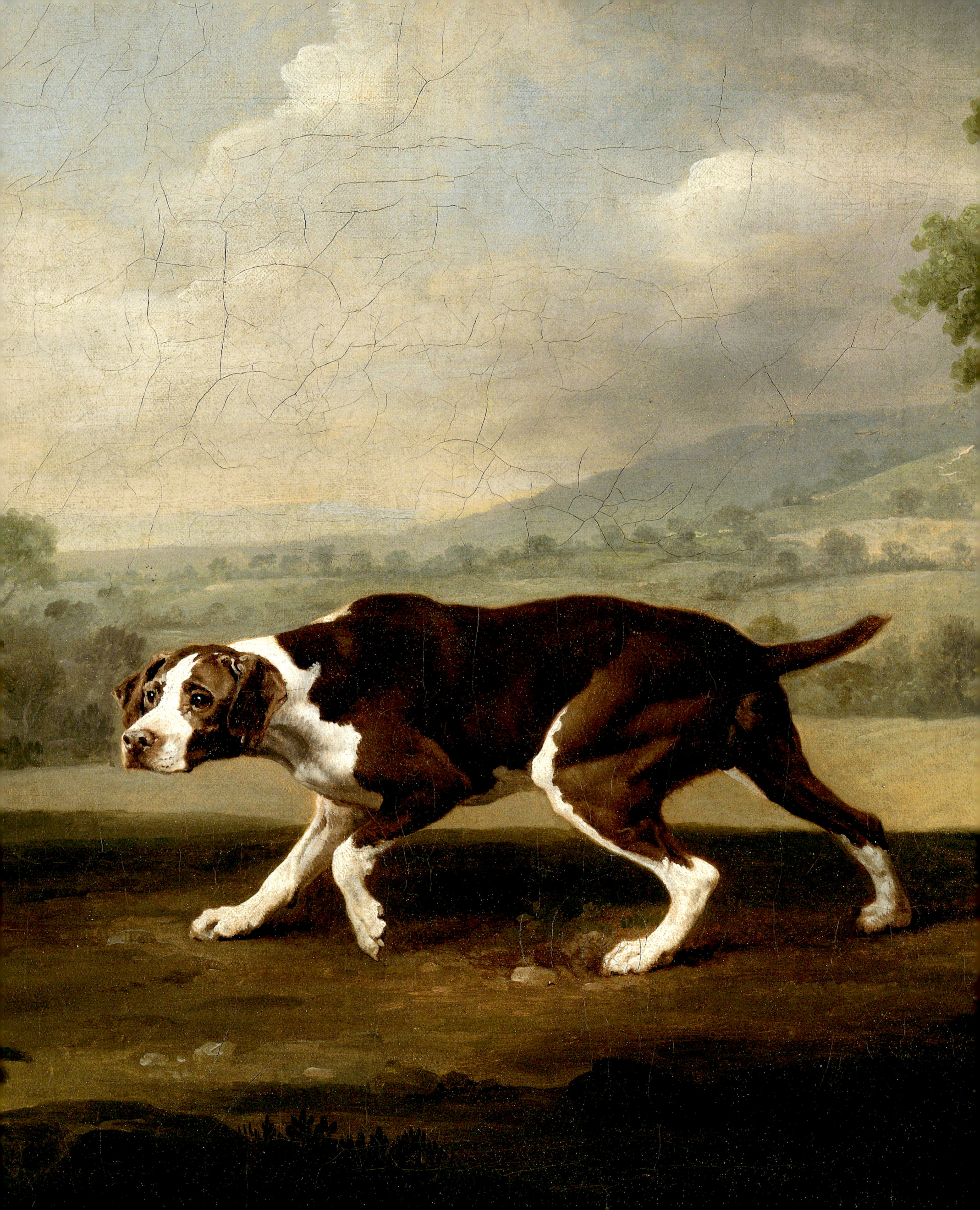

Herbert W. Rott

SOME EARLY GERMAN COLLECTORS OF BRITISH ART

There were a number of reasons why England seemed particularly attractive to German intellectuals in the second half of the eighteenth century. Its political system appeared to present an alternative to the absolutist rule practised in the German states, and the economic upswing and first stirrings of the industrial revolution demonstrated the advantages of giving market forces a free rein—even if this rising prosperity tended to widen the gap between those at the top of the social scale and those at the bottom. In the arts too, profound changes were underway. England ousted France in matters of taste and style. This was especially evident in the area of garden design, where rigidly formal French gardens were increasingly being replaced by English-style landscape gardens—not least in Germany. Soon those artists and intellectuals who considered themselves progressive were no longer looking to Rome or Paris for inspiration, but rather to London. It was in London more than anywhere else, or so it seemed to them, that artists addressed the issues raised by modern life. The art of close observation—empiricism as the foundation of visual culture—was more advanced in Britain than anywhere else in Europe. In the capital the enlightened and thoroughly modern individual encountered a world of paintings and prints that not only attributed a new importance to real life, the subjective emotions and feelings of the individual but also to the most pressing social problems of the day.

The growing demand for paintings in Great Britain—whether portraits or landscapes to adorn interiors or the portraits of animals with which the nobility liked to surround themselves—had given rise to an art market in which individual artists were afforded some licence. Within only a few decades of William Hogarth a quintessentially English school of art had grown up that was not only able to set itself apart from its European antecedents but also to determine the pace on the Continent. Printmaking was of crucial importance in this and the medium underwent some dramatic improvements in quality as artists became more skilled and their methods more sophisticated. Prints became big business and as export items were another source of income for painters, engravers and publishers. These advances were closely watched in Germany, where journals, annuals and almanacs reported at length on life, literature and art in England, and where reviews of the latest prints from England were more detailed and more up-to-date than anywhere else in Europe, including England itself.[1] Around 1800, therefore, it was not so much paintings as prints which were making their way to Germany, to be snapped up by collectors as proof of both their modern taste in art and the technical accomplishment of England's engravers.

ENGLISH PAINTING IN MUNICH

This exhibition project was sparked by a rather unassuming picture in Munich's Neue Pinakothek: George Stubbs's painting *The Spanish Pointer* from the mid-1760s (cat. no. 29). The engraving after this motif by William Woollett (cat. no. 72) is not based on the Munich picture as has long been assumed, but rather on a second version (Egerton no. 88) then in the possession of Thomas Bradford. We do not know who commissioned the work in the Neue Pinakothek, but we do know that it must have arrived in Bavaria around 1800. Its first documentary mention was in 1810 when it is listed in the catalogue of the Schleissheimer Gemäldegalerie, drawn up by the gallery's then director Johann Christian von Mannlich.[2]

The painting was thus probably purchased by King Max I Joseph (1756–1825) (fig. 1). Bavaria's first regent has tended to be overshadowed as a collector by predecessors such as Prince-Elector Maximilian I and Prince-Elector Max Emanuel, who brought paintings by Dürer and Rubens to Munich, and not least by his own son,

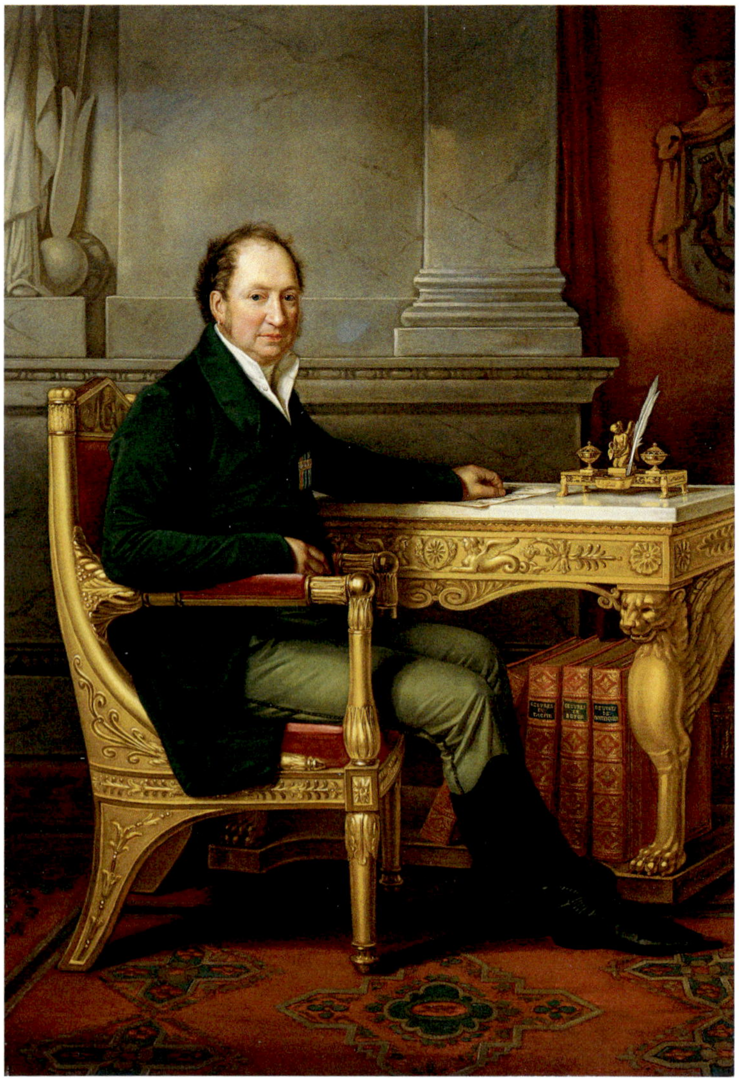

1 Joseph Stieler, *King Max I Joseph of Bavaria at his Writing Desk,* 1814
Oil on canvas, 200 x 133 cm
Private collection

King Ludwig I, who implemented the building of the Alte Pinakothek and had the Neue Pinakothek built to house his own private collection of contemporary painting. Max I Joseph was, however, also responsible for setting the tone of future developments to a certain extent; his personal interest in seventeenth-century Dutch painting, as well as contemporary genre and landscape painting bolstered the position of Realist painters and ensured the future influence of this strand of painting in Munich. Max I Joseph not only added to the electoral collections (the royal collections from 1806 onwards); he also built up a private collection of his own which was auctioned off after his death in 1826, with certain lots being purchased for the royal collections.[3] Seventeenth-century Dutch painters like Jacob van Ruisdael and Philips Wouwerman were among the king's preferred artists. His collection also included Jan Vermeer's *Woman Holding a Balance*—in those days believed to be the work of Gabriel Metsu—which now hangs in the National Gallery in Washington, having similarly been sold in 1826.[4] Among his acquisitions of contemporary works there is no mistaking the king's fondness for genre and landscape painting made for those from a bourgeois background. While his son and successor Ludwig I promoted the emotional, highly idealized history painting of the young Nazarenes, Max I Joseph preferred the realism of such local painters as Johann Georg von Dillis, Max Joseph Wagenbauer and Albrecht Adam, which paved the way for the first realistic landscape paintings in Munich.

2 David Wilkie, *Reading of a Will,* 1820
Oil on panel, 78 x 116.5 cm
Munich, Bayerische Staatsgemäldesammlungen, Neue Pinakothek

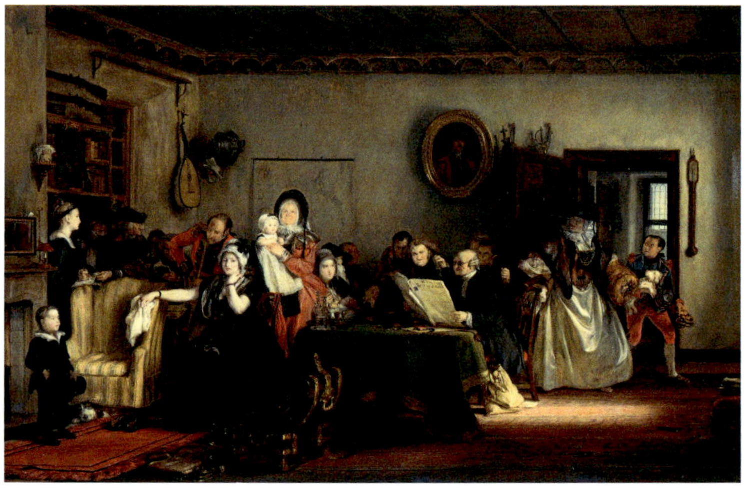

The most important work by a British artist, indeed by any contemporary artist, to ever be purchased by Max I Joseph is David Wilkie's *Reading of a Will*, a painting which the king himself commissioned through the British envoy in 1820, explicitly leaving the choice of subject to the artist (fig. 2). Another work by an English artist was George Morland's *Fishermen Pushing a Barge into the Water*, which found its way to Munich along unknown paths (fig. 3). Both paintings were in the king's private collection and hung in the Munich Residenz, where visitors could see them: Wilkie's in the salon and Morland's in the study.[5] Both were also later purchased for the royal collections, where—together with Stubbs's *Spanish Pointer*—they form the rootstock of the collection of eighteenth- and nineteenth-century British painting now in the Neue Pinakothek. Wilkie's *Reading of a Will*, in particular, has not only come to be regarded as a shining example of its type—genre painting which is modern, subtle and realistic—but it has also proved itself to have exerted considerable influence over the development of this style of painting since its arrival in Munich.[6]

The acquisition of a painting by England's most highly regarded animal painter fits well with this picture. Stubbs's *Spanish Pointer* built on the Dutch tradition of painting animals in a realistic way, as exemplified by the works of Paulus Potter and others already in the collection. At the same time it was also an excellent, if modest example, of the intrinsically British genre of "sporting art", which made its influence felt in Germany through the medium of print. When he acquired Wilhelm von Kobell's *Two Horsemen*, Max I Joseph also added the work of a Munich painter who was influenced by English models to his collection (fig. 4).

Yet hanging in Schloss Schleissheim the impact of Stubbs's portrait of the dog was limited. This palace was used as a repository for those works which, owing to lack of space, could not be presented in the Hofgartengalerie, which had been erected between 1777 and 1783 near the Residenz. It languished in this out-of-town residence long after the Alte Pinakothek opened its doors in 1836, nor was it given a place in the Neue Pinakothek when the latter opened in 1853. The work was simply not spectacular enough to earn it a more prominent place, nor was the name Stubbs as well known as it had once been. Not even after the First World War, when the Neue Pinakothek was reorganized and endowed with a whole gallery of eighteenth- and nineteenth-century English painting, was Stubbs's work deemed worthy of display alongside Gainsborough's *Portrait of Uvedale Tomkyns Price* (purchased in 1909), Opie's *Portrait of a Lady* and, of course, Wilkie's *Reading of a Will* (on show at the Neue Pinakothek since its inauguration). Only in 1981, when the present building was opened in place of its bombed-out predecessor, was the *Spanish Pointer* finally given a place in the Neue Pinakothek alongside the many British paintings purchased in the 1970s and 1980s.

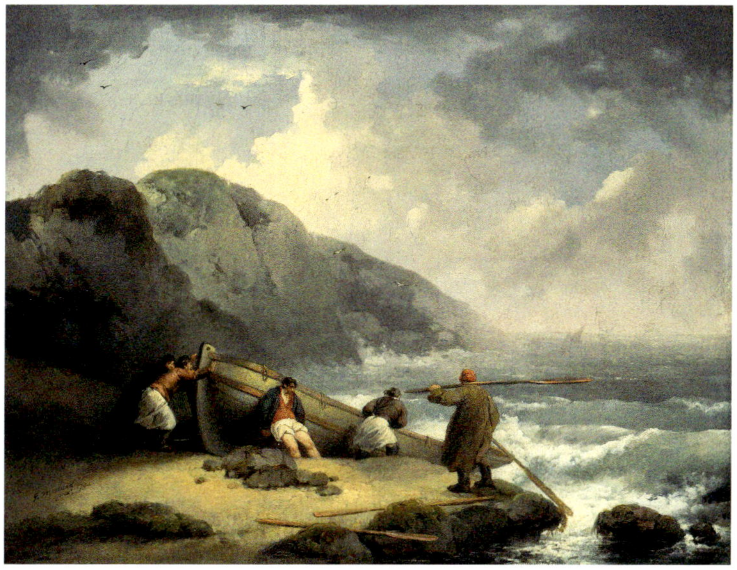

3 George Morland, *Fishermen Pushing a Barge into the Water*, 1793
Oil on canvas, 40.1 x 51.7 cm
Munich, Bayerische Staatsgemäldesammlungen, Neue Pinakothek

4 Wilhelm von Kobell, *Two Horsemen*, c. 1791
Oil on canvas, 103.8 x 97.9 cm
Munich, Bayerische Staatsgemäldesammlungen, Neue Pinakothek

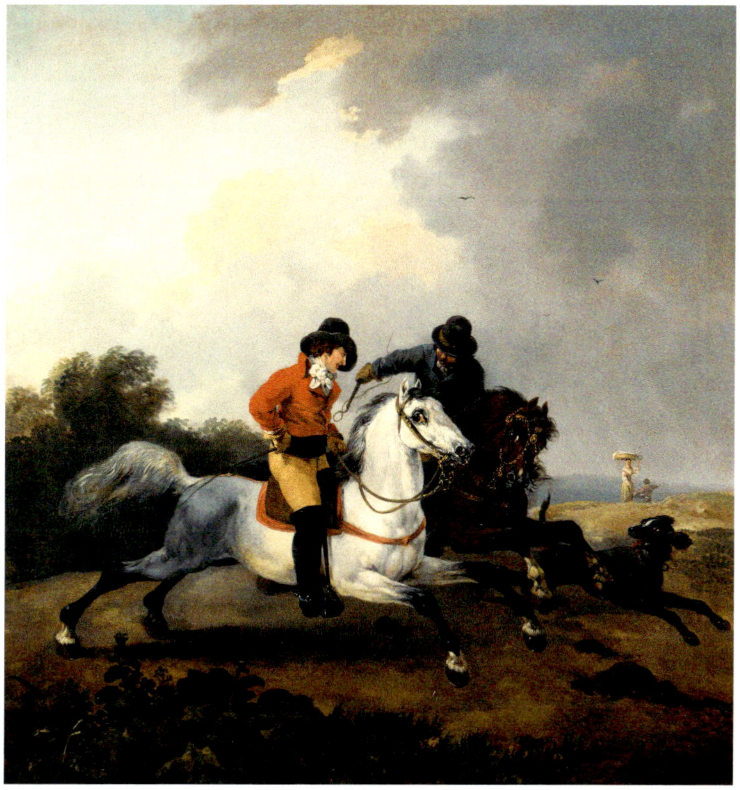

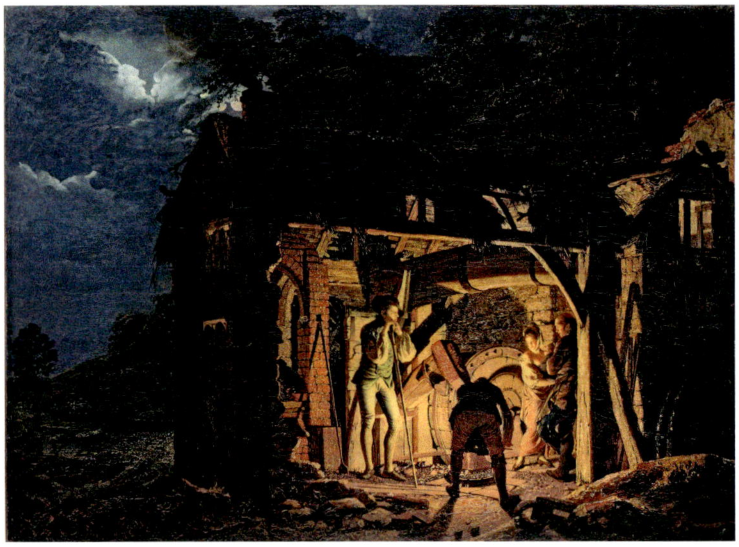

5 Joseph Wright of Derby, *An Iron Forge*, 1773
Oil on canvas, 105 x 140 cm
St. Petersburg, The State Hermitage Museum

Though this painting has spent most of its German life on the margins of the Munich collection, the very fact that a work by England's most important animal painter was purchased at such an early date is in itself remarkable. To this day it has remained the only work by George Stubbs to be found in a German museum and is one of only three works by this artist in collections on the Continent (the others are in the Louvre, Egerton no. 131, and in the Musée d'art et d'histoire in Geneva, Egerton no. 66). It is also worth noting that these early purchases of British art were motivated by genuine curiosity regarding the art being produced on the other side of the Channel. At that time English paintings, unlike English prints, were still a rarity in German collections. What paintings there were tended to be portraits which owed their presence to familial and dynastic connections; take, for instance, the *Portrait of William Pitt the Younger* by John Hoppner (formerly attributed to Thomas Lawrence) and the *Portrait of Charles Manners-Sutton* by Thomas Lawrence, which are both in Hanover today and which were once in the possession of the Hanoverian royals.[7] Hanover is also home to a rural genre painting in which William Beechey clearly demonstrates the influence of similar scenes in the work of Thomas Gainsborough.[8] So too, there is a historical justification for Gainsborough's life-size *Portrait of Queen Charlotte* (a replica of the original in the Royal Collection),[9] formerly in the grand-ducal collections in Schwerin: Charlotte, after all, was a princess of the House of Mecklenburg-Strelitz. In all of this the artist Thomas Lawrence presents an exception, for during his stay in Vienna in 1818/19 he was commissioned to paint works not only for the Prince-Regent but also for members of the imperial family and Viennese high society, including a portrait of Metternich's daughter Clementine.[10]

In Munich, on the other hand, English paintings were collected first and foremost on account of their artistic merits. We have to look much further afield to find a comparable love of British art and then on an infinitely larger scale: the Russian Empress Catherine the Great (1729–1796), a scion of the House of Anhalt-Zerbst who spent her childhood in Stettin, purchased the collection of Robert Walpole in 1779, in which there were not only numerous Dutch and Flemish works and other Old Masters but also seven works by British artists. She had already acquired *An Iron Forge*, a major work by Joseph Wright of Derby, five years earlier (fig. 5) and added to this with the acquisition of his *The Annual Girandola at the Castel d'Angelo in Rome* in 1779.[11] Especially noteworthy, however, is her decision to commission Joshua Reynolds with a history painting whose subject the artist was at liberty to choose, resulting in *The Infant Hercules Strangling the Serpents* (1789), and a second large history painting by Reynolds, *The Continence of Scipio*, was acquired from the estate of Prince Grigory Potemkin in 1792.[12] With these and other works, Catherine II had amassed what was the largest collection of English painting anywhere on the Continent by 1800. In Munich, in contrast, Max I Joseph's son and heir Ludwig I missed a unique opportunity to add William Turner's breathtaking *Opening of the Walhalla* to his father's collection. Turner submitted this work to the exhibition of the Munich Academy, enclosing a verse encomium to the Bavarian king in the hope that Ludwig, then the best-known collector of contemporary painting in Germany, might buy the canvas.[13] His hopes were dashed, however, for when the work was unveiled the people of Munich responded with consternation. The king for his part was not inspired to buy.

ENGLISH PRINTS IN GERMAN COLLECTIONS

If British paintings were something of a rarity in German collections, the same cannot be said of prints. The advances made in both the technical and artistic quality of prints, especially in the various techniques used to create etchings, turned English prints into much sought-after, cutting-edge commodities. Especially in the later eighteenth century no self-respecting aficionado with a collection that included contemporary prints could afford to dispense with English examples. Mezzotint, in particular, proved ideal for the reproduction of paintings so that, starting in the 1760s, the exhibition of paintings at London art shows frequently went hand in hand with their marketing in this form. Most Continental collectors were first introduced to contemporary British painting in this way. Sales structures were so advanced that German collectors could get their hands on British prints with relative ease thanks to such major art dealers as Bremer und Sohn in Brunswick, Rost in Leipzig, Frauenholz in Nuremberg and Artaria in Vienna and Mannheim.[14]

In Dresden Prince-Elector Frederick Augustus III, who became King Frederick Augustus I of Saxony (1750–1827) in 1806, had a vast collection of some 6,000 prints, a large number of which were British, and which passed to the Kupferstich-Kabinett in Dresden on his death. When deciding what to purchase Augustus was able to rely on the knowledge and judgment of Carl Heinrich von Heinecken (1707–1791). The latter's highly influential *Idée générale d'une collection complette d'estampes* published in 1771 prophesied the pre-eminence of the British school of printmaking, which although still relatively young was full of vigour and potential even then.[15]

In Karlsruhe Margravine Caroline Louise of Baden-Durlach (1723–1783) had a collection of paintings with which she laid the foundations of the collections of the margraves and later grand dukes of Baden. As an educated and intelligent woman with an inquiring mind, she even produced drawings and etchings of her own. When it came to paintings, her main interest was in Dutch and French art. Nonetheless her collection of prints—today in the Kupferstichkabinett of the Staatliche Kunsthalle Karlsruhe—contained an impressively large number of British works.[16]

What has not survived is the remarkable body of European, primarily English, prints brought together by Duke Charles II Augustus of Palatinate-Zweibrücken (1746–1795) at Schloss Karlsberg near Homburg in Saarland. A scion of the Palatinate-Birkenfeld line of the Wittelsbach dynasty, Charles Augustus was the brother of the very same Max I Joseph who was to become prince-elector and later king of Bavaria. The palace that he had built between 1778 and 1788 on Buchenberg Hill near Homburg was one of the largest and most ambitious palace projects of the eighteenth century. Its architect, the painter Johann Christian von Mannlich (1741–1822), also acted as director of the Karlsberg art collections and later, in the service of Max I Joseph, went on to play a key role in the consolidation and enlargement of the Wittelsbach collections in Munich. In Karlsberg he wasted no time in piecing together a comprehensive collection of paintings. This included numerous works by Dutch and French painters such as Claude Lorrain, Jean-Siméon Chardin and François Boucher, which now rank among the highlights of the collection in the Alte Pinakothek. Two landscapes by Philippe-Jacques de Loutherbourg, a native of Strasbourg who moved to London in 1771, were also in Karlsberg before making their way to Munich. The palace was destroyed by French troops in 1793 only a couple of years after its completion, but fortunately the art collections had previously been removed from Charles Augustus's palace to safety and Mannlich was able to ensure that many of the paintings could be taken to Munich. A different fate befell the print collection. It was broken up and most works were sold at auction in Mannheim in 1795. Thanks to two inventories drawn up in that same year listing some 4,500 prints, scholars have nevertheless been able to reconstruct the collection.[17] We now know that it contained engravings of Italian and Dutch paintings as well as numerous works by French and German artists. Especially striking and most unusual, however, is the contingent of English prints which numbered around 500 works and represented a special focus of the collection. Among them were a number of mezzotints, including some in colour, of paintings by Richard Wilson, Joshua Reynolds, Thomas Gainsborough, Benjamin West and George Stubbs.

Another Wittelsbach prince, Prince-Elector and Count Palatine Charles Theodore (1724–1799), had begun collecting in 1758 and amassed an even larger collection of drawings and prints at his palace in Mannheim. An inventory drawn up in 1780 lists nearly 60,000 prints, categorized according to school. While the Italian, French, Dutch and German holdings each contributed some 10,000 pieces to that total, there were few works of British origin in comparison. 2,000 is nonetheless a considerable figure.[18] Originally housed in the Mannheimer Schloss, the prints collection was moved to Munich in 1794, where Charles Theodore had been resident becoming prince-elector of Bavaria in 1777. Once in Munich the Mannheim collection formed the core of what would later become the Königliches Kupferstichkabinett and is now the Staatliche Graphische Sammlung. The collection of British prints, most of which came from Mannheim originally, were destroyed in the Second World War.

Another major collection of English prints, also from southwest Germany, was more fortunate. This is the collection that originally belonged to Lothar Franz von Erthal (1717–1805) and which was transferred to Schloss Johannisburg in Aschaffenburg in 1792 when its owner was forced to relocate following the French occupation of Mainz. Lothar Franz was the brother of the ruling Frederick Charles von Erthal (1719–1802), archbishop and prince-elector of Mainz and arch-chancellor of the Holy Roman Empire, who had himself amassed an impressive collection of paintings, most of them by seventeenth-century Dutch and eighteenth-century German painters. In 1786 he commissioned Ferdinand Kobell of Mannheim to paint a cycle of fifteen views of Aschaffenburg and the surround-

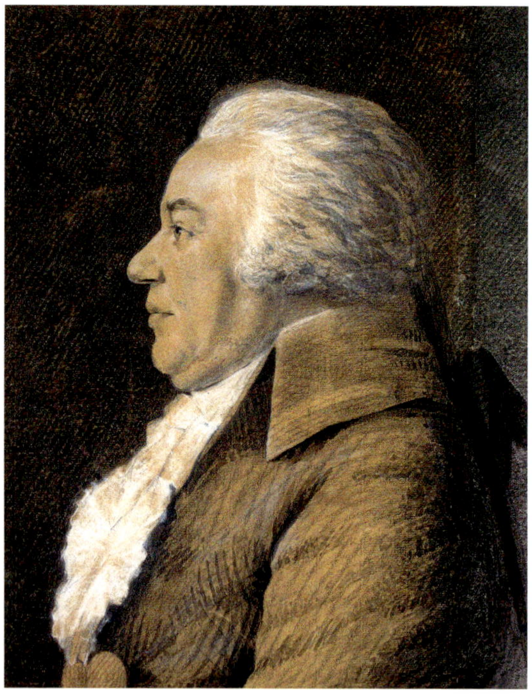

6 Daniel Nikolaus Chodowiecki, *Duke Francis Frederick of Saxe-Coburg-Saalfeld*, Chalk with wash and white heightening, 48.9 x 37.9 cm Kunstsammlungen der Veste Coburg, Kupferstichkabinett

ing countryside, which now ranks among the first examples of landscape painting in Germany to free itself from the fetters of Baroque convention and take on a more realistic style. In Mainz, as would also be the case in Aschaffenburg, the library with its collection of prints was entrusted to the care of Wilhelm Heinse, one of the most original German writers of the period.

Lothar Franz's collection of prints, like his brother's collection of paintings, focused on what was then modern art. His main interest was in French and British prints, although he also collected Old German and Dutch prints of the seventeenth century. An inventory of the engravings dated 1806 lists 14,000 numbered works, although there were some 20,000 single sheets altogether, of which 7,300 have survived.[19] It is the eighteenth-century English prints above all which make this collection so important today. It includes significant bodies of work by engravers such as Francesco Bartolozzi, Giovanni Battista Cipriani, Maria Cosway, Richard Earlom, Gavin Hamilton, Sylvester Harding and William Woollett, as well as numerous engravings of paintings by Thomas Gainsborough, George Morland, Allan Ramsay, Joshua Reynolds (well over 200), George Romney, Benjamin West, Joseph Wright of Derby, Johann Zoffany and several others, giving a vivid and varied impression of the contemporary British visual arts. Included in this exhibition are thirteen reproductive engravings after George Stubbs from the collection in Aschaffenburg, among them a complete series of the *Prints of Horses* engraved by Benjamin Green between 1767 and 1770 (cat. nos. 65–70).

When Lothar Franz von Erthal died his collection became the property of the state and was integrated in the Hofbibliothek. Then, in 1814, the Principality of Aschaffenburg fell to Bavaria and with it the Hofbibliothek and the collection of engravings and paintings. The latter had been augmented with several very valuable works from the Stiftskirche in Aschaffenburg after secularization, including those by Grünewald and Cranach. Today the Aschaffenburger Graphische Sammlung falls under the aegis of the Munich-based Staatliche Graphische Sammlung and is in the custodial care of the Museen der Stadt Aschaffenburg.

A good deal larger and more comprehensive is the collection of prints initiated by Duke Francis Frederick Anthony of Saxe-Coburg-Saalfeld (1750–1806) (fig. 6) initiated in the 1770s in Coburg. The duke was one of the first collectors to focus on early German prints and the work of other printmaking schools of the sixteenth to the eighteenth century, although contemporary German prints formed his main interest. With this broadminded approach he built the foundations of what is now the Kupferstichkabinett of the Veste Coburg, one of the largest collections of its kind in the world. British prints are extremely important to this collection, which boasts no fewer than 1,000 mezzotints among its holdings, including around 100 by John Smith and Valentine Green respectively, as well as others by Richard Earlom and William Ward, John Raphael Smith and James McArdell. The aquatints include some excellent prints by James Barry.[20]

In closing, let us not overlook an impressive collection of British prints assembled by the local merchant John Jacob Hertel (1782–1851) now on permanent loan to the Germanisches Nationalmuseum in Nuremberg from the Museen der Stadt Nürnberg. A patrician rather than a prince, Hertel was not just interested in paintings and prints but also in natural history and scientific instruments.[21] The nineteen paintings in his collection include several Old German Masters as well as an authentic self-portrait by Rembrandt. Meanwhile his collection of prints numbered more than 6,000, among which are a complete set by Daniel Chodowiecki and others of German, Dutch, French and English origin. John Dixon's famous engraving after Stubbs's *Tigress*, dated 1772 (cat. no. 78), is exhibited here alongside offprints from the *Shooting* series.

This short overview could be extended by the names of several more figures.[22] One collector of note would be George Frederick Brandes (1719–1791) of Göttingen. A lawyer and official of the Hanoverian state, Brandes amassed an encyclopaedic collection of more than 40,000 prints, including one of the most comprehensive collections of British prints then in existence, which—after being painstakingly catalogued—was sold at auction in Leipzig in 1796.[23] Collections like his attest to the exceptionally eclectic, unprejudiced culture of collecting that prevailed in Germany in the late eighteenth and early nineteenth centuries—a culture in which British prints had a significant role to play.

---

1 Timothy Clayton, "Reviews of English Prints in German Journals 1750–1800," in: *Print Quarterly* 10, 1993, pp. 123–37; Anne-Marie Link, "'Papierkultur'. The British Print, History and Modernity in Enlightenment Germany," in: Christiana Payne and William Vaughan (eds.), *English Accents. Interactions with British Art c. 1776–1855*, Aldershot 2004, pp. 29–50.

2 Johann Christian von Mannlich, *Fortgesetzte Beschreibung der Königlich-Baierischen Gemälde-Sammlungen. Enthaltend die Gemälde zu Schleisheim und Lustheim*, Munich 1810, p. 101, no. 1870: "Georg Stabbs. / Ein Hünerhund besteht kleines Wildpret."

3 Barbara Hardtwig, "König Max Joseph als Kunstsammler und Mäzen," in: Hubert Glaser (ed.), *Krone und Verfassung. König Max I. Joseph und der neue Staat. Beiträge zur bayerischen Geschichte und Kunst 1799–1825*, Munich 1992, pp. 423–38.

4 *Vermeer in München. König Max I. Joseph von Bayern als Sammler Alter Meister*, Markus Dekiert (ed.) Exhib. Cat. Alte Pinakothek, Munich 2011.

5 Hardtwig 1992 (see note 3), p. 431, no. 32 (Morland) and p. 432, no. 84 (Wilkie).

6 Cf. the entry on Wilkie's painting by Barbara Hardtwig in *Spätklassizismus und Romantik* (*Neue Pinakothek, Gemäldekataloge*, vol. 5), Munich 2003, pp. 537–41. The art collector Franz Erwin Graf von Schönborn commissioned a painting from Wilkie at the same time as King Max I Joseph of Bavaria. The work for the former, *The Unexpected Visitor*, was widely disseminated as a popular print entitled *Guess My Name*. Schönborn was also in possession of a number of British prints, including some after Stubbs and Wilkie. Cf. Katharina Bott, *Ein deutscher Kunstsammler zu Beginn des 19. Jahrhunderts. Franz Erwein von Schönborn (1776–1840)*, Alfter 1993, pp. 177–80. Rudolf Arthaber in Vienna also possessed a work by Wilkie from 1838; this was *The Bride at Her Toilet on the Day of Her Wedding*, which has been at the National Gallery of Scotland in Edinburgh since 1920. Cf. the entry by Hamish Miles on this work in *Sir David Wilkie of Scotland*, Exhib. Cat. North Carolina Museum of Art, Raleigh 1987, no. 41.

7 *Die deutschen, französischen und englischen Gemälde des 17. und 18. Jahrhunderts sowie die spanischen und dänischen Bilder. Kritischer Katalog mit Abbildungen aller Werke (Niedersächsisches Landesmuseum Hannover, Landesgalerie)*, Angelica Dülberg (ed.), Hanover 1990, nos. 188 and 194.

8 Already listed in *Verzeichniss der Bildhauerwerke und Gemälde, welche sich in den Königlich Hannoverschen Schlössern und Gebäuden befinden*, Hanover 1844, no. 1; Dülberg 1990 (see note 7), no. 182.

9 *George III and Queen Charlotte. Patronage, Collecting and Court Taste*, Jane Roberts (ed.), Exhib. Cat. The Royal Collection, London 2004, no. 11.

10 Kenneth Garlick, *Sir Thomas Lawrence. A Complete Catalogue of his Oil Paintings*, Oxford 1989, nos. 543, 552, 559; Michael Levey, *Sir Thomas Lawrence*, New Haven and London 2005, pp. 212–22.

11 Elizaveta Renne, *Sixteenth- to Nineteenth-Century British Painting (State Hermitage Museum Catalogue)*, New Haven and London 2011, nos. 122–123.

12 Ibid, nos. 86–87.

13 *XI. Kunstausstellung der königlich bayerischen Akademie der bildenden Künste*, Munich 1845, p. 20, no. 155: "Die feierliche Eröffnung der Walhalla bei Regensburg, in allegorischer Darstellung." Cf. Martin Butlin and Evelyn Joll, *The Paintings of J.M.W. Turner*, 2 vols., New Haven and London 1977, no. 401.

14 Timothy Clayton, *The English Print 1688–1802*, New Haven and London 1997, p. 280.

15 Karl Heinrich von Heinecken, *Idée générale d'une collection complette d'estampes*, Leipzig 1771, p. 4: "… & alors, étant encouragée par des recompenses, elle surpassera peut-être un jour toutes les autres."

16 Lilli Fischel, "Notizen zur Geschichte des Karlsruher Kupferstichkabinetts," in: *Zeitschrift für die Geschichte des Oberrheins* 105, 1957, pp. 265–94.

17 Wilhelm Weber, *Schloß Karlsberg. Legende und Wirklichkeit. Die Wittelsbacher Schloßbauten im Herzogtum Pfalz-Zweibrücken*, Homburg 1987, pp. 475–81.

18 *Künstler zeichnen, Sammler stiften. 250 Jahre Staatliche Graphische Sammlung München*, Michael Semff and Kurt Zeitler (eds.), 3 vols., Munich 2008, vol. 1, pp. 91 f.

19 Ingrid Jenderko-Sichelschmidt, "Notizen zur Geschichte Aschaffenburgs und seiner Staatlichen Graphischen Sammlung," in: Wilhelm Weber (ed.), *Englische Schabkunstblätter aus ehemaligem kurfürstlichen Besitz in Mainz*, Exhib. Cat. Mittelrheinisches Landesmuseum, Mainz 1983, pp. 15–26, here p. 23. Cf. most recently Frithjof Schwartz, "Englische Schabkunstblätter in der kurmainzischen Sammlung Erthal in Aschaffenburg," in: Eva-Maria Hanebutt-Benz and Isabella Fehle (eds.), *"Die also genannte Schwarze Kunst, in Kupfer zu arbeiten." Technik und Entwicklung des Mezzotintos*, Exhib. Cat. Gutenberg-Museum and Landesmuseum, Mainz and Städtische Kunstsammlungen, Albstadt, Berlin and Munich 2009/10, pp. 177–84.

20 Christiane Wiebel, *Aquatinta, oder "Die Kunst mit dem Pinsel in Kupfer zu stechen." Das druckgraphische Verfahren von seinen Anfängen bis Goya*, Exhib. Cat. Kunstsammlungen der Veste Coburg and Suermondt-Ludwig Museum, Aachen, Munich and Berlin 2007/08, pp. 212–19.

21 *Die Sammlungen des Handelsgerichts-Assessors Joh. Jac. Hertel aus den Gebieten der Kunst und Wissenschaft, des Gewerbefleisses und der Natur*, Nuremberg 1841; Wilhelm Schwemmer, "Aus der Geschichte der Kunstsammlungen der Stadt Nürnberg," in: *Mitteilungen des Vereins für Geschichte der Stadt Nürnberg* 40, 1949, pp. 97–206, here pp. 152ff.

22 Cf. Clayton 1997 (see note 14), p. 272, which mentions, among others, the collections of Christian Ludwig von Hagedorn in Dresden and Johann Melchior von Birckenstock in Vienna.

23 Michael Huber, *Catalogue raisonné du Cabinet d'Estampes de feu Monsieur Brandes … contenant une collection des pieces anciennes et modernes de toutes les ecoles dans une suite des artistes depuis l'origine de l'art jusqu'à nos jours*, 2 vols., Leipzig 1794.

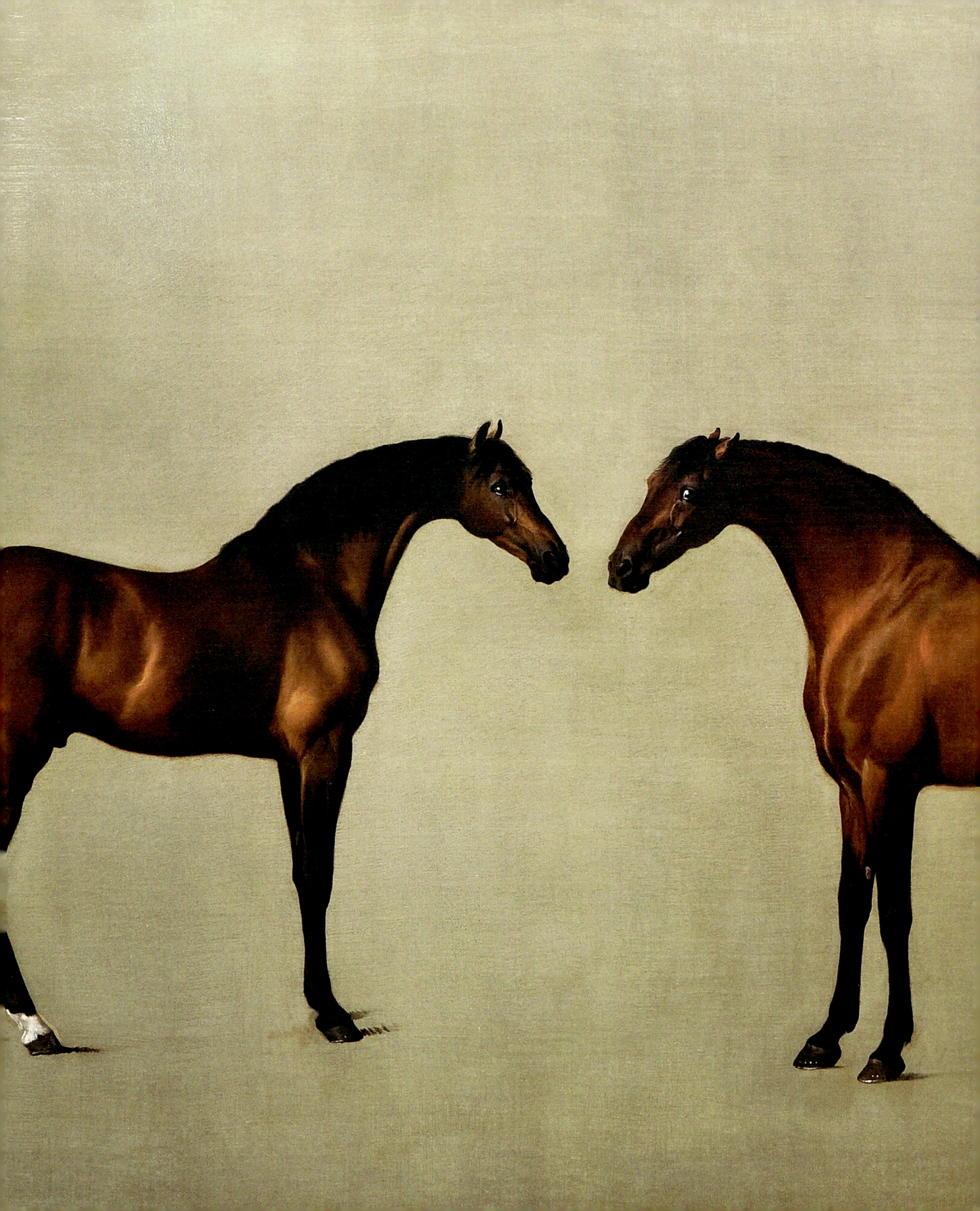

CATALOGUE

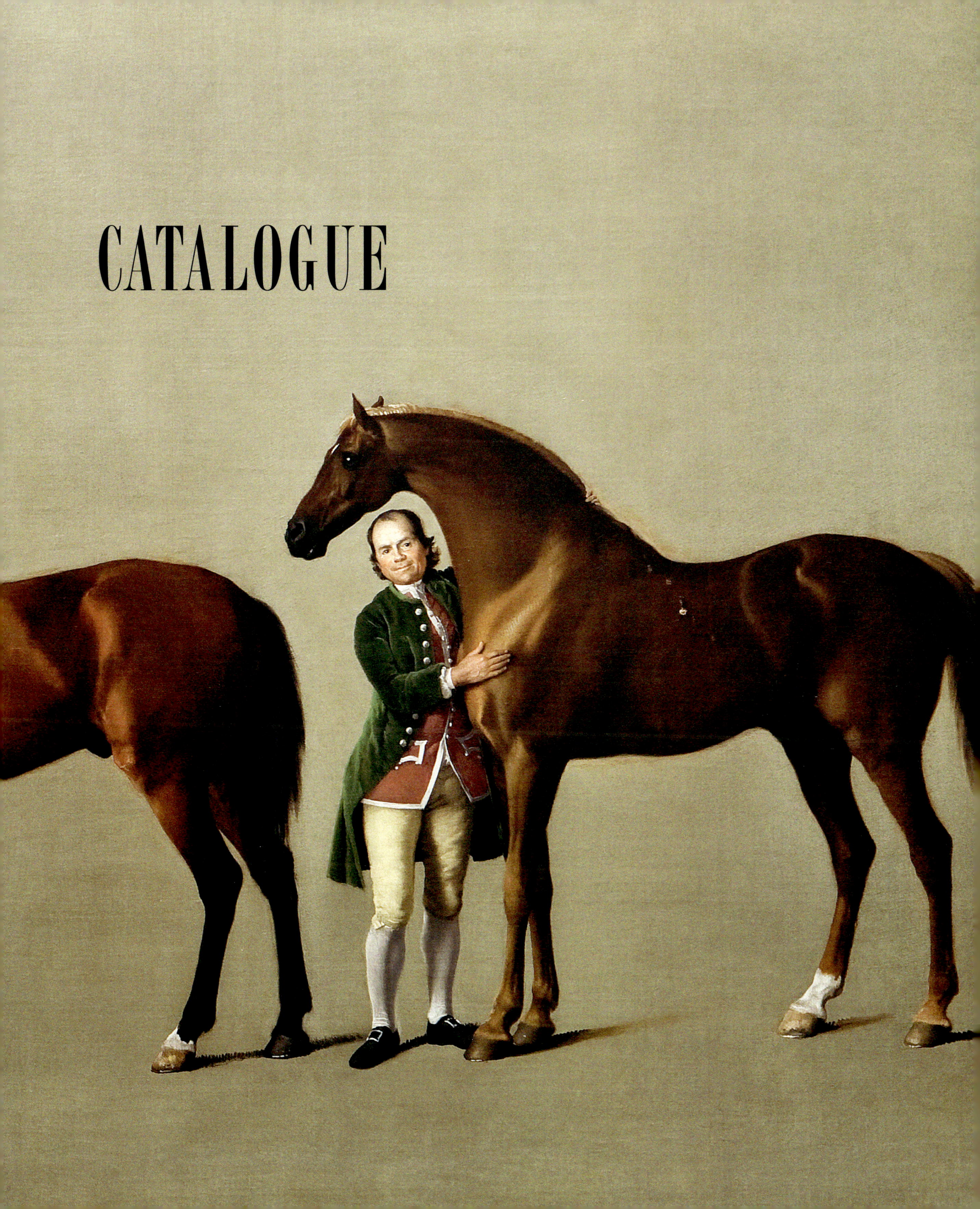

THE ANATOMY OF THE HORSE

PAINTINGS

PRINTS

PRINTS AFTER STUBBS

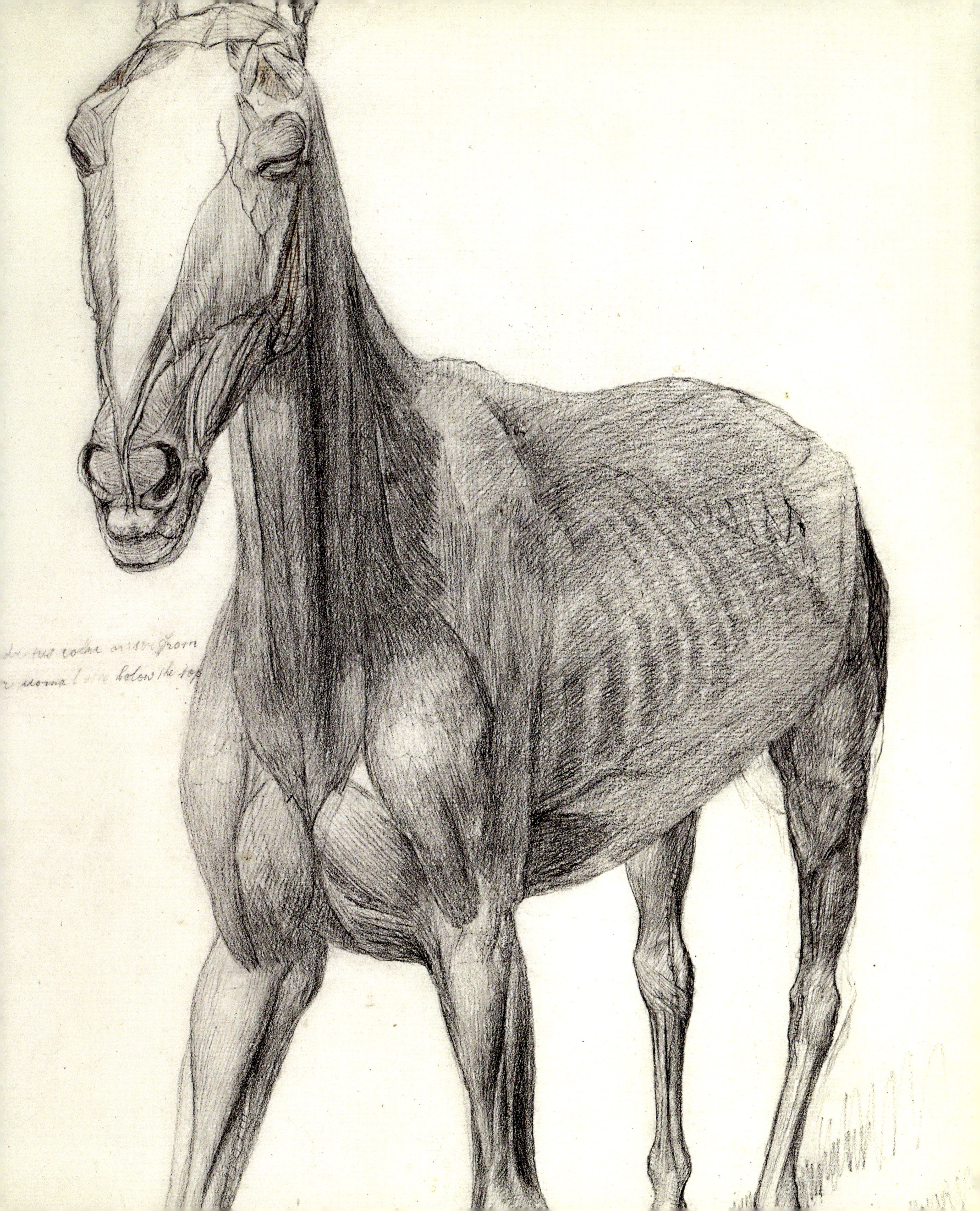
arising from
below the top

THE ANATOMY OF THE HORSE

George Stubbs's *Anatomy of the Horse* is one of the great anatomy projects of the past 500 years in Western art history. Even today it is both scientifically and aesthetically convincing and the exceptional graphic and anatomical accuracy of his drawings and etchings is impressive. They mark the acme of the interaction between art and science that characterized the Age of Enlightenment. Never before had so much care and attention been lavished on the anatomy of the horse in the pursuit of art; never before had a single artist or anatomist undertaken such an ambitious project and single-handedly seen it through to completion from inception to publication. Stubbs's achievement is an artistic, physical, intellectual and technical tour de force. It entailed dissecting, preparing, describing and drawing horses and then making etchings from the drawings with which to illustrate his treatise. His only assistant in all of this was his common-law wife Mary Spencer.

The project took ten years to complete from start to finish, although it is likely that the planning and conception lasted a good deal longer. Even as a child, Stubbs had shown a passion not only for drawing but also for anatomy, and he followed up on this when he later took up the study of human anatomy at York County Hospital. The idea of producing a proper study of equine anatomy probably gained ground in the circle of Stubbs's York colleagues in around 1751 or perhaps a little later. The surgeon Charles Atkinson, who taught Stubbs human and veterinary anatomy, could well have been the initiator—in 1834 Atkinson's son James described how Stubbs had told him as much when he visited the painter at his studio in London. Be that as it may, there is no doubt that Stubbs began his study of equine anatomy independently of his fellow students shortly after returning from Italy in 1756. The only support he received was from his patroness Lady Nelthorpe, who, after having commissioned a portrait of herself and her husband, arranged for a barn at Horkstow in northern Lincolnshire to be placed at Stubbs's disposal. The hamlet of Horkstow belonged to the dilettante Charles Gore, scion of a wealthy family of merchants, who presumably made the property available as a favour to Nelthorpe.

Stubbs was thirty-two when he installed himself at Horkstow. He spent the next eighteen months dissecting horses after bleeding them to death by severing the jugular vein. Since the ever-advancing process of putrefaction meant that each animal could be used for only six to seven weeks, it seems likely that he dissected some twelve animals altogether. As the son of a currier, Stubbs was doubtless inured to the less pleasant aspects of anatomical practice —the stench of rotting flesh, for example, and the secretion of putrid bodily fluids. Before the advent of antiseptics the risk of infection was high, yet Stubbs managed to remain healthy, probably by relying on vinegar solutions. Using a tried and tested embalming method, the artist injected the blood vessels, muscles and nerves of the beast with liquid wax or tallow so as to conserve its natural shape for as long as possible. He devised a contraption that enabled him to fix the horses in a 'natural', life-like pose and that aided him in drawing them. Consisting of several hooks suspended from an iron beam in the ceiling, these gripped the horses between the ribs and steadied their spines. The hooves were affixed to board or plank which had been nailed to the floor. Stubbs began each dissection by slitting open the abdominal cavity. After removing the entrails he proceeded from there to the thoracic cavity and the head. After cleaning and preparing each anatomical specimen, he made drawings of it, which he supplemented with verbal descriptions. This constant back and forth between scalpel, pencil and pen resulted in a large number of working drawings, twenty-four of which have been preserved (cat. nos. 1–6). In order to be able to standardize the position of the various muscles, blood vessels and other anatomical features irrespective of the size of each beast, Stubbs first drew a standard skeleton—complete with dimensions—from three different perspectives. Using tracing paper, he then transferred this skeleton to his other drawings so that he could enter the results of his dissections there.

Stubbs's three general views of the horse show it standing in profile and in mid-trot from both front and rear. After drawing the skeleton in red, brown and black inks, he pencilled in the muscles, sinews, tendons, veins and arteries, sometimes making local use of red chalk in his working studies. Executed entirely in pencil, the eighteen finished drawings are considerably more detailed and graphically much more subtle than these pen-and-ink drawings (cat. nos. 7–15). Once the skeleton had been presented from the three

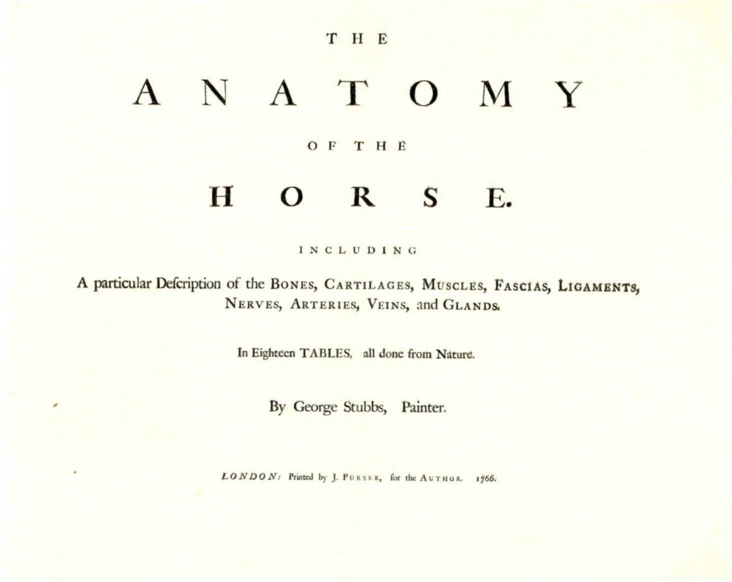

THE

ANATOMY

OF THE

HORSE.

INCLUDING

A particular Defcription of the BONES, CARTILAGES, MUSCLES, FASCIAS, LIGAMENTS, NERVES, ARTERIES, VEINS, and GLANDS.

In Eighteen TABLES, all done from Nature.

By George Stubbs, Painter.

LONDON: Printed by J. PURSER, for the AUTHOR. 1766.

1 *The Anatomy of the Horse*, London 1766,
Title page
London, The British Museum

standard perspectives, the drawings followed the progress of the dissection through all five layers, from the outermost subcutaneous muscles to the muscles deep inside the body. These drawings form the basis for the book illustrations which Stubbs began preparing after moving to London in 1758/59. Humphry reports that established printmakers and experienced engravers such as Charles Grignion and Arthur Pond refused to take on the task of rendering them for printing purposes because they were unable to make sense of them, reacting to the request with smirking and bewilderment. Yet it is hard to lend much credence to this account, bearing in mind that Stubbs's drawings soon made him so famous in London that he received numerous commissions for both horse portraits and hunting scenes. It seems much more likely that the artist himself was put off by the exorbitant costs involved in just such a project; his determination to maintain the anatomical accuracy and graphic precision of his drawings, which might otherwise be jeopardized by entrusting the work to another, may have compelled him to carry out the work himself. Stubbs taught himself to etch—doubtless with the help of experienced printmakers—and devoted henceforth much of his spare time to producing the printing plates for his *Anatomy*. The ensuing prints are so artfully nuanced as to put them on a par with the drawings. The call for subscriptions issued in 1765 heralded the work as the result of the author's own dissections and keen powers of observation. The *Anatomy* was published by J. Purser of London in 1766 as the work of "George Stubbs, Painter."

It was certainly not a matter of course that an anatomical project of such unprecedented complexity should have been conceived and completed by a painter with no outside assistance at all. What, then, was Stubbs's purpose in publishing such a work? Who was it aimed at? His foreword leaves us in no doubt that he targeted other artists, whose ability to depict animals, Stubbs believed, would benefit greatly from a better understanding of animal anatomy. The horse as a motif was more important than ever before in eighteenth-century England, where a keen interest in horse-breeding, equestrian sports and hunting had put a premium on painters with a natural talent for representing horses. Stubbs's anatomical atlas put such works on a new scientific footing and so paved the way for a revolution in horse painting in England, as well as beyond. Above all, however, the *Anatomy* told of Stubbs's own aesthetic aspirations. The anatomical accuracy of the plates is matched by the self-assured artfulness of what they show. By presenting each animal with all of its limbs intact, they generate a sense of vitality which has the effect of preserving the horse's innate beauty and dignity. And although the purpose of the book was to afford its readers a glimpse inside this noble beast, it also keeps them at a respectful distance. The depiction of the horse in mid-trot and the sculptural modelling of its muscles and sinews are redolent of vitality and vigour. The body of the horse is thrown into relief by the light which floods in consistently and uniformly from the front and above. The anatomical elements cannot only be clearly recognised and differentiated; they also follow the light-dark modelling of the entire body. Stubbs masters not only aesthetic challenges such as these but also the trickiest examples of the foreshortening needed to represent complex structures like the cranial spine and foot joints. The extraordinary depth and plasticity achieved by Stubbs in his two-dimensional drawings not only aids our understanding of equine anatomy; it also makes these works an aesthetic pleasure to behold.

The extent to which the drawings are a product of Stubbs's artistic imagination and synthesis becomes apparent when the *Anatomy of the Horse* is compared with other anatomical atlases and illustrated treatises (see pp. 49–52). Stubbs clearly distanced himself from the apparently brutal, purportedly 'naturalistic' anatomical works of his age. With his impartial, anatomical abstraction of the whole horse and his focus on the connectedness and proportions of every part of the body he based his work on the 'idealistic' tradition of human anatomy. Stubbs's transference of this idealistic, essentially aesthetic approach to veterinary anatomy was certainly not so

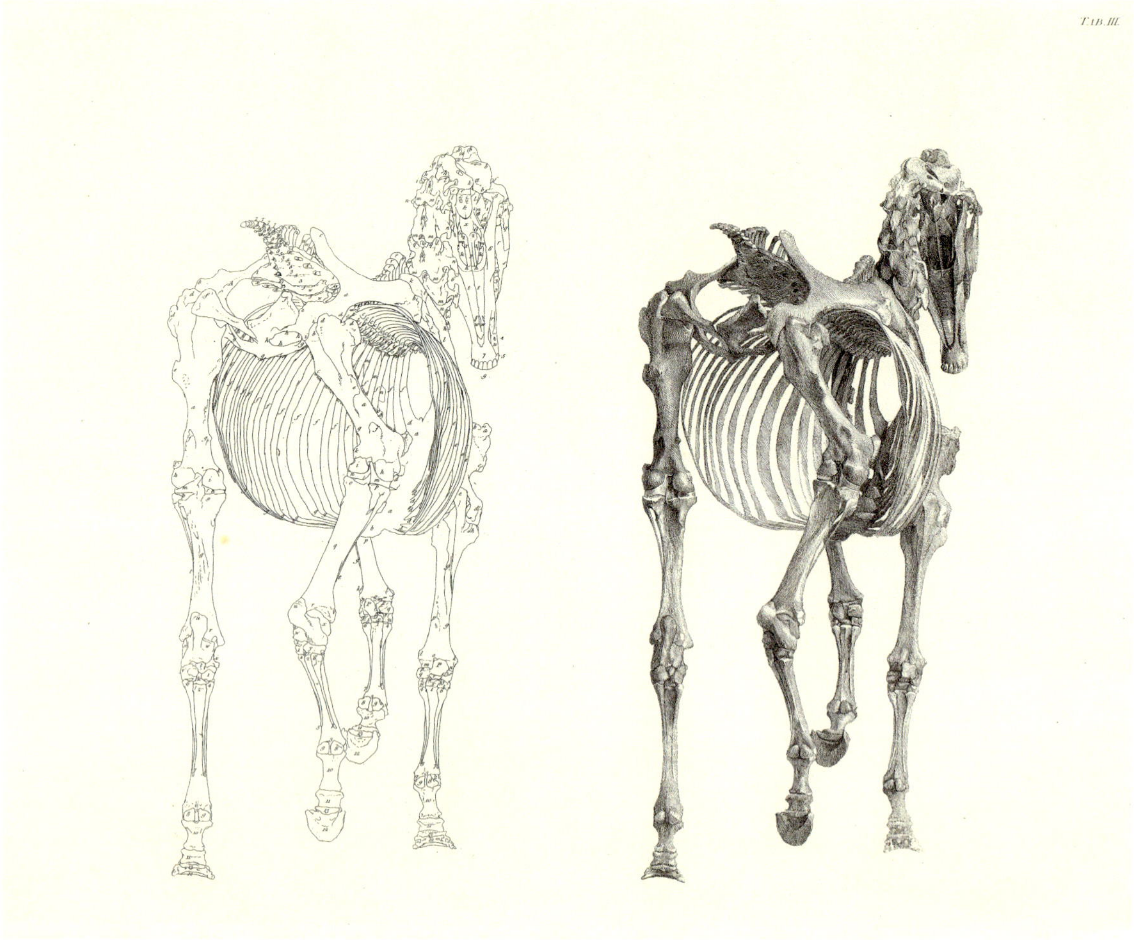

2 *The Anatomy of the Horse*, London 1766, The Third Anatomical Table of the Skeleton of the Horse, etching London, The British Museum

impartial as to be indifferent. On the contrary, it can be read as an emphatic declaration of his own belief in the horse as a beast just as worthy of anatomical analysis as man. Stubbs's faith in the capacity of comparative anatomy to visualize the horse as a noble, sentient creature is borne out by his painstakingly detailed reproduction of the nervous system and the blood vessels, which would surely have been of only secondary importance to horse painters.

Stubbs's *Anatomy* consciously differentiates itself from an exclusively veterinary atlas by dispensing with the depiction of the entrails altogether. Yet his drawings of the blood vessels, nerves, sinews, tendons and cartilage are also explicitly aimed at non-artists. Horse-breeders, horse surgeons and horse lovers were also to be introduced to anatomical details as part of gaining a better understanding of equine physiognomy and the possible causes of disease or injury. The increased importance afforded and popularization of anatomy evident in this work marks an important milestone in the history of science. The first state schools of veterinary medicine based on the examination and understanding of animal anatomy were founded in France in the 1760s, just as Stubbs was putting the finishing touches to his *Anatomy*. Prior to this, only old wives' remedies and obscure concoctions had been handed down or passed on. The scientists of the Enlightenment demanded that traditional practices pass the test of rationality and called for veterinary medicine to be based on the dissection of real animals. By regarding painting as a kind of science, scrutinizing it critically and using experimentation to provide it with a firm foundation, Stubbs himself adopted much the same approach to inherited wisdom. Keen observation and visual absorption went on to become the cardinal virtues of all empirical disciplines. Not only surgeons and natural historians profited from powers of observation but artists and art lovers too. It is likely that Stubbs's anatomical drawings and etchings became so rapidly well known because they so persuasively demonstrated his 'art of observation'.

3 *The Anatomy of the Horse*, London 1766, The Ninth Anatomical Table of the Muscles … of the Horse, etching London, The British Museum

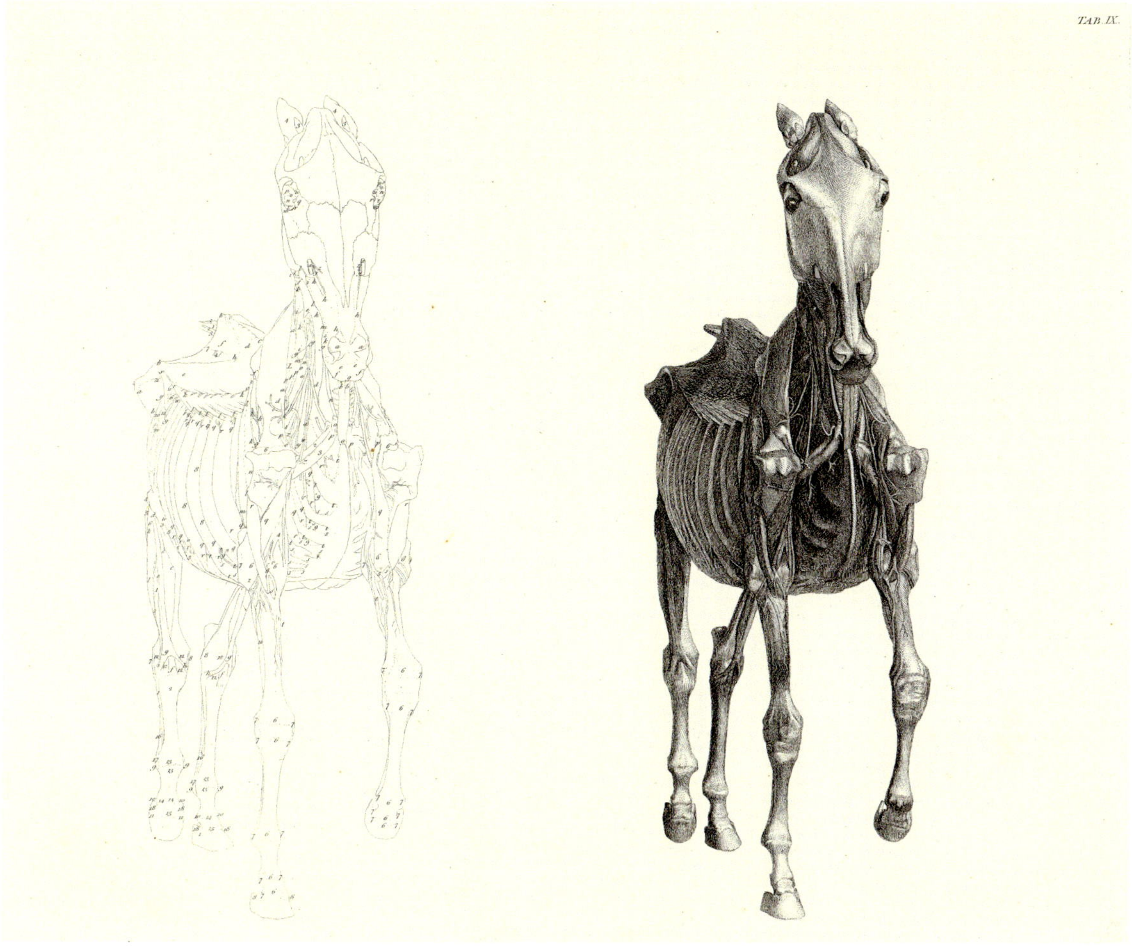

The perspicacity that made Stubbs receptive to the smallest nuances and variations also manifests itself in the sophistication of his style, specifically in his method of singling out certain elements while at the same time depicting them naturalistically as part of a larger whole. The *Anatomy of the Horse* thus reconciles the implicit contradiction between the brutally destructive process of anatomical dissection and the creative process of bringing a living creature to life through art. This outstanding achievement of idealistic anatomy made Stubbs's original drawings ideal teaching materials long after he himself had died. They were purchased by the successful English animal painter Edwin Landseer (1802–1873) and after his death passed to the Royal Academy in 1879 where they were used as models for drawing exercises.

OK

Lit.: Basil Taylor, "Stubbs as Anatomist", in: Exhib. Cat. *George Stubbs,* 1976, pp. 10–19 (first 1958) – Terence Doherty, *The Anatomical Works of George Stubbs*, London 1974 – Exhib. Cat. *George Stubbs,* 1984/85, nos. 6–25 – *Mehr Licht. Europa um 1770. Die bildende Kunst der Aufklärung*, Herbert Beck, Peter C. Bol and Maraike Bückling (eds.), Exhib. Cat. Städelsches Kunstinstitut und Städtische Galerie Frankfurt am Main, Munich 1999, nos. 39–40. – Exhib. Cat. *Stubbs and the Horse*, 2004/05, nos. 1–32 – Egerton, *George Stubbs,* 2007, pp. 112–29, no. 7 – Andrew Cunningham, *The Anatomist Anatomis'd. An Experimental Discipline in Enlightenment Europe*, Farnham, Burlington 2010, pp. 340–54

For conservational reasons, cat. nos. 1–4 and 7 cannot be shown in the exhibition.

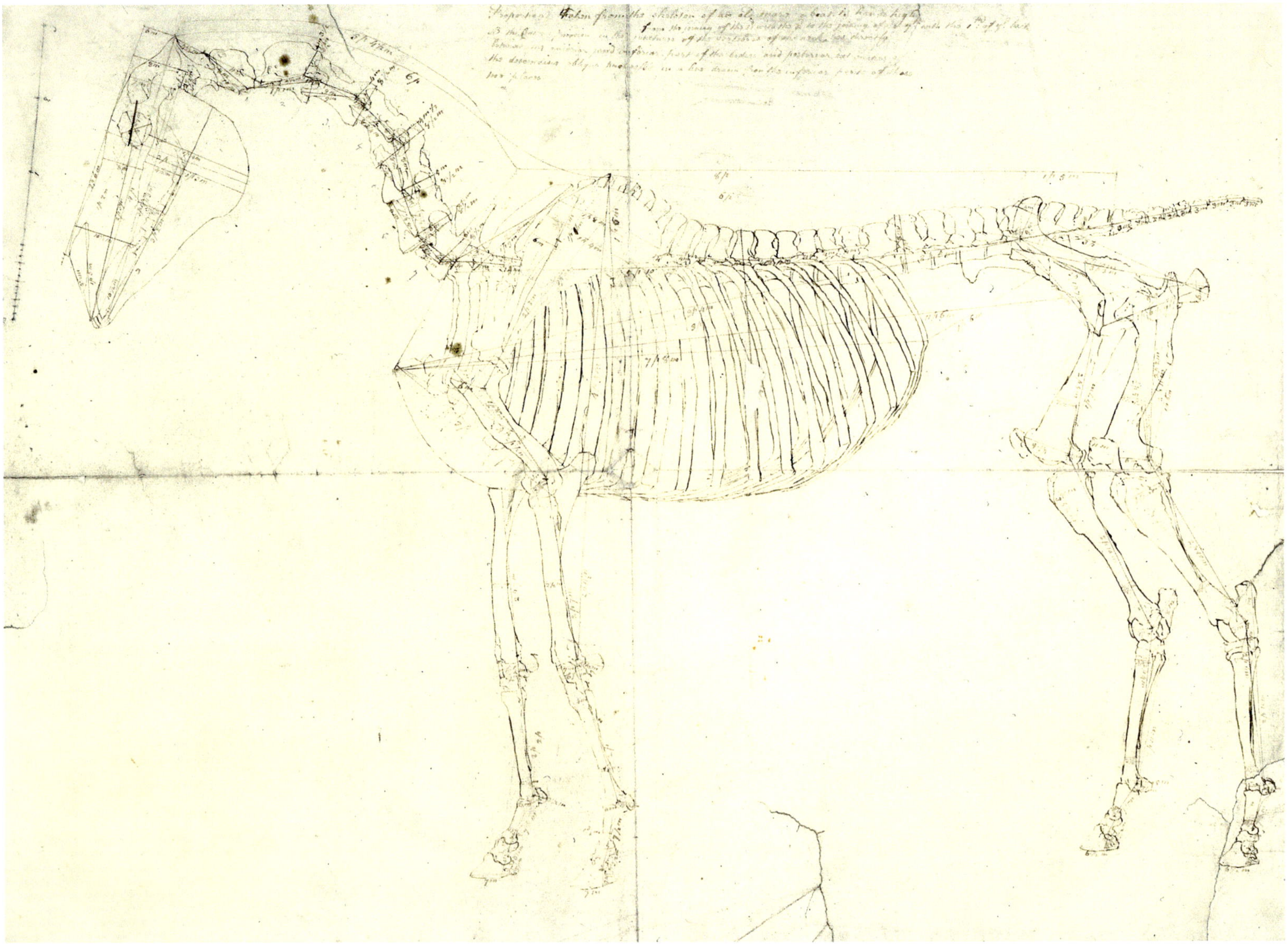

1

Measured working drawing for 'The First Anatomical Table of the Skeleton of the Horse'

Pen and brown ink, pencil, 36.7 x 50.4 cm
London, Royal Academy of Arts, Inv. no. 03/1589 (RA 36)

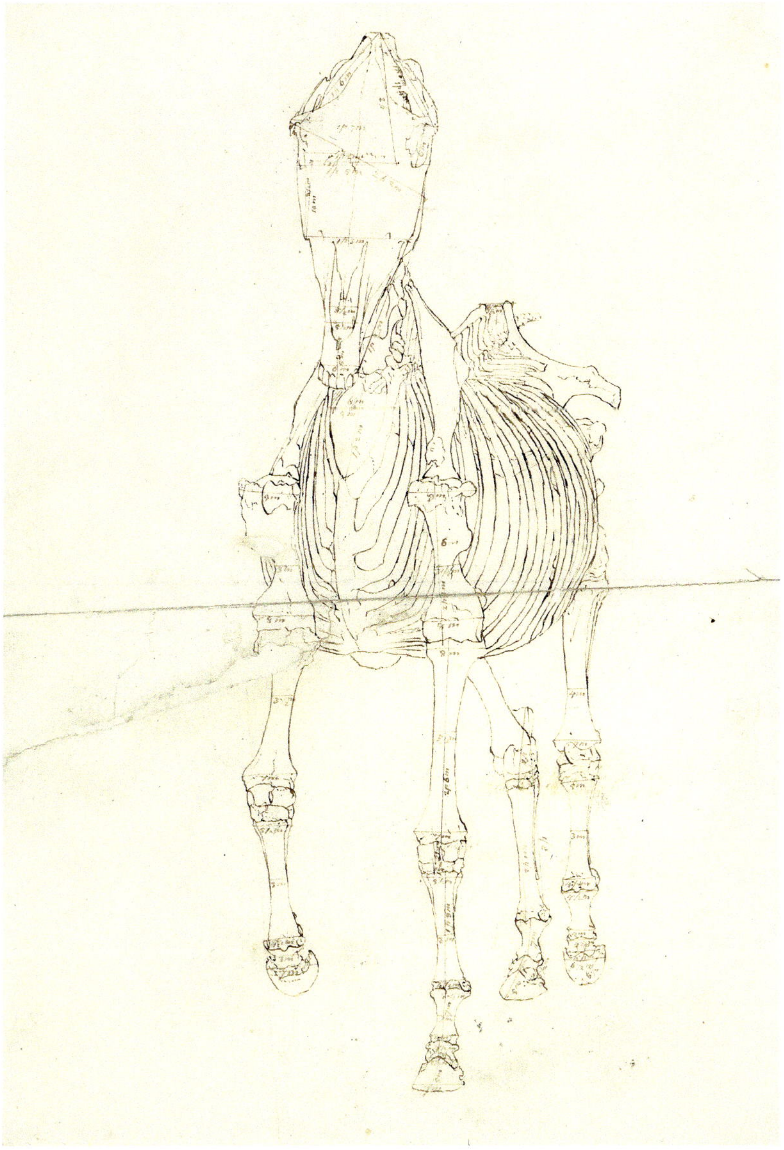

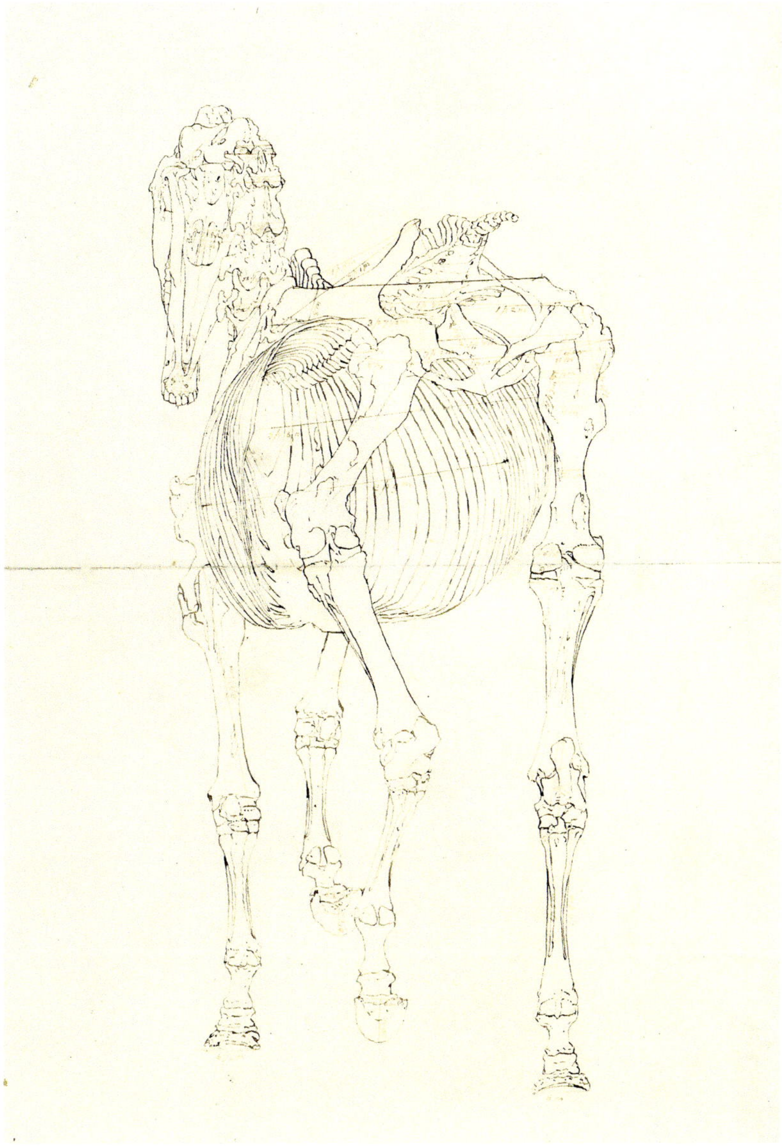

2

Measured working drawing for 'The Second Anatomical Table of the Skeleton of the Horse'

Pen and brown ink, 36.7 x 25.0 cm
London, Royal Academy of Arts, Inv. no. 03/1588 (RA 36)

3

Measured working drawing for 'The Third Anatomical Table of the Skeleton of the Horse'

Pen and brown ink, 36.7 x 25.0 cm
London, Royal Academy of Arts, Inv. no. 03/1587 (RA 34)

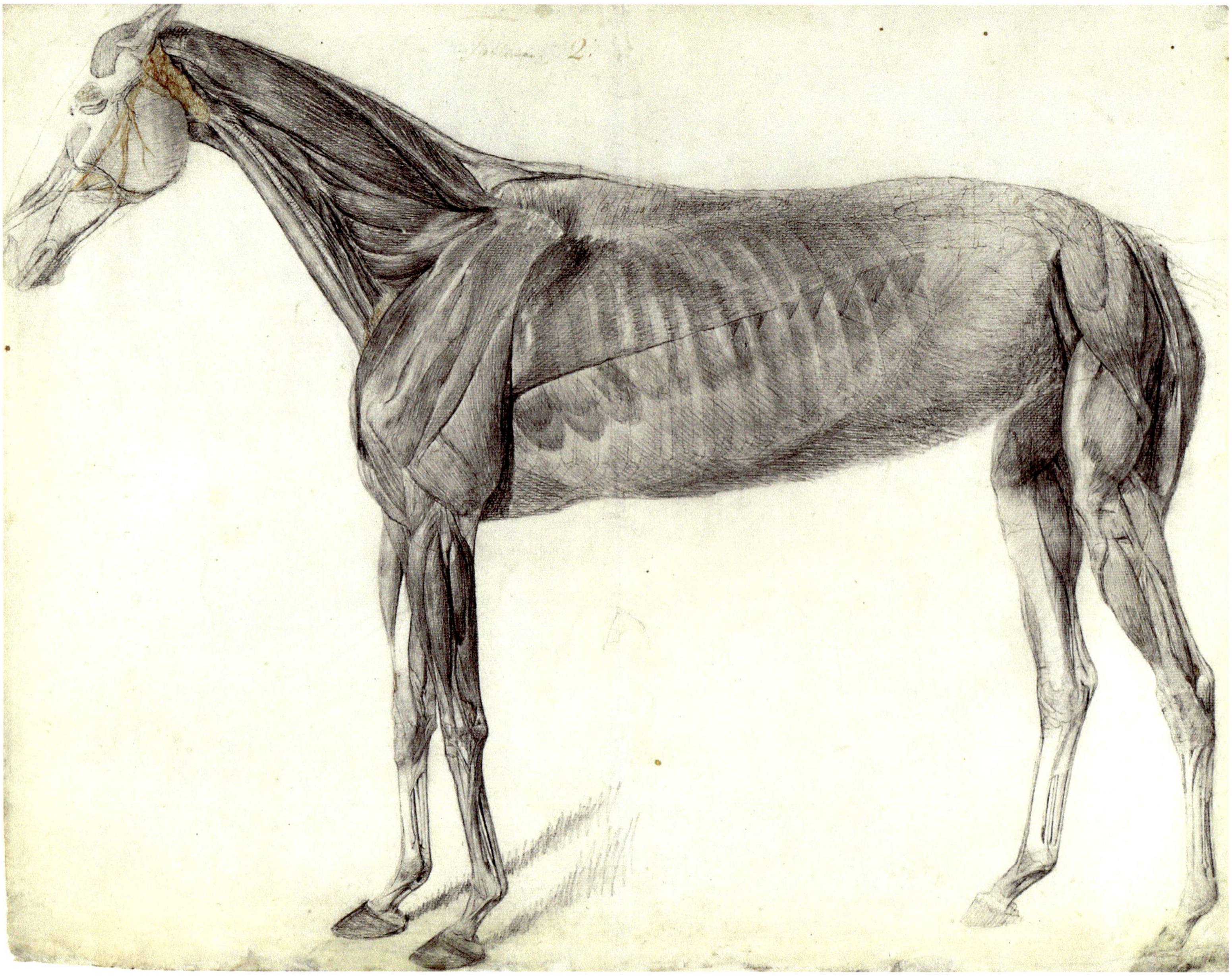

4

Working drawing for 'The Second Anatomical Table of the Muscles ... of the Horse'

Pencil, red chalk, red and brown ink, 48.4 x 61.0 cm
London, Royal Academy of Arts, Inv. no. 03/1584 (RA 31)

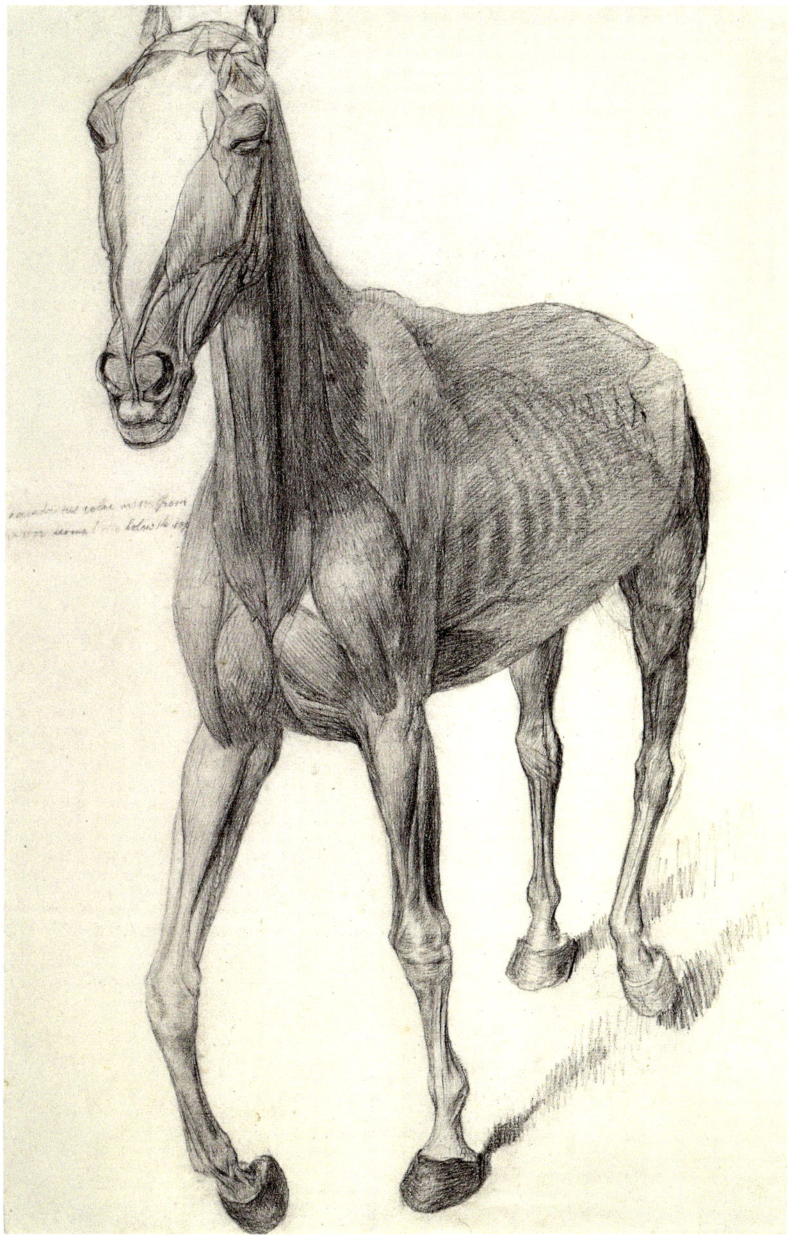

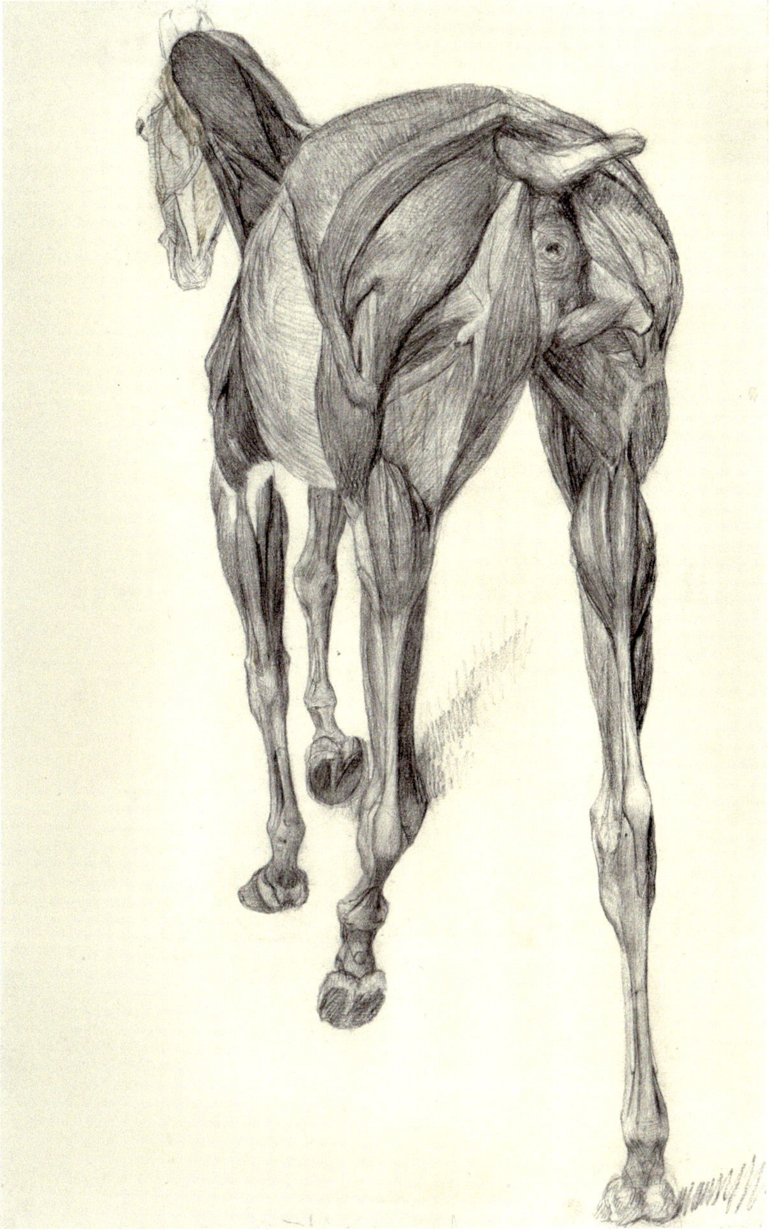

5

Working drawing for 'The Seventh Anatomical Table of the Muscles ... of the Horse'

Pencil, black and red chalk, 47.0 x 29.8 cm
London, Royal Academy of Arts, Inv. no. 03/5731 (RA 6)

6

Working drawing for 'The Thirteenth Anatomical Table of the Muscles ... of the Horse'

Pencil, black and red chalk, 47.0 x 29.2 cm
London, Royal Academy of Arts, Inv. no. 03/5719 (RA 2)

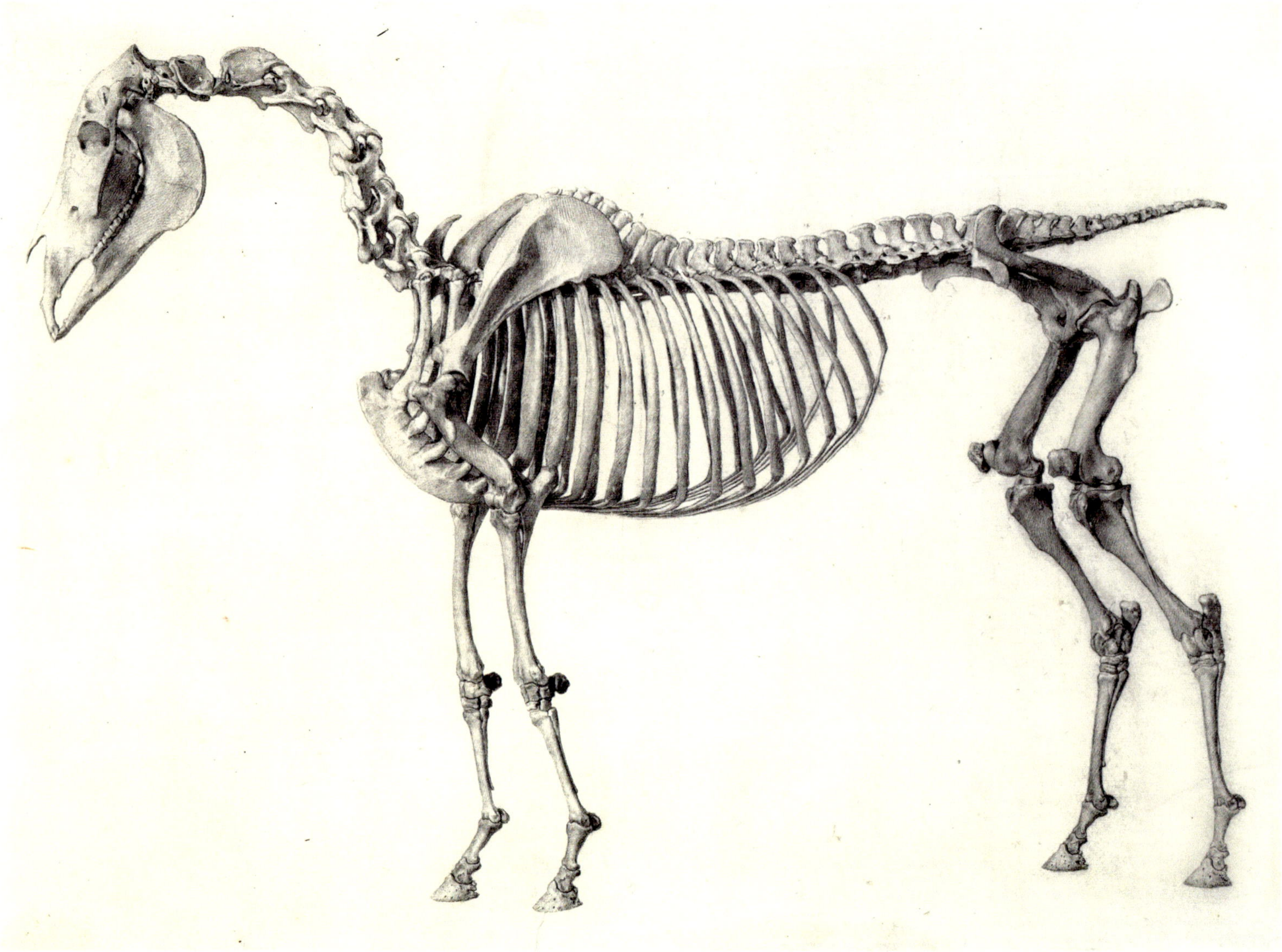

7

Finished study for 'The First Anatomical Table of the Skeleton of the Horse'

Black chalk, 36.1 x 48.3 cm
London, Royal Academy of Arts, Inv. no. 03/5720 (RA 5)

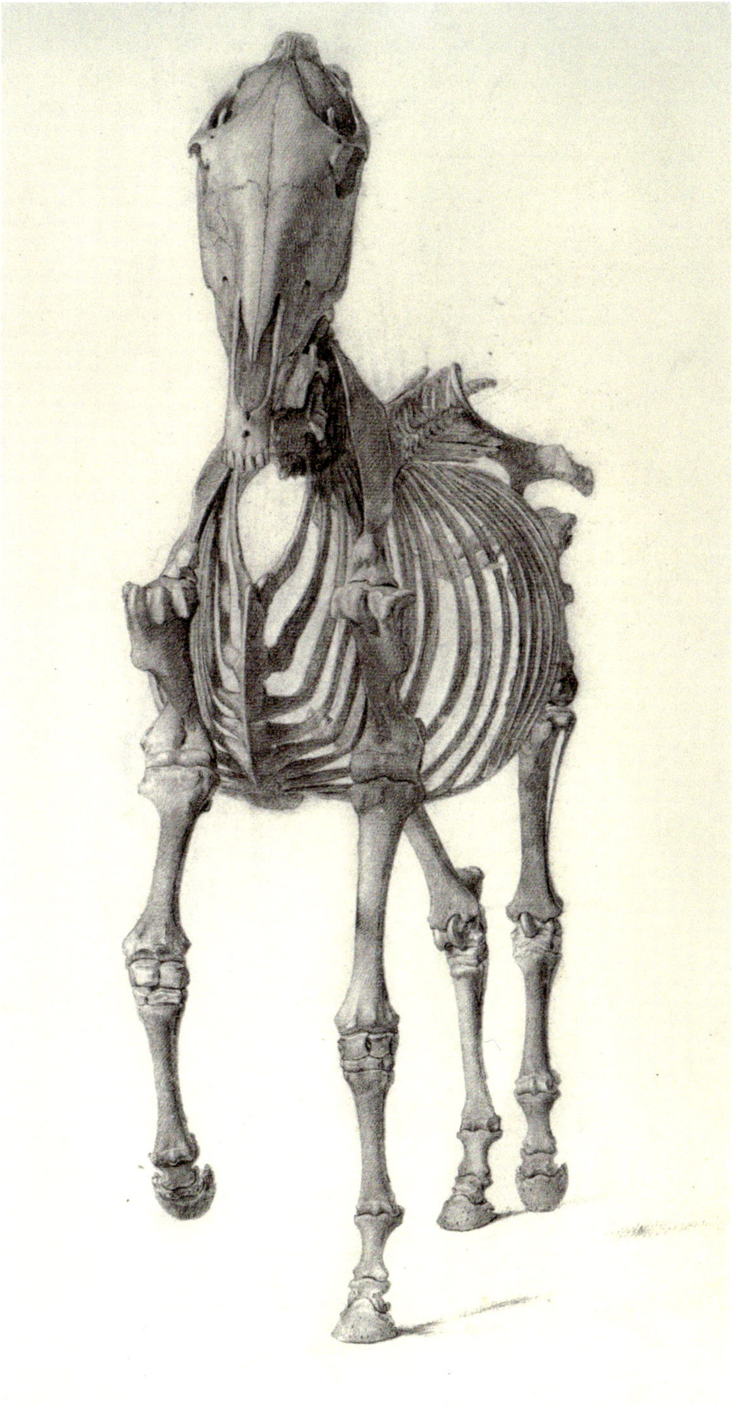

8

Finished study for 'The Second Anatomical Table of the Skeleton of the Horse'

Pencil and black chalk, 35.6 x 18.4 cm
London, Royal Academy of Arts, Inv. no. 03/5716 (RA 10)

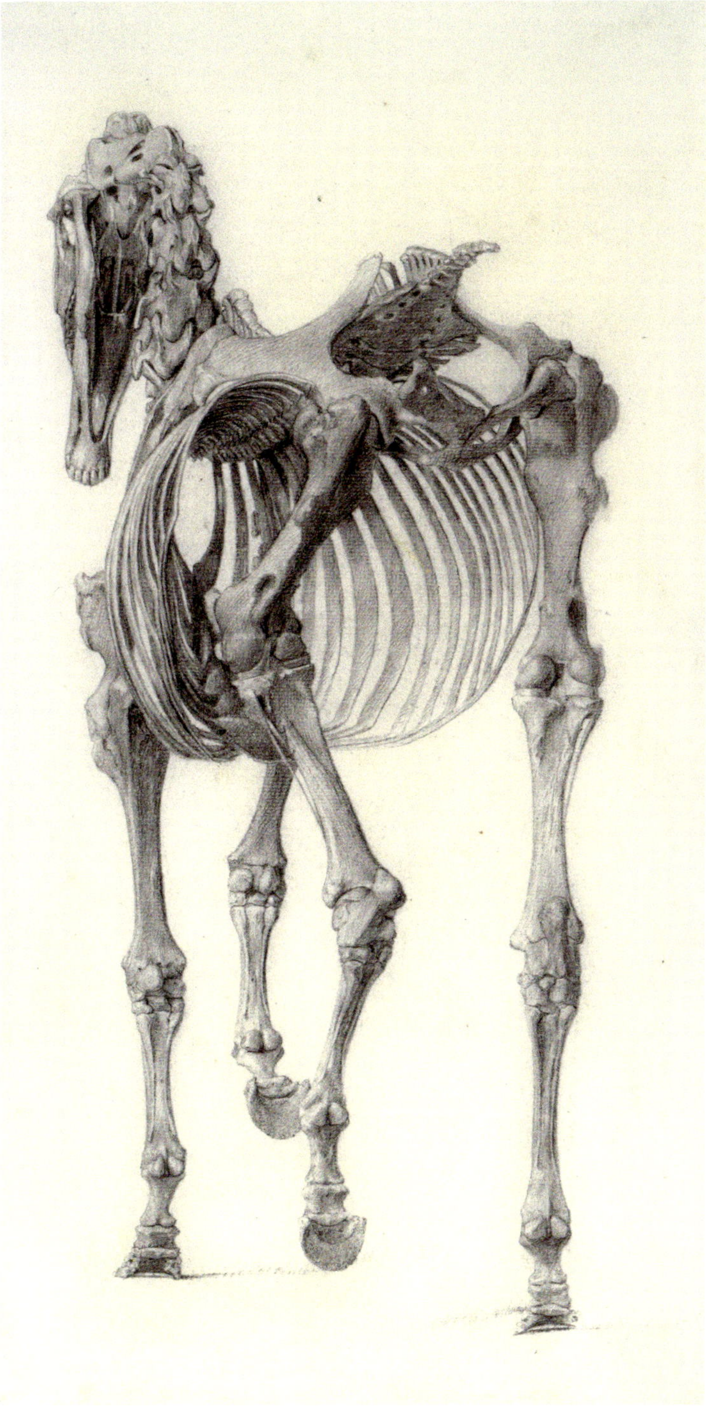

9

Finished study for 'The Third Anatomical Table of the Skeleton of the Horse'

Pencil, 35.4 x 18.0 cm
London, Royal Academy of Arts, Inv. no. 03/5718 (RA 18)

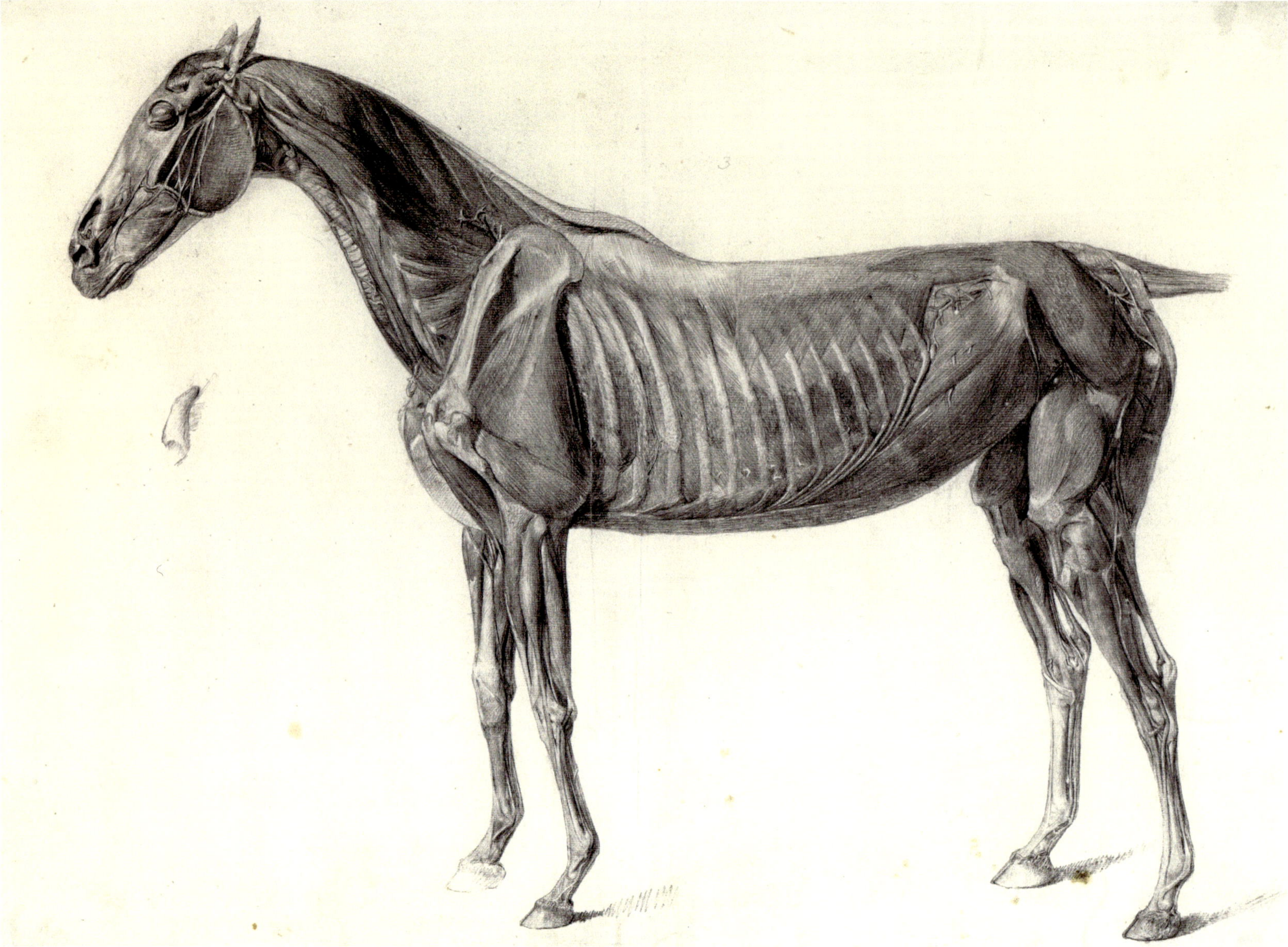

10
Finished study for 'The Third Anatomical Table of the Muscles ... of the Horse'

Pencil, 36.6 x 50.5 cm
London, Royal Academy of Arts, Inv. no. 03/1580 (RA 28)

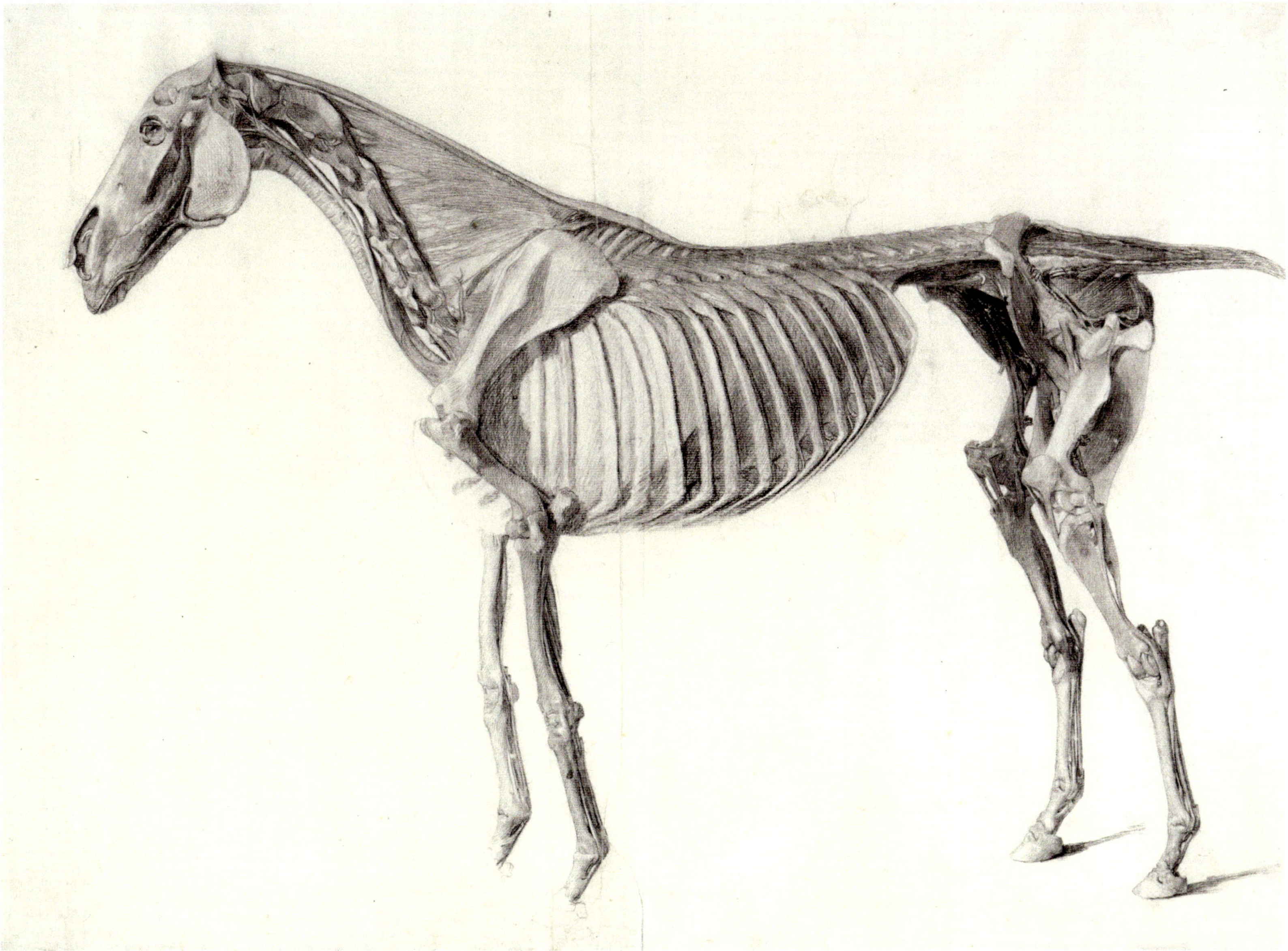

11

Finished study for 'The Fifth Anatomical Table of the Muscles ... of the Horse'

Pencil and black chalk, 36.7 x 50.5 cm
London, Royal Academy of Arts, Inv. no. 03/1583 (RA 30)

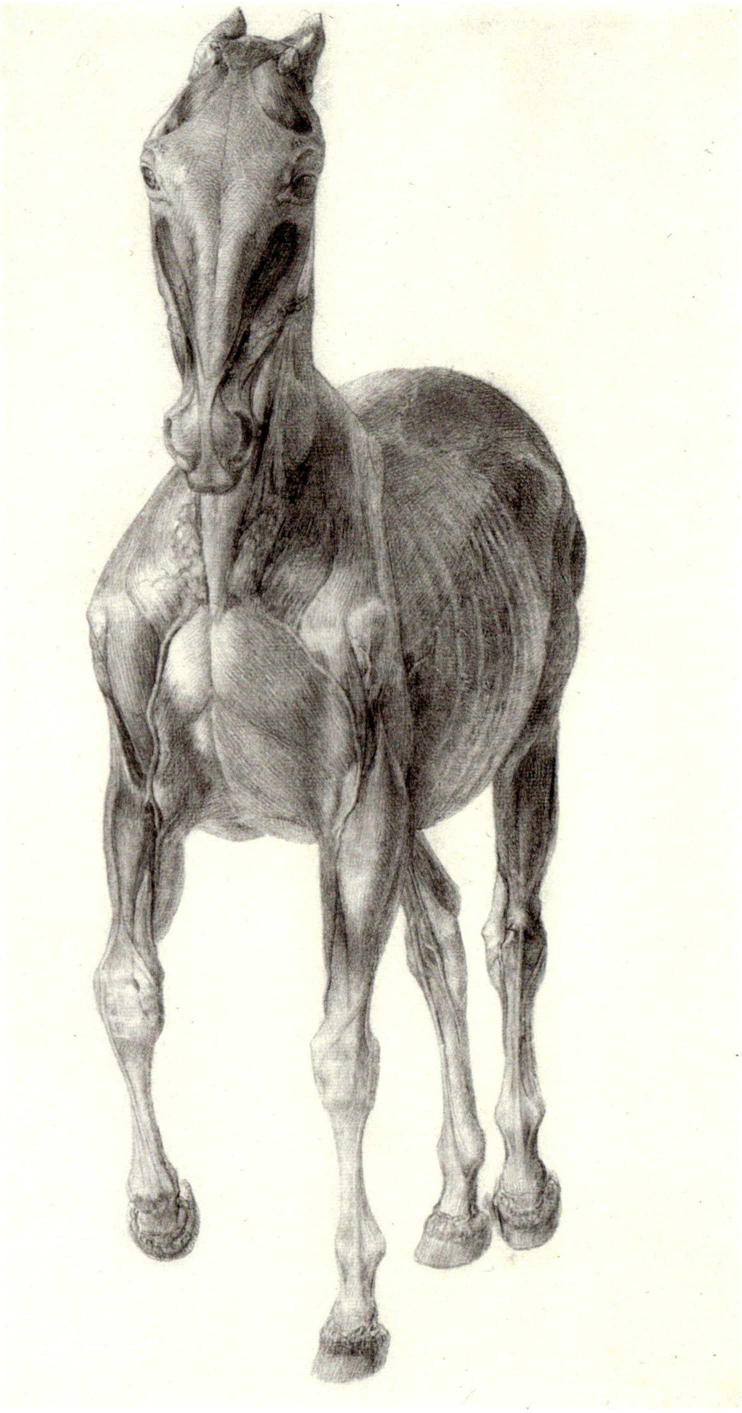

12

Finished study for 'The Seventh Anatomical Table of the Muscles ... of the Horse'

Black chalk, 35.9 x 18.3 cm
London, Royal Academy of Arts, Inv. no. 03/5710 (RA 13)

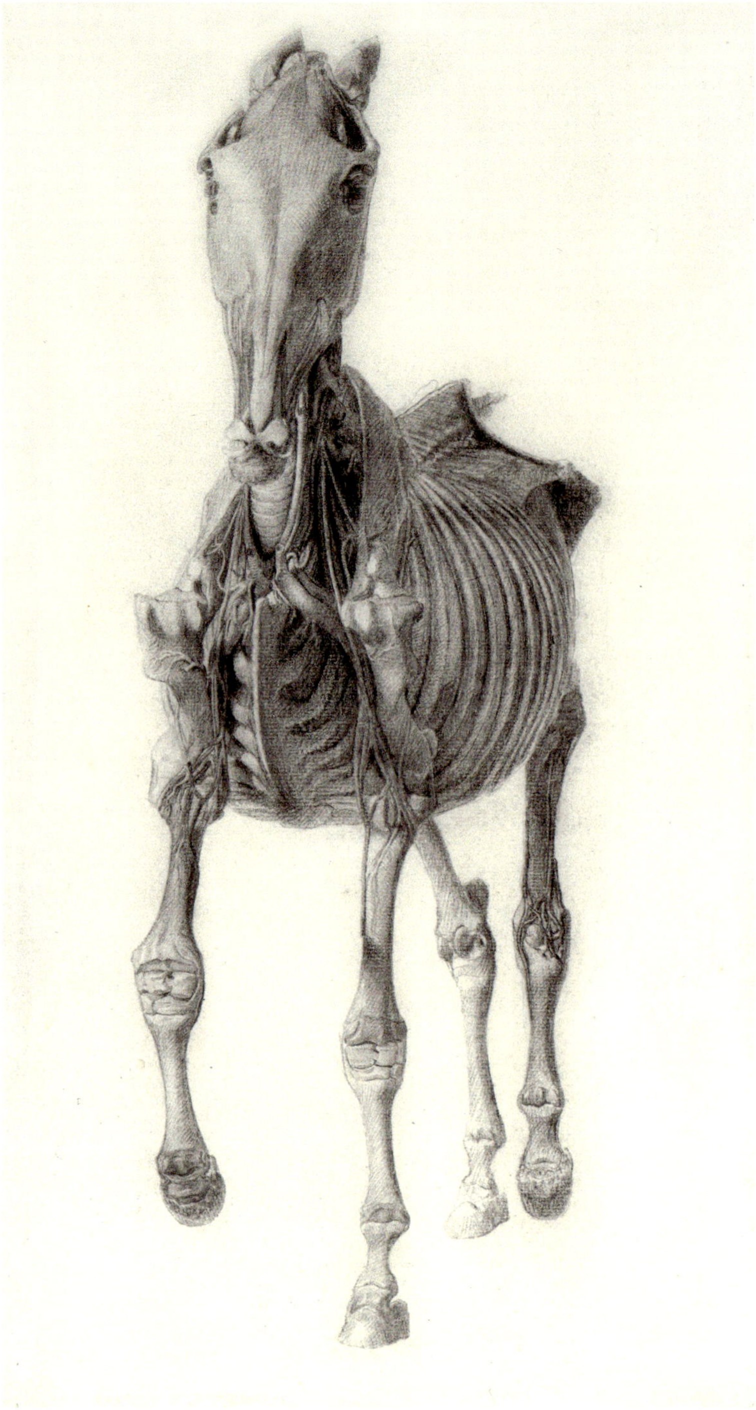

13

Finished study for 'The Tenth Anatomical Table of the Muscles ... of the Horse'

Pencil, 35.5 x 19.5 cm
London, Royal Academy of Arts, Inv. no. 03/5717 (RA 17)

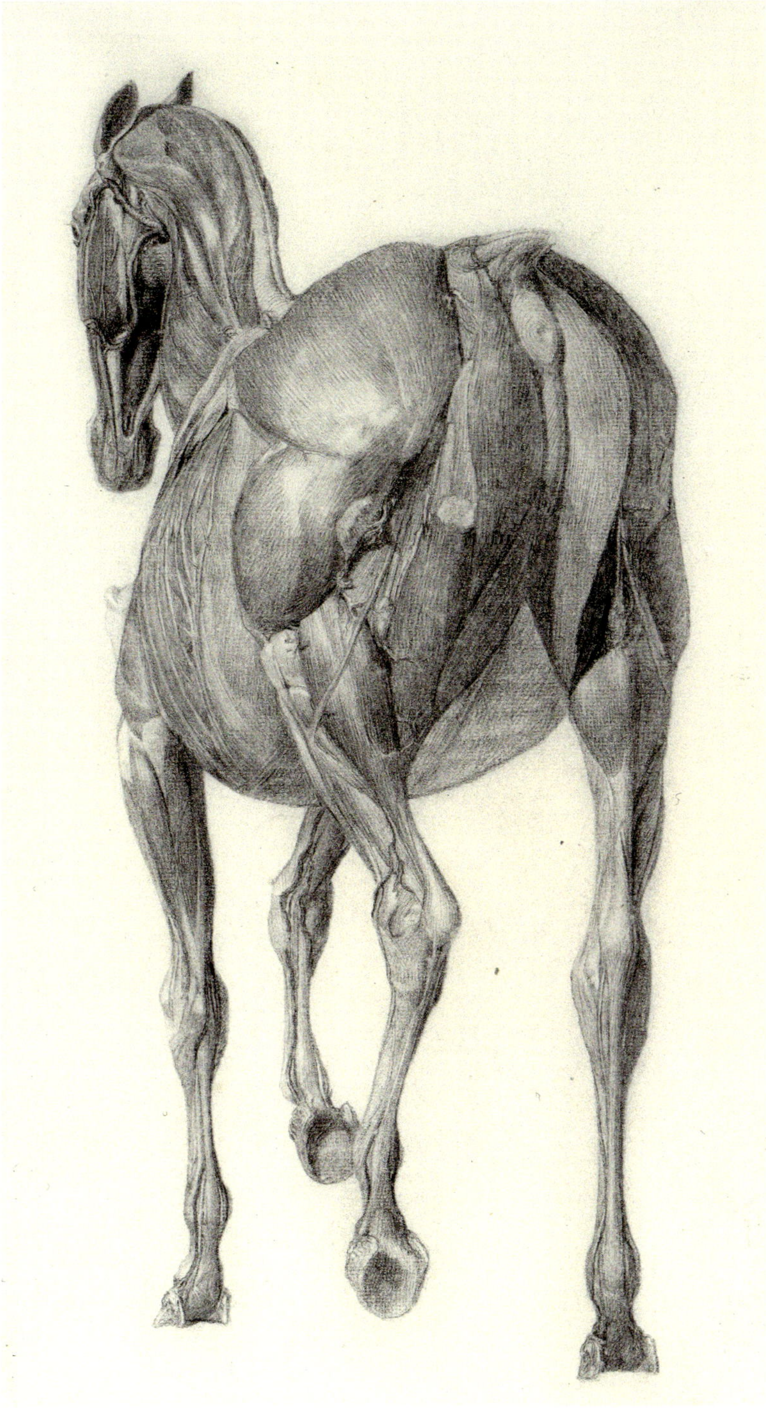

14

Finished study for 'The Thirteenth Anatomical Table of the Muscles ... of the Horse'

Pencil and black chalk, 34.7 x 18.7 cm
London, Royal Academy of Arts, Inv. no. 03/5714 (RA 7)

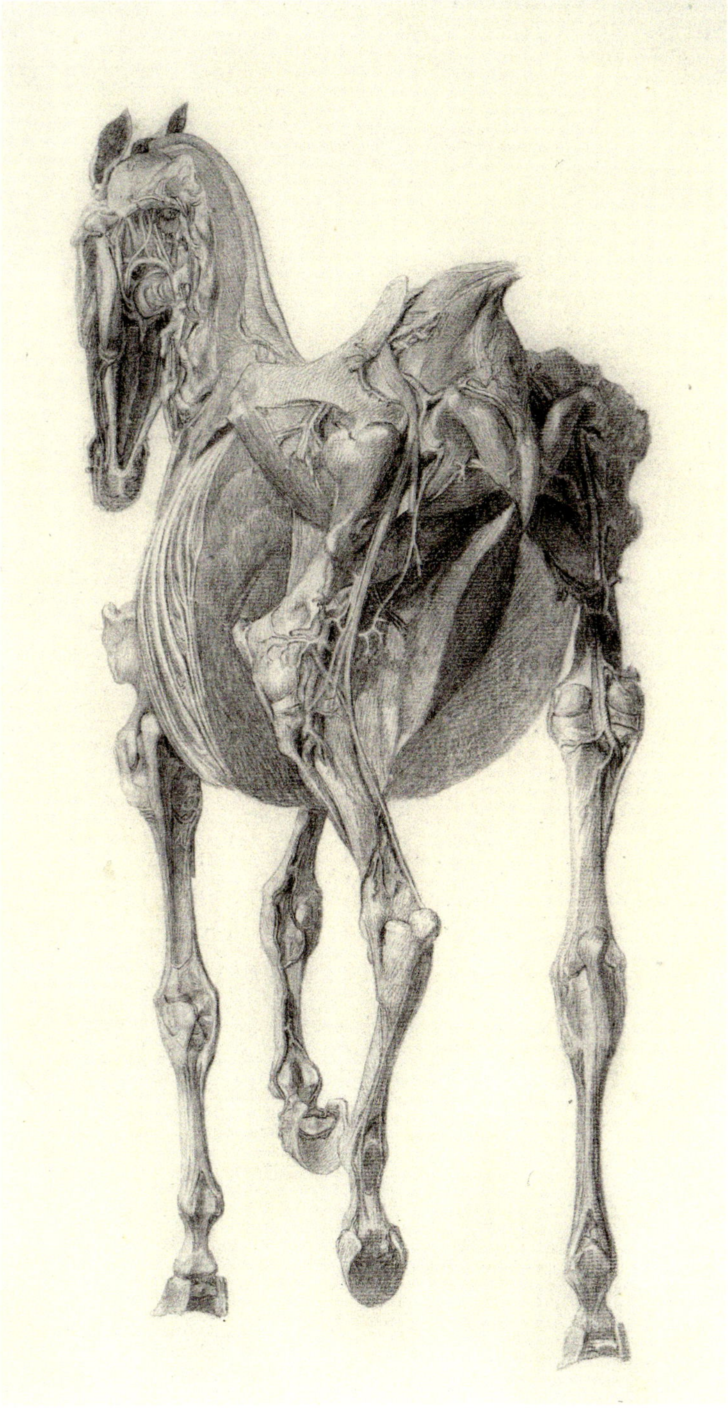

15

Finished study for 'The Fifteenth Anatomical Table of the Muscles ... of the Horse'

Pencil, 36.2 x 19.1 cm
London, Royal Academy of Arts, Inv. no. 03/5712 (RA 16)

THE ANATOMY OF THE HORSE

PAINTINGS

PRINTS

PRINTS AFTER STUBBS

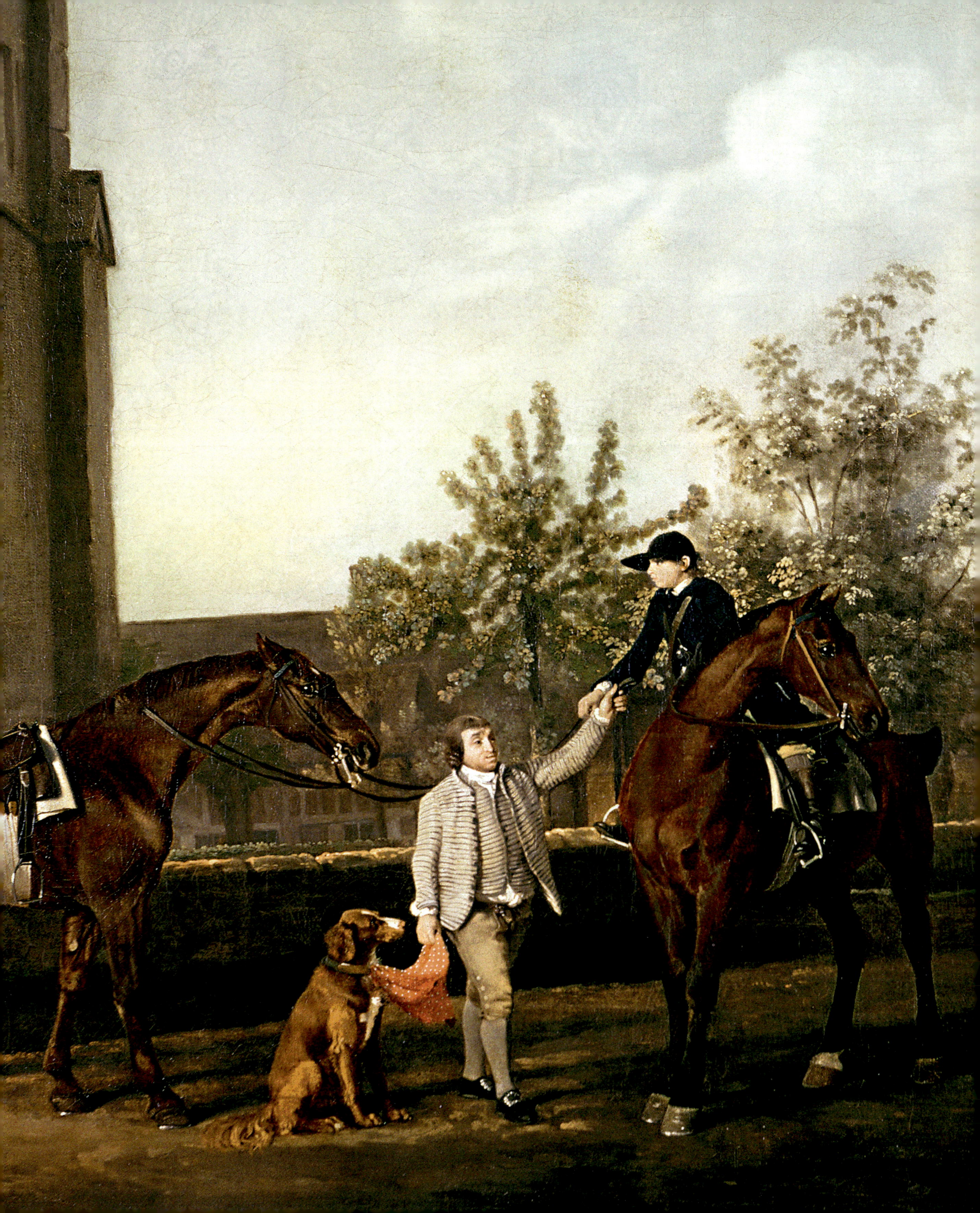

16
Self-Portrait c. 1759

Oil on copper, 14.0 x 10.8 cm
Inscribed in a different hand on verso: *Stubs*

New Haven, Yale Center for British Art, Paul Mellon Fund

George Stubbs began his career as an artist not with horses, but with portraits of people. The few works that are known from the period before his tour of Italy in 1754/55 and his study of equine anatomy in 1756/57 are all portraits of members of the landed gentry in Lincolnshire and Yorkshire, where the artist was then living. In them Stubbs is still bound by Baroque convention; yet a determination to capture the individuality of each subject is evident in his treatment of both faces and gestures, and the same determination clearly anticipates his later works.

This charming little portrait painted on copper only came to light in 1976. A comparison with later likenesses and an old inscription on the verso—admittedly not in Stubbs's own hand—suggest that it is a self-portrait. Judging by the posture and the direction of the gaze, the artist painted himself looking in the mirror. He must have been about thirty-five at the time and Judy Egerton has dated the painting between 1756 and 1759, that being the period which Stubbs devoted to dissecting and drawing horses in Horkstow in Lincolnshire. The cautiously inquiring look directed at the viewer and, of course, at the artist himself betrays the curiosity and interest in impartial observation by which Stubbs was invariably guided, including in his study of anatomy.

HWR

Lit.: Michael Jaffé, "Stubbs. A Self Portrait," in: *The Burlington Magazine* 127, 1985, p. 85 – Egerton, *George Stubbs*, 2007, no. 1

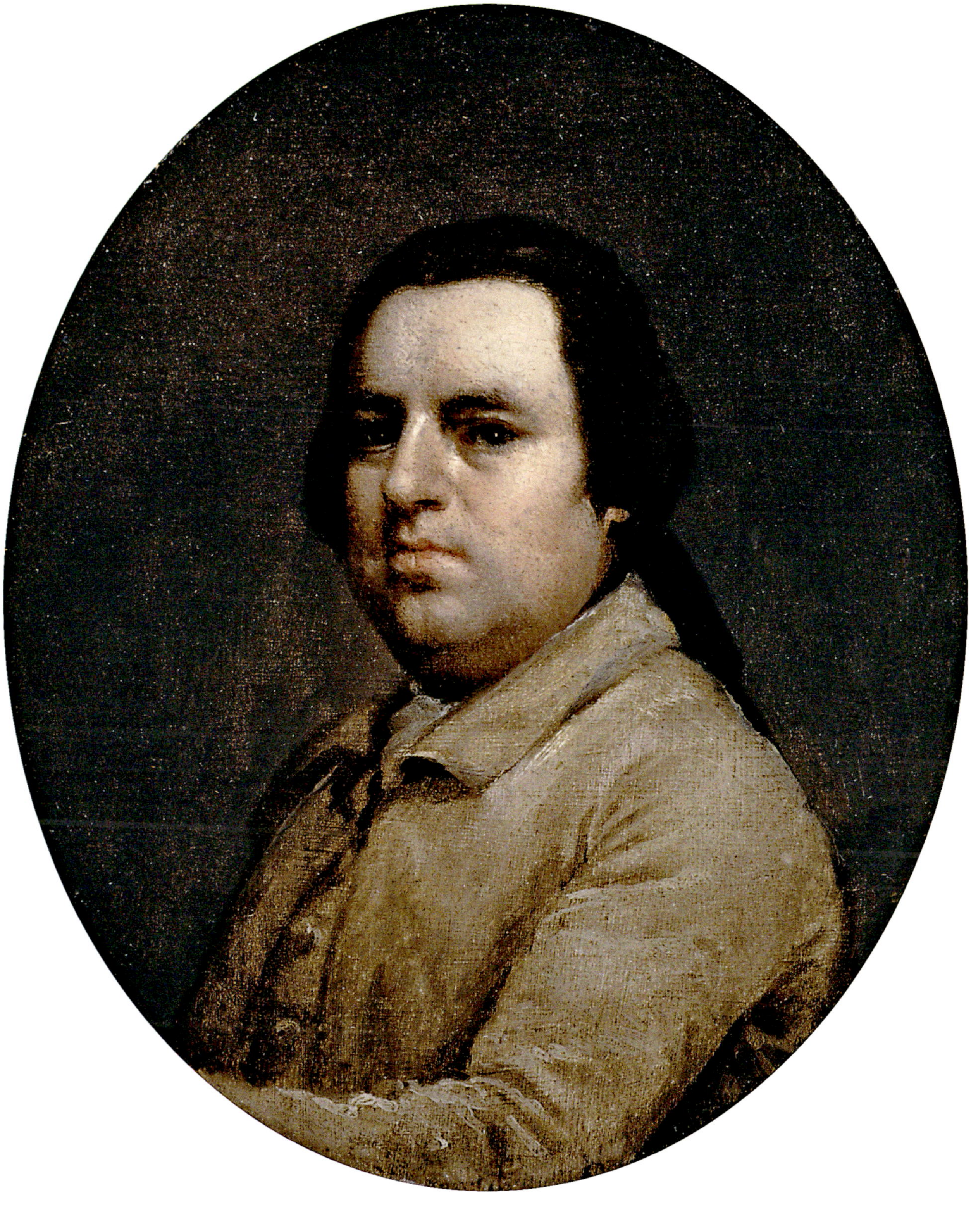

17

The Duke of Ancaster's Bay Stallion Blank with Old Parnam, his Groom c. 1761

Oil on canvas, 100.4 x 125.8 cm
Inscribed in a different hand at bottom right: *DUKE OF ANCASTER'S / BLANK*

Commissioned by Peregrine Bertie, 3rd Duke of Ancaster and Kesteven (1714–1778), Grimsthorpe, Lincolnshire – private collection

After moving to London in 1758/59, Stubbs soon made a name for himself among the horse-breeding and horse-racing nobility as an artist who knew all about equine anatomy. His ability to portray individual animals so realistically that they were instantly recognizable made him the leading exponent of British sporting art. Among his earliest and most important patrons was the Duke of Ancaster, whose famous stud at Grimsthorpe Castle produced numerous thoroughbreds.

Blank, the stallion depicted here, was foaled in 1740 at a stud belonging to the Earl of Godolphin. After a brief career as a racehorse with a win at Newmarket in 1748, he was sold to the Duke of Ancaster whom he served as a stud right up to his death in 1769. Blank is paraded in front of the viewer as if on a stage. His flailing forelegs and rearing body typify him as a spirited beast. This is unusual for Stubbs, who generally preferred to paint his horses in calm, static poses. The groom holding the stallion in check is not only named but his facial features are also rendered with painstaking detail. The almost cloudless sky, combined with the silvery green of the trees dotting the gently undulating landscape in the background, lends a sunny aspect to the work. Judy Egerton has proposed a dating of the early 1760s for this painting, of which nothing else is otherwise known.

HWR

Lit.: Exhib. Cat. *George Stubbs*, 1984/85, no. 44 – Egerton, *George Stubbs*, 2007, no. 46

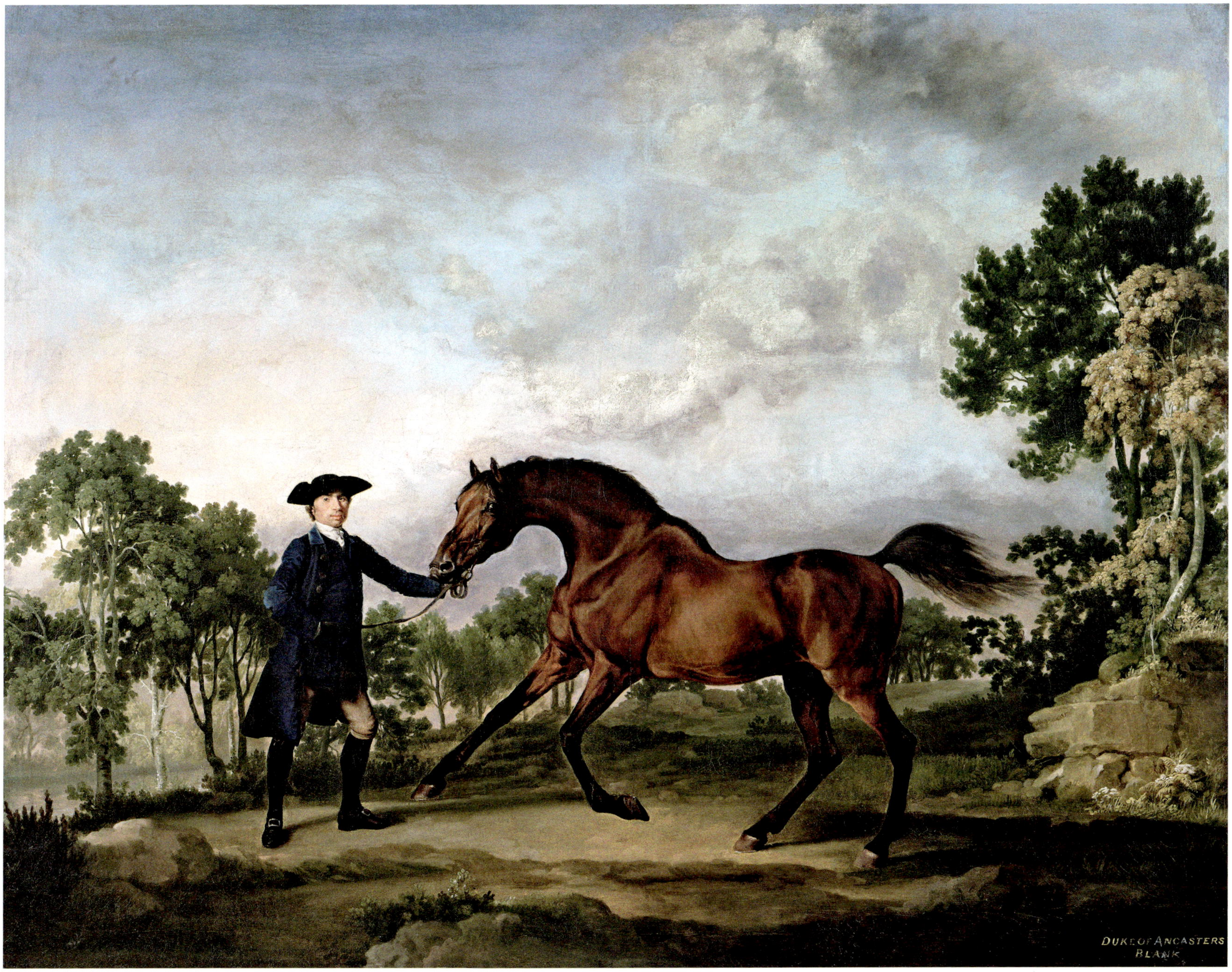
DUKE OF ANCASTERS
BLANK

18
Bay Racehorse, probably King Herod 1767 (?)

Oil on canvas, 94 x 127.5 cm

Probably commissioned by Sir John Moore, Nether Hall, Suffolk – private collection

This picture belongs to a group of masterly portraits of horses painted in the early and mid-1760s, when Stubbs took traditional horse painting to new artistic heights. The noble animal is paraded in full length before the viewer. The finely-tuned body, on which the paths of the muscles and blood vessels (the prominence of the latter probably emphasizing the known weakness in King Herod) stand out clearly in the light streaming in from the side, are proof of Stubbs's knowledge of anatomy acquired through his study of nature. The groom, clad in grey livery with a tricorn and wig, takes on a supporting role. The calm and balanced composition is bisected across the middle by the line of the horizon, while an expansive coastal landscape with a gently undulating coastline can be made out in the background.

According to David Oldrey, the horse portrayed is King Herod, one of the most famous racehorses in the history of equestrian sports and breeding. He was bred by Prince William Augustus, Duke of Cumberland (1721–1765), the third son of King George II and Princess Caroline of Brandenburg-Ansbach. Foaled in 1758, King Herod was an outstanding racehorse between 1763 and 1767. After retiring he became one of the three stallions from which every thoroughbred in the world now descends in the male line. When the duke died in 1765 both this horse and Eclipse (cat. no. 77), one of the other two founding fathers, were sold—King Herod to Sir John Moore of Nether Hall, whose livery is being worn by the groom in this painting. The same tall groom appears in a similar grey-green livery coat in other pictures of the horse after his sale and, as David Oldrey also points out, the rural background implies the date of 1767, immediately after the horse had been retired to stud in late April. Although Judy Egerton has adduced stylistic grounds for a dating of around 1761/62, similar silvery landscapes are also to be found amongst Stubbs's later works.

HWR

Lit.: Egerton, *George Stubbs*, 2007, no. 21

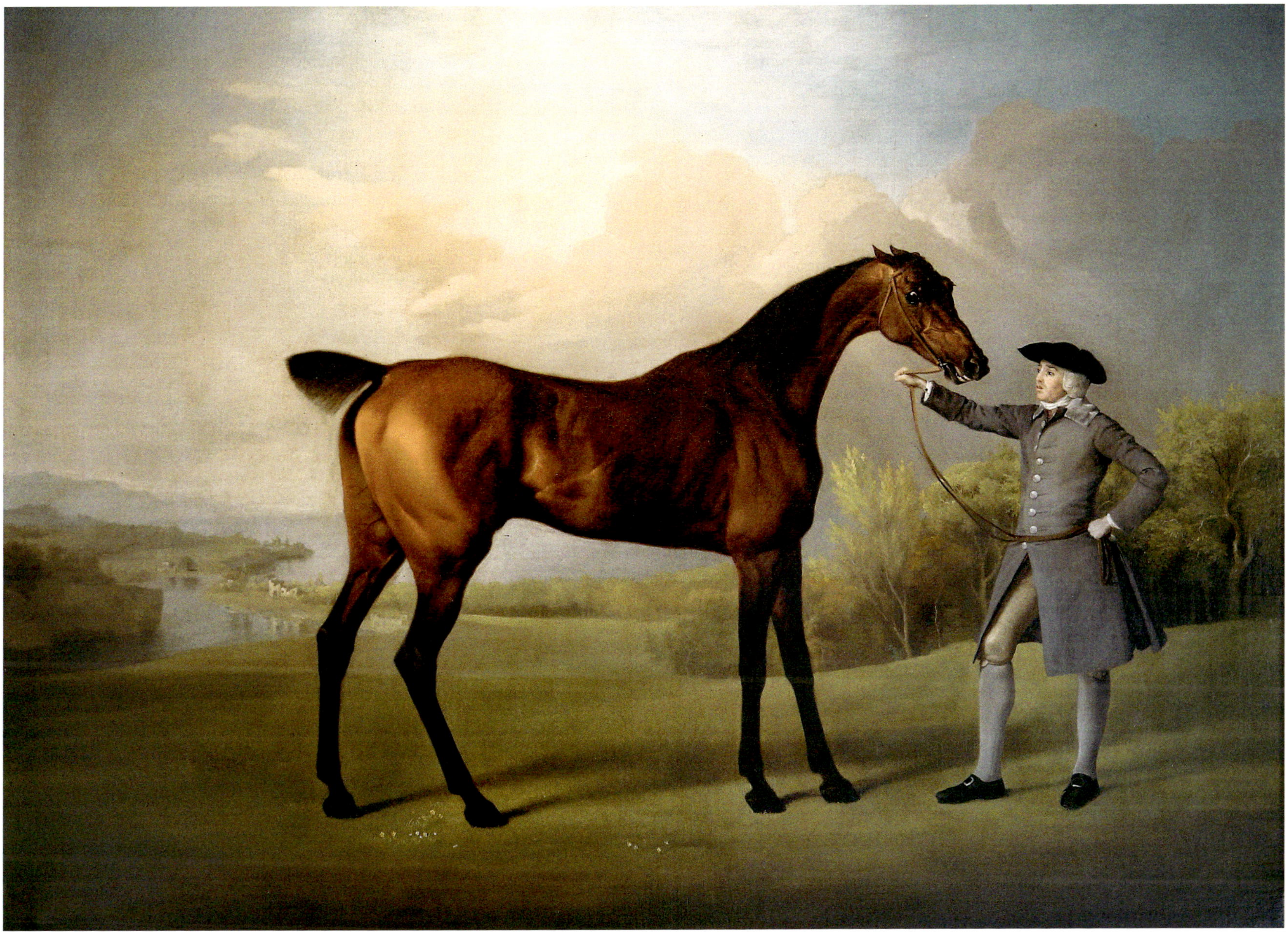

19

Whistlejacket and Two Other Stallions in the Wentworth Stud with Joshua Cobb, the Head Groom 1762

Oil on canvas, 99 x 187 cm

Commissioned by Charles Watson-Wentworth, 2nd Marquess of Rockingham (1730–1782), Wentworth Woodhouse, Yorkshire – The Trustees of the Rt. Hon. Olive, Countess Fitzwilliam's Chattels Settlement, by permission of Lady Juliet Tadgell

The five paintings that Stubbs produced for Lord Rockingham in 1762 belong to an exceedingly small group of actually documented works. We know from receipts and an entry in the Wentworth ledger that Stubbs received a sum of £192 5s "for a Picture of five brood-Mares and two foles one picture of three Stallions and one picture of a figure on Horseback one picture of five Dogs and another of one Dog with one Single Horse." Four of the five paintings are still in family hands; three of them form part of this exhibition (cat. nos. 19, 20 and 28).

This portrait of three stallions in Lord Rockingham's Wentworth stud serves as a pendant to the painting *Mares and Foals* (cat. no. 20). Unlike the larger and livelier group of mares, the male beasts are viewed from the side, lined up seriously and austerely. This frieze-like arrangement, combined with the absence of a background landscape, lends the work a compelling, monumental quality.

Depicted are Godolphin Hunter and Godolphin Colt, both of them young stallions from the Wentworth stud. Whistlejacket, marked out by his long mane and by the attention lavished on him by the groom Joshua Cobb, stands to their right. Stubbs portrayed Whistlejacket in a second, life-size portrait, which is also thought to have been painted in 1762 (p. 32, fig. 8). Although one might assume otherwise based on the figure he cuts in the 1762 portrait, Whistlejacket, who had been at Wentworth since 1759, never performed with consistent greatness on the racetrack.

HWR

Lit.: H. F. Constantine, "Lord Rockingham and Stubbs. Some New Documents," in: *The Burlington Magazine* 95, 1953, pp. 236–38 – Exhib. Cat. *George Stubbs*, 1984/85, no. 33 – Exhib. Cat. *Stubbs and the Horse*, 2004/05, no. 38 – Egerton, *George Stubbs*, 2007, no. 31

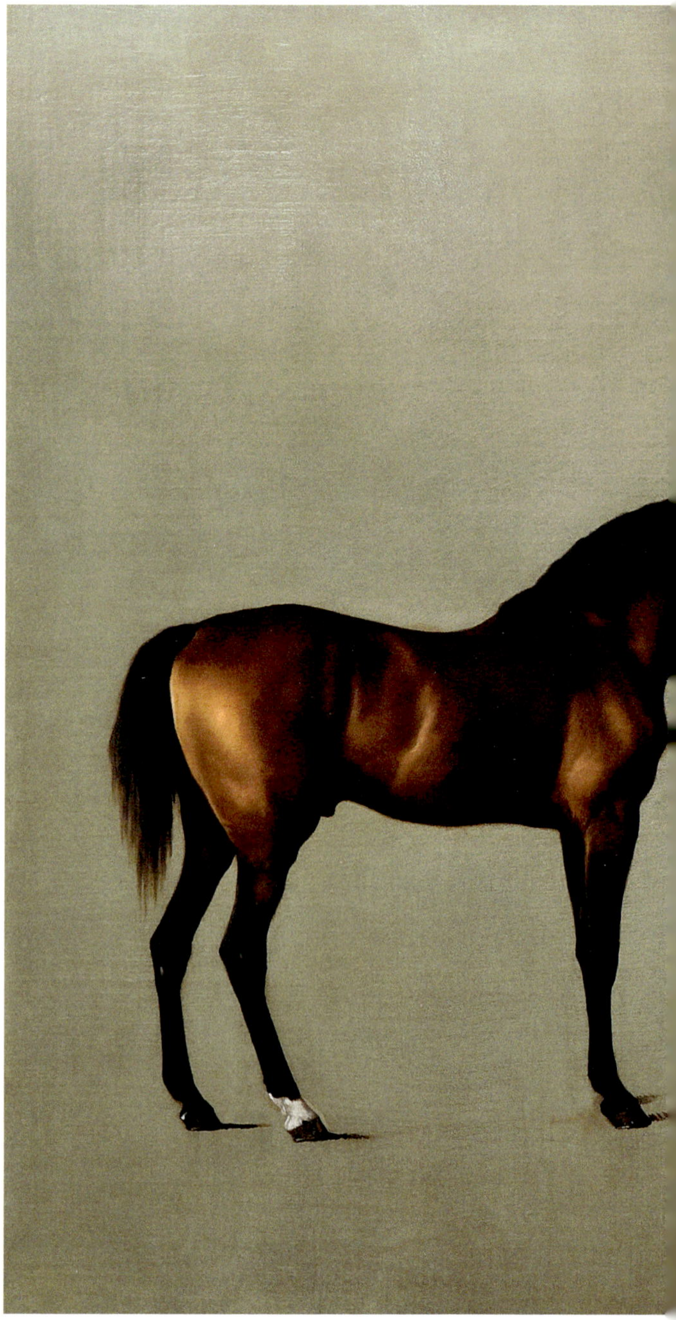

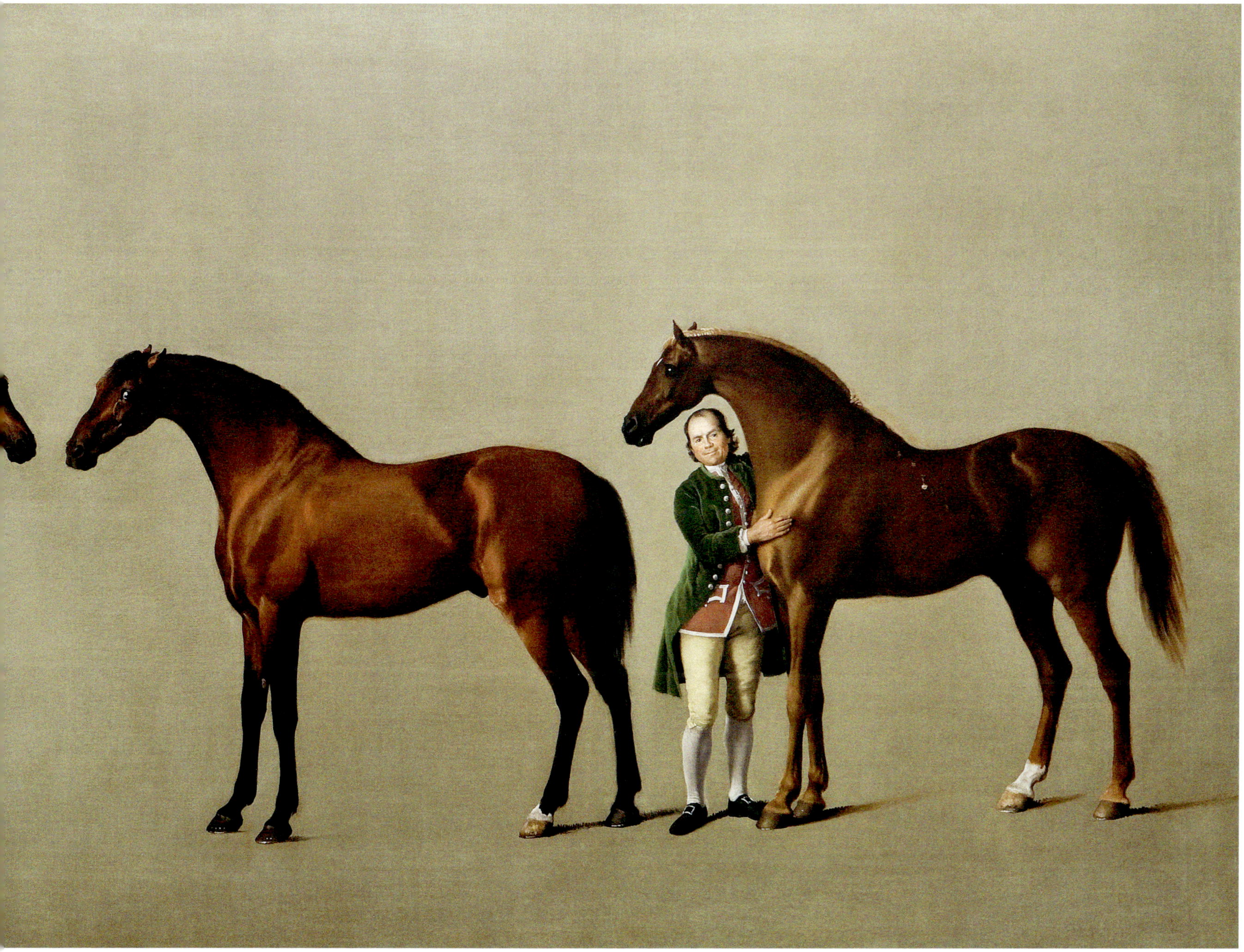

20

Mares and Foals 1762

Oil on canvas, 99 x 190.5 cm

Commissioned by Charles Watson-Wentworth, 2nd Marquess of Rockingham (1730–1782), Wentworth Woodhouse, Yorkshire – The Trustees of the Rt. Hon. Olive, Countess Fitzwilliam's Chattels Settlement, by permission of Lady Juliet Tadgell

The painting *Mares and Foals* shows five brood-mares and two foals in a seemingly casual grouping which, on closer inspection, turns out to be an artfully balanced composition. The beasts are viewed either from the side, obliquely from behind, or from the front, the anatomical splendour of their appearance being just as masterfully handled as the foreshortening required by the different angles. The work derives much of its understated, classicistic elegance from the background. This is an almost monochrome foil rendered in oscillating shades of brown and ochre and vitalized by just enough shading to bring out the animals in all of their plasticity. The painting belonged to the interior of Wentworth Woodhouse, as did the remarkable collection of sculptures which Lord Rockingham had begun amassing after his tour of Italy in 1756–58. Surrounded by sculptures both ancient and modern, Stubbs's contemporary horse portraits must have acquired an almost sculptural presence of their own.

Lord Rockingham, who as leader of the Whigs twice served briefly as Prime Minister (in 1765/66 and 1782), ran Wentworth Woodhouse in Yorkshire as a model estate, making full use of innovative farming methods. The stud with stables which he had built for him by John Carr in 1768 became famous as an architecturally accomplished and self-contained part of the demesne. The portrait of himself by Joshua Reynolds, Stubbs's portraits of his finest horses, and his inherited Palladian mansion, which is reproduced in three plates of volume IV of *Vitruvius Britannicus* (1739), should be very much understood as a unity that articulated 'enlightened nobility'. After the sale of Wentworth Woodhouse in 1948 following the death of the 8th Earl Fitzwilliam the pictures were removed to another location and the power of this statement compromised for ever.

HWR

Lit.: Exhib. Cat. *George Stubbs*, 1984/85, no. 88 – Exhib. Cat. *Stubbs and the Horse*, 2004/05, no. 37 – Blake, *George Stubbs and the Wide Creation*, 2005, pp. 147 f. – Egerton, *George Stubbs*, 2007, no. 30

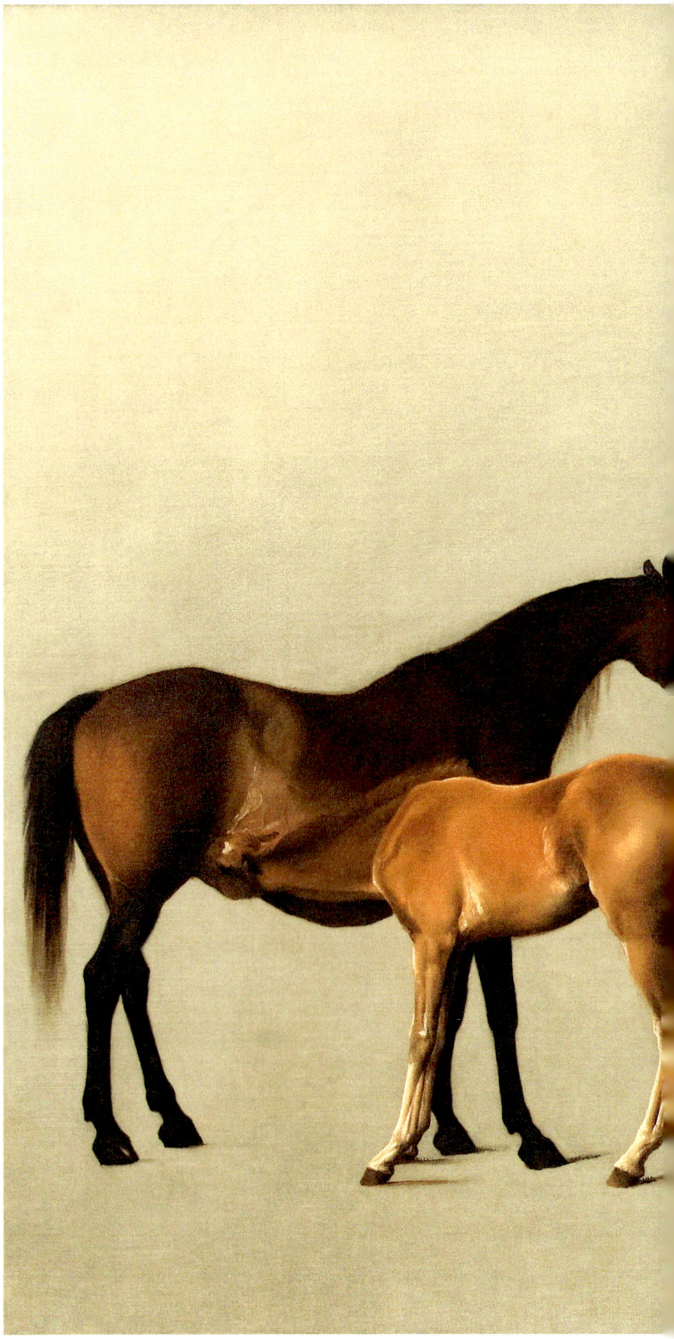

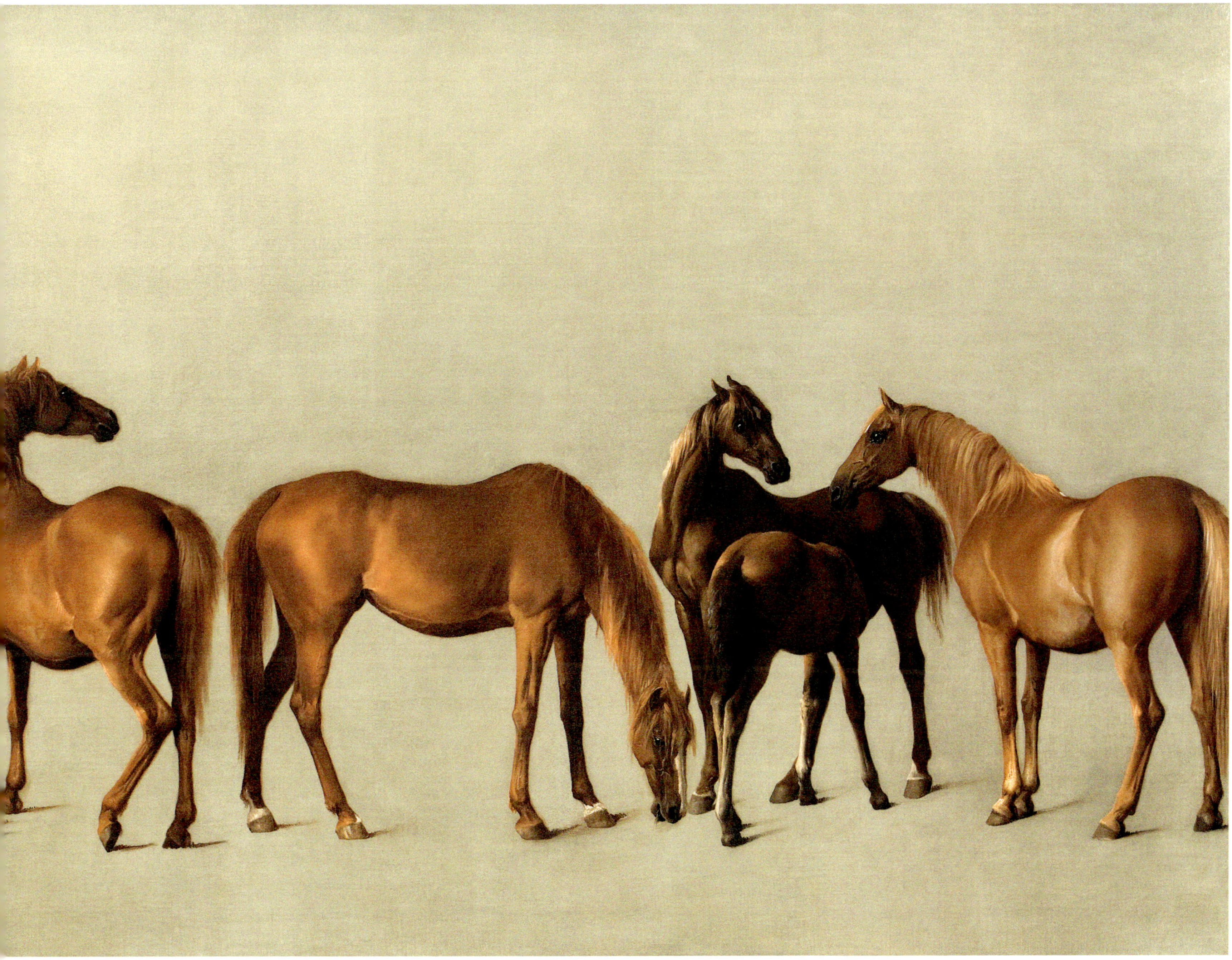

21

Mares and Foals in a River Landscape c. 1763–65

Oil on canvas, 101.6 x 161.9 cm

Probably commissioned by George Brodrick, 3rd Viscount Midleton (1730–1765), Peper Harow, Surrey – London, Tate (purchased with assistance from the Pilgrim Trust 1959)

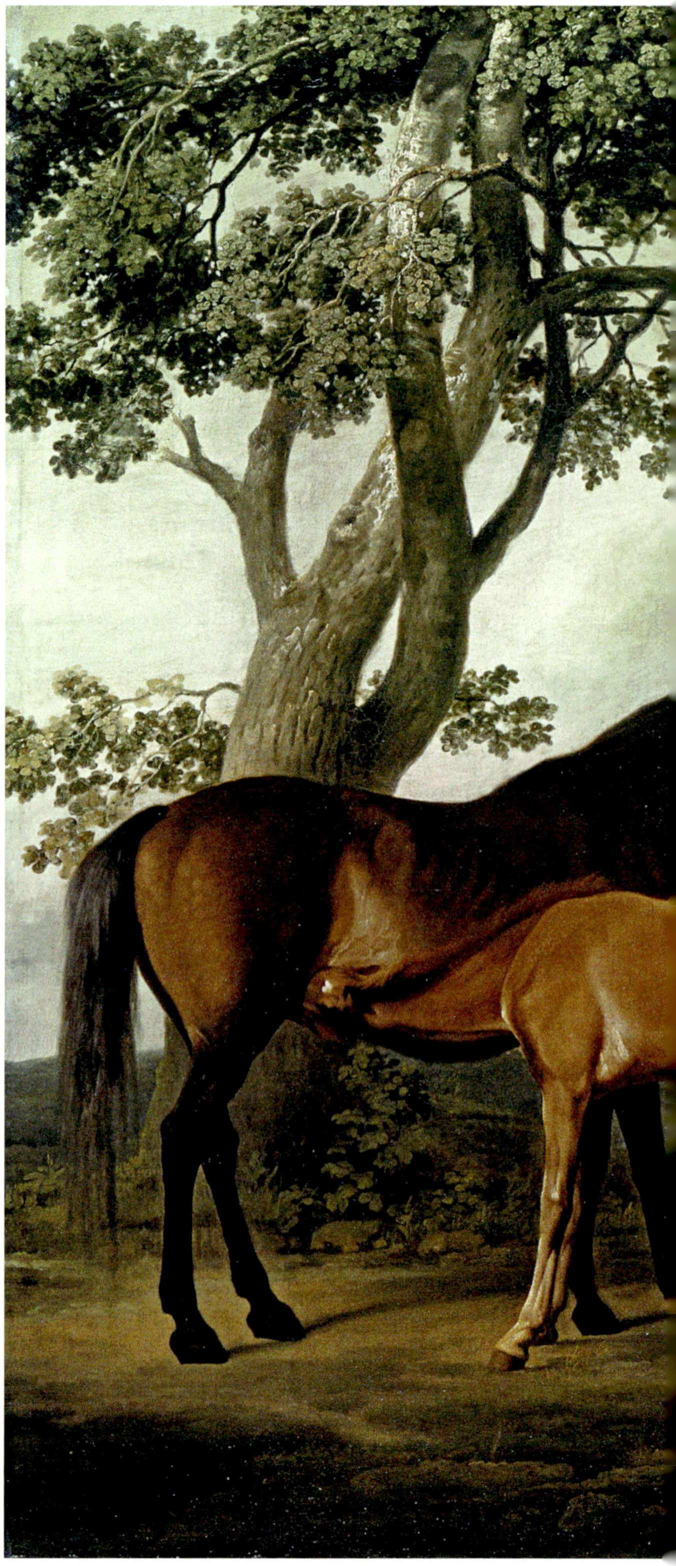

The painting is a variant of Lord Rockingham's *Mares and Foals* (cat. no. 20), of which the left and right groups are reproduced here, albeit with the mare on the right depicted as a grey horse in this work. Unlike the earlier version, this painting portrays the horses against a background landscape with a huge tree on the left, the branches of which splay out over the animals like a parasol, and a park with a tree-lined river on the right.

The painting belonged to the family of Viscount, later Earl, Midleton and was commissioned by George Brodrick, 3rd Viscount Midleton, who sat in the House of Commons for the Whigs from 1754 to 1765. Having decided to modernize his Peper Harow estate in Surrey, he engaged Lancelot 'Capability' Brown to landscape it in 1762/63 and had a Palladian mansion erected three years later, designed by William Chambers. The Viscount's premature death shortly after the work on Peper Harow House began did not prevent its completion. Like two other works by Stubbs, the painting could well have been purchased for the new house, where in a photograph taken in 1925 it can be seen hanging above the mantelpiece of the drawing room.

'Mares and Foals' was Stubbs's most successful horse motif alongside the 'horse-and-lion' groups. In the course of the 1760s, he created nearly a dozen variations on this theme, all of them for patrons of note, such as Lord Bolingbroke, Lord Rockingham, the Duke of Grafton, Lord Grosvenor and the Duke of Cumberland. A print of one of them by Benjamin Green (cat. no. 67) helped to disseminate the motif.

HWR

Lit.: Exhib. Cat. *George Stubbs*, 1984/85, no. 89 – Exhib. Cat. *Stubbs and the Horse*, 2004/05, no. 43 – Egerton, *George Stubbs*, 2007, no. 62

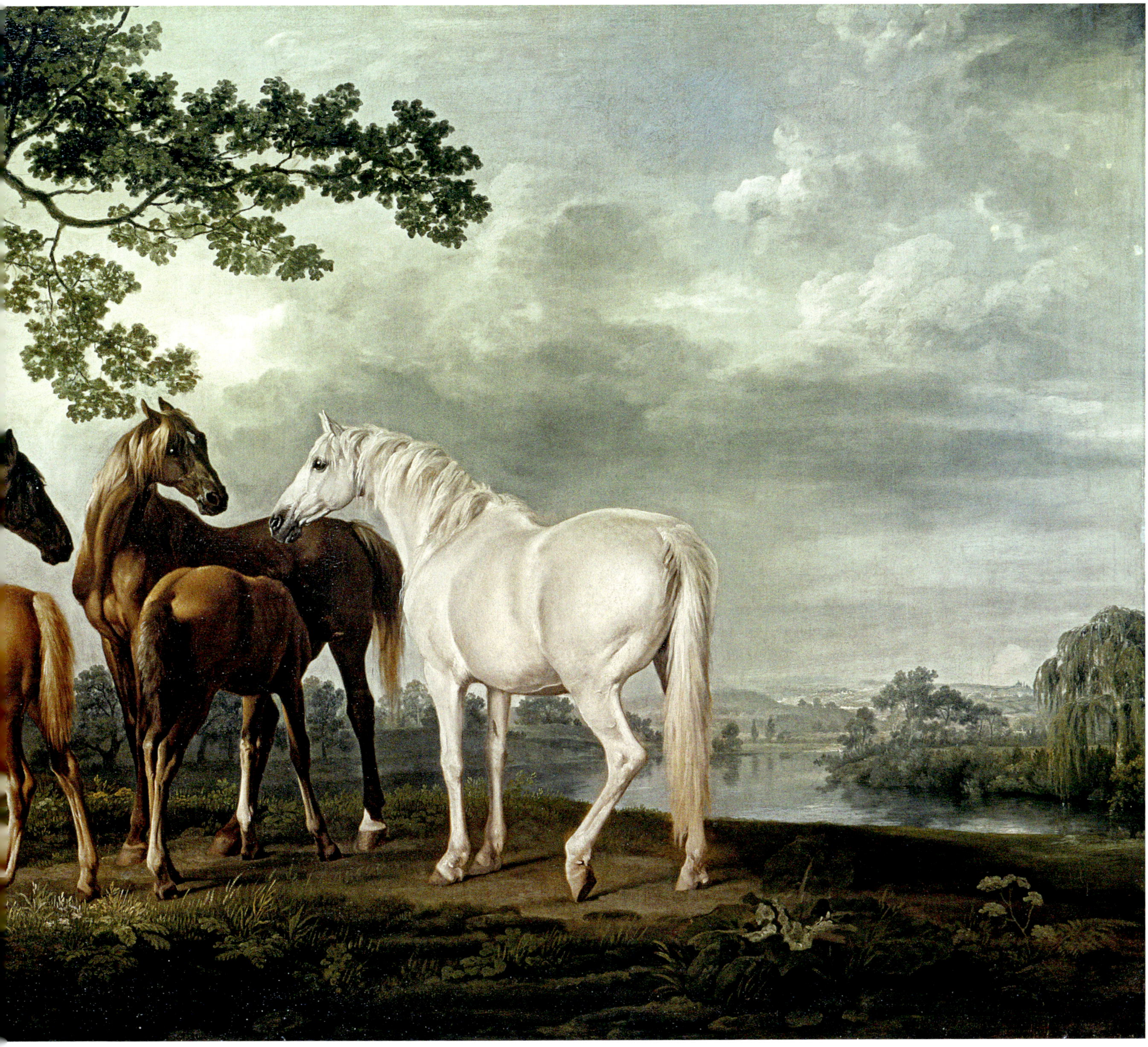

22

Gnawpost and Two Other Colts 1768

Oil on canvas, 100.4 x 125.7 cm
Signed and dated at bottom centre: *Geo: Stubbs pinxit 1768*

Probably commissioned by Jenison Shafto (c. 1728–1771), West Wratting Park, Cambridgeshire – private collection

This painting of three colts in a meadow is a variation on the 'mares-and-foals' motif. The landscape does not afford any long views into the distance as the meadow is curtailed by a wood and stable at the back, while a huge tree blocks off the composition to the right. One of the foals, aptly named Gnawpost, is depicted gnawing at the bark of the tree. Stubbs painted another version of this work in 1793 for the Turf Gallery, a gallery showing portraits of the most famous horses in the history of racing (Egerton no. 316). This later version remained in the possession of the artist himself and was advertised in the auction catalogue of his estate as "Three portraits in an interesting landscape, one of a Colt, named Gnaw Post, and two others—beautifully painted throughout and highly finished."

Foaled in 1767, Gnawpost and the two other colts are shown here as yearlings. All three came from Jenison Shafto's stud at West Wratting near Newmarket. Gnawpost began racing at Newmarket as well as elsewhere in 1770 and won several trophies before being retired to stud. The painting was almost certainly commissioned by Jenison Shafto, an enthusiastic horse breeder, racehorse owner and speculator, who after losing a fortune in bad bets at Newmarket in 1771 took his own life. The portrait of himself he had painted by Joshua Reynolds dates from 1755.

HWR

Lit.: Egerton, *George Stubbs*, 2007, no. 93

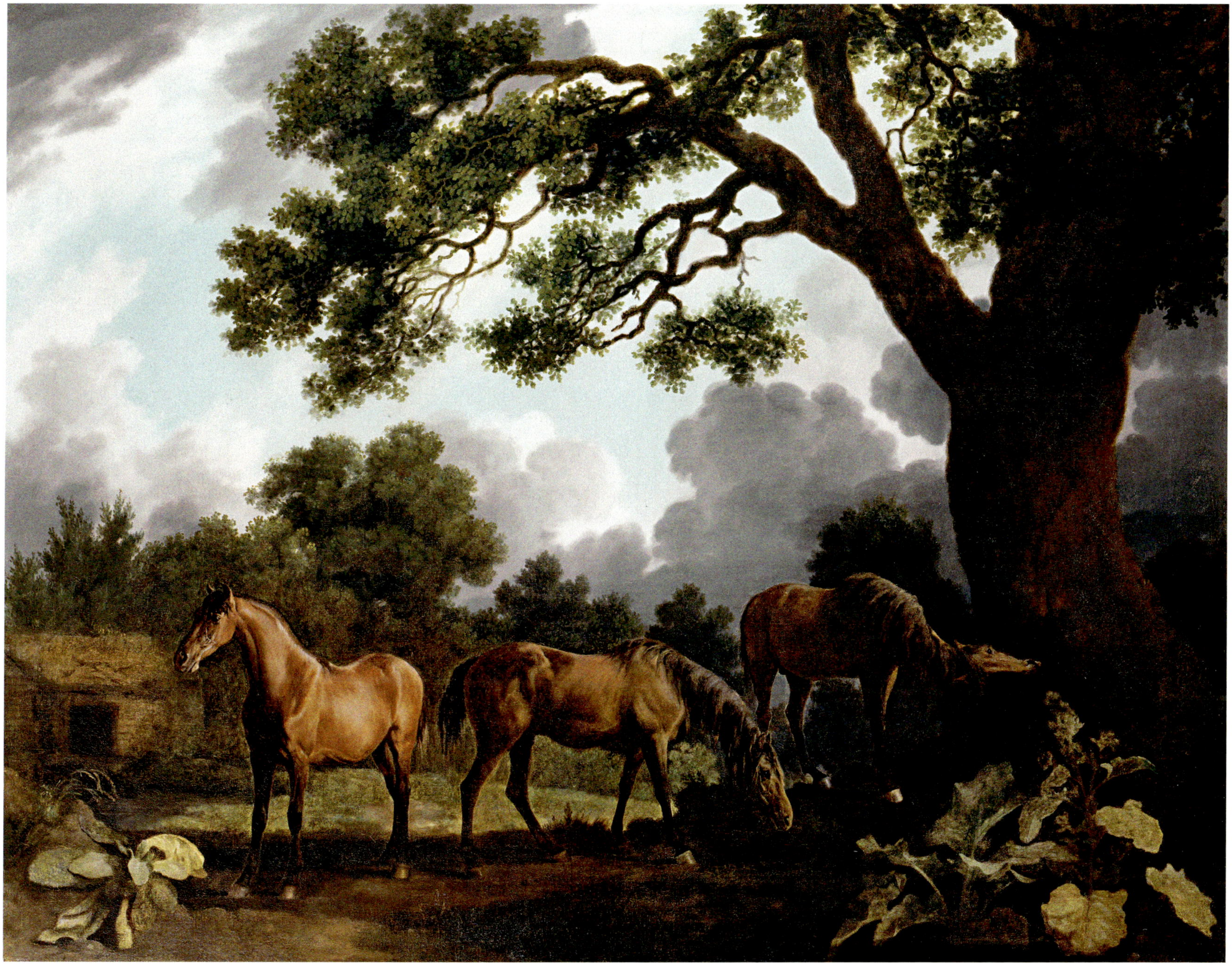

23

Jenison Shafto's Brown Horse Ascham with a Groom at Newmarket c. 1765/66

Oil on canvas, 71.2 x 104.2 cm

Probably commissioned by Jenison Shafto (c. 1728–1771), West Wratting Park, Cambridgeshire – private collection

This painting is one of the earliest horse portraits by Stubbs to show a racehorse at Newmarket. The early eighteenth century had seen the racecourse there, approximately 100 kilometres north of London in Suffolk, advance to become England's horse-racing capital. It was there, under the auspices of the Jockey Club founded in 1750, that the rules were developed that would make horse-racing one of the first competitive disciplines of modern sports. Visible in the background is the spire of St. Mary's Church, while the building on the right is the rubbing house the 'King's Stables', whose plain brick exterior makes for a curious contrast with the shimmering dark-brown coat of the superbly built horse, which is being led by the bit by his groom. Stubbs's modelling of the horse's musculature bathed in soft light recalls the drawings made to illustrate his treatise *The Anatomy of the Horse* published in 1766.

Ascham, who was foaled in Sir James Lowther's stud in 1759, had already had some success at Newmarket when he was bought by Jenison Shafto, who had a stud of his own at West Wratting near Newmarket. Shafto presumably commissioned the portrait before he sold Ascham again in 1768. After Shafto's death in 1771, both this painting and several others by Stubbs passed into the hands of Thomas Parker, the 3rd Earl of Macclesfield (1723–1795). This has led Judy Egerton to hypothesize that, like other paintings by Stubbs once owned by the notoriously indebted Shafto, it was pledged in settlement of betting debts following his death. The sale could well have been negotiated by George Lane Parker, younger brother of the Earl of Macclesfield, who was also an equestrian sports enthusiast and a founding member of the Jockey Club.

HWR

Lit.: Egerton, *George Stubbs*, 2007, no. 61

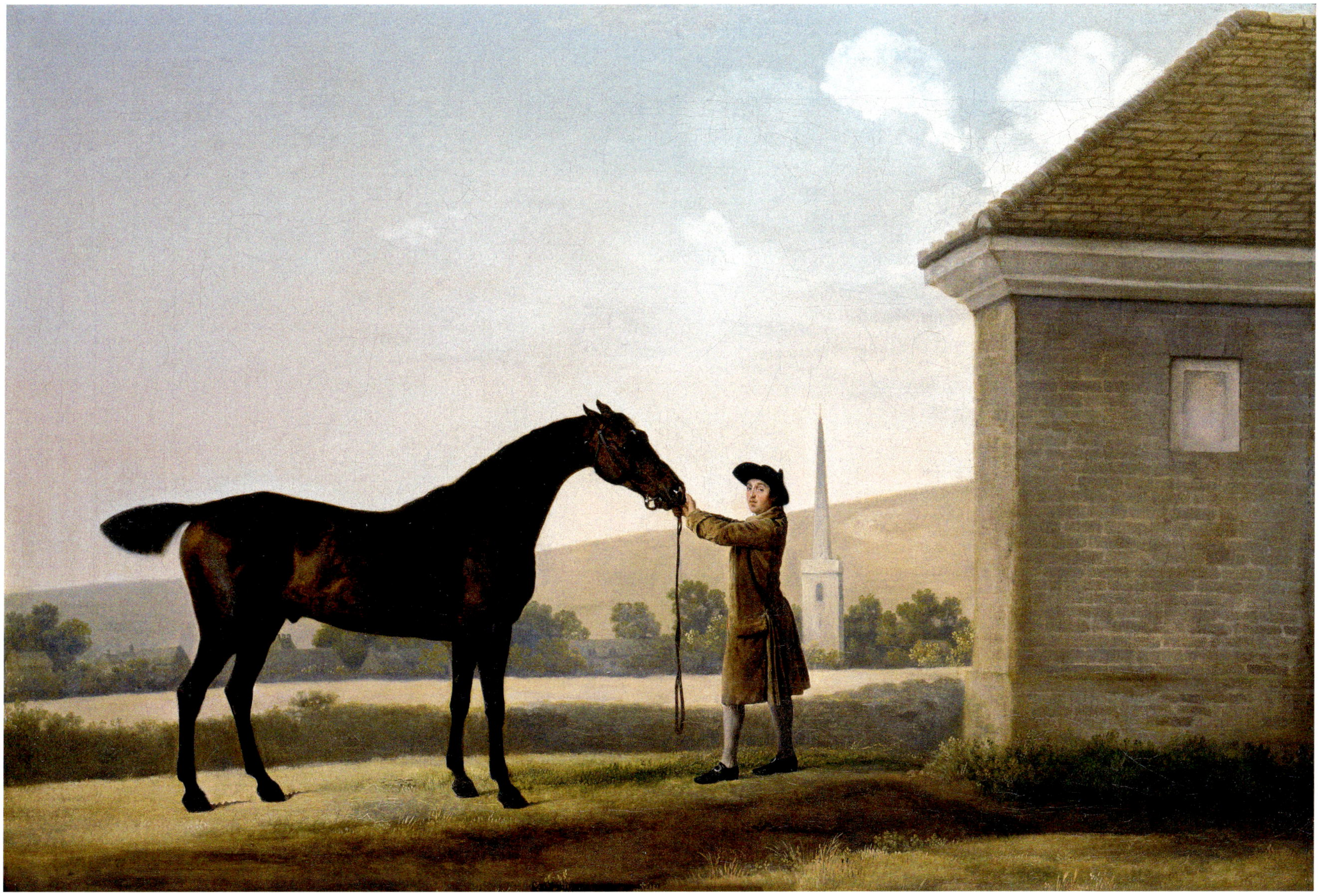

24

Newmarket Heath, with a Rubbing House c. 1765

Oil on canvas, 30.2 x 41.9 cm

1807 in the artist's estate – London, Tate (purchased 1979)

Only two pure landscapes by George Stubbs have survived and both are studies of the landscape and buildings on Newmarket Heath, the scene and centre of English thoroughbred horse-racing. They show the rubbing houses where the horses were saddled and prepared for the race and where they were rubbed dry afterwards.

Shown here is the rubbing house known as the 'King's Stables' near the finish of the four-mile-long Beacon Course. Stubbs chose to frame the scene in such a way that the simple structure—a rectangular brick building with windows and doors punctuating its long side—would only be glimpsed on the canvas's left edge. Visible in the background are more stables, the 'King's Stand' and, in the distance further to the right, the 'Duke's Stand'.

The viewpoint is daring, but carefully chosen and prescient. Clearly this is not a sketch painted in situ but rather an assiduously composed landscape that was most likely executed in the studio. That Stubbs used the same study virtually unaltered for his large painting *Gimcrack on Newmarket Heath* (p. 14, fig. 3) supports this supposition. The rubbing house, which all racing enthusiasts would have instantly recognized as the one on Newmarket Heath, serves both as a landmark and as a source of authenticity and is thus rendered with the same meticulous attention to detail as Stubbs was wont to lavish on his horses, grooms and riders. More than thirty years later, he used the same study yet again as the background for one of his most famous paintings, *Hambletonian, Rubbing Down* of 1800 (p. 19, fig. 7).

HWR

Lit.: Exhib. Cat. *George Stubbs*, 1984/85, no. 52 – Egerton, *George Stubbs*, 2007, no. 68 – *George Stubbs A.R.A, Gimcrack on Newmarket Heath*, Auct. Cat. Christie's, London 2011, p. 26

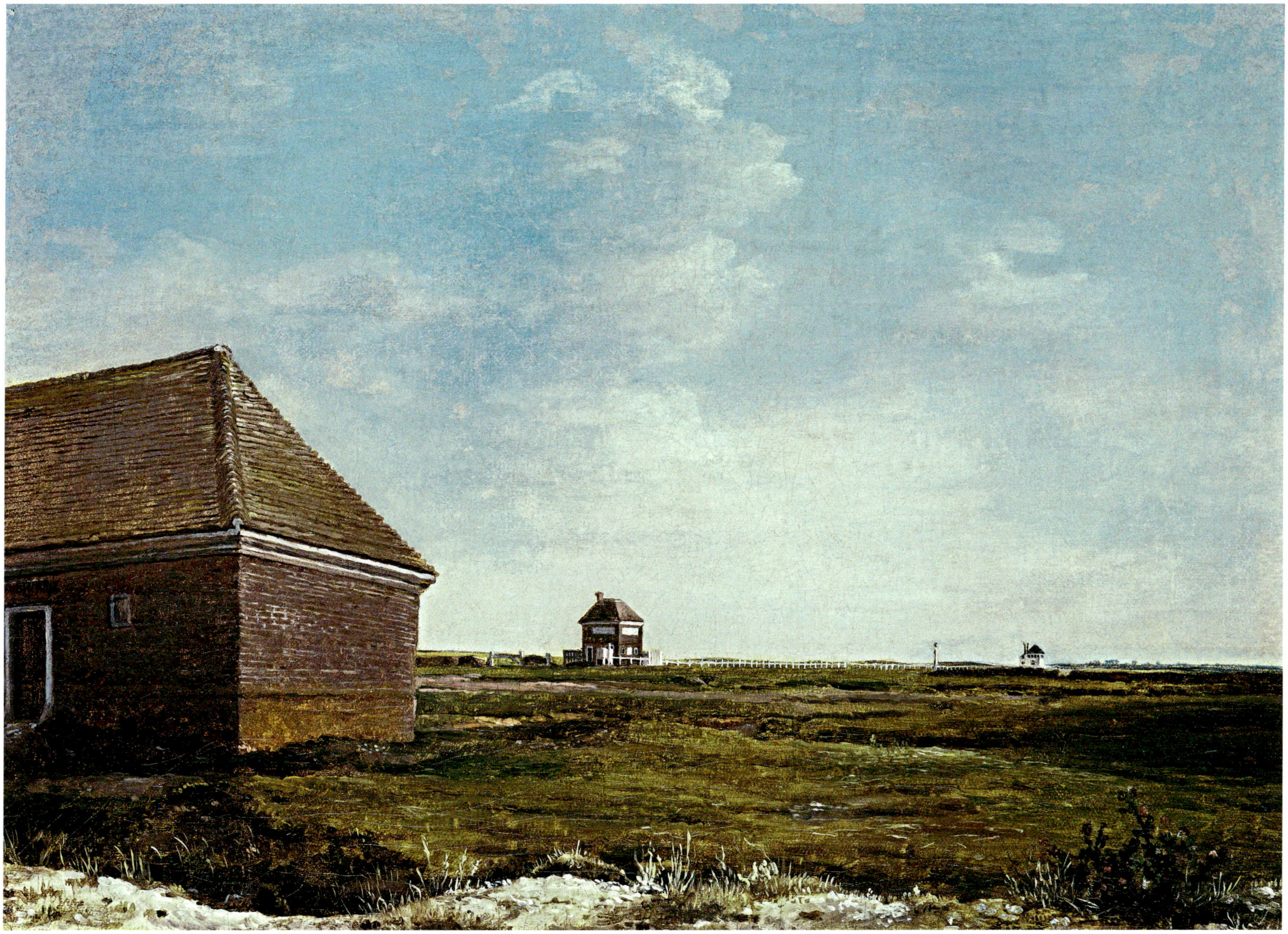

25

Turf, with Jockey up, at Newmarket c. 1766

Oil on canvas, 96.5 x 124.5 cm
Inscribed in a different hand at bottom left: *Turf*

Commissioned by Frederick St. John, 2nd Viscount Bolingbroke (1732–1787) –
New Haven, Yale Center for British Art, Paul Mellon Collection

The brown stallion in this painting is portrayed facing left, perfectly centred. The horizon is so low that both horse and jockey are thrown into relief against the pale blue sky. The scene is circumscribed and the stage set by two architectural elements, one of them obtrusive, the other barely noticeable at all. While the windowless, monolithic stable wall at right contrasts sharply with the finely modelled figure of the horse, the element opposite it, close to the left edge of the canvas, is a mere post such as was used to stake out the racecourse. The post is positioned so as to leave just enough room for a tiny strip of landscape to the left of it. It is in details such as these that Stubbs's intuitive sense of tension and balance is most apparent. Although the painting seems serene and immobile, the building on the right and the expansiveness of the racecourse on the left, towards which the horse is looking, invest the composition with a latent dynamism.

The horse is Turf, a stallion born in 1760 who raced successfully at Newmarket until sustaining an injury in 1767. His greatest triumph was in 1766 when he beat King Herod to the finish. Turf's owner was Lord Bolingbroke, who probably commissioned this portrait in honour of that win.

It is in his greatest horse portraits such as this one that Stubbs's superiority over his predecessors and contemporaries is most clearly in evidence. There is nothing at all superficial about his subtle, finely drawn and anatomically precise depiction. Both intense and keenly observed, it expresses Stubbs's own estimation of the horse as a paragon of beauty, power and strength, and as a creature in which spirit and character coexist in perfect harmony with physical elegance and grace.

HWR

Lit.: Exhib. Cat. *George Stubbs*, 1984/85, no. 57 – Exhib. Cat. *George Stubbs in the Collection of Paul Mellon*, 1999/2000, no. 8 – Exhib. Cat. *Stubbs and the Horse*, 2004/05, no. 46 – Egerton, *George Stubbs*, 2007, no. 72

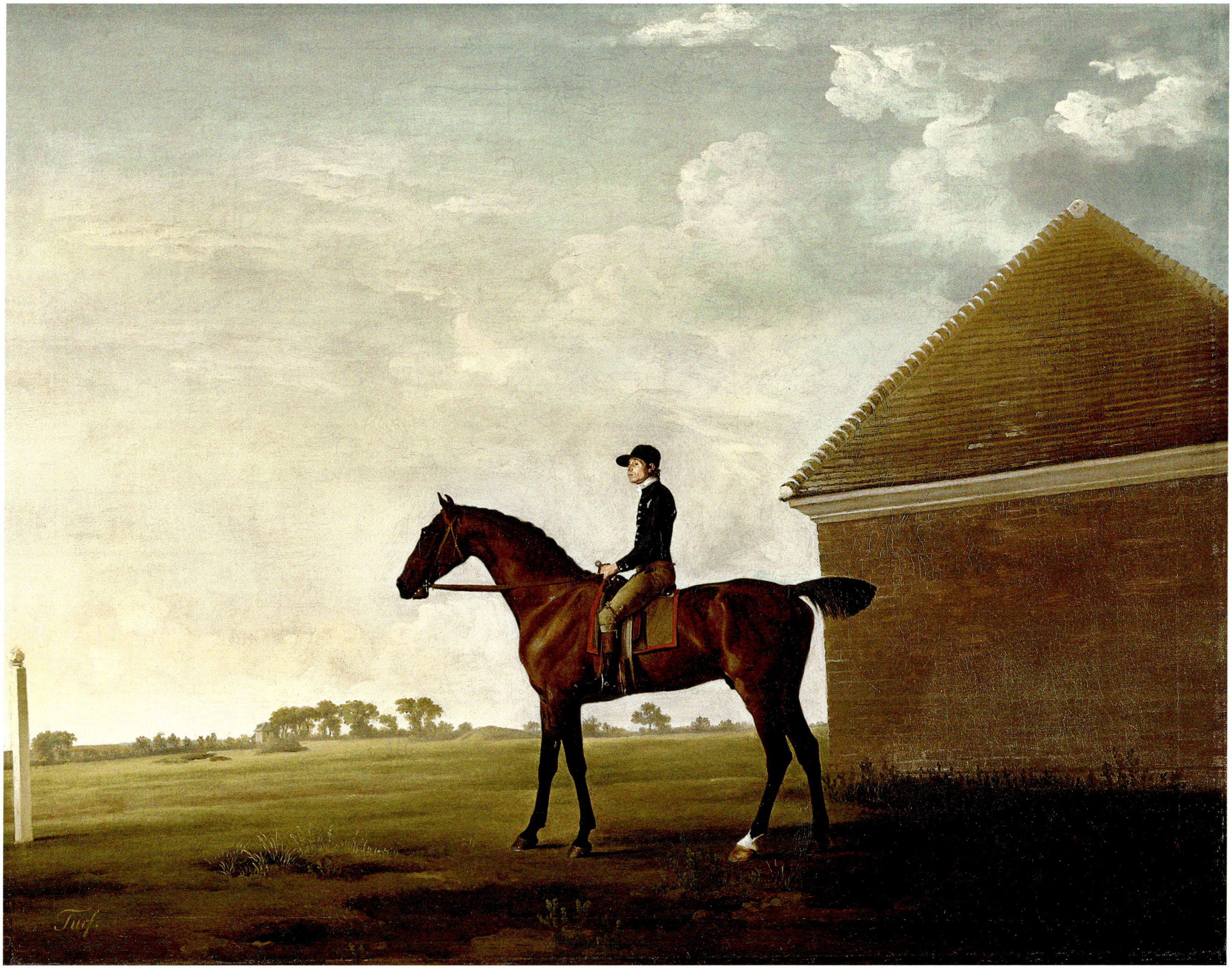
Turf.

26

Otho at Newmarket, with John Larkin up 1768

Oil on canvas, 101.3 x 127.0 cm
Signed and dated at bottom right: *Geo: Stubbs pinxit / 1768*;
inscribed in a different hand underneath the horse: *Otho*

Commissioned by John Fitzpatrick, 2nd Earl of Upper Ossory (1745–1818), Ampthill Park, Bedfordshire – London, Tate (presented by Paul Mellon through the British Sporting Art Trust 1979)

Despite its almost identical format, the horse and rider in this work are larger than in *Turf* (cat. no. 25). The stallion Otho is depicted at rest, facing right, with a jockey sitting upright in the saddle. The setting of Newmarket Heath is similar to that in the portrait of Ascham which Stubbs painted for Jenison Shafto (cat. no. 23). The façade of the King's Stables looms large to the right, while the town of Newmarket and tower of St. Mary's Church are visible behind it in the distance.

Otho was a product of Richard Vernon's stud at Newmarket. Foaled in 1760, he began his successful racing career on his home turf in 1764. After suffering his first defeat against Lord Rockingham's bay Malton in 1766, he was sold to Lord Ossory, who raced him with somewhat mixed fortunes for another two years before retiring him to stud. The painting was probably commissioned by Lord Ossory—possibly to mark Otho's retirement from the racetrack.

What is striking about this horse portrait by Stubbs is his unusual handling of light, which lends the work its vitality and drama. The dark clouds that have gathered in the sky make for an ominous atmosphere and both foreground and stable are deep in shadow. Only Otho and his rider are bathed in sunshine, which throws them into sharp relief against the glowering sky. A quiet melancholy hangs over the work, which manifestly shows the horse at a time when his career at Newmarket was nearing its end. Unlike other more traditional painters of the sporting art, Stubbs does not depict the races themselves. Not even the most famous and most successful racehorses are ever shown in action; instead they are captured somewhere near the stable either immediately before or straight after a race. This lends his horse portraits their serene grandeur and puts them, in turn, on a par with human portraiture.

HWR

Lit.: Exhib. Cat. *George Stubbs*, 1984/85, no. 58 – Exhib. Cat. *George Stubbs in the Collection of Paul Mellon*, 1999/2000, no. 7 – Egerton, *George Stubbs*, 2007, no. 73

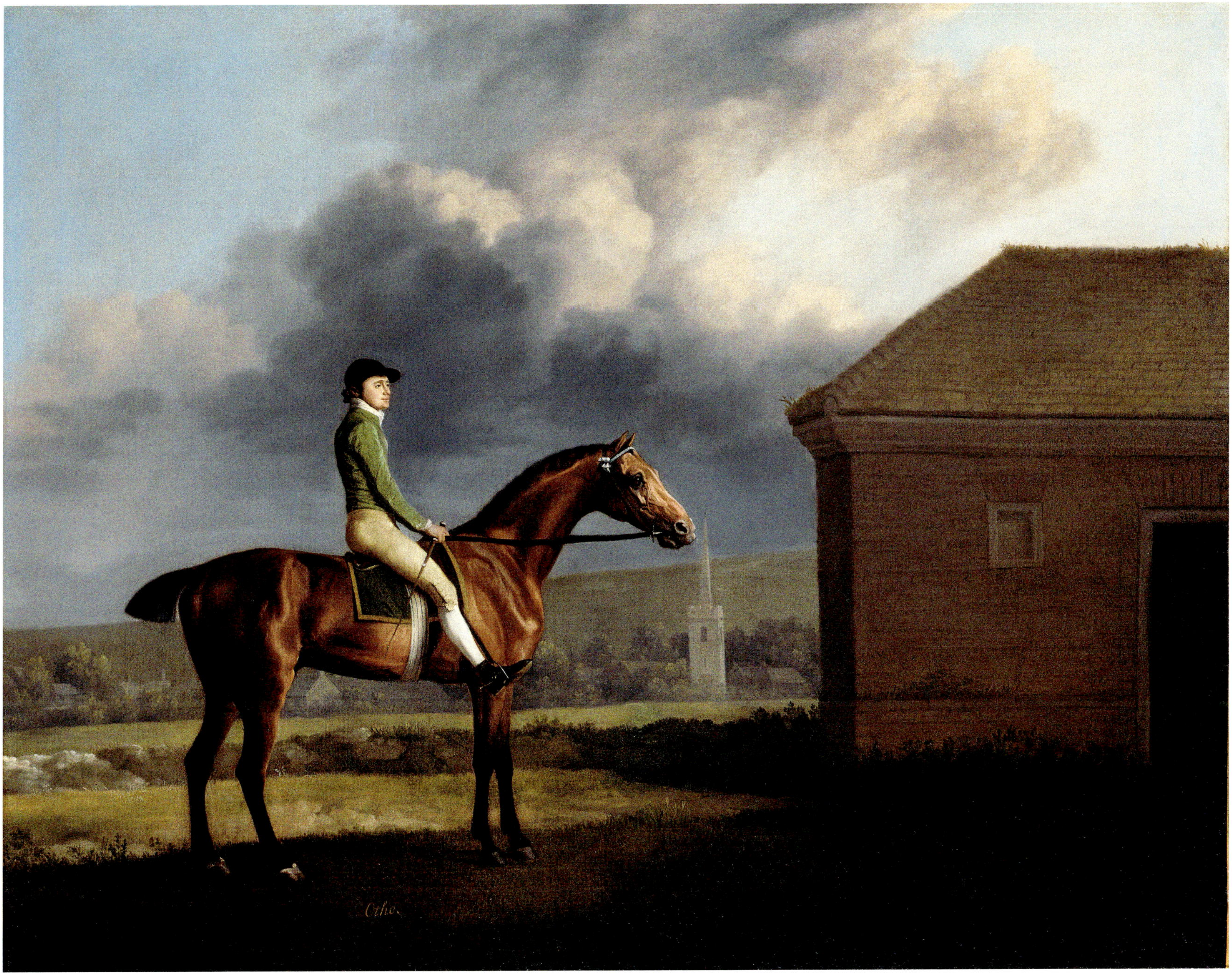
Otho

27

The Marquess of Rockingham's Arabian Stallion, with a Groom c. 1766

Oil on canvas, 97.8 x 123.2 cm

Commissioned by Charles Watson-Wentworth, 2nd Marquess of Rockingham (1730–1782), Wentworth Woodhouse, Yorkshire – Edinburgh, National Gallery of Scotland (accepted by HM Government in lieu of inheritance tax 2002)

This painting varies the theme of a horse in a landscape by showing a highly unusual location. The scene is Creswell Crags, a picturesque limestone gorge in the Peak District. Stubbs explored this wild, inaccessible place in the early 1760s and it became his backdrop of choice for the 'horse-and-lion' paintings (cat. no. 42). The crags have all the hallmarks of an ancient, primordial landscape as yet untouched by human hand.

The horse portrayed is an anonymous Arabian stallion from Lord Rockingham's Wentworth Woodhouse stud. Clearly not a famous racehorse, this stallion with striking white fetlocks must have served primarily as a sire. The work also exemplifies Stubbs's skill as a master of landscape painting. While the crags dominate the right of the scene, heavy clouds are gathering above the low horizon at left. This juxtaposition of a geological and a meteorological formation not only makes for an atmosphere of sublime grandeur but also provides a highly advantageous foil for what is clearly a noble, superbly-built beast. The wildness of the landscape recalls man's prehistoric origins and reminds us that the history of civilization is a history of human intervention. One such successful intervention was the crossbreeding of Arabian and native breeds which in the eighteenth century produced the first English Thoroughbred—an accomplishment that Charles Darwin cited as a shining example of how selective breeding might improve on nature itself. The painting is probably the one listed in 1766 as "A Picture of an Arabian," for which Stubbs received a sum of £40.

HWR

Lit.: Exhib. Cat. *George Stubbs*, 1984/85, no. 72 – Exhib. Cat. *Stubbs and the Horse*, 2004/05, no. 51 – Egerton, *George Stubbs*, 2007, no. 49

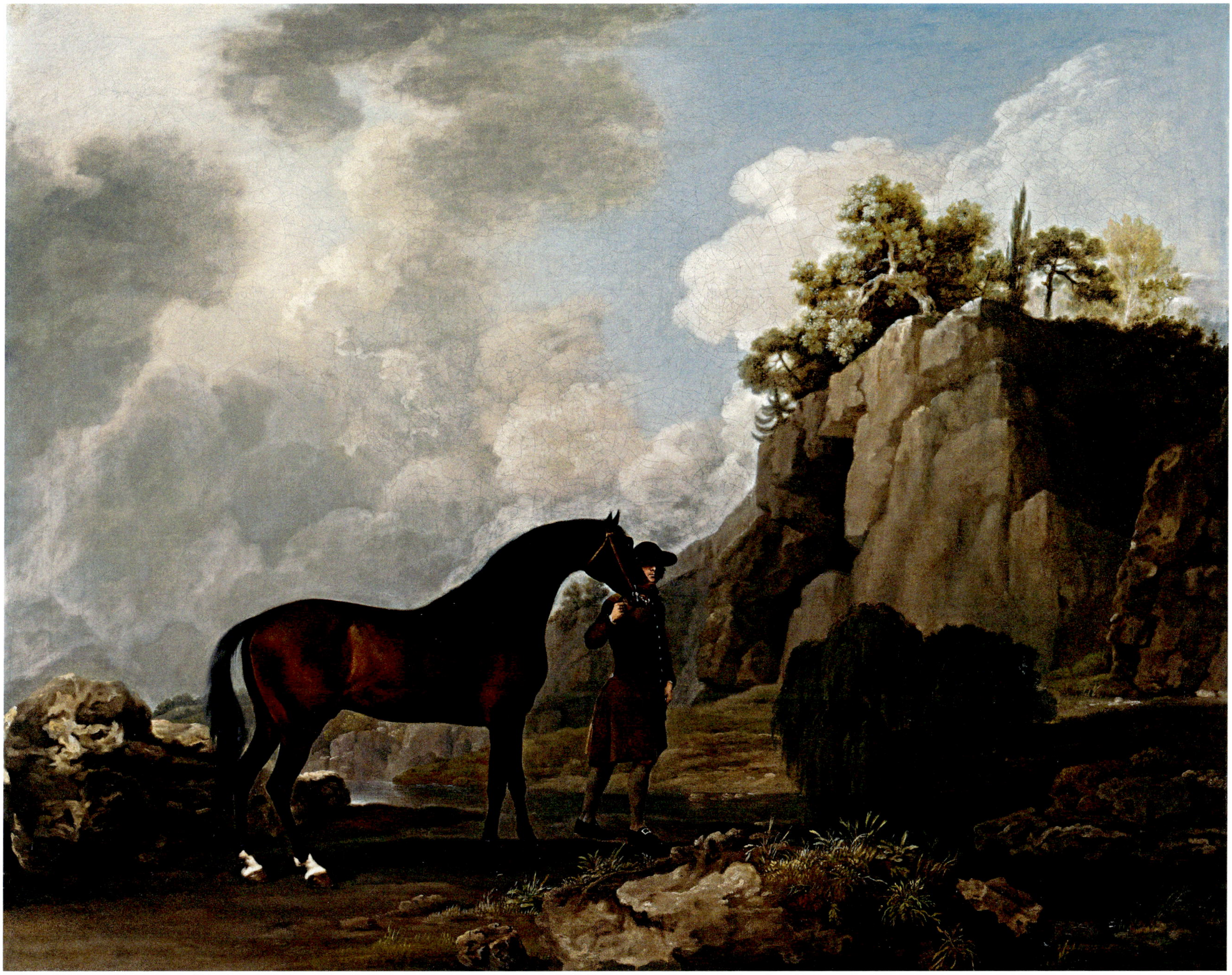

28

Five of Lord Rockingham's Hounds in a Landscape 1762

Oil on canvas, 101.5 x 127 cm

Commissioned by Charles Watson-Wentworth, 2nd Marquess of Rockingham (1730–1782), Wentworth Woodhouse, Yorkshire – The Trustees of the Rt. Hon. Olive, Countess Fitzwilliam's Chattels Settlement, by permission of Lady Juliet Tadgell

The simplicity of the composition and unpretentiousness of the subject are deceptive: this portrait of the 2nd Marquess of Rockingham's hunting hounds is, in fact, a masterpiece of animal painting. The hounds are carefully lined up along the lower edge of the canvas so that the dogs alternate with the bitches, their distinguishing features in each case reproduced with portrait-like precision. The background landscape, with its rolling hills and atmospherically dense trees and cliffs, which are rendered in finely nuanced shades of green and brown, opens up onto a cloudy sky in the far distance. Meanwhile the hounds in the foreground are bathed in soft sunlight which sets off their fine white coats and modelled bodies to excellent advantage.

The hounds belonged to the pack that Lord Rockingham kept at Wentworth Woodhouse for hunting foxes and stags. Breeding hunting hounds, like keeping a stud, was a source of prestige for the preeminent members of the nobility for whom the hunt was a way of asserting their privileged social status and dominion over the land and all the living creatures it sustained.

The painting was commissioned by Lord Rockingham, who paid for it together with four other paintings—including *Whistlejacket and Two Other Stallions* (cat. no. 19) and *Mares and Foals* (cat. no. 20)—in August 1762.

HWR

Lit.: H. F. Constantine, "Lord Rockingham and Stubbs. Some New Documents," in: *The Burlington Magazine* 95, 1953, pp. 236–38 – Exhib. Cat. *George Stubbs*, 1984/85, no. 36 – Egerton, *George Stubbs*, 2007, no. 33

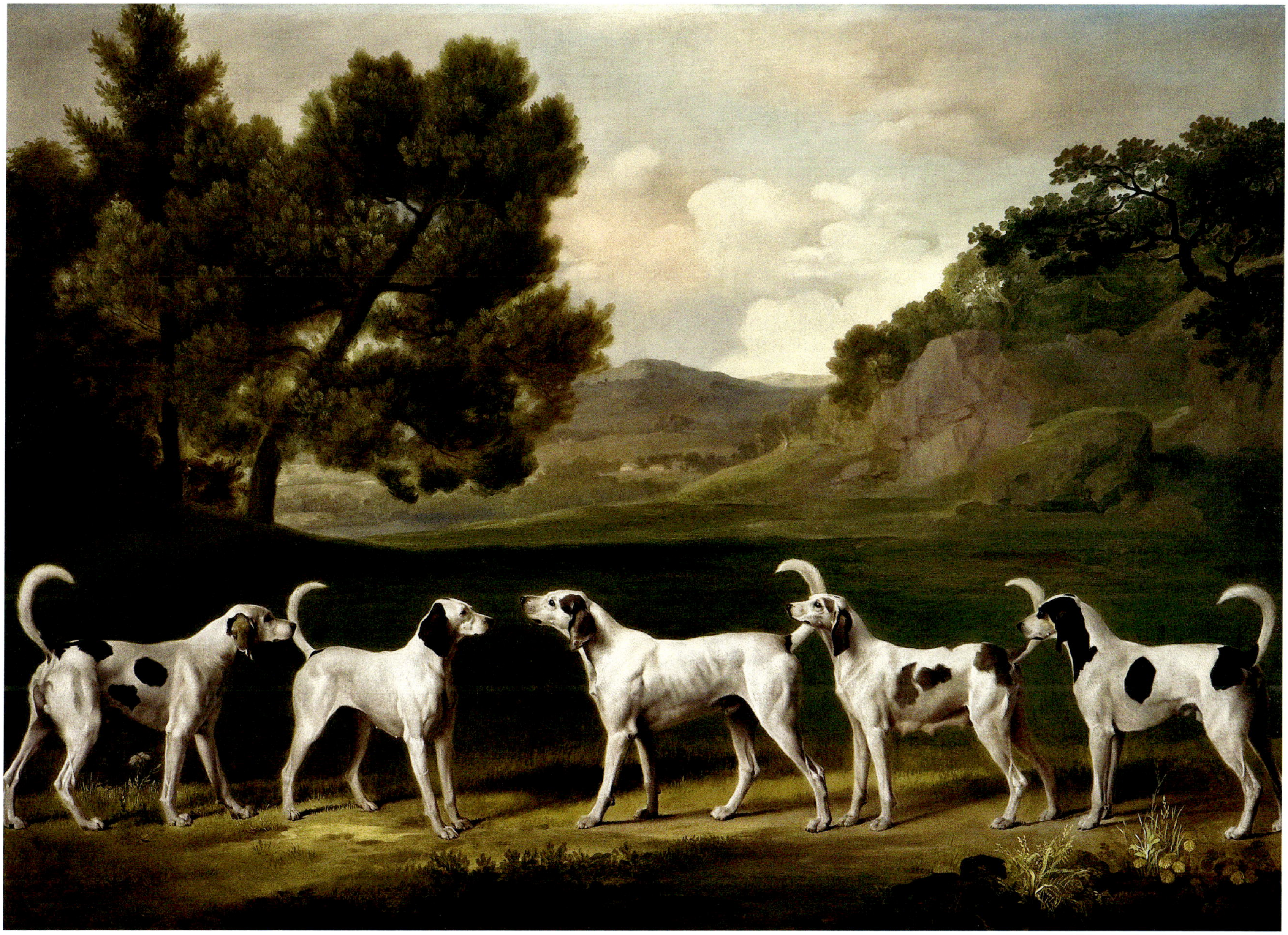

29

Spanish Pointer c. 1766

Oil on canvas, 60.5 x 69.5 cm
Signed at bottom right: *Geo: Stubbs pinxit*

Munich, Bayerische Staatsgemäldesammlungen, Neue Pinakothek

Crossbreeding not only brought forth new breeds of horse but also new breeds of hound optimized for specific purposes. The pointer is a gun dog used to sniff out and point to small game such as pheasants and partridges. The name Spanish Pointer indicates that the breed was imported from Continental Europe and then perfected by still more crossbreeding.

Stubbs portrays an exceptionally handsome animal against an expansive, hilly landscape dotted with small clusters of trees. The dog has frozen in mid-run and is shown in an alert position with his left foreleg bent and his head slightly cocked to one side. He has clearly picked up a scent and is showing his master where the game is hiding so that it can be flushed out.

The two versions of this composition that Stubbs painted are almost identical in size and differ only in a few details. In 1768 the publisher Thomas Bradford commissioned the engraver William Woollett to produce a print of the version then in Bradford's possession (cat. no. 72). A comparison of this print with the two paintings suggests that the painting in question was indeed the second version, which is now in private hands (Egerton no. 88). Bradford also possessed four paintings of hunting scenes, and commissioned Woollett to make engravings of these works too (cat. nos. 73–76).

The early provenance of this version of the *Spanish Pointer* is unclear. Documents indicate that it hung in Schloss Schleissheim near Munich from 1810 onwards. It therefore seems likely that it was purchased around 1800 by Prince-elector Maximilian Joseph, who would later become King Max I Joseph of Bavaria and who is known to have possessed paintings by other British artists such as George Morland and David Wilkie as well. The painting was thus the only work by Stubbs to be held in a collection outside of the British Isles at this early date.

HWR

Lit.: *Nach-Barock und Klassizismus (Bayerische Staatsgemäldesammlungen/Neue Pinakothek, Gemäldekataloge,* vol. 3), edited by Barbara Hardtwig, Munich 1978, pp. 344–46 – Egerton, *George Stubbs*, 2007, no. 87

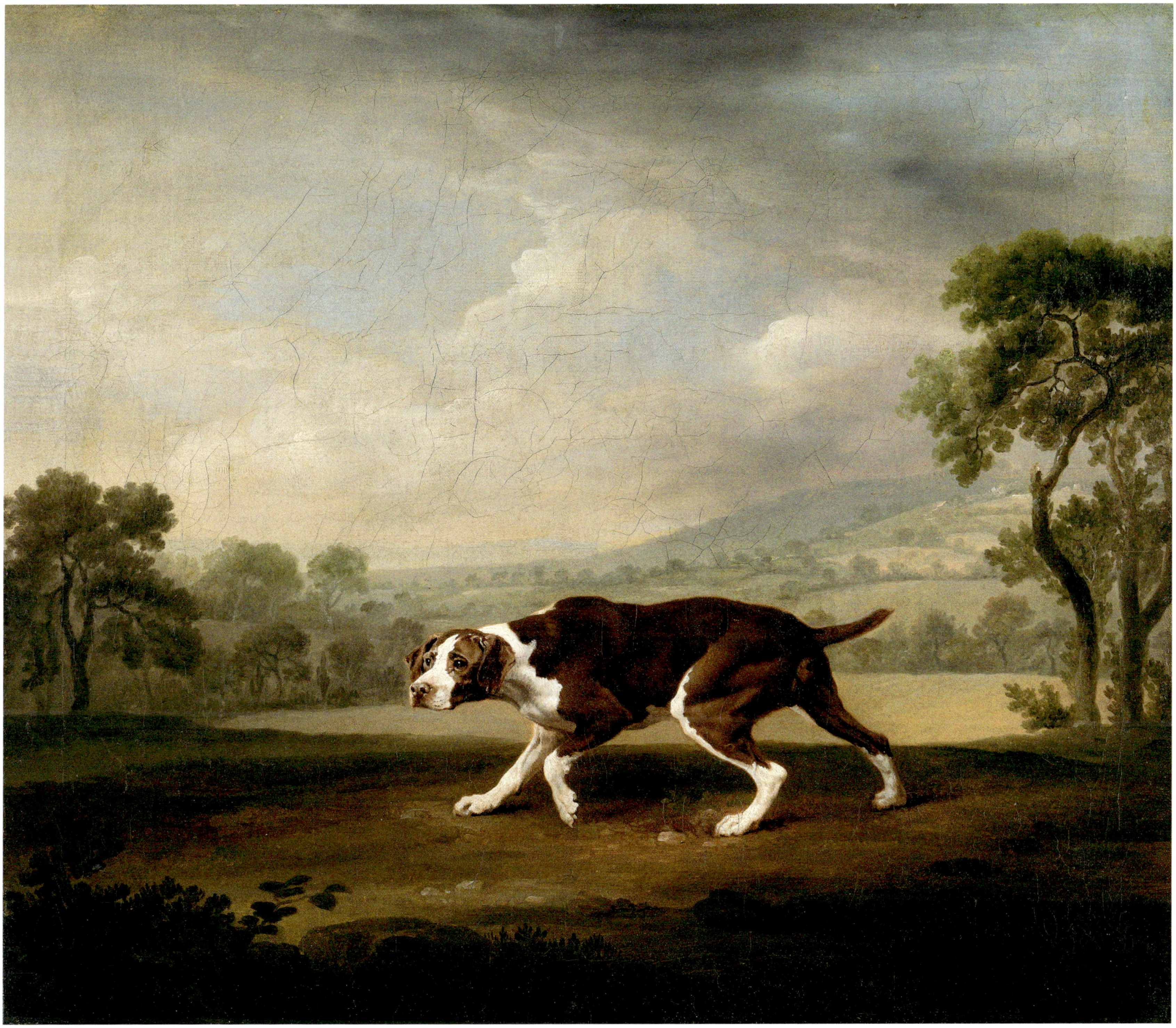

30
A Brown and White Dog Formerly Belonging to William Pitt, 1st Earl of Chatham 1788

Oil on panel, 81.3 x 100.3 cm
Signed and dated at bottom left: *Geo: Stubbs pinxit / 1788*; inscribed on the dog's collar: *William Earl of Chatham / Hayes 1777*

Commissioned by John Pitt, 2nd Earl of Chatham (1756–1835), Hayes, Kent – private collection

Stubbs's patrons wanted their horses to be portrayed in a way that made them instantly recognizable. Occasionally, he was asked to perform a similar service for their dogs, whose names and pedigrees have likewise been recorded. Here, too, Stubbs was unsurpassed. The high esteem in which his work was held is evident from the fact that some of his dog portraits were reproduced as engravings. The technique used to produce both paintings and prints alike was an extremely subtle one.

Stubbs seems to have specialized in spaniels and foxhounds. The finest example of such a hound, albeit a crossbred in this case, is the one portrayed here, whose collar tells us that he belonged to William Pitt. Since the painting is dated 1788, the date of 1777 on the collar is presumably the dog's year of birth. Painted on wood, the work is more than a metre wide. The hound is viewed from the side so that we can admire him in all his glory. His head is turned towards the viewer and he looks out of the painting at us. Because the landscape with foliage in the background is essentially a dark foil, it does not detract from the panel-filling subject at all.

Here, as in his horse portraits, Stubbs positions his subject with great care: while the dog's left foreleg accentuates the central vertical axis and his belly follows the lower line of the golden section, the right vertical of this aesthetically pleasing, compositional principle runs right through the inscribed collar and right foreleg.

WB

Lit.: Exhib. Cat. *George Stubbs*, 1984/85, no. 102 – Egerton, *George Stubbs*, 2007, no. 271

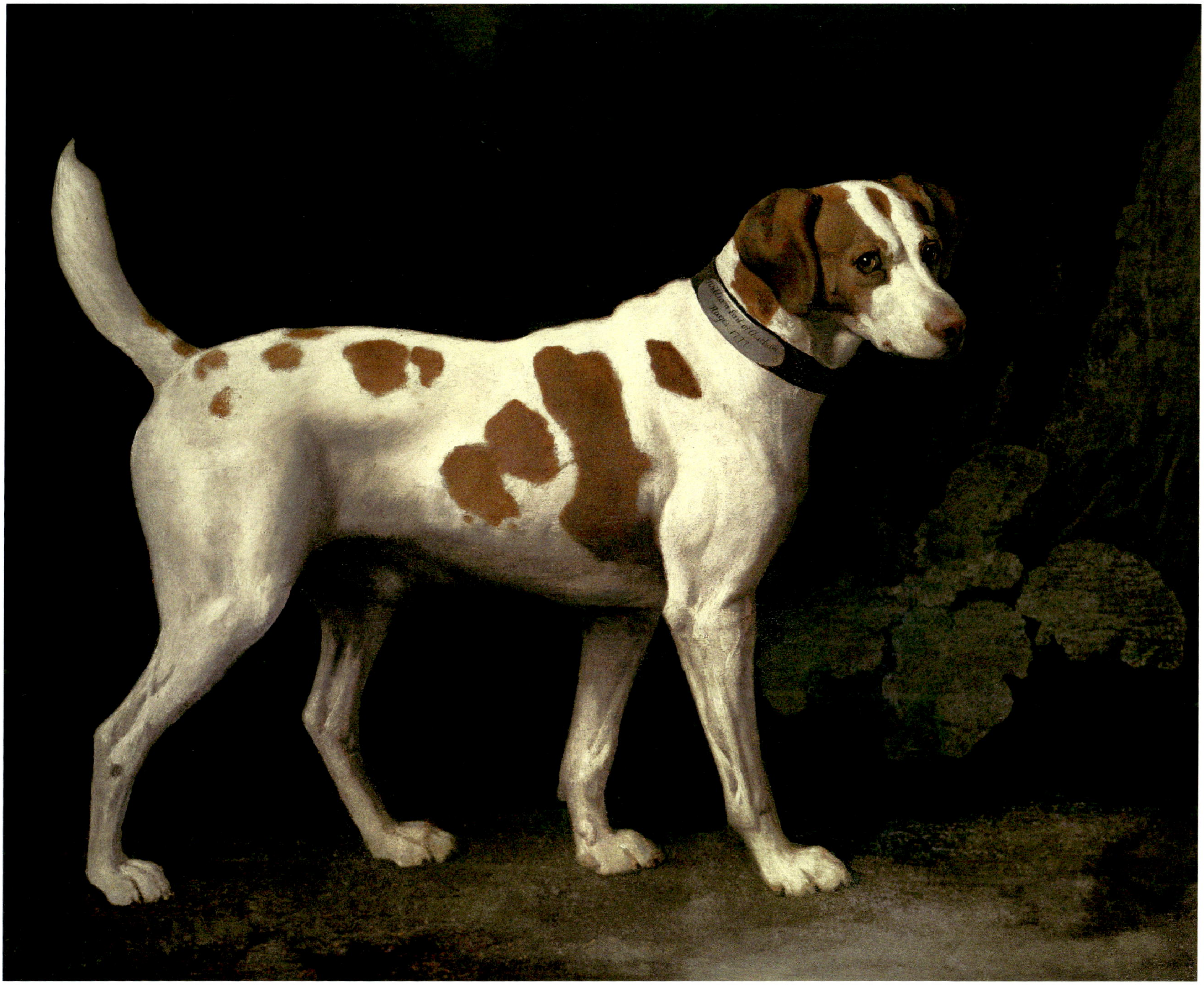

31

Lord Torrington's Hunt Servants Setting Out from Southill, Bedfordshire c. 1767

Oil on canvas, 61 x 105 cm

Commissioned by George Byng, 4th Viscount Torrington (1740–1812), Southill Park, Bedfordshire – private collection

With their realistic renderings of the local topography and stylistic appropriation of seventeenth-century Dutch models, the three pictures that Stubbs painted for Lord Torrington around 1767 (Egerton nos. 99–101) surely rank among the most remarkable works in his entire oeuvre. Views of country estates are here combined with pastoral scenes or preparations for the hunt.

Stubbs spent several weeks at Southill as a guest of Lord Torrington preparing and possibly even painting all three works. While his patron is notably absent, several of his servants and even some of the farmhands who worked on Lord Torrington's estate are included in the various scenes. This particular painting, a carefully balanced composition showing three men, three horses and two dogs about to set off on the hunt in a landscape with a village in the background, is described in Ozias Humphry's *Memoir* as a hunting scene showing "his Lordship's Coachmen, Grooms, Hunters, a few dogs and his Whipper-in." According to Judy Egerton, the scene is Southill, in front of All Saint's Church, whose tower is clearly visible at left. The coachman wearing a striped jacket and light-coloured breeches is captured in the act of handing over the reins of a saddled but riderless horse to one of the hunters, while a second hunter, who has already turned his horse, sets off to the right. The whip on the saddle and hunting hound next to this second hunter mark him out as the 'whipper-in' of the pack.

Stubbs reproduces the scene with cool precision. The houses, gardens and medieval church tower are rendered with an almost photographic attention to detail. No less care has been bestowed upon the horses, which are presented in a range of postures and positions.

HWR

Lit.: Francis Russell, "Lord Torrington and Stubbs. A footnote," in: *The Burlington Magazine* 122, 1980, pp. 250–53 – Exhib. Cat. *George Stubbs*, 1984/85, no. 46 – Exhib. Cat. *Stubbs and the Horse*, 2004/05, no. 56 – Egerton, *George Stubbs*, 2007, no. 99

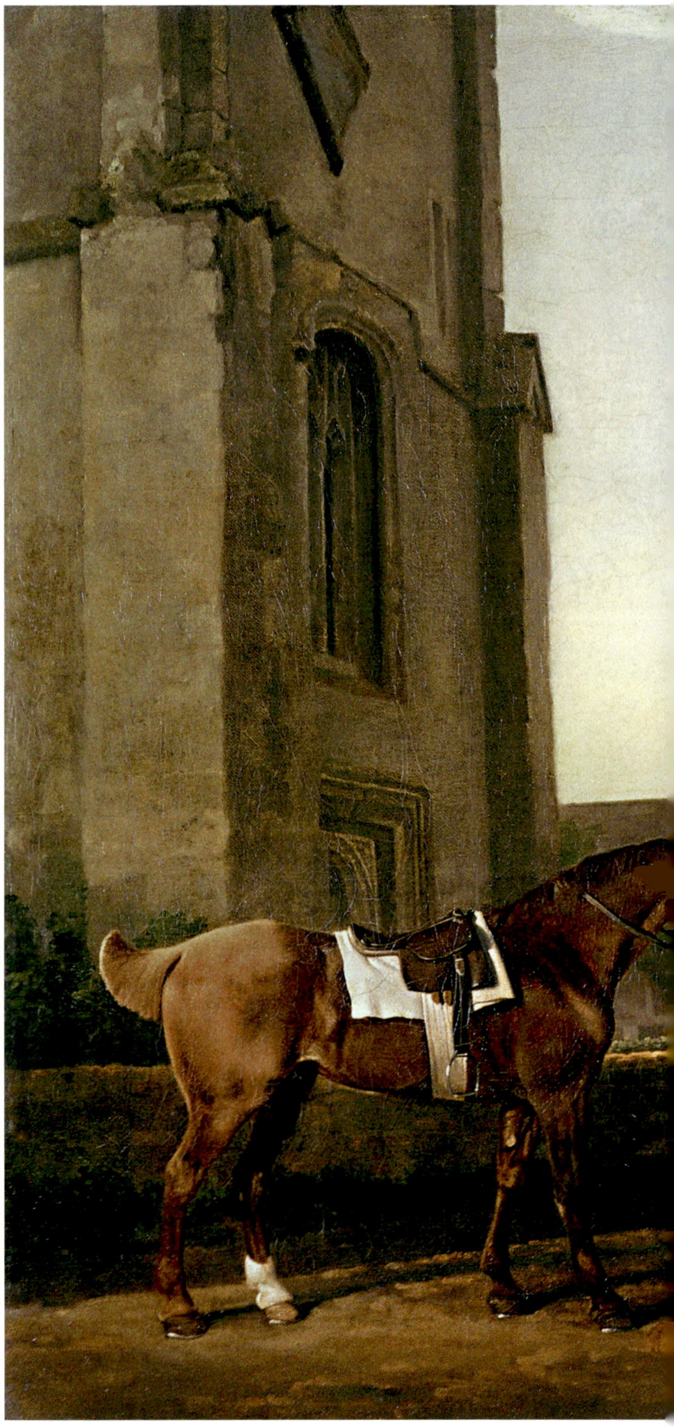

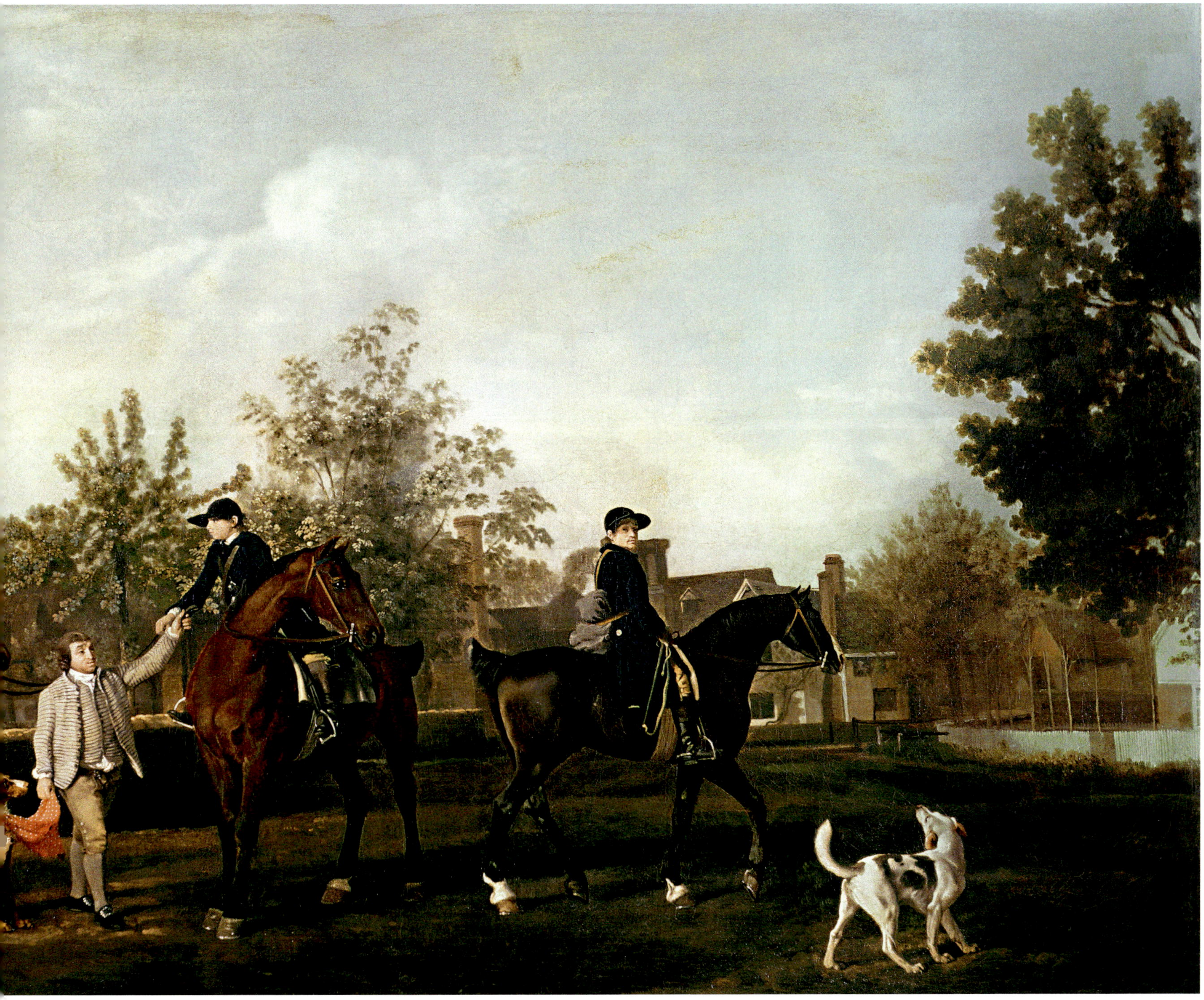

32

Lord Torrington's Steward and Gamekeeper, with Dogs c. 1767

Oil on canvas, 61 x 107 cm

Commissioned by George Byng, 4th Viscount Torrington (1740–1812), Southill Park, Bedfordshire – private collection

The second painting that Stubbs painted for Lord Torrington shows "an old man, his Steward, on an aged horse with the Game Keeper, followed by a Pomeranian dog" (Humphry, *Memoir*). The setting is a dense wood where the two men specified in the title are shown acting out their respective roles: the steward on horseback and the gamekeeper on foot, holding a gun and accompanied by three dogs. It was the job of the gamekeeper to assert his lord's hunting rights and to catch poachers. The Game Laws of 1671, which remained in force until 1831, envisaged stiff penalties for anyone caught poaching. To ensure that hunting remained attractive as a privilege of the nobility, all landowners kept gamekeepers to maintain the necessary stocks of game and to take action against those poor country folk who resorted to hunting to feed their families. Yet the painting cannot be read as either condoning or condemning the game laws of the day or those who benefited from them. Stubbs depicts the two elderly men with the same meticulous attention to detail as he lavished on Lord Torrington's other personnel.

In 1778, when financial necessity compelled Lord Torrington to part with his collection of paintings, this work by Stubbs passed into other hands. When in 1790 B. B. Evans published engravings of the *Labourers* and *Game Keepers* (cat. nos. 85–86), the paintings belonged to Andrew Harrison.

HWR

Lit.: Exhib. Cat. *Stubbs and the Horse*, 2004/05, no. 55 – Blake, *George Stubbs and the Wide Creation*, 2005, pp. 166–69 – Egerton, *George Stubbs*, 2007, no. 101

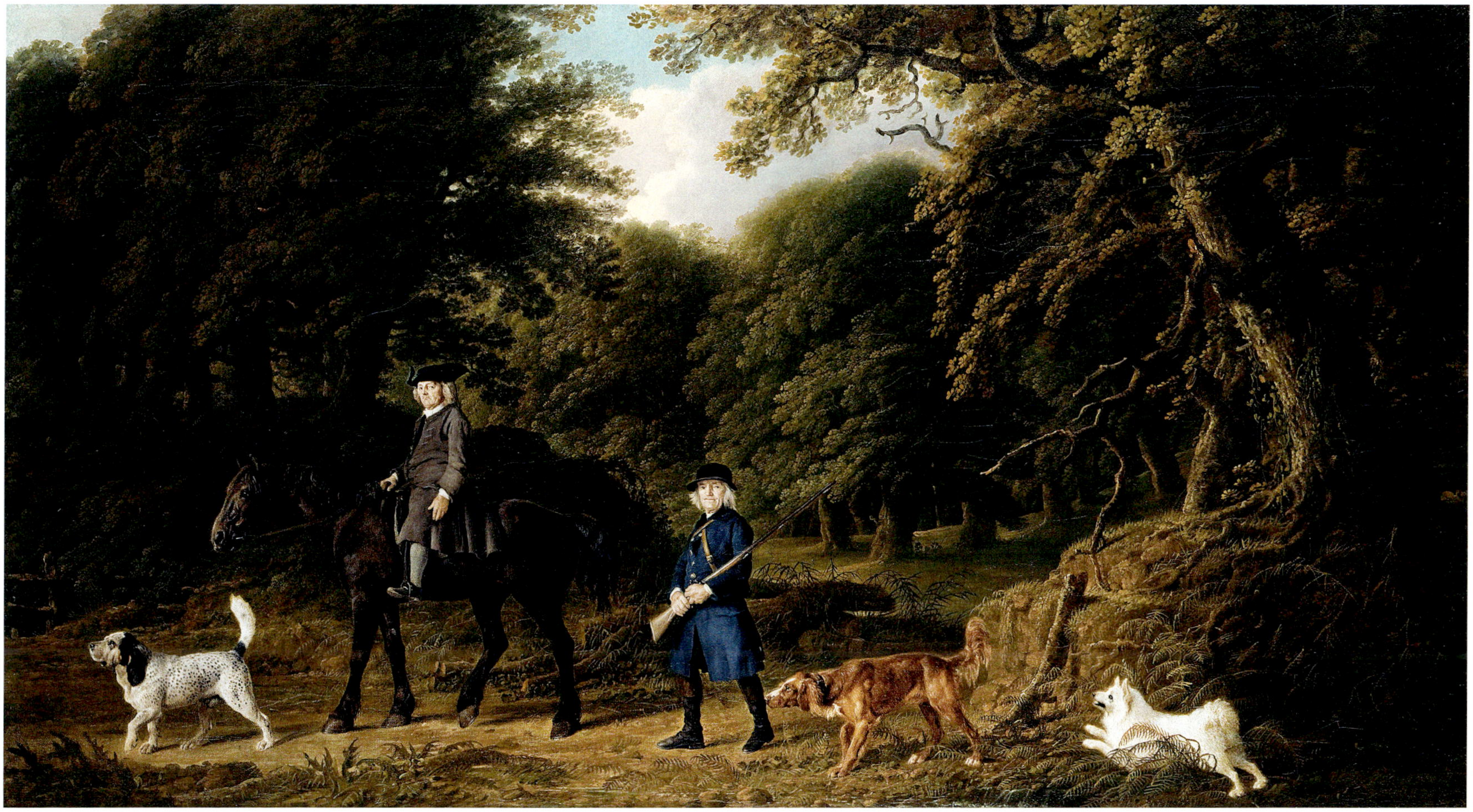

33

Labourers 1779

Oil on panel, 92 x 137.1 cm
Signed and dated at bottom centre: *Geo: Stubbs p: 1779*

Upton House, Warwickshire, The Bearsted Collection (The National Trust)

This painting is a somewhat larger version of the example painted for Lord Torrington by Stubbs in 1767, which is now at the Philadelphia Museum of Art (Egerton no. 100). The labourers of the title are working on Lord Torrington's estate at Southill in Bedfordshire. The façade of the new Palladian lodge designed by Isaac Ware depicted in the background adds a distinctive touch.

Thanks to Ozias Humphry's *Memoir*, we are surprisingly well informed about the circumstances in which the first version of this work was painted. Lord Torrington, who as a collector had a marked preference for seventeenth-century Dutch genre painting and possessed works by Philips Wouwerman, Aelbert Cuyp and Jan Steen among others, had frequently observed his labourers at work and was fascinated by these scenes which had the effect of "appearing like a Flemish subject." When commissioned to capture just such a picture, Stubbs selected the moment in which the men interrupted their labours to discuss what to do next. He then made sketches from models as well as various studies, none of which has survived. Also lost is the compositional study listed in the inventory of Stubbs's estate on which both the first version of 1767 and this second version painted twelve years later were based.

The charm of this painting resides in its sympathetic portrayal of labourers whose individual facial features and plain, but clean clothes are reproduced with great precision. No less attention is paid to the horse harnessed to the wooden cart. The animal has been identified as Lord Torrington's old hunter—a horse he is known to have prized highly and hence wanted to have immortalized in a painting. Stubbs portrays the horse as a creature of great spirit which, in its dutiful rendering of a service, radiates dignity and nobility. Two generations later, the French painter Théodore Géricault depicted working horses in such a similarly sympathetic style that it seems at least conceivable that he was inspired by Stubbs's own engraving of *Labourers* of 1791 (Lennox-Boyd no. 86), or perhaps by the print of the first version of the painting published by B. B. Evans in 1790 (cat. no. 85).

HWR

Lit.: Francis Russell, "Lord Torrington and Stubbs. A footnote," in: *The Burlington Magazine* 122, 1980, pp. 250–53 – Egerton, *George Stubbs*, 2007, no. 211

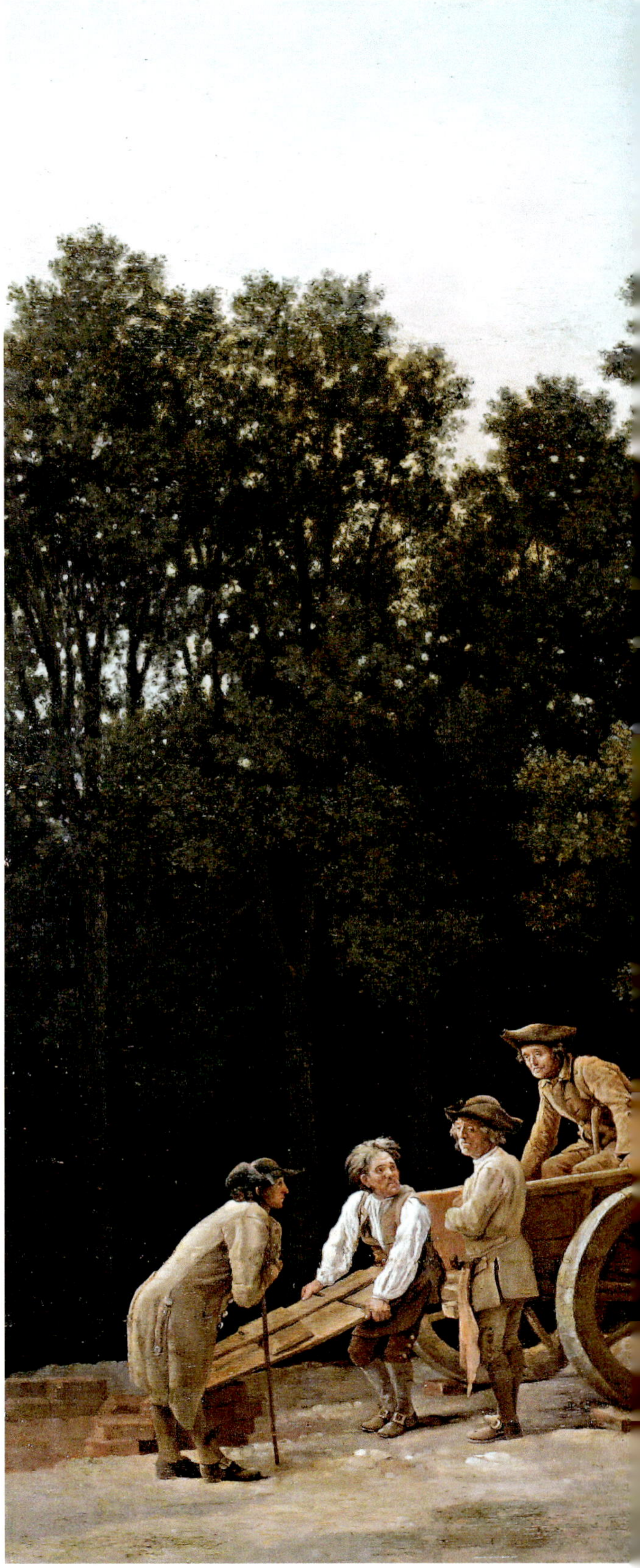

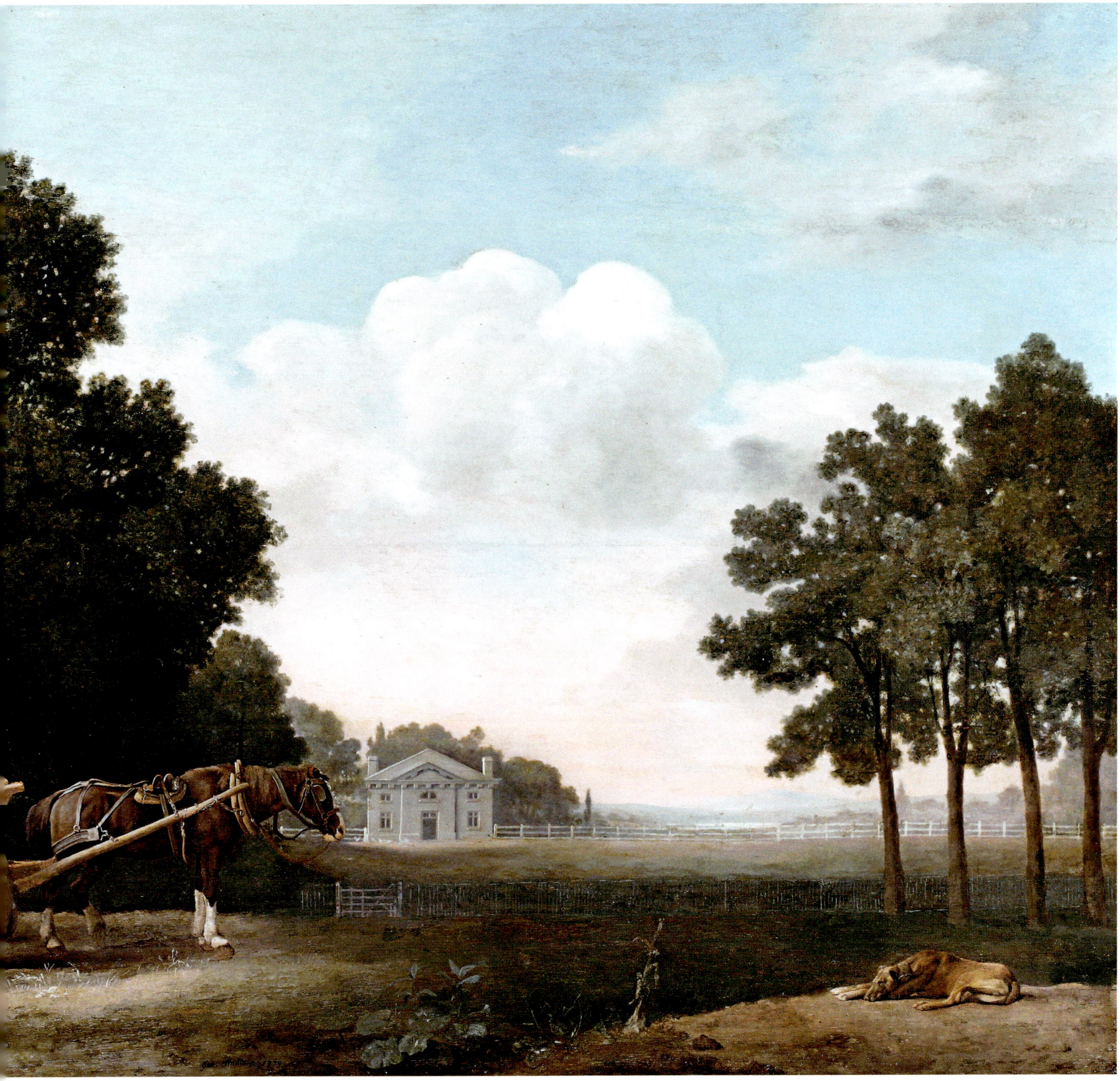

34

A Lady Reading in a Park c. 1767–70

Oil on canvas, 62.2 x 76.2 cm

Private collection

This portrait of a lady in a wooded park is the only work of its kind in George Stubbs's oeuvre. Clad in a magnificent floral gown made of the finest silk with a string of pearls wound twice around her neck and with flowers decorating her hair, the young woman of the title is portrayed sitting on a bench to the right of centre, engrossed in a book. Soft sunlight from above illuminates her figure, accentuating it against the much darker surroundings. The park with its old deciduous trees opens out onto a sunny clearing in the background which makes for a similarly bright counterweight to the figure of the young woman in the foreground. Absorbed in her reading in the peace and tranquillity of tamed nature, the woman is enveloped by a special, dreamy aura.

The identity of the young woman is unknown. When the painting's anonymous owner put it up for auction in 1811, it was described merely as "A Park Scene with a Lady Sitting." Noting its special place in the artist's work and the peaceful intimacy of the scene, Judy Egerton has suggested that it is a portrait of someone from Stubbs's own circle of acquaintances and has named Charlotte Nelthorpe as a possible candidate. Charlotte was the daughter of Sir Henry Nelthorpe and his wife Elizabeth, who in Stubbs's early years ranked among his most important patrons. As the early provenance of the painting is still swathed in mystery and it does not contain any concrete clues, this suggestion is bound to remain hypothetical. Charlotte Nelthorpe was born in 1742, married Robert Carter Thelwall in 1767 and was painted by Stubbs together with her husband and daughter in 1776 (Egerton no. 183).

HWR

Lit.: Exhib. Cat. *George Stubbs*, 1984/85, no. 109 – Egerton, *George Stubbs*, 2007, no. 97

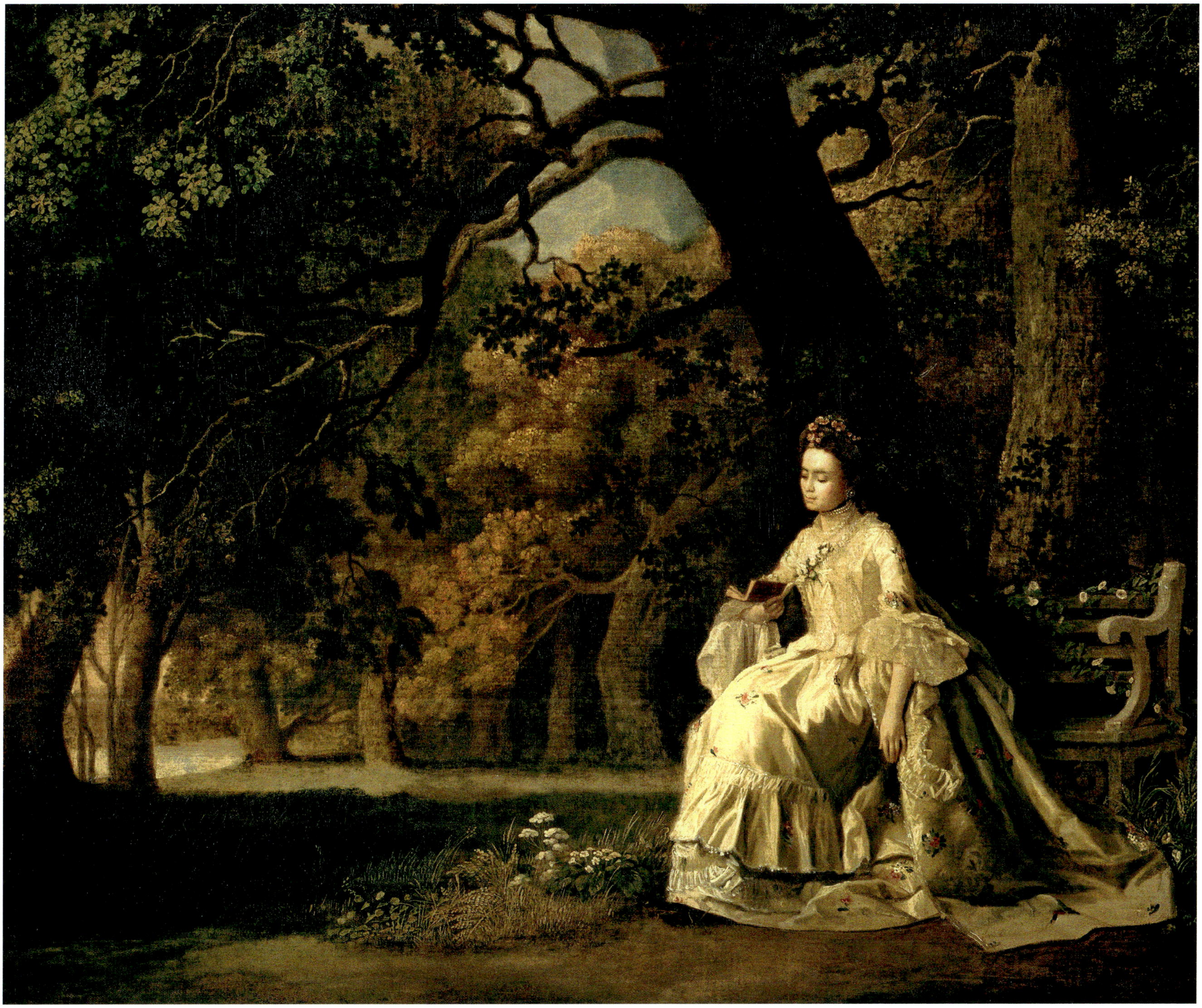

35

Sir Peniston and Lady Elizabeth Lamb, later Lord and Lady Melbourne, with Lady Lamb's Father, Sir Ralph Milbanke (The Milbanke and Melbourne Families) c. 1769

Oil on canvas, 97.2 x 147.3 cm

Commissioned by Peniston Lamb, 1st Viscount Melbourne (1745–1828), Brocket Hall, Hertfordshire – London, The National Gallery

This portrait of the Milbanke and Melbourne families is one of Stubbs's few 'conversation pieces' and is in fact the most important work in this group. It shows Elizabeth Lamb, née Milbanke—sitting in a coach on the left—and the man she has just married, Sir Peniston Lamb, mounted on a magnificent Arabian stallion on the right. Standing next to the young woman—she was just sixteen at the time of her marriage—is her father Sir Ralph Milbanke. The most striking figure in the group, however, is the young man at the centre of the composition, Elizabeth's younger brother John Milbanke, who ironically had only a minor role to play in family affairs. The landscape in the background is not a portrait of the family estate, but more a combination of set pieces. The huge oak features in other paintings by the artist, as do the crags on the right which look strikingly similar to Creswell Crags.

The painting was probably commissioned in honour of the marriage that took place in the spring of 1769. It was an alliance between two families of different social backgrounds: the Milbankes, who had long belonged to the landed gentry, and the Lambs, who represented 'new money'. The young couple had an eventful life ahead of them. Sir Peniston Lamb, from 1770 Lord Melbourne, had a decidedly unspectacular career as a member of parliament and invested his money in property and paintings, amassing a collection which included some of the finest works by Joseph Wright of Derby. Lady Melbourne relished her meteoric rise and had numerous extramarital affairs with men of high rank, including the Prince of Wales, later becoming a confidante of Lord Byron. The lack of interaction between the figures in the painting and their apparent indifference to each other might almost be read as auguring the tensions that would later afflict their marriage.

HWR

Lit.: Exhib. Cat. *George Stubbs*, 1984/85, no. 110 – *The British School (National Gallery Catalogues)*, edited by Judy Egerton, London 1998, pp. 248–55 – Exhib. Cat. *Stubbs and the Horse*, 2004/05, no. 59 – Egerton, *George Stubbs*, 2007, no. 130

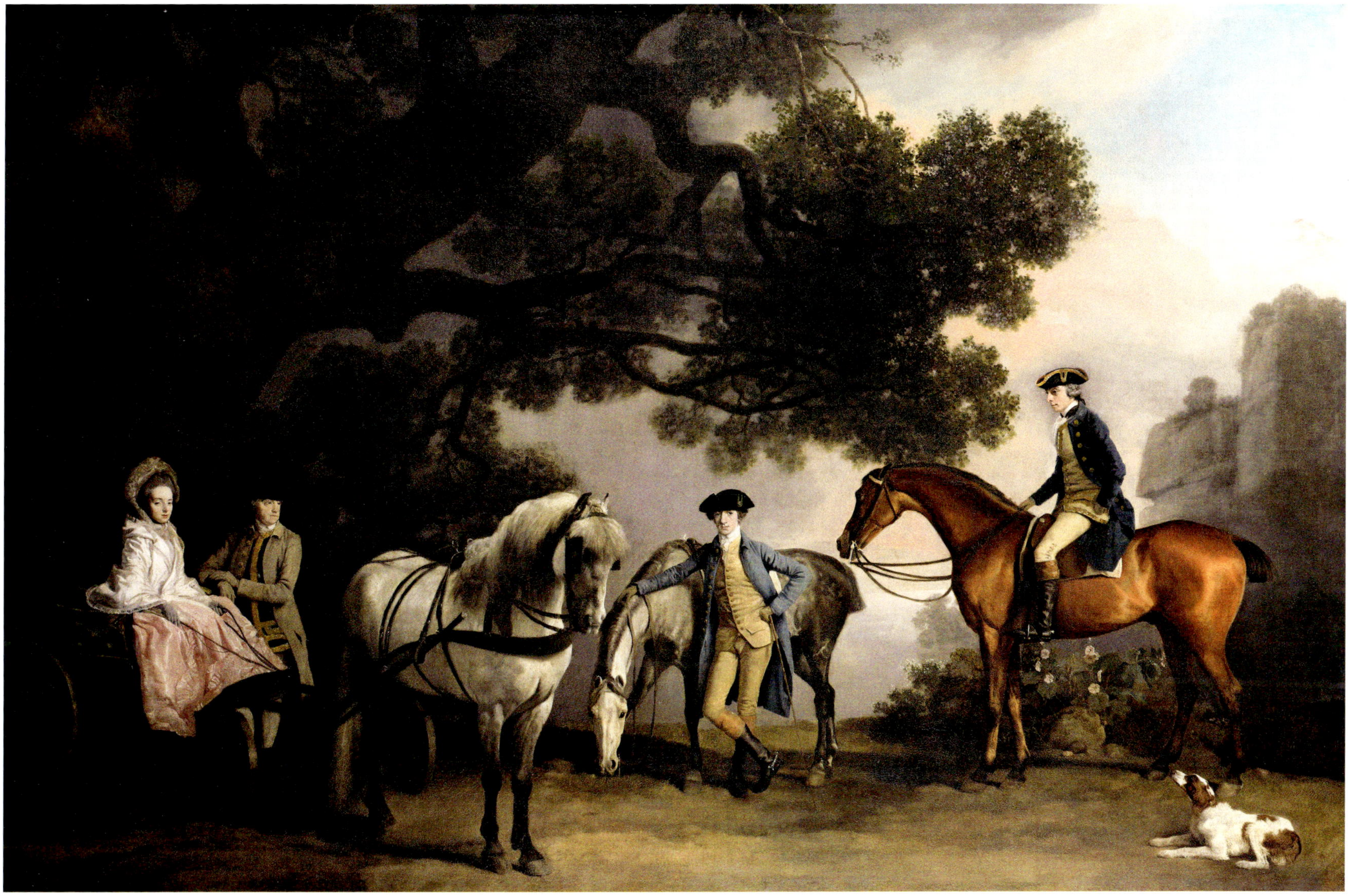

36

Joseph Smyth, Lieutenant of Whittlebury Forest, Northamptonshire c. 1762–64

Oil on canvas, 64.2 x 76.9 cm

Commissioned by Joseph Smyth (1710–1799) or Augustus Henry Fitzroy, 3rd Duke of Grafton (1735–1811) – Cambridge, Fitzwilliam Museum

This painting belongs to a group of works by Stubbs in which the focus is on the rider rather than the horse, in this case not a thoroughbred but a dapple grey. The subject is Joseph Smyth, who held the office of Lieutenant of Whittlebury Forest for fifty-two years, that is to say he was chief forester and steward of Whittlewood Forest in Northamptonshire. Like all forests in Great Britain, Whittlewood Forest belonged to the Crown, although responsibility for appointing the said Lieutenant lay with the Duke of Grafton, who had tutelage over the forest and owned the stately hunting lodge Wakefield Lodge in it. It is thus conceivable that this portrait was commissioned either by the sitter himself or by his lord, the Duke of Grafton, for whom Stubbs is known to have painted a version of his mares and foals in a river landscape (Egerton no. 42) and a portrait of the duke's racehorse Antinoüs (Egerton no. 43) in the early 1760s.

Horse and rider are placed squarely in the foreground, leaving very little room for views of the open countryside beyond. Surprisingly, the landscape is not woodland, but a river and floodplain viewed from an elevated vantage point. The subject is wearing his lieutenant's uniform consisting of a green coat with gold trimmings and has adopted a pose and facial expression that signify vigour and determination.

HWR

Lit.: Exhib. Cat. *George Stubbs*, 1984/85, no. 32 – Exhib. Cat. *Stubbs and the Horse*, 2004/05, no. 42 – Egerton, *George Stubbs*, 2007, no. 44

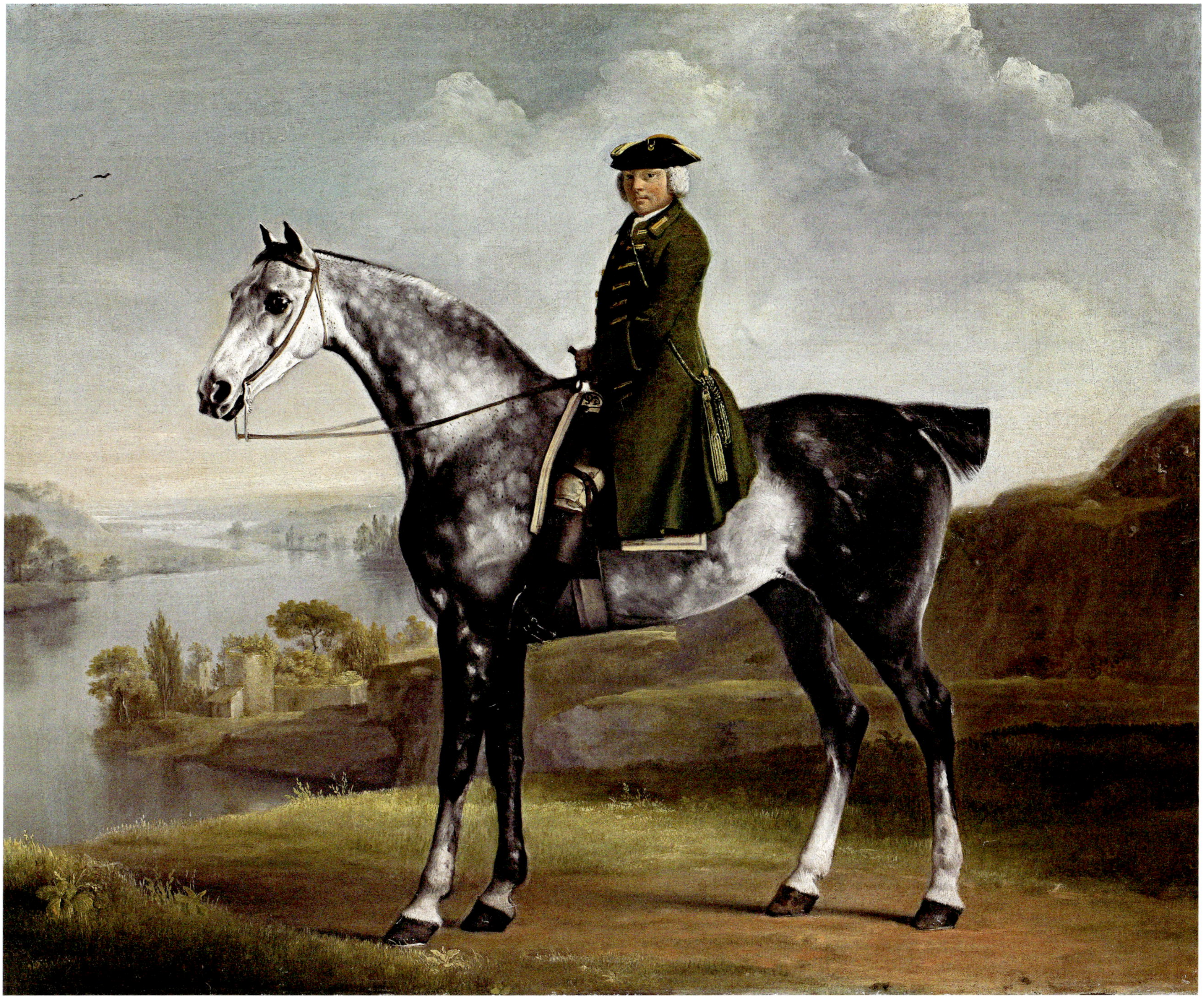

37

John Warde of Squerryes Court with an Imported Bay Stallion 1770 (?)

Oil on canvas, 64.8 x 73.7 cm
Signed at bottom right: *Geo. Stubbs pinxit*

Commissioned by John Warde (1721–1775), Squerryes Court, Kent – private collection

George Stubbs so excelled as a painter of horses and animals that his accomplishments as a portraitist and landscape painter are often overlooked. Yet as far as we know, most of the works he produced before the mid-1750s were portraits. In the course of the 1760s he painted several outstanding works showing tender portraits of patrons with or without their families, horses and views of their estates. One good example of these is this portrait of John Warde in front of the pond at Squerryes Court in Kent. The young man is shown standing just to the left of a large tree whose huge, dark trunk dwarfs his slim figure. His folded arms and casually crossed legs lend him the air of a daydreamer with a touch of melancholy in his facial expression. Standing next to him, held loosely by the reins, is a powerfully built Arabian bay stallion whose dark body is thrown into relief by the light expanse of water and the slightly cloudy sky behind him.

The young man portrayed is either John Warde III (1721–1775) or his son John Warde IV (1755–1838). Yet Judy Egerton's dating of the painting to the early 1760s is not compatible with the ages of either father or son: the former would have been over forty by then, while the latter would have still been a child. Assuming the subject is the younger John Warde at the age of, say, sixteen, the painting would have to be dated around 1770 and there do not appear to be any stylistic factors that might rule out such a dating. John Warde III tried his hand as a horse breeder—the stallion shown here was doubtless one of his studs—and was a keen collector of art, especially of paintings by Italians such as Guido Reni and Salvator Rosa purchased from art dealers in London.

HWR

Lit.: Egerton, *George Stubbs*, 2007, no. 126

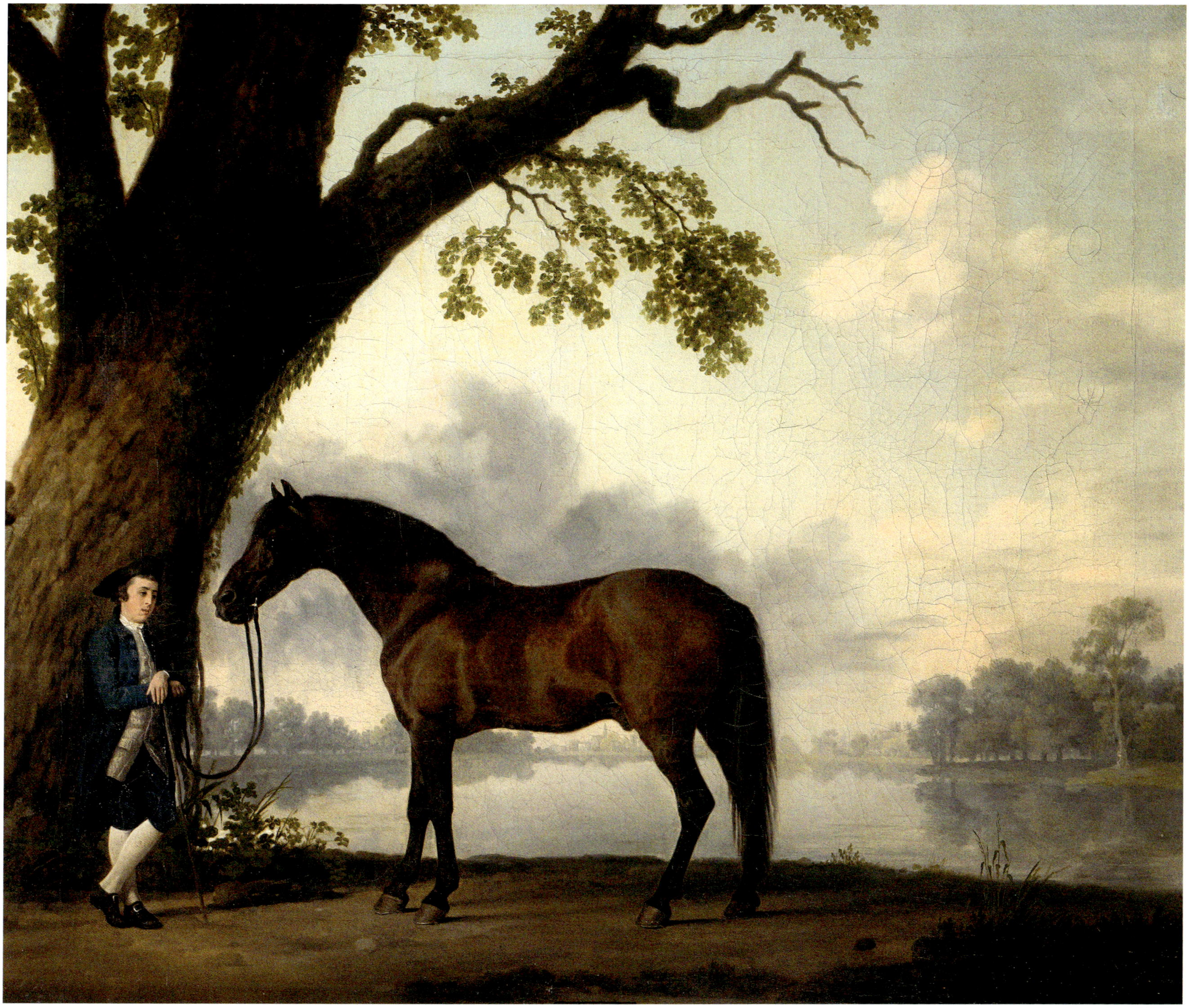

38

A Gentleman (Alexander Brymer?) in Riding Dress with a Chestnut Hunter 1768

Oil on canvas, 61 x 71 cm
Signed and dated at bottom right: *Geo: Stubbs pinxit / 1768*

Probably commissioned by Alexander Brymer (1729?–1822) – private collection

This painting was in the hands of the Brymer family until 1968. According to family tradition, the man portrayed is Alexander Brymer, who spent part of his life in Nova Scotia. Brymer came from Dundee in Scotland and emigrated to Halifax in the early 1770s, where he made a considerable fortune as a merchant and entrepreneur and as Deputy Paymaster to the British troops stationed there. He returned to England in 1801 and after starting out in London eventually settled in Ramsgate, where he died in 1822 (James S. Macdonald, *North British Society, Halifax, Nova Scotia. Annals 1768–1903*, Halifax, N. S. 1903, pp. 24–27). An engraving made after a contemporary portrait of Brymer does indeed bear a resemblance to the gentleman in Stubbs's painting.

The painting shows a stocky man standing next to a saddled horse. The surrounding landscape is unusually picturesque—possibly at the express wish of the patron. The massive trunk of an oak whose branches arch over both man and horse frames the composition at right, while a lush river landscape with a little town in the distance opens up at left. Arcadian scenery such as this is very much the exception in Stubbs's oeuvre.

HWR

Lit.: Egerton, *George Stubbs*, 2007, no. 127

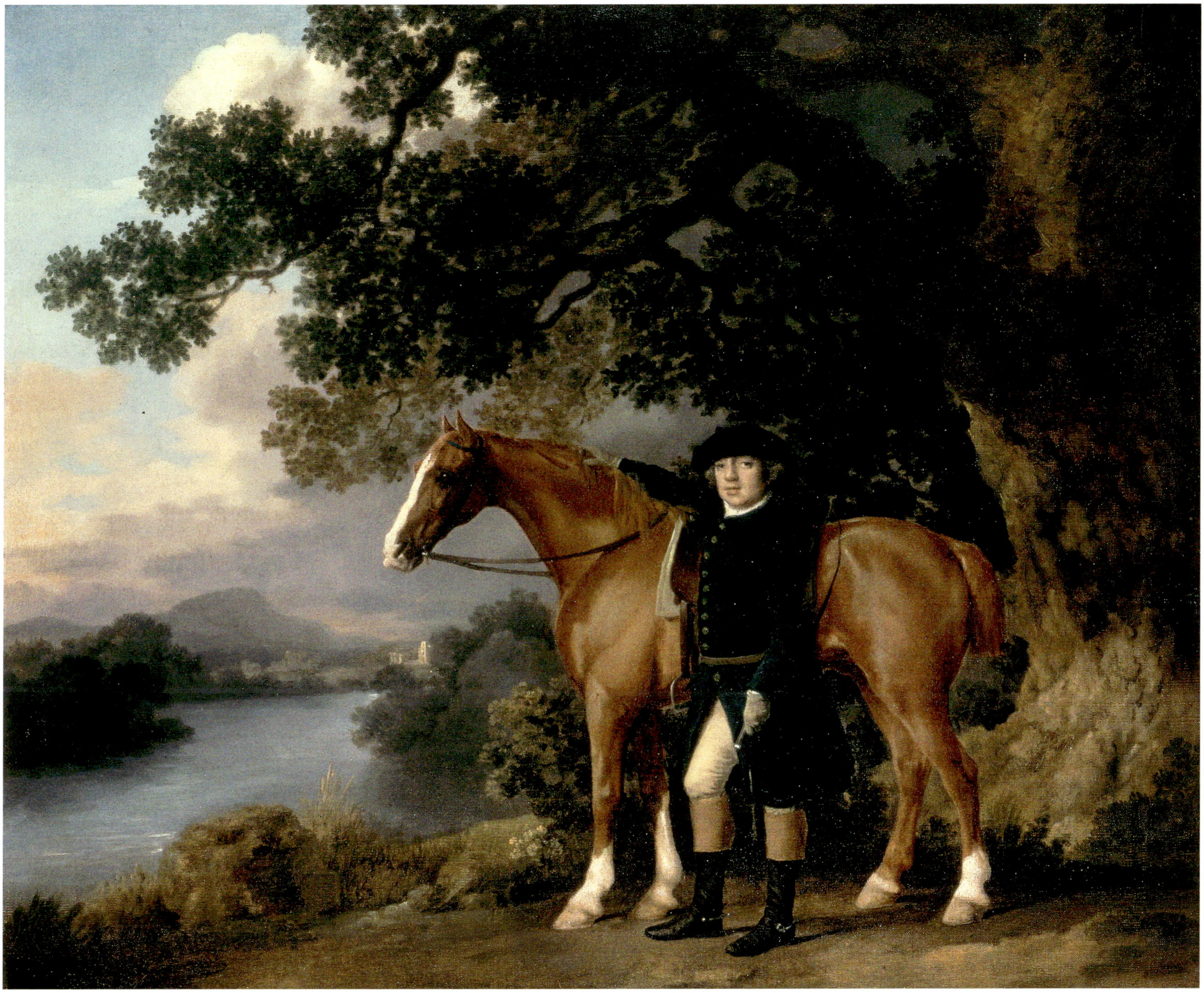

39
Self-Portrait 1781

Enamel on Wedgwood earthenware, 67.6 x 51.1 cm
Signed and dated on the palette: *Geo: Stubbs / pinxit 1781*; inscribed on verso: *Geo Stubbs painted by himself for his friend Richard Thorold / of the Inner Temple London. 1781.*

London, The National Portrait Gallery (purchased with help from The Art Fund 1967)

This self-portrait was one of five enamel paintings done on Wedgwood earthenware that Stubbs submitted to the Royal Academy exhibition in 1782. Like several of his other works in enamel, this too was intended as a gift for a friend, in this case Richard Thorold, a lawyer by profession who also made a name for himself as an inventor. Stubbs was clearly confident that the new painting method would meet with approval in this quarter.

Stubbs's large enamels measuring more than one metre across were made possible by Wedgwood's invention of biscuit porcelain plaques, which in turn were the result of endless experiments with new kilns and various methods of controlling firing temperatures. Stubbs and Wedgwood shared a determination to trial new materials and manufacturing methods and to explain the science behind them.

Stubbs planned his self-portrait in a finely squared preparatory drawing which is now in the Paul Mellon Collection. It is about half the size of the painting and was easily transferred thanks to the squaring. Painting in enamels is an exceedingly slow and painstaking process which is executed in stages and therefore necessitates a grid. The composition of the half-figure portrait follows the classical (self-)portrait form. The subject's body is shown in three-quarter profile, while his head is turned slightly so that he appears to be looking over his shoulder at the viewer. Because the study for the work was almost certainly done in front of a mirror, the pupils have ended up in the corners of the eyes—which accounts for the rather stiff look that so many self-portraits have. The head turned over the shoulder, on the other hand, had been highly prized as an iconographic signifier of artistic inspiration in England ever since the days of van Dyck. The positioning of the right eye on the vertical central axis is also very much in keeping with portrait convention and has the effect of fixating the viewer and forcing him to engage with the subject.

WB

Lit.: Exhib. Cat. *George Stubbs*, 1984/85, no. 4 – *Mid-Georgian Portraits 1760–1790 (National Portrait Gallery)*, edited by John Ingamells, London 2004, pp. 449 f. – Exhib. Cat. *Stubbs and the Horse*, 2004/05, no. 66 – Egerton, *George Stubbs*, 2007, no. 232

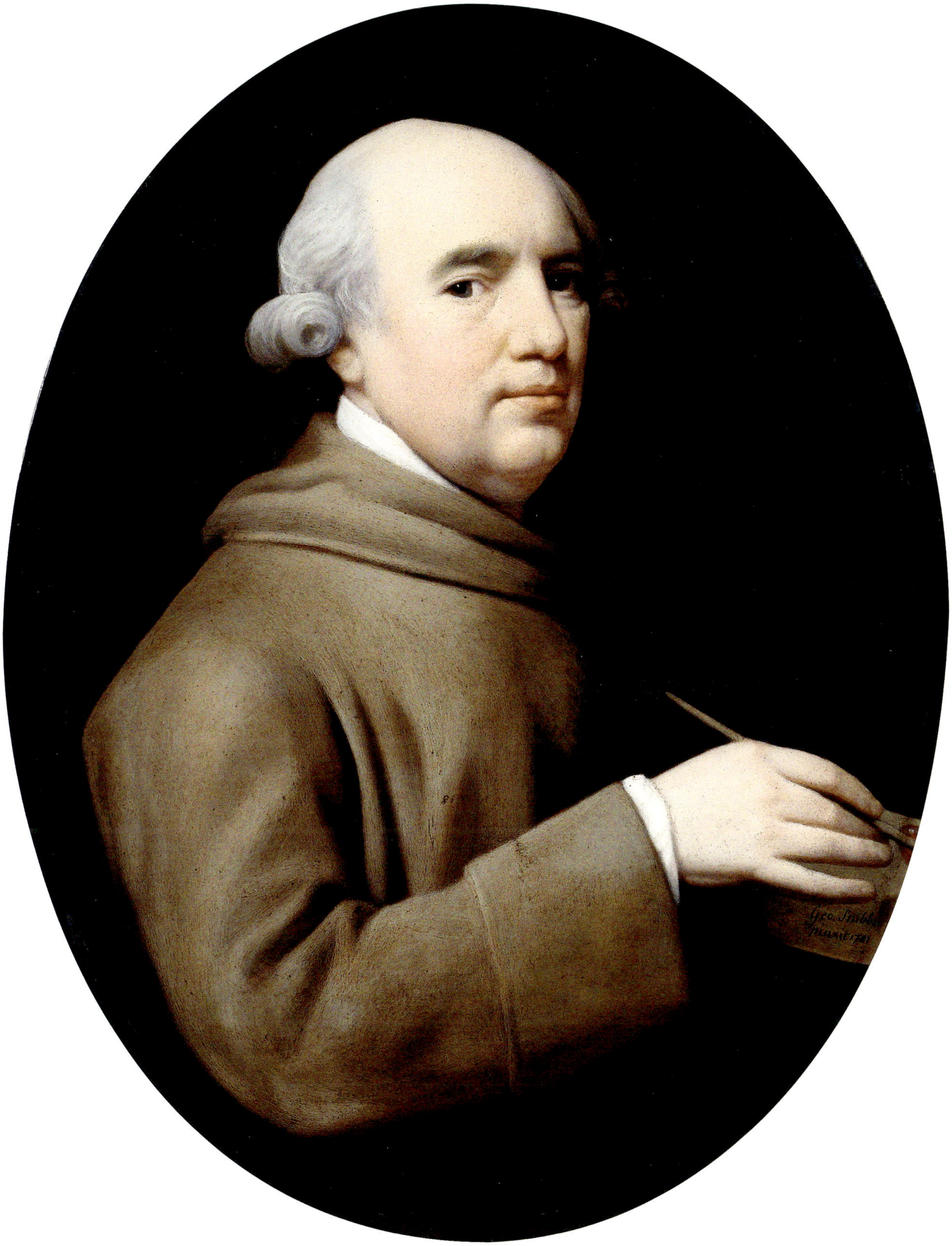

40
Horse Frightened by a Lion c. 1762/63

Oil on canvas, 70.5 x 104.1 cm

New Haven, Yale Center for British Art, Paul Mellon Collection

A remarkably large number of works in George Stubbs's oeuvre belong to the 'horse-and-lion' group. They capture three key moments that can be read in sequence: 1. A horse rears back in horror at the sight of an approaching lion. 2. The lion pounces onto the petrified horse, digging its claws deep into the horse's flanks and sinking its teeth into its back. The horse throws back its head, with its mouth wide open and tongue agonizingly outstretched. 3. The lion brings the horse to its knees and proceeds to tear the flesh from its back. Stubbs produced several different versions of all three types in a range of formats and techniques.

His first group of 'horse-and-lion' paintings dates to approximately 1762/63, while a second probably followed in 1769/70. The first prints were made in 1767 and were such an instant success that Stubbs's son, George Townley Stubbs, launched a series of his own in 1770. Stubbs himself did not make engravings after his own works until much later, in 1777, when his reproductions included an etching of a 'horse-and-lion' motif (cat. no. 65). Most of these early reproductions were done in mezzotint, which Stubbs later dropped in favour of the new 'mixed method,' so called because it combines engraving and etching. The great advantage of this new method was that it bathed the image in a veil of soft, finely-nuanced light—an effect that Stubbs sought to generate in his paintings too. It was thus an optical means of bringing an image to life.

In addition to the engravings, there are several small replicas painted in enamel colours on copper and Wedgwood's earthenware tablets, as well as some done on wood. Stubbs, it seems, experimented with a range of techniques and effects to find those that would show off his compositions to best advantage. The work in the Paul Mellon Collection shows the first type of 'horse-and-lion' motif and presumably belonged to the first group painted in 1762/63, since after 1769 the horses under attack were invariably grey.

WB

Lit.: Exhib. Cat. *George Stubbs in the Collection of Paul Mellon*, 1999/2000, no. 25 –
Exhib. Cat. *Stubbs and the Horse*, 2004/05, no. 40

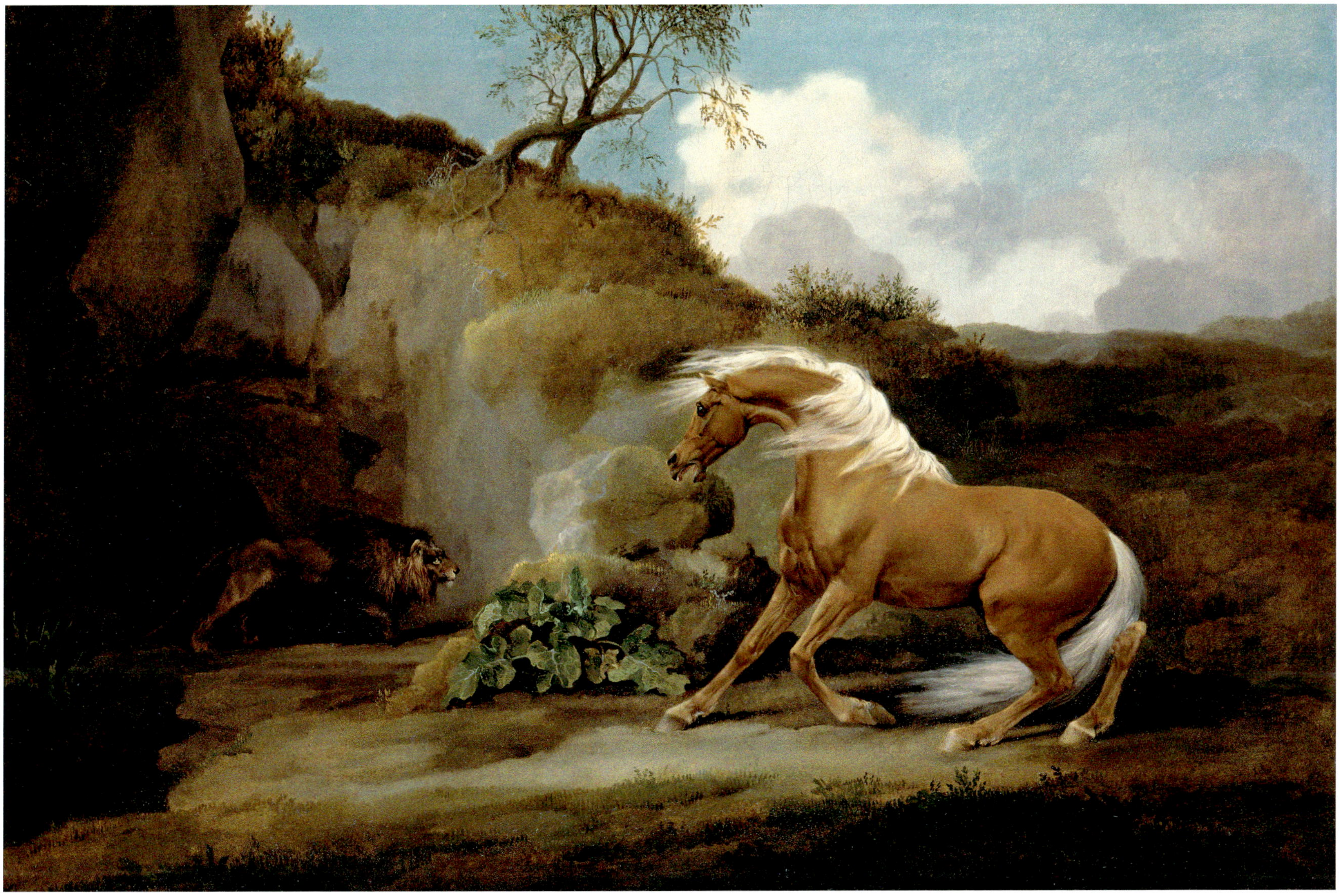

41

Lion Attacking a Horse 1769

Enamel on copper, 24.1 x 28.3 cm

Purchased in 1770 by Peniston Lamb, 1st Viscount Melbourne (1745–1828), Brocket Hall, Hertfordshire – London, Tate (purchased with assistance from the Friends of the Tate Gallery 1970)

* Not exhibited

The second type of 'horse-and-lion' motif, showing a lion attacking a horse, is represented here by this small painting dating from 1769 done in enamel colours on copper. Compared with the huge original—it is nearly three metres wide—commissioned by Lord Rockingham (p. 33, fig. 9), this version is indeed tiny, being less than thirty centimetres across. The dramatic expressiveness of the motif has been nonetheless retained. Stubbs wisely decided to concentrate on the essentials of the piece and by minimizing the landscape and cutting off the corners created a work in which the motif appears to be bursting out of its octagonal format.

Lord Melbourne, for whom Stubbs also painted a family portrait (cat. no. 35), bought this piece from the artist, but apparently had some difficulty persuading Stubbs to part with it. This may have to do with Stubbs's fear of being branded a minor master since enamels were liable to be regarded more as a product of the applied arts than of High Art. Such a reputation would have run counter to his determination to charge his own sure grasp of reality to such an extent that it became High Art. All the same he continued to take a considerable interest in enamel painting and in the expressive potential which he believed it promised. Horace Walpole's description of the work in his copy of the 1769 Society of Artists' catalogue as "very pretty" can be read as both complimentary and condescending. Walpole's sense of a classical hierarchy of genres was clearly unshakable.

Stubbs once again uses aesthetic means to anchor his work inside of its octagonal format. The vertical black line leading from the point where the lion's head and horse's neck and mane meet extends all the way down to the knee of the left foreleg. It is also taken up by the precipitous cliff face in the background and so marks the central axis on which the drama of the whole scene turns.

WB

Lit.: Exhib. Cat. *George Stubbs*, 1984/85, no. 64 – Exhib. Cat. *Stubbs and the Horse*, 2004/05, no. 60 – Egerton, *George Stubbs*, 2007, no. 112

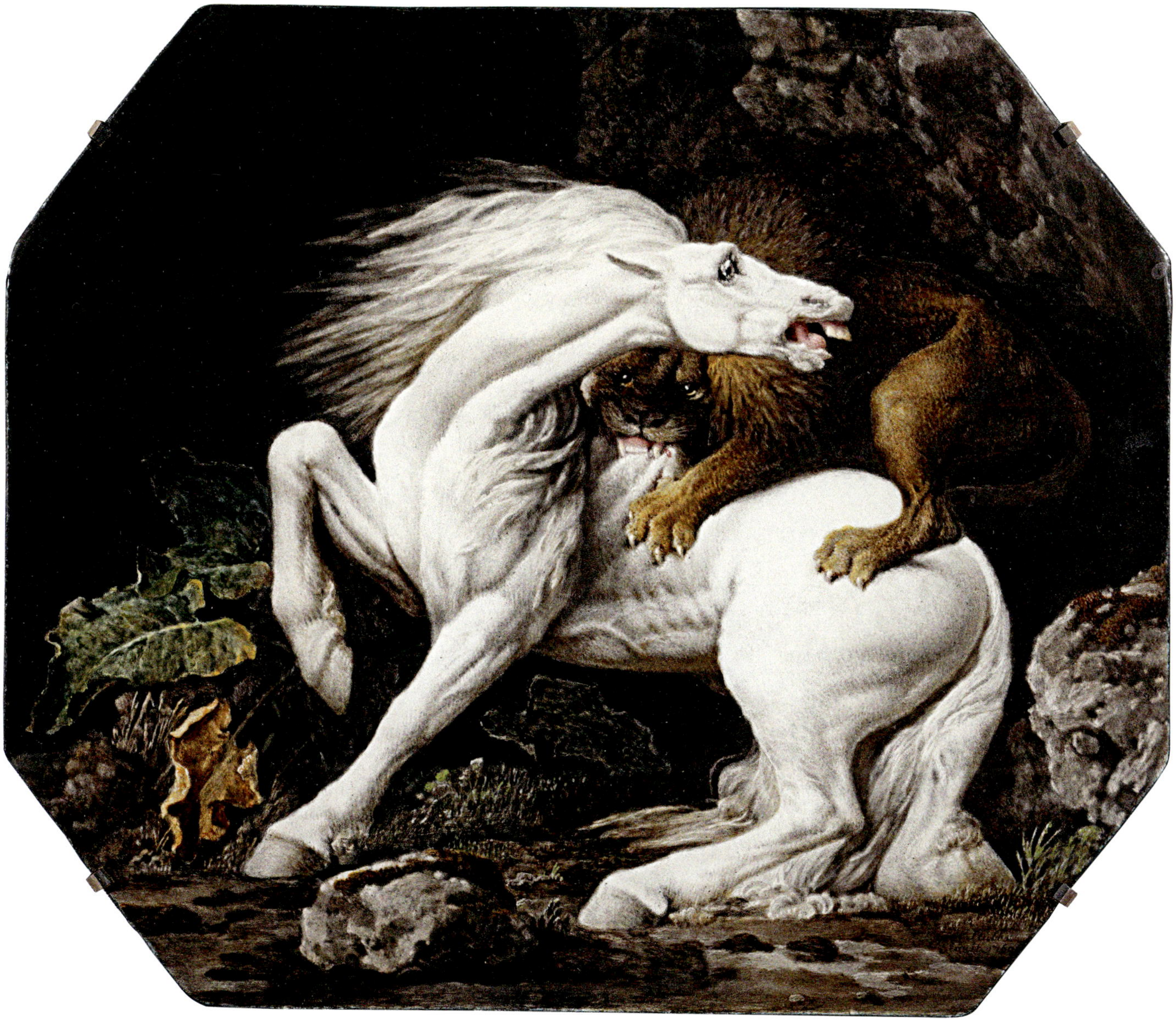

42

Horse Devoured by a Lion 1763

Oil on canvas, 69.2 x 103.5 cm

London, Tate (purchased 1976)

This painting in the Tate Gallery shows the third type of the 'horse-and-lion' motif, in which the lion has already brought the horse down. The topography of both this work and its pendant (Egerton no. 38) is much more vividly drawn than in the example of the first type also exhibited here (cat. no. 40). Stubbs apparently discovered Creswell Crags in the Peak District on the border of Nottinghamshire and Derbyshire in the early 1760s and was instantly captivated by the wild, primordial character of the place. With its limestone crags and prehistoric caves it not only made an ideal backdrop for his 'horse-and-lion' paintings but also shifted the scene of the action to a time in the distant past when fighting tooth and claw was essential to survival. As the Arabian breeds that sired the first thoroughbred racehorses appeared to have retained their fighting spirit and English horse breeders regarded it as their mission to preserve and to perpetuate this ancient life force while simultaneously refining it, Stubbs's paintings can also be said to be about the ennobling power of history; they are images of an ideal.

The past is present in another form, too, since all of these paintings of a fallen horse being devoured by a lion were most likely modelled on an antique marble sculpture in the garden of the Palazzo dei Conservatori in Rome, which Stubbs presumably saw on his visit to Italy in 1754. In the restored condition in which Stubbs would have seen it, however, the marble is rather lacking in tension. This is because instead of being violently thrown back, as it is in Stubbs's painting, the horse's head added by the overzealous restorers stares straight ahead. The Renaissance artists who reproduced the marble must have noticed this shortcoming themselves, since their bronze paraphrases of it—or at least those stemming from the circle of Giambologna—all render the horse with its head thrown back. So Stubbs's model might well instead have been one of those bronzes, especially as some of them are known to have been in England at the time, including in the collections of Lord Rockingham and others among Stubbs's patrons. A sixteenth-century print of Adamo Scultori's marble which greatly enhances the drama of the piece is also known to have been in circulation.

WB

Lit.: Exhib. Cat. *George Stubbs*, 1984/85, no. 63 – Exhib. Cat. *George Stubbs in the Collection of Paul Mellon*, 1999/2000, no. 17 – Exhib. Cat. *Stubbs and the Horse*, 2004/05, no. 41 – Egerton, *George Stubbs*, 2007, no. 39

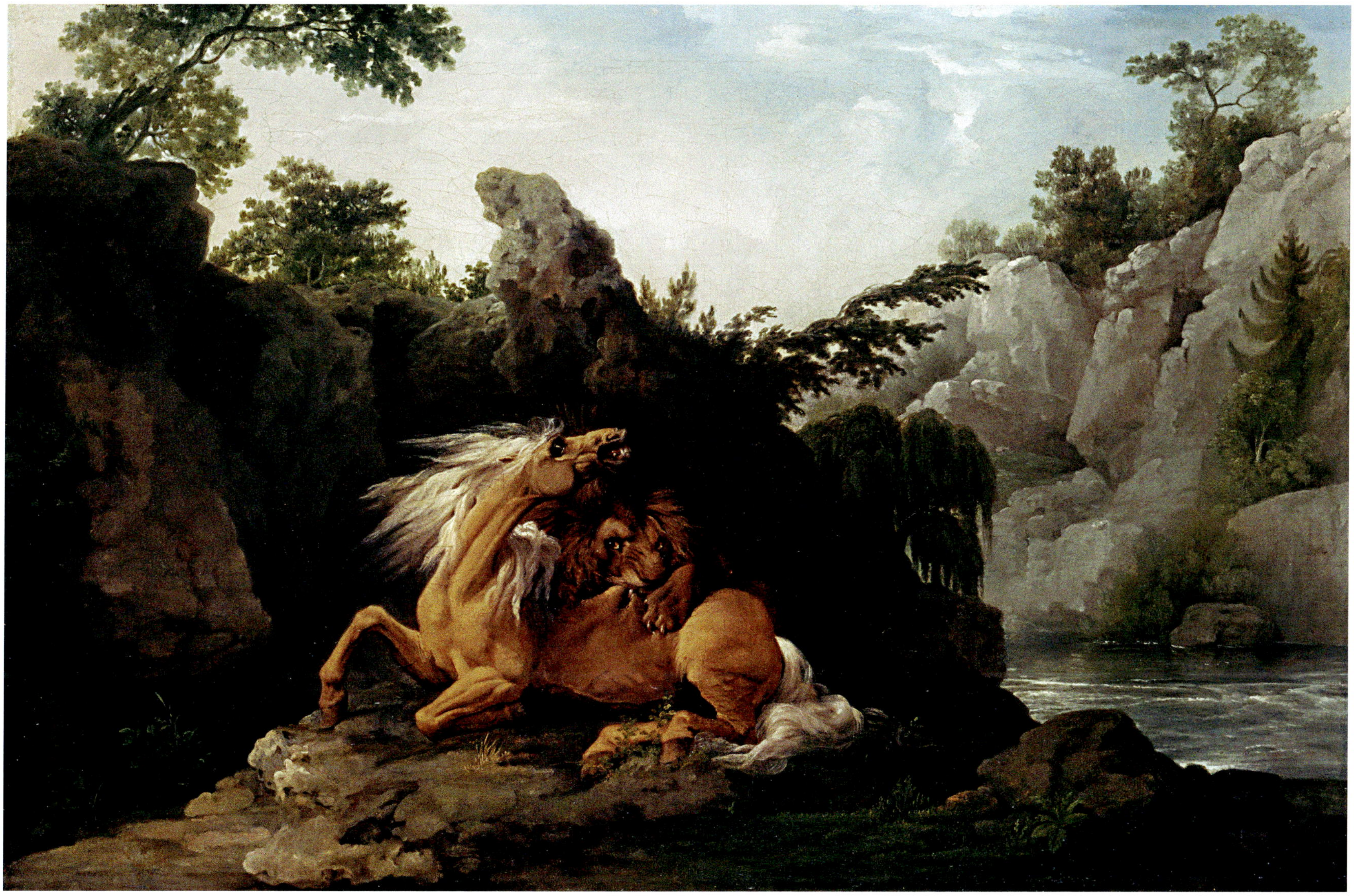

43
Lion Devouring a Stag 1769

Oil on canvas, 101.7 x 127.6 cm

Probably purchased by Charles Manners, 4th Duke of Rutland (1754–1787), Belvoir Castle, Leicestershire – private collection

This depiction of a lion sinking its teeth into a felled stag marks a significant deviation from the 'horse-and-lion' theme. The type can again be traced back to 1765 when Lord Rockingham commissioned a pendant piece to his monumental original of the 'horse-and-lion' typology (Egerton no. 111). While Lord Rockingham's 'lion and stag' was equally monumental (2.43 x 3.33 m), this version—first exhibited in 1769—is both smaller and better than the original in a number of different respects. As Walpole with his typically fine feelers instantly noticed, the latter was strangely lacking in tension, mainly because the stag has become a mere attribute of the lion, which itself seems like a separate portrait. Stubbs's treatment of the two beasts in the work shown here is much more convincing: the lion has turned the stag over and sunk its teeth into its back so that what we are looking at is the belly of the stag, which is rigid in desperation and held down by the lion crouching behind it.

There is something slightly statuesque about this group positioned in front of a flat cliff face. Stubbs actually enhanced this effect by using a method we also see elsewhere in his work: first by marking the vertical central axis—this runs right down the lion's nose and is then taken up by the shadow cast by the cliffs—and then by adding a long, pale-grey cloud which, corresponding in length to the central group, floats above the cliff in front of the mountainous backdrop. It is a method that works almost imperceptibly and which Stubbs repeated in a variation of the first type of 1770 (Egerton no. 120).

WB

Lit.: Egerton, *George Stubbs*, 2007, no. 119

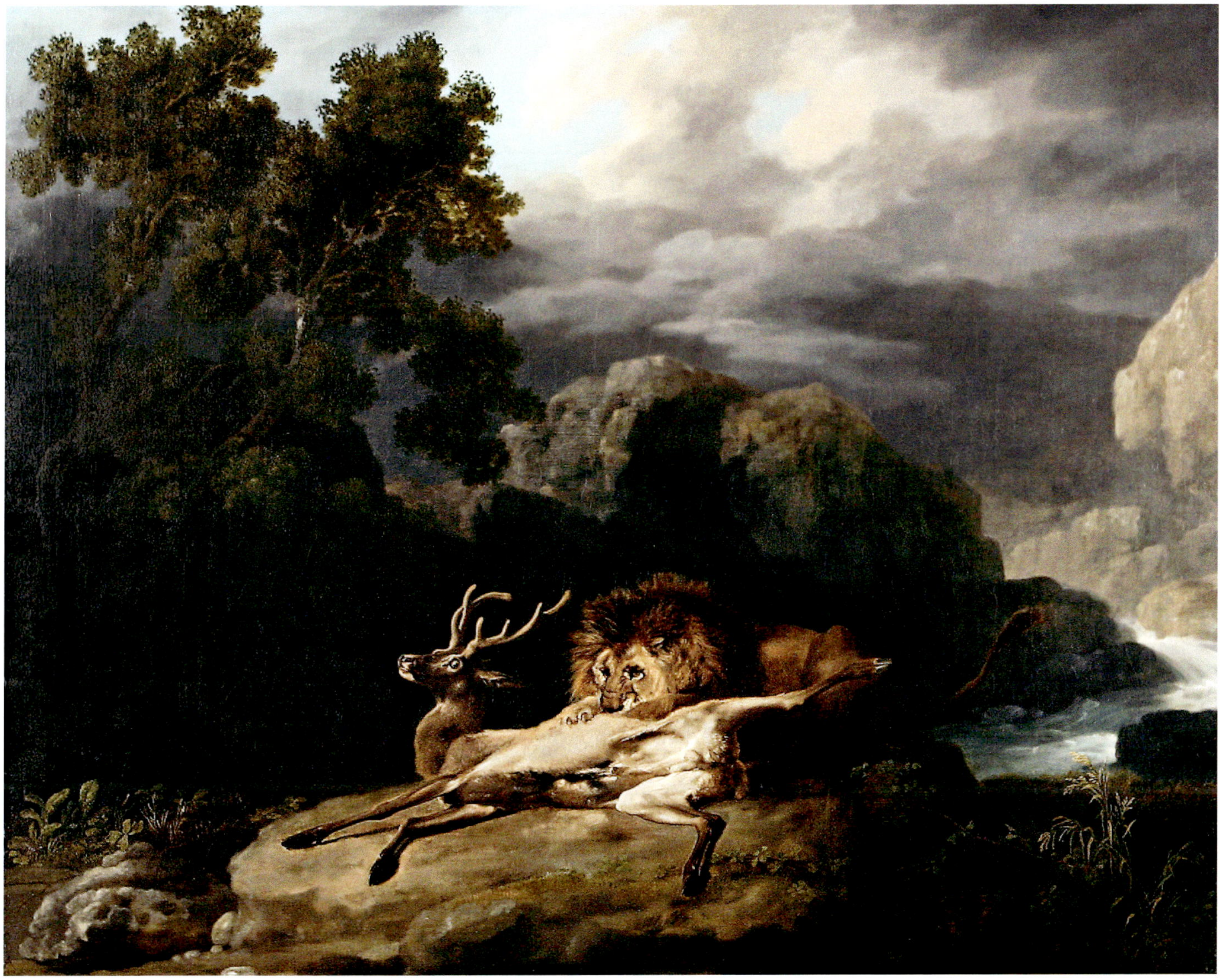

44

Cheetah and Stag with Two Indian Attendants 1765

Oil on canvas, 180.7 x 273.3 cm

Commissioned by George Pigot, 1st Baron Pigot (1719–1777), Patshull Hall, Staffordshire – Manchester Art Gallery (purchased with the assistance of the Victoria and Albert Museum Purchase Grant Fund and The Art Fund)

This magnificent painting dates from a time when Stubbs, having already had some success as a painter of equine and hunting scenes, was endeavouring to establish a reputation as a painter of exotic creatures as well. Exhibited at the Society of Artists in 1765, it was listed in the catalogue as a "Portrait of a hunting tyger". Legend has it that the painting shows the very same cheetah that the Governor of Madras, Sir George Pigot, brought with him to England as a gift for King George III in 1764. After the ship had docked in Plymouth on 6 June, the cheetah was taken to Windsor where the Duke of Cumberland, uncle to the king, had a menagerie. According to the *London Chronicle* of 3 July 1764 and several other newspapers, a select group of guests was to be treated to the spectacle involving the introduction of a stag into the cheetah's cage, where it was to be torn to pieces before their eyes. The stag, however, proved to be more than a match for the hapless cheetah, which after being raked up on the stag's antlers and hurled through the air, fled into the woods where it brought down a rather less resilient fallow deer.

This, or some similar event, is taken up by Stubbs's painting. The splendid full-length cat is presented life-size. Next to it are two men whose skin colour and clothes identify them as being from India, like the cheetah itself. One of the two has just removed the animal's blindfold, while the other is gesturing towards the stag behind him. The landscape is difficult to localize with any certainty, although there can be no doubt that Stubbs painted the cheetah from life and that the two Indian attendants are also authentic portraits. The silky sheen of the predator's coat and the finely-woven cloth in which the two men are clad lend the work an exotic and sensuous charm. They are also an impressive, if ambivalent, allusion to Great Britain's role as a colonial power.

HWR

Lit.: George Clutton, "The Cheetah and the Stag," in: *The Burlington Magazine* 112, 1970, pp. 536–39 – Blake, *George Stubbs and the Wide Creation*, 2005, pp. 184 f. – Exhib. Cat. *George Stubbs*, 1984/85, no. 79 – Egerton, *George Stubbs*, 2007, no. 76 – Eric Frederick Gollannek, *"Empire Follows Art." Exchange and the Sensory Worlds of Empire in Britain and its Colonies, 1740–1775*, PhD thesis, University of Delaware 2008, pp. 246 f.

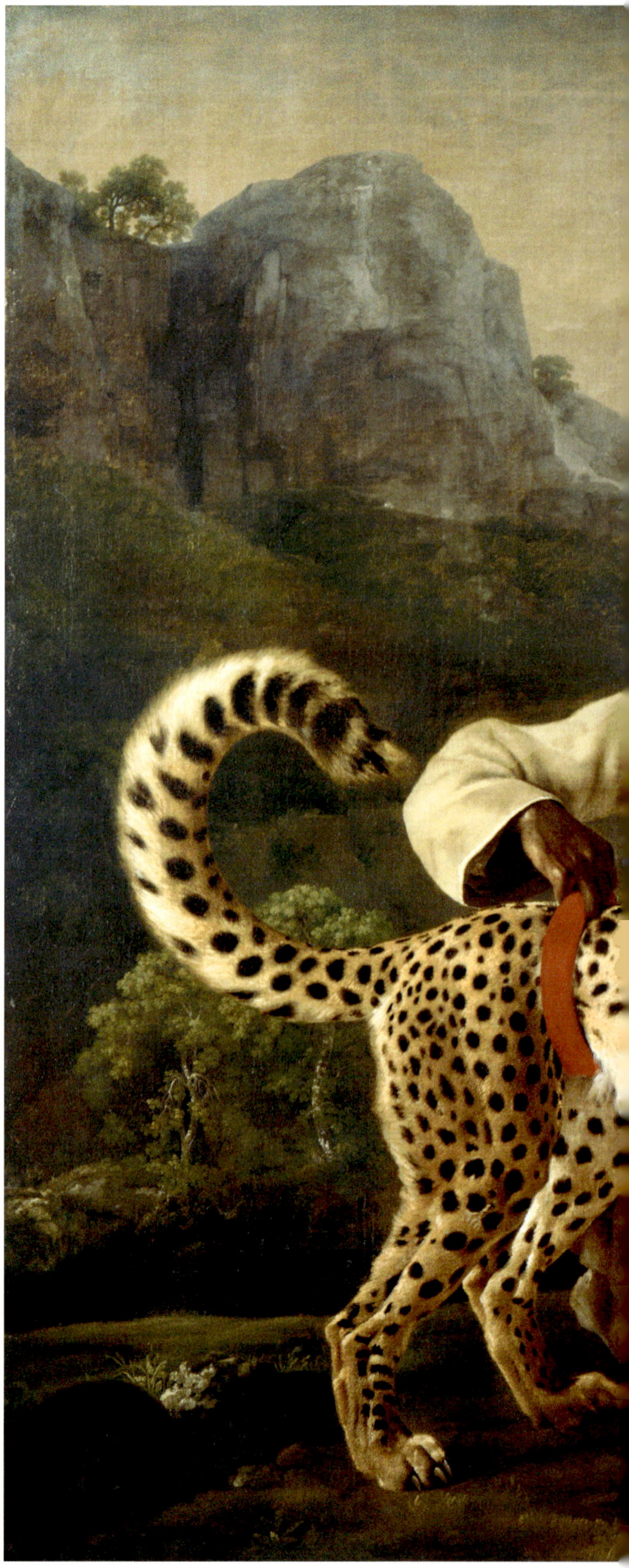

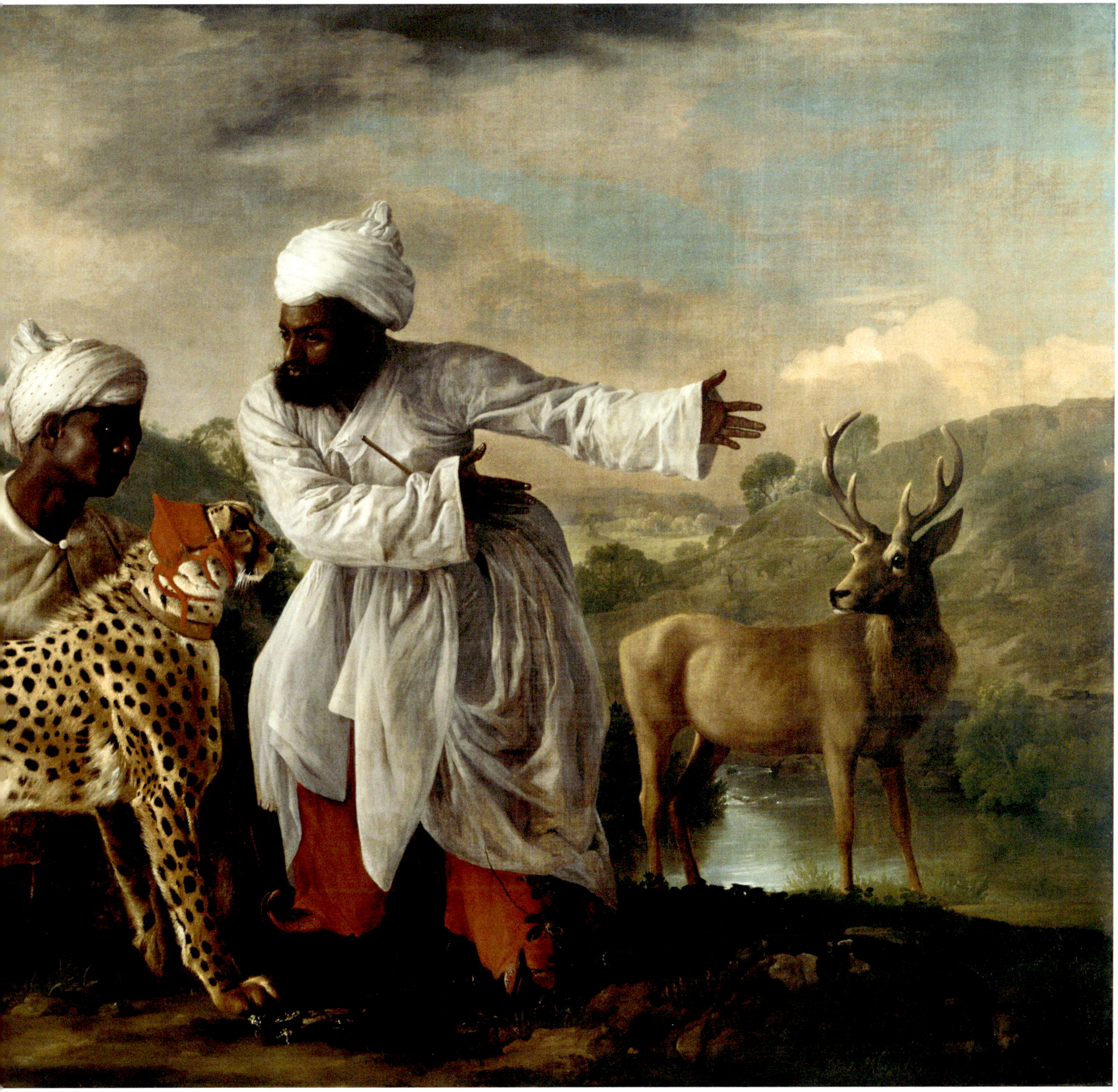

45

Zebra 1763

Oil on canvas, 102.9 x 127.6 cm

1807 in the artist's estate – New Haven, Yale Center for British Art, Paul Mellon Collection

The *Zebra* is one of Stubbs's most famous works and a pioneering achievement as the first of his portraits of exotic animals. A belated wedding gift from King George III to the young Queen Charlotte, the female zebra was the first of its kind to be imported into England on its arrival from the Cape of Good Hope in July 1762.

Menageries of exotic animals had existed since the Middle Ages and in the age of Absolutism were one of the many means by which European royal courts demonstrated the extent of their power and influence in the world—as well as being a source of exclusive entertainment. This particular zebra, however, was kept in a public paddock near Buckingham House where, known affectionately as "the queen's ass", it became a major attraction as well as the subject of numerous political satires and derisory poems in which the queen was ridiculed. Stubbs, in contrast, takes his subject very seriously and goes to great lengths to reproduce the animal with anatomical accuracy and in a way that does justice to its exotic beauty. Thanks to the artist's keen powers of observation, zoologists have been able to identify the animal as a Cape Mountain Zebra.

Although the exact circumstances under which Stubbs painted his *Zebra* are obscure, we do know about one royal commission for such a portrait. Queen Charlotte ordered that a likeness should be painted after realizing that public interest in the animal was so great that not everyone would be able to see it (John Watkins, *Memoirs of Her Most Excellent Majesty Sophie-Charlotte*, London 1819, p. 185). And since we also know that Stubbs's own painting, which on his death was found in his estate, was exhibited at the Society of Artists in 1763, we are bound to ask whether Stubbs was deliberately competing with the artist commissioned by the queen—presumably in hopes of attracting the attention of potential patrons?

OK

Lit.: Exhib. Cat. *George Stubbs*, 1984/85, no. 77 – Exhib. Cat. *George Stubbs in the Collection of Paul Mellon*, 1999/2000, no. 19 – Blake, *George Stubbs and the Wide Creation*, 2005, pp. 214 f. – Egerton, *George Stubbs*, 2007, no. 40 – Christopher Plumb, *Exotic Animals in Eighteenth-Century Britain*, PhD thesis, University of Manchester 2010, p. 172

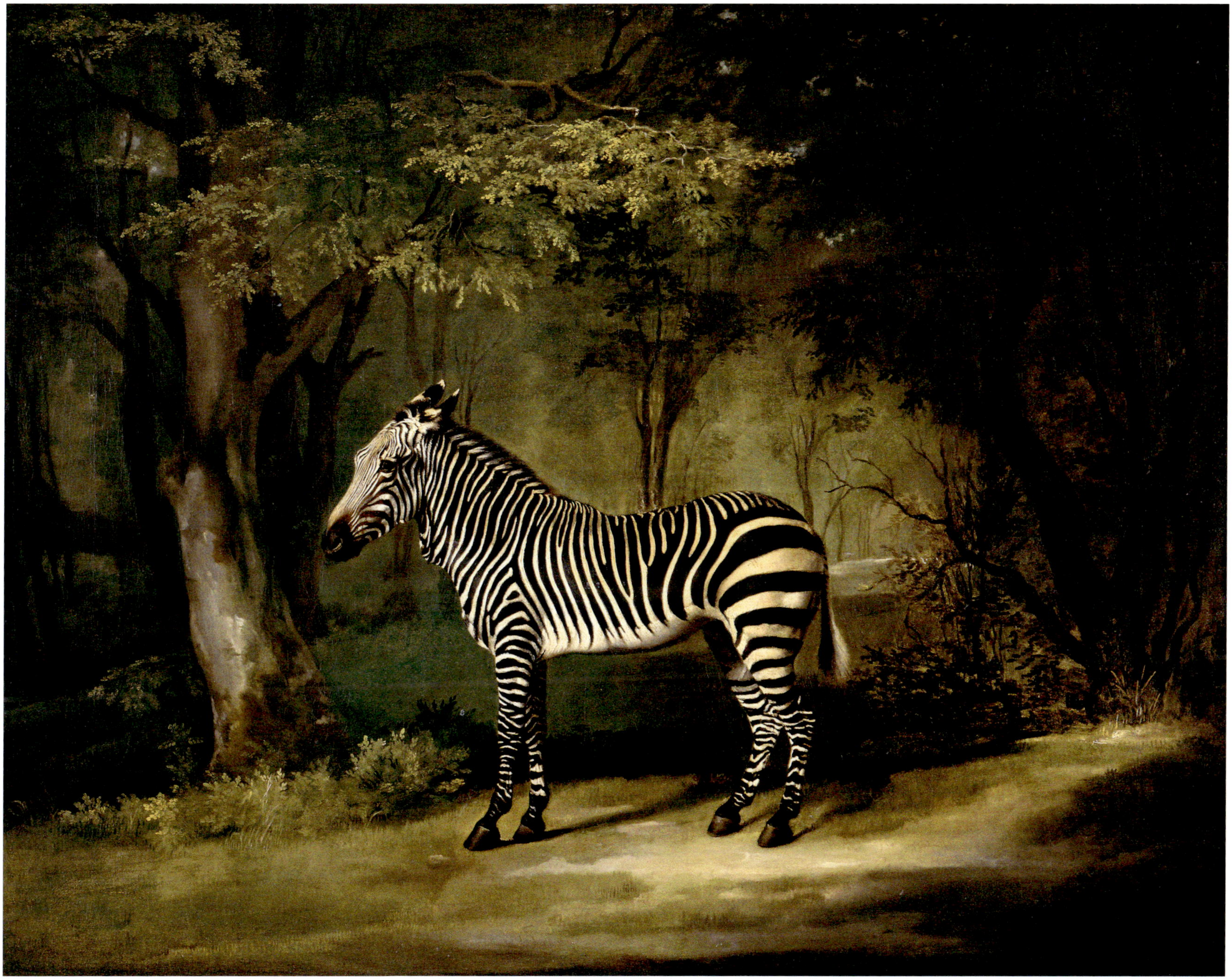

46
Bull Moose 1770

Oil on canvas, 61 x 70.5 cm
Signed and dated at bottom right: *Geo: Stubbs pinxit / 1770*

Commissioned by the physician and natural philosopher William Hunter (1718–1783) –
The Hunterian, University of Glasgow

It was doubtless Stubbs's *Zebra* that brought him to the attention of William Hunter, who, as physician-extraordinary to the Queen, had been granted a royal privilege to study a pair of her nilgais (Indian antelopes). As a scientist who often had to make do with vague verbal descriptions and fantastical pictures, Hunter knew the value of accurate paintings both as a visual aid and as a source of information. He therefore commissioned Stubbs to paint a nilgai (1769) and a Canadian bull moose (1770).

As with so many other exotic creatures, there were hopes that both the nilgai and the bull moose might be successfully domesticated and even bred. Hunter's interest in them was very different, however, and in those days controversial too: Stubbs's painting of a yearling bull moose was intended to add weight to his theory that entire species could become extinct. In 1697 the discovery of the fossilized antlers of a giant stag or 'Irish elk' had been published. Hunter was intent on showing that these antlers were clearly different from the mature antlers of the Canadian elk. Stubbs thus took care to place the precisely rendered antlers in the foreground of his painting. Yet to argue that the 'Irish elk' had become extinct—a theory of which not even Hunter was ultimately convinced—would have meant challenging the dogma of the Great Chain of Being, which, being preordained by God, had no room for either extinction or evolution. The antlers in the lower left of Stubbs's painting look strangely pointless. Earlier animal painters would have had no qualms about simply endowing the young moose with the antlers of a fully-grown beast. Stubbs, however, confined his aesthetic licence to the fictional landscape in the background, providing his moose with an evocative setting.

OK

Lit.: W. D. Ian Rolfe, "William Hunter (1718–1783) on Irish 'Elk' and Stubbs's Moose," in: *Archives of Natural History* 11, 2, 1983, pp. 263–90 – Exhib. Cat. *George Stubbs*, 1984/85, no. 82 – W. D. Ian Rolfe, "William and John Hunter: Breaking the Great Chain of Being," in: William F. Bynum and Roy Porter (eds.), *William Hunter and the Eighteenth-Century Medical World*, Cambridge 1985, pp. 297, 319 – *"My Highest Pleasures". William Hunter's Art Collection*, edited by Peter Black, Exhib. Cat. Hunterian Art Gallery, University of Glasgow, London 2007, no. 43 – Egerton, *George Stubbs*, 2007, no. 106

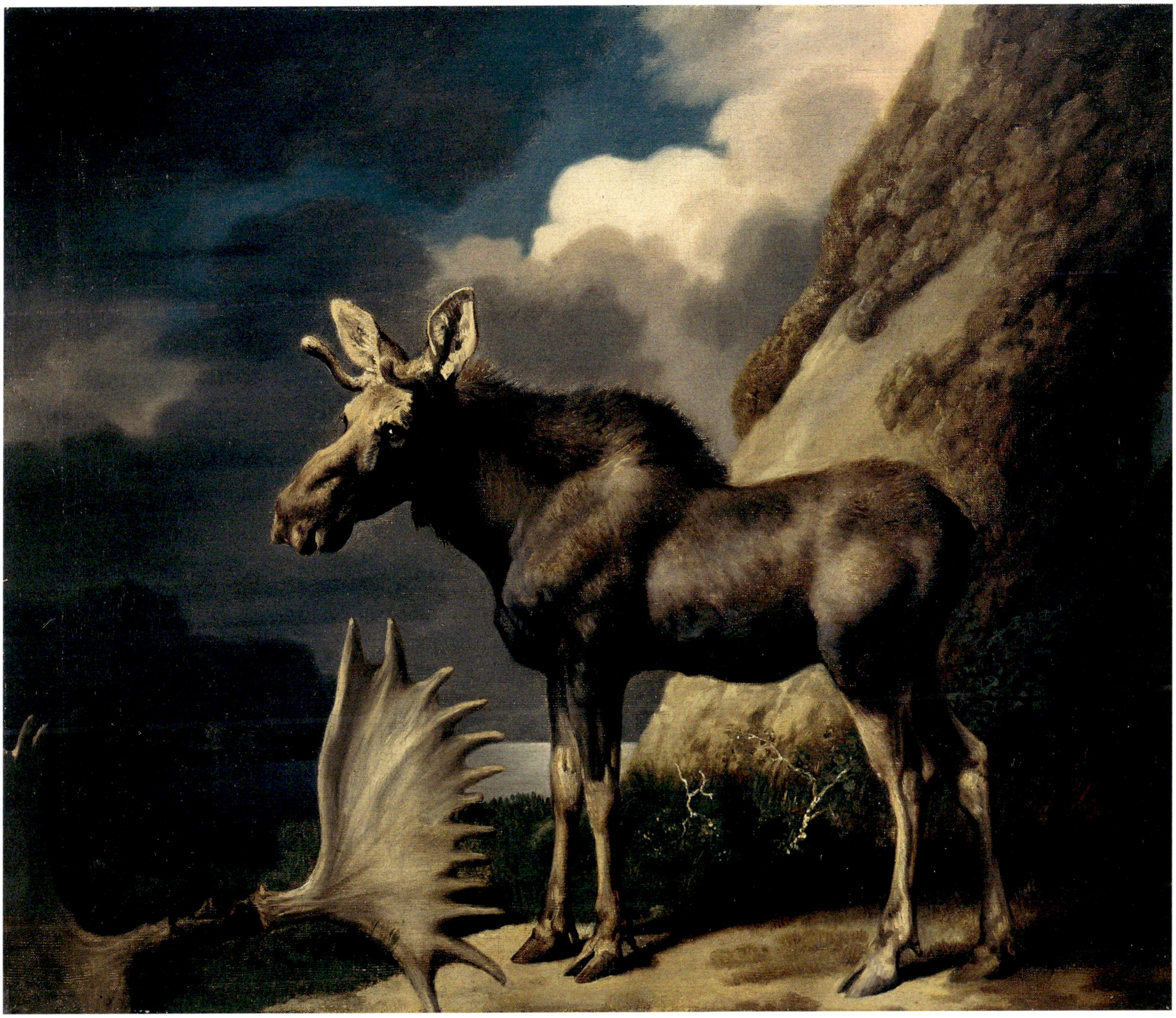

47

Rhinoceros c. 1790/91

Oil on canvas, 69.9 x 92.7 cm

Commissioned by the physician and natural philosopher John Hunter (1728–1793) – London, Hunterian Museum at the Royal College of Surgeons

Both William Hunter and his brother John commissioned Stubbs to make paintings of exotic animals. His painting of a male and female monkey was done in 1770–75 (Egerton no. 141), while the two last commissions, *Warren Hastings's Yak* (Egerton no. 285) and the *Rhinoceros* shown here, date from 1790/91. When John Hunter died in 1793, the *Rhinoceros* was found in his teaching collection, which went on to form the basis of today's Hunterian Museum at the Royal College of Surgeons in London. The house on Leicester Square, home to Hunter since 1783, held the 14,000 specimens and preparations of some 500 different species of plant and animal that he had amassed for his museum of natural history. These were essential to his study of comparative anatomy and inspired Stubbs to embark on his last great drawing project: a *Comparative Anatomical Exposition of the Structure of the Human Body with that of a Tiger and a Common Fowl.*

In Hunter's museum the *Rhinoceros* had a purely scientific function as an exact reproduction of a real creature. The aesthetic aspects of the composition thus had to take second place to the work's potential as a scientific source. Stubbs therefore filled the canvas with a view of a rhinoceros in profile, paying special attention to the texture and folds of its thick, protective skin. Profile views of animals at rest had come to be regarded as the most neutral and informative means of visualizing them ever since being presented this way in the plates of Buffon's *Histoire naturelle* in 1750. Stubbs even goes so far as to dispense with all background details and narrative elements such as might detract from the rhinoceros itself. This objectivity of depiction contrasted greatly with the idea of the animal as a crowd-puller at annual fairs, which was the role played by the bizarre creature for most Londoners. Having arrived in England in 1790 as only the third of its species to set foot there, the rhino first went on show at the Lyceum on the Strand. In 1793 it was taken to Windsor and the Ascot Races as entertainment for the royal family and died there of an infected leg later that same year.

OK

Lit.: Exhib. Cat. *George Stubbs*, 1984/85, no. 87 – T. H. Clarke, *The Rhinoceros from Dürer to Stubbs, 1515–1799*, London 1986, pp. 70–75 – Egerton, *George Stubbs*, 2007, no. 278

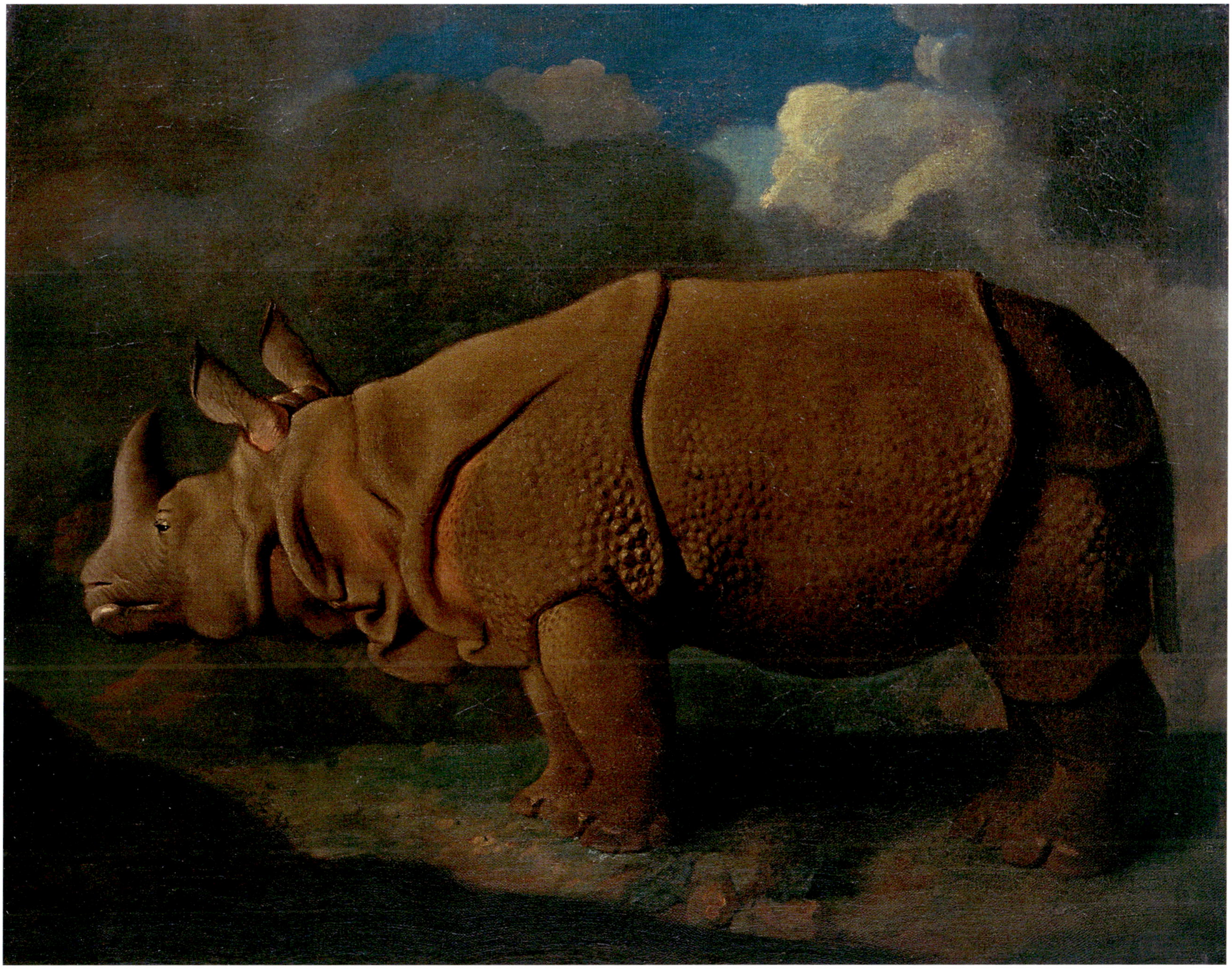

48

King Charles Spaniel 1776

Oil on canvas, laid on panel, 59.7 x 69.8 cm
Signed and dated bottom right: *Geo: Stubbs / pinxit 1776*

Private collection

A domestic animal in England since the sixteenth century, and improved by cross-breeding, the King Charles Spaniel was the royal dog par excellence. It owes its name to the kings Charles I and Charles II of England, who surrounded themselves with such dogs and were enthusiastic breeders. Anthony van Dyck included two such dogs in his 1635 portrait of the young Charles in *The Five Children of King Charles I* (in the Royal Collection). Stubbs shows the dog walking to the left with its head turned to face the viewer. It is one of the artist's most touching dog portraits. As Judy Egerton appropriately remarked in her description of this work in the catalogue of the London Stubbs exhibition: "The picture has much charm, but no sentimentality."

Having come to light only in 1973, the painting's provenance and the patron who commissioned it are unknown. The only clue provided by the work itself is the thistle in the left foreground, which could perhaps suggest Scotland.

HWR

Lit.: Exhib. Cat. *George Stubbs*, 1984/85, no. 100 – Egerton, *George Stubbs*, 2007, no. 169

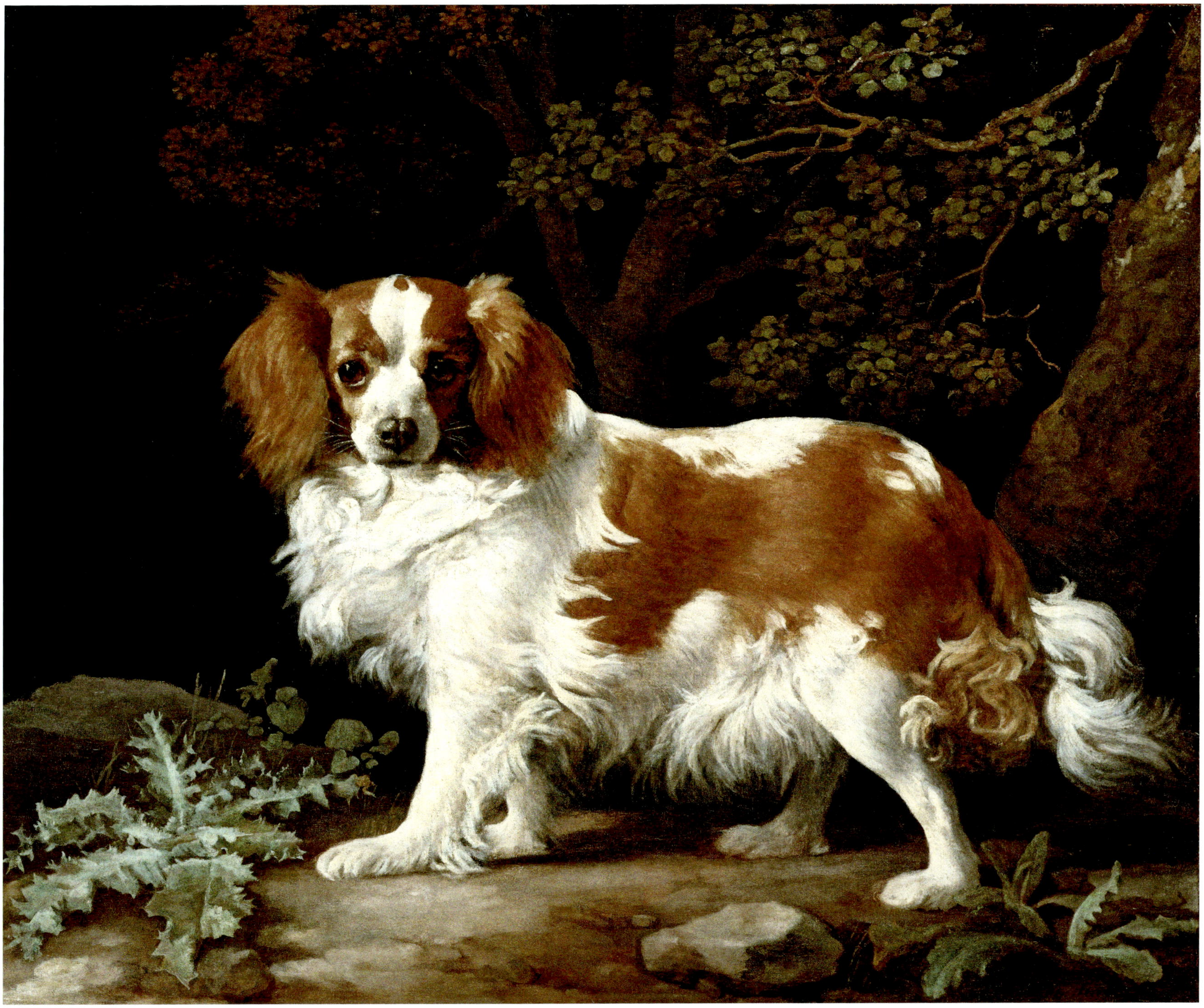

49
Turk, a Dog Belonging to the Duke of Rutland 1778

Oil on panel, 96.5 x 121.9 cm
Signed and dated at bottom right: *Geo: Stubbs pinxit 1778*

Commissioned by Charles Manners, 4th Duke of Rutland (1754–1787), Belvoir Castle, Leicestershire – private collection

Exhibited at the Royal Academy in 1778, Stubbs's painting of Turk the dog, commissioned by the Duke of Rutland, was widely praised for its verisimilitude and technical finesse. Thanks to the fact that it has remained in family hands, the painting is remarkably well preserved. Turk was what is now known as a keeshond or Dutch barge dog, a subspecies of the Pomeranian breed. The work derives its monumentality from the fact that Stubbs allowed the dog to fill the whole panel.

Those who study Stubbs's dog portraits in detail and compare them with his 'mixed method' (that is, partly etched) engravings of foxhounds dating from 1788 (cat. no. 56 and 57) will be struck by his use of frayed contours to generate a barely perceptible but all-enveloping and above all vitalizing veil of light. This technique, made possible in part by a toned-down palette and reserve when it comes to the blurring of colour, reached its apogee in his portrait of the *Milbanke and Melbourne Families* of 1769 (cat. no. 35). Though I am unable to prove it conclusively, I am inclined to believe that Stubbs first encountered such atmospheric effects when looking through a *camera obscura*. Light phenomena such as these—the bundling of light in areas bathed in sunlight and its fading away in areas of shade—have to be seen before they can be painted. We can nevertheless find them described in various popular treatises, including those on the camera obscura written by manufacturers such as Benjamin Martin or James Ferguson, both of whom had close ties to the Lunar Society and worked for the advancement of science in the provinces.

WB

Lit.: Egerton, *George Stubbs*, 2007, no. 196

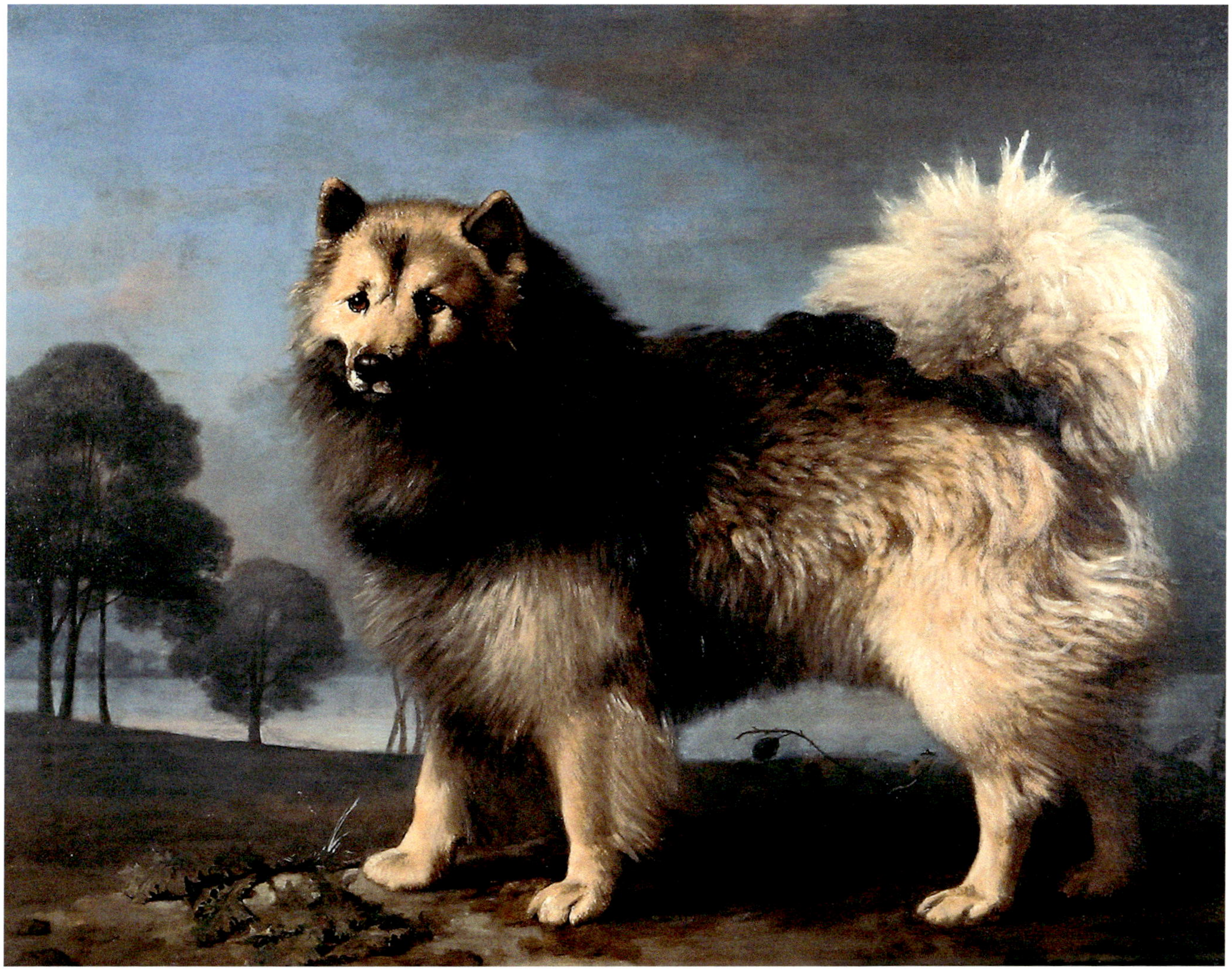

50

The Prince of Wales's Phaeton, with the Coachman Samuel Thomas and a Tiger Boy 1793

Oil on canvas, 102.2 x 128.3 cm
Signed and dated at bottom right: *Geo: Stubbs pinxit / 1793*

Commissioned by George Augustus, Prince of Wales (later King George IV, 1762–1830), Carlton House, London – The Royal Collection, lent by Her Majesty Queen Elizabeth II

Stubbs did not receive any royal commissions until very late in his career. It was not until 1790 that George Augustus, Prince of Wales, commissioned him to paint a series of pictures dedicated to the Prince's interest in sporting art and rural life to adorn his new townhouse, Carlton House on Pall Mall. The twelve paintings that Stubbs produced for the prince between 1790 and 1793, all in the same format, count among the finest works of his late phase.

As is often the case with Stubbs, the patron himself and master of the depicted people, animals and equipage does not appear in the painting. On the contrary, the scene owes its tension to the fact that the coach is being prepared in expectation of the Prince of Wales's imminent arrival. Desmond Shawe-Taylor has described in vivid detail the subtlety with which Stubbs eschews the usual pomp and ceremony and instead gives visible shape to the new set of values—speed, glamour and elegance—with which the heir to the throne wished to be associated. The phaeton is a 'high-flyer' whose large wheels, light superstructure and sprung suspension were intended to make it suitable for travelling at high speeds. It was the fastest and sportiest vehicle of the age and was generally driven by its owner. The only other person on board was the unfortunate 'tiger boy', whose job it was to risk life and limb cowering behind the seat, ready to intervene in the case of an emergency. The two stallions being prepared for harnessing by the state coachman Samuel Thomas epitomize both speed and strength, their black, shiny coats making for a pleasing harmony with the leather-upholstered coach. Although each of its constituent elements stands for a modern aesthetic of speed and elegance the scene as a whole is curiously static. Only the Pomeranian Fino, who is shown here barking at one of the horses, adds an element of active spontaneity and unrest.

HWR

Lit.: Exhib. Cat. *George Stubbs*, 1984/85, no. 135 – Exhib. Cat. *Stubbs and the Horse*, 2004/05, no. 74 – Egerton, *George Stubbs*, 2007, no. 306 – Desmond Shawe-Taylor, *The Conversation Piece. Scenes of fashionable life*, London 2009, pp. 156–59

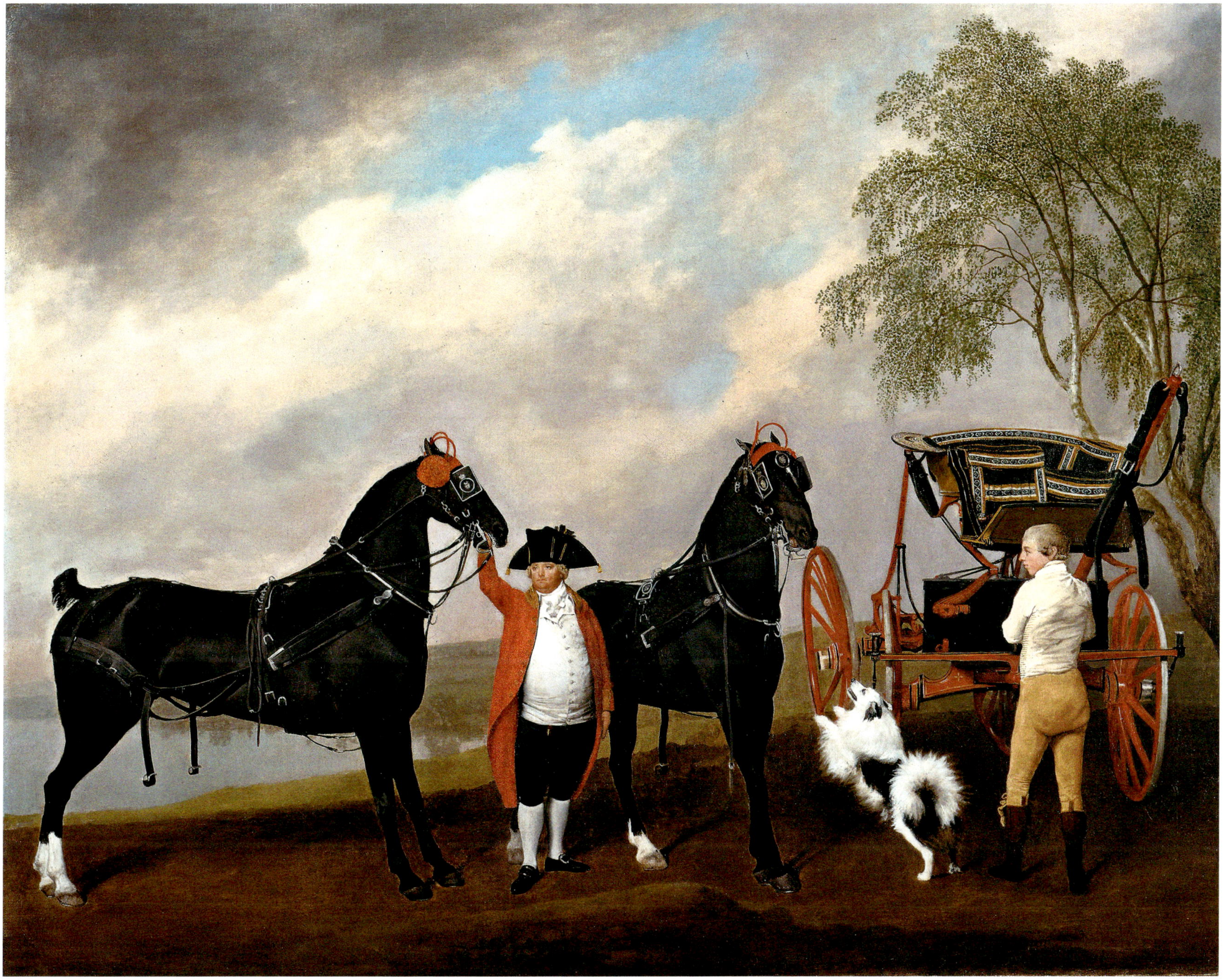

51

Soldiers of the 10th (Prince of Wales's Own) Regiment of Light Dragoons 1793

Oil on canvas, 102.2 x 128.1 cm
Signed and dated at bottom right: *Geo: Stubbs p: / 1793*

Commissioned by George Augustus, Prince of Wales (later King George IV, 1762–1830), Carlton House, London – The Royal Collection, lent by Her Majesty Queen Elizabeth II

Another of the works that Stubbs painted for the Prince of Wales's townhouse between 1790 and 1793 was the *Soldiers of the 10th Regiment of Light Dragoons.* George Augustus, Prince of Wales, was made Colonel Commandant of the regiment on 26 January 1793, and thereafter liked to have himself portrayed in full regimental dress. Although he commanded the regiment on various manoeuvres, including that in August 1793 when he celebrated his thirty-first birthday at a military encampment near Brighton, he never went to battle with them—against France, for example, with which Great Britain had been at war since 1792.

As in *The Prince of Wales's Phaeton* (cat. no. 50), here, too, the patron himself is missing from the painting. Shown instead are four soldiers belonging to his regiment: on the left a sergeant on horseback parading with sable held high, then a trumpeter, followed by a sergeant and a foot soldier, both of whom are standing to attention with bayonets fixed. Stubbs's characteristically laconic approach to his subjects is taken to an extreme in this work. The four, utterly immobile figures are lined up next to each other, staring straight ahead. The effect is not just unnatural, it is almost surreal. Central to the concept of the work, however, is Stubbs's descriptive rendering of his models, whose uniforms and weapons are reproduced in inordinate detail, even down to the Prince of Wales's feathers on the horse's saddlecloth. The composition is so carefully balanced that not a single element could be moved without upsetting the whole and forfeiting its coherence. Stubbs treats each of the four soldiers as a portrait subject in his own right, so that the individual facial features of each are clearly recognizable.

HWR

Lit.: Exhib. Cat. *George Stubbs*, 1984/85, no. 136 – Christopher Lloyd, *The Queen's Pictures. Old Masters from the Royal Collection*, London 1994, pp. 84 f. – Egerton, *George Stubbs*, 2007, no. 307

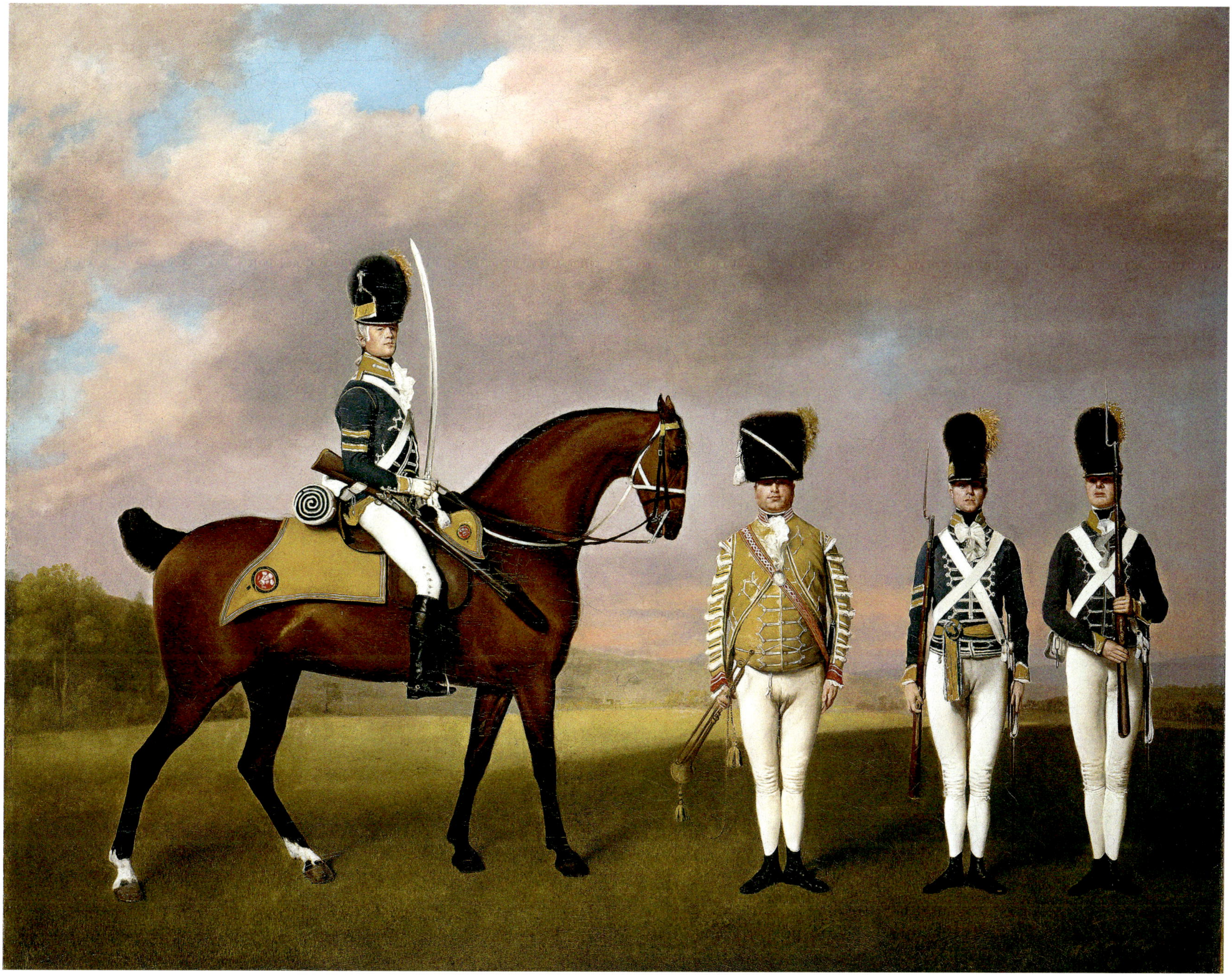

THE ANATOMY
OF THE HORSE

PAINTINGS

PRINTS

PRINTS AFTER STUBBS

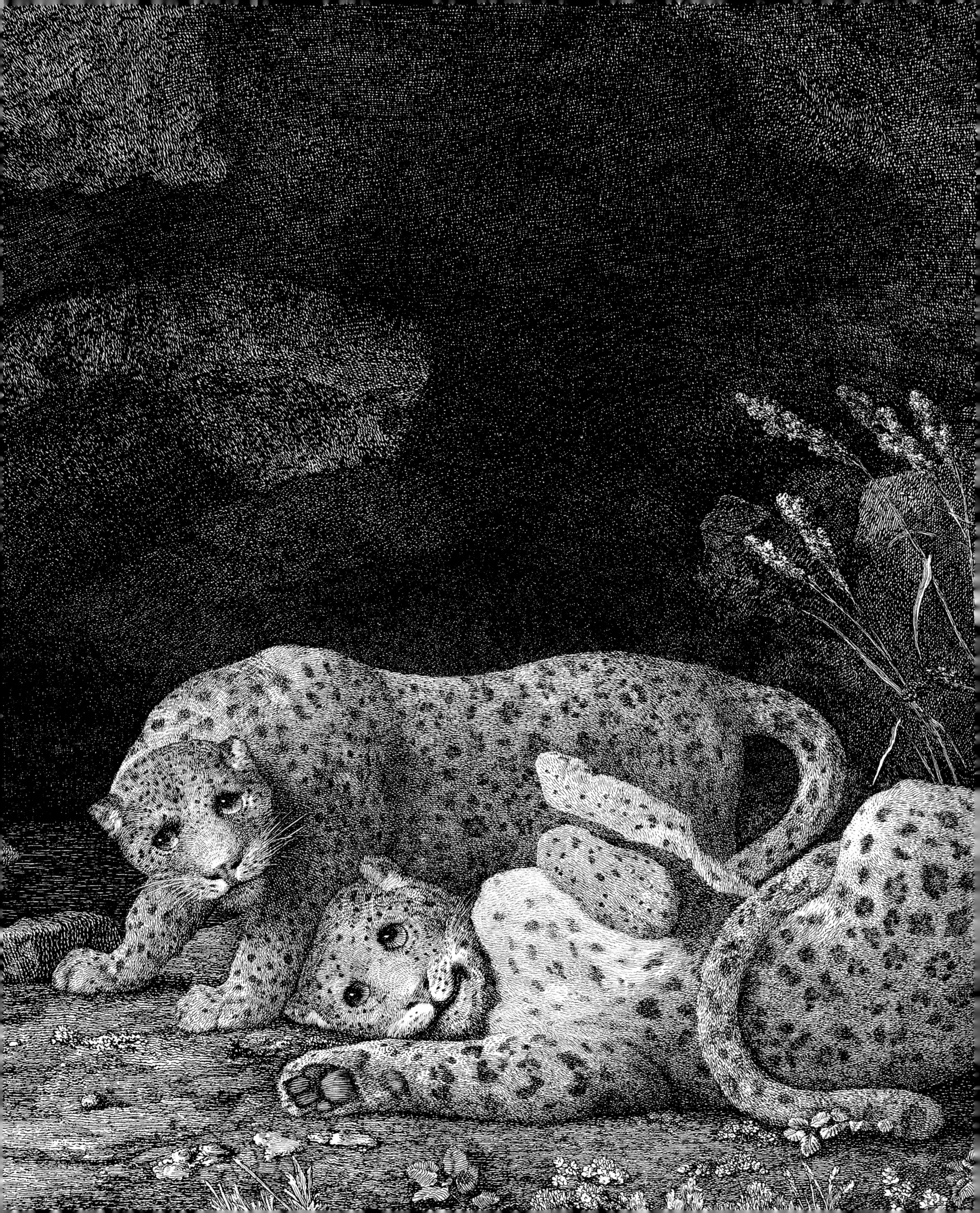

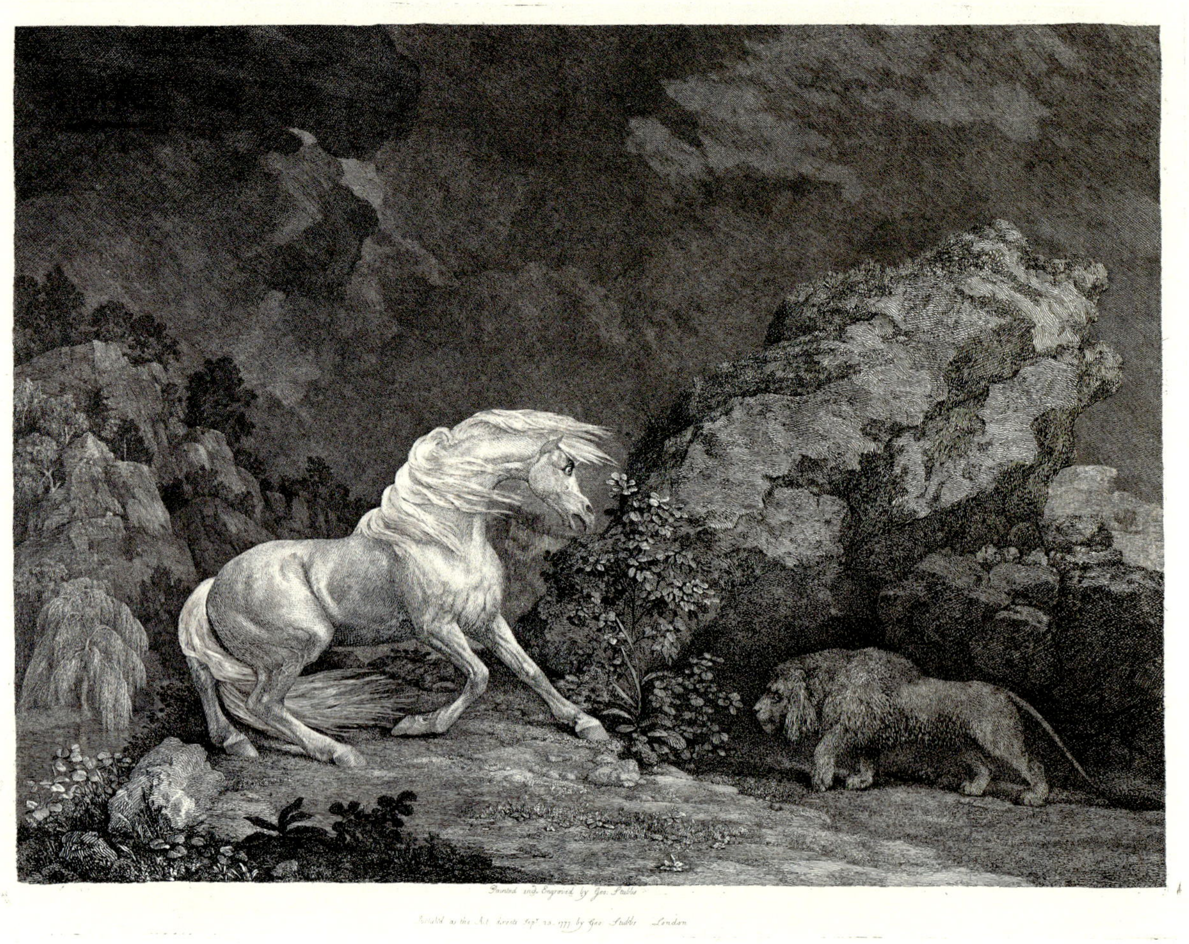

52

A Horse Affrighted by a Lion 1777

Etching, 37.3 x 47.8 cm (Plate), 49.2 x 67.9 cm (Sheet)
Ins. bottom: *Painted and Engraved by Geo: Stubbs / Publish'd as the Act directs Sep:*^{r} *25. 1777 by Geo: Stubbs London*
London, The British Museum, Inv. no. 1865-1-14-909

A Horse Affrighted by a Lion from 1777 is the first print published separately by Stubbs, possibly based on the painting that was exhibited under the same title at the Society of Artists in 1763 (Egerton no. 38). In this print, the scene of a horse shrinking in terror from a lion is strongly dramatized and its execution is far more expressive than in the painting. Thin and smooth lines have been used to suggest delicate leaves and the tense muscles of the horse, while bold and frilly lines indicate sharp rocks and shadows. This variety of evocative textures is illustrative of Stubbs's unconventional way of engraving, which was due to the fact that he was not trained as a professional engraver.

Stubbs's fascination with the 'Horse and Lion' theme might have been instigated during his trip to Rome in 1754, where he must have seen the restored version of the antique *Lion and Horse* group located at the Capitol. After that, Stubbs painted and engraved many variations on this emotionally powerful theme, like his painting from c. 1762/63 in the Paul Mellon Collection (cat. no. 40).

SG

Lit: Taylor, *The Prints of George Stubbs*, 1969, no. 1 – Exhib. Cat. *George Stubbs*, 1984/85, no. 172 – Lennox-Boyd et al., *George Stubbs*, 1989, no. 59 II

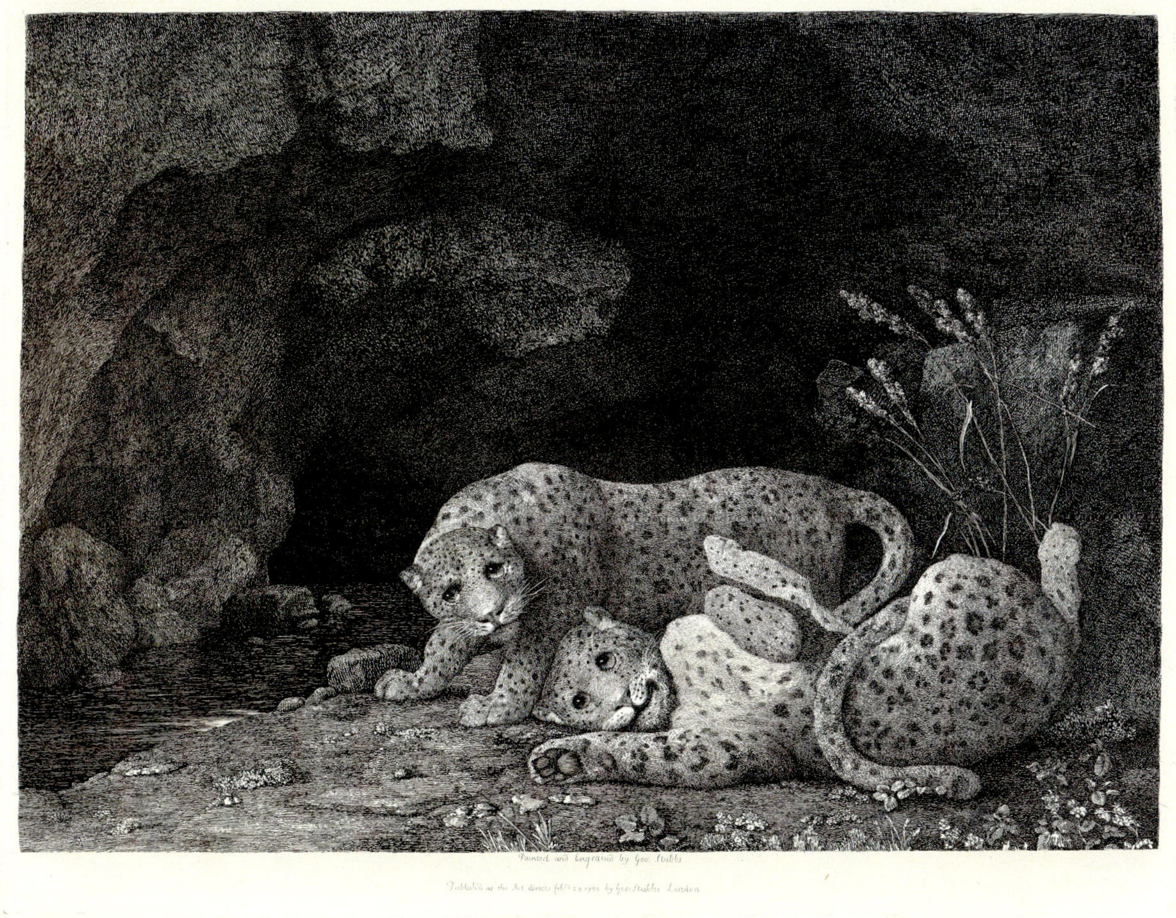

53

Tygers at Play 1780

Etching, 37.3 x 47.7 cm (Plate), 48.3 x 65.7 cm (Sheet)
Ins. bottom: *Painted and Engraved by Geo: Stubbs / Publish'd as the Act directs feb:ry 25. 1780 by Geo: Stubbs London*
London, The British Museum, Inv. no. 1865-1-14-912

Stubbs's etching of *Tygers at Play* was sold as a companion to *A Horse Affrighted by a Lion* (cat. no. 52). It presents the image of two leopards against a sober, cave-like background, their glassy eyes focused on the viewer. The source of this etching is difficult to determine, but it shows most resemblances with the painting *Tygers at Play* (Egerton no. 123).

Stubbs's interest in the subject of exotic animals, which was novel at that time, developed against the background of a growing general interest in and demand for empiric depictions of natural phenomena. The accurate and sometimes dispassionate way in which Stubbs rendered animals was much favoured among natural historians, who often hired him for this purpose (cat. nos. 46 and 47). These leopard cubs look as if they have been studied from life in an English menagerie, where Stubbs might have considered their playful movements and spotted furs as a challenge to depict.

SG

Lit: Taylor, *The Prints of George Stubbs*, 1969, no. 2 – Exhib. Cat. *George Stubbs*, 1984/85, no. 173 – Lennox-Boyd et al., *George Stubbs*, 1989, no. 60 II

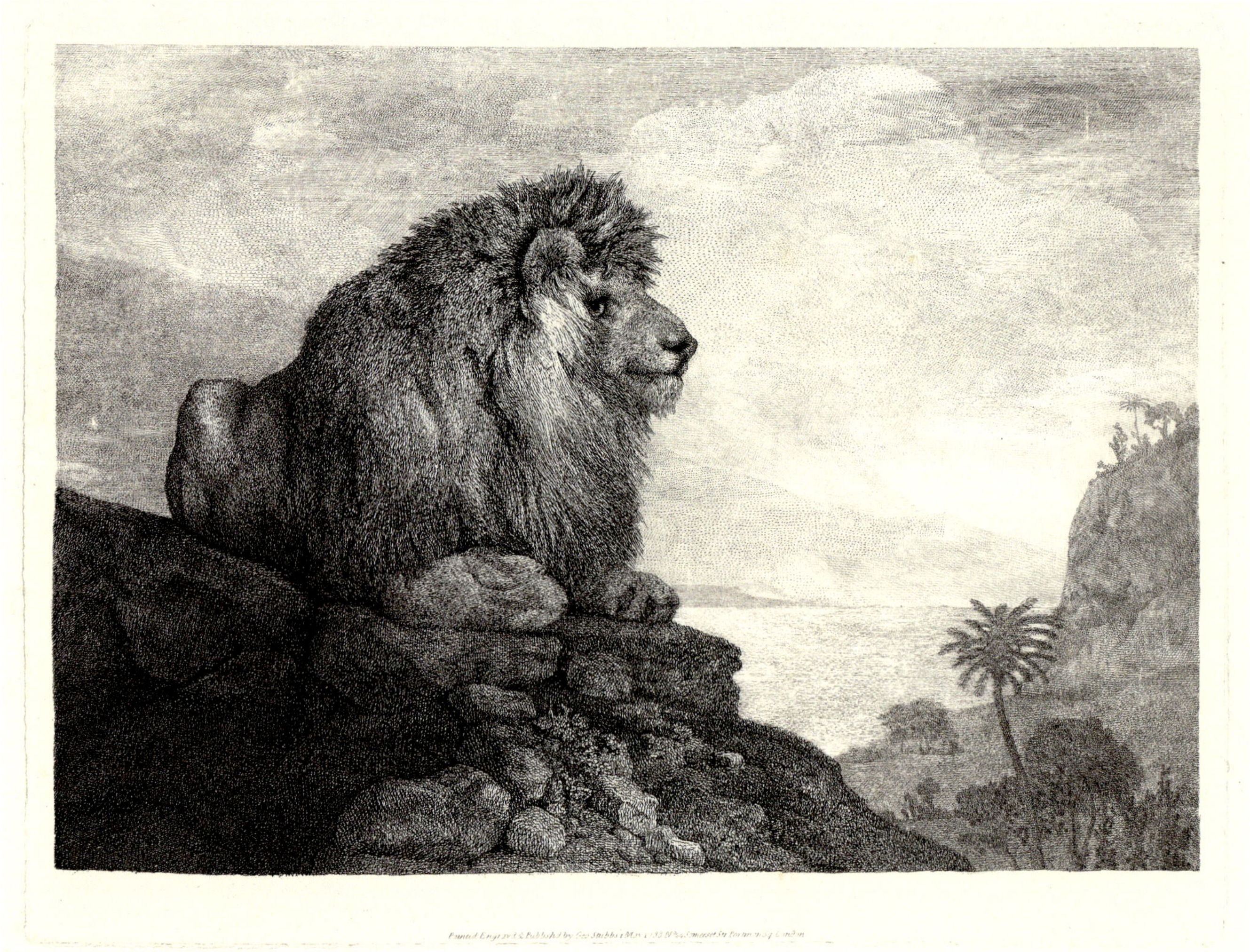

54

A Lion 1788

Etching with roulette work, 25.2 x 32.8 cm (Plate), 31.8 x 40.1 cm (Sheet)
Ins. bottom: *Painted Engravd & Publishd by Geo Stubbs 1 May 1788*
N° 24 Somerset Str Portman Sq London
London, The British Museum, Inv. no. 1865-1-14-917

The exotic scene of this print is exceptional in Stubbs's oeuvre, showing a reclining lion against the background of an African bay. The print formed a pair with *A Tyger* (cat. no. 55) and was probably based on the enamel *Lion Seated Overlooking a Rocky Coast* from 1775 (Egerton no. 201). It is not known whether Stubbs has also painted oil paintings depicting this subject.

Stubbs's main concern in this print was clearly the interplay between the dark lion on the rock in the foreground and the sunlit bay in the distance, which strongly contrast with each other. The lion's fur seems to have been drawn hair by hair with frilly lines and the sea is rendered skilfully with a striped texture, suggesting the reflection of sunlight on waves. Although Stubbs has depicted the lion accurately, in combination with the evocative background of the scene, the print provides an attractive and imaginative impression of a rare exotic animal.

SG

Lit: Taylor, *The Prints of George Stubbs*, 1969, no. 7 – Exhib. Cat. *George Stubbs*, 1984/85, no. 178 – Lennox-Boyd et al., *George Stubbs*, 1989, no. 73 I

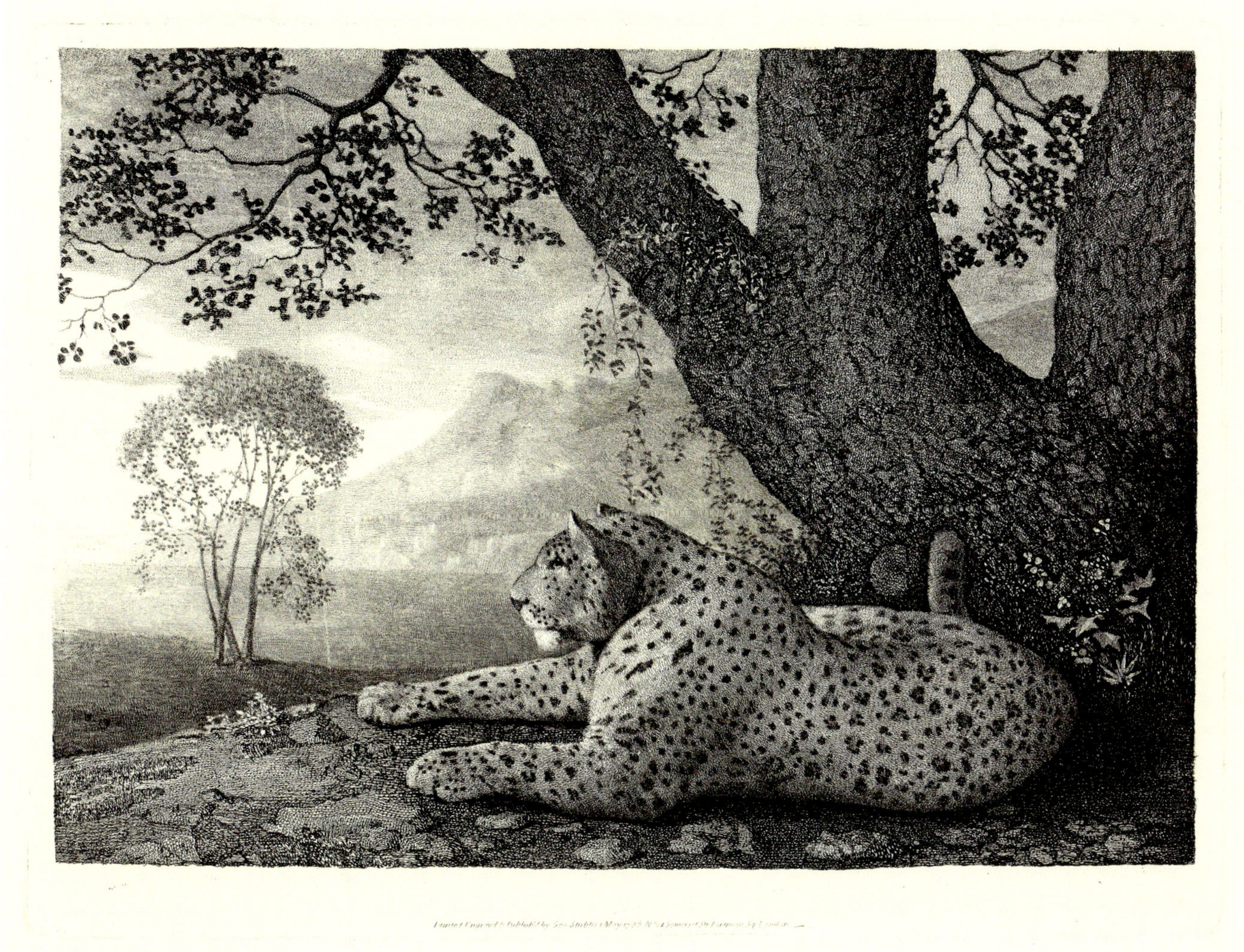

55

A Tyger 1788

Etching with roulette work, 25.2 x 32.8 cm (Plate), 29.4 x 38.4 cm (Sheet)
Ins. bottom: *Painted, Engravd & Publish'd by Geo Stubbs 1 May 1788*
N° 24 Somerset Str Portman Sq London
London, The British Museum, Inv. no. 1865-1-14-918

A Tyger formed a pair with *A Lion* (cat. no. 54) and shows a leopard gazing over a coastal scene. Like its companion, this engraving originates in an enamel picture, *Recumbent Panther* from 1778 (Egerton no. 204). The engraving combines a dark arrangement with a reclining panther beneath an oak tree in the foreground and a sunlit bay in the background. Eye-catching is the softly fading light of the setting sun in the distance. Its reflection upon the water and the way in which it extends towards the leopard provide the print with a hint of warmth and radiance. Furthermore, the bark of the curiously English-looking oak tree is skilfully rendered. As is the case with *A Lion*, this scene's combination of a lifelike leopard with an evocative landscape distinguishes it from Stubbs's more authentic likenesses of exotic animals, such as *A Recumbent Lion* (cat. no. 58).

SG

Lit: Taylor, *The Prints of George Stubbs*, 1969, no. 6 – Exhib. Cat. *George Stubbs*, 1984/85, no. 177 – Lennox-Boyd et al., *George Stubbs*, 1989, no. 74 I

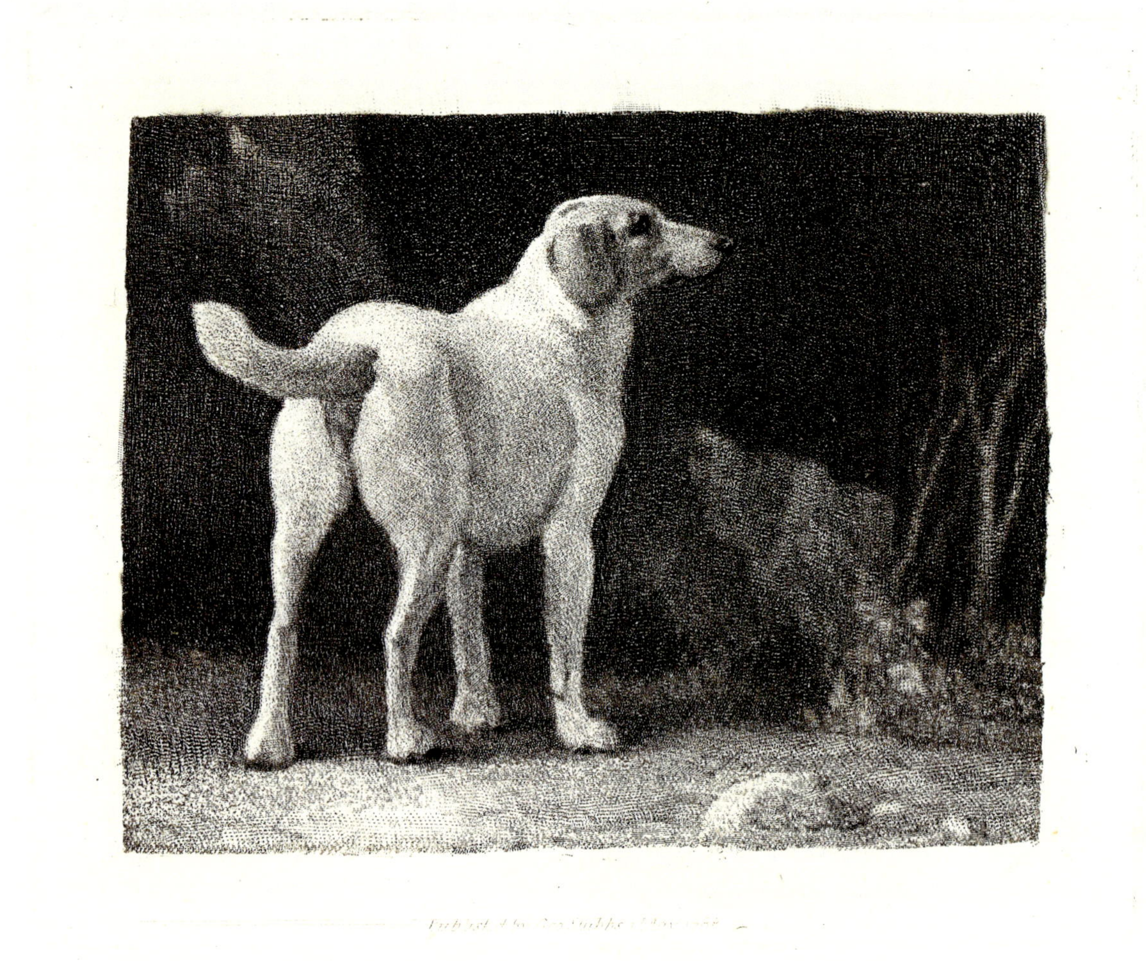

56

Dog (Foxhound) 1788

Roulette work with etching, 10.6 x 12.7 cm (Plate), 16.5 x 21.1 cm (Sheet)
Ins. bottom: *Publishd by Geo Stubbs 1 May 1788*
London, The British Museum, Inv. no. 1865-1-14-919

This small print of a dog is one of the 'Three prints of single Dogs' engraved in 1788. All three designs of this small series are included in the painting *The 3rd Duke of Richmond with the Charlton Hunt* from c. 1759 (p. 12, fig. 1). In addition, individual oil studies for or after the dogs in this painting are known and a detailed pencil study might have served as a model for this small series (Exhib. Cat. *George Stubbs*, 1984/85, no. 170).

The accuracy and naturalism with which Stubbs has depicted the dog in this print suggest that he has studied his subject closely from nature with the intention of providing an image that is dismissive of any narrative. The pose of the dog and the chosen angle of the image provide the print with an impression of immediacy that is complemented by the soft execution of the print in roulette work, making the print almost photo-like.

SG

Lit: Taylor, *The Prints of George Stubbs*, 1969, no. 11 – Exhib. Cat. *George Stubbs*, 1984/85, no. 182 – Lennox-Boyd et al., *George Stubbs*, 1989, no. 79 I

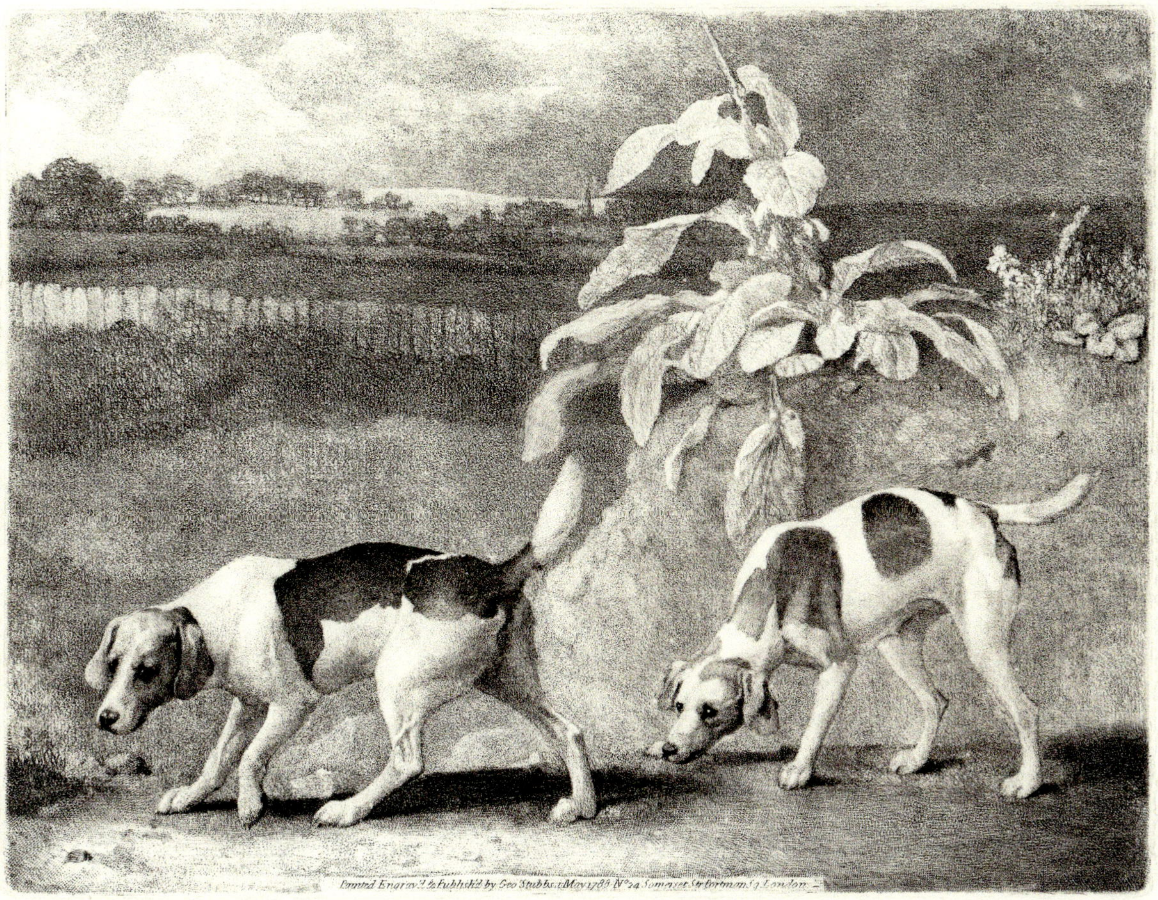

57

Two Dogs (Foxhounds) 1788

Soft-ground etching with roulette work, 18.1 x 23.3 cm (Plate), 25.0 x 31.4 cm (Sheet)
Ins. bottom, within image:
Painted Engrav'd & Publish'd by Geo Stubbs 1 May 1788
N° 24 Somerset Str Portman Sq London
London, The British Museum, Inv. no. 1865-1-14-922

Two Dogs from 1788 presents two foxhounds on a scent against the background of a softly rendered landscape. Paintings with this scene are not known by Stubbs. As remarked by Taylor, however, a drawing of '2 Pointers in a Landscape' that was sold in 1807 possibly relates to it.

This print does not contain many firm lines. Instead it is very tonal, providing the scene with an unusual drawing-like impression. Much emphasis is put on the natural poses of the dogs and great care has been bestowed to their surroundings. The large plant in the background, for example, seems to have been recorded from nature. Although the print is rendered very skilfully, it was sold for the relatively cheap price of only 2s 6d because of its small size.

SG

Lit: Taylor, *The Prints of George Stubbs*, 1969, no. 13 – Exhib. Cat. *George Stubbs*, 1984/85, no. 184 – Lennox-Boyd et al., *George Stubbs*, 1989, no. 75 I

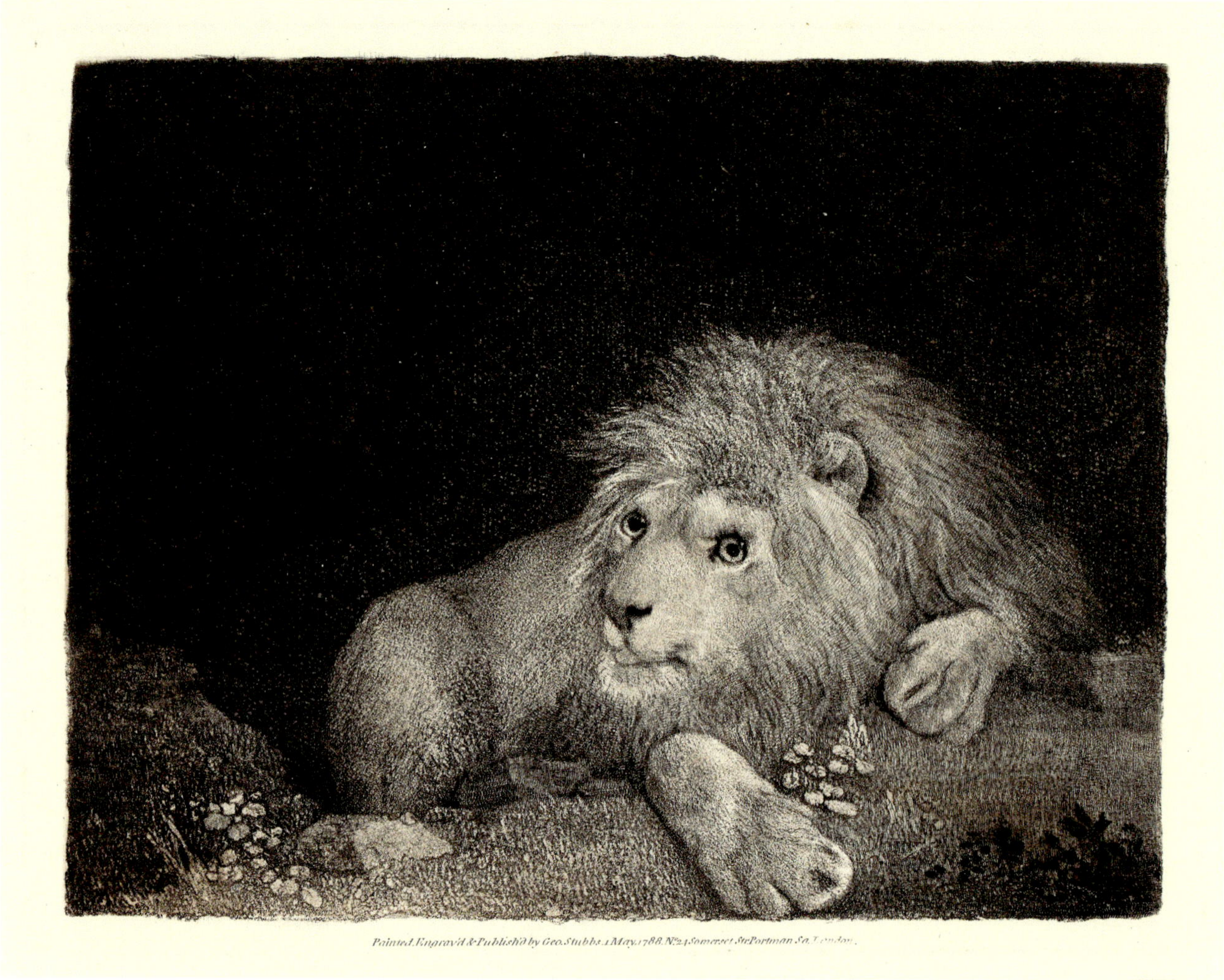

58

A Lion 1788

Soft-ground etching with roulette work, 17.4 x 22.4 cm (Plate), 25.2 x 33.1 cm (Sheet)
Ins. bottom: *Painted, Engrav'd & Publish'd by Geo. Stubbs, 1 May, 1788. N.° 24 Somerset Str. Portman Sq. London.*
London, The British Museum, Inv. no. 1865-1-14-915

This etching shows another lion by Stubbs, based on an unknown painting. Usually, lions in Stubbs's designs are accompanied by other animals or complemented with sophisticated surroundings (like cat. no. 52), but in this print, the lion is shown against a background of pure darkness. This strengthens his figure and emphasizes his fierce look and tremendous claws. Apart from the carefully rendered lion, the scene does not contain many details. Only a few little flowers and leaves are suggested in the grass.

Stubbs's interest in depicting lions—especially growling, attacking and feeding lions—might have been connected to their sublime quality to arouse terror in the beholder by presenting a violent side of nature. This lion, however, is not portrayed in a dramatic way. It owes its strength to its naturalism and the complete absence of any anthropomorphic features, illustrating Stubbs's interest in the depiction of subjects in an honest way.

SG

Lit: Taylor, *The Prints of George Stubbs*, 1969, no. 9 – Exhib. Cat. *George Stubbs*, 1984/85, no. 180 – Lennox-Boyd et al., *George Stubbs*, 1989, no. 76 III

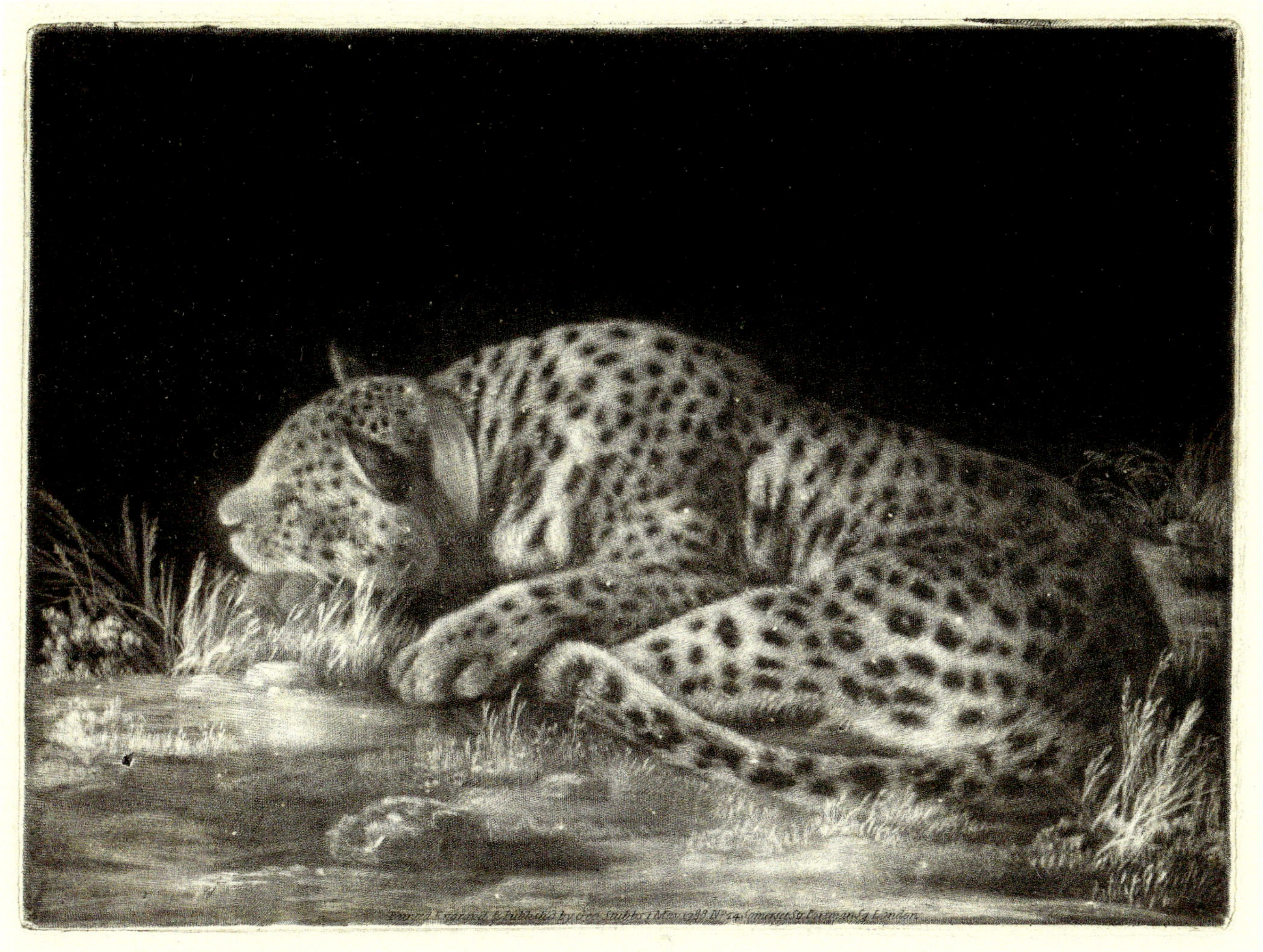

59

A Tyger (A Sleeping Leopard) 1788

Mezzotint, 15.3 x 20.3 cm (Plate), 25.1 x 33.8 cm (Sheet)
Ins. bottom, within image: *Painted Engrav'd & Publish'd by Geo Stubbs 1 May 1788 N.° 24 Somerset Str Portman Sq London*
London, The British Museum, Inv. no. 1865-1-14-916

This *Sleeping Leopard* is the only print by Stubbs that was completely executed with certainty in mezzotint. Its source cannot be safely determined, but its origin should perhaps be sought in the enamel *Sleeping Leopard* from 1777 (Egerton no. 202). This leopard was previously connected with a cheetah owned by Lord Pigot (see cat. no. 44), but because it does not show the specific features of a cheetah, it might be better to consider it as a leopard which Stubbs may have studied during a visit to a menagerie.

The background of the print is left fully black, so as not to distract the viewer's gaze from the sleeping leopard, which is executed in a neutral, accurate way. The animal's velvety fur shows a remarkably delicate transition from light to darker tones, providing depth to its body. Soft wrinkles in its skin are suggested in the same manner. Impressions of this print were usually printed on white wove paper, but this version from the British Museum is printed on cream laid paper of high quality.

SG

Lit: Taylor, *The Prints of George Stubbs*, 1969, no. 8 – Exhib. Cat. *George Stubbs*, 1984/85, no. 179 – Lennox-Boyd et al., *George Stubbs*, 1989, no. 77 II

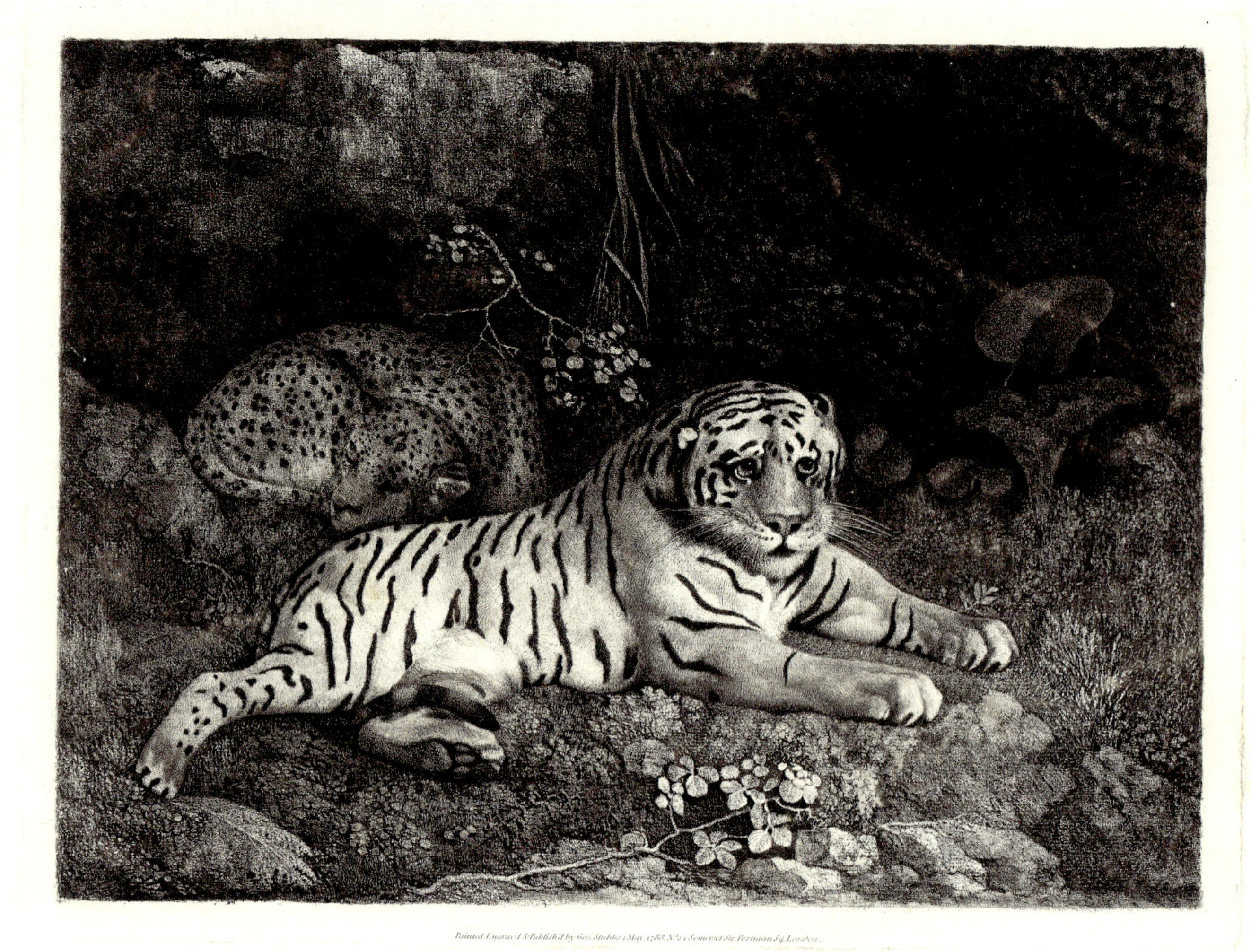

60

Two Tygers 1788

Soft-ground etching with roulette work, 25.3 x 32.8 cm (Plate), 32.1 x 40.6 cm (Sheet)
Ins. bottom: *Painted, Engrav'd & Publish'd by Geo. Stubbs. 1 May, 1788.*
N.° 24 Somerset Str. Portman Sq. London.
London, The British Museum, Inv. no. 1865-1-14-913

This print showing a resting tiger with a leopard asleep in the background is taken from an unknown painting or a combination of the *Tigress* from 1769 and the enamel *Sleeping Leopard* from 1777 (Egerton nos. 77 and 202).

The pair of 'tygers' are shown lying on a bed of minutely executed vegetation, surrounded by sharply rendered branches. The use of delicate lines and soft transitions of grey tones to shape the animals makes them look lively. After the first state of the print, an impression of which can be found in the Rijksmuseum in Amsterdam, the plate was edited by means of roulettes. It is not known whether these adjustments were made in order to touch the plate up after various uses, or whether Stubbs had always meant to provide more depth and details to the scene in that way.

SG

Lit: Taylor, *The Prints of George Stubbs*, 1969, no. 5 – Exhib. Cat. *George Stubbs*, 1984/85, no. 176 – Lennox-Boyd et al., *George Stubbs*, 1989, no. 72 III

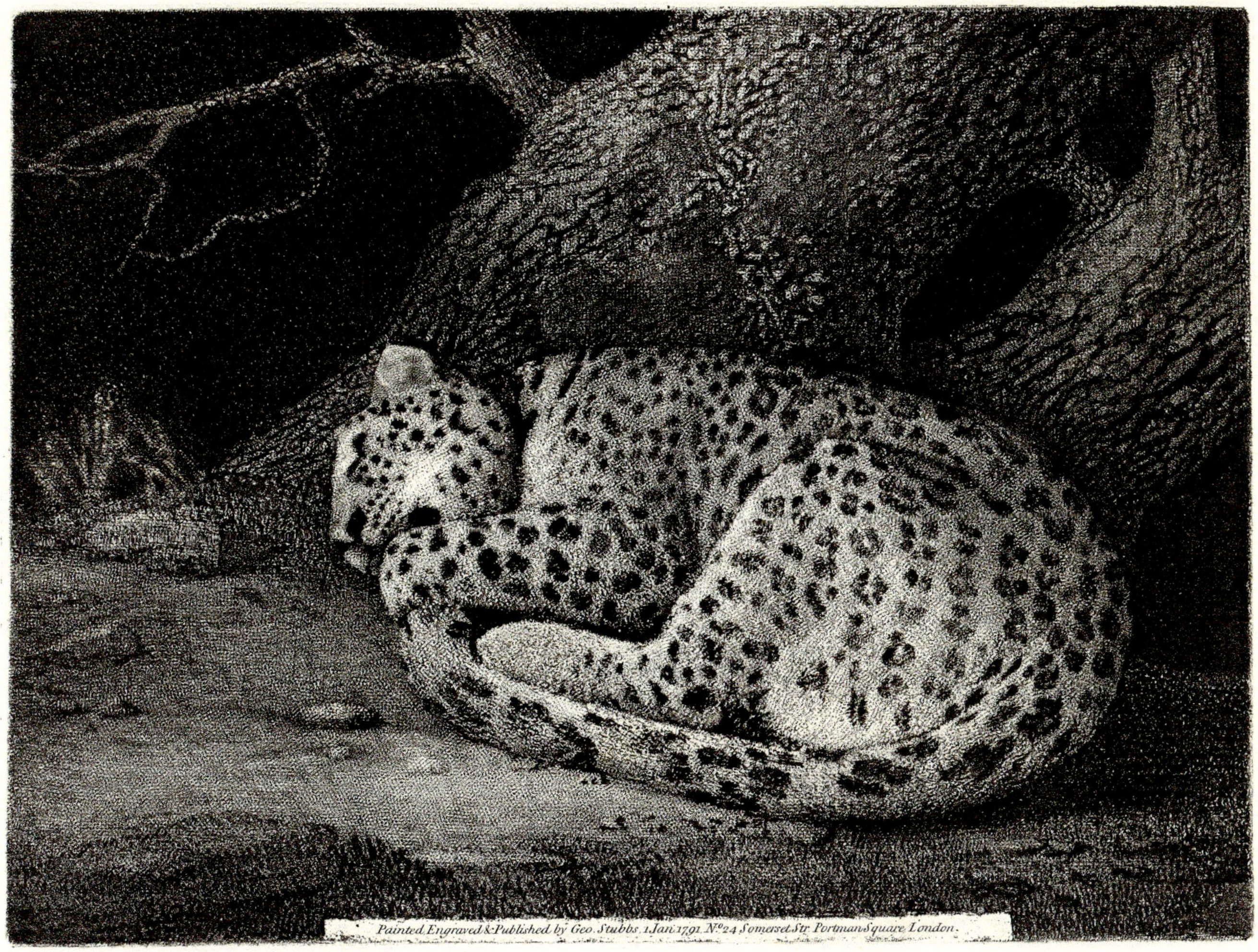

61

A Sleeping Leopard 1791

Soft-ground etching with roulette work, 18.0 x 23.7 cm (Plate), 24.7 x 31.9 cm (Sheet)
Ins. bottom, within image: *Painted, Engraved & Published by Geo. Stubbs, 1 Jan 1791, N.° 24 Somerset Str. Portman Square London.*
London, The British Museum, Inv. no. 1865-1-14-914

This *Sleeping Leopard*, the original title of which is not known, is perhaps the most touching of the two that Stubbs engraved, showing a softer side of nature than his growling lions. The design of this print is probably taken from a currently unknown painting, although the enamel *Sleeping Leopard* from 1777 is often associated with it (Egerton no. 202) and the motif can also be found in the print *Two Tygers* (cat. no. 60).

Stubbs's depiction of the leopard is enchanting and vulnerable—rolled up, clutching the end of its tail with its forepaw. The monochrome tone of the print and the sparing use of highlights dramatize this portrayal even further, providing the scene with a nocturnal atmosphere. The charming quality of the image is complemented by the tiny strokes and small dots with which the leopard's fur is rendered, providing a hint of softness.

SG

Lit: Taylor, *The Prints of George Stubbs*, 1969, no. 18 – Exhib. Cat. *George Stubbs*, 1984/85, no. 189 – Lennox-Boyd et al., *George Stubbs*, 1989, no. 91 II

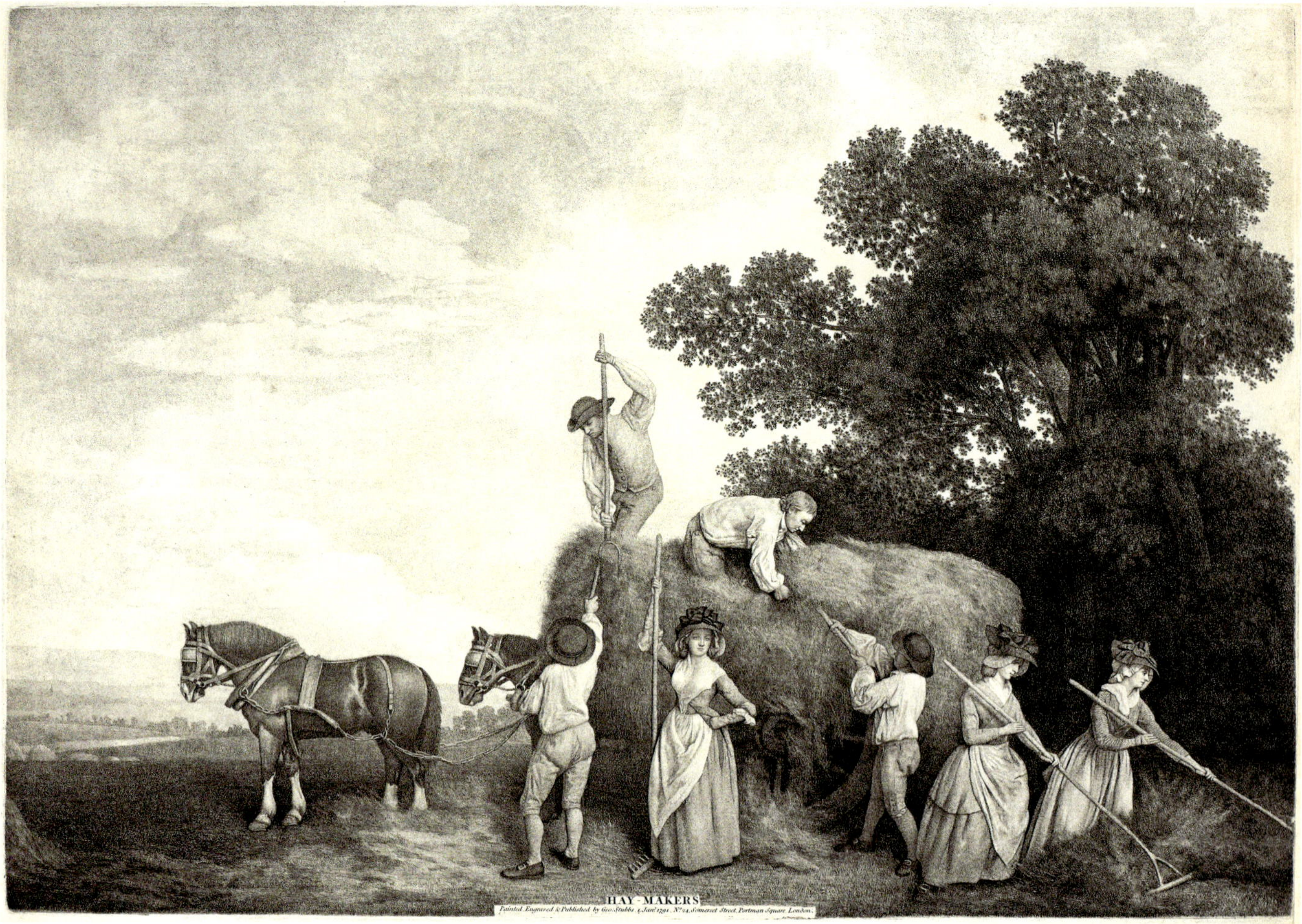

62

Haymakers 1791

Stipple with roulette work, 48.2 x 68.3 cm (Plate),
52.4 x 69.9 cm (Sheet)
Ins. bottom, within image: *HAY-MAKERS / Painted, Engraved & Published by Geo: Stubbs, 1. Jan.y 1791. N.° 24, Somerset Street, Portman Square, London.*
London, The British Museum, Inv. no. 1865-1-14-907

During the 1780s, Stubbs produced a pair of panel paintings called *Haymakers* and *Reapers* (Egerton nos. 248–249). With these paintings, he departed from his usual subject of human and animal portraits by depicting common workers performing the task of harvesting corn and making hay in the English countryside. A second, more elaborate version of this pair was painted in 1785 and exhibited in 1786 at the Society of Artists (Egerton nos. 250, 252; pp. 16 f., figs. 5–6). Stubbs's prints from 1791 are based on this pair.

Reapers shows a rural scene with workers performing the various steps of harvesting corn, supervised by a farmer on horseback. In *Haymakers*, six workers are loading hay on a cart, while one woman is leaning on her rake in front of it, looking straight at the viewer. Both prints are very detailed, with for example jugs and pots in the foreground of *Reapers*, and a precise rendering of foliage, clothes and faces in *Haymakers*.

There has been much debate as to the sources or ideas that might underlie this pair of paintings. It is clear that the subject of harvesting can be traced back to fifteenth-century illuminated manuscripts that contain step-by-step illustrations of the process. In the course of the sixteenth century, this tradition was developed

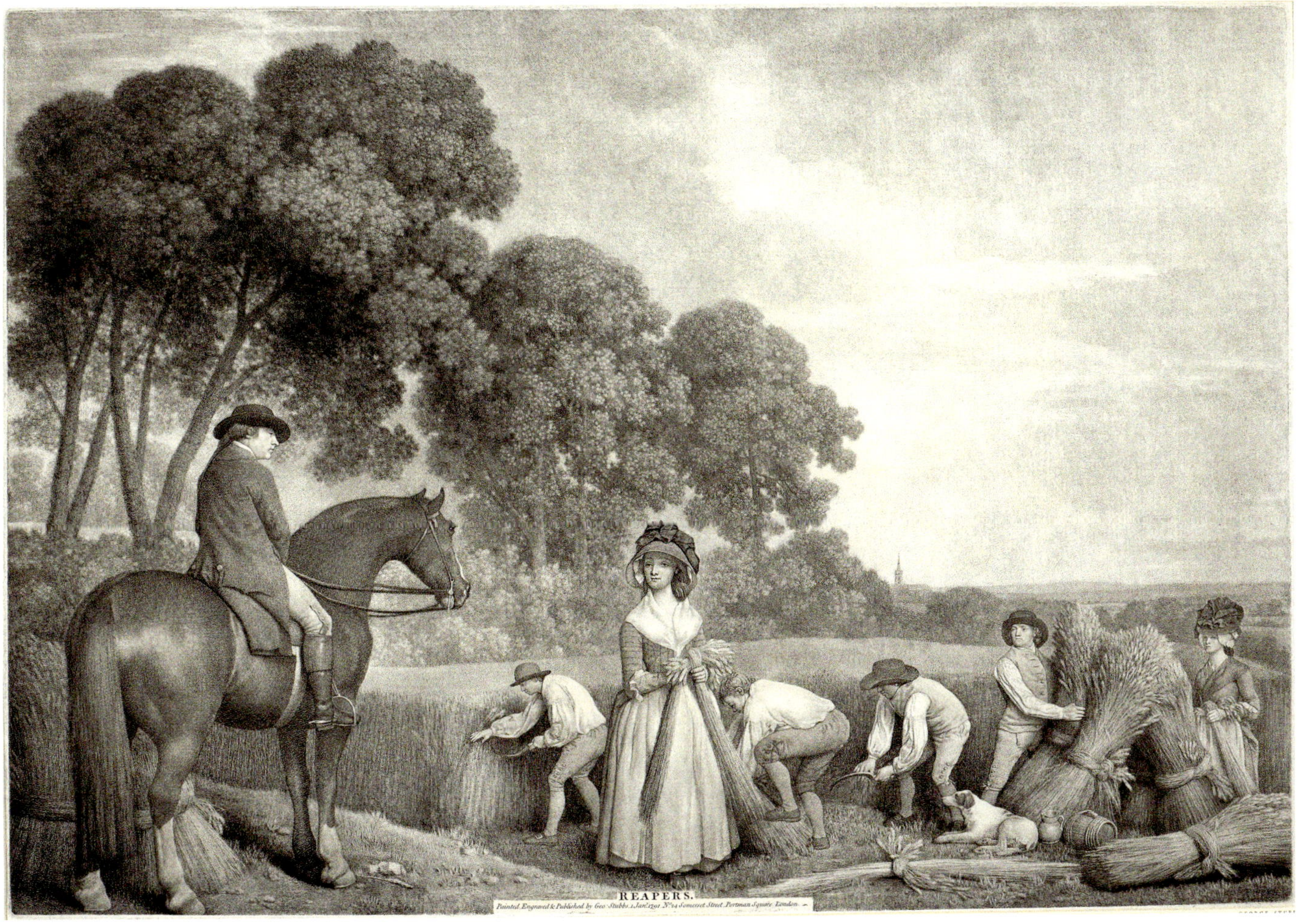

63

Reapers 1791

Stipple with roulette work, 48.3 x 68.3 cm (Plate),
51.8 x 72.8 cm (Sheet)
Ins. bottom, within image: *REAPERS. / Painted, Engraved & Published by Geo: Stubbs, 1 Jan.y 1791. N.° 24 Somerset Street, Portman Square. London.*
London, The British Museum, Inv. no. 1856-10-11-99

further in Flemish painting by Pieter Bruegel the Elder (1525–1569). By the seventeenth century, the preoccupation with subjects like farmers, shepherds and cattle culminated in the rich tradition of apparently naturalistic and spontaneous rural scenes in Flemish and Dutch painting, like Philips Wouwerman's *Peasants in the Fields: Hay Harvest* from c. 1655 (London, Dulwich Picture Gallery).

Haymakers and *Reapers* have earlier been described as idyllic and timeless, because their compositions were considered rigid and the clothes of the labourers far too immaculate and proper with regard to their activities. As such, they have for example been connected to the formal and classical landscapes of Nicolas Poussin (1594–1665) and James Thomson's lyrical poem *The Seasons* from 1726–30, by Barrell. As argued by Egerton, however, Stubbs's scenes are much more natural than they might appear at first sight—especially for their time. They are not sentimentalized and present individuals in natural poses, performing real tasks. Questioning the apparent immaculateness of their clothes, Egerton points out that one of the labourers has a rip in his sleeves and another is wearing a humble, hand-sewn apron (in the 1785 picture of *Haymakers*). These documental aspects give the impression that Stubbs has studied his subjects from life in the countryside, relating *Haymakers* and *Reapers* perhaps more to sixteenth- and seventeenth-century Flemish and Dutch painting than to the idyllic landscapes of Poussin.

Already from the early seventeenth century onwards, English collectors developed a strong taste for Flemish and Dutch landscapes. By the middle of the eighteenth century, works by Aelbert Cuyp (1620–1691), Nicholaas Berchem (1620–1683), Theobald Michau (1676–1756) and many others had found their way into the collections of Lord Fitzwilliam, Charles Jennens of Holborn, and Stubbs's most prominent patrons the Dukes of Rutland and Richmond, the Duchess of Marlborough and Lord Torrington (Frank Simpson, 'Dutch Paintings in England before 1760', *The Burlington Magazine* 95, 1953, pp. 39-42).

Although the influence of Flemish and Dutch seventeenth-century landscapes on English painting grew strong especially in the early nineteenth century, Stubbs was undoubtedly aware of the work of his Flemish and Dutch predecessors, which was eagerly collected by his fellow-countrymen. His picture of *Lord Torrington's Brickmakers* (cat. no. 33) suggests that he must at least have been familiar with its particularities, since the picture originates in the idea of having the labourers painted 'like a Flemish subject'. The cart, dog and contemporarily dressed workers depicted in this picture are elements that occur frequently in the work of for example Wouwerman and Michau, of whom Lord Torrington possessed multiple 'landscapes' with 'figures' (Christie's sales catalogue 23–24 January 1778). Other works by Stubbs, such as *Landscape with Cattle* from 1768 (Egerton no. 107), showing a piping boy next to a herd of cows, are unmistakably reminiscent of Aelbert Cuyp (see for example Stephen Reiss, *Aelbert Cuyp*, London 1975, no. 78), of whom Lord Torrington possessed 'a landscape, with a shepherd attending cattle' and 'a girl, milking a cow on the side of a river'. It is imaginable that the accurate depictions of cows, dogs, and horses in the work of Wouwerman and Cuyp have influenced Stubbs.

It goes without saying that Dutch and Flemish painting will not have been the only or even the most prominent source that might have been relevant for Stubbs's *Haymakers*, *Reapers* and other rustic scenes. Stubbs's formal style and straightforward compositions depart from Flemish and Dutch painting, but the common subjects and documental quality of these works clearly relate to it. They connect Stubbs to artistic traditions that extend beyond the borders of England and expand his already celebrated versatility as a painter of portraits, landscapes and animals.

SG

Lit: Taylor, *The Prints of George Stubbs*, 1969, nos. 16–17 – John Barrell, *The Dark Side of the Landscape. The Rural Poor in English Painting 1730–1840*, Cambridge 1980, pp. 25–31 – Exhib. Cat. *George Stubbs*, 1984/85, nos. 187–188 – Lennox-Boyd et al., *George Stubbs*, 1989, nos. 89 II, 90 II – Blake, *George Stubbs and the Wide Creation*, 2005, pp. 239–245 – Egerton, *George Stubbs*, 2007, pp. 468–477

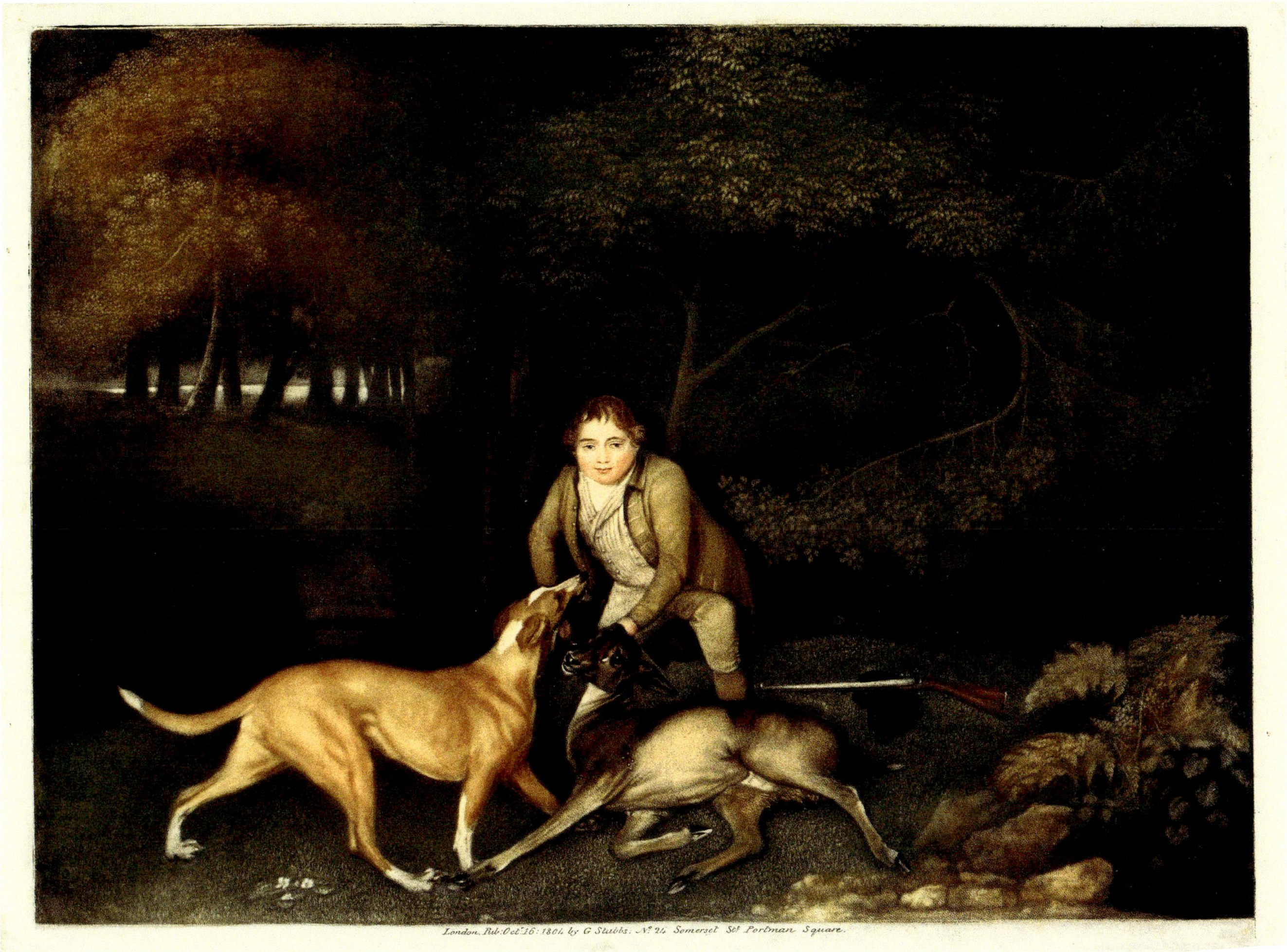

64

Thomas Freeman, the Earl of Clarendon's Gamekeeper, with a Dying Doe and a Hound 1804

Mezzotint printed in colour, 36.8 x 49.8 cm (Plate), 39.3 x 52.7 cm (Sheet)
Ins. bottom: *London. Pub: Oct.ʳ 16: 1804 by G Stubbs: N.° 24 Somerset St.ᵗ Portman Square.*
London, The British Museum, Inv. no. 2010-7081-2217

This coloured print is taken from the painting *Freeman, the Earl of Clarendon's Gamekeeper, with a Dying Doe and a Hound* from 1800 in the Paul Mellon Collection (Egerton no. 335). It shows the gamekeeper Thomas Freeman, who is looking straight at the viewer and is about to give the *coup de grace* to a shot doe. Although the print is generally attributed to George Stubbs, it is also thought to be a case of close collaboration between him and his son. Egerton refers for example to the smirking face of the gamekeeper as the work of George Townley Stubbs, because it is inconsistent with the mysterious appearance of the man in the painting.

The print shows a strong contrast between highlights and shadows. As a central group, Freeman, the dog and the doe are executed with almost photographic qualities. They are brightly lit against the dark tones of the forest, while it is only in the upper left corner that fading sunlight is shown slipping between the trees.

SG

Lit: Taylor, *The Prints of George Stubbs*, 1969, no. 19 – Exhib. Cat. *George Stubbs*, 1984/85, no. 190 – Lennox-Boyd et al., *George Stubbs*, 1989, no. 145 I

THE ANATOMY OF THE HORSE

PAINTINGS

PRINTS

PRINTS AFTER STUBBS

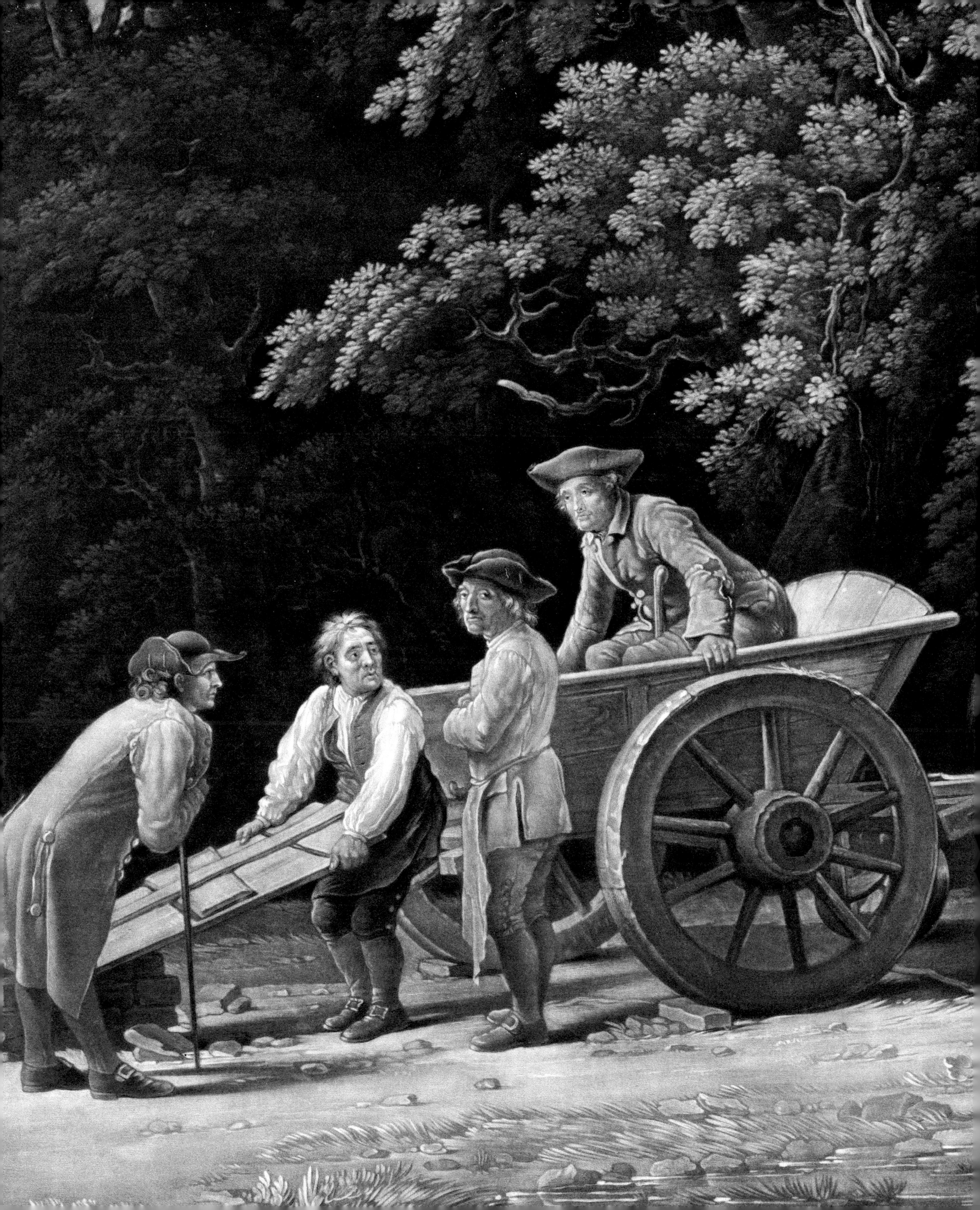

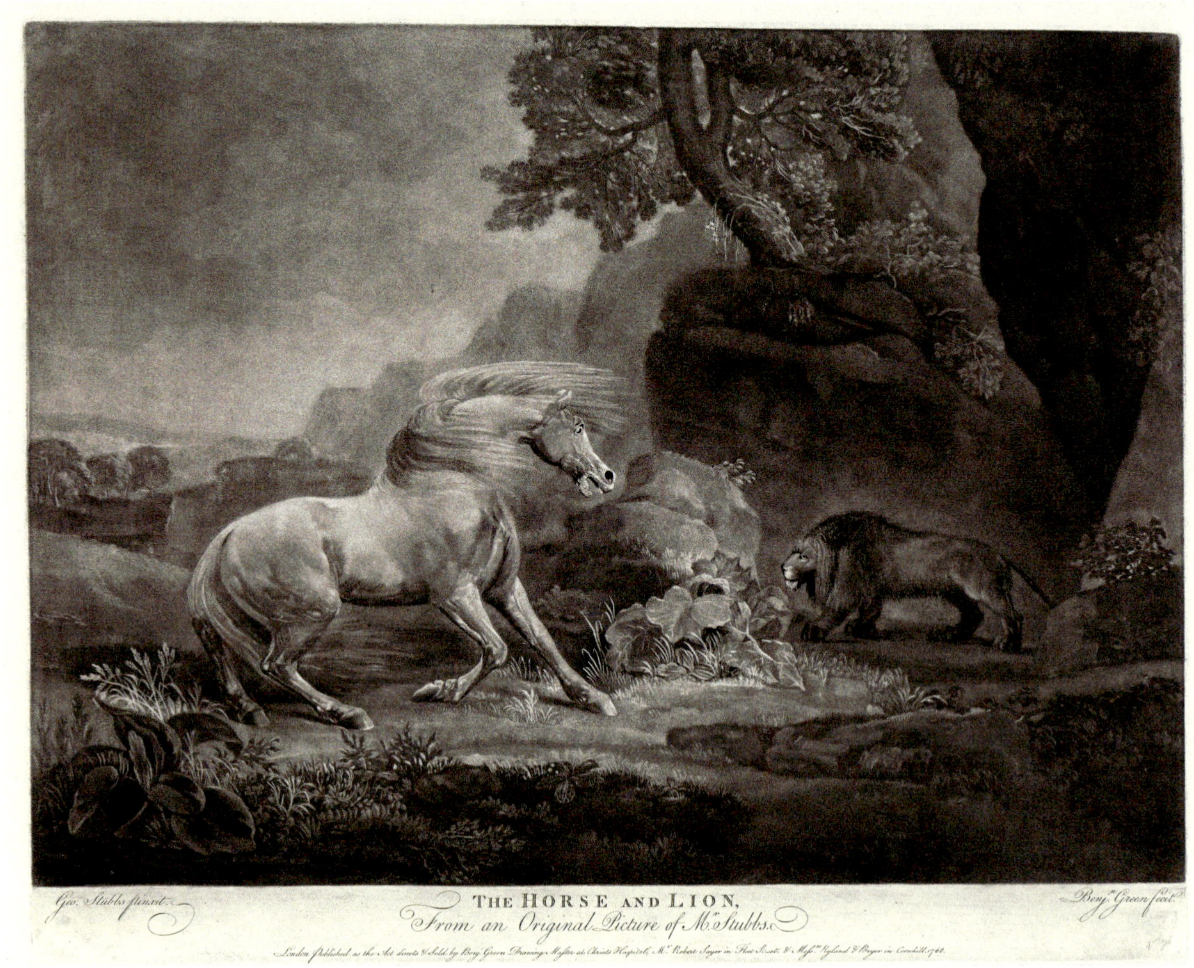

65

The Horse and Lion 1767

Benjamin Green (1739–1798) after George Stubbs

Mezzotint, 45.1 x 55.5 cm (Plate), 47.1 x 58.5 cm (Sheet)
Ins. bottom left: *Geo. Stubbs pinxit.*, right: *Benjn Green fecit.*
Aschaffenburg Collection, Staatliche Graphische Sammlung München, Inv. no. 111 E 5/4

Benjamin Green was the first to engrave a series of prints after paintings by Stubbs. His series, called *Prints of Horses*, was meant to promote Stubbs's work and talent as an artist and includes six prints (cat. nos. 65–70), of which *The Horse and Lion* was the first. Central to this print is a horse shrinking in terror at the sight of a lion, communicated by the animal's sudden backwards move, the highlighted tension of its muscles and veins, and its widely opened eye. In addition to the gracious figure of the horse and the threatening posture of the lion, much care has been bestowed on the vegetation with which the scene is adorned and a sense of naturalism is provided.

Stubbs received his inspiration for the subject of this print from the antique *Lion and Horse* group in Rome (cat. nos. 40–42). He explored this theme in many of his paintings and enamels and even in a Wedgwood relief (Egerton no. 223), but the exact picture from which Green has taken his print cannot be named with certainty.

SG

Lit.: Lennox-Boyd et al., *George Stubbs*, 1989, no. 4 II

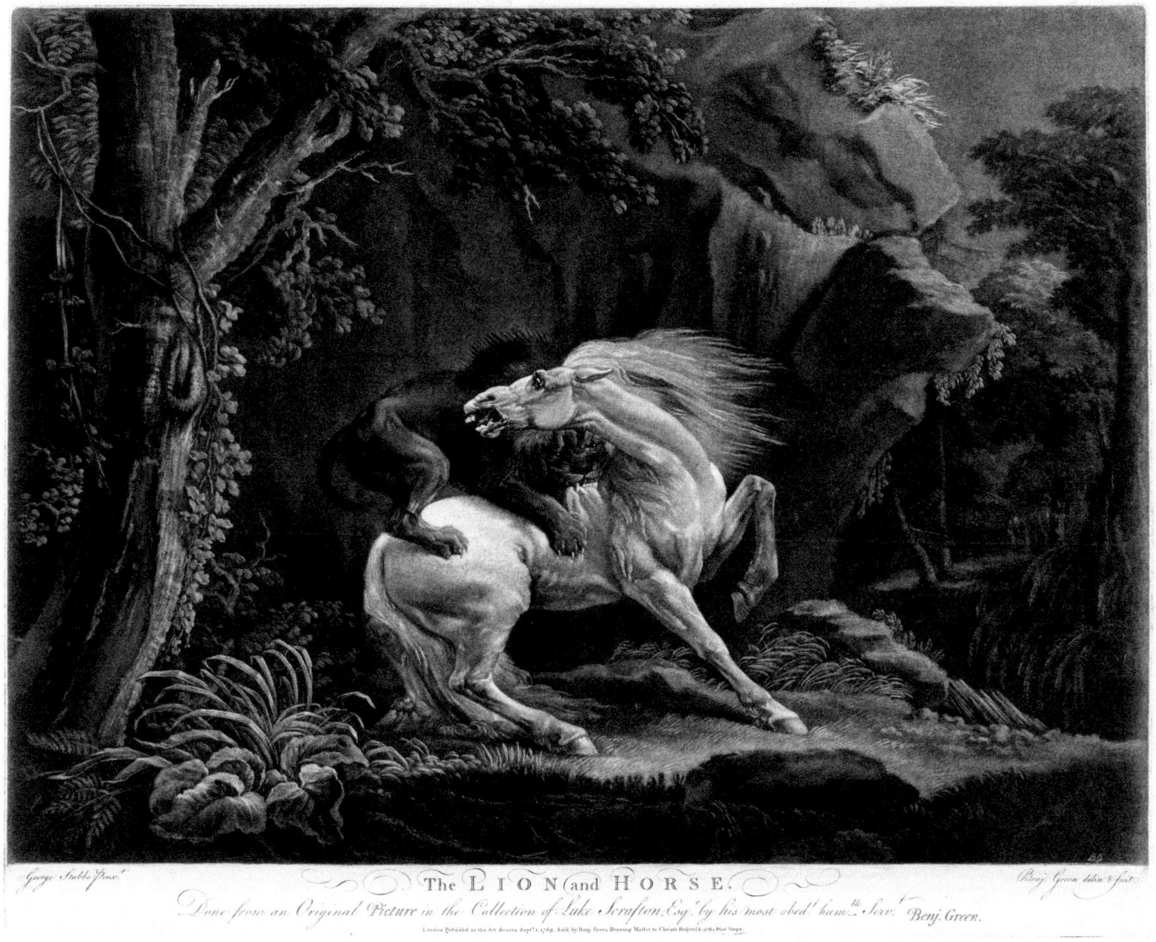

66

The Lion and Horse 1769

Benjamin Green (1739–1798) after George Stubbs

Mezzotint, 45.6 x 55.7 cm (Plate), 47.7 x 58.4 cm (Sheet)
Ins. bottom left: *George Stubbs Pinx.*[t], right: *Benj. Green delin & fecit.*
Aschaffenburg Collection, Staatliche Graphische Sammlung München, Inv. no. III E 5/7

The Lion and Horse is taken from an unknown picture that was probably bought in 1769 by the attorney Luke Scrafton (1732–1769/70). The painting was presumably destroyed during that same year, when Scrafton moved to India with his possessions and his ship was lost with all hands in a storm en route.

The print presents the image of a lion attacking a horse and shows a broad range of textures, from the shining curves of the horse to the rough bark of the tree to the left. It is detailed down to the shiny tongue of the horse, the small curly hairs around its hoofs, and the teeth and nails of the lion. Also indicative of the careful execution of the print is the foliage in the lower left corner, which is represented with an almost imperceptible transition of grey tones and white accents. The design reproduced in this print was clearly inspired by the antique *Horse and Lion* group and Stubbs's oeuvre contains many variations of it, such as *Horse Devoured by a Lion* from 1763 (cat. no. 42).

SG

Lit.: *Englische Schabkunstblätter,* Wilhelm Weber (ed.), Exhib Cat. Mittelrheinisches Landesmuseum, Mainz 1983, no. 22 – Lennox-Boyd et al., *George Stubbs*, 1989, no. 7 III

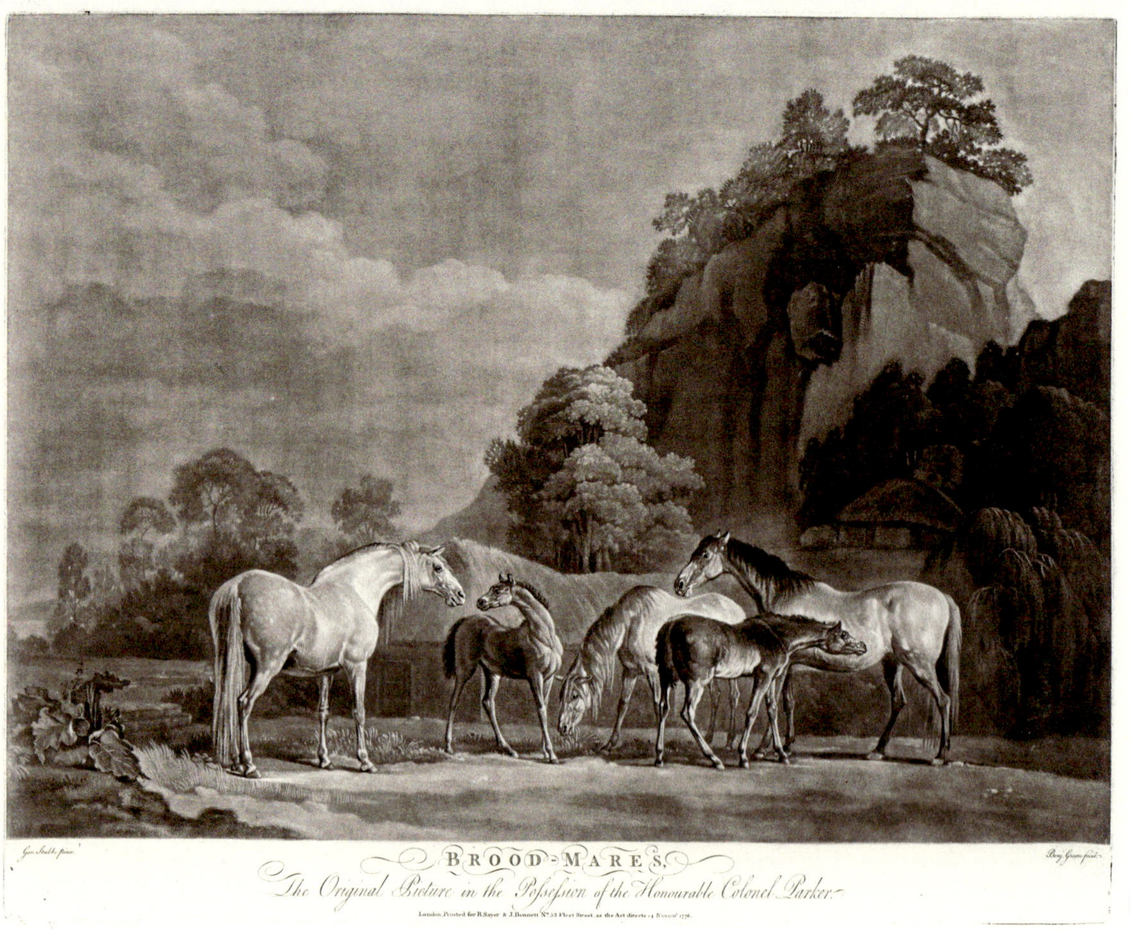

67

Brood Mares 1768

Benjamin Green (1739–1798) after George Stubbs

Mezzotint, 45.6 x 55.6 cm (Plate), 47.5 x 57.5 cm (Sheet)
Ins. bottom left: *Geo. Stubbs pinx.*, right: *Benj. Green fecit.*
Aschaffenburg Collection, Staatliche Graphische Sammlung München, Inv. no. III E 5/6

Brood Mares is based on a painting that was presumably commissioned by Colonel George Lane Parker (1724–1791) and sold by Sotheby's in December 2010 (Egerton no. 89). The print is thought to have been exhibited together with the painting at the Society of Artists in 1768. It shows a group of three mares and two foals grazing against the background of some farmer's huts and a cliff. The landscape is probably based on Creswell Crags, an area that Stubbs often turned to for the landscapes of his designs. All horses are executed in great detail and shaped with shadows and highlights that gradually merge into each other. The subtlety of their execution provides the animals with a convincing sense of depth and liveliness.

Stubbs painted many variations on the 'Mares and Foals' theme, mostly commissioned by particular patrons who wanted to have their estate and horses depicted. An example of such a variation is *Mares and Foals in a River Landscape* from 1763–65 (cat. no. 21). This print may have functioned as an advertisement to attract more similar commissions.

SG

Lit.: Lennox-Boyd et al., *George Stubbs*, 1989, no. 5 III

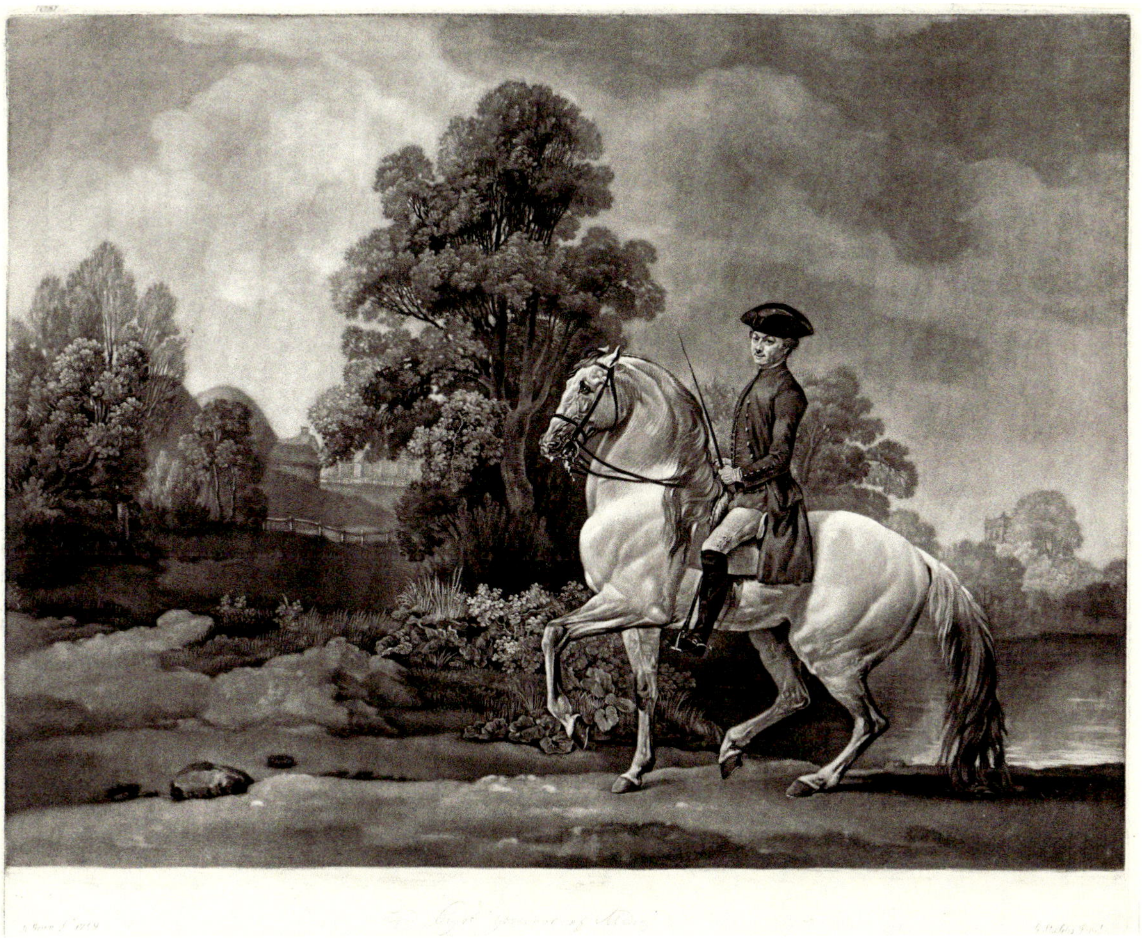

68

Lord Pigot 1769

Benjamin Green (1739–1798) after George Stubbs

Mezzotint, 45.9 x 55.5 cm (Plate), 46.6 x 57.1 cm (Sheet)
Ins. bottom left: *B Green ft 1769*, right: *G. Stubbs Pinx.*[1]
Aschaffenburg Collection, Staatliche Graphische Sammlung München, Inv. no. III E 5/1

This print is taken from Stubbs's portrait of *Lord Pigot of Patshull Riding a Spanish-Bred Charger* from c. 1768 (Egerton no. 78). The portrait was probably commissioned in 1765 by Lord Pigot, but the print was engraved in 1768 and exhibited at the Society of Artists in 1769 as a 'mezzotinto print of a gentleman on horseback'. It depicts Lord Pigot on horseback against the background of an English-looking estate. The horse is displayed in a tight pose, its body rendered with thin lines following the contours of its muscles. Like Lord Pigot's personal features, those of the horse are shown very clearly, its face exhibiting a strained but disciplined expression, with foam dripping from its mouth.

Lord Pigot seems to have had a profound influence on the design of this portrait. The way in which he is depicted on his obedient horse is reminiscent of portraits of a century earlier, in which such a representation referred to the sitter's qualities to govern. As suggested by Egerton, the perhaps unflattering representation of Lord Pigot, grinning and controlling his horse with cruel spurs and bit, might not have been far from reality in view of his reputation as an opportunist and despot.

SG

Lit.: Lennox-Boyd et al., *George Stubbs*, 1989, no. 6 II

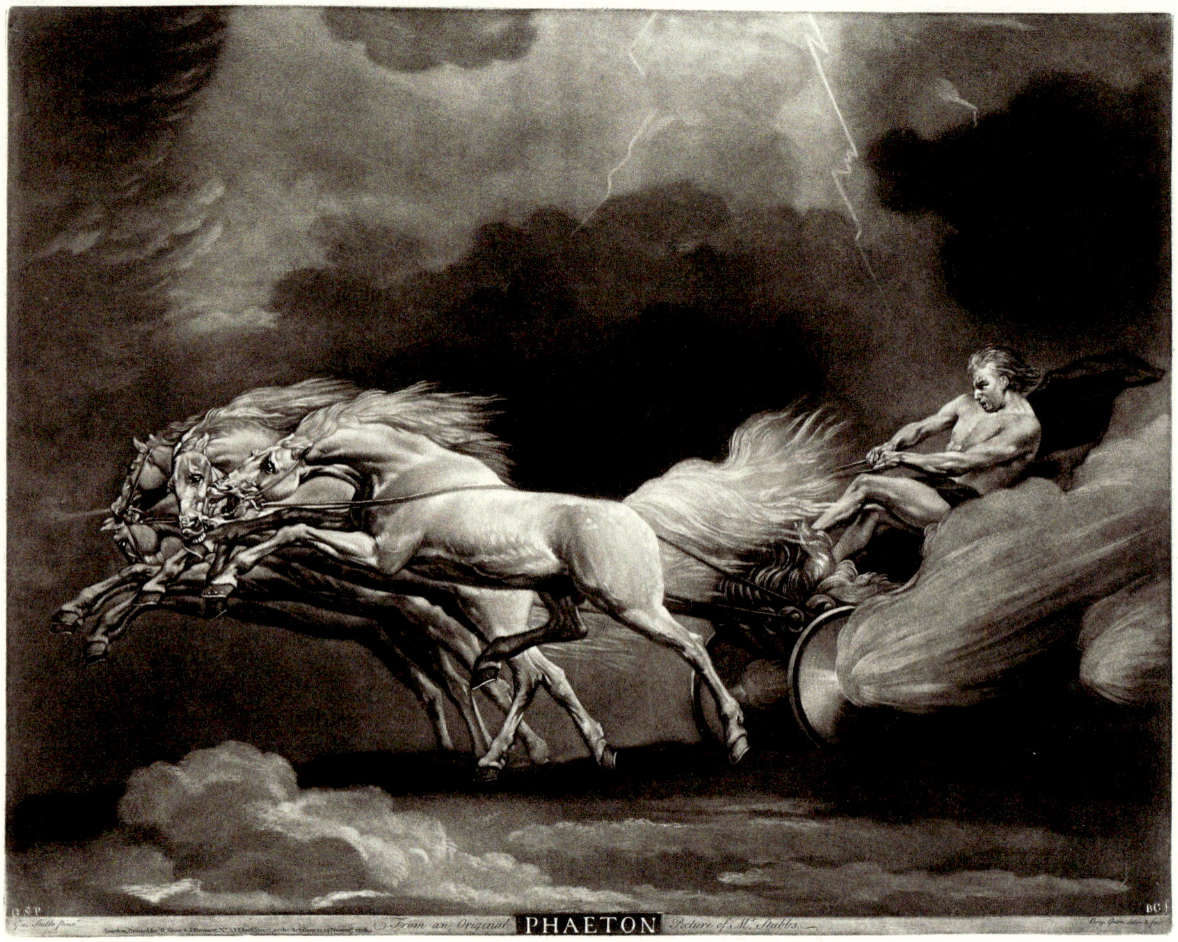

69

Phaeton 1770

Benjamin Green (1739–1798) after George Stubbs

Mezzotint, 56.1 x 44.4 cm (Plate), 46.8 x 58.4 cm (Sheet)
Ins. bottom left: *Geo. Stubbs pinx.*^{t}, right: *Benj. Green delin & fecit.*
Aschaffenburg Collection, Staatliche Graphische Sammlung München, Inv. no. III E 5/2

This print depicts the disastrous flight of Phaeton in the chariot of his father Helios. It was probably taken from an untraced painting of this scene that was exhibited at the Society of Artists in 1764 and shows the only mythological scene by Stubbs that is reproduced in print (Egerton no. 52). In view of the relative frequency with which Stubbs used this design, he clearly considered it to be an important one. It exists among other forms in an enamel from 1775, in a model for Wedgwood from 1780, and in multiple paintings. Furthermore it is shown in his portrait originally by Ozias Humphry (Exhib. Cat. *Fearful Symmetry*, 2000, no. 30).

In the print, attention is drawn to the four horses, whose troubled expressions are highlighted dramatically. Steam escapes from one of their noses. The fatal character of the situation is underlined by the two thunderbolts cutting the sky and the way in which Green has provided depth to the clouds by using surfaces of sharp lines, placed at right angles to each other. Like the *Lion and Stag*, *Phaeton* was not displayed at the Society of Artists and Green seems not to have advertised it.

SG

Lit.: Lennox-Boyd et al., *George Stubbs*, 1989, no. 8 II

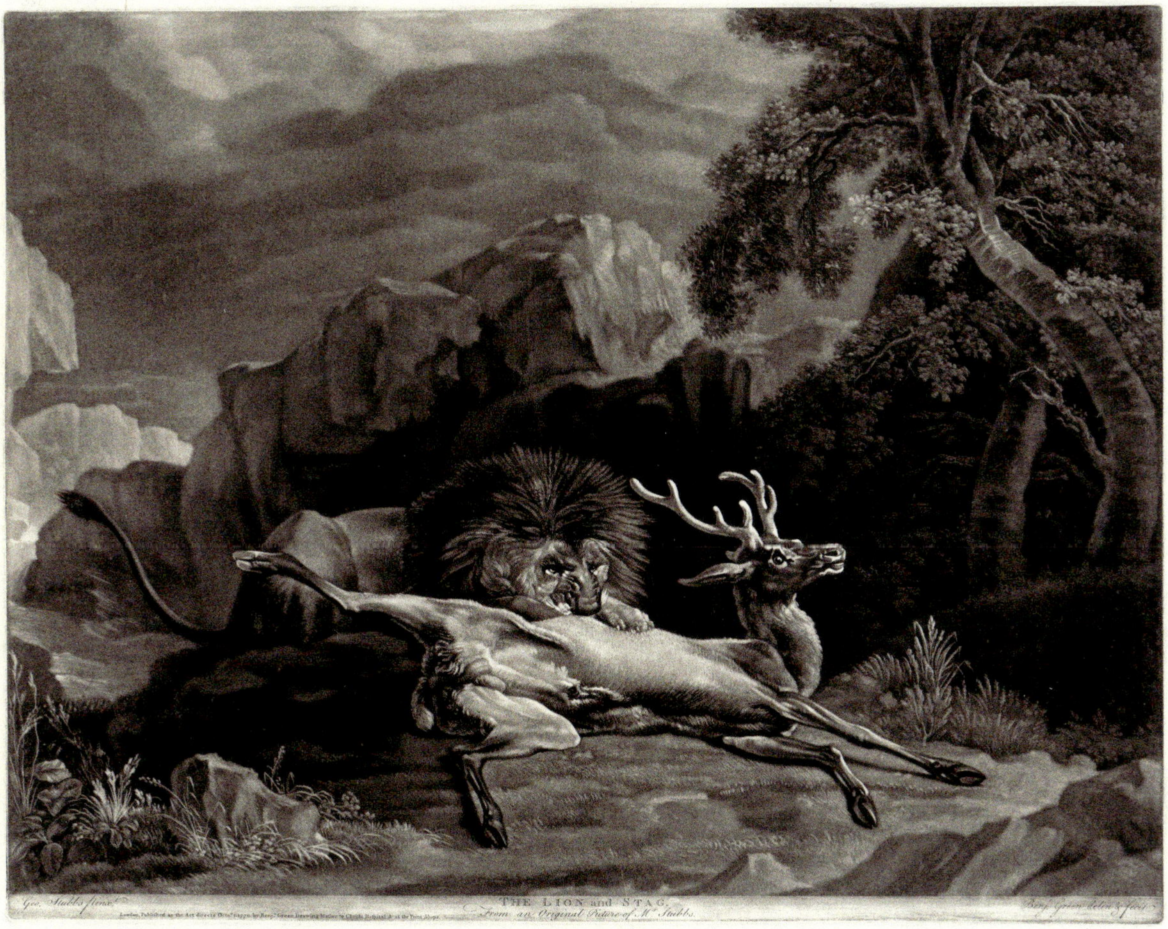

70

The Lion and Stag 1770

Benjamin Green (1739–1798) after George Stubbs

Mezzotint, 44.6 x 56.2 cm (Plate), 47.3 x 59.0 cm (Sheet)
Ins. bottom left: *Geo. Stubbs pinx.*[1], right: *Benj. Green delin & fecit*
Aschaffenburg Collection, Staatliche Graphische Sammlung München, Inv. no. III E 5/3

This print of Green's series depicts a lion devouring a stag. It is probably based on a painting that was on display at the Society of Artists in 1769 and was later bought by the 5th Duke of Rutland (cat. no. 43), but other works by Stubbs showing this subject (Egerton nos. 111 and 115) are also known.

The design of the print follows its source closely and incorporates many dramatic elements, such as an overcast sky and a wild river. It also shows a highly articulated contrast between light and dark, with an emphasis on the anxious look in the eye of the stag and the ferocious head of the feeding lion. The different textures that are shown are blended in a subtle way. Note for example the way in which the shiny skin of the stag's legs passes almost invisibly into its furry body.

SG

Lit.: Lennox-Boyd et al., *George Stubbs*, 1989, no. 9 II

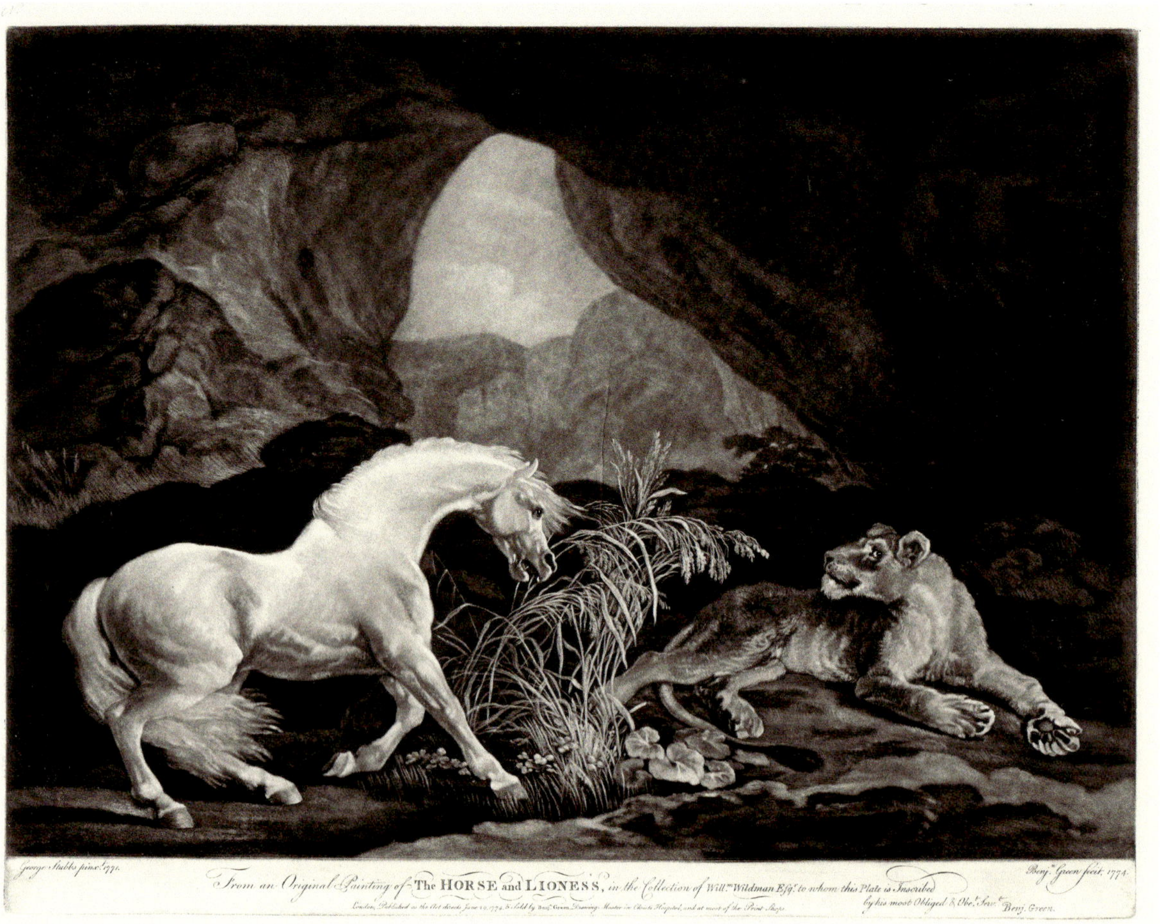

71

The Horse and Lioness 1774

Benjamin Green (1739–1798) after George Stubbs

Mezzotint, 44.8 x 57.0 cm (Plate), 47.1 x 59.0 cm (Sheet)
Ins. bottom left: *George Stubbs pinx.^{t} 1771.*, right: *Benjn Green fecit. 1774.*
Aschaffenburg Collection, Staatliche Graphische Sammlung München, Inv. no. III E 5/5

The Horse and Lioness was advertised in 1774 as a substitute for the plate of *The Horse and Lion* (cat. no. 65), which appears to have been worn out at the time. The choice for a similar subject, but a new design, might have been made in order to satisfy new buyers of the series, as well as interesting current owners of a set.

The print is based on a painting from 1771 that was owned by William Wildman at the time and bought in 1787 by the Polygraphic Society, where it remained until at least 1793. It shows another image of a pale, frightened horse, this time alarmed by a lioness. Shadowy cliffs provide the scene with a dark background, while the tiny strokes with which the lioness is shaped suggest a deeply golden coloured fur. Canes of reed separate the two animals, rendered with such meticulous detail that their individual leaves and seeds can be perceived.

SG

Lit.: Lennox-Boyd et al., *George Stubbs*, 1989, no. 37 II

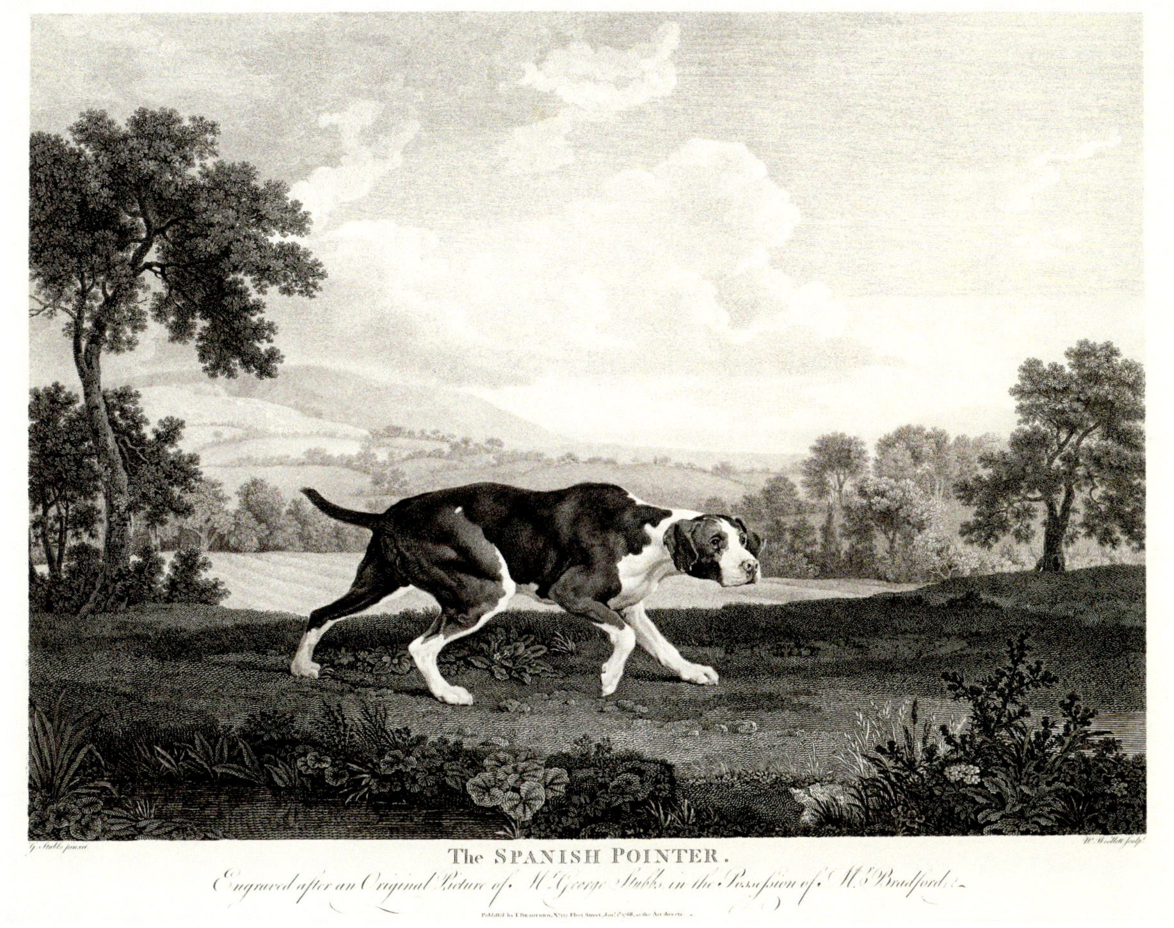

72

The Spanish Pointer 1768

William Woollett (1735–1785) after George Stubbs

Engraving with etching, 44.7 x 56.0 cm (Plate), 45.0 x 56.0 cm (Sheet)
Ins. bottom left: *G. Stubbs pinxit.*, right: *W. Woollett sculp.*[1]
Nuremberg, Germanisches Nationalmuseum (long-term loan from the Graphische Sammlung, Museen der Stadt Nürnberg), Inv. no. St. N. 5652, Kapsel 1530

William Woollett's line engravings after Stubbs are very different from the subtle etchings by George Stubbs himself or the soft mezzotints by Benjamin Green, showing a variety of profound line textures. Woollett produced five of them, all published and probably also commissioned by Thomas Bradford, who owned most of the paintings that Woollett reproduced. *Spanish Pointer* was the first of these engravings and might have been based on the painting in the Neue Pinakothek (cat. no. 29). But it also features elements that are different from this painting and can only be found in a second version of it sold by Sotheby's in 1972 (Egerton no. 88), such as the sharp-edged foliage in the lower right corner and the singular tree to the left of the print. Perhaps this last painting is therefore a more likely source of the engraving.

Although the main focus of the picture is clearly on the pointer, with its shimmering eyes and muscular body, Woollett has also bestowed great care on the landscape. Noteworthy are for example the variety of vegetation in the foreground, which is mirrored in the water, and the way in which the voluptuous trees and sloping hills gradually dissolve into the background.

SG

Lit.: Lennox-Boyd et al., *George Stubbs*, 1989, no. 10 IV

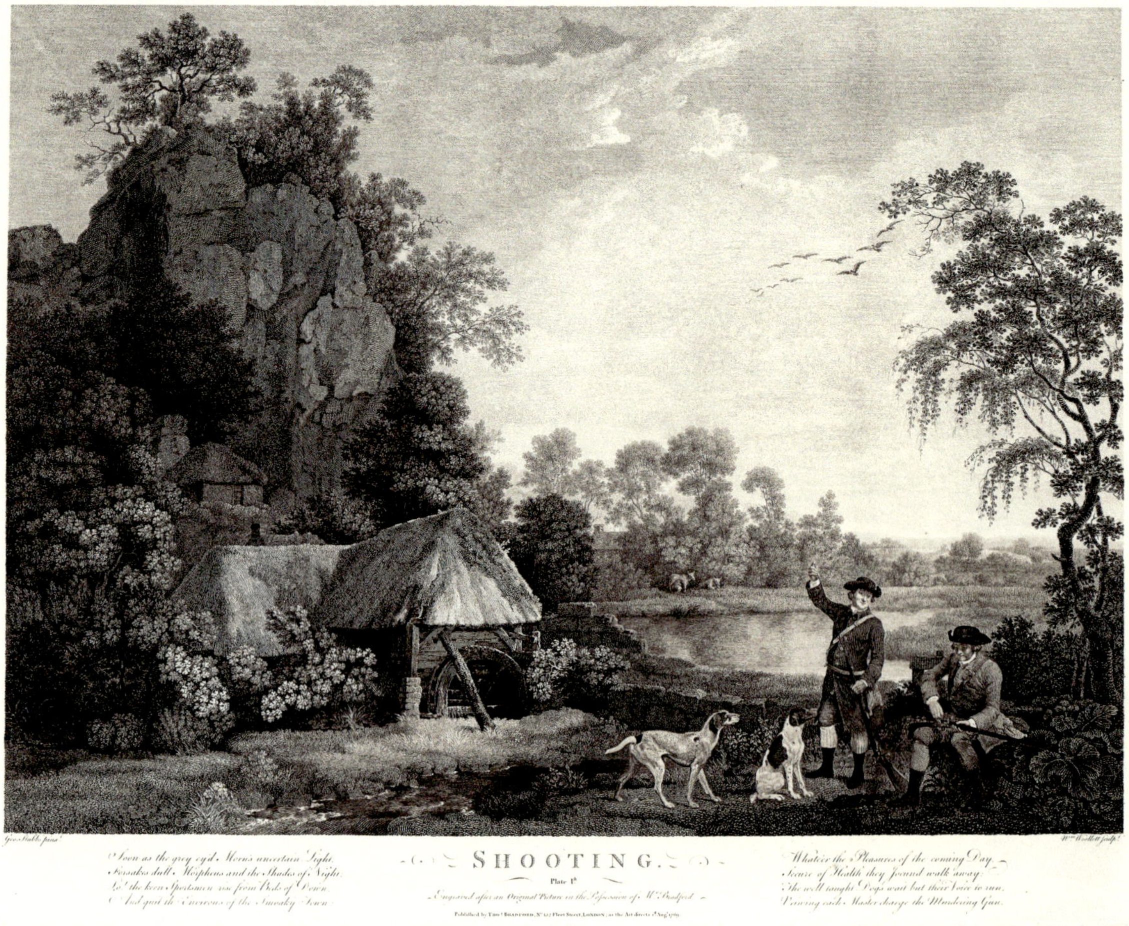

73

Shooting I 1769

William Woollett (1735–1785) after George Stubbs

Engraving with etching, 44.2 x 54.9 cm (Plate), 52.1 x 64.5 cm (Sheet)
Ins. bottom left: *Geo. Stubbs pinx.t*, right: *W.m Woollett sculp.t*
Nuremberg, Germanisches Nationalmuseum (long-term loan from the Graphische Sammlung, Museen der Stadt Nürnberg), Inv. no. St. N. 9326, Kapsel 1019 c

After *The Spanish Pointer* was finished Woollett engraved a set of four shooting scenes which was based on four paintings commissioned by William Wildman (possibly in association with Thomas Bradford) in 1767. The paintings were exhibited individually from 1767 to 1770 and are now in the Paul Mellon Collection (Egerton no. 82–85). As suggested by Egerton, they can be interpreted as 'friendship portraits', showing two middle-aged men out hunting with their two dogs. In her view, the fuller-faced man might be identified as William Wildman, after which Lennox-Boyd et al. surmised that the other might represent Thomas Bradford, but that cannot be determined with certainty (see Clayton p. 67).

Because the original paintings are in essence landscapes, it is hardly surprising that Woollett, who specialized in landscapes, was appointed to reproduce these pictures. *Shooting I* is the first of the set,

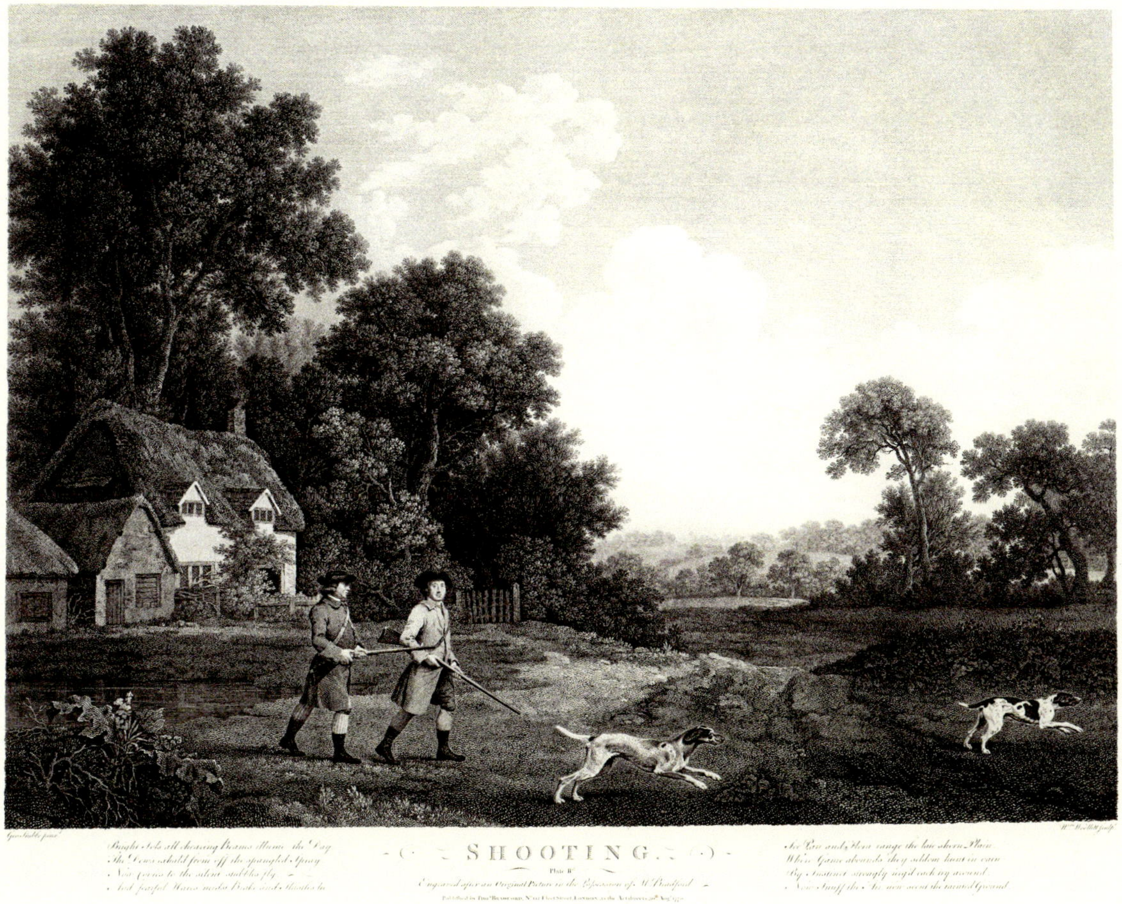

74

Shooting II 1770

William Woollett (1735–1785) after George Stubbs

Engraving with etching, 44.1 x 55.2 cm (Plate), 52.1 x 64.6 cm (Sheet)
Ins. bottom left: *Geo. Stubbs pinx.*^{t}, right: *W.*^{m} *Woollett sculp.*^{t}
Nuremberg, Germanisches Nationalmuseum (long-term loan from the Graphische Sammlung, Museen der Stadt Nürnberg), Inv. no. St. N. 9347, Kapsel 1019 c

showing a view of the countryside around Creswell Crags. In this engraving, Woollett carefully combined textures of small leaves, woolly clouds and smooth surfaces of water into an evocative landscape. The print also includes many details, from the two cows emerging from the bushes near the waterfront to the flight of birds adorning the sky.

The landscape in *Shooting II* is somewhat different from its predecessor, providing the viewer with a wide, hilly outlook. To the left of the image, a house is depicted in detail. Its straw roof contains holes and is in some places lightened by the sun. The frames around its windows are engraved minutely and smoke is shown emerging from the chimney. This level of detail can also be found in the vegetation that occupies the foreground, of which the leaves and branches each seem to have been defined individually.

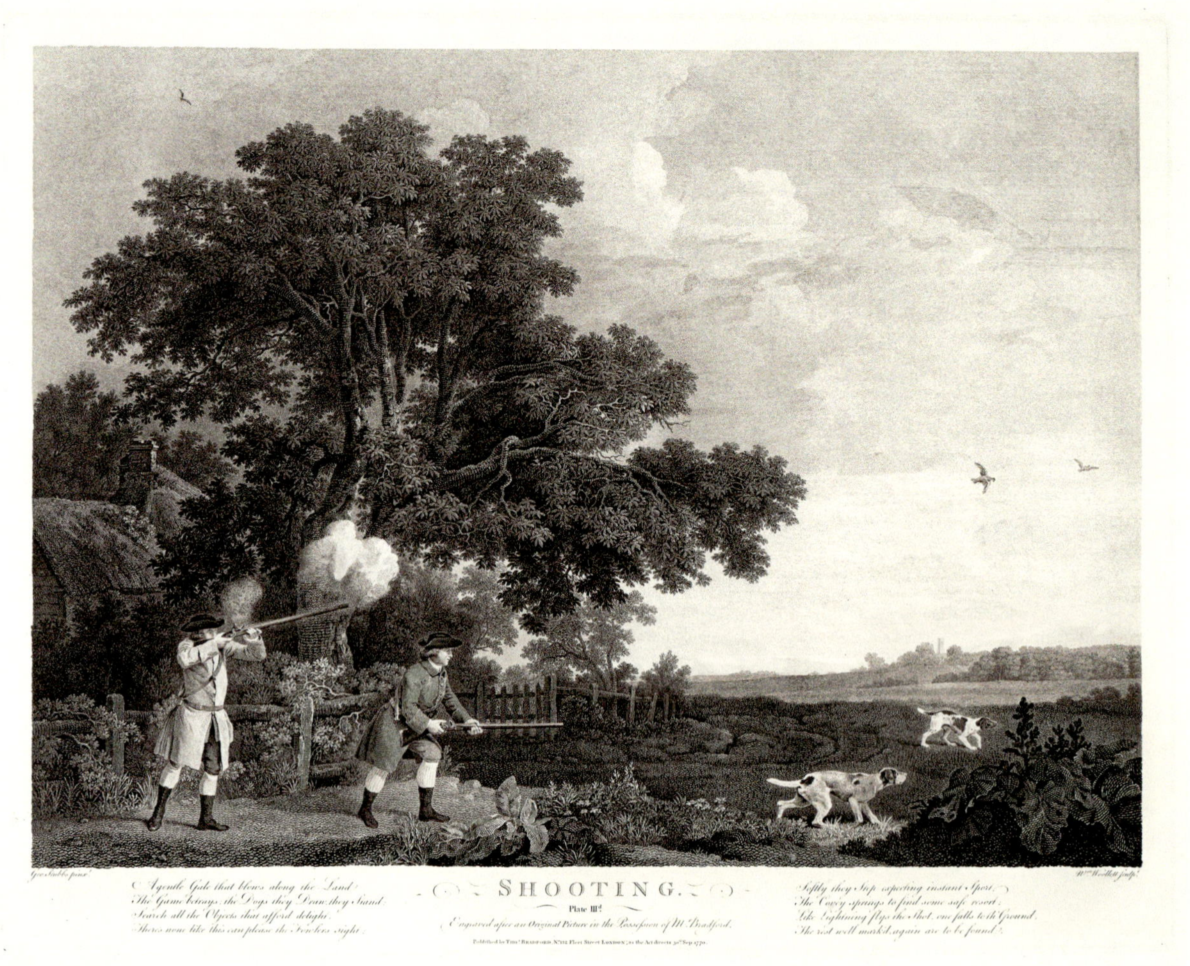

75

Shooting III 1770

William Woollett (1735–1785) after George Stubbs

Engraving with etching, 44.1 x 55.1 cm (Plate), 52.1 x 64.6 cm (Sheet)
Ins. bottom left: *Geo. Stubbs pinx.ᵗ*, right: *W.ᵐ Woollett sculp.ᵗ*
Nuremberg, Germanisches Nationalmuseum (long-term loan from the Graphische Sammlung, Museen der Stadt Nürnberg), Inv. no. St. N. 9348, Kapsel 1019 c

In *Shooting III* the viewer is provided with yet other fresh elements. One of the two hunters fires a shot at a bird. Softly rendered smoke rises from the barrel of his gun. What is interesting about this print is again the subtle manner in which alternating textures provide depth to the cloudy sky. Again, Woollett has depicted the landscape with a great sense of detail. Even a tiny village can be discerned between the hills in the distance.

Finally, contrasting the wide views of the first three shooting scenes, *Shooting IV* presents the two hunters discussing a hare in a forest. The trees that surround them fill almost the entire picture plane, their branches, leaves and bark suggested by myriad delicate lines. The vista to the left of the image, showing a river with a small group of houses, is very striking. Despite the suggested distance, it is even possible to count the number of windows.

Although Woollett's prints present four very sophisticated landscapes, they also present a considerable number of differences when compared with the set of paintings in the Paul Mellon Collection. Trees, bushes, and elements such as the two cows in *Shooting I*

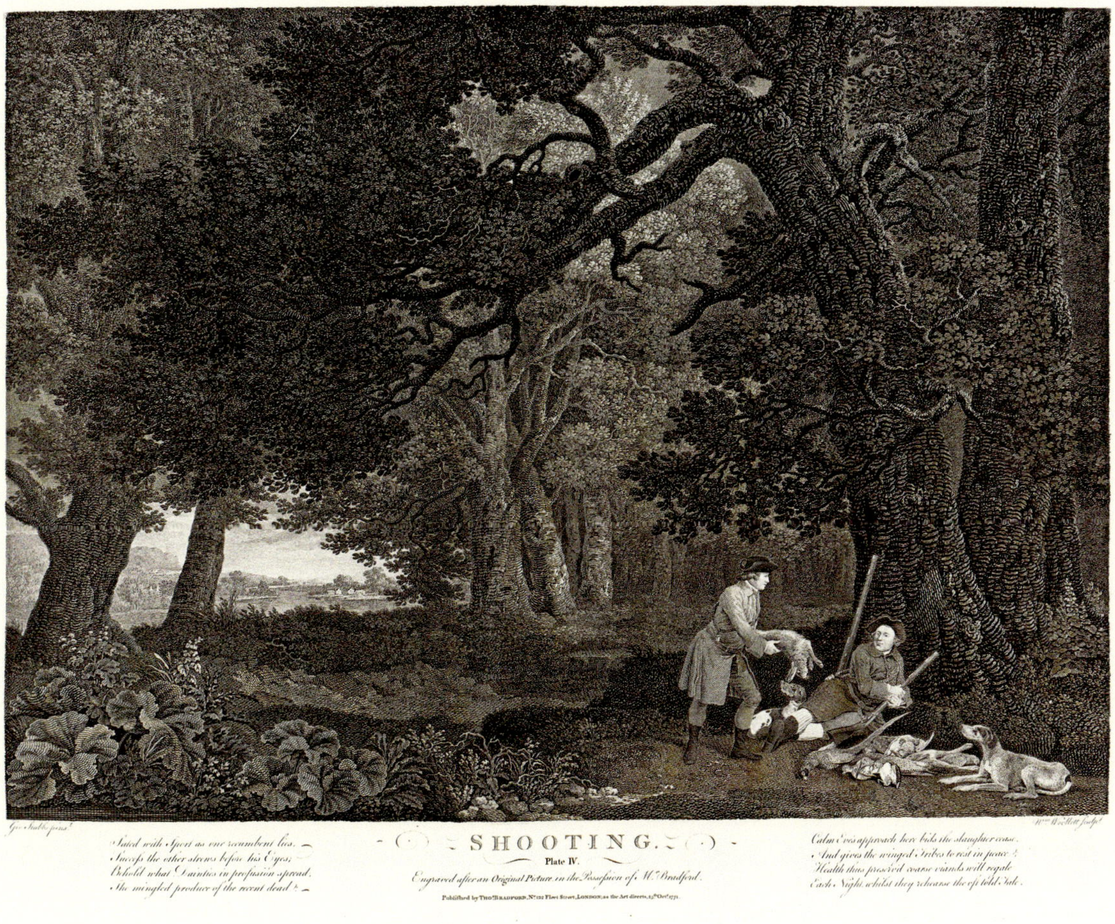

76

Shooting IV 1771

William Woollett (1735–1785) after George Stubbs

Engraving with etching, 45.2 x 55.7 cm (Plate), 55.8 x 77.8 cm (Sheet)
Ins. bottom left: *Geo. Stubbs pinx.*^{t}, right: *W.*^{m} *Woollett sculp.*^{t}
Kunstsammlungen der Veste Coburg, Kupferstichkabinett,
Inv. no. XI.109.55

are added to the original composition and others are replaced or omitted. As argued by Lennox-Boyd et al., this might suggest that the set of paintings in the Paul Mellon Collection is not the one from which Woollett's engravings were taken, but it could also indicate that Woollett took, or was granted, more pictorial license than for example Benjamin Green—perhaps because he had already established a good reputation as an engraver.

The engravings were in any case highly successful. They were sold until 1829 and copied for Thomas Gosden in 1825, showing the two men wearing updated costumes. By that time, the engravings were even used to decorate tableware and tiles.

SG

Lit.: Lennox-Boyd et al., *George Stubbs*, 1989, no. 11 v, 12 v, 13 v, 14 v – Exhib. Cat. *George Stubbs in the Collection of Paul Mellon*, 1999, no. 45, 46, 51, 52 – Blake, *George Stubbs and the Wide Creation*, 2005, pp. 170–176

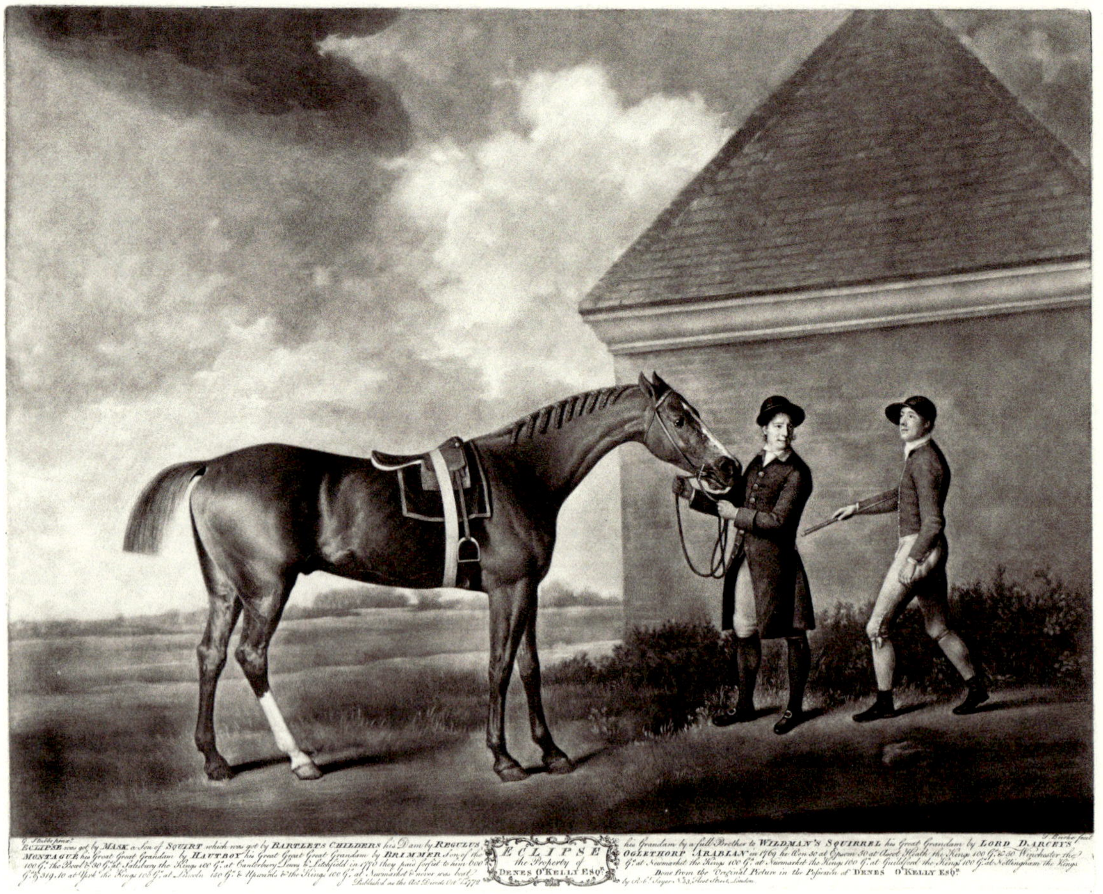

77

Eclipse 1772

Thomas Burke (1749–1815) after George Stubbs

Mezzotint, 45.7 x 56.2 cm (Plate), 47.5 x 58.5 cm (Sheet)
Ins. bottom left: *G. Stubbs pinx.*[t], right: *T. Burke fecit*
Aschaffenburg Collection, Staatliche Graphische Sammlung München, Inv. no. 11 E 16/27

Thomas Burke's print of the racehorse Eclipse was printed and reprinted up to the twentieth century. Its immense popularity was due to the fact that it showed the most famous, undefeated racehorse of the eighteenth century. The image is probably taken from a painting that was owned by the family of Colonel O'Kelly and was sold by Christie's in November 1987 (Egerton no. 96). The painting was commissioned by Denis O'Kelly on the occasion of his purchase of the horse from its former owner William Wildman in 1770. It shows the likeness of Eclipse with his jockey Samuel Merrit, approaching as if he is about to mount. They are positioned in front of a rubbing house in Newmarket, where Eclipse raced most of his races. When he retired in 1771, Eclipse became a popular sire at Clay Hill near Epsom and sired 334 winners. He died on 27 February 1789 in Canons, near Edgware.

Burke has engraved a very soft rendition of Stubbs's painting. The horse is modelled with a subtle transition of grey tones, while bright highlights accentuate the contours of its muscles. Its hind legs show almost photographic qualities, while the background of the image is kept very sober so as not to distract the viewer's gaze from the horse.

SG

Lit.: Lennox-Boyd et al., *George Stubbs*, 1989, no. 32 II – Exhib. Cat. *Stubbs and the Horse,* 2004, no. 63 – Exhib. Cat. *George Stubbs in the Collection of Paul Mellon*, 1999, no. 12

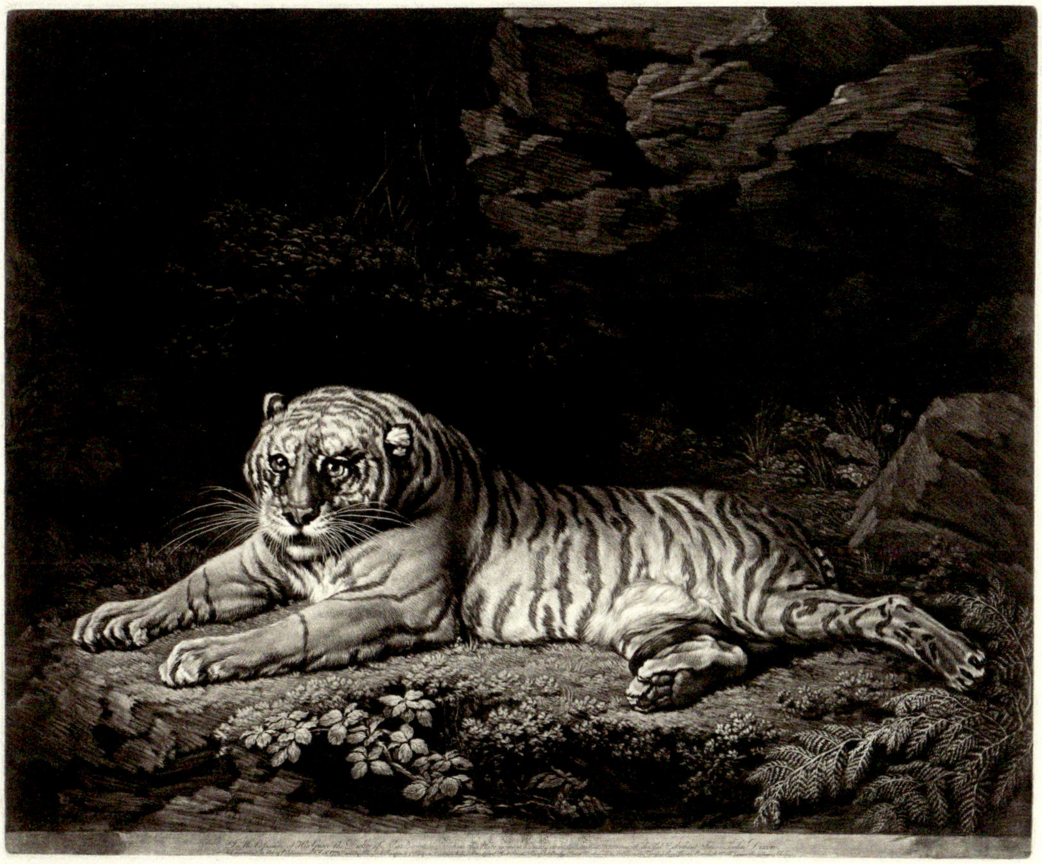

78

A Tigress 1772

John Dixon (1740–1811) after George Stubbs

Mezzotint, 48.1 x 58.0 cm (Plate), 54.5 x 74.0 cm (Sheet)
Ins. bottom, within image: *G Stubbs pinxit*, right: *J Dixon fecit*
Nuremberg, Germanisches Nationalmuseum (long-term loan from the Graphische Sammlung, Museen der Stadt Nürnberg),
Inv. no. St. N. 5326, Kapsel 1019 c

This print by John Dixon is based on Stubbs's *Tigress* from 1769, which can be found in the collection of the Duke of Marlborough (Egerton no. 77). It shows a spectacular image of a reclining tigress which was presented to George Spencer, the 4th Duke of Marlborough by Robert Clive, Governor of Bengal. The tigress was kept in the Duke's menagerie at Blenheim Palace and multiple portraits were made of her, but Stubbs's portrait can undoubtedly be considered as the most true to nature.

In Dixon's mezzotint, the tigress is placed against a dark background, making the animal stand out of the image. Every single hair of the tigress's fur seems to have been drawn separately, following the curves of her body in a most natural way. The bold use of highlights and shadows provides the fur with an intense glow that is only surpassed by the brightness of her crisp white whiskers. It is not hard to believe that this print was the most highly praised reproduction of a painting by Stubbs in its time and that it was put forward as an example that demonstrated the skills of contemporary mezzotinters (see Clayton p. 69).

SG

Lit.: Lennox-Boyd et al., *George Stubbs*, 1989, no. 33 IV

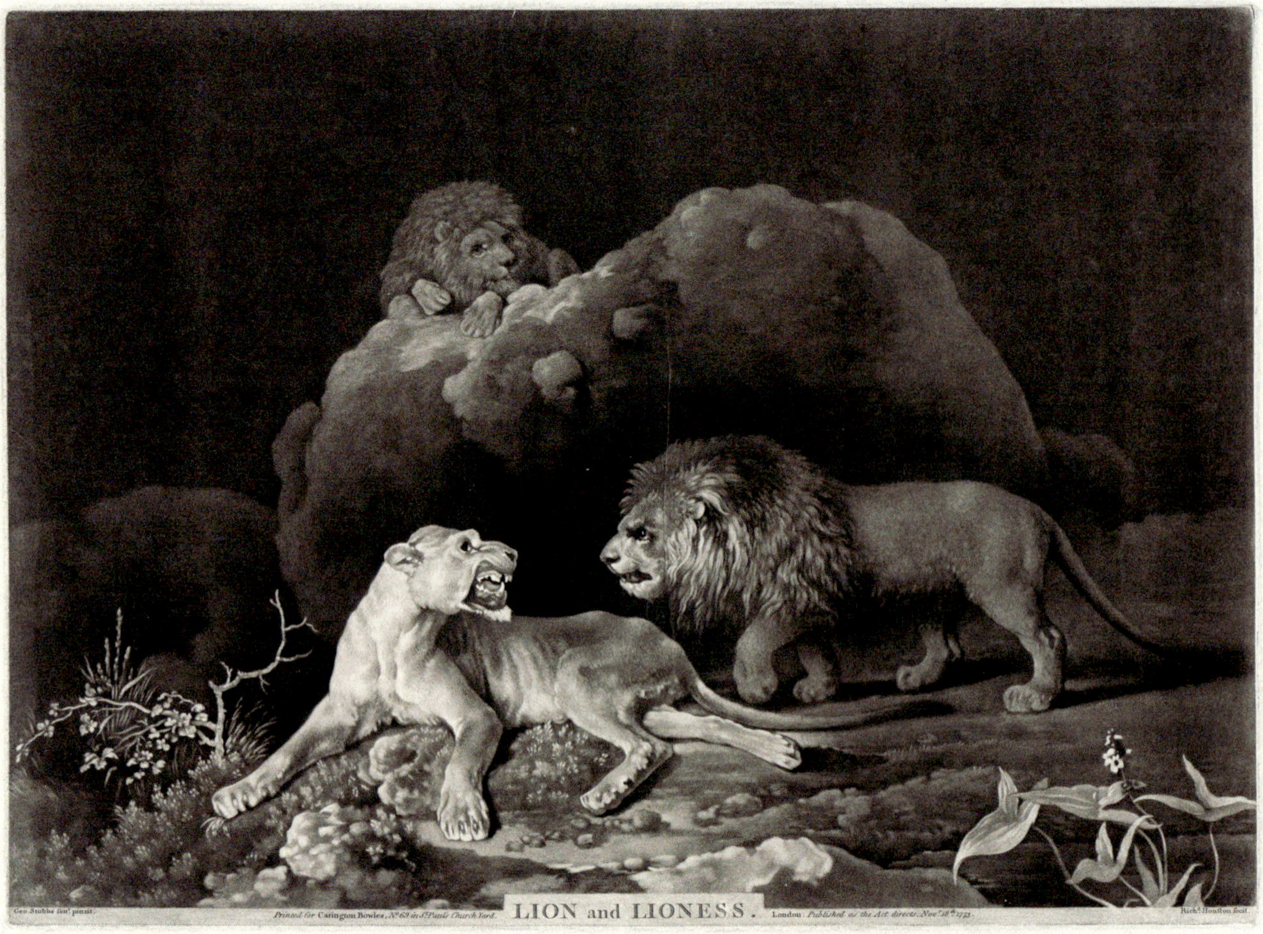

79

Lion and Lioness 1773

Richard Houston (1722–1775) after George Stubbs

Mezzotint, 35.5 x 48.2 cm (Plate), 38.5 x 51.3 cm (Sheet)
Ins. bottom left: *Geo. Stubbs sen.ʳ pinxit.*, right: *Rich.ᵈ Houston fecit.*
Aschaffenburg Collection, Staatliche Graphische Sammlung München, Inv. no. 11 E 19/55

This print by Richard Houston is most probably based on the *Lion and Lioness* from 1772 that was exhibited at the Society of Artists in 1773 (Egerton no. 161). The painting was probably commissioned by Sir John Nelthorpe in Lincolnshire and is still in his original collection. Central to the print is a lioness, growling fiercely at an approaching lion. All the light is focused on her, her deep blond and shiny fur contrasting with the frilly manes of her male counterpart. Because of the relative emptiness of the scene and the lioness's deep black eye and white teeth, she stands out of the image strongly.

Stubbs is known to have painted multiple images with the 'Lion and Lioness' subject. Under the title *A Den of Lions* (Egerton no. 162), a painting by Stubbs was exhibited at the Society of Artists in 1772, showing a design that is strongly related to that of the painting in Lincolnshire. An enamel in the Paul Mellon Collection also shows this design (Exhib. Cat. *George Stubbs in the Collection of Paul Mellon*, 1999, no. 20).

SG

Lit.: Lennox-Boyd et al., *George Stubbs*, 1989, no. 36 I

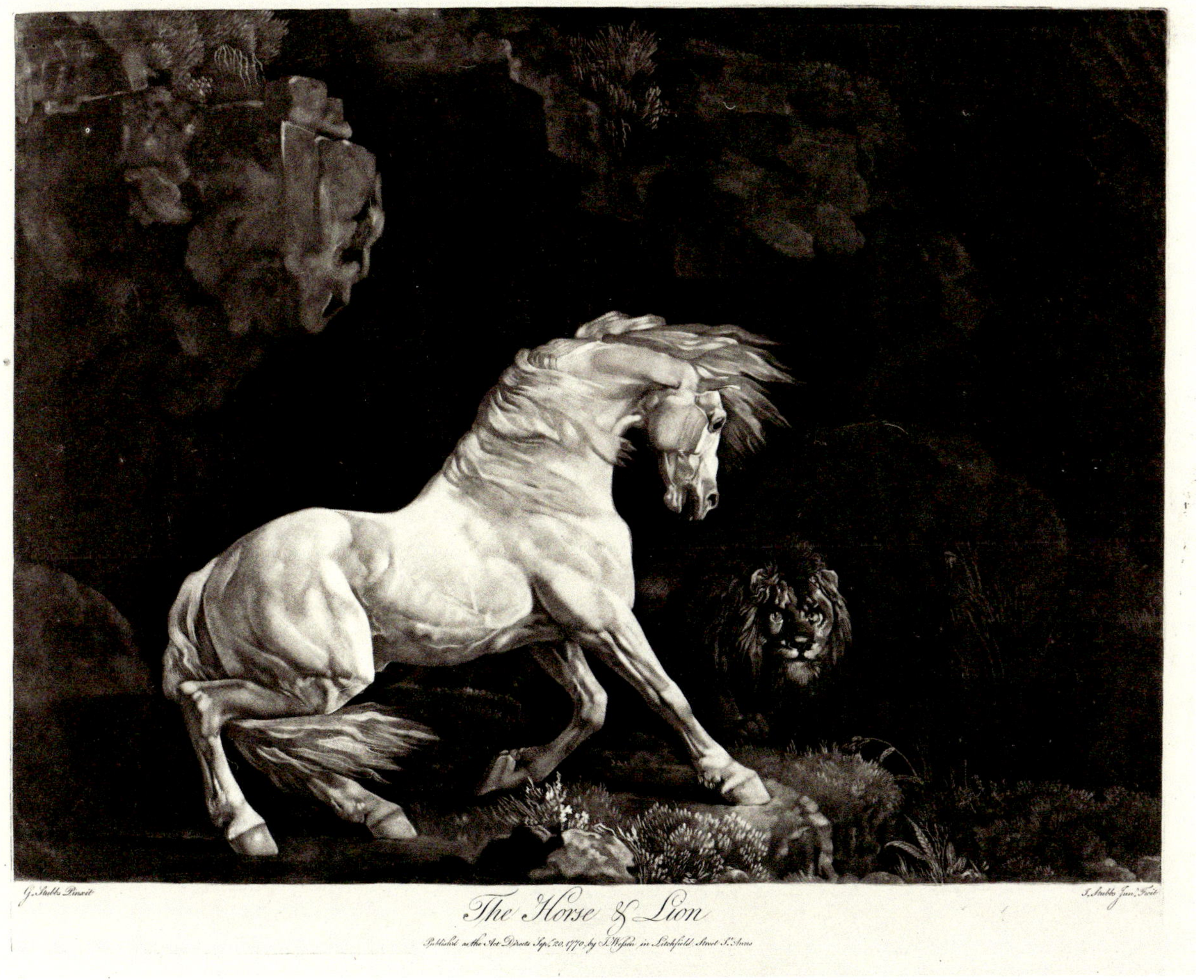

80

The Horse and Lion 1770

George Townley Stubbs (1748–before 1816) after George Stubbs

Mezzotint, 45.6 x 55.2 cm (Plate), 52.2 x 65.8 cm (Sheet)
Ins. bottom left: *G. Stubbs Pinxit*, right: *J. Stubbs Jun. Fecit*
Kunstsammlungen der Veste Coburg, Kupferstichkabinett, Inv. no. XI.162.1

This print by Stubbs's son George Townley Stubbs was his second published engraving after work of his father. It is based on the painting *Horse Frightened by a Lion* from 1770 in the Walker Art Gallery in Liverpool (Egerton no. 120), or the enamel from 1770 in a private collection (Egerton no. 114). Because George Townley Stubbs's print shows and omits aspects from both these images, the exact source is, however, difficult to determine.

The print presents a large white horse, terrified at the sight of an approaching lion. As in Green's print of this subject, the horse is shown making a backwards move, but its body is rendered in a much more modern and sculptural way, with sharp transitions of grey and white tones and a rather angular anatomy that also features in the above-mentioned painting and enamel. Striking is also the head of the lion that emerges from the dark background with large, accentuated eyes, ready to attack.

SG

Lit.: Lennox-Boyd et al., *George Stubbs*, 1989, no. 16 II

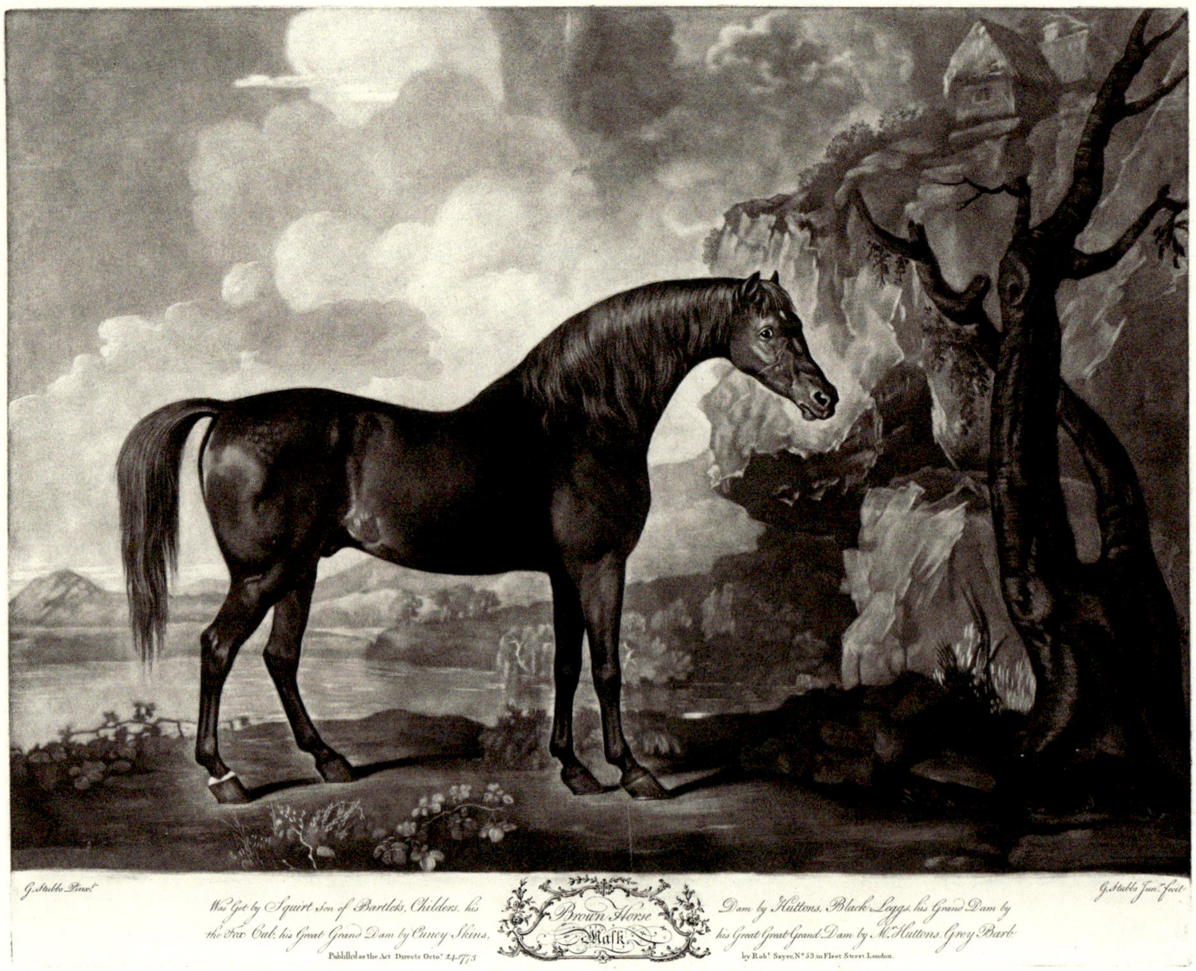

81

Brown Horse Mask 1771

George Townley Stubbs (1748–before 1816) after George Stubbs

Mezzotint, 45.5 x 55.8 cm (Plate), 47.8 x 58.6 cm (Sheet)
Ins. bottom left: *G. Stubbs Pinx.*[t], right: *G. Stubbs Jun.*[r] *fecit*
Aschaffenburg Collection, Staatliche Graphische Sammlung München, Inv. no. III E 7/29

This mezzotint by George Townley Stubbs is based on the painting *Marske, the Sire of Eclipse* from 1770 (Egerton no. 95). It shows the famous brown colt Marske, or Mask that was foaled in 1750 and bred by John Hutton, a famous breeder from Yorkshire. In 1764, Mask sired the unbeatable Eclipse and became very popular as a stud horse. Townley Stubbs's print was published at the time when Eclipse started to dominate the turf. When the plate was acquired by Sayer and Bennett in 1773, the engraving was sold as a companion to Burke's *Eclipse* (cat. no. 77).

Following Stubbs's portrait, George Townley Stubbs has paid much attention to the individual features of the horse, such as the small star on his head and the white coronet on his right hind leg. Because the contours of the horse are surrounded by a soft halo, its figure is strongly accentuated, focusing the viewer's attention on its appearance.

SG

Lit.: Lennox-Boyd et al., *George Stubbs*, 1989, no. 25 III

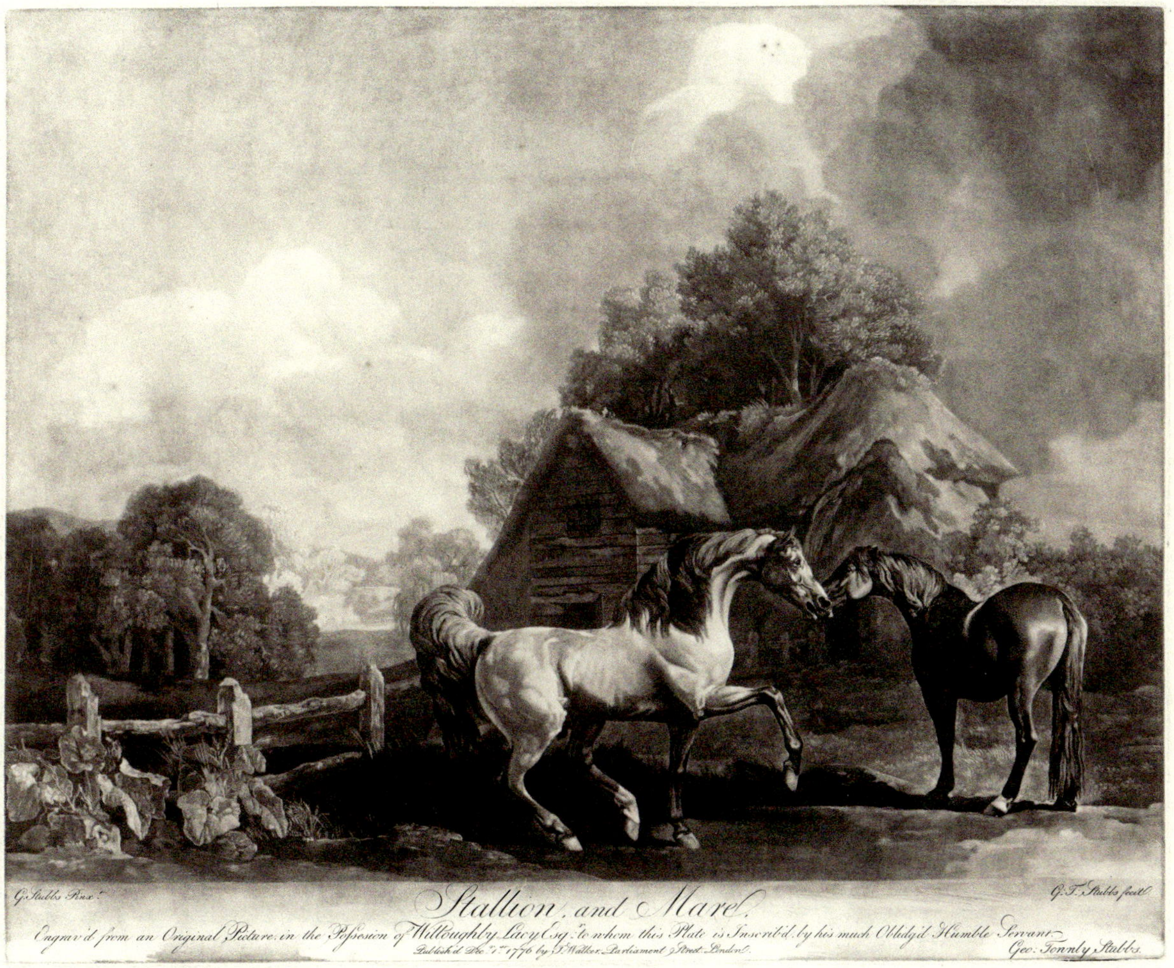

82

Stallion and Mare 1776

George Townley Stubbs (1748–before 1816) after George Stubbs

Mezzotint, 48.2 x 58.2 cm (Plate), 50.5 x 60.5 cm (Sheet)
Ins. bottom left: *G. Stubbs Pinx.*^{t}, right: *G: T: Stubbs fecit.*
Aschaffenburg Collection, Staatliche Graphische Sammlung München, Inv. no. III E 7/30

This print depicts an interacting stallion and mare. It is taken from the painting *Stallion and Mare* from 1769, which was exhibited at the Society of Artists in the same year and is now in a private collection (Egerton no. 92). With the painting, Stubbs probably aimed to capture the 'animal passions', a popular theme among animal painters at the time. Central to the image is the sexual tension between the stallion and the mare, communicated by the stallion's restless pose and the wild movement of its tail.

The print shows many details which are articulated by thin dark lines and strong white highlights, like the manes of the stallion and the leaves in the lower left corner. It also incorporates features that are suggested more subtly, including the ribs of the stallion and the texture of the wooden fence. Townley Stubbs has adequately adopted the dramatic lighting of the painting, providing the hind legs of the mare with a powerful glow and depth.

SG

Lit.: Lennox-Boyd et al., *George Stubbs*, 1989, no. 48 II

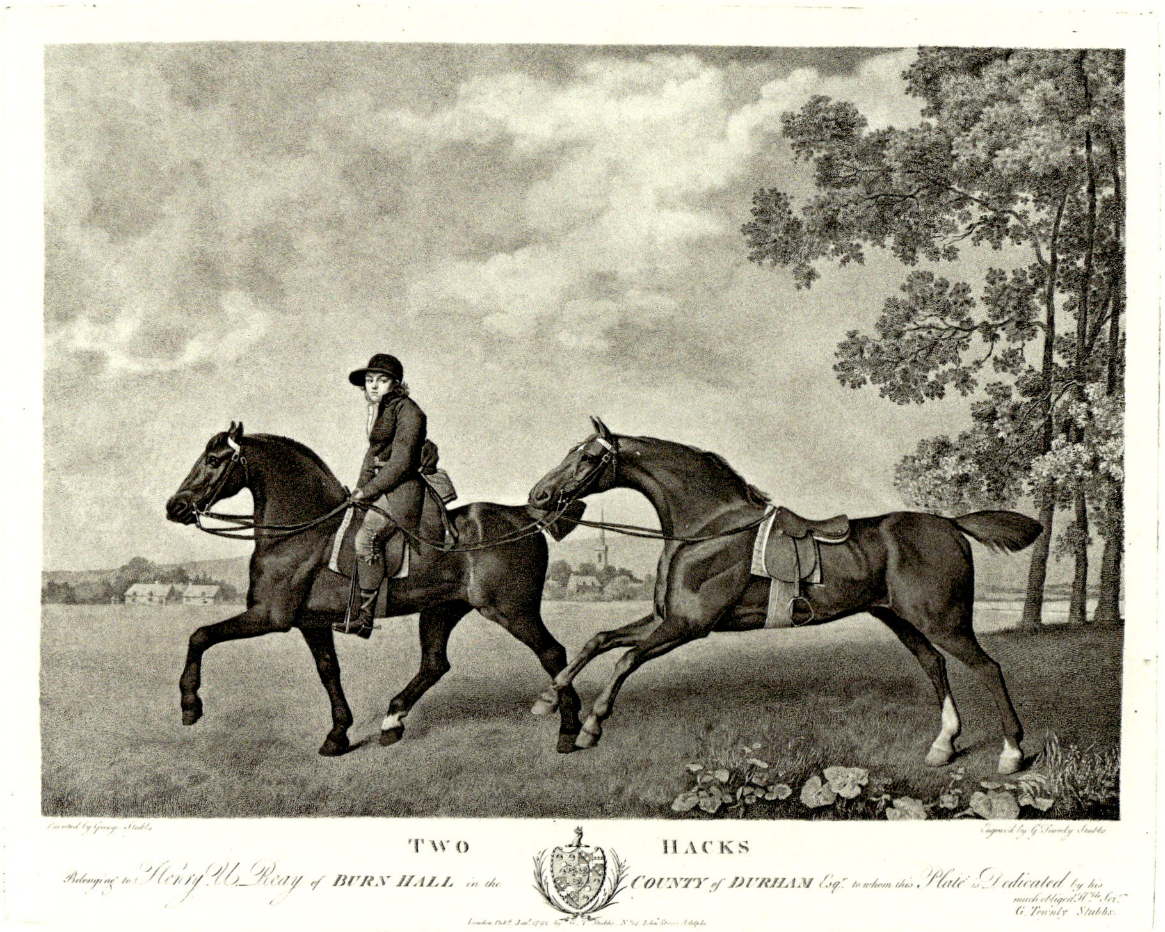

83

Two Hacks 1792

George Townley Stubbs (1748–before 1816) after George Stubbs

Mezzotint with roulette work, 40.3 x 50.4 cm (Plate), 48.0 x 60.4 cm (Sheet)
Ins. bottom left: *Painted by George Stubbs.*, right: *Engraved by G. Townly Stubbs*
Kunstsammlungen der Veste Coburg, Kupferstichkabinett, Inv. no. XI.210.2

The source of this print by George Townley Stubbs was the painting *Two Saddled Horses, one Ridden by a Groom* from 1789 in the Huntington Library (Egerton no. 275). The painting was commissioned by Henry Utrick Reay, a wealthy landowner and colliery proprietor in Northumberland, as a companion to the painting from which the print *Two Hunters* is taken (cat. no. 84). Reay had a preference for the use of ponies as hacks, horses for local riding, which explains the subject of the painting.

Townley Stubbs's use of roulette work has provided this print with an impression that strongly differs from that of his mezzotints. It does not, however, affect its quality. The small dots with which the scene is drawn give the print a grainy impression, but also present some convincing textures. Much depth has been provided to the anatomy of the horses. A great deal of detail is shown in the foliage of the trees to the right, the leaves in the foreground and the village in the background of the print. In addition to general black-and-white impressions of this plate, Townley Stubbs also sold colour-printed impressions of it (see Clayton p. 73).

SG

Lit.: Lennox-Boyd et al., *George Stubbs*, 1989, no. 94 II

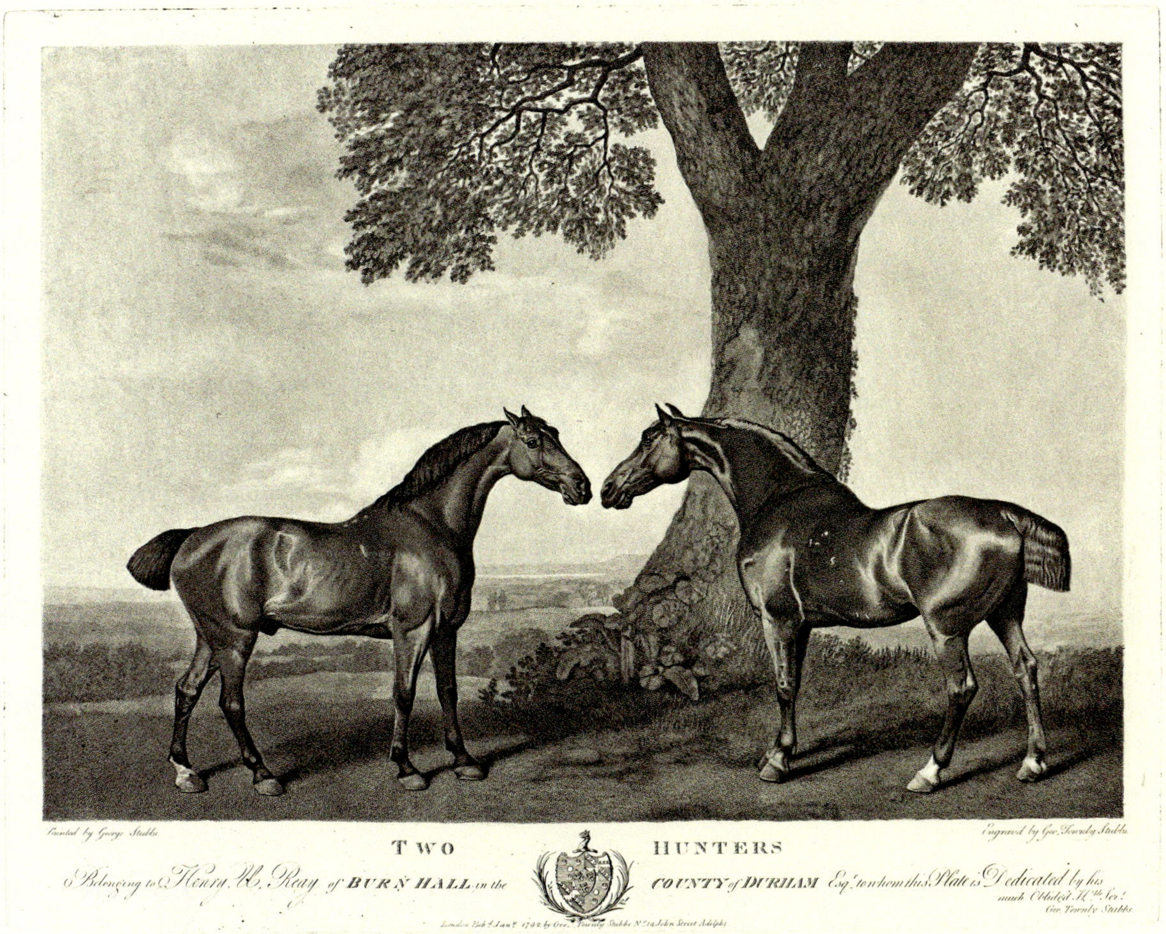

84

Two Hunters 1792

George Townley Stubbs (1748–before 1816) after George Stubbs

Mezzotint with roulette work, 40.3 x 50.6 cm (Plate), 48.5 x 60.8 cm (Sheet)
Ins. bottom left: *Painted by George Stubbs.*, right: *Engraved by G. Townly Stubbs*
Kunstsammlungen der Veste Coburg, Kupferstichkabinett, Inv. no. XI.210.1

This print by George Townley Stubbs is taken from Stubbs's painting *Two Bay Hunters* from 1786 in Cape Town (Egerton no. 264). Like the painting from which *Two Hacks* was taken, this painting was commissioned by Henry Utrick Reay, showing two hunters almost touching noses.

Like *Two Hacks* (cat. no. 83), *Two Hunters* is an example of George Townley Stubbs's use of the roulette technique. In particular the suggestion of the healthy coats of the horses catches the eye, but also the bark of the tree in the background is executed with a sense for naturalism. As was the case with *Two Hacks*, Townley Stubbs sold colour-printed impressions of *Two Hunters* in addition to black-and-white ones.

SG

Lit.: Lennox-Boyd et al., *George Stubbs*, 1989, no. 95 II

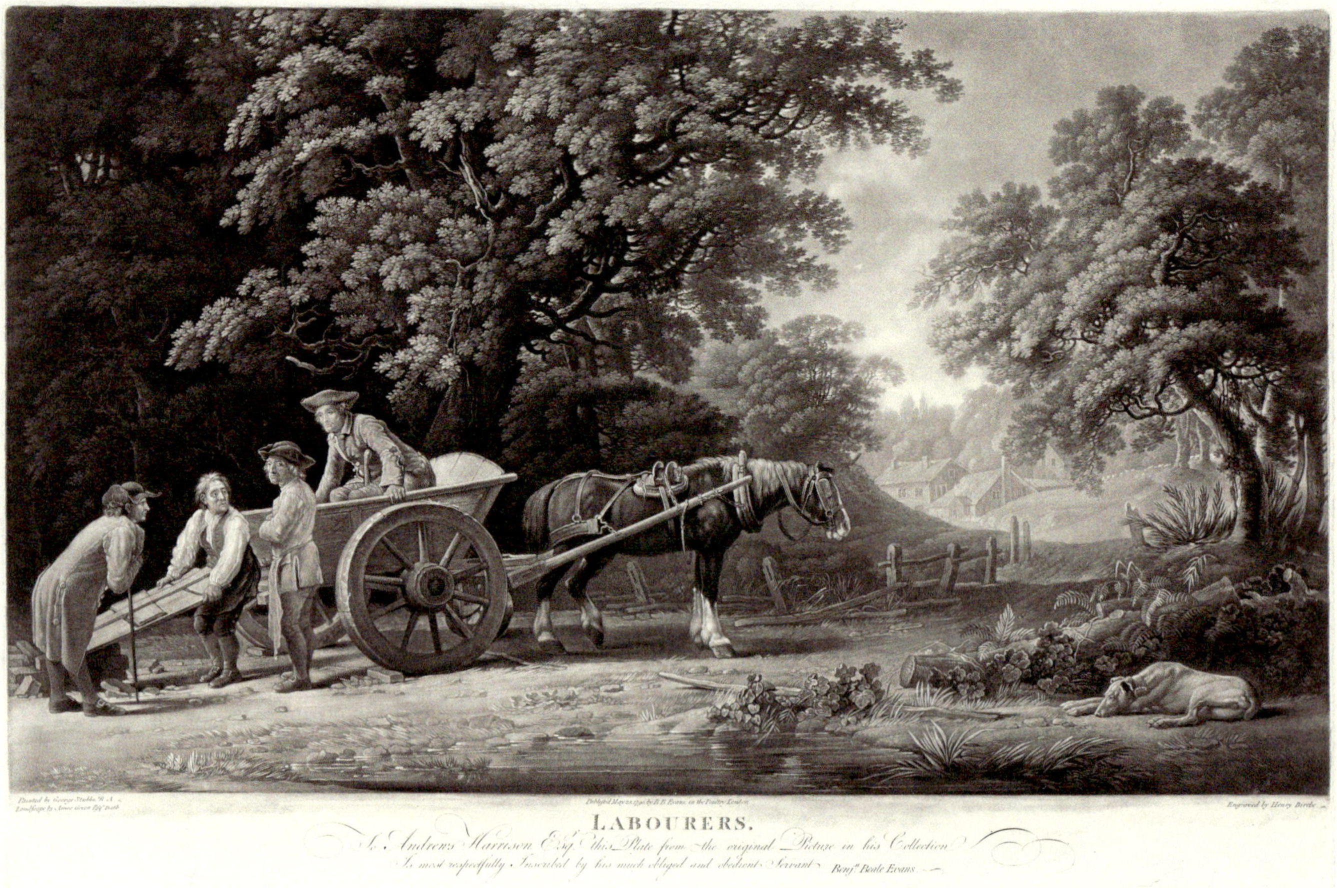

85

Labourers 1790

Robert Laurie (1755–1836) and Richard Earlom (1743–1822) after George Stubbs

Mezzotint, 43.9 x 65.4 cm (Plate), 45.8 x 67.2 cm (Sheet)
Ins. bottom left: *Painted by George Stubbs. R. A. / Landscape by Amos Green. Esq.ʳ Bath*, right: *Engraved by Henri Birche.*
Aschaffenburg Collection, Staatliche Graphische Sammlung München, Inv. no. 11 E 16/1

This mezzotint by Robert Laurie and Richard Earlom was made under the pseudonym of Henry Birche. Earlom used this name in order to engrave for B. B. Evans while he was actually exclusively contracted by John Boydell (1720–1804) (see Clayton p. 73). The engraving is based on *Lord Torrington's Brickmakers* from 1767 in Philadelphia (Egerton no. 100). This painting was commissioned by Lord Torrington, who often spent his time watching his labourers at work in his garden, 'appearing like a Flemish subject', and asked Stubbs to paint them as such.

The print presents a scene with a cart and four labourers against the background of a wooded countryside. Highlighted are the personal features of the men, the gear of the workhorse and the sleeping dog in the lower right corner. The vista in the upper right corner also catches the eye, providing a glimpse of a sunlit house in the woods that is accompanied by a flock of tiny white sheep. The motif of the labourers, with the cart and sleeping dog, has been re-used in a painting from 1779 (cat. no. 33) which is now in the Bearsted Collection.

SG

Lit.: Lennox-Boyd et al., *George Stubbs*, 1989, no. 87 IV

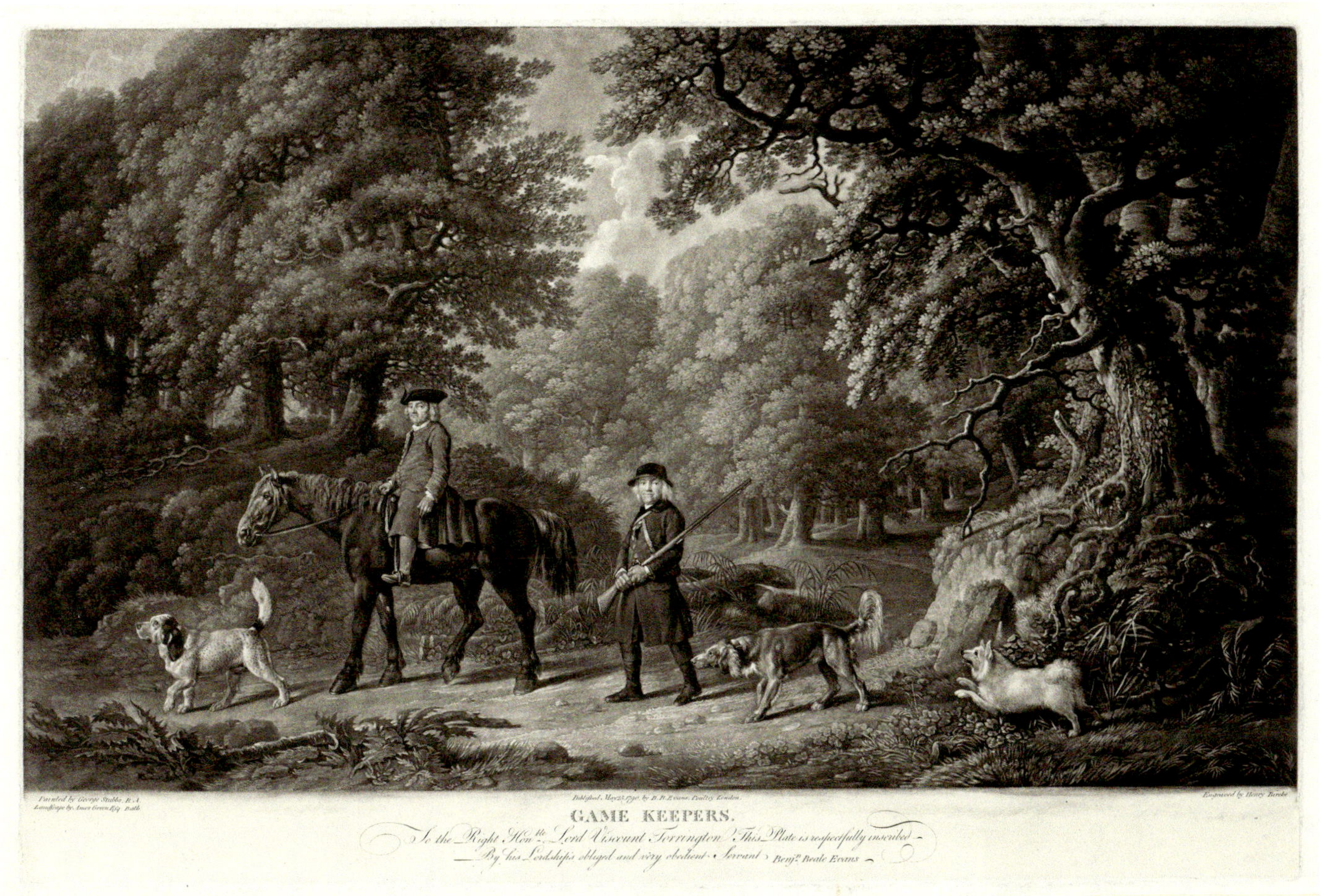

86

Game Keepers 1790

Robert Laurie (1755–1836) and Richard Earlom (1743–1822) after George Stubbs

Mezzotint, 43.6 x 65.3 cm (Plate), 45.8 x 67.9 cm (Sheet)
Ins. bottom left: *Painted by George Stubbs. R. A. / Landscape by Amos Green. Esq: Bath.*, right: *Engraved by Henri Birche.*
Aschaffenburg Collection, Staatliche Graphische Sammlung München, Inv. no. 11 E 16/2

Another print by Laurie and Earlom features Lord Torrington's steward and gamekeeper. Although the two depicted men and their dogs are the subject of the print, the forest that surrounds them has been rendered with equal effort. This holds particularly for the right part of the image, where a prominent oak tree with clutching branches and a blanket of ivy fills the picture plane. Like *Labourers*, *Game Keepers* features a vista in the background, revealing a sunlit open space that provides the print with a great sense of depth.

Like *Labourers*, this print is taken from a painting commissioned by Lord Torrington, *Lord Torrington's Steward and Gamekeeper with Dogs* from 1767 (cat. no. 32). The man with the gun can be identified as the gamekeeper Joseph Mann, who had already been working for the Lords Torrington for 34 years when George Byng, the 4th Viscount, commissioned this portrait of him.

SG

Lit.: Lennox-Boyd et al., *George Stubbs*, 1989, no. 88 IV

GEORGE STUBBS—BIOGRAPHICAL NOTES

1724

The son of a tradesman, George Stubbs was born on 25 August 1724 in Liverpool, a city then on the threshold of a boom that would transform it into the biggest port in Great Britain within only a couple of decades. The family had been involved in the leather processing industry for generations and even at the tender age of eight Stubbs is said to have made sketches of bones and remains given to him by a friendly neighbouring doctor. Following the death of his father in 1741 Stubbs was either apprenticed to or employed by a local painter, Hamlet Winstanley, who apparently taught him the art of painting in oils. The young Stubbs, however, broke with the older artist and pursued his training alone. "From this period," wrote his first biographer, Ozias Humphry, "Nature was his only study, and experience his master."

1744

Very little is known about the next stations in Stubbs's career. He painted portraits for a short time in Wigan and Leeds before moving to York, where he lived for several years. There he appears to have founded a family, or at least fathered several children; including George Townley Stubbs (born 1748), who later collaborated with his father and worked as an engraver. In York Stubbs pursued his anatomy studies and dissected the bodies of both humans and animals. His expertise in this area qualified him to hold lectures at the town's County Hospital. In 1751 Stubbs provided illustrations based on the autopsies of pregnant women for John Burton's obstetrical treatise *An Essay Towards a Complete New System of Midwifery*. Having learned how to etch, Stubbs rendered these ready for print himself.

1754

Stubbs travelled to Italy in order to continue his artistic education, spending several months in Rome. Later he would maintain that he had been unaffected by the sight of antiquities and the art of past eras, and that he had neither made copies of them nor other drawings while there. At the end of his life, Stubbs recounted his version of the voyage to Ozias Humphry, who summarized it thus: "His motive for the voyage was to convince himself that Nature is superior to all art, whether Greek or Roman, ancient or contemporary." By the end of 1755 Stubbs had returned to England.

1758

Stubbs withdrew from society to an isolated farmstead at Horkstow, near to Barton upon Humber in Lincolnshire, where he spent eighteen months conducting studies of equine anatomy with the help of no one but Mary Spencer, his common-law wife. Stubbs developed a sophisticated procedure which allowed him both to prepare the horses' bodies for study and to draw them in life-like poses. Forty-two drawings passed into the possession of Edwin Landseer after the death of the artist and are preserved today in the Royal Academy of Arts in London. In 1758, or in spring 1759, Stubbs relocated to London, where—at the age of thirty-five—he vaulted to success. Occupying an artistic position for which there were few competitors, he made his name as a painter of horses in no time at all. There was also considerable demand: the import of Arabian, Turkish and Barb horses to England in the seventeenth century had inspired owners to cross them with native breeds. In the eighteenth century impressive successes were achieved by exercising systematic selection. As luxury commodities with a high price tag, the thoroughbreds this produced became the subjects of portraits. Charles Lennox, 3rd Duke of Richmond, commissioned Stubbs to produce three paintings showing scenes of hunting and riding at Goodwood, his property in Sussex. Stubbs spent several months there making preparatory studies for the pictures and painting them. In 1761 Stubbs showed his work at the Society of Artists (founded two years before, in 1759) for the first time. Between 1761 and 1774 Stubbs exhibited more than sixty paintings at its annual exhibition of members' work.

1762

Stubbs painted *The Grosvenor Hunt*—his largest and most important painting of a hunt—and also the first of many compositions showing mares and foals. *The Grosvenor Hunt* for Richard Grosvenor and *The Charlton Hunt* for the Duke of Richmond are not only astonishing proof of his mastery when it comes to representing horses and dogs in movement but also brilliant visualizations of the status of the men who commissioned them, the powerful lords of inconceivably vast swathes of land. In the same year Stubbs received a number of commissions from Charles Watson-Wentworth, 2nd Marquess of Rockingham, who was at the centre of a circle of politically active, wealthy, young nobles with a passion for horse-breeding and horse-racing. Rockingham owned large estates, above all in Yorkshire, where he was also the owner of one of England's largest country piles in the Palladian style: Wentworth Woodhouse. His property was home to a renowned stud which had brought forth famous thoroughbreds, like the stallion Whistlejacket, immortalized by Stubbs in a painting of monumental size. For Lord Rockingham's London residence on Grosvenor Square Stubbs painted two enormous pictures of lions attacking their prey: *A Lion Attacking a Stag* and *A Lion Attacking a Horse*.

1763

George Stubbs acquired a property at 24 Somerset Street, near to Oxford Road in London's West End. Specially adapted to meet his needs with spaces for both living and working, the artist resided at this address until his death (in 1909 the building was torn down to make way for Selfridge's Department Store on Oxford Street). In addition to his paintings of horses, Stubbs began to produce likenesses of exotic animals. Stubbs found his 'sitters' in the menageries at the royal court and on the country estates of the English nobility. In 1763 he painted Queen Charlotte's zebra followed in 1764 by a cheetah for the British Governor of Madras, Lord Pigot. He was commissioned by the doctor and natural philosopher William Hunter to paint an elk and a nilgai (Indian antelope), pictures which Hunter used to illustrate his lectures on natural history.

1766

The Anatomy of the Horse was published in 1766 after having been in preparation for many years. Having tried in vain to find an engraver for his drawings, Stubbs had finally undertaken the work of rendering them for print himself. Moreover, he had also written an extensive accompanying text in which the plates are explained and his own mastery of equine anatomy is documented. Signalling the heights he had reached as a painter of animals, the first engravings of Stubbs's paintings began to appear in the mid 1760s. Beginning in 1767 Benjamin Green published a series of six large-format mezzotints after works by Stubbs. From 1770 onwards, Stubbs's son, George Townley Stubbs, became a member of this circle of engravers, publishing plates made after his father's paintings.

1775

In the 1770s Stubbs began to paint on wood panels and to experiment with enamel colours on copper and Wedgwood earthenware. His aim was to achieve a smooth, homogenous and precise application of colour, which would be more durable than painting on canvas. In 1775 he submitted several panel paintings for the exhibition at the Royal Academy of Arts (founded 1768)—an institution with which he had a fraught relationship. The five enamel paintings on Wedgewood plaques entered by Stubbs for the Academy Exhibition in 1782 were badly hung and barely noticed. After being absent for several years, Stubbs returned to the RA Exhibition again in 1786, when he showed his *Haymakers* and *Reapers*.

1778

In the 1780s Stubbs retired from exhibiting and turned his attention to new subjects as well as experimenting with printing processes. He had already issued his first autograph print of a painting in 1777, a large-format reproduction of his *Horse Affrighted by a Lion* of 1762. He went on to publish twelve sheets (dated 1 May 1778), comprising largely etchings and soft-ground etchings. He made use of a number of different techniques and tools in order to achieve soft and delicate tones. He primarily depicted cats of prey, but some dogs—going back to studies made for the *Charlton Hunt*—are also represented. These are among the most beautiful English prints of the eighteenth century.

1790

It was some time before Stubbs received his first commission from the royal family. In 1790 George Augustus, the Prince of Wales, handed the artist the task of producing a series of paintings for his London residence, Carlton House in Pall Mall. These were to be dedicated to the interests of the prince: country life, sports and animals. Following their completion Stubbs received a commission from another patron for a much larger project. Painted portraits were to capture 145 of the most famous racehorses and thoroughbreds of past decades. The paintings were intended for public exhibition—following the example of the Boydell Shakespeare Gallery—and were to be made more widely available in the form of prints. Known only as "Mr Turf", the patron remained anonymous. Though the Prince of Wales also appears to have been involved, the man behind "Mr Turf" was actually Andrew O'Kelly, the nephew and heir of the gambler and horse owner Denis O'Kelly. With seventeen paintings by Stubbs, the Turf Gallery in Conduit Street opened to visitors in 1794—its success, however, was not as great as had been hoped. Stubbs was never to be remunerated as had been promised and withdrew from the project.

1800

Stubbs exhibited his late masterpiece and last great work, *Hambletonian Rubbing Down,* at the Royal Academy exhibition. The commission came from Sir Harry Vane-Tempest, Hambletonian's owner. In spring 1799, Hambletonian had triumphed over the rival horse, Diamond, in a memorable race at Newmarket. This victory by the most famous racehorse of the time was to be immortalized in a pair of paintings. Stubbs's decision to dedicate the painting—the composition of which is quite extraordinary—to the rubbing down of the horse after the race, rather than the running itself, or the moment in which it crossed the line, irritated his patron, who did not take delivery of the painting and refused to pay. A lawsuit ensued, which ended in Stubbs's favour.

1806

In later years, Stubbs retired from public life to concentrate on researching and making etchings for his final large project: a comparative anatomy illustrated by thirty plates and explanatory texts to be published under the title *A Comparative Anatomical Exposition of the Structure of the Human Body, with that of a Tiger and a Common Fowl.* He was able to complete fifteen engravings which were published in three batches between 1804 and 1806. The text, however, stayed unprinted. Towards the end of Stubbs's life, one of his closest friends was the portrait painter Ozias Humphry, who recorded the artist's reminiscences, producing thereby one of the few sources of information on Stubbs's life. The Earl of Clarendon was among the last patrons to commission work from Stubbs. The dozen paintings executed for him include the gloomy *Freemann, the Earl of Clarendon's Gamekeeper*, which hunting scene Stubbs also rendered as an etching. George Stubbs died on 10 July 1806 and was interred in the graveyard of St Marylebone in London, though his grave no longer exists. He named his common-law wife Mary Spencer as his heir. The executor of his estate was to be Lady Isabella Saltonstall, who had helped him in the financial difficulties he experienced in old age.

1807

Stubbs apparently died in debt; the house in Somerset Street had to be sold and the remains of his artistic career were put up for auction. Administered by Peter Cox, the sale of the 26 and 27 May 1807 saw paintings, drawings and prints from his estate being offered in eighty-nine lots, the sale of which achieved around £3,500. The catalogue accompanying the auction gives a taste of what was left behind after Stubbs's death and, moreover, with a few notable exceptions, how much has since been lost. Almost entirely missing today are Stubbs's drawings and sketch books, as well as almost all of his painted studies and preparatory works. The materials Stubbs had assembled for the *Comparative Anatomy* were excluded from the post-mortem sale and sold by Mary Spencer to the printer and art dealer Edward Orme in 1817. His unusually large library with 1,800 volumes was sold to the book dealer William Stewart in November 1807. In no time at all Georg Stubbs was forgotten entirely.

Compiled using Ozias Humphry, *Memoir*; Blake, *George Stubbs and the Wide Creation*, 2005; and Egerton, *George Stubbs*, 2007.

BIBLIOGRAPHY

Barrell, John, *The Dark Side of the Landscape. The Rural Poor in English Painting 1730–1840*, Cambridge 1980

Belsey, Hugh, "A Newfoundland Dog by George Stubbs," in: *The Burlington Magazine* 129, 1987, pp. 735 f.

Belsey, Hugh, "Stubbs' Exacting Art," in: *Apollo* 165, 2007, pp. 88 f.

Belsey, Hugh, "George Stubbs. Welbeck," in: *The Burlington Magazine* 151, 2009, pp. 115 f.

Blake, *George Stubbs and the Wide Creation*, 2005
Blake, Robin, *George Stubbs and the Wide Creation. Animals, People and Places in the Life of George Stubbs 1724–1806*, London 2005

Brewer, John, *The Pleasures of the Imagination*, London 1997

Busch, Werner, *Das sentimentalische Bild. Die Krise der Kunst im 18. Jahrhundert und die Geburt der Moderne*, Munich 1993

Bynum, William F. and Roy Porter (eds.), *William Hunter and the Eighteenth-Century Medical World*, Cambridge 1985

Clarke, T. H., *The Rhinoceros from Dürer to Stubbs, 1515–1799*, London 1986

Clayton, Timothy, *The English Print 1688–1802*, New Haven and London 1997

Constantine, H. F., "Lord Rockingham and Stubbs. Some New Documents," in: *The Burlington Magazine* 95, 1953, pp. 236–38

Cormack, Malcolm, *Country Pursuits. British, American, and French Sporting Art from the Mellon Collections in the Virginia Museum of Fine Arts*, Charlottesville et al. 2007

Cunningham, Andrew, *The Anatomist Anatomis'd. An Experimental Discipline in Enlightenment Europe*, Farnham, Burlington 2010

Deuchar, Stephen, *Sporting Art in Eighteenth-Century England. A Social and Political History*, New Haven and London 1988

Doherty, Terence, *The Anatomical Works of George Stubbs*, London 1974

Donald, Diana, *Picturing Animals in Britain 1750–1850*, New Haven and London 2007

Egerton, Judy and Dudley Snelgrove, *British Sporting and Animal Drawings, c. 1500–1850. Sport in Art and Books*, New Haven 1978 *(The Paul Mellon Collection)*

Egerton, Judy, *British Sporting and Animal Paintings, 1655–1867. Sport in Art and Books*, New Haven 1978 *(The Paul Mellon Collection)*

Egerton, Judy, "George Stubbs and the Landscape of Creswell Crags," in: *The Burlington Magazine* 126, 1984, pp. 738–43

Egerton, *George Stubbs*, 2007
Egerton, Judy, *George Stubbs, Painter. Catalogue raisonné*, New Haven and London 2007

Egerton, Judy, "'So good with the humbler persons.' Stubbs as Portraitist," in: *The Burlington Magazine* 149, 2007, pp. 672–77

Exhib. Cat. *Fearful Symmetry*, 2000
Fearful Symmetry. George Stubbs, Painter of the English Enlightenment, Nicholas H. J. Hall (ed.), Exhib. Cat. Hall & Knight Ltd., New York 2000

Fierce Friends. Artists and animals, 1750–1900, Louise Lippincott and Andreas Blühm (eds.), Exhib. Cat. Van Gogh Museum Amsterdam and Carnegie Museum of Art, Pittsburgh, London 2005

Fordham, Douglas, "George Stubbs's 'Zoon Politicon,'" in: *Oxford Art Journal* 33, 1, 2000, pp. 1–23

Fountain, R. B., "George Stubbs (1724–1806) as an Anatomist," in: *Proceedings of the Royal Society of Medicine* 61, 1968, no. 7, pp. 639–46

Fountain, Robert and Alfred Gates, *Stubbs' Dogs. The Hounds and Domestic Dogs of the Eighteenth Century as seen through the Paintings of George Stubbs*, London 1984

George Stubbs. Anatomist and Animal Painter, Judy Egerton (ed.), Exhib. Cat. Tate Gallery, London 1976

Exhib. Cat. *George Stubbs*, 1984/85
George Stubbs 1724–1806, Judy Egerton (ed.), Exhib. Cat. Tate Gallery, London and Yale Center for British Art, New Haven, London 1984/85

Exhib. Cat. *George Stubbs in the Collection of Paul Mellon*, 1999/2000
George Stubbs in the Collection of Paul Mellon. A Memorial Exhibition, Exhib. Cat. Yale Center for British Art, New Haven and Virginia Museum of Fine Arts, Richmond 1999/2000

George Stubbs. A Celebration, Alex Kidson (ed.), Exhib. Cat. Walker Art Gallery, Liverpool, Tate Britain, London and The Frick Collection, New York, London 2006/07

Gilbey, Walter, *Life of George Stubbs, R.A.*, London 1898

Godfrey, Richard, *Printmaking in Britain. A General History from its Beginnings to the Present Day*, Oxford 1978

Godfrey, Richard, "George Stubbs as a Printmaker," in: *Print Collector's Newsletter* 13, 1982, 4, pp. 114–6

Kemp, Martin, *Visualizations. The Nature Book of Art and Science*, Oxford et al. 2000

Lennox-Boyd et al., *George Stubbs*, 1989
Lennox-Boyd, Christopher, Rob Dixon and Tim Clayton, *George Stubbs. The Complete Engraved Works*, Abingdon 1989

MacEwen, John, "The Instinct for Abstraction. Long known for the anatomical authority of his sport paintings, 18th-century artist George Stubbs was also, as a recent show testifies, peculiarly modern in his freedom of formal invention," in: *Art in America* 73, 3, 1985, pp. 109–17

McKendrick, Neil, John Brewer and J. H. Plumb (ed.), *The Birth of a Consumer Society. The Commercialization of Eighteenth-Century England*, London 1982

Mehr Licht. Europa um 1770. Die bildende Kunst der Aufklärung, Herbert Beck, Peter C. Bol and Maraike Bückling (eds.), Exhib. Cat. Städelsches Kunstinstitut and Städtische Galerie Frankfurt am Main, Munich 1999

A Memoir of George Stubbs by Ozias Humphry and Joseph Mayer, with an introduction by Anthony Mould, London 2005

Mills, John and Raymond White, "The Mediums Used by George Stubbs. Some Further Studies," in: *National Gallery Technical Bulletin* 9, 1985, pp. 60–4

Milner, Frank, *George Stubbs. Paintings, Ceramics, Prints & Documents in Merseyside Collections, Liverpool (Walker Art Gallery, Lady Lever Art Gallery, Liverpool City Libraries)*, Liverpool 1987

Morrison, Venetia, *The Art of George Stubbs*, London 1989

"My Highest Pleasures". William Hunter's Art Collection, Peter Black (ed.), Exhib. Cat. Hunterian Art Gallery, University of Glasgow, London 2007

Myrone, Martin, *George Stubbs*, London 2002

Parker, Constance-Anne, *Mr Stubbs. The Horse Painter*, London 1971

Paul Mellon's Legacy–A Passion for British Art. Masterpieces from the Yale Center for British Art, Exhib. Cat. Yale Center for British Art, New Haven and Royal Academy of Arts, London, New Haven and London 2007

Paulson, Ronald, *Emblem and Expression. Meaning in English Art in the Eighteenth Century*, London 1975

Plumb, John H., *The Commercialisation of Leisure in Eighteenth-Century England*, Reading 1973

Potts, Alex, "Natural Order and the Call of the Wild. The Politics of Animal Picturing," in: *Oxford Art Journal* 13, 1990, pp. 12–33

Rolfe, W. D. Ian, "A Stubbs Drawing Recognised," in: *The Burlington Magazine* 125, 1983, pp. 738–41

Rolfe, W. D. Ian, "William Hunter (1718–1783) on Irish 'Elk' and Stubbs's Moose," in: *Archives of Natural History* 11, 2, 1983, pp. 263–90

Rolfe, W. D. Ian, "William and John Hunter. Breaking the Great Chain of Being," in: Bynum and Porter 1985, pp. 297–319

Rump, Gerhard Charles, *Pferde- und Jagdbilder in der englischen Kunst. Studien zu George Stubbs und das Genre der 'Sporting Art' von 1650–1830*, Hildesheim, Zurich and New York 1983

Russell, Francis, "Lord Torrington and Stubbs. A footnote," in: *The Burlington Magazine* 122, 1980, pp. 250–53

Snelgrove, Dudley, *British Sporting and Animal Prints, 1658–1874. Sport in Art and Books*, New Haven and London 1981 *(The Paul Mellon Collection)*

Exhib. Cat. *Stubbs and the Horse*, 2004/05
Stubbs and the Horse, Malcolm Warner and Robin Blake (eds.), Exhib. Cat. Kimbell Art Museum, Fort Worth, The Walters Art Museum, Baltimore and The National Gallery, London, London and New Haven 2004/05

Stubbs and Wedgwood. Unique Alliance between Artist and Potter, Bruce Tattersall (ed.), Exhib. Cat. Tate Gallery, London 1974

Taylor, Basil, *Animal Painting in England from Barlow to Landseer*, London 1955

Taylor, Basil, *George Stubbs 1724–1806*, Exhib. Cat. Whitechapel Art Gallery, London 1957

Taylor, Basil, "Stubbs as Anatomist," in: *George Stubbs. Rediscovered anatomical drawings from the Free Public Library Worcester, Massachusetts*, Exhib. Cat. The Arts Council of Great Britain, London 1958, pp. 3–18

Taylor, Basil, "George Stubbs. 'The Lion and Horse' Theme," in: *The Burlington Magazine* 107, 1965, pp. 81–86

Taylor, *The Prints of George Stubbs*, 1969
Taylor, Basil, *The Prints of George Stubbs*, Exhib. Cat. The Festival Gallery, Aldeburgh and The Victoria and Albert Museum, London, London 1969

Taylor, Basil, "George Stubbs and a Drawing by Carle Vernet," in: *Notes on British Art* 13, 1969, p. 4

Taylor, Basil, *Stubbs*, London 1971

Waterhouse, Ellis, "Lord Fitzwilliam's Sporting Pictures by Stubbs," in: *The Burlington Magazine* 88, 1946, p. 199

Waterhouse, Ellis, *Painting in Britain 1530 to 1790*, 3rd ed., London 1969 *(The Pelican History of Art)*

Worsley, Giles, *The British Stable*, New Haven and London 2004

Vamplew, Wray, *The Turf. A Social and Economic History of Horse Racing*, London 1976

LENDERS TO THE EXHIBITION

Her Majesty Queen Elizabeth II: cat. nos. 50, 51

The Trustees of the Rt. Hon. Olive, Countess Fitzwilliam's Chattels Settlement, by permission of Lady Juliet Tadgell: cat. nos. 19, 20, 28

The Syndics of the Fitzwilliam Museum, Cambridge: cat. no. 36

Kunstsammlungen der Veste Coburg: cat. nos. 76, 80, 83, 84

The National Gallery of Scotland, Edinburgh: cat. no. 27

The Hunterian, University of Glasgow: cat. no. 46

The Duke of Rutland, Belvoir Castle, Grantham: cat. nos. 43, 49

Minerva Kunststiftung, Lachen, Switzerland: cat. no. 48

The Trustees of the British Museum, London: cat. nos. 52–64

Hunterian Museum at the Royal College of Surgeons, London: cat. no. 47

The National Gallery, London: cat. no. 35

The National Portrait Gallery, London: cat. no. 39

Royal Academy of Arts, London: cat. nos. 5–6, 8–10, 12–15

Tate, London: cat. nos. 21, 24, 26, 42

Manchester City Galleries: cat. no. 44

Private collections: cat. nos. 17, 18, 31, 34

Private collection, c/o Guy Morrison, London: cat. no. 32

Private collection, c/o Konrad Bernheimer, Munich: cat. no. 38

Staatliche Graphische Sammlung München, Munich: cat. nos. 65–71, 77, 79, 81, 82, 85, 86

Yale Center for British Art, New Haven: cat. nos. 16, 25, 40, 45

The Earl of Macclesfield, North Stoke: cat. nos. 22, 23

Germanisches Nationalmuseum, Nuremberg: cat. nos. 72–75, 78

The Lord Langford, Bodrhyddan, Rhuddlan: cat. no. 30

Upton House, The Bearsted Collection (The National Trust): cat. no. 33

John Warde, Squerryes Court, Westerham: cat. no. 37

This book is published on the occasion of the exhibition

George Stubbs (1724–1806)
Science into Art – Tiermalerei zwischen Wissenschaft und Kunst
Neue Pinakothek, Munich
January 26 – May 6, 2012

Bayerische Staatsgemäldesammlungen

General Director
Klaus Schrenk

Curator of the exhibition, editor of the catalogue
Herbert W. Rott

Assistance with the preparation of the exhibition and catalogue
Sophie Goldhagen

Assistance
Nicole Losch-Maute

Registrar
Ingrid Huber

Conservation
Renate Poggendorf, Carola Sauter

Installation
Heino Kahrs and team

Public Relations and Marketing
Tine Nehler, Christine Kramer

Events
Barbara Siebert and team

Education
Jochen Meister and team

Photography
Haydar Koyupinar and team

Administration
Robert Kirchmaier, Roland Weiß

This publication was supported by *The Paul Mellon Centre for Studies in British Art.*

Authors of catalogue texts

WB Werner Busch
SG Sophie Goldhagen
OK Oliver Kase
HWR Herbert W. Rott

Photograph Credits

Humboldt-Universität zu Berlin, Universitätsbibliothek: Essay Kase, figs. 12–14; The Bridgeman Art Library: Essay Busch, figs. 2, 5, 7, Essay Myrone, fig. 7, Essay Russell, figs. 1, 5, cat. nos. 30, 31, 33 (Chris Titmus), 34, 49; Fitzwilliam Museum, Cambridge: cat. no. 36; Kunstsammlungen der Veste Coburg: Essay Rott, fig. 6, cat. no. 76, 80, 83, 84; Country Life Picture Library (IPC Media Ltd): Essay Russell, fig. 3; Christie's Images Limited: Essay Myrone, fig. 3, Essay Russell, fig. 4; Edinburgh, National Gallery of Scotland: cat. no. 27; Forget/Sagaphoto.com: Essay Kase, fig. 2; The Hunterian at the University of Glasgow: cat. no. 46; London, The Trustees of the British Museum: Essay Busch, figs. 1, 11, Essay Clayton, figs. 1–7, 9–13, pp. 107–109, figs. 1–3, cat. nos. 52–64; London, Hunterian Museum, The Royal College of Surgeons: cat. no. 47; London, The National Gallery: Essay Busch, fig. 8, cat. no. 35; London, The National Portrait Gallery: cat. no. 39; London, Royal Academy of Arts: cat. nos. 1–15; London, Tate: Essay Myrone, figs. 5, 6, Essay Busch, fig. 6, cat. nos. 21, 24, 26, 41, 42; London, Victoria and Albert Museum: Essay Busch, fig. 3; Manchester Art Galleries: cat. no. 44; Munich, Bayerische Staatsbibliothek: Essay Kase, figs. 3, 7–10; Munich, Bayerische Staatsgemäldesammlungen: Essay Rott, figs. 2–4, cat. no. 29; Staatliche Graphische Sammlung München, Aschaffenburg Collection: Essay Clayton, fig. 8, cat. nos. 65–71, 77, 79, 81, 82, 85, 86; The National Library of Medicine: Essay Kase, figs. 4, 5, 15; New Haven, Yale Center for British Art: Essay Myrone, figs. 4, 8–10, Essay Busch, figs. 4, 10, Essay Kase, fig. 16, Essay Clayton, fig. 8, cat. nos. 16, 25, 40, 45; New Haven, Yale University Art Gallery: Essay Busch, fig. 10; Nuremberg, Germanisches Nationalmuseum: cat. nos. 72–75, 78; Paris, Bibliothèque nationale de France: Essay Kase, fig. 1; Paris, RMN, Musée du Louvre (bpk): Essay Kase, fig. 6 (Thierry Le Mage); St. Petersburg, The State Ermitage Museum: Essay Rott, fig. 5; The Royal Collection, Her Majesty Queen Elizabeth II: cat. nos. 50, 51; The Trustees of the Rt. Hon. Olive, Countess Fitzwilliam's Chattels Settlement, by permission of Lady Juliet Tadgell: Essay Russell, fig. 2, cat. nos. 19, 20, 28 (Martin Apps); The Trustees of the Goodwood Collection: Essay Myrone, figs. 1, 2.

Library of Congress Control Number: 2011945123
Publication Data: a catalogue record for this book is available from the British Library; Deutsche Nationalbibliothek holds a record of this publication in the Deutsche Nationalbibliografie; detailed bibliographical data can be found under: http://dnb.d-nb.de

Cover: Mares and Foals, 1762 (detail from cat. no. 20)
Frontispiece: Cheetah and Stag with Two Indian Attendants, 1765 (detail from cat. no. 44)

Prestel Verlag, Munich
A member of Verlagsgruppe Random House GmbH

Prestel Verlag
Neumarkter Strasse 28
81673 Munich
Tel. +49 (0)89 4136-0
Fax +49 (0)89 4136-2335
www.prestel.de

Prestel Publishing Ltd.
4 Bloomsbury Place
London WC1A 2QA
Tel. +44 (0)20 7323-5004
Fax +44 (0)20 7636-8004

Prestel Publishing
900 Broadway, Suite 603
New York, NY 10003
Tel. +1 (212) 995-2720
Fax +1 (212) 995-2733
www.prestel.com

Editorial Direction: Anja Besserer
Copy-editing: Jane Michael, Munich
Translation from the German: Philippa Hurd, London, and Rachel King, Munich: contributions by Werner Busch, Oliver Kase; Bronwen Saunders, Frankenthal: catalogue text The Anatomy of the Horse, catalogue texts Paintings; contribution by Herbert W. Rott; Rachel King, Munich: foreword, biographical notes, cover texts
Design: WIGEL, Munich
Layout: Meike Sellier, Eching/Munich
Production: Andrea Cobré
Art Direction: Cilly Klotz
Origination: Reproline mediateam, Munich
Printing and Binding: Appl, Wemding

FSC www.fsc.org MIX Paper from responsible sources FSC™ C004592

Verlagsgruppe Random House FSC-DEU-0100
The FSC-certified paper *BVS matt/Drive Silk* was supplied by Deutsche Papier

ISBN 978-3-7913-5169-8 (German trade edition)
ISBN 978-3-7913-6384-4 (German museum edition)
ISBN 978-3-7913-5170-4 (English edition)